Mexi

James and Oliver Tickell

C000154275

Mitchell Beazley

THE AMERICAN EXPRESS ® TRAVEL GUIDES

Published by Mitchell Beazley, an imprint of Reed Consumer Books Ltd, Michelin House, 81 Fulham Road, London SW3 6RB and Auckland, Melbourne, Singapore and Toronto

Edited, designed and produced by Castle House Press, Llantrisant, Mid Glamorgan CF7 8EU, Wales

First published 1984 as *The American Express Pocket Guide to Mexico*. Second edition 1988. Third edition 1991. This edition, revised, updated and expanded, published 1993.

A cataloguing-in-publication record for this book is available from the British Library.

ISBN 1 85732 159 6

The editors thank Neil Hanson and Alex Taylor of Lovell Johns, David Haslam, Fred Midwood, Sally Darlington and Sylvia Hughes-Williams for their help and co-operation during the preparation of this edition. Special thanks are due to Herbert Bailey Livesey for his contribution to the GUIDE TO MEXICAN SPANISH, and to Mauricio Ribes of the Mexican Ministry of Tourism, London, a constantly helpful source of information and advice.

The authors would like to thank: Raúl Ortiz, Cultural Attaché at the Embassy of Mexico, London; Oriana Tickell, who writes for Mexico City's *Tiempo Libre* magazine, for her invaluable help with the chapter on Mexico City; William Blackburn and Douglas Cullen.

Thanks are due to the following for their kind permission to reprint the following extracts: Laurence Pollinger Ltd and the Estate of the late Mrs Frieda Lawrence Ravagli (UK) and Alfred A. Knopf Inc. (US) for the quotation from *Mornings in Mexico* and *Etruscan Places* by D.H. Lawrence; William Heinemann Ltd and The Bodley Head (UK) and Viking Penguin Inc. (US) © Graham Greene 1939, 1978 (UK), and 1939 © renewed 1967 (US) for the quotation from *The Lawless Roads* (published in the USA under the title *Another Mexico*) by Graham Greene.

Contents

Practical information

Maps

How to use this book

Few guidelines are needed to understand how this book works:

- For the general organization of the book, see CONTENTS on the pages preceding this one.
- Wherever appropriate, chapters and sections are arranged alphabetically, with headings appearing in **CAPITALS.**
- Often these headings are followed by location and practical information printed in *italics.*
- As you turn the pages, you will find subject headers, similar to those used in telephone directories, printed in CAPITALS in the top corner of each page.
- If you still cannot find what you need, check in the comprehensive and exhaustively cross-referenced INDEX at the back of the book.
- Following the index, a LIST OF STREET NAMES IN MEXICO CITY provides map references for all roads and streets mentioned in the book that are located within the areas covered by the main Mexico City maps.

CROSS-REFERENCES

These are printed in SMALL CAPITALS, referring you to other sections or alphabetical entries in the book. Care has been taken to ensure that such cross-references are self-explanatory. Often, page references are also given, although their excessive use would be intrusive and ugly.

FLOORS

We use the American convention in this book: "first floor" means the floor at ground level.

PUBLISHING CREDITS

FOR THE SERIES:
Series Editor:
  David Townsend Jones
Map Editor: David Haslam
Indexer: Hilary Bird
Gazetteer: Anna Holmes
Cover design:
  Roger Walton Studio

FOR THIS EDITION:
Edited on desktop by:
  Sharon Charity
Art editor:
  Eileen Townsend Jones
Illustrators: Jeremy Ford (David Lewis Artists), Oxford Illustrators Ltd, Sylvia Hughes-Williams, David Evans
Cover photo: Tony Stone Worldwide

FOR MITCHELL BEAZLEY:
Art Director: Tim Foster
Production: Katy Sawyer
Publisher: Sarah Bennison

PRODUCTION CREDITS:
Maps by Lovell Johns, Oxford, England
Mexico City metro map by TCS, Aldershot, England
Typeset in Garamond and News Gothic
Desktop layout in Ventura Publisher
Reproduction by M & E Reproductions, Essex, England
Linotronic output by Tradespools Limited, Frome, England
Printed and bound in Great Britain by Clays Ltd, St Ives plc

KEY TO SYMBOLS

☎	Telephone	☐	TV in each room
Fx	Facsimile (fax)	☎	Telephone in each room
★	Recommended sight	🐕	Dogs not allowed
☆	Worth a detour	≋	Swimming pool
i	Tourist information	♨	Garden/terrace
⬅	Parking	⋐	Good view
⏛	Building of architectural interest	⚓	Good beach nearby
		♂	Tennis
🔟	Free entrance	♐	Golf
📷	Entrance fee payable	⚓	Riding
▪	Entrance expensive	⬲	Fishing
📷	Photography forbidden	♈	Gym/fitness facilities
⌡	Guided tour	⚲	Bar
⬛	Cafeteria	⬥	Sauna
✳	Special interest for children	⚱	Spa
⚲	Hotel	👥	Conference facilities
⏛	Luxury hotel	⫤	Restaurant
♣	Good value (in its class)	▬	Simple restaurant
▭	Cheap	⚱	Luxury restaurant
▥	Inexpensive	▭	A la carte available
▥	Moderately priced	▬	Good wines
▥	Expensive	⚭	Open-air dining
▥	Very expensive	●	Disco dancing
▣	Secure garage	♩	Nightclub
⌂	Quiet hotel	♫	Live music
♿	Facilities for disabled people	♪	Dancing

HOTEL AND RESTAURANT PRICE CATEGORIES

These are denoted by the symbols ▭ (cheap), ▥ (inexpensive), ▥ (moderately priced), ▥ (expensive) and ▥ (very expensive). They correspond approximately to the following actual local prices, which give a guideline **at the time of printing**. Note that this is only a rough guide: prices go up and down with currency fluctuations and economic swings. Mexico's new-found economic stability has brought steadier but higher prices, as inflationary increases have not been fully matched by currency depreciation, and this trend may continue.

Price categories		Corresponding to approximate **US$** prices
		for **hotels** / for **restaurants**
		double room with / *meal for one with*
		bath; singles are / *service, taxes and*
		slightly cheaper / *house wine*

		for **hotels** double room with bath; singles are slightly cheaper	for **restaurants** meal for one with service, taxes and house wine
▥	very expensive	over $100	over $40
▥	expensive	$75-100	$20-40
▥	moderately priced	$45-75	$10-20
▥	inexpensive	$20-45	$5-10
▭	cheap	under $20	under $5

About the authors

James and **Oliver Tickell** were brought up in Mexico, and since then have been frequent visitors to the country and to the rest of Central America. **James Tickell**, author of the original *American Express Pocket Guide to Mexico* (1984), is an architect by training, who has worked in Chiapas, Southern Mexico on agricultural improvements and housing projects for the Tzeltal Indians. He is now a well-known and successful figure in London's voluntary housing sector.

This fourth edition in the series' new, larger format was extensively revised, updated, reorganized and expanded by **Oliver Tickell**, a free-lance writer on travel, science and the environment. He has written for many newspapers including *The New York Times, The Times, The Independent, The Guardian* and *The Daily Telegraph* and for a number of periodicals including *New Scientist, The New Statesman and Society, Green Magazine, Country Life* and *BBC Wildlife*.

The two brothers are co-authors of *Cusco, Peru* and *Tikal, City of the Maya* in the *Travel to Landmarks* series (Tauris-Parke).

The authors' sister, **Oriana Tickell,** who writes for Mexico City's *Tiempo Libre* magazine, made a major contribution to the WHERE TO STAY and EATING AND DRINKING sections of the chapter on Mexico City.

A message from the editors

Months of concentrated work were dedicated to making this edition accurate and up to date when it went to press. But time and change are forever the enemies, and between editions we are very much assisted when you, our readers, write to tell us about any changes you discover.

Please keep on writing — but please also be aware that we have no control over restaurants, or whatever, that take it into their heads, after we publish, to move, or change their telephone number, or, even worse, close down. Our authors and editors aim to exclude trendy ephemera and to recommend places that give every indication of being stable and durable. Their judgment is rarely wrong. Changes in telephone numbers are something else. We apologise for the world's telephone authorities, who seem to change their numbers like you and I change shirts.

My serious point is that we are striving to tailor the series to the very distinctive tastes and requirements of our discerning international readership, which is why your feedback is so valuable. I particularly want to thank all of you who wrote while we were preparing this edition. Time prevents our responding to most such letters, but they are all welcomed and frequently contribute to the process of preparing the next edition.

Please write to me at **Mitchell Beazley**, an imprint of Reed Illustrated Books, Michelin House, 81 Fulham Road, London SW3 6RB; or, in the US, c/o American Express Travel Guides, **Prentice Hall Travel**, 15 Columbus Circle, New York, NY 10023.

David Townsend Jones, Series Editor, American Express Travel Guides

Mexico

Viva México!

Most visitors to Mexico arrive well equipped with preconceptions. Incredible though it seems to those who know the country, some still expect to find a land of big-hatted *bandidos* snoozing in the sun under a cactus, rising only to wash down red-hot chilies with tequila. The Mexico they find both embraces and defies such preconceptions. Extremes are common: wealth and poverty, beauty and squalor, baking deserts and lush rainforest, friendly efficiency and surly incompetence.

If anything, these contrasts are increasing. Mexico is now experiencing a time of rapid change: social, political and economic. As Mexico opens its markets to foreign trade, opens its companies to outside investment and converts community-held lands *(ejidos)* into private property, this is a time of promise and fear for the people of Mexico. Promise, as the stock market booms, investment floods in and corporate profits soar. Fear, as small farmers and industries are forced into unequal competition with large, efficient US producers; as investment in new technology creates fewer, not more jobs; as the minimum wage shrinks to a third of its 1978 value; and as peasants *(campesinos)* are forced off the land their forefathers have farmed for generations, into a harsh and uncertain future.

In the words of a once-popular car sticker: "Mexico, ámalo o déjalo" — Mexico, love it or leave it. Faced with soaring prices and declining incomes at home, ever-increasing numbers of Mexicans are opting for the latter option. Hundreds of thousands migrate across the US border and multiply their earnings as cheap labor in farms, industries and the service sector. For tourists, the choice is less stark: they can both love Mexico *and* leave it, after a few weeks of well-spent vacation.

And indeed most visitors do love it. With all that Mexico has to offer, it is no surprise that it is a prime tourist destination. Fortunately, the country is so vast in size that tourist invasions can easily be accommodated. There is plenty for everybody: hundreds of miles of palm-shaded beaches and azure seas — some deserted, others with vibrant, luxury resorts; awesome ruins of ancient civilizations, which crop up everywhere from the heart of Mexico city to the deepest jungle; and a wealth of charming colonial towns and remote Indian villages.

Today's tourists can spend a vacation in Mexico without speaking a word of Spanish. But this not only limits them to the tourist circuits, but cuts them off from the greatest attraction of all — the Mexicans themselves. They are a complex but always warm and vital people, with a long, often painful, but unique and fascinating history.

THE MEXICANS

The traumatic birth of Mexico occurred in 1521 with the bloody fall of Aztec Tenochtitlán to the Spanish Conquistadors. Originally named New Spain, the pre-independence infancy of the nation consisted of three centuries of harsh Spanish exploitation and domination of the native peoples. Even now, despite revolutions, social changes and much bloodshed, inequalities survive from this period, transmuted into the modern structures of political and economic power.

In crude but distressingly accurate terms, wealth and power is concentrated in the hands of a tiny élite of pure European ancestry who dominate political life — the so-called "thousand families." At the bottom of the heap are the Indians, Mexico's native people. Defined as those who speak an indigenous language, they account for some 10 percent of the population.

The vast majority of Mexicans are "*mestizos*," of mixed European and Indian race in varying proportions. As their race is mixed, so is their culture and their economic standing, with the many tensions and contradictions this brings. The strong sense of national identity that has been formed over recent decades is very much one of *mestizo* people: the élite maintains its social and family ties with Spain, and develops lucrative economic relationships with the US. As for the millions of non-Spanish-speaking Indians, only marginally integrated into national life, most would be amazed to hear themselves described as Mexican.

For the Indians, the Conquest is not a historical event but a continuing reality; grinding poverty and the theft of their ancestral land continues to be their lot. And for those who attempt to resist, assassination and imprisonment without trial are common occurrences. The Ministry of the Interior has recently admitted that 10 percent of the prison population, some 8,000, are Indians who do not even know why they are there.

BEFORE THE CONQUISTADORS

Today's Indians are the direct descendants of the ancient Aztecs, the Maya and the many other peoples whose civilizations were so rapidly overthrown by the Conquistadors. One of history's great tragedies is the wholesale destruction by the Conquistadors of Pre-Hispanic societies and cultural achievements. The sad legacy of this catastrophe is that, with the exception of the Aztecs, very little is known of Pre-Hispanic history, music or daily life; the few painted scrolls *(códices)* that do survive have until recently defied translation, and even now provide only isolated if fascinating glimpses of long-extinct societies.

Still, the archeological evidence alone leaves no doubt that in many ways Pre-Hispanic societies of Mexico were socially and culturally more advanced than their European counterparts. Tenochtitlán in 1521 was the largest city in the world, controlling a domain the size of modern France. Since neither the wheel nor metal implements were in everyday use, this achievement seems all the more striking.

Despite their backwardness in certain respects, it is hard to understand how such powerful and brilliant civilizations came to be defeated by a mere handful of adventurers. The reasons are complex. Certainly, Aztec society was so hierarchical, and preoccupied with the observance of intricate religious ceremonies and dictates, that it was unable to respond imaginatively to an entirely new threat. Had the Aztec warriors concentrated on killing the intruders rather than revering them as gods or trying to capture them for sacrifice, their victory would have been certain.

Spanish technological superiority — guns, horses and swords — also played a part, as did the Aztecs' superstitious fear that their invaders might be gods. But more important still was the effect of new European diseases, such as smallpox, measles and the common cold, all potentially lethal to the Indians, who had no immunity to them. Civilizations were destroyed by epidemics before a European even got to see them. Also crucial was the assistance given to the Spanish by rebellious tribes, formerly subject to Aztec domination.

Within years, or even months, of the fall of Tenochtitlán, the other societies of Mesoamerica had undergone a similar fate, a rare exception being the Maya kingdom of Tayasal, on the site of Flores in modern-day Guatemala, which held out until 1697. On all sides, Indian priests and rulers were executed and their ancient legends, theology and customs outlawed as witchcraft, while the people suffered compulsory conversion to Christianity and virtual enslavement.

For many years the Indians, who were widely believed to have no souls, were regarded as beasts of burden and treated worse. The result was that the population collapsed from an estimated 16-to-22 million to just 1.5 million in a mere 20 years.

And yet, even today, one can still trace a strong Pre-Hispanic influence, not only in the native areas but in everyday Mexican life. A good example is the prevailing attitude to death. Mexicans are fatalistic at the best of times, but in fiestas such as the Day of the Dead the idea of death is embraced with macabre relish. This derives directly from Pre-Hispanic religions, which glorified death and sacrifice, and for whom the world of the dead was an ever-present reality.

But modern Mexico has an ambivalent attitude toward its indigenous heritage; the speaking of Maya languages in schools on the Yucatán peninsula is forbidden, while the ancient Maya ruins are the focus of a lucrative tourist industry.

FROM CONQUEST TO REVOLUTION

After the Conquest, the country was divided out among the conquistadors into vast "*encomiendas*." Parcels of land, together with the Indians residing on them, were granted to a Spaniard (the *encomendero*) in trust for the emperor, in return for converting the Indians to Christianity and safeguarding their moral welfare. In practice, this meant that the *encomendero* had total power to exploit both land and Indian with uncontrolled savagery, which was often precisely what happened.

Over time, the *encomiendas* turned into heritable estates, known as "*haciendas*." Land was also granted for the domains of monasteries, for towns, laid out to a grid plan, and for "*reducciones*," smaller centers of population into which Indians were concentrated in order to maintain control over them. Such were the principal tools of Spanish colonization, which recreated the feudal social and political structures of medieval Spain in the New World.

The economic relationship of New Spain with its mother country was entirely one-way: it was a place for Spaniards, often of lowly birth, to come and get rich, and even acquire a title, before retiring to Spain. Still, a growing number of Spaniards, known as "*criollos*," were born in Mexico, and began to resent the inferior treatment they received from the European Spanish. Their demand to be treated as equal citizens of the

Spanish Crown eventually developed a momentum that led ultimately, in 1821, to independence.

As for the unfortunate Indians, they died in their thousands in armies on both sides of the war, not to mention fighting for their own land and rights. But their position in the independent Mexico was not merely unimproved, but worse. Indeed the whole idea of independence, as opposed to equal rights, was inspired not only by the French and American revolutions, but by the growing insistence of the Spanish Crown on better treatment of its indigenous subjects, thus eroding the *criollos'* wealth and privilege.

The independence era of the 19th century was a time of upheaval in Mexican history, with Mexico losing its northern states to the US in a series of unequal battles, which led to US forces occupying Mexico City; it was only because US diplomatic messages became garbled that Mexico even held onto Baja California. All the time, the Indians remained disenfranchised and their lands up for grabs by a developing plantocracy producing sugar, coffee and other agricultural export commodities.

Some semblance of hope for the common people emerged in 1861, when the Zapotec Indian Benito Juárez became President. But his rule was interrupted by the intervention of colonial powers, including the imposition by the French of Maximilian, Archduke of Austria, as Emperor of Mexico. Maximilian was dislodged and Juárez restored to power, but in the chaos his attempts at land reform were never able to take root.

After a brief interregnum, he was succeeded by the brutal but charming dictator Porfirio Diáz, who gave his name to a whole era of Mexican history: the 34-year-long reign of terror known as the "*Porfiriato*." Diáz was one of the earliest exponents of the Latin American military state, suppressing political dissent, cornering economic power, cultivating foreign influence by attracting overseas investment on favorable terms, and placing himself at the center of a vast web of patronage.

On one level, the rule of Diáz transformed Mexico into a modern state, accelerating investment, development and industrialization. But the cost to ordinary Mexicans was enormous, and his indifference to the sufferings of Mexican peasants, robbed of their lands and working as near-slaves on grim *haciendas,* led inevitably to the Mexican Revolution, which broke out in 1910 when the moderate Francisco Madero overthrew Diáz.

The Revolution is misleadingly named, as it was no single event, but a series of civil wars among conflicting parties, joined in fleeting alliances and divided by murderous betrayals. Suffice it to say that the great peasant leader of the revolution, Emiliano Zapata, and the charismatic bandit-warrior of the north, Pancho Villa, ended up being murdered by the conservatives; that their demands for land reform remained unfulfilled; and that there was hardly a family in Mexico that survived it intact.

The Revolution ended only in 1917, with the enactment of the Constitution of Querétaro. Another 17 years were to go by before President Lázaro Cárdenas, in 1934, implemented the land reform provisions contained in the new constitution, returning millions of hectares of land to their cultivators; in 1938 he went on to assert sovereignty over foreign corporations in Mexico by nationalizing the entire oil industry.

MODERN MEXICO

Mexico is an interesting example of that apparent contradiction, the one-party democracy. Since 1929 it has been continuously ruled by another apparent contradiction, the Party of Institutional Revolution, universally known as the PRI. With the PRI identified by the red, white and green of the Mexican flag, its equation with the Mexican state is almost absolute, and the boundaries between PRI, government and state are at best ill-defined, at worst nonexistent. There are opposition parties, but until recently they have failed to gain significant electoral success for a variety of reasons — not least of which are widespread electoral fraud and political intimidation.

The 1988 presidential election was a watershed in Mexican politics. Despite resorting to all kinds of electoral trickery — including the removal of opposition voters from electoral rolls; larger turnouts in PRI strong-holds than the entire electoral register; an 8–day computer failure; and refusal to publish results from 25,000 electoral districts — the PRI candidate, Carlos Salinas de Gortari, won only 50.7 percent of the votes, the narrowest majority ever recorded in a Mexican presidential election.

His opponent was Cuauhtémoc Cárdenas, the son of the revered President Lázaro Cárdenas, standing on a strongly reformist manifesto with the support of all major opposition parties. It is widely accepted that Cárdenas was the winner: in the electoral results that *were* published, he led the field by 39 to 34 percent; in those that were not published, Salinas supposedly led by 67 to 20 percent.

The result, catastrophic for the PRI, has triggered deep changes. Reforms to the party structure have taken place, and the PRI has recently been forced to begin fund-raising from business to pay for its election campaigns, rather than helping itself to government funds. However, its new policy commitment — reversing all the old nationalist rhetoric — to the neoliberal economics of free trade, privatization and cost-cutting, remained undiminished. And it likewise pursued its "Article 27" constitu-tional reforms on land tenure, opening the way for the dismemberment of the *ejidos,* the communal farms that since the reforms of Lázaro Cárdenas have occupied some 43 percent of Mexico's farmland.

Rather than adjust his policies in response to the widespread dissatis-faction, Salinas launched a new "solidarity" social funding initiative to mitigate some of their heavy social costs. Known as Pronasol, it is an excellent example of the PRI's capacity to absorb and neutralize dissent, by convincing opponents — through reasoned argument backed up with an assemblage of carrots and sticks — that they can best meet their objectives within the PRI's far-reaching framework. The distribution of Pronasol funds, under the control of local PRI organizers, is targeted at areas of political dissent.

In this way much of the opposition has been absorbed or stifled, and in the 1991 mid-term congressional elections the PRI vote bounced back up above the 60 percent mark.

It is hard to overestimate the ability of the PRI to hold onto power: for example it is certain that the next President of Mexico, to be elected in 1994, will be the "official" candidate, as picked personally by Salinas de

Gortari. But in the longer term, the future is less certain. Some critics are likening the rule of the PRI to the *Porfiriato,* and indeed the similarities of policy and direction are more than skin-deep. One big difference is that now the dictator is not an individual but a party, which has to change its leader every six years, and is thus more adaptable and better equipped to survive the long haul. But just as Díaz was deposed by bloody revolution after his 34-year rule, so the PRI may, ultimately, face a similar fate if it does not heed the deeper causes of discontent.

Other important centers of power in Mexico include the army, incorporated by Lázaro Cárdenas into the PRI structure, the Roman Catholic Church, trade unions and business sectors. The role of the army in politics has been limited ever since the Revolution, and Mexico commits relatively little to arms expenditure: no matter how much Mexico spent, it would be unable to challenge the US; and as for the risk that trouble in Central America might spill over its southern borders, even its modest level of expenditure is more than enough to counter that. Although generally respected and preferring to remain in the background, the army is always ready to suppress internal dissent, as when it turned its guns on student protestors in Tlatelolco in 1968.

Like the army, the Church is constitutionally hemmed in; but there have been recent indications of change and a coming-together of Church and state. In 1991 Salinas sponsored constitutional amendments reversing bans on the Church owning property or being involved in education and politics, and on priests wearing clerical garb in public. Then, in 1992, Mexico re-established diplomatic relations with the Vatican. These changes are generally popular, with more than 90 percent of the country expressing allegiance to the Church.

The emblem of the country's patron saint, the Virgin of Guadalupe, has been used as a battle symbol in popular uprisings ever since 1810, and her image is to be seen in every home, factory and vehicle across the land. The power of the Church in Mexico is dormant, like the snow-capped volcanoes towering over Mexico City.

Not so that of the trade unions, who are officially part of the PRI. They are in a strong position to enforce the demands of organized labor, often against the wishes of the government and indeed the majority of people. One of the first acts of the Salinas presidency was a crackdown on union violence and corruption in the oil industry, to almost universal approval. The disappointment is that this was not followed up by further significant reforms; but, with the unions forming a fundamental part of the PRI system, this was no cause of surprise.

On the other hand, the government has confronted the unions by privatizing the nationalized industries they dominate, in most cases by direct sale to large private industrial groupings. These combines, based in the north, have historically complained much of the taxation, expropriations and barriers to investment imposed by the government in the south. But now they have decisively won the argument, with the government lifting numerous controls and committed to pursuing Mexico's membership of NAFTA, the North American Free Trade Agreement with the US and Canada.

At the same time, the so-called "*maquiladora*" industries along the US border have boomed, importing raw materials and parts for assembly into finished products for re-export, using cheap Mexican labor and escaping from the unions, costly health-and-safety regulations, and troublesome US environmental controls. The sector now accounts for a quarter of Mexico's manufacturing exports and employs half a million people. A similar boom is taking place in the agro-export sector, as out-of-season fruits, vegetables and flowers are flown or trucked up to the US from corporate farms; and investment from multinational food-processing corporations is now creating a new *"agro-maquila"* sector.

Increasingly, therefore, the north of the country is identifying its interests with the US. Here and in the southern US a new Anglo–Hispanic society seems to be emerging, encouraged by the massive flow of goods and people across the frontier, both legal and illegal. Many Mexicans regard the flow of illegal emigration northward as Mexico's answer to the land lost to the US in 1848 — an invasion without armies. Interestingly, many of those working in the US are indigenous people, for example Mixtecs and Nahuas, who are learning English without ever having spoken Spanish, and who are now preserving their culture and language in the suburbs of Los Angeles, Chicago and New York.

The modern industrial boom in Mexico was made possible by the discovery of huge oil reserves. Ironically, this good fortune was a significant factor in bringing about the financial crisis of 1982, when Mexico's $86 billion foreign debt was for a short time the largest in the world, and Mexico went into default on $24 billion of capital and interest repayments. The combined evils of falling oil prices, widespread corruption, excessive public expenditure, protectionism and runaway inflation led to a drastic drop in the value of the peso. Things were not helped by the widespread disillusionment with politicians and public officials, generally perceived as being ineffective and concerned solely with personal gain, from the humblest clerk right up to the president of the time himself.

López Portillo's successor, Harvard-educated President Miguel de la Madrid, was elected in 1982 and instituted harsh austerity programs. But the downturn in world markets and the severe economic effects of the 1985 earthquake prevented any real recovery.

More recently, President Salinas de Gortari won widespread international approval for his free-market reforms, winning new loans and debt renegotiation. He has been successful: debt has been stabilized at around $100 billion, business is booming, and the peso has settled at roughly three to the dollar. But he is far from having swept out the Aegean stables he inherited, and many of the most fundamental and long-term problems of Mexico are not merely unsolved but have been exacerbated.

For example, population: where Mexico had 30 million people in 1950, more than 100 million are projected for the year 2000. The combination of population growth and the neglect of subsistence agriculture has resulted in the phenomenal expansion of cities, now home to 75 percent of Mexicans as against 40 percent in 1950, most of whom live without piped water or sewers. So, even while the rate of population increase has been brought down to under 2 percent, from 3.5 percent in the 1960s, it still outstrips economic growth, not to mention the capacity of the environment to sustain more than a million new people a year.

In environmental terms, there is little scope for optimism. Control over polluting industries and the disposal of hazardous wastes is almost nonexistent. Water supplies are both over-exploited and contaminated with industrial waste and raw sewage. Mexico is the most deforested country in Latin America: 98 percent of its tropical jungles are already lost, and 1.5 million acres of all types of forest are destroyed every year; unfortunately, Mexico is unable to protect even most of its national parks.

Even as Mexico becomes a proportionally more urban country, actual numbers in the countryside continue to rise, putting extra pressure on the land. In the absence of investment in sustainable farming, the rivers run with mud every rainy season, and nearly one million acres of agricultural land and pasture are rendered unproductive every year. In the closing decade of the century, the prospect of effective solutions to these problems, which must ultimately determine the future of Mexico, appears increasingly remote.

A nation of vast inequalities, looking over the edge of an environmental and demographic abyss, may not seem the obvious choice for a vacation. But Mexico still has some of the planet's most stupendously beautiful scenery and some of its last true wildernesses, from the stark vastness of the Baja California deserts, to the cloud-forests of the Sierra Madre Sur. Their very size and remoteness has preserved some of these places. Others hang by a thread.

Mexico still has thousands of solid reminders of its Pre-Hispanic peoples, in the ruined temples, pyramids and cities that dot every part of the country, in the wealth of art and sculpture housed in the museums of Mexico City. Despite hundreds of years of massacres, enslavement and brutality, the rich indigenous heritage is a tangible underpinning to the structure of a pulsating modern society. And, in glorious defiance of its sorrowful history, Mexico is the country of *tacos* and tequila, of *machismo* and *mariachis,* where every minor saint's day is an excuse for a fiesta, a joyous explosion of color and fun.

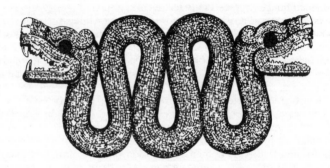

Aztec pectoral ornament, inlaid with turquoise,
in the form of a double-headed serpent.

Culture, history and background

Landmarks in Mexico's history

c.30000BC: The first men to enter the Americas cross the Bering Straits from Siberia and spread s in search of game. **c.2500BC**: Cultivation of corn, enabling evolution to more settled societies.

THE PRE-CLASSIC ERA *(c.1500-c.200BC)*

c.1000BC: Flowering of Olmec civilization in se of Mexico. Trade and war carry their culture and religion throughout Mesoamerica. **c.800BC**: Under Olmec influence, the agricultural communities of the Valley of Mexico grow more sophisticated, developing the Tlatilco culture.

c.700BC: The Izapa culture develops in the jungles of modern Guatemala under Olmec influence. **c.400BC**: Violent destruction of the Olmec capital of La Venta; gradual disappearance of the Olmecs. Some possibly migrate to Monte Albán in the Valley of Oaxaca, where a powerful Pre-Zapotec culture is emerging.

THE CLASSIC ERA *(c.200BC-c.AD900)*

Characterized by the blossoming of minor Pre-Classic cultures into major urban civilizations. The two most important are the Teotihuacán culture of the Valley of Mexico and the brilliant Maya culture, which starts in the jungles of Central America and spreads to the Yucatán.

c.300AD: The highly centralized Teotihuacán state reaches the height of its power, with trading colonies as far s as modern Guatemala. Its influence has been traced in the Totonacs of the Gulf, the Zapotecs of Oaxaca, the cultures of the w and even the Maya farther s.

c.600-c.900: The collapse of Teotihuacán and the end of its predominance. Civil unrest, soil exhaustion, plague, drought and barbarian invasion from the N all appear to play a part. During the next 300 years all the Classic civilizations collapse. The Maya civilization of the Mesoamerican rainforest is no exception, but the loss is far from complete as the focus of Maya culture shifts N to the Yucatán peninsula.

THE POST-CLASSIC ERA *(c.900-1521)*

Repeated barbarian invasion from the N and the adoption of civilized ways by the invaders lead to the growth of new cultures. The most important of these is the civilization of the warlike Toltecs, who dominate the Valley of Mexico from their capital of Tula. In the se, the outstandingly artistic Mixtecs supplant the Zapotecs.

c.980: Occupation of the Yucatán peninsula by Toltecs, and spread of the cult of Quetzalcóatl, the Plumed Serpent. This leads to the birth of a new Toltec–Maya culture known as the Itzá.

1168: Tula destroyed by marauders from the N, followed by the dispersal of the Toltecs. Coincidentally, it is also in this year that the Aztec (or Mexica) tribe are thought to have left their unknown island home in search of a new capital, to be pointed out to them by their gods.

1345: After nearly two centuries of wandering, the Aztecs settle in their city of Tenochtitlán in the swamps of the Valley of Mexico. It rapidly becomes the center of a powerful trading empire, exacting tribute from coast to coast and from as far s as the Valley of Oaxaca.

1492: Christopher Columbus discovers the New World. **1512–18**: Spanish explorers from Cuba reconnoiter the coast of the Yucatán and the Gulf of Mexico. **1519**: Hernán Cortés lands near modern Veracruz on April 21, with artillery, horses and some 500 soldiers. He capitalizes on resentment of the Aztecs to recruit first the local Totonacs and later, after some resistance, the Tlaxcalans, in his march on Tenochtitlán. Cortés enters the city peacefully on November 12, but imprisons the Emperor Moctezuma. Resistance is tempered by the widespread belief among the Aztecs that he is the reincarnation of the god Quetzalcóatl.

1520: Cortés leaves Tenochtitlán to defeat a rival expedition led by Diego Velasquez, and returns to find his garrison under Aztec attack. He manages to reunite his forces, but after a month the Spaniards are forced to flee; in the fight to escape, many are killed and much treasure is lost.

1521: After a three-month siege, Cortés regains Tenochtitlán from the Aztecs, decimated by famine and European diseases. The city is razed, its people killed or enslaved. Conquest of Central Mexico quickly follows.

THE COLONIAL ERA *(1521-1821)*

1522: Cortés appointed ruler of "New Spain" by Carlos V. Reconstruction of Tenochtitlán starts, under the new name of México. **1524**: Franciscan friars arrive to evangelize the native peoples, followed by the Augustinians and Dominicans. New Spain is soon covered with monasteries and missions. **1535**: The first Spanish Viceroy reaches Mexico.

1598: With the colonization of New Mexico complete, all of modern Mexico and much of the southern US is now under Spanish rule. The native population is used as slave labor on the vast estates and in the mines. For two centuries, there is little change in the status quo, and the Spanish settlers grow rich and keep the native population in subjugation.

1808: Bonaparte's invasion of Spain sparks off rebellion of Creoles (Mexican-born Spaniards) against Spanish rule, which is crushed. **1810**: Inspired by the American War of Independence and the French Revolution, a group of Creoles plots another rebellion, led by Father Miguel Hidalgo, a priest, and Ignacio Allende, an officer in the royalist army. On September 16, Hidalgo delivers the *grito* (call to arms) at Dolores Hidalgo. Guanajuato and San Miguel are soon taken and sacked; uprising spreads.

1811: Royalist forces defeat Hidalgo, who is executed. José Mariá Morelos continues the struggle. **1813**: Morelos declares independence at Congress of Chilpancingo. **1815**: Morelos defeated and executed.

1821: Former royalist officer, Agustín de Iturbide, proclaims Constitution of Iguala, offering peace to Spain and freedom to all. On August 24, Treaty of Córdoba is signed, confirming Mexican independence.

THE ERA OF INTERVENTIONS *(1821-1914)*

1822: Iturbide proclaimed Emperor of Mexico. US citizens given permission to settle in Texas. **1823**: Iturbide forced to resign, and eventually executed by soldiers of ambitious young general Santa Ana.

1824: New constitution declares Mexico a federal republic, under the presidency of former soldier Guadalupe Victoria. **1829**: A small Spanish army arrives on the Gulf coast, intending to repeat Cortés' success, but is defeated at Tampico by Santa Ana. **1831**: Santa Ana becomes President.

1836: American colonists in Texas rebel; after an initial Mexican success at the Alamo, Santa Ana is captured at the Battle of San Jacinto and forced to recognize Texan independence. **1838**: As a result of indignities suffered by French citizens in Mexico, the French mount a brief punitive expedition, in the course of which Santa Ana loses a leg.

1845: Texas annexed by US. **1846**: US declares war on Mexico. **1847**: Mexico defeated at Angostura. US Army arrives in Veracruz and takes Mexico City. **1848**: Mexico cedes the states of Arizona, California, Nevada, New Mexico, Utah and part of Colorado to the US in exchange for $15 million.

1855: Final fall of Santa Ana, followed by the election of President Comonfort, committed to change Mexican society by reducing the power of the Church and the military. **1858**: Comonfort is overthrown by conservatives who have taken Mexico City. A civil war between conservatives and reformist liberals ensues. **1860**: The liberal Benito Juárez triumphs, and becomes Mexico's first Indian President. **1861**: Juárez is at once faced with a massive foreign debt, and suspension of payments leads to a military intervention in Veracruz by Spain, Great Britain and France.

1862: Alarmed by France's warlike stance, the Spanish and the British withdraw their troops. On May 5, a French army is defeated at Puebla. **1863**: A reinforced French army takes Mexico City, and the Imperial Crown of Mexico is given to Maximilian, Archduke of Austria and a cousin of the French Emperor Napoleon III. **1866**: French troops withdraw to face the Prussian threat in Europe. Benito Juárez resumes government.

1867: Maximilian captured and executed at Querétaro. **1872**: Death of Juárez. **1876**: Juárez's popular general, Porfirio Díaz, takes over, apparently committed to democratic rule. However, he amends the constitution and rules for 34 years, with one short break (1880–84). He encourages foreign investment, and brings an industrial infrastructure to the country. However one percent of the people gain control of 70 percent of all land, and the lower classes get poorer.

1910–11: Mexican Revolution begins as Díaz is overthrown by the idealistic reformer Francisco Madero, aided by revolutionary armies of Emiliano Zapata in the s and Pancho Villa in the n. Díaz is exiled to France, and Madero becomes President. **1913**: Madero fails to carry out promised land reforms and is murdered by General Huerta, who proclaims himself

President. He is at once opposed by the "Constitutionalist" armies of Zapata, Villa, Venustiano Carranza and Alvaro Obregón.

1914: Brief American intervention in Veracruz to cut off Huerta's arms supply. Huerta is defeated, and Venustiano Carranza becomes President with US support. Zapata and Villa continue to fight for land reforms, but many of their followers revert to banditry.

THE MODERN ERA

1917: The Constitution of Querétaro is enacted, strongly anticlerical and promising labor and land reforms. Carranza remains President. **1919**: Carranza arranges Zapata's assassination. **1920**: Carranza is assassinated on orders from Obregón. Villa ends his rebellion. Obregón assumes the presidency, instigating only limited reforms. **1923**: Pancho Villa assassinated by unknown gunmen.

1927: Popular religious uprising led by the "Cristeros" ("Christians") is savagely repressed by the anticlerical government of Plutarco Calles. **1929**: The National Revolutionary Party, the forerunner of the PRI, is founded. **1934**: The first large-scale land reforms are carried out by the new President, Lazaro Cárdenas. **1938**: Nationalization of the oil industry; US imposes economic sanctions. **1942**: Mexico enters World War II on the side of the Allies, but takes little part.

1946: Election of President Miguel Alemán. Redistribution of land continues, accompanied by rapid industrial growth. The PRI assumes its present name. **1954**: Women win the vote.

1968: Social unrest. Suppression of student protest: hundreds killed by the army in the "Tlatelolco massacre" in Mexico City before the Olympic Games. **1970**: Luis Echeverría becomes President, with a policy of inward investment and closed markets. **1976**: President López Portillo elected at a time of record oil revenues. However over-borrowing, economic mismanagement and large-scale corruption hinder development and create the debt crisis. **1980**: López Portillo keeps Mexico out of GATT, the General Agreement on Tariffs and Trade.

1981: Oil prices collapse. **1982**: Mexico defaults on its foreign debts, López Portillo nationalizes the banks in response to speculation against the peso. The newly elected President de la Madrid institutes a program of national austerity in response to the foreign debt crisis. **1985**: Mexico City hit by massive earthquake. Tourism not seriously affected, but long term economic damage caused. **1986**: World Cup in Mexico City. Mexico joins GATT.

1987: Economy remains weak; Mexico and US sign trade agreement. Serious divisions surface within the PRI, and Cuauhtémoc Cárdenas leaves the PRI to contest the forthcoming election. **1988**: Carlos Salinas de Gortari becomes President, with smallest ever electoral majority, barely in excess of 50 percent, and widespread electoral fraud. Generally accepted that Cárdenas is the rightful winner.

1989: Economy and peso stabilize, but declining living standards and democratic aspirations cause continuing challenges to political orthodoxy; widespread political violence erupts in areas of declining PRI support. Cárdenas founds the Party of Democratic Revolution (PRD).

1990: Banco de México successfully renegotiates much of its foreign debt, but resulting strength of peso undermines competitiveness of exports. Presidents Bush and Salinas commence free-trade negotiations. Reformist movement within the PRI gains strength. **1991**: PRI restores its standing in mid-term elections. Constitutional constraints on Catholic Church relaxed. Canada, the US and Mexico join in talks for the North American Free Trade Agreement (NAFTA). Privatization of state assets gives Mexico its first ever budget surplus.

1992: Article 27 constitutional reforms passed, permitting the breakup of *ejido* communal farms into private holdings. Mexico remains committed to NAFTA, but reservations emerge in US. **1993**: Accession of US President Clinton puts stumbling block on NAFTA progress; US concern mounts as Far Eastern investment floods into Mexico to establish bridgehead for US markets. The New Peso is issued, knocking three zeros off the old, devalued currency. Presidential elections scheduled for **1994**.

Who's who in Mexico

This list represents just some of the key figures in Mexican history. See also ART AND ARCHITECTURE, on pages 26-39, and the INDEX.

Alemán, Miguel *(1900-83)*
President from 1946–52, in a period of spectacular economic growth. Despite major public works, his regime's suppression of workers' movements and the spread of corruption alienated popular support.

Allende, Ignacio *(1769-1811)*
A nationalist hero, he left the Spanish Royal Army to join the rebellion of 1810. As General of Hidalgo's army he achieved some important victories, but was eventually captured and executed near Chihuahua.

Cabrera, Miguel *(1695-1768)*
The best-known painter of the colonial era, born an Indian peasant. His religious works are in churches all over Mexico.

Cárdenas, Cuauhtémoc *(1934-)*
The son of Lázaro Cárdenas, and the leader of the social-democratic opposition in Mexico. Having risen through the PRI, he hoped to be chosen as the 1988 presidential candidate, but was passed over in favor of Salinas de Gortari. After losing the election, in which he is widely believed to have won the most votes, he founded the Democratic Revolutionary Party (PRD).

Cárdenas, Lázaro *(1895-1970)*
Perhaps the only post-1917 president to effect both economic success and the reformist principles of the Revolution. During his Presidency (1934–40) he initiated the first agrarian reforms, covering 49 million acres, and the nationalization of the foreign oil companies.

Carranza, Venustiano *(1859-1920)*
A shrewd politician who emerged from the internal fighting following the 1910 Revolution to become president in 1914. War between the

former revolutionary comrades continued, and he was assassinated in 1920. He is still regarded as one of the fathers of modern Mexico.

Cortés, Hernán *(1485-1547)*

The leader of the small band of Spanish adventurers who landed in Mexico in 1519. By a combination of luck, guile, skill, ruthlessness and great courage, they subjected the powerful native civilizations to the Spanish crown within three years. Cortés died in Spain, but his remains were brought to Mexico in accordance with his wishes.

De las Casas, Bartolomé *(1474-1566)*

A leading Spanish churchman, who by simple Christian example achieved the peaceful conquest of many Indian tribes. In 1544 he became Bishop of Chiapas, where he was shocked by the brutal treatment of the Indians by the Spanish. Returning to Spain, he championed their cause at court, eventually persuading the king to grant them certain civil rights.

De la Madrid, Miguel *(1934-)*

A brilliant Harvard-trained administrator, President of Mexico from 1982–88. He instituted a program of austerity to deal with Mexico's massive foreign debt, but with limited success.

De Quiroga, Vasco *(1470-1565)*

The first bishop of Michoacán, he saw the suffering of the Indians as analogous to those of Christ, and made great efforts to defend them from exploitation. In each village of his see, he encouraged the development of a different craft. Many still thrive.

Díaz, Porfirio *(1830-1915)*

A popular general under Juárez, he took power in 1877 after a succession of short-lived governments. He ruled, with one brief break, until the 1910 Revolution, bringing stability and an industrial infrastructure to Mexico, but dividing the country: the wealthy and powerful thrived, but the common people suffered cuts in income and the expropriation of lands. In recent years there have been attempts by the government to emphasize his positive achievements.

Hidalgo, Father Miguel *(1753-1811)*

A philanthropic and learned parish priest, who became the leader of the 1810 rebellion against Spanish rule when he gave the famous *grito* (call to arms) at Dolores Hidalgo. Captured and executed in 1811, he is regarded as the "Father of Independence."

Iturbide, Agustín *(1783-1824)*

An ambitious and opportunistic soldier, who led royalist armies against the 1810 revolutionaries. In 1821, he proposed the Plan of Iguala for Mexican Independence, and signed the Treaty of Córdoba by which Spain recognized the new nation. He was then proclaimed Emperor of Mexico, but was later executed by General Santa Ana.

Juárez, Benito *(1806-72)*

The first Indian president, often known as "Mexico's Abraham Lincoln." His greatest achievement was the overthrow of the interventionist French regime of 1861-67. Despite good intentions, the troubled state of the country prevented him from carrying out his proposed social and land reforms.

Madero, Francisco *(1873-1913)*
A mild idealist, who led the 1910 Revolution against the iron rule of Porfirio Díaz. After becoming president, he proved incapable of controlling the country and was murdered by his former colleague, General Huerta.

Maximilian of Hapsburg *(1832-67)*
A cousin of Napoleon III, Emperor of France. After the French intervention of 1861, he was made Emperor of Mexico, but when the French troops were withdrawn to meet the Prussian threat, he was defeated and executed by Benito Juárez.

Moctezuma *(1480-1520)*
Moctezuma, the penultimate Aztec emperor, began his career as a great warrior general. However, by the time of the arrival of Cortés (see page 24), he had grown weak, timid and indecisive, and allowed the Spanish to occupy Mexico and take him prisoner. He was killed by an unknown assailant in the *"noche triste"* Aztec uprising of 1520.

Morelos y Pavón, José María *(1765-1815)*
A revolutionary priest who joined Hidalgo's uprising of 1810. He led an insurgent army in the south of the country, and became a martyr of Independence when captured and shot.

Netzahualcoyotl *(1402-72)*
The enlightened and humane poet-king of the Pre-Hispanic kingdom of Texcoco. He was a legal and social reformer, but is best remembered for his poems, which stress the beauty of life and the inevitability of death.

Paz, Octavio *(1914-)*
Mexico's foremost man of letters and poet laureate; his works have been widely translated and have won international awards. His best-known work is a penetrating prose study of the Mexican mind, entitled *The Labyrinth of Solitude*.

Salinas de Gortari, Carlos *(1948-)*
Mexico's president since 1988, a US-trained technocrat and a vigorous free-market reformer. His rule has marked a decisive shift in the whole direction of government, from left-wing nationalism to neoliberalism reminiscent of that of Ronald Reagan or Margaret Thatcher.

Villa, Pancho *(1878-1923)*
A sadistic but charismatic bandit who rose to fame as leader of a 1910 revolutionary army in the north of Mexico. After victory was achieved he attempted to seize power, and continued his career of looting and terrorism until bribed into submission. He was eventually assassinated to prevent further revolts.

Zapata, Emiliano *(1879-1919)*
The most famous and flamboyant of all the 1910 revolutionaries, and Mexico's great champion of land reform, Zapata, a peasant from Morelos, led a victorious army in the south. The violence of his followers and his radical idealism were troublesome to President Carranza, who ordered his assassination. His name, which is revered among the impoverished peasantry of the south, is still a potent symbol of popular protest.

Art and architecture

It may not often seem so to the traveler, but the similarities and continuity between the various Mesoamerican civilizations are much more important than the differences. The common trends and the continuous cultural, military and trading links that emerge from the thousands of years of Pre-Hispanic history have been amply demonstrated by archeological evidence. Common to all were the sacred ball game, human sacrifice, gods (under different names) and the framework of religious belief, the construction of ceremonial pyramids, hierarchical social organization, and the cultivation of corn as a staple crop.

All the Mesoamerican cities on which kingdoms were based were in fact ceremonial centers for the complex, animistic religions; these religions dominated all artistic achievement, and also governed many aspects of everyday life, leading to a highly regimented totalitarian society.

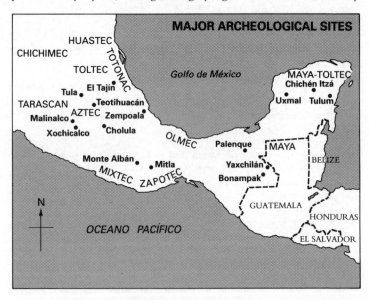

The rulers were priest-kings, and beneath them was a strict hierarchy, a system that blocked innovation and social, artistic and technological evolution, but also gave potters, metalworkers and sculptors the chance to develop their skills, freed of the need to grow or gather their own food.

In ancient Mesoamerica, art was highly circumscribed by convention and ceremonial function, yet that imaginative self-expression that characterizes art in the modern sense emerges with a surprising frequency, especially in informal ceramic works, resulting in many wonderful pieces.

Yet in the long term, development was slow and mainly confined to style and elaborate decoration, while the underlying technologies remained stagnant over centuries. This is true of metalworking, for example, and of building: while the Pre-Hispanic Maya sculptors and stonemasons carved extraordinary *stelae* and built colossal pyramids, they never discovered the true arch. It is intriguing to consider the architectural possibilities that the arch, the technological breakthrough behind the European cathedrals, could have opened up if discovered by the builders of Palenque.

Innovation is a product of the inventive individual in a society that is ready to accept change; the nonindividualistic, largely static societies of Mesoamerica failed to provide the soil in which the seed of innovation could take root and flourish. This failure not only limited the achievements of Mesoamerican civilizations, but may be seen as one of the reasons for their collapse when confronted with a wholly new challenge — the devious, adaptable and ever-inventive Europeans.

The three main periods are the **Pre-Classic era** (c.1500–c.200BC), when urban culture developed; the **Classic era** (c.200BC–c.AD900), the golden age of powerful theocratic civilizations; and the **Post-Classic era** (c.900–1521), a more troubled and militaristic age, although not deficient in artistic achievement.

Three distinct areas are of major importance: the Valley of Mexico; the Valley of Oaxaca; and the southeast, including the Yucatán peninsula and most of modern Guatemala. Farther from the influence of the great cities are the two coasts of Central Mexico, and the northern states.

THE PRE-CLASSIC ERA

The **Olmecs** from the Gulf coast dominate Pre-Classic art. Little is known of their origins or language, but it is certain that they were the first Mesoamerican people to build pyramid bases for temples, to work precious stones, to carve large stone altars, sculptures and *stelae* (low-relief tablets), and to evolve a calendar system.

From the symbolism of their art it would seem that they were a religious people, with the **jaguar-god** prominent. The most famous Olmec art form is the **giant monolithic head**, often mingling the features of a jaguar with a human face, typically with the negroid features that have led to speculation about the origins of the Olmecs (see illustration in VILLAHERMOSA on page 273).

They also produced **miniature carvings** of exquisite beauty in jade and other precious stones, matching the work of any later Classic civilization for sophistication. Architecturally, the Olmecs were

Miniature of the
Olmec Jaguar God

less advanced. Like most other Pre-Classic civilizations, their pyramids were simply mounds of earth faced with loose stone or adobe blocks.

With the discovery of major Pre-Classic Maya sites such as **El Mirador** near Guatemala's northern frontier with Mexico, the distinction between the **Maya Classic** and Pre-Classic becomes somewhat blurred. The Maya are now known to have created complex societies and ceremonial centers at a far earlier date than previously imagined, around 500BC, although the use of commemorative *stelae* and hieroglyphs is thought to have been a later phenomenon.

The other Pre-Classic civilizations remained at the village stage. Little more than pottery survives of their art, as they generally worked in

perishable materials and not in stone. Some of this pottery, although technically crude, shows imagination and even humor — especially fine are the **Tlatilco Venuses** (pictured left), plump but graceful ladies from the Valley of Mexico, now in the MUSEO NACIONAL DE ANTROPOLOGÍA in Mexico City. Pre-Classic pottery deals with all aspects of daily life but rarely with religion, which at this period lacked the all-embracing importance it had in later cultures.

The Pre-Classic pottery style developed furthest along the west coast, in modern Colima and Nayarit, where figurines of great realism were produced. However, these cultures of the west remained essentially Pre-Classic in character throughout the Classic era, despite some adoption of techniques such as stone-working, and this style is known as "**Evolved Pre-Classic**."

Tlatilco Venus

THE CLASSIC ERA

Teotihuacán

The main Classic civilization of the Valley of Mexico was based at an enormous ceremonial center outside Mexico City. Traces of its artistic influence are found throughout Mesoamerica.

The architecture of Teotihuacán itself is on a massive scale. The main **pyramids** have stepped sloping sides, but many of the surrounding buildings are constructed on the *talud y tablero* principle of **stepped terraces**, with stucco reliefs, murals, and carved heads of gods and animals, all showing a high level of craftsmanship. The murals are not preoccupied with the violence and sacrifice associated with later cultures. The religious symbolism, rather, revolves around the rain-god **Tlaloc** and the peaceful, plumed serpent-god, later known as **Quetzalcóatl**.

Early Teotihuacán **pottery** resembles Pre-Classic work; but later on, the figurines become more individualized, often wearing tall feather headdresses. Functional pottery vessels become fine and delicate, decorated with fresco painting or with intricate inlaid glazing; the predominant colors are red and green, with designs mostly resembling those of the mural paintings.

Perhaps the finest artistic products of Teotihuacán are the beautifully inlaid **masks** of stone, using such precious materials as jade, mother-of-pearl and garnet, which were probably used as death masks (pictured right). Their restrained and powerful creativity place them among the highest achievements of Mesoamerican art.

Teotihuacán **funerary mask**, inlaid with jade

The Zapotecs

From their great hilltop city at **Monte Albán**, the Zapotecs dominated the Valley of Oaxaca during the Classic era. Their art and architecture show the influence of Teotihuacán, of the Olmecs, and of the Maya.

The architecture is austere and well-ordered, using columns to create large internal spaces. The famous **low-relief panels** of Monte Albán are probably of Pre-Zapotec origin, and show Olmec influence; the Zapotec **calendar glyphs** (symbols) on them were added later date. These glyphs are found on *stelae* and murals throughout the Zapotec area, for the calendar was central to their religion. The best Zapotec murals are found in tombs and resemble those of Teotihuacán in subject matter and style.

The Zapotecs were superb potters; even functional items were decorated with intricately modeled or incised motifs. More interesting still are the ornamental and ritual vessels, which were developed into a unique and accomplished art form. They are incorrectly known as **funerary urns**; although usually found in tombs, their actual purpose is unknown.

A typical urn has only a small receptacle and is in the form of a god, sometimes the rain-god Tlaloc (known here as Cocijo) whose clothing, jewelry and headdresses are shown in superb detail. These urns (see picture, right) are by far the most intricate product of Mesoamerican ceramic art.

Zapotec ceramic urn, in the form of a goddess

The Maya

The Maya culture was spread across a large area, including the Yucatán peninsula and much of the Central American rainforests and highlands. Although its development was parallel to the other Classic civilizations, it was more directly derived from the Olmec culture, but subject to influences from Teotihuacán and Tula in Central Mexico. The Maya built well over a hundred large ceremonial centers linked by a network of wide causeways of crushed limestone, and countless smaller centers. They were much the most advanced Mesoamerican culture, in mathematics, astronomy, calendrical computation, and architecture.

Architecture, their greatest art, developed regional variations over the large area of Maya culture. There are three main building types: the **pyramid**, usually steeper than those of Central Mexico, with a stone temple and roof-comb at the summit; the **palace**, consisting of chambers around courts; and the **ball-court**, for playing the sacred ball game.

The original Maya style, the "**Petén**," after the region of modern Guatemala in which the civilization reached its greatest peak, is characterized by especially steep pyramids, low-relief decoration on all wall surfaces, and extensive use of corbel vaulting and the "**Maya arch**," with sloping sides and a lintel. It is also in the Petén area that the finest sculptured *stelae* are to be found. It is now clear that the great temples and pyramids were erected to the glory of warrior kings whose histories are related in the hieroglyphs.

Pyramid of the Inscriptions, at the
Maya city of **Palenque**, unusual in
having a burial chamber inside.

Simultaneously, in the Yucatán, the "**Puuc**" style developed. This was distinguished by its more elaborate facades, decorated with stone and stucco masks; palaces often had two stories, with great monumental doorways. If this was the Maya Baroque, then the later "**Chenes**" and "**Río Bec**" styles of the south were the Maya Churrigueresque. The graceful proportions of the "Puuc" are completely lost under great masses of ornamentation, in a way strangely reminiscent of the proportions of 17thC Mexican churches.

Of other Maya art forms, the *códices*, painted scrolls with hieroglyphic writing, were almost all destroyed by the Spaniards, who thought them the Devil's work. The few *códices* that survive have only recently been deciphered by teams of Mexican and US scholars, and one of the best-known Maya writings, the *Popol Vuh,* only survives in Western script. (An English edition is available.)

Weaving is one craft that has survived centuries of cultural assault, especially in the Maya highlands of Chiapas and Guatemala. Many designs and motifs in everyday use represent a direct heritage from Pre-Hispanic times.

Like the Olmecs, the Maya were skilled jade workers, and also bone engravers. Functional pottery was decorated with stylized painted and appliquéd motifs. In some areas the art of **figurine modeling** reached great heights of realism, despite the predominance of symbolism and ritualism; the finest figurines come from the island of **Jaina** off the coast of Campeche. The same realistic tendency is found in some mural painting; the famous **murals of Bonampak**, in particular, must rank among the world's great works of art.

The Gulf coast

After the dispersal of the Olmecs, the Gulf area lost its importance. In Classic times, the central Gulf was occupied by a people referred to as the **Totonacs**, although it is not known whether they spoke the Totonac language now used in this area. Farther north lived the **Huastecs**, believed by some to be an isolated branch of the Maya.

The Totonac pyramids were unique in their construction, using rows of niches in place of the usual vertical panels. The finest of the Totonac sites is at **El Tajín**, in the state of Veracruz (see the illustration of the **Pyramid of the Niches**, on page 126). The Totonacs were also accomplished potters; but their most notable art forms were the strange "yokes," "palmate stones" and "votive axes," of smooth, sculpted stone with incised designs; no convincing explanation has been given for their use, and the names are speculative, but the designs show a consummate blend of realism and abstraction.

Maya temple in the older part of Chichén Itzá, known to the Spanish as **La Iglesia** ("The Church"), although its true purpose remains unknown.

Much of the southern Gulf Coast was occupied during the late Classic period by the **Chontal** or **Putun Maya**, who traded with the Yucatán, Oaxaca and Central Mexico. One theory is that their northward expansion around AD800 helped to introduce Central Mexican traits into cities of the northern lowlands such as **Uxmal** and **Chichén Itzá**. Their southerly expansion may also have been a trigger for the collapse of the Classic centers of the Petén, a theory based on archeological evidence from sites along the Usumacinta river.

THE POST-CLASSIC ERA

The Toltecs

After the decline of the great Classic civilizations, the Toltecs were among the first invading tribes to settle in the Valley of Mexico. Although they assumed many of the civilized customs and the religion of their predecessors, the emphasis of Toltec culture was more violent and militaristic. The Tula economy appears to have been based on the far-reaching trade in green obsidian, of which they controlled important sources.

Toltec architecture is less impressive than that of Teotihuacán, but in comparison is innovative in its complex planning and use of columns. The decoration of the buildings — murals, carvings and low-reliefs — is highly accomplished. Typical themes are eagles and jaguars representing the two military orders, human sacrifice, processions of warriors, and plumed serpents; this last symbolizes here a more malevolent aspect of Quetzalcóatl, as one who demanded continual human sacrifice. The

Toltec *Chac-mool*,
Chichén Itzá

dominant image in their sculpture is the warrior, of which the best examples are the four vast **atlantes** (spear-throwers) on the Temple of the Morning Star at their capital of TULA (see illustration on page 93). Another typical form is the *chac-mool*, the reclining figure with a receptacle for sacrificial offerings (a much-photographed example, from Chichén Itzá, is pictured left). Examples of this figure have been found all over Mesoamerica, indicating widespread Toltec influence.

The Toltecs were among the first cultures to start working precious metals, and were probably skilled engravers of jade and precious and semiprecious stones; however, little of their jewelry has been found. Toltec pottery, with the exception of some very fine hollow **figurines** of the gods, is functional and uninteresting.

The Maya–Toltecs

After the fall of Tula in 1168, a group, probably of Toltec origin, known as the **Itzá**, migrated to the Yucatán peninsula. Their new skills and knowledge were the impetus for a revival of the declining Maya culture.

Although they appear to have come as conquerors, the "**Itzá Renaissance**" that resulted is a genuine fusion of Maya and Toltec traditions, best represented by their capital, Chichén Itzá. All the main themes of Toltec architecture are present in the buildings here, and the decoration is similarly military. At the same time, the use of such Maya techniques as **arch and corbel vaulting**, and the workmanship itself, leaves no doubt that the craftsmen were Maya, directed, perhaps, by a ruling Itzá warrior-class.

In many ways the Maya–Toltec civilization offers us little of interest. For example, the murals, although energetic and vivid, do not rival those of the Classic Maya, and very little of note has been found in the way of pottery. **Metalworking**, on the other hand, became highly advanced; especially fine are the *repoussé* gold discs found at the bottom of the sacred well or *cenote* at Chichén Itzá.

Maya–Toltec culture fell into decadence about a century before the arrival of the Spaniards, and subsequent artistic production was negligible. By the time of the Conquest, most of the large ceremonial centers had long since been abandoned, and the flame of Maya culture had retreated to lesser centers such as **Mayapan** and **Tulum**.

The Mixtecs

Simultaneously, a mountain tribe called the Mixtecs established dominance over the Zapotecs in the Valley of Oaxaca, and across a large area to the north, including much of the modern state of Puebla. Mixtec craftsmanship was unequaled in such fields as metalwork, pottery, carving, and hieroglyphic scroll painting *(códices)*. The best finds of Mixtec work come from the tombs of **Monte Albán**, where the treasures include jade and crystal statues, mosaics of semiprecious stones, and exquisite gold and silver jewelry cast by the "lost wax" method.

Mixtec architecture is known for large areas of **geometric decoration**, using thousands of small carved stones. The later Zapotecs adopted this technique, under Mixtec direction, for the famous palaces of **Mitla** (see illustration on page 156).

Mixtec polychrome pottery was so highly prized that it is found all over Mesoamerica. It has elegant and restrained forms, with stylized religious themes for decoration.

The Purépecha (Tarascans)

In western Mexico, the Pre-Classic styles followed an independent evolution throughout the Classic period, reaching a level of considerable sophistication. In the Post-Classic era, there was a minor flowering of the Purépecha culture in the area around Lake Patzcuaro. Although only semiurbanized, the Purépecha became expert metalworkers and potters rivaled only by the Mixtecs. The art of the **feather mosaic** was also developed here, and these works were highly valued by the Aztecs; unfortunately no examples survive.

The Aztecs

In the early 15thC, the Mexica, a semibarbaric Nahua tribe, achieved social and political dominance in the Valley of Mexico. The influence on the Mexica (or Aztecs), of their predecessors, the Toltecs, was strong, as was that of their neighbors such as the Mixtecs. All of these elements they combined in a new and dynamic way, but sadly, of all the cultures thriving at the time of the Conquest, the art of the Aztecs suffered the greatest destruction by the Spanish.

The general appearance of Aztec architecture was massive and somber, with palaces and very steep **pyramids** similar to the early "Puuc" Maya style, although larger. The decoration, with the insistent themes of war and sacrifice, is more reminiscent of the Toltecs. Aztec religious beliefs were highly complex, since whenever they conquered a people, their gods were assimilated into the pantheon. Indeed, when the Aztecs themselves were conquered, they were surprised to discover that the Spanish would not do the same.

Sculpture of Coatlicue,
Aztec goddess of earth
and death

33

Mask of **Aztec**
God of darkness

The Aztec **sculptures** that have survived show great inventiveness in depicting the gods, sometimes realistic, at other times symbolically abstract, but never over-decorated; gruesome subjects are frequent; human sacrifice was practiced more by the Aztecs than by any other people. Only with the discoveries at the **Templo Mayor** in MEXICO CITY (see page 58) did the extent of Aztec skill in such arts as jewelry, pottery and engraving become apparent.

POST-CONQUEST ARCHITECTURE

After the Spanish Conquest of 1521, the architectural traditions of millennia disappeared almost without trace. In many cases, the Spanish used the foundations and stones of pyramids to build their own places of worship. An era of ecclesiastical building began, with styles influenced by developments in Europe, especially Spain. Throughout the colonial period, secular building, derivative of church building in style, remained of secondary importance.

But the evolution of Mexican architecture was not a mere imitation of the Spanish. The cultural relationship of the two countries was a complex interaction, producing a separate mode of Mexican architectural expression, which reached its highest point with the dramatic flowering of the Mexican **Ultra-Baroque** or **Churrigueresque** in the 18thC.

The naming of the different styles is a matter of continuous debate, with each academic school discerning different periods and devising particular names for them. This is further complicated by the fact that many churches include elements of various styles incorporated over a long period of building.

The first colonial architecture (1521–80)

Immediately after the Conquest, the four orders of friars (Augustinian, Dominican, Franciscan and Jesuit) built fortified **monasteries** to act as centers for the conversion and domination of the native peoples. Each order had its own characteristics, but the basic pattern was constant: a simple basilical church, looking onto a walled forecourt or "atrium."

The monastery, with its chambers grouped around a two-story cloister, was characteristically beside the church, with the main door also on the atrium. A third element, unique to Mexico, is the open chapel or *posa* on one side of the atrium, used for outdoor ceremonies involving unbaptized Indians, who could not be admitted to consecrated ground. In the center of the atrium was usually a **carved stone cross**, early examples of which often show Pre-Hispanic decorative motifs.

The earlier monasteries are of simple **Spanish Romanesque** style, with some Gothic touches added to fortifications. The **Renaissance** eventually came to Mexico in a form far removed from the Classical purity of the Italian High Renaissance. Both in Spain and Mexico, the Renaissance inspired the development of the **Plateresque** style, which retained elements of the Gothic and the Mudéjar (Islamic) styles. The term derives from the Spanish word for silversmith, as the style is reminiscent of decorated silverwork.

Typical of the Plateresque are flat surfaces decorated with medallions, simple Classical orders with minor variations, and restrained ornamentation. The Gothic influence is seen in pointed crenellations, and more occasionally in pointed arches. The Islamic influence is confined to such features as exquisitely carved and fitted woodwork, as well as flat, rich areas of geometric ornamentation. However, despite these other elements, the Plateresque is essentially a product of the Renaissance.

Mexican Baroque (1580–1730)

Toward the end of the 16thC the first phase of monastery building came to an end, and work started on the great three-nave **cathedrals**, such as those at MEXICO CITY (illustrated on page 59) and PUEBLA. Meanwhile, the growth of Spanish Baroque was reflected in Mexico. However, the first phase of Mexican Baroque architecture neglects the dynamic organization of space typical of its European original, and consists of little more than a decorative fashion for enrichment of facades and altar screens with Plateresque ornamentation. The Classical orders are more or less preserved, although with a certain liberty of proportion.

Loreto Chapel,
San Luis Potosí

The development of Mexican Baroque from the late 17thC is associated with the use of the two architectural elements whose names are used to describe the periods of their popularity. The first to appear is the "**Solomonic**" **column** (see the picture of the **Loreto Chapel** at San Luis Potosí), either twisted or helical, with a Corinthian capital. This phase, corresponding to the European High Baroque, is characterized by rich Renaissance-inspired decoration.

Churrigueresque (1730–80)

This second phase is known as the **age of the *estípite*** (after the characteristic architectural element), **Mexican Churrigueresque**, or **Ultra-Baroque**. The *estípite* is a complex form of pilaster, with a Classical capital and a curious collection of parts, including square and circular blocks with medallions, and an inverted obelisk base. Ironically, the Spanish architect Churriguera was not known for his use of this form.

The most important feature of the Churrigueresque style is the amazing profusion and richness of ornamentation, which often submerges structural elements in a stone froth of foliage, statues, medallions, garlands and cherubs.

Especially striking is the polychromatic tile decoration of the **Puebla Churrigueresque**. The artistic and religious passion of the craftsmen who elaborated the style is arguably the most impressive phenomenon in the history of Mexican architecture. In some places, strong traces of Pre-Hispanic influence can be discovered in the details of carvings.

Neoclassical and the *Porfiriato* (1780-1910)

The intensity of the Churrigueresque was short-lived, and it was succeeded by the rational calmness of the Neoclassical, which arrived in Mexico 50 years after its European emergence. The final prosperous years of the colonial era saw the erection of some fine Neoclassical buildings by architects trained at the **Academy of San Carlos** (opened 1781).

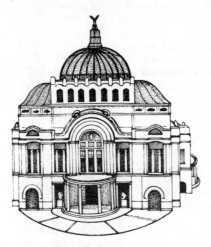

Palacio de Bellas Artes, Mexico City

After independence was achieved in 1821, the turbulent conditions and poverty of the country precluded significant building projects. It was only when stability and prosperity returned, under Porfirio Díaz (1876–1911), that a revival of architecture took place. Typical of the *Porfiriato* were grandiose public buildings in an eclectic variety of cosmopolitan styles, ranging from Italianate Art Nouveau (**Palacio de Bellas Artes**, in Mexico City, pictured left), to the Parisian architecture of Mérida, to Spanish/Islamic Gothic (the **main post office**, also in the capital). The emphasis lay on following European trends to prove that Mexico was a modern, advanced nation. The Revolution of 1910, however, put another halt to building.

Modern architecture

When building resumed in the 1920s, the styles more or less reflected contemporary fashions in the US and Europe. There were attempts to create a Mexican neocolonial style, and even a native or Pre-Hispanic-inspired style, but the functionalism of steel and reinforced concrete won the day for large-scale projects and housing. The work of the muralists (see pages 38-9) gave a marked Mexican flavor to public buildings, but only recently has it become possible to speak of Mexico's separate architectural identity.

At its best, this is represented by buildings such as the **Museo Arqueológico** at JALAPA or the **Museo Nacional de Antropología** in MEXICO CITY. Here one can see bold treatment of volume, mass and light, imaginative use of local materials, and an integration of interior and exterior space. The style is eclectic, but among others, motifs from Mexico's architectural past are apparent.

Mexican architects lead the world in the use of very lightweight concrete shell structures; these graceful parabolic forms are frequently used to roof large single spaces, such as churches. A good example is the **church** in **Coyoacán**, Mexico City, designed by the leading exponent of the technique, **Felix Candela**.

With the boom in the construction of enormous **luxury hotels**, architects are developing new ways of combining traditional forms and motifs with the engineering potential of reinforced concrete. Colonial-style patios and verandas are juxtaposed with acres of curvaceous palm-shaded pools; air-conditioned pyramids re-create the structures of the Ancient Maya; surfaces are softened with ornamental arches and balconies that reflect Moorish influences.

The purpose is to create human-scale and attractive spaces out of massive thousand-room buildings — to impress hotel guests with the grandeur of soaring lobbies complete with waterfalls, while reassuring them that it is a place they can consider home, not just an inhuman monument. Thus the more modern luxury hotels have come a long way from the crudely functional concrete boxes of the 1960s, in livability and in all-round attractiveness. And in the process a whole new architectural style has come into being.

POST-CONQUEST PAINTING AND SCULPTURE

During the early colonial period almost all sculpture and painting dealt with religious subjects. At first the artists were all Spanish immigrants, such as **Cristóbal de Villalpando**; as time passed, professionally trained Mexican-born Spaniards, and even some Indians, emerged, among them **Cabrera**, **Ibarra**, **Alcibar** and **Tinoco**. Mexican painting followed Spanish fashions even more slavishly than did Mexican architecture. The **Mexican Baroque**, with its emphasis on *chiaroscuro* and formal elaboration, reached its height in the early 18thC; a reaction of simplification followed.

The **Progressive Academy of San Carlos**, the first fine art school in Mexico City, was founded in 1781, a landmark in the development of Mexican art. Famous academicians included **Manuel Tolsa**, **Jerónimo Gil** and **José María Vasquez**. Even so, it was only after Independence that Mexican art began to reflect immediate reality. The most famous painter of this period is **José María Velasco**, whose grandiose landscapes, which are now national treasures, contrast nature's immensity with the beauty of man's creation. After the upheavals of the 1910 Revolution, artistic endeavor was concentrated on mural painting (see pages 38-9).

Considerable interest has also re-awakened in the surrealist portraitist **Frida Kahlo**, who was married to Diego Rivera, the greatest of the muralists. More recently, many of the most exciting contemporary Mexican artists, for example the painter-sculptor **Feliciano Béjar** and the sculptor **Helen Escobedo**, have adopted strong environmental themes in their work.

National University Library, Mexico City,
with **wall mosaics** by **Juan O'Gorman**

Mexico City today is one of the most artistically active capitals of Latin America, and a visit to the permanent collection of the **Museo de Arte Moderno** (see MEXICO CITY, page 65) will give a good idea of the current scene. The new and excellent **Museo Nacional de Arte** (see MEXICO CITY, page 64) shows the entire broad sweep of Mexican art history, from Pre-Hispanic to the 20thC.

The muralists

Throughout Pre-Hispanic and colonial times, religious buildings were decorated with large, colorful murals. The tradition disappeared after Independence in 1821, but was revived by the post-Revolution government, which began the practice of commissioning murals for public buildings. The intention was to capture the hearts of the largely illiterate population, while encouraging a new sense of national identity and an appreciation of the indigenous artistic heritage. As a result, the murals can seem rather didactic, with titles such as *Workers United* and *Pan-American Unity*. Despite this, the boldness and imagination of the artists usually transcends the subject matter.

Today the mural is Mexico's finest and most distinctive national art form, and remains a potent tool of mass communication.

The three great muralists were **Diego Rivera** (1886–1957), **Clemente Orozco** (1883–1949) and **David Siqueiros** (1898–1974). Rivera was perhaps the most politicized of the three; he felt strongly that his art should reject foreign influence and create a new national symbolism. The result was a heady blend of historical mysticism, with pagan, native,

Christian and Marxist themes. Rivera's greatest murals are on the **Palacio de Cortés** (in Cuernavaca), the **Palacio Nacional** (in Mexico City) and the **University** in Chapingo (see page 99). Of artistic and architectural note is the **Rivera Museum** in Mexico City, designed by the artist and housing Pre-Hispanic collections, as well as his own work.

Clemente Orozco was based in Guadalajara; his work relies more on creating a sense of dynamic movement, where Rivera was statically decorative. Among Orozco's best works are the murals at the **Casa de Azulejos** and the **Museum of National History** in Mexico City, and in public buildings throughout Guadalajara.

David Siqueiros was more innovative, experimenting with new paints, multiple perspectives, and abstraction. He remained committed to social reform throughout his life, and even spent some time in prison as a result. His best-known works are at the **Poliforum Siqueiros** in Mexico City.

Later muralists have generally tended to produce more commonplace work, painting to order for bureaucrats and politicians and rarely emerging from the shadow of the great masters. Honorable exceptions include **Rufino Tamayo**, who decorated the **Museo Nacional de Antropología**, and **Juan O'Gorman**, whose wall mosaics combine art and architecture in an exciting and unique way, relying heavily on Pre-Hispanic symbolism. The walls of the **National University Library** in the capital (pictured opposite; see page 73) are his largest and most interesting work.

Music and dance

The Mexicans have music and dance in their blood, and in no other area is the richness and diversity of their cultural origins more apparent. In many areas, the native people have retained their songs and dances almost unchanged since Pre-Hispanic times, with stringed instruments added to traditional flutes and drums.

One reason why so much native music has survived is the early missionaries' policy of encouraging the Indians to perform their traditional dances in honor of the new God. In remote areas this custom has survived, and ancient war and fertility dances are still performed in front of churches on fiesta days.

Other dances were invented by the missionaries to educate their flocks; a good example is the ***moros y cristianos*** dance, which illustrates the early wars in Spain between the Moors and the Christians. The strongest influence on the music, of course, is that of Spain, but African rhythms predominate in some coastal areas, while in the north of the country the influence of the United States is noticeable.

The best way to experience the full range of regional dances is to see a performance by the **Ballet Folklórico**, either in Mexico City or on tour. Numerous varied and well-choreographed dances are performed in the correct costumes, including stately flamenco-inspired dances from Spain and, at the other end of the spectrum, the Yaqui Deer Dance from the north of Mexico, in which dancers enact the hunting and killing of a deer.

Perhaps the most impressive of all the native dances still performed is that of the **Voladores**, the Totonac flying pole-dance (see page 126), from the eastern coast. The brightly costumed dancers whirl down through space, spiraling around a tall tree trunk to which they are tied by a long rope. Like all the native dances, it has its origins in religious ceremony; the Spanish missionaries believed it to be nothing more than a dangerous game.

It is still possible to see native dances performed in some villages, where they play an important part in the strange mixture of paganism and Catholicism that is the usual native religion. In some places these customs are slowly dying out, but in others they represent an important reassertion of traditional values, and are continuing to evolve and retain their relevance in a changing society. Some dances may be performed mainly by professional dance companies at hotels as a folkloric tourist spectacle, but the underlying indigenous cultures are far from extinct.

Among the traditional sounds of Mexico is the **marimba**, an instrument of resonant hardwood bars that vibrate with a clear, bell-like note when struck with a small rubber mallet. At times deeply mournful, or suddenly light and cheerful, the *marimba* is the most popular sound of the Indians of southern Mexico and Guatemala. At fiestas, as many as six huge instruments may be gathered in one place — usually the plaza outside the church — where, accompanied by rockets and firecrackers and a generous flow of cane alcohol mixed with Coca-Cola, festivities can continue all day and night.

Even more typical is the cheerful sound of **mariachi** music, originating in the state of Jalisco and now common all over Mexico. *Mariachis* are professional musicians, available for hire, who dress in silver-studded black uniforms and accompany their songs with guitars, violins and trumpets. Traditionally, they are employed by young men to serenade their loved ones, or on special occasions such as weddings or birthdays.

Today the two main centers are the **Plaza Garibaldi** in **Mexico City** and the **Plaza de los Mariachis** in **Guadalajara**, where they congregate and play songs while awaiting customers, the songs varying from the hauntingly sad to the bright and brassy. For the price of a few drinks, *mariachis* will compose and sing a ditty on the subject of your choice.

Serenading in the small hours was once banned by a mayor of Mexico City, but was reinstated by his successor to massive public acclaim within hours of his taking office. However customs may change, it seems the Mexicans will never lose their passionate love of music and dance.

SUGGESTIONS FOR FURTHER READING

Fiction

A visit to Don Octavio (1990), Sybille Bedford

Aztec (1980), Gary Jennings

Confabulario (1976), Juan José Areola

Journey to Ixtlán: The Lessons of Don Juan (1973) and Tales of Power (1974), Carlos Castaneda

The Nine Guardians, Rosario Castellanos

Pedro Paramo (1972), Juan Rulfo

The Plumed Serpent (1926), D.H. Lawrence

The Power and the Glory (1940) and The Lawless Roads (1939), Graham Greene

Under the Volcano (1947), Malcolm Lowry

Where the Air is Clear (1960) and Burnt Waters (1981), Carlos Fuentes

Travel writing

Incidents of Travel in the Yucatán (1841), John L. Stephens

Life in Mexico (1843), Frances Calderón de la Barca

Mornings in Mexico (1930), D.H. Lawrence

Time among the Maya (1991), Ronald Wright

Travels in the Mexique Bay (1934), Aldous Huxley

Viva Mexico: A Traveller's Account of Life in Mexico (1908), Charles Macomb Flandrau

Arts

The Art and Architecture of Mexico, Pedro Rojas

Arts of Ancient Mexico, Jacques Soustelle

Aztec Art (1983), Lois Smith and Mitch Tuchman

Costumes of Mexico (1985), The Day of the Dead (1990), Mexican Textiles (1990), Arts and Crafts of Mexico (1990), Chloë Sayer

Diego Rivera (1986), Cynthia Newman Helms

Folk Treasures of Mexico (1990), Marion Oettinger

Frida Kahlo: The Brush of Anguish (1990), Martha Zamora

Frida Kahlo: The Paintings (1992), Hayden Herrera

Mexican Masks (1985), Donald Cordry

Mexico: Splendor of Thirty Centuries (1990) Metropolitan Museum

Sculpture of Ancient West Mexico (1989), Esher Pasztory

The Skeleton at the Feast (1991), Elizabeth Carmichael and Chloe Sayer.

A Treasury of Mexican Folkways (1967), Frances Toor

Pre-Hispanic Mexico

The Ancient Kingdoms of Mexico (1982)

The Ancient Maya (1983), Sylvanus Morley and Robert Sharer

Aztecs (1991), Inga Clendinnen

The Aztecs (1973), Nigel Davies

The Blood of Kings: Dynasty and Ritual in Ancient Maya Art (1986), Linda Schele and Mary E. Miller

The Cities of Ancient Mexico (1989), Jeremy Sabloff

Daily Life of the Aztecs (1961), The Ancient Civilizations of Mexico (1969), The Four Sins (1971), The Olmecs (1985), Jacques Soustelle

Mexico (1984), The Maya (1987), Breaking the Maya Code (1992), Michael D. Coe

Mexico before Cortés: Art, History and Legend, Ignacio Bernal

View from the Top of the Temple (1984), Kenneth Pearce.

Mexican history

A Compact History of Mexico (1985), Ignacio Bernal

The Conquest of New Spain, Bernal Díaz del Castillo

The Course of Mexican History (1990), Michael Meyer and William Sherman

Five Letters / Letters from Mexico (1519–26), Hernán Cortés

History of the Conquest of Mexico (1843), William H. Prescott

A History of Mexico (1962), Henry Bamford Parkes

The Mexican Revolution (1986), Alan Knight

Mexico since Independence (1991), Leslie Bethell

Mission to Mexico (1992), Henry Mackenzie-Johnston

Sons of the Shaking Earth (1959), Eric Wolf

Triumph and Tragedy: A History of the Mexican People (1992), Ramón Eduardo Ruíz

The Wind that Swept Mexico (1971), Anita Brenner

Zapata and the Mexican Revolution (1968), John Womack.

Modern Mexico

The Children of Sanchéz (1962), Five Families (1959), Oscar Lewis

Distant Neighbors (1984), UK edition, Inside the Volcano (1985), Alan Riding

The Labyrinth of Solitude (1950), Selected Poems (1979), Collected Poems (1989), The Monkey Grammarian (1989), Octavio Paz

Mexican and Central American Mythology (1967)

The Mexicans: A Personal Portrait (1989), Patrick Oster

Mexico: A Country Guide (1992), Tom Barry

Mexico: Feast and Ferment, Tom Owen Edmunds

Where the Air is Clear (1960), Carlos Fuentes

The X in Mexico, Irene Nicholson

Mexico
region by region

Planning your visit

Planning
your visit

Where and when to go

GEOGRAPHY

Mexico is a vast country, covering nearly 2 million sq.km ($\frac{3}{4}$ million sq. miles) and surrounded by more than 10,000km (6,250 miles) of coastline. Within, it is a land of enormous contrast, with steamy coastal jungles, vast deserts, volcano-top glaciers, mountain pine forests and temperate central highlands. As for the coast, it varies between surf-battered rocks, forbidding mudflats, wildlife-rich mangrove swamps — and some of the world's most magnificent beaches, mostly spread along the E **Yucatán peninsula**, **Baja California** and the **Pacific mainland** W of the **Isthmus of Tehuantepec**.

Mexico is really defined by its mountains, known generically as the **Sierra Madre** — the Mother Mountains. The most important range is the **Sierra Madre Occidental**, which runs in an unbroken chain of mountains more than 2,000km (1,250 miles) long, from the US border to the Isthmus of Tehuantepec, rarely less than 2,000m (6,560 feet) in height. To the E of these mountains, much of the N of Mexico consists of arid high plains, breaking to the E into the smaller **Sierra Madre Oriental**, which falls, steeply in parts, into the hot, damp coastal plains of the Gulf of Mexico. The two ranges join in the **Central Highlands**, the volcanic heartland of Mexico, with Mexico City at its center.

To the S and E of the heartland, the **Sierra Madre Sur** bears the high ground through to the **Isthmus of Tehuantepec**, a low, flat strip of land, some 50km (31 miles) wide, that links the Atlantic and Pacific Oceans at a height little above sea level. The Isthmus, the natural location for a second interoceanic canal, is also the true continental divide between North and Central America. Its flatness is only broken, on the N coastal plain, by the small, free-standing **Tuxtla mountains**.

Farther E in the state of Chiapas rise up the twin ranges of the Sierra Madre Sur, which continue unbroken into Guatemala to the SE. To the NE lies the low-lying **Yucatán peninsula**, a 100,000 sq.km (62,500 sq.mile) block of free-draining limestone that juts N into the ocean, defining the boundary between the pea-soupy **Gulf of Mexico** to the N and W and the clear-watered **Caribbean** to the E.

CLIMATE

The temperature of any location in Mexico depends less on latitude than on altitude, which can vary between sea level and 5,714m (18,741 feet) at the tip of **Citlaltépetl** (also known as the **Punta de Orizaba**). At sea level, it is warm right through the year in every part of the country; and the highest volcano tops are guaranteed to be permanently freezing, at least when the sun isn't shining.

Many cities, including **Mexico City**, **Morelia**, **San Luis Potosí**, **San Miguel de Allende**, **Guanajuato** and **San Cristóbal de las Casas**, are located at about 2,000m (6,560 feet). Here it is cold enough to catch a rare touch of winter frost, although days are typically warm and sunny. Still, the central and western uplands — Mexico City and the colonial towns — are more visited during the milder, pleasant summer months.

Perhaps the perfect altitude is 1,500m (4,920 feet), roughly the height of **Cuernavaca**, **Taxco**, **Guadalajara** and **Jalapa** — low enough for the evenings to stay warm and the vegetation to take on a tropical color and exuberance, but high enough to enjoy cool nights throughout the year, with a crisp freshness in the morning air and a gentle fall of dew.

These cities are blessed with "eternal spring," with temperatures nearly always in the region of 19-29˚C (68-80˚F). Only in the **rainy season** are the blue skies covered for an hour's rain in the afternoon — but then the landscape is at its greenest and loveliest.

Across the country, the rainy season has lost its former clockwork regularity, but lasts approximately from June to September. In the s, the rains are longer and heavier, and in the high plains of the N it may not rain at all. However, even in the N, the Sierra Madre Occidental and Oriental enjoy abundant rains, nourishing their high-altitude pine forests, and forming rivers that support large areas of irrigated agriculture.

There are other geographical distinctions. The climate is drier to the N and W and wetter to the s and E. Thus, most of **Baja California** has a desert climate broken only by isolated, unpredictable tropical storms, while the **rainforests** of the se get some 2.5m (98 inches) of rain a year.

All the **coastal resorts** are especially pleasant during the winter high season (December to April); however, this is also when they are at their most expensive and crowded, especially over public holiday weekends. The central Pacific coast averages 20-27˚C (68-80˚F) during the winter and stabilizes at the upper end of the range in the summer; in late fall there are occasional tropical storms, some reaching hurricane force.

The **South–East** is popular throughout the year, but the heat and humidity build up to uncomfortable levels during the heavy rainy season. Along the Gulf and Pacific coasts, for instance, temperatures above 33˚C (91˚F) are common, and tropical conditions persist throughout the year. The **Yucatán peninsula** can get especially hot in still, summer weather. Only the **Chiapas highlands** have noticeable winters; and in summer, the cool air offers a welcome break from the torrid lowland heat, even though the sunshine is burning hot.

Northern Mexico is sunny and dry throughout the year, with average daytime temperatures around 25˚C (77˚F). Seasonal variations are small, but winter still brings frost to Monterrey and heavy snowfalls to the Sierra Madre. There is only a short and light winter rainy season, heavier in the mountains. Apart from a few high-altitude oases, most of **Baja California** is rainless desert, struck only by rare and unpredictable flash floods. The

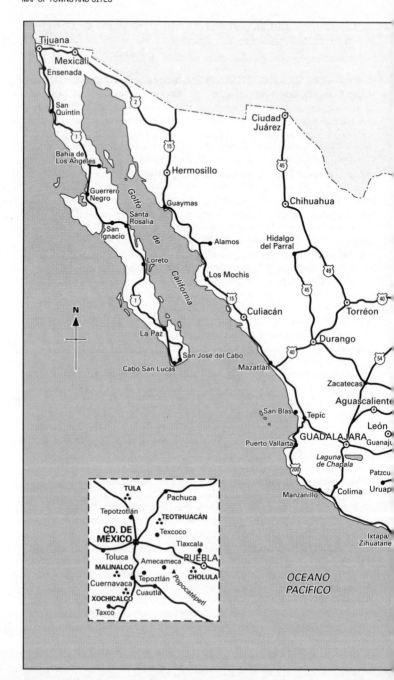

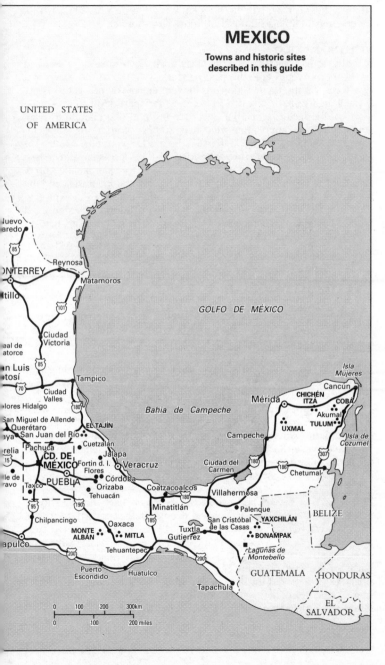

MEXICO

**Towns and historic sites
described in this guide**

UNITED STATES
OF AMERICA

Nuevo
Laredo

MONTERREY

Reynosa

Matamoros

tillo

Ciudad
Victoria

GOLFO DE MÉXICO

eal de
atorce

n Luis
tosí

Tampico

Isla
Mujeres

Ciudad
Valles

Mérida

CHICHÉN
ITZÁ

Cancún

lores Hidalgo

Bahia de Campeche

COBÁ

San Miguel de Allende

EL TAJÍN

Akumal

Querétaro

San Juan del Río

UXMAL

TULUM

aya

Cuetzalán

Campeche

*Isla de
Cozumel*

relia

Pachuca

Jalapa

CD. DE
MÉXICO

Fortin d. l.
Flores

Veracruz

Ciudad del
Carmen

lle de
ravo

Taxco

PUEBLA

Córdoba

Chetumal

Orizaba

Coatzacoalcos

Tehuacán

Minatitlán

Villahermosa

Chilpancingo

Oaxaca

MONTE
ALBÁN

MITLA

Tuxtla
Gutiérrez

Palenque

San Cristóbal
de las Casas

YAXCHILÁN

BELIZE

BONAMPAK

apulco

Tehuantepec

*Laguñas de
Montebello*

GUATEMALA

HONDURAS

Puerto
Escondido

Huatulco

Tapachula

EL
SALVADOR

| 0 | 100 | 200 | 300km |

| 0 | 100 | 200 miles |

47

summer heat can be baking, frequently soaring beyond 40°C (104°F); indeed, much of Baja simply closes down for summer.

VISITING MEXICO

A "grand tour" consisting of a brief visit to all the destinations described in this book would take the best part of a year. So in the space of a two-week vacation, your choice is limited: either you can get to know a small area well, or you can jet between far-apart destinations seeing many of the major sights, but never staying put long enough to relax and enjoy the country. But whichever strategy you adopt, some advance planning will help you to make the most of your time in Mexico.

Visitors who are new to Mexico and speak little Spanish would do best to limit themselves to the more touristic areas — for example the s tip of Baja California, the major Pacific resorts, the Yucatán peninsula and the vicinity of Mexico City. The more adventurous, interested in exploring the country in greater depth, can head off in virtually any direction, each with its own unique character and fascination. To find out more, read on through the regional introductions.

Events in Mexico

For more information, contact the **Secretariat of Tourism** in Mexico City ☎(5) 250 8555. See also NATIONAL HOLIDAYS on page 325 and EVENTS throughout the book.

JANUARY • **New Year's Day**. Good at MITLA, with all-night Zapotec dancing around bonfires. • Jan 6: **Day of the Kings**. Native dancing at MALINALCO with pilgrimage to nearby Chalma. This, not Christmas, is the day of gift-giving; a special cake is baked and whoever gets the baby doll inside it hosts a party on Feb 2. • Jan 11: **Immaculate Conception** religious fiesta. Celebrated in MORELIA with lights and flowers. • Jan 17: **San Antonio Abad**. In the country, and at the Plaza de las Tres Culturas (MEXICO CITY), animals are blessed outside churches. • Jan 18: **Santa Prisca** religious fiesta. See TAXCO.

FEBRUARY • **Carnival week** (dates vary): fairs, flower shows, masquerades, street theater, cultural events. Best at MAZATLÁN, MÉRIDA and VERACRUZ. Other good ones are at COZUMEL, ACAPULCO, CUERNAVACA, **Huejotzingo** (see PUEBLA, pages 111-5), TAMPICO, TEPOZTLÁN, **Chamula** (see SAN CRISTOBAL DE LAS CASAS, pages 262-7) and LA PAZ. • Feb 1-8: **Our Lady of Rescue** religious fiesta. Celebrated at **Tzintzuntzán** (see MORELIA). • Feb 2: **Candlemas** (**Candalería**). Best are the colorful semiaquatic celebrations at **Tlacotalpán** (see VERACRUZ), and at **Santa María del Tule** (see OAXACA) • Feb 5: **Constitution Day**.

MARCH, EASTER • **Holy Week**. Celebrated all over, with parades and Passion Plays; best at PATZCUARO, TAXCO, SAN CRISTÓBAL DE LAS CASAS,

MALINALCO and SAN LUIS POTOSÍ. • Mar 21: **Birthday of Benito Juárez**. Celebrated with special gusto at his birthplace, **Gueletao** (OAXACA).

APRIL • Apr 1-7: **Indian fair** at SAN CRISTÓBAL DE LAS CASAS, attended by Indians from all over Chiapas. • Apr 15: **Flower festival**, FORTÍN DE LAS FLORES. • Apr 15-26: **Fiesta de San Marco** at AGUASCALIENTES, with rodeos.

MAY • May 1: **Labor Day parades** in all major cities. • May 3: **Holy Cross** (**Santa Cruz**). Dancing at VALLE DE BRAVO; fireworks and picnics on building sites. • May 5: **Fiestas** to celebrate Battle of Puebla at ACAPULCO and PUEBLA. • May 15: **San Isidro** (patron saint of animals). Oxen are decorated with flowers and ribbons, and blessed.

JUNE • June 1: **Navy Day**. Parades at ports. • **Corpus Christi** (Thurs, 60 days after Easter, date varies): **Ritual blessing** of children; **Totonac flying pole dance** at Papantla (see EL TAJÍN). • June 24: **San Juan Bautista** religious fiesta. Celebrated at SAN JUAN DEL RÍO with a procession of the saint from the church to bathe in the river. • June 29: **St Peter and St Paul**, fisherman's festival. Celebrated everywhere named after San Pedro or San Pablo; particularly lively at **San Pedro Tlaquepaque** (see GUADALAJARA).

JULY • July 1: **Fiesta** begins at GUANAJUATO. • July 16: **Virgin of Carmen** fiesta. Celebrated at **Catemaco** (see VERACRUZ), and at **San Angel** (see MEXICO CITY) with flower fair. • July 25: **Santiago** (**St James**) fiesta. Celebrations at URUAPÁN and SAN LUIS POTOSÍ. • Last two Mondays in July: **Guelaguetza fiesta**, with Indian dances, at OAXACA.

AUGUST • Aug 8: **Fiesta** with a pagan flavor at Paracho (see URUAPÁN). • Mid-Aug, for one week: **Copper fair** at Santa Clara del Cobre (see PATZCUARO). • Aug 15 and 16: **Assumption** (**Asunción**). Religious processions — in state of Tlaxcala over carpets of flowers; particularly good at **Huamantla**. Also good at **Santa Clara del Cobre**. • Aug 25: **San Luis** fiesta. Celebrated at SAN LUIS POTOSÍ. • Aug 27-31: **Fiesta de la Morísima**, including **Dance of the Moors and Christians**, (see MUSIC AND DANCE, on page 39) at ZACATECAS. • Aug 28: **San Augustín**. PUEBLA has the best fiesta.

SEPTEMBER • Sept 6-9: **Virgen de los Remedios**. Native dancing at CHOLULA. • Sept 15 and 16: **Independence Day**. In every Zócalo the mayor gives the *grito* (revolutionary call to arms) on the 15th, followed by celebrations all night and next day; best at DOLORES HIDALGO and MEXICO CITY, where crowds of 500,000 gather in the Zócalo for the fireworks; military parade next day. • Sept 29: **San Miguel**. Lively fiesta at SAN MIGUEL DE ALLENDE, starting the previous night.

OCTOBER • **Arts festival**, GUADALAJARA and **Cervantino festival** in GUANAJUATO, all month. • Oct 4: **San Francisco** fiesta. Celebrated in

URUAPÁN. • Oct 4-12: **Virgin of Zapopán** fiesta. Parades through GUA-DALAJARA and Zapopán, culminating on Oct 12. • Oct 12: **Columbus Day (Día de la Raza)**, celebration of Mexico's indigenous identity, plus the discovery of the Americas by Christopher Columbus.

NOVEMBER • Nov 1 and 2: **Day of the Dead (Día de los Muertos)**. Candlelit vigils in cemeteries, most notably at **Janitzio** (see PATZCUARO, page 165), **San Gabriel Chilac** (see TEHUACÁN, page 118) and CUETZA-LAN (pages 118-9). • Nov 20: **Anniversary of the 1910 Revolution**, celebrated with nationwide patriotic events.

DECEMBER • Dec 12: **Virgen de Guadalupe**. Celebrated all over Mexico; the largest and most fervent worship of Mexico's patron saint is at MEXICO CITY basilica. • Dec 16: Start of **Christmas** with *posadas* (processions, then parties); all the usual fiesta events, up until Christmas Day. • Dec 23: **Fiesta de los Robonos**, OAXACA; competitions of **giant radishes** carved into amazing shapes.

Using this guide

Destinations are grouped in ten regions roughly corresponding to state and geographical boundaries, plus Mexico City. Each section begins with an introduction, which provides a general description of the region and what it has to offer the visitor. The sequence of destinations that follows is designed to coincide with likely routes. It is hoped that this will make the guide easy to use, both in advance planning and on the ground.

Information on the main towns, cities and cultural sites in Mexico is arranged under these headings: **What to see**: archeological sites, museums, beaches; **Where to stay**: luxury resorts and budget accommodation; **Eating and drinking**: the best restaurants, regional specialties; **Nightlife**: beach bars, folkloric happenings, chic nightclubs; **Shopping**: what to look for, and where to find it.

Sights are grouped either alphabetically or, where the geography of a city permits, in the order in which you are most likely to visit them. In some cases, this means starting with the town's **Zócalo** (main square) and radiating outwards.

Look out for the ★ symbol against outstanding sights, the ⌂ symbol, which highlights places of special architectural interest, and the ✳ symbol, indicating places likely to appeal to children. Throughout, **bold** type is used to show highlights of any sort. Cross-references to other destinations in the book are printed in SMALL CAPITALS.

Charge/credit cards are in such widespread use across Mexico that their acceptability is assumed here. Instead, we indicate the rare exceptions. Full details are given in CHARGE AND CREDIT CARDS, page 309.

Commonly-used abbreviations, such as those in addresses, are also explained in ADDRESSES, on page 319.

Mexico City

Birthplace of a nation

Mexico City, one of the world's largest and most populous cities, is a dirty, ugly, energetic and fascinating monster that sprawls over the once-lovely face of the Valley of Mexico. Where Hernán Cortés gasped with wonder at the beauty of the Aztec capital, Tenochtitlán, its sunlit temples and palaces reflected in the shimmering waters of a vast blue lake, today's visitors gasp instead at the thin, smog-laden air polluted by contaminating industries and more than 4 million smoking vehicles. From the Paso de Cortés, the high pass between the twin volcanoes of Popocatépetl and Ixtaccihuatl that offered the conquistadors their first magical view of the valley, today's city is invariably hidden under an impenetrable, immovable, yellow-gray blanket of smog.

Angel of Independence,
Mexico City

Down in the city, the picture is little more alluring. The lake, drained in the 19th century to facilitate urban expansion, has now been reduced to a few minute remnants, themselves threatened by water pollution and continued urbanization. In its place is a great, roaring metropolis, a seemingly endless expanse of concrete, tarmac and traffic with a curiously insistent life of its own, which makes few concessions to its citizens or the environment they live in. Levels of carbon monoxide, oxides of nitrogen, hydrocarbons, dust and ozone in particular are alarmingly high for most of the time.

At last, schemes are afoot to make the future more bearable. Since the late 1980s, for example, all vehicles have been banned from the city for one working day each week. More recently, some of the worst-offending industries, such as cement works and oil refineries, have been forced to move out of the valley. The buses that once used to belch out thick black diesel

51

smoke are gradually being tamed, and all new cars now come fitted with catalytic convertors.

However, even these measures are proving to be of limited effectiveness. A rise in the total car population is nullifying the effect of the ban, so now two-day bans are declared when the smog is especially severe, and a permanent two-day ban may soon be announced. Another problem is the large number of very old, highly polluting vehicles.

One novel suggestion has been to install giant gas burners at strategic points around the city, to puncture the thermal inversion layer and thus allow the hot, dirty air to rise out of the valley. But this, say the city's environmentalists, is madness: it would generate even more pollution of its own (at fabulous expense), allow the underlying problems to carry on growing unchecked, and dump all the pollution somewhere else. No doubt something will eventually be done; too little and too late, but just enough to stop the city choking on itself.

But Mexico City is not all doom and gloom: life, in a chaotic, spontaneous and surprisingly joyful way, goes on. As well as smog, there is a unique energy and excitement in Mexico City's air, arising out of the sheer vastness of its scale and the vitality of its people. Downtown, the city seethes with cultural and artistic life, making it an intellectual focus for all of Hispanic America. There are multitudes of historic sights, museums, Aztec ruins, colonial monuments and charming villages hidden away behind the main roads; and the city's hotels, restaurants and shops rank among the world's best. Hold your breath and who knows, you might even love the place.

Underlying Mexico City's problems is the phenomenal growth it has experienced, transforming it from a gracious city of barely 4 million to its present 22 million, in a matter of three or four decades. This is the result of the immigration of hordes of *campesinos* (small farmers), forced out of their villages by land grabs, low farm prices and rural population growth. The cheap labor they provide has fueled the country's rapid economic growth, but in the process, Mexico City has become home to a quarter of all Mexicans, many of them living with no mains services. Some predict that the city's numbers will increase to 25 million in the early 21st century, to make it the biggest in the world.

Every day the outlying slums inch out across the dried-up lake bed, over farmland and up the foothills of the encircling volcanoes: already the shanty town of Netzahualcoyotl, east of the city, is the country's second largest center of population, with uncounted millions of inhabitants. But bleak although life is in such places, there is often a high level of local organization. And just as the outward uniformity of a rainforest can disguise the ecological uniqueness of its every part, so the monotony of Mexico City's urban desert conceals the diverse identities of its people and their communities.

Expeditions of Indian or mestizo (mixed-race) *campesinos,* no longer able to survive on agriculture in the countryside, often join together to create new urban settlements, retaining their customs, extended families, fiestas and native tongues. The secret of Mexico City is that it is home, not to a deculturalized 22-million-strong proletariat, but to thousands of interlinked social, cultural and ethnic groups creating their own order out of the chaos that surrounds them, so weaving a complex fabric that replicates the structure of Mexico as a whole.

In a historic resonance, Mexico City reproduces the function of the Aztec city of Tenochtitlán: it is a center of political and military power, dominating a vast area and sucking in prodigious wealth and resources.

The history of the city is neatly encapsulated in the Plaza de las Tres Culturas (Square of the Three Cultures), built around the restored remains of the Aztec center of Tlatelolco. To one side is a dark, cavernous colonial church, to another the modern offices of the Ministry of Foreign Affairs, on a third side a busy eight-lane highway, and a modern housing development completes the square. In the middle of the plaza is a plaque inscribed, "On the 13th of August 1521, defended by the heroic Cuauhté-moc, Tlatelolco fell under the power of Hernán Cortés. It was neither a triumph nor a defeat, but the painful birth of the mixed race that is the Mexico of today."

As recently as 1968, hundreds of protesting students were killed in the square, in a Tienanmen-style massacre directly preceding the Mexico City Olympics. Hundreds of people were again killed here in the 1985 earthquake, when a nearby housing complex collapsed, the result of faulty design and inadequate materials. The painful birth continues.

What a scene to burst upon the first eyes that beheld it: the great city of Tenochtitlán, standing in the midst of the five great lakes, upon verdant and flower covered islands, a Western Venice, with thousands of boats gliding swiftly along its streets, and its long rows of low homes diversified by the multitude of its pyramidal temples . . . the profusion of water now so wanting to the landscape.
(Frances Calderón de la Barca, *Life in Mexico*, 1843)

Mexico City: facts and figures

In everyday conversation, the capital is often referred to as *México*, while the country is called *La República*. The city is also called the "Distrito Federal," usually abbreviated to the initials "DF," pronounced "De-Efe." Its inhabitants, somewhat derogatorily, are often known as "Chilangos," as a result of their fabled fondness for chili.

Some useful points of information:
- 1,820km (1,375 miles) SE of US border at Ciudad Juárez.
- Altitude: 2,240m (7,347 feet)
- Population: 10 million in Federal District, 22 million in total metropolitan area.
- See color maps **13–15** and maps on pages 60 and 70-71.

INTERNATIONAL AIRPORT   In the E of the city, served by Metro (Terminal Aerea station, *not* Aeropuerto).

RAILROAD STATION   Estación Buena Vista, Insurgentes Norte near Revolución Metro (☎ *(5) 547 6270/5240)*.

BUS STATIONS   Terminal del Norte, Av. de los Cien Metros 4907 *(☎(5) 587 5973/67),* for the N to the US border; **Terminal Oriente** (TAPO), Calzada Ignacio Zaragoza 200 (by San Lazaro Metro) *(☎(5) 762 5977),* for the E including Oaxaca and Yucatán; **Terminal Central Poniente**, Río Tacubaya 102 *(☎(5) 271 0481),* for the W Pacific coast; **Terminal del Sur**, Taxqueña 1320 *(☎(5) 544 2101),* for the S Pacific coast.
- For bus reservations and tickets in the Zona Rosa, go to **Mexicorama** *(Plaza del Angel arcade, Londres 161, map14D4 ☎(5) 525 2050).*
- For connecting buses to the US, there is a **Greyhound** office *(Reforma 27, map14C5 ☎(5) 535 4200/2618).*

TOURIST INFORMATION   The main city office is in the **Zona Rosa** at Amberes 54 and Londres, map **14**D4 *(☎(5) 528 9469);* there are also offices in the **airport** and at **Buenavista railroad station**; you could also call the INFOTUR multilingual tourist telephone service *(☎(5) 525 9380-7; 9am-9pm)* for information on Mexico City.
- SECTUR, from its office in **Polanco** at Presidente Masaryk 172, map **13**C2 *(☎(5) 250 8555),* runs a similar toll-free 24-hour service *(☎(5) 250 0123/8601/8419)* that covers the entire country.
- Another source of information is the **Mexico City Chamber of Commerce** *(Reforma 42, Zona Rosa, map14C5* ☎(5) 546 0585).

AMERICAN EXPRESS TRAVEL SERVICE   Reforma 234 at Havre, Zona Rosa, map **14**C4 *(☎(5) 207 7204/7049/6950).* Also at:
- Campos Eliseos 204, Local 5, map **13**D2 *(☎(5) 280 1111/281 4533)*
- Patriotismo 635, near Patriotismo Metro, off map **13**F3 *(☎(5) 326 2500, ext. 2117/8/9)*
- Centro Comercial Perisur, Local 231 *(☎(5) 606 3333/2606)*

Mexico City: planning

ORIENTATION

The colonial heart of Mexico City is the **Zócalo**, the great main square, with the PALACIO NACIONAL and the CATEDRAL METROPOLITANA. Here, and in the surrounding area, it is only necessary to raise your eyes above the commercial bustle at street level, to catch a glimpse of the gracious capital of the viceroys of New Spain.

The center of the Aztec capital of Tenochtitlán was also here, built on artificial islands in the lake that then filled the Valley of Mexico. When Cortés and his men first marched across the mountains and caught sight of the silver-glinting pyramids, they were entranced by such beauty. Yet they tore it down stone by stone and used the temples as quarries for their own churches and palaces.

Behind the cathedral, some colonial buildings were recently demolished, and archeologists reconstructed the base of the Aztec Great Temple, the TEMPLO MAYOR. Cortés would have turned in his grave, but this bold homage to the past was proof of the Mexicans' belief in the mixed origins of their race and culture.

Mexico City's main avenue, the grandiose and tree-lined **Paseo de la Reforma**, passes a few blocks from the colonial area, on a curving trajectory between the w and the NE. It was laid out in the 19thC as a new Champs-Élysées, although at the time it passed mostly through country-side. Since then, the explosive growth of the city has vindicated the planners: it takes more than an hour to drive out of the city in either direction to reach the open fields.

To the NE, Reforma leads to the holiest shrine in the country, the BASILICA DE NUESTRA SEÑORA DE GUADALUPE, shrine of the Virgin, patron saint of all the country. To the w, it first passes the **Zona Rosa** (Pink Zone), the smartest commercial area, near where the best shops, restaurants and hotels are concentrated. Then it arrives at the city's long-suffering green lung, **Bosque de Chapultepec** (Chapultepec Park), where every visitor should spend a day looking around the stunning MUSEO NACIONAL DE ANTROPOLOGÍA, seeing the best of Pre-Columbian art amid the finest of modern Mexican architecture.

What with the pollution and other traumas of Mexico City, the affluent prefer to live well away from the center. Many luxurious villas have been built on the wooded hills to the w, out past Chapultepec Park on Reforma, known as **Las Lomas**. Others prefer the old houses of the charming colonial villages to the s of the city, reached down the freeway-style **Periférico**, or the seemingly endless **Insurgentes Sur**: Avenida Insurgentes stretches for a total length of 34km (21 miles).

San Angel and **Coyoacán** have retained a distinctive character, despite being serious pollution hotspots, and are well worth a visit.

GETTING AROUND

Mexico City presents quite a challenge to the visitor, because of its great size. Fortunately, most places of touristic interest are concentrated in relatively small areas. However, the distances are still too large to allow you to walk everywhere, and some engagement with taxis or public transport is inevitable. Fortunately the city is well-provided with public transport, as indeed it has to be to cater to the needs of its citizens, most of whom do not own cars.

Using the Metro

For sheer efficiency and value, there is nothing to compete with the Metro, at least in those parts of the city it serves. It is modern, clean, quiet, extensive and generally safe, and its biggest fault is that you have to walk a surprisingly long way at some interchanges. You should also note that those with heavy luggage are not admitted — a rule enforced with particular severity in the **rush hours** *(roughly 8-9am and 5-6pm)*. In general, rush hours are best avoided anyway as the system gets very crowded; one compensation of rush-hour travel for women and children is that special carriages are set by for their use.

Buy as many **tickets** as you will need during your visit (and a few extra) at one go, to avoid standing in line. At the automatic gate, push your ticket into the hole and the gate opens; it keeps the ticket, and you have the freedom of the network.

Lines are numbered from **one** to **nine**, but the easiest way to get around is to remember the name of the station at the end of the line in the direction you are going in, and follow the signs pointing to it. By contrast with other networks, such as the London Underground, missing a train in Mexico City is no disaster: there really will be another one along soon. The entire network is open between 6am and 12.30pm.

A color **map** of the Mexico City Metro system can be found at the back of the book. A free map can be picked up when you buy your tickets.

By bus

Buses are another vital and inexpensive way of getting around, particularly on those routes not adequately served by the Metro. Bus routes often coincide with the major arterial roads; thus most buses along **Insurgentes** (the main avenue running N–S across the Zona Rosa) or **Reforma** (the main avenue running E–W through the center, which forms the backbone of Mexico City) are likely to carry on doing so. Check the destination on the front of the bus, and if in doubt consult the driver or your fellow passengers, who will invariably be helpful.

By Colectivo/Pesero

Once run along the lines of communal taxis, *colectivos* (also called *peseros*) have now become very much like a slightly informal species of bus: no longer are they converted motorcycles or VW Combis, but substantial Mercedes minibuses that run along pre-set routes, often the same as those of the buses.

The main differences between buses and *colectivos* is that the latter are more expensive (but still very cheap) and far more frequent. And where buses are run by companies, most *pesero* drivers are freelance operators who own their own vehicle and operate the route under franchise. The best rule is to take whichever comes first.

By car

If you're not a resident, or trying to escape via the most direct route, don't even *think* of driving a car in Mexico City. If in doubt, take a taxi. Remember that all cars, even foreign ones, are banned from the city's roads for one day a week according to the license (number) plate, and this may go up to two days.

By taxi

On arrival in Mexico City airport, the disoriented tourist has the protection of a standard fee into the center, payable in advance at a ticket office. Otherwise, you're on the meter. Unless you've come to some special deal, make sure that your driver sets his meter when you enter, and carefully examine any charge sheets he might show you to justify multiplying up your fare. Some meters seem to clock up the pesos much faster than others, but that's the luck of the draw.

One problem with Mexico City's taxis is that there is no qualifying examination, so many drivers simply don't know their way around; compounding this difficulty, many drivers also exhibit a total inability to read maps. If you find yourself going nowhere, be firm: get out and try again. Note that there are different kinds of taxis: the most common is a VW Beetle with its front passenger seat taken out, less expensive than the shiny black ones that hang around outside hotels.

EVENTS IN MEXICO CITY

As well as the usual national events (see pages 48-50), the following are celebrated with particular gusto in Mexico City:

• January 17, **San Antonio Abad**: Animals are blessed in the Plaza de las Tres Culturas, outside the colonial church of Santiago.

• July 16: **Virgin of Carmen flower fair** at San Angel.

• September 15 and 16, **Independence Day**. Crowds of 500,000 gather on the evening of the 15th for the President's traditional *grito* (shout) at 11pm, followed by fireworks and throwing of flour and eggs (which can get rough); there is a 5-hour military parade the following morning. There are good views of both from the terrace restaurant of the HOTEL MAJESTIC.

• December 12, **Día de Guadalupe**: vast crowds gather at the BASILICA DE NUESTRA SEÑORA DE GUADALUPE for the colorful feast of Mexico's patron saint. Celebrations throughout the night.

What to see in Mexico City

Mexico City's sights are concentrated in distinct areas that are most conveniently explored separately, so destinations are grouped together in these areas.

Most of the sights in central Mexico City are marked on maps **13-15** at the back of the book, and for each sight in this area a map reference is given that will help to locate it. The SIGHTS IN MEXICO CITY map on page 60 pinpoints the sights that fall outside the central area, and on pages 70-71 there is a map of the San Angel and Coyoacán districts.

THE CENTER

Map **15**C6-7; served by ample public transport.

Zócalo
Map 15C7.

At the center of every town of New Spain, the main church and government buildings were built around a wide parade ground. In the middle was a pedestal (*zócalo* in Spanish) waiting to receive a statue of the Spanish monarch. When the statues failed to arrive on time, *Zócalo* became universal slang in Mexican Spanish for the whole square.

Mexico City's Zócalo *(map 15 C7),* officially **Plaza de la Constitución**, is the largest and most grandiose in the country, and on a world scale is second in size only to Red Square in Moscow. It was built over the great Aztec marketplace of Tenochtitlán, whose stones were used to construct the **cathedral** and the original **Palacio Nacional**.

When it's not full of people, as it is on **May Day** or **Independence Day** (September 15), the Zócalo can be bleak and forbidding; the vast paved area is unbroken by so much as a blade of grass. It was once planted with trees, but these were all cut down during the revolution to give more space for patriotic events.

Templo Mayor (Teocalli) ▥ ☆
Map 15C7. Calle Republic de Guatemala, behind the cathedral ☛ To reserve an English-speaking guide ☎(5) 542 1717. Open 9am–5pm. Closed Mon.

After the Conquistadors destroyed the Aztec city of Tenochtitlán and built over the ruins using the same stones, it was thought that the old city had disappeared forever. Descriptions by Spanish chroniclers, and their inaccurate sketches, enabled archeologists to make theoretical reconstructions.

It was known that the main temple enclosure was nearly $\frac{1}{2}$ km ($\frac{1}{4}$ mile) square, and contained around a hundred buildings, including temples on pyramid bases, altars of skulls *(tzompantli),* ball-courts for the sacred game, houses for pilgrims, and the palaces of nobles. The city was on a largely manmade island in a lake, and was linked to the mainland by wide causeways.

The **main temple** was surmised to be under the cathedral. It was therefore a great discovery when, in 1977, workmen of the electricity company uncovered the base of the temple while excavating. The surrounding buildings were compulsorily purchased and demolished, and the work of reconstruction then started in earnest, ending in 1982.

The base of the pyramid was about 80 by 100m (262 by 328 feet). It had steep, stepped sides, with two parallel staircases up the w front, leading to a terrace at a height of 30m (98 feet). Set back from the stairs were two tall temples, one dedicated to the god of fertility and rain, Tlaloc, the other to the Aztec tribal god of war and the sun, Huitzilopochtli. This dualism was fundamental to Aztec beliefs.

The archeological finds during excavations far surpassed anything previously known, and included statues, jewelry and everyday objects from all over Mesoamerica. They have led to a major reappraisal of the importance of the Aztecs in the development of Pre-Hispanic art.

A spacious **museum** has been built on site to house these finds. It comprises eight halls leading through the phases of Tenochtitlán's history from foundation to conquest, and exploring the different aspects — cultural, commercial, ecological and religious — of the civilization that flourished there.

Catedral Metropolitana ▥ ☆
Map 15C7. n side of the Zócalo.

The largest church in Mexico, the cathedral was originally designed for Lima, Peru, but the plans got mixed up and, once the mistake had been discovered, it was decided to leave things as they were. The cathedral then took 240 years (1573–1813) to complete, and thus encompasses a wide variety of architectural styles.

Built with some 3,000 tonnes of stone, the cathedral has sunk into the mud to a depth of about 3m (10 feet) and is still moving, despite the support of an estimated 55 Aztec temples that serve as its foundations.

The facade has both Neoclassical and Baroque elements, while altars inside are in the heavily ornamented Churrigueresque style. Many of these were destroyed in a disastrous fire in 1967.

The adjacent 18thC church, the **Sagrario**, was built to house sacred relics, vestments and treasures from the archbishopric, and possesses one of the finest Churrigueresque facades in the country.

Palacio Nacional ⅲ ☆

Map 15C7. On the Zócalo ◙ *Open irregularly 10am–1pm. Closed Mon.*

Frequently rebuilt through the centuries, the Palacio Nacional has been used by all Mexico's rulers from Cortés onward. The central courtyard, passing under the **Bell of Liberty** (see DOLORES HIDALGO, pages 201-2), is open to visitors. On Independence Day (September 15), the President rings the bell at 11pm to signal the start of celebrations.

Around the grand stair and galleries of the courtyard are **murals** by the mature Diego Rivera, illustrating various scenes from Mexican history. The vast pictures on the stairway depict the class struggles of post-Conquest Mexico, and six on the upper floor celebrate the country's Pre-Hispanic cultures; the depiction of Cortés as a syphilitic hunchback is based more on ideology than historical evidence.

In the left-hand courtyard is a small **museum** (▧ *open Mon-Sat 10am-8pm, Sun 10am-1pm)* dedicated to the memory of Benito Juárez.

Monte Nacional de Piedad (National Pawnshop)

Map 15C7. On the NW corner of the Zócalo ◙ *Open Mon–Fri 10am–2pm, 5–7pm; Sat 10am–2pm. Closed Sun.*

This 18thC building is a giant pawnshop. Stroll around the amazing variety of objects, left by the needy to secure loans. These are mostly jewelry, antiques and furniture; larger items such as cars and washing machines are handled elsewhere. Unredeemed objects are surprisingly

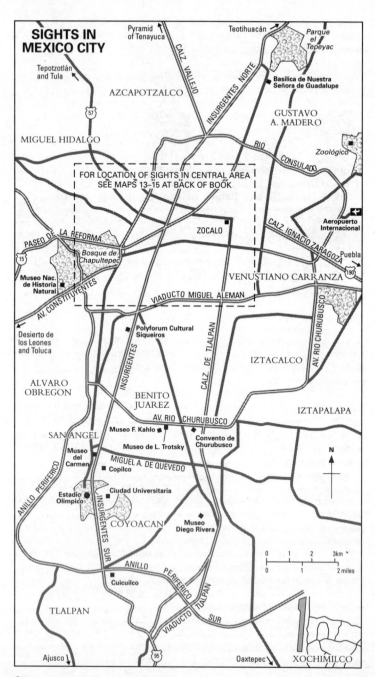

costly, not that this deters an army of bargain-hunters; but you may have some luck at one of the occasional, widely-advertised sales.

North and east of the Zócalo

Map 15C7. Allow 1½–2hrs.

This and the following two areas of the center are each most conveniently explored on foot. Leaving the Zócalo with the cathedral on your right, walk N up Brasil three blocks to the charming little **Plaza Santo Domingo**. Colonial mansions line the S and E sides, with the SE corner occupied by the 1731 **Customs House**, its interior decorated with Siqueiros murals that depict the betrayals of the Mexican revolution.

On the W side of the square stands a gallery occupied by *evangelistas* (professional letter-writers), while to the N is the 18thC Baroque church of **Santo Domingo**, on the site of two earlier buildings. On the square's NE corner is the former **Palace of the Inquisition**, the Dominican institution that sought out and burned alive tens of thousands of heretics and other sinners between 1571 and 1808.

Go back a block, turn left into Donceles, and on the left is the church of **La Enseñanza**, notable for its exuberantly ornamented Churrigueresque high altar. Near the corner with Argentina is the **Secretariat of Public Education** *(Argentina 28, three blocks N of the Templo Mayor),* the former Convent of the Incarnation, which has an astonishing 239 Rivera **murals** from the 1920s on the patio and staircase up to the 3rd floor; admittance is not guaranteed, but try your luck.

A little farther down Donceles, on the left, is the former Jesuit college of **San Ildefonso** (**🏛**), which now contains a school. In the courtyards *(**🔲** open 9am–2pm; closed Sat, Sun)* are **murals** from the early 1920s by Rivera, Orozco and Siqueiros. Orozco's cynicism about the failure of the revolution to bring about social change makes a refreshing contrast to Rivera's sometimes naive idealism.

Continue E down Donceles (here called Justo Sierra), then turn left into Loreto, thereby reaching the nearby Plaza Loreto. Inside the elegant Neoclassical church of **Santa Loreto**, be sure to see the religious **oil paintings** (**☆**) by the Zapotec Indian painter Miguel Cabrera (died 1768). The other church on the plaza, **Santa Teresa**, is also worth a visit.

Walking back down Loreto, turn left after three blocks into the pedestrian mall Moneda to visit the gracious church of **La Santísima Trinidad**, the bell tower of which is fashioned to resemble a papal crown. Then head W for the Zócalo. On the left after two blocks is the **Museo de San Carlos** (**🔲** *open 10am–6pm; closed Mon),* known also as the Academy of the Three Noble Arts. This contains works by colonial artists, and some lesser-known paintings by European masters such as Bosch, Rubens and Murillo.

Finally, by the Zócalo on Calle Moneda, in the same block as the Palacio Nacional, on the left, is the great carved wooden door of the **Museo Nacional de las Culturas** (**🏛 🔲** *open 9am–6pm; closed Fri).* The collections are of no great interest, being mostly reproductions. However, the old mansion in which they are housed, with its arcaded court, fountain and flowers, is a cool and agreeable place to sit and recover from your walk.

South of the Zócalo
Map 15C6-7. Allow 1–1½hrs.

Leave the Zócalo with the Palacio Nacional immediately to the left, and head s down Pino Suarez, past the Supreme Court of Justice on your left. On the left, at the end of the third block from the Zócalo, is the old 18thC mansion of the Counts of Santiago, now the **Museo de la Ciudad de Mexico**, or Museum of the City of Mexico *(▨ open 10am-5.30pm; closed Mon)*. Here can be seen assorted memorabilia and a model of the center of Tenochtitlán. On one corner of the building, reused stones bear Aztec carvings.

A block farther down the street, on the right, is the church of **Jesús de Nazareth**, burial place of Hernán Cortés, whose vault displays an alarming 1944 mural by Orozco illustrating the Book of Revelations. Five minutes' walk away is the **Metro station of Pino Suarez**, where Aztec ruins were found during construction; these are worth a look.

To continue, turn right, walk three blocks w, then turn right again up Isabel la Católica. Four blocks away is the **Biblioteca Nacional**, the National Library *(▥ ▣ open 9am-1.30pm; closed Sun)*, housed in the huge old Baroque church of San Agustín. Two blocks farther n is the busy shopping street of 16 de Septiembre. Turn right to return to the Zócalo.

West toward the Alameda Central
Map 15C6. Allow 1½–2hrs.

Leave the Zócalo on Madero, with the Merchants Arcade on the left. At the beginning of the third block on the right is the 18thC Jesuit church of **La Profesa**, with a fine Baroque doorway. Another two-and-a-half blocks on the left is the magnificent 1784 **Palacio Iturbide** *(▥ Madero 17),* where the hapless would-be Emperor of Mexico, Agustín Iturbide, lived in 1821–22. It is now used by the Banco de México. Visitors are allowed into the courtyard during office hours, and paintings are sometimes on show.

Next, on the right, is the unmistakable 16thC **Casa de los Azulejos** or House of Tiles *(▥ ✩ ▣ open during shopping hours).* The facade of this pretty colonial residence is entirely covered in blue-and-white Puebla tiles. The great **courtyard**, roofed in amber-colored glass, is used as a restaurant by SANBORN'S; be sure to stop for a coffee (see SHOPPING on page 86).

Opposite is the equally unmistakable **Torre Latino Americana** *(▥ ▨ ◁ open 10am-11pm);* from the observation deck on the 44th floor there are good views of the city (or of the smog). This is the tallest building in any earthquake zone, the veteran of some mighty shakes.

Next to the tower, also on Madero, is the church of **San Francisco**, built over Moctezuma's zoo. It was once part of a monastery, the Franciscan headquarters for all New Spain, demolished during the anticlerical period in the 19thC. The church was gutted, but the very fine **Churrigueresque doorway** remains. The Alameda Park is a block away.

Alameda Central (Alameda Park)
Map 15C6. Allow 4hrs.

This pleasantly shaded park was laid out in the 16thC on the site of a drained marsh, as a suitable venue for burning heretics. Standing at the western end, the former monastery of San Diego, now the **Pinacoteca Virreinal museum** *(🖸 open 10am-7pm; closed Mon)*, houses a collection of colonial paintings, and the chapel contains a 1959 **mural** by Cantú depicting monastic life.

On Juárez, facing the middle of the Alameda, is the **Museum of Popular Arts** *(🖸 open during shopping hours)*, in the old church of Corpus Christi; many of the crafts exhibited are for sale. Cross the park to see the two adjacent 17thC churches of **Santa Veracruz** and **San Juan de Díos**.

Museo del Mural de Diego Rivera

Map 15C6. Jardin de la Solidaridad, by Alameda 🖾 *Open Tues–Sun 10am–6pm. Closed Mon.*

When the Hotel Del Prado (originally Regis) was destroyed in the 1985 earthquake, among the survivors was Diego Rivera's magnificent mural *Dream of a Sunday Afternoon in the Alameda*, which portrays the grand sweep of Mexican history and culture integrated into a single view of the Alameda. One of Rivera's greatest masterpieces, it was painted in 1947 amid considerable controversy, caused by the atheistic statement "Dios no existe" (God does not exist), now removed.

The site of the hotel has now been transformed into the **Garden of Solidarity** as a memorial to the indomitable spirit of the Mexican people at the time of the 1985 earthquake. A new building has been erected to house the 15m by 4m (50-foot by 13-foot) mural, almost miraculously moved undamaged from the hotel lobby to its new location.

Museo Franz Mayer 🏛

Map 15C6. Hidalgo 45 in the Old Hospice of San Juan de Díos ☎(5) 518 2265 🖾 *Open Tues–Sun 10am–5pm. Closed Mon.*

This Aladdin's Cave was opened in 1986 in a beautifully restored colonial hospice to house the huge and diverse private collection of Franz Mayer, who died in 1975. The collection includes paintings, sculpture, furniture, silver and ceramics from the 16thC to the present day.

Museo Nacional de la Estampa (National Print Museum)

Map 15C6. Hidalgo 39, next to Museo Franz Mayer 🖸 *Open Tues–Sun 10am–6pm. Closed Mon.*

This new gallery contains four main exhibition areas for prints, lithographs, etchings and other printed works of art.

Palacio de Bellas Artes (Palace of Fine Arts) 🏛 ☆

Map 15C6. At E end of the Alameda Park ☎(5) 510 1388 🖸 *Open Mon–Sat 10am–5.30pm; Sun 10am–1.30pm.*

A grandiose Italianate palace (pictured on page 36), containing an opulent theater, recital room and collections of paintings and murals by David Alfaro Siquieros. It also contains a single mural by Diego Rivera, a reproduction of one painted for the Rockefeller Center in New York City, which was destroyed for its communist sentiments.

The building, completed in weighty Italian marble in 1934, has sunk an average of 9cm (3$\frac{1}{2}$ inches) every year into the soft soil. It is the home of the **Ballet Folklórico** (see MEXICO CITY BY NIGHT, page 84), which every visitor to Mexico should try to see at least once. Those who cannot go to a performance should at least see the remarkable **Tiffany mother-of-pearl curtain** in the proscenium arch.

Museo Nacional de Arte ★

Map 15C6. Calle de Tacuba 8, near the Alameda Park ☎*(5) 521 7320* 🖭
Open 9am–7pm. Closed Mon.

The 1911 building that houses this museum was until 1982 merely the Ministry of Telegraphs, yet it is so grandiose that it might have been a presidential palace; the site was formerly occupied by a hospital for syphilitics. The collections range from Pre-Columbian to the present, with examples of the very best from each epoch. It is fascinating to see the broad sweep of Mexican cultural history under one roof, and it is worthwhile coming here more than once.

Start on the third floor, where the first room is devoted to the history of the building itself. In the other rooms, the works are divided by period and also, more imaginatively, by theme and technique. The small **Pre-Hispanic rooms** (**2** and **3**) have some well-chosen pieces, such as the exquisitely carved **Maya altar**, and a large **Aztec carving of a snail** from the ruins of the TEMPLO MAYOR. **Colonial art** is well represented (rms **4–7**), mostly by religious works that once hung in churches. On the same floor, a 19thC room has **landscapes** by foreign artists traveling in Mexico, all straining to capture the country's wild splendor and great open skies.

With the exception of engravings, all 20thC art is on the second floor. A room is given over to popular or folk art, and its influence on modern Mexican art is easily seen by comparing the works in other rooms.

WEST OF THE CENTER

From the heart of Mexico City, the **Paseo de la Reforma** sweeps w to the enormous **Bosque de Chapultepec** (Chapultepec Park), and its numerous sights *(map 13D2* 🖭 ▣ ✴ ▭*)*. The largest park in the city, it contains several museums, an amusement park, zoo, boating lake and luxury restaurant. If you like seeing thousands of people enjoying themselves and creating mounds of litter and a fair bit of noise in the process, come on a Sunday; otherwise come during the week. It is inadvisable to enter the park after dark.

Museo Casa de Carranza (Museum of the House of Carranza) 🏛

Map 14C4. Lerma 35, next to Maria Christina Hotel ☎*(5) 286 6519* 🖭 *Open Tues–Sat 9am–7pm; Sun 11am–3pm. Closed Mon.*

This pleasant 1908 house, in the style of a French villa, was the home of President Venustiano Carranza (1859–1920). Although revered as a revolutionary hero, it was Carranza who ordered the betrayal and murder of his rival, peasant leader Emiliano Zapata. The house retains its original decor and furnishings, and a library of revolutionary history.

Museo de la Cera (Wax Museum)

Map 14D4. Londres 6, Zona Rosa. Open 11am–7pm.

A small but very enjoyable museum, with all the main icons of Mexican myth and history including a sacrificial Aztec virgin, as well as a rather out-of-place John Lennon and Hammer Horror imports. The Art Nouveau mansion in which it is housed is worth a visit in its own right.

Castillo de Chapultepec (Chapultepec Castle) ★

Map 13D2. Chapultepec Park ☎*(5) 553 6242* 🖭 ➳ ◄€ *Castle, museum and gallery open Tues–Sat 9am–5.30pm; Sun 10am–1.30pm. Closed Mon.*

This imposing 18thC building up on the hill in Chapultepec Park houses the **Museum of National History** (**⚅**), containing a collection of memorabilia and bric-a-brac from the Conquest up to the 1910 Revolution. There are also vivid 1930s **frescoes** by the muralists Siqueiros, Orozco and O'Gorman, showing their polemically Marxist interpretation of Mexican history.

The **Emperor Maximilian**, during his short and ill-starred reign, had rooms here, which can be visited. His richly decorated **Imperial Coach** is on display, a striking contrast to the simple coach used by his rival, **Benito Juárez**, as the actual seat of the provisional government during Juárez' evasion of Maximilian's troops. Beneath the castle, these and other important episodes in Mexico's history are depicted in the three-dimensional son-et-lumière **Gallery of History**, also known as the **Museo del Caracol** (Museum of the Snail) due to its spiral design (☆ **⚅ ⚄**).

Museo de Arte Moderno ▥ ☆
Map 13D3. Chapultepec Park ☎(5) 553 6211 ⚅ ⚄ Open 10am–5pm. Closed Mon.

An interesting modern building at the end of the park next to the impressive marble monument to the **Niños Héroes** (Child Heroes). In 1847, these six cadets leaped to their deaths from Chapultepec Castle after fighting against the invading Americans. The museum's good permanent collection of Mexican art is augmented by frequent visiting exhibitions by major foreign artists.

Museo Rufino Tamayo ▥
Map 13D3. Reforma, opposite Museo de Arte Moderno ⚅ Open 10am–7pm.

The design of this museum is boldly modern, but the permanent art collection is disappointing. Excellent temporary exhibitions are staged from time to time, however; they are advertised in the press and on large boards that can be seen from Reforma.

Museo Nacional de Antropología ▥ ★
Map 13D2. Reforma, opposite Chapultepec Park ☎(5) 553 6266 ⚄ ⚄ ⚄ ⚄ Open Tues–Sat 9am–7pm; Sun 10am–6pm. Closed Mon.

This unique museum, itself a stunning work of modern architecture, designed by Pedro Ramírez Vázquez, has an outstanding collection of Pre-Hispanic treasures. The **mural decorations** by Rufino Tamayo, not actually part of the exhibitions, also deserve thorough attention. So many cultures and civilizations are represented in this museum, including those of the indigenous peoples of modern Mexico, that it is impossible to do them all justice in a single visit.

The entrance off Reforma is guarded by a **giant statue** found near the capital, thought to be of the **rain god, Tlaloc**: on the day that it was moved here, Mexico City was drenched by unseasonal rain. The galleries are on two floors around the courtyard; the first floor houses the Pre-Hispanic collections, with one room given over to each main cultural group; upstairs are the modern native items. In each case, it makes sense to concentrate on areas of the country that you plan to visit.

On the left of the foyer is the **bookstall**, which has an excellent selection of maps, cards, and books on archeology. Across on the right are the temporary exhibition rooms, where the latest finds from various excavations are on display. To get to the permanent galleries, head into the central court under the unusual **umbrella fountain**.

Start on the right with the three small galleries containing an introduction to anthropology and the development of Mesoamerican civilization: omit these if you are in a hurry. The next three rooms are devoted to the three main periods of civilization in the Valley of Mexico: the Pre-Classic, Classic (Teotihuacán) and Post-Classic (Toltec and Aztec).

In the **Pre-Classic** Room, see especially the **pottery figurines** from Tlatilco, and the "**Acrobat's Vase**" from near the same site. The life and imagination in these simple pieces remain fresh after hundreds of years. In the **Teotihuacán Room**, the inlaid **funerary masks** are the main attraction. The **Toltec Room** is smaller and less interesting, but the adjacent **Aztec Room** is not to be missed. The centerpiece is the **Aztec calendar** (pictured left), a 25-ton circle of basalt, with engravings symbolizing the Aztec system for measuring time, a vital part of their cosmology and religion.

Aztec calendar

The Aztec room is at the end of the courtyard. Back down the other side are the rooms dealing with civilizations from other parts of Mexico. First come the civilizations of the Valley of Oaxaca: the Classic **Zapotecs**, and the Post-Classic **Mixtecs**. The latter were famous for their especially fine pottery and jewelry.

The next room goes back in time to the **Olmecs** of the Gulf coast, the first important culture of Mesoamerica, whose sculpture was highly accomplished at all scales, from giant monolithic heads down to beautifully carved miniature jade figurines. Next door is the room of the **Maya** people, once the most advanced civilization of Mesoamerica.

Outside the room, in the garden, is a full-sized reproduction of the famous **Painted Temple of Bonampak**, complete with its three painted chambers. Finally comes a room of artifacts from N and W Mexico; both areas were remote from the more advanced cultures but, in the W especially, a high artistic level was reached. See the delightful little **pottery figurines**, illustrating all aspects of everyday life.

The second-floor galleries are devoted to the modern descendants of the Pre-Hispanic master-craftsmen. In much of the country the indigenous ways of life and ancient customs are being undermined, and traditional costumes are invariably an early casualty of cultural change; these displays at least preserve an outward impression of the societies that are so fast disappearing.

Free guided tours of the museum are available in Spanish, but a small fee is charged for other languages. The large **catalog** serves not only as a guide, but as a reference book for all the Mesoamerican cvilizations.

Centro Cultural de Arte Contemporáneo ⅢⅢ

Map 13D1. Overlooking Chapultepec Park, with entrance on Campos Eliseos and Jorge Eliot ▧ *Open Tues–Sun 10am–6pm; Wed 10am–9pm. Closed Mon.*

This dramatic new building houses Mexico's newest major gallery, financed entirely from private sources. It consists of three large floors of display space, holding at any time one major exhibition and up to five others in various media, at least one of them photographic. It also houses a permanent collection by the Mexican photographer Manuel Alvarez Bravo, as well as a section on Pre-Hispanic art. The center has an exchange program with Madrid's Prado museum.

Other museums

There are two museums in the "second section" of Chapultepec Park, along Constituyentes beyond the Periférico junction: the **Museum of Natural History** *(open 10am-5pm, 10am-6pm on Sun; closed Mon),* and the **Technological Museum** *(open 9am-5pm, 9am-1pm on Sun; closed Mon).*

Oriented toward the education of the young, they are very popular among Mexican families, but little visited by tourists. Both are worth avoiding on weekends, when they can be excessively busy.

NORTH OF THE CENTER

The following principal sights in the N of the city are all within easy reach of the center and can all be fitted into a single day's excursion.

Plaza de las Tres Culturas (Square of the Three Cultures) ☆

Map 15A6. Reforma Norte, 3km (1$\frac{1}{2}$ miles) N of the city center near Tlatelolco Metro station on line 2.

The symbolic importance of this place, the heart of the secondary Aztec center of Tlatelolco where the Aztecs met their final defeat, is discussed on page 53. This is the site of the notorious "Tlatelolco massacre" before the 1968 Olympic Games.

A peaceful student occupation of the square, protesting at the suppression of democratic rights, was brought to an abrupt end when the dissenters found themselves blocked into the square by security forces. Then, on orders that can only have come from the President, rooftop snipers and helicopter gunships opened fire, leaving uncounted hundreds dead. The government's calculated gamble paid off: the world's media ignored the massacre, the Olympic games passed unmolested by political protest, and the opposition movement was terrorized into silence for the next decade.

Both the **Aztec ruins** and the 1609 colonial church of **Santiago Tlatelolco** are interesting.

Basilica de Nuestra Señora de Guadalupe (Shrine of the Virgin of Guadalupe) ☆

At the N end of Calzada de Guadalupe, a short walk from the Basílica Metro station on Line 3.

Reforma Norte continues N of the PLAZA DE LAS TRES CULTURAS, becoming Calzada de Guadalupe and ending in front of this huge modern basilica.

The dark-skinned Virgin of Guadalupe, Mexico's patron saint, first manifested herself in 1531 when — according to the well-established

67

legend — she appeared to a humble peasant, informing him of her wish to have her shrine built on this spot. The local bishop was skeptical, but the Virgin appeared again, telling the peasant to return to pick the roses that would be miraculously growing there. This he did, wrapping them in his cloak to show the bishop. When he arrived, the cloak was found to bear an image of the Virgin, and a church was built to house it.

The Virgin rapidly gained popularity, partly because of her Indian features and partly because she had appeared on Cerrito Tepeyac, a site sacred to the Pre-Columbian mother goddess Tonantzin. But despite the immediate upsurge in conversions to Catholicism, it still took more than two centuries of theological debate before the Virgin received papal approval, in 1754. The Virgen de Guadalupe was the symbol of the 1810 revolutionaries, and millions of reproductions of the miraculous image are to be found in cars, homes, factories and churches.

Every year on December 12, vast crowds of pilgrims gather to venerate the Virgin with fervent all-night religious devotions punctuated by magnificent firework displays. But the basilica is very active throughout the year, with hordes of sellers of religious items congregating on the wide paved area in front and a regular flow of pilgrims, many of them on their knees. One disturbing sight is the old women who have vowed never to walk again, shuffling around on their knees with their feet up in the air as they beg for alms. The result of their penance is permanent deformity, as their knees flatten into pads and their lower legs wither away.

Next door is the **old basilica**, a large colonial church of no great intrinsic merit but housing a fine collection of religious paintings, sculptures and porcelain objects. Behind it the **Capilla del Pocito** marks the place where a well materialized miraculously during one of the Virgin's appearances. The **Capilla de las Rosas**, where the roses were gathered, can also be visited. In the **Capilla del Tepeyac**, on the hill, are murals depicting all these miraculous episodes. The roses themselves, needless to say, have long since disappeared.

Pyramid of Tenayuca 🏛 ☆
4km (2 miles) E of Calzada Vallejo 🚌 🚶 *Open 10am–6pm. Closed Mon.*
Calzada Vallejo forks left from Insurgentes Norte at the Monumento a la Raza; the ruins are then signposted to the right.

These are smaller than the ruins of TEOTIHUACÁN but much closer to the center of the city, and can be combined with a visit to the BASILICA DE GUADALUPE. The main **pyramid** contains no less than five earlier pyramids, and was itself built over once, although this seventh layer has disappeared. The first pyramid, dating from about the 13thC, was built by the predecessors of the Aztecs. Of particular interest is the **row of serpents' heads** along the base of the pyramid: there were originally about 750, but over the years some have disappeared.

SOUTH OF THE CENTER

Where Insurgentes Sur passes between the wealthy suburbs of San Angel and Coyoacán, nearly 10km (6 miles) S of the intersection with Reforma, the granite **Monumento Obregón** provides a useful reference point for visiting the many interesting sights nearby. It marks the spot where General Alvaro Obregón was assassinated in 1928, and contains the General's arm, which was shot off in battle in 1915, carefully preserved in formalin.

There is a **map** of the San Angel and Coyoacán areas on the following pages. See also the SIGHTS IN MEXICO CITY map on page 60.

Poliforum Cultural Siqueiros ☆
Insurgentes Sur 700 at Filadelfia, 3km (1½ miles) s of center ▨ ═

On your way s, stop and visit this strange modern building, which provides space for a great variety of cultural performances. It has a good selection of folk art on display, most of it for sale, but is distinguished by the passionately Marxist **murals** of David Siqueiros, paid for by the wealthy capitalist who financed the center.

Coyoacán
Foot-weary visitors should take a taxi. Coyoacán's Zócalo lies 2.5km (1½ miles) E of the Monumento Obregón, on Insurgentes Sur, and 2km (1 mile) E of Quevedo Metro station.

Like SAN ANGEL to the w of the Monument, Coyoacán was once an independent village. Although swallowed up by the city, it retains its charm and distinctive character, and is now a popular place to live, even though pollution is bad here. The history of Coyoacán goes back a great deal further than colonial times: originally founded by the Toltecs in the 10thC, it was a thriving Aztec community of 20,000 when the Spanish arrived. It then served Cortés as a base for the siege of Tenochtitlán, the Aztec capital, and some of its buildings date from these turbulent times.

The best approach to Coyoacán is along **Av. Francisco Sosa**, a narrow street of low-rise colonial houses inhabited by affluent Mexicans. At the beginning of the street, near Quevedo Metro station, is an interesting modern **church** designed by Mexico's well-known modern architect, **Felix Candela**. Opposite, across Francisco Sosa, is an 18thC **Baroque chapel**. From here it is 1km (½ mile) E to the Plaza de Santa Catarina, with the attractive 16thC **church of Santa Catarina**, and another 1km (½ mile) to Coyoacán's Plaza Hidalgo, the Zócalo.

If you need another rest, stop off at the **Casa de Jesús Reyes Heroles** (Sosa 202), a convincingly colonial 20thC building that serves as a cultural center. On the Zócalo, see the early colonial church of **San Juan Bautista** (1582); and the 18thC **Palacio Municipal**, on the site of Cortés's palace in which Cuauhtémoc was held prisoner. On Saturday and Sunday there is a lively **market**, with bookstalls, on the adjacent Jardín Centenario.

From the plaza, head N up Centenario for six blocks, then turn right into Londres. The **Museo Frida Kahlo** (☆ *Londres 127* ☎ *(5) 554 5999* ▨ *open 10am–6pm; closed Mon)* is the studio of the extraordinary woman and notable artist who for many years was married to Diego Rivera. It contains a large number of Kahlo's works, many of them self-portraits, some of them portraits of Rivera, and a large collection of Pre-Columbian, colonial and folk art including some charming little pictures commemorating lucky escapes from disaster.

The former home of another extraordinary woman, yet more pivotal in Mexico's history, is also in Coyoacán: Cortés built a house here that

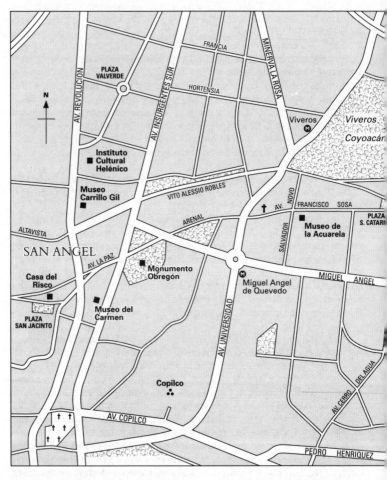

was briefly inhabited by his wife, who conveniently died to make room for La Malinche, his native mistress whose linguistic skills and local knowledge were vital to the success of the Conquest. The **Casa de la Malinche**, built of reddish stone, stands to this day *(Higuera 57 and Vallarta, two blocks E of the Zócalo)* but, perhaps not altogether surprisingly, remains uncommemorated.

In the northern part of Coyoacán is the **Museo de Léon Trotsky** (☆ *1.5km/1 mile NE of the Zócalo at Av. Río Churubusco 410* ☎ *(5) 554 0687* 🚾 *open 10am–5pm; closed Mon).* This fortress-like building was the home of Leon Trotsky, the Russian revolutionary, who endured his many years of exile here under constant threat from Stalinist ideological adversaries who were determined to kill him. After surviving a number of assassination attempts, Trotsky was finally murdered on August 20,

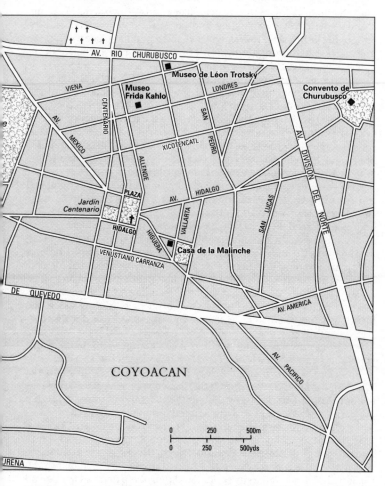

1940 by a former friend, who stuck an ice-axe into his head as he fed his pet rabbits in the garden. The house is a shrine to Trotsky's memory, frozen in time just as it was on that fateful day.

From the Trotsky museum it is about 1km ($\frac{1}{2}$ mile) E along Río Churubusco to the **Convento de Churubusco** *(between División del Norte and Calzada Tlalpán* ![icon] *open 9am–1pm, 3–5pm; closed Mon)*, an old Franciscan monastery in well-kept grounds. A battle took place here in 1847 between Mexican and US troops, and it has been turned into a museum dedicated to the history of foreign interventions in Mexico, which turn out to be surprisingly numerous.

San Angel

The colonial center of San Angel lies $\frac{1}{2}$ km ($\frac{1}{4}$ mile) w of the Monumento Obregón on Insurgentes Sur along Av. de la Paz, and 1km ($\frac{1}{2}$ mile) w of the Quevedo Metro.

71

This charming colonial village has, like nearby Coyoacán, been surrounded by the ever-expanding and endlessly polluting Mexico City. Although a fashionable residential area and a popular place to visit, San Angel lacks the historic distinction of its more illustrious neighbor; its oldest buildings date from the 17thC.

Approaching San Angel from the Monumento Obregón along Av. de la Paz, the first building of note is a Carmelite convent dating from 1617, now the **Museo del Carmen** (☎ *(5) 548 5312* ◪ *open 10am–5pm; closed Mon),* which is on the left just before the traffic artery of Revolución. The courtyard is full of trees and flowers, with a tiled fountain at its center. Somewhat gruesome, by contrast, is the **crypt** full of mummified bodies. In the church, see the colonial oil paintings, especially the *Marriage of the Virgin* by Cristóbal de Villalpando.

Cross over Revolución, keeping the flower market on your right, and carry on w up Av. de la Paz into San Angel proper, maybe stopping at the large FONART shop on Av. de la Paz (see SHOPPING, page 86). Several fine houses are passed on the way to the **Plaza San Jacinto**. In 1847, 50 Irish soldiers who sided with Catholic Mexico in the Mexican–American war, in which the US annexed much of the country, were hanged here as traitors by invading US forces; they are fondly remembered in Mexico, however, and there is a small plaque in their honor in the square.

The best day to visit Plaza San Jacinto is Saturday, when there is a lively arts and crafts market (see BAZAR SÁBADO on page 86). At #15 is the luxuriously furnished 18thC mansion known as the **Casa del Risco** or "House of Broken Porcelain" (⏧ ☎ *(5) 548 2329* ◪ *open 9am-3pm; closed Sun),* now a museum of colonial and European art. In the courtyard stands a fountain whose decoration gives the house its name.

From here, go down Alvaro Rivera, then turn right up Santísima to Alta Vista. On the left is the restored 18thC hacienda of San Angel, known as the **San Angel Inn**. It is now a luxury restaurant, but even those on a budget should at least have a drink in the beautiful **courtyard**.

To return to the Monumento Obregón, head back E down Alta Vista. From here fork left into Desierto de los Leones. On the left is Rivera's former studio, the **Museo Estudio Diego Rivera** *(open 10am-6pm; closed Mon).* Designed by architect Juan O'Gorman in 1930, the studio has now been restored to its condition during the painter's lifetime and retains a strong sense of his frenetic, larger-than-life character.

Crossing over Revolución, it is worth stopping at the excellent **Museo Alvar y Carmen Carrillo Gil** *(Revolución 1608 at Alta Vista* ☎ *(5) 548 6467* ◩ *open 10am-6pm; closed Mon),* an interesting gallery of mostly modern art where the works of Klee, Picasso and Kandinsky rub shoulders with homegrown masters including Rivera, Siquieros and Orozco, not to mention Maya pieces from Jaina Island. To the E of here is Insurgentes Sur, where a right turn takes you back to the monument.

Copilco ☆

◪ ➡ *Open 10am–6pm. Closed Mon. Take Insurgentes Sur 1km (mile) s of the Monumento Obregón, turn left (s) into Av. Copilco, then left again following signposts to the site; or take a taxi from Copilco Metro station on line 3.*

Under the thick layer of lava that covers most of this archeological site, various tombs — some of them 3,500 years old — have been discovered. The **tunnels** used for the excavation now form a museum in which pottery, obsidian tools and skeletons from the graves arc displayed. The great heat and pressure from the volcanic eruption has twisted and deformed the bones.

University City (UNAM) 🏛 ☆

📷 *2km (1 mile) s of the Monumento Obregón, turn left off Insurgentes Sur.*

The 1950s architectural styles are bold and diverse, the buildings heavily decorated, and the whole complex is surrounded by gardens and squares in the twisted lava fields of the Pedregal. Most famous of the buildings is the ten-floor **Library** (illustrated on page 38), covered in mosaics by Juan O'Gorman. On the E wall is his vision of Mexico's future; the theme of the other three walls is historical.

Behind the Library is the Plaza Mayor. At the **Faculty of Science**, on the far side of the plaza, see the mural, *Conquest of Energy*, by José Chavez.

Cross the small plaza behind this building to reach the **Faculty of Medicine**, where another enormous mural is appropriately titled *Life and Death*. Then turn right for the short walk to the dome of the **tropical greenhouse**, full of interesting botanical specimens from all over Mexico. The **Museum of Art and Science** is passed on the way back to Insurgentes Sur. By the bus stop are a small bookstore and a post office, while on the far side of Insurgentes Sur is the **Olympic Stadium** (🏛), designed by Felix Candela, with an enormous mural by Rivera.

The rest of the University is 2km (1 mile) farther s down Insurgentes Sur, on the left. Behind the buildings is a collection of huge open-air sculptures by some of Mexico's leading sculptors. The centerpiece of the **Espacio Escultórico** (☆), designed jointly by a group of six sculptors, is a great ring of tilted white monoliths surrounding a tortured sea of lava. The frozen violence of the rocks contrasts with the tranquility of the setting, giving an almost supernatural atmosphere. Also worth a visit are the **Botanical Gardens**, next to the Institute of Ecology, w of Insurgentes, with an extensive cactus garden laid out among the lava outcrops.

Cuicuilco ☆

To the E of Insurgentes Sur, after intersection with the Periférico 1.5km (1 mile) s of the University City ↠ ✗ Site and museum. Open 9am–6pm. Closed Mon.

The archeological site of Cuicuilco, a circular pyramid more than 100m (328 feet) across, dating from around 500BC, lay covered by lava following an eruption of Xitli volcano for thousands of years until excavations began in 1922. On the site is a small museum containing artifacts from Cuicuilco and from contemporary sites all over central Mexico.

Xochimilco ☆

24km (15 miles) s of center at SE end of the Periférico; by public transport, take Metro line 2 s to Tasqueña, then transfer to bus or the light railroad (under construction at time of writing) ✳ ◁€

The floating gardens of Xochimilco come to life on Saturday and Sunday, when the canals, filled with flower-covered boats and *mariachi* bands, become the scene of a languid water-borne carnival. Just as the gardens of Babylon were not hanging, however, these gardens are not actually floating, but are little artificial islands. The Aztec word for them was *chinampas,* and all of Tenochtitlán's fruit and vegetables were grown on these islands.

Even today, Xochimilco meets a proportion of Mexico City's needs in this respect, although this may not be true for much longer. Already the extent of the *chinampas* has been reduced to just 800 hectares (1,976 acres) from the original 20,000 (49,400).

The problems are many: pressure on land for housing; falling water levels; and infestations of water hyacinths, siltation and health problems caused by sewage runoff and direct sewage flows into the canals. Despite Xochimilco's 1987 designation by UNESCO as a Human Cultural Heritage site, this highly productive example of Pre-Hispanic agricultural technology, along with the boating canals, may well be doomed.

Boats, each with a gondolier, can be rented (▓ *in daylight hours)* at a fixed hourly rate. Take a picnic and some cold drinks, and go off to explore some of the quieter backwaters.

Museo Anahuacalli ▥ ★

Calle del Museo 150, near Division del Norte, best reached by taxi from Tasqueña Metro station ▓ Open 10am–6pm. Closed Mon; Dec 15–Jan 5. A visit can be combined with an excursion to Xochimilco (above).

This massive, somber pyramidal building of solidified lava was designed by Diego Rivera to house his magnificent Pre-Hispanic collection. In the entrance hall, a stone plaque bears Rivera's dedication of the museum: "I return to the people the artistic heritage which I was able to redeem from their ancestors."

The first floor has exhibits from the three main civilizations of the Valley of Mexico: Teotihuacán, Toltec and Aztec. Especially fine are the life-sized Teotihuacán **funerary stone masks**. Some of the rooms are devoted to Pre-Hispanic gods common to all three cultures, emphasizing the importance of ancient religious symbolisms to Rivera's art.

The second floor is dominated by the great central room that Rivera intended to use as a studio, although he died before the building was completed. It contains charcoal studies for murals, unfinished paintings, and Pre-Hispanic pieces from the cultures of western Mexico, which also fill the other rooms on the second floor.

It is in this area that Rivera's collection surpasses all others, even that in the MUSEO NACIONAL DE ANTROPOLOGÍA. The most important exhibit in the main room is the **ball-game** from the state of Nayarit, a model of players, spectators and the actual court of the sacred ball-game; its vivid realism is rare in Mesoamerican art. See also the charming little **pot-bellied dogs** from Colima. Known as *escuintles,* they were highly valued as a delicacy by all Pre-Hispanic peoples.

On the smaller top floor are further Aztec pieces, and some Totonac work from the E coast. Although their region was isolated from the mainstream of civilization, the items in this collection show the artistic accomplishment of the Totonacs. The most remarkable piece is a **head of a coyote**, with a collar and enormous ears. Among the other works are several small "**smiling faces**"; such joyous expressions are a rarity in Mesoamerican art, which tended to reflect an austere, dramatic view of the world.

On the Sunday nearest to December 8, Rivera's birthday is celebrated with Indian dancing all day on the patio of the museum.

WALKS NEAR THE CITY

Perhaps surprisingly, within an hour's drive of the capital there are quiet mountains and forests where the air is fresh and clear, all deserted on weekdays. See also AROUND MEXICO CITY (pages 87-108).

Ajusco ☆
Take the road sw toward the village of Ajusco (a continuation of Paseo del Pedregal beyond the Periférico Sur), and park at the Albergue Alpinista hostel, about 12km (7 miles) from the Periférico.

One of the tallest of the volcanoes near the city. It is a stiff climb of $1\frac{1}{2}$ hours to the top; avoid the cliffs over to the left. In the rainy season, the climb is best undertaken early in the day, in order to be back before the start of the afternoon downpours. The views and solitude make all the effort worthwhile.

Desierto de los Leones
Leave the city w along Reforma; follow signposts for Toluca and after 22km (13 miles) take the mountain road left, signposted to Parque Nacional Desierto de los Leones. Alternatively, leave the city s along Altavista, which becomes Av. Desierto de los Leones after crossing the Periférico.

The parking lot is by a beautiful half-ruined **monastery** (☆ 🔲 *open standard hours)* surrounded by tranquil pine forests. There are no maps of the area, but it is hard to get lost if you stick to the forest paths. The name ("Desert of the Lions") refers to the pumas that used to haunt the area. Five kilometers (3 miles) farther w along the Toluca road, another left turning leads s to the area known as **La Marquesa**. All along this road are picnic spots with paths snaking off into the forests on the foothills of the Ajusco mountain range. The area is very quiet during the week, but gets busy on weekends.

Lagunas de Zempoala
Take the old free road s toward Cuernavaca; just past Tres Cumbres, 51km (31 miles), turn right heading w. See also AROUND MEXICO CITY, page 106.

A region of mountain lakes surrounded by forests is reached after 11km (6 miles). There are numerous paths, popular on weekends. Horses may be hired, and there is pleasant riding among the alpine scenery. Mexico City's demand for water has unfortunately led to some of the lakes drying out, especially in the dry season.

Where to stay in Mexico City

There are hundreds of hotels in Mexico City, ranging from international luxury palaces to rock-bottom boarding houses, where rooms can be rented by the hour.

RESERVATIONS: Tourists never have to sleep on the street, but it is best to reserve in advance, as demand is unpredictable and the more popular hotels can fill up quickly. If you arrive late without a reservation, take the first reasonably decent room you can afford for the first night, and hunt for something better the next day.

PRICES: Hotels in Mexico City are generally more expensive than in the rest of the country. The top international-style hotels are as expensive as anywhere, but middle- and lower-range hotels can be significantly cheaper than their equivalents in the US and Europe.

APARTMENT HOTELS: Visitors planning a longer stay, and aiming at comfort without financial ruin, may prefer to stay in a full-service apartment hotel, recognizable by names containing the word "Suites."

LOCATION: There are two main hotel areas, both convenient for sightseeing and shopping. Most of the luxury hotels are on **Reforma** near the Zona Rosa (the triangular shopping district off Reforma by the Angel of Independence) and along toward the center, while many of the more traditional and less pricey establishments are around the **Zócalo**.

AIR CONDITIONING: As a result of the pollution, virtually all hotels have **air conditioning**, so our listings do not repeat this.

CHARGE AND CREDIT CARDS: These are accepted so widely that we refer to them only in those exceptional cases where they are not; see CHARGE AND CREDIT CARDS on page 309.

USING OUR SYMBOLS: Symbols are used to show which hotels are particularly luxurious (🏨) and those that represent good value (♣). Other symbols show price categories (see HOW TO USE THIS BOOK on page 7), and give a resumé of the facilities that are available. A key to all symbols used can be found in HOW TO USE THIS BOOK on page 7.

SEE ALSO: Useful hints on choosing a place to stay in Mexico City can be found in WHERE TO STAY on pages 326-7. TIPPING on pages 322-3 takes the strain out of the fraught business of gratuities. Our essential guide to MEXICAN SPANISH includes a sample hotel booking letter, as well as many useful phrases dealing with accommodation.

HOTELS A TO Z
Zona Rosa and Reforma area:

ARISTOS
Map **14**D4. Paseo de la Reforma 276 CP06600 ☎(5) 211 0112 ☒(5) 525 6783 ▥ 360 rms ⬛ ⬒ 🍴 ♉ ➹ ⚓
♈ ⊙ ♫
Location: Zona Rosa. This is a large, tastefully furnished and decorated hotel, which offers its clientele a wide range of amenities. These include a sauna, gymnasium, travel agency and beauty parlor.

CAMINO REAL 🏨 ♣ 🏛
Map **13**D3. Mariano Escobedo 700 CP11590 ☎(5) 203 2121 ☒(5) 250 6897 ▥ 713 rms ⬛ ⬒ ⬒ 🍴 ⚓ ≋
♫ ⚓ ♈ ⊙ ♫
Location: By Chapultepec Park. People

have been known to come to Mexico just to stay at this luxurious self-contained neo-Aztec city, spread across 8 acres (3.2 hectares). With its wild disco, smart restaurants, rooftop tennis courts and poolside gardens, it entertains and pampers residents and Mexican high society around the clock. The guest rooms are large, and service is rapid, if a little impersonal.

CENTURY ZONA ROSA 🏨
Map **14**D4. Liverpool 152 CP06600 ☎(5) 584 7111 ☒(5) 525 7475 ▥ 194 rms ⬛ ⬒ 🍴 ≋ ⚓ ♈ ⊙ ♫
Location: Zona Rosa. This modern hotel offers expensive elegance on a circular theme that extends to the beds, the balconies and even to the marble bathtubs.

GALERIA PLAZA
Map **14**D4. Hamburgo 195 CP06600
☎(5) 211 0014 [Fx](5) 528 9583
▥ 433 rms ◢ ☰ 𝆓 ⌘ ☲ ♈ ○ ♫
Location: Zona Rosa. Part of the Westin Camino Real chain, this smooth-running hotel offers a welcome haven from the noise and bustle on the streets below, and an excellent restaurant.

HOLIDAY INN CROWNE PLAZA 🏨
Map **14**C5. Reforma 80 CP06600 ☎(5)
705 1515 [Fx](5) 546 1706 ▥ 610 rms
◢ ☰ 𝆓 ⌘ ☲ ♈ ○
Location: Zona Rosa. With a wide choice of restaurants, nightclubs and other entertainments, the only thing lacking here is a swimming pool.

KRYSTAL ZONA ROSA 🏨
Map **14**D4. Liverpool 155 CP06600 ☎(5)
211 3460 [Fx](5) 211 3490 ▥ 324 rms
◢ ☰ 𝆓 《 ☋ ☲ ♈ ○ ♫
Location: Zona Rosa. This renovated high-rise hotel can boast a superb rooftop swimming pool, in addition to efficient service, good restaurants and a lively nightlife.

MARCO POLO 🏨
Map **14**D4. Amberes 27 CP06600 ☎(5)
207 1893, or toll-free ☎(800) 90060
[Fx](5) 533 3727 ▥ 60 rms ☰
Location: Half a block s of Reforma in the Zona Rosa. A comfortable, upmarket hotel with an excellent restaurant. The four penthouse suites, each with its own Jacuzzi and roof terrace, offer the ultimate in luxury.

MARÍA CRISTINA ♣ ⏛
Map **14**C4. Lerma 31 CP06500 ☎(5) 546
9880 [Fx](5) 566 9194 ▥ 150 rms
☰ ◢ ♈
Location: N of the Zona Rosa, overlooking the Jardín del Arte. This 1930s-built hotel is renowned for excellent value, considering its quality and location.

MARIA ISABEL SHERATON 🏨
Map **14**D4. Paseo de la Reforma 325
CP06500 ☎(5) 207 3933 [Fx](5) 207
0684 ▥ 747 rms ◢ ☰ 𝆓 《 ☋ ☲
♈ ○ ♫

Location: Near the Zona Rosa, overlooking the Angel of Independence. After enjoying the restaurants and nightclubs, get back in shape in the Turkish bath and gymnasium. The upper five floors have been converted into a super-luxurious hotel-within-a-hotel, the **Sheraton Towers**, with fine views over the city. The daily buffet lunch is recommended for hungry shoppers from the Zona Rosa.

MARQUIS REFORMA 🏨
Map **14**D4. Paseo de la Reforma s/n
CP06500 ☎(5) 211 3600, or toll free
(800) 90176 [Fx](5) 211 5561 ▥ 210
rms ◢ ☰ 𝆓 ☲ ♈ ♫
Location: Near Zona Rosa. A new pink granite-and-marble palace that caters to business travelers by providing full office facilities as well as all the usual comforts of a top-notch hotel.

NIKKO
Map **13**D2. Campos Elíseos 204 CP11560
☎(5) 203 4800, or toll-free (800) 90888
[Fx](5) 254 6980 ▥ 750 rms ◢ ☰ ☋
♈ ○ ♨
Location: near Chapultepec Park. Part of the Japanese Nikko chain, this towering hotel occupies a prime position overlooking the Bosque de Chapultepec. Its excellent facilities, including a modern health club and restaurants serving French, Japanese and Mexican cuisine, put it at the top of many people's choice of hotels in the city; but to others the atmosphere remains curiously impersonal.

PLAZA FLORENCIA
Map **14**D4. Florencia 61 CP06600 ☎(5)
211 0064 [Fx](5) 511 1542 ▥ 148 rms
◢ ☰ 𝆓 ☲ ♈ ○ ♫
Location: Zona Rosa. This ultramodern hotel has the misfortune of being on the very busy shopping street that runs s off Reforma from the Angel monument; fortunately the pleasant rooms are well soundproofed.

QUALITY INN CALINDA GENEVE ♣ ⏛
Map **14**D4. Londres 130 CP06600 ☎(5)
211 0071 [Fx](5) 208 7422 ▥ 347 rms

━ ⇌ 🍴 👔 ♈ 🎵

Location: Zona Rosa. The cocktail bar is reminiscent of a rainforest and the lobby spacious and well-furnished, but the rooms are small and uninteresting.

SEVILLA PALACE 🏨

Map **14**C5. *Reforma 105 CP06030* ☎(5) *566 8877* [Fx](5) *535 3842* ▥ *414 rms*
━ ⇌ ⇚ 👔 ♈ 🅾 🚹 🎵

Location: Near Zona Rosa. One of Mexico City's newest luxury hotels: dizzying glass elevators travel the 23 floors to the panoramic nightclub.

STOUFFER PRESIDENTE 🏨

Map **13**D2. *Campos Elíseos 218 CP11560* ☎(5) *327 7700* [Fx](5) *327 7730* ▥ *750 rms* ━ ⇌ 🍴 🛥 ⇚ 👔 ♈ 🅾 🎵

Location: By Chapultepec Park. The spacious rooms of this modern luxury hotel offer some of the city's finest views, while the soaring inverted-pyramid lobby offers even more dramatic interior perspectives. Guests can take their pick of shops, restaurants and live music at the lobby bar.

In the Zócalo area:

DE CORTÉS BEST WESTERN ♣ 🏛

Map **15**C6. *Hidalgo 85 CP06030* ☎(5) *518 2182* [Fx](5) *518 3466* ▥ *29 rms*
━ ⇌ 🍴 🛥 🅾 🎵

Location: By the Alameda. This small but delightful hotel occupies a renovated colonial building of 1780, with pleasantly airy rooms surrounding a tree-shaded courtyard, complete with fountain. One thing to bear in mind: the *mariachi* fiesta that takes place every Saturday makes an early night out of the question.

GRAN HOTEL HOWARD JOHNSON ♣ 🏛

Map **15**C7. *16 de Septiembre 82 CP06000* ☎(5) *510 4040* [Fx](5) *512 2085* ▥ *125 rms* ━ ⇌ 🏠 🍴 👔 ♈ 🅾

Location: On the Zócalo. The magnifi-

cent lobby of this traditional luxury hotel is worth a visit in its own right, with its stained-glass dome by Tiffany, chandeliers and smoothly gliding 19thC cage-elevators all reflected in an abundance of mirrors. The hotel has its own, typically excellent, branch of DEL-MONICO'S restaurant, with a panoramic view of the downtown area.

MAJESTIC BEST WESTERN

Map **15**C7. *Madero 73 CP06000* ☎(5) *521 8600* [Fx](5) *518 3466* ▥ *85 rms* ⇌ ♈

Location: On the Zócalo. Handsome, comfortable neocolonial hotel with a magnificent **rooftop restaurant** that swings into life with live *mariachi* music accompanying the all-afternoon Sunday buffet.

RITZ BEST WESTERN

Map **15**C6. *Madero 30 CP06000* ☎(5) *518 1340* [Fx](5) *518 3466* ▥ *140 rms* ⇌ ♈

Location: Two blocks w of the Zócalo. The largest of the three Best Westerns in downtown Mexico City, this pleasant hotel is also the least special; but the classical piano music in the bar can make a refreshing change from too many *mariachis.*

In the south:

REAL DEL SUR 🏨

División del Norte 3640 at junction with Tlalpán CP04620 ☎(5) *678 1133* [Fx](5) *678 0427* ▥ *120 rms*
⇌ ♈ 🅾 🎵

Location: In the s of the city, near Coyoacán. This is the first, and so far the only luxury hotel in the s of the city. With its soaring glass-roofed lobby, spacious guest rooms, restaurants, shops and the full range of facilities, the Real del Sur is certainly the equal of any of its more established rivals in the central areas.

ALSO WORTH CONSIDERING . . .

The principal hotels listed above are but a small selection out of an immense number. Quite a few others are also worth considering, especially for the more economically inclined.

In and around the Zona Rosa:

Additional hotels in the fashionable Zona Rosa area *(map 14D4, CP06600)* include:

- **Royal** *(Amberes 78* ☎*(5) 525 4850* [Fx]*(5) 514 3330* ▥ to ▥ *162 rms* ═ ♈*)*.
- **Suites Amberes** *(Amberes 64* ☎*(5) 533 1306-9* [Fx]*207 1509* ▥ to ▥ *28 rms* ☎ ☎ ♈*)* has a range of spacious apartments, all with a small kitchen, balcony and modern colonial-style furniture.
- **Vasco de Quiroga** *(Londres 15* ☎*(5) 546 2614* ▥ *52 rms* ═*)*.

On the E fringes of the Zona Rosa:

- **El Ejecutivo** *(Viena 8* ☎*(5) 566 6422* [Fx]*(5) 705 5476* ▥ to ▥ *118 rms* ═*)*.
- **Internacional Havre** *(Havre 21* ☎*(5) 211 0082* ▥ *48 rms* ♈ ═*)*.
- **Prim** *(Versalles 36 near General Prim, map 14C5* ☎*(5) 592 4600* [Fx]*(5) 592 4835* ▥ *180 rms* ═ ♈*)*.
- **Suites Havre** *(Havre 74, map 14C4* ☎*(5) 533 5670-74* ▥ to ▥*)*, another apartment hotel.
- **Viena** *(Marsella 28* ☎*(5) 566 0700* [Fx]*(5) 592 7302* ▥ *71 rms* ♈ ═*)*.

South of the Zona Rosa:

- **Misíon Park Plaza** *(map 14D4, Nápoles 62* ☎*(5) 533 0535* ▥ ═*)* is comfortable and well placed.
- **Reforma** *(♣ map 14C5, Reforma at Paris CP06470* ☎*(5) 546 9680* ▥ *269 rms* ☎ ═ ▨ ☻ ♈ ●*)*, set among the high-rise glass towers along Reforma, is still recommended for its 1930s decor and good service.

There are also many hotels in the streets N of the Zona Rosa across Paseo de la Reforma. Overlooking the Jardín del Arte are:

- **Mallorca** *(map 14C4, Serapio Rendon 119 CP06470* ☎*(5) 566 4833* ▥ *124 rms* ═*)*.
- **Stella Maris** *(map 14C4, Sullivan 69 CP06470* ☎*(5) 566 6088* [Fx]*(5) 592 5904* ▥ *116 rms* ═*)*.

Others include:

- **Bristol** *(map 14C4, Plaza Necaxa 17 CP06500* ☎*(5) 208 1717* ▥ *134 rms* ═ ♈*)*.
- **Del Angel** *(map 14C4, Lerma 154 CP06500* ☎*(5) 533 1032* ▥ *100 rms)*, near the Angel of Independence.
- **Jardín Amazonas** *(Río Amazonas 73 CP06500, map 14C4* ☎*(5) 533 5950* [Fx]*(5) 514 2440* ▥ *50 rms* ♈ ═ ☎*)*.
- **Michelangelo Suites** *(Río Amazonas 78, map 14C4* ☎*(5) 566 9877* ▥ *40 rms* ═ ♈*)*.

Zócalo area:

Other hotels in the central area include:

- **Ambassador** *(map 14C5, Humboldt 38 CP06050* ☎*(5) 518 0110* [Fx]*(5) 510 9645* ▥ ═*)*, two blocks SW of the Alameda.
- **Catedral** *(map 15C7, Donceles 95* ☎*(5) 521 6183* ▥ *116 rms* ♈ ═*)*, a traditional hotel near the cathedral.

On Uruguay, two blocks s of the Zócalo:
- **Monte Carlo** *(#69, map 15 C6* ☎ *(5) 521 2559* ▥ *)*, spacious.
- **Roble** *(#109, map 15 C6* ☎ *(5) 522 7830* ▢ *)*, cheap if charmless.

On Av. 5 de Mayo, between the Zócalo and the Alameda:
- **Canada** *(* ♣ *#47, map 15 C6* ☎ *(5) 518 2106* ▥ *)*, clean, modern and popular.
- **Juárez** *(* ♣ *Callejón de 5 de Mayo 17, N off Av. 5 de Mayo, map 15 C6* ☎ *(5) 512 6929/0568* ▢ *38 rms)* has a touch of elegance.
- **San Antonio** *(* ♣ *Callejón 5 de Mayo 29, S off Av. 5 de Mayo, map 15 C6* ☎ *(5) 512 9906* ▥ *44 rms)*, another good choice.

Handy for travelers . . .

For those who need to spend a night near the airport there are three expensive hotels: the luxurious **Fiesta Americana Aeropuerto** *(*🏨 *Fundidora de Monterrey 89 CP15520* ☎ *(5) 762 0199* Ⓕⓧ *(5) 785 1034* ▨ *481 rms* ≋ ☿ ⫸ *)*; the neo-colonial **Holiday Inn Aeropuerto** *(*🏨 *Blvd. Puerto Aéreo 502 CP15500* ☎ *(5) 762 4088* Ⓕⓧ *(5) 762 9934* ▨ *324 rms* ≋ ♠ ⫸ *)*, with its own shops and travel agency; and the **JR Plaza** *(Blvd. Puerto Aéreo 390* ☎ *(5) 785 5200 or toll-free (800) 70242* Ⓕⓧ *(5) 784 3221* ▨ ⫸ ☿ ● *125 rms)*.

For those catching an early bus from the Terminal del Norte, the **Brasilia** *(Cien Metros 4823, CP07770* ☎ *(5) 587 8577* ▥ ⫸ *)* is recommended.

Dining out in Mexico City

Mexicans love eating out, and nowhere is this more true than in Mexico City. Every national cuisine is represented, as is the enormous diversity of Mexican cooking. The cost of a meal can vary enormously, but prices are lower than in the US or Europe, while the standard of cooking and service is comparable. Visitors new to the city can thus afford to avoid the lower-priced restaurants. The menu of gastronomic opportunities is so extensive that those who venture no farther than hotel dining rooms and fast-food bars are missing an important part of the Mexican experience.

There are two contenders for that one unforgettable evening: the **San Angel Inn** and the **Hacienda de los Morales**. The colonial atmosphere, sophisticated cooking and excellent wines available in both establishments place them firmly among the world's greatest restaurants.

Every neighborhood has its small family restaurants, but the smarter establishments are concentrated mostly in the fashionable **Zona Rosa**. The southern district of **San Angel** and the areas around the **Zócalo** also have a good selection. For luxury restaurants, telephone reservations are advisable a day ahead.

The subtleties of Mexican cuisine are explained in FOOD AND DRINK, pages 327-31; the MENU GUIDE in MEXICAN SPANISH should prove useful to those whose gastronomic lexicon is less than perfect.

The following selection concentrates on places offering Mexican food and ambience, with a few notable exceptions. Symbols show which restaurants are particularly luxurious (⚱) or simple (♨). Price categories are explained in HOW TO USE THIS BOOK, on page 7.

ALIMENTATIO

Off map 13D1. Prado Nte 560, Lomas de Chapultepec ☎*(5) 520 6343* ▥▢
This small Parisian-style restaurant is nearly always full and accepts no reservations, but it is worth waiting to get in. Be sure to leave space for dessert, as the choice is mouthwatering.

ANDERSON'S

Map 13D3. Reforma 400, Zona Rosa ☎*(5) 525 1006/511 5187* ▥▢ ♫
The menu may be written to amuse, the decor offbeat, the waiters relaxed and casual; but the food in this lively, crowded restaurant is usually reliable. There is a sister branch in the southern suburb of San Angel *(Calzada Desierto 67* ☎*(5) 548 1265)* serving the same international menu; steaks here are very good. Music and clamor!

ARROYO

Insurgentes Sur 4003, Tlalpán ☎*(5) 573 7745* ▥▢ ⚱
South of University City, Arroyo is an excellent place for *al fresco* barbecue lunches on weekends. It is justifiably popular with families, who can include it in a visit to Xochimilco or any of the other sights to the s of the city center. The food is reliable, if perhaps a touch unadventurous.

BELLINGHAUSEN

Map 14D4. Londres 95, Zona Rosa ☎*(5) 207 6149* ▥▢
This well-established hotel is one of the few in the Zona Rosa area that is not a tourist trap. The cooking is traditional, and there is a lovely outdoor patio. It tends to get very crowded at lunchtimes on weekends.

CHAMPS-ÉLYSÉES ⚱

Map 14D4. Amberes 1 on Reforma ☎*(5) 514 0450* ▥▢ ➦
One of Mexico City's best French restaurants. Watch top politicians and businessmen wheeling and dealing over lunch. The evenings are quieter and more intimate.

CHEZ WOK

Map 13C1. Tennyson 117 and Masaryk, Polanco ☎*(5) 281 3410/2921* ▥▢
A very classy, upmarket Chinese restaurant; the Peking Duck and Sichuan dishes are particularly authentic, although all the food has acquired a slightly Mexican aroma.

CICERO'S ⚱ ▥

Map 14D4. Londres 185, Zona Rosa ☎*(5) 525 6130* ▥▢ ➦ ⚘
Very fashionable, this is a beautifully furnished old mansion in the Zona Rosa, crammed with antiques. It serves seafood specialties.

CIRCULO DEL SURESTE ⚘

Map 14C5. Lucerna 12 ☎*(5) 535 2704* ▥▢ ♫
To sample the aromatic spicy food of the Yucatán peninsula, very different from typical Mexican cuisine, try this simple and unpretentious restaurant. A must if you don't intend to travel to the Yucatán itself.

LA CIRCUNSTANCIA

Map 15B6. Honduras 17, by Plaza Garibaldi ☎*(5) 529 4140/4258* ▥▢
This is perhaps the best exponent of the *nueva cocina Mexicana,* and the number one choice for eating in the downtown area; it is especially lively at night. One special delicacy to try is the *mole de zarzamora* — chicken *mole*, but made with raspberries in place of the usual chocolate.

DARUMA ⚘

Map 14C4. Río Tiber 50, Colonia Cuauhtémoc ☎*(5) 511 8115* ▥▢
This reliable, centrally located Japanese restaurant is especially recommended for its well-stocked *sushi* bar.

DEL LAGO ⊜ 🏛
Map 13D2. Chapultepec Park 2nd Section
☎(5) 515 9585 ▥ ➴ ⵣ 𝅘 ⵣ
A flamboyant, modern glass-and-shell-concrete fantasy on the lakeside, providing international cuisine in a formal atmosphere.

DELMONICO'S ⊜
Map 14D4. Londres 87, Zona Rosa ☎(5)
528 7530/514 7003 ▥ ⵣ 𝅘
The menu is international and the service superb in this elegant restaurant. There is another branch at the GRAN HOTEL HOWARD JOHNSON (see WHERE TO STAY IN MEXICO CITY).

FONDA DEL RECUERDO
Map 13C3. Bahía de las Palmas 39A, Colonia Anzures ☎(5) 545 1652 ▥ 𝅘
Seafood is the specialty here, and the cooking is typical of the state of Veracruz. There is always a party atmosphere, with at least five bands playing all at once.

FONDA DON CHON ♣
Map 15C6. Regina 159, Colonia Centro
☎(5) 522 2170 ▯▢
This unobtrusive establishment must have one of the most exotic menus in Mexico — come here for iguana, grasshopper and wild boar in mango sauce. There are some unusual vegetable dishes.

FONDA EL REFUGIO ♣ ⊜
Map 14D4. Liverpool 166, Zona Rosa
☎(5) 525 8128 ▥ ➡
Traditional Mexican food is supplemented by regional specialties, and by one of the capital's best wine cellars.

LA GALVIA
Map 13D1. Campos Elíseos 247 ☎(5)
281 0560/2310 ▥
This *nueva cocina* restaurant is a great favorite of politicians and businessmen, who appreciate its organic lettuces and Mediterranean decor.

HACIENDA DE LOS MORALES ⊜ 🏛
Off map 13C1. Vázquez de Mella 525, Polanco ☎(5) 540 3225 ▥ ➡ ⵣ

This beautifully restored 16thC hacienda provides impeccable international and Mexican specialties. Dress is formal. A favorite venue for riotous high-society parties.

HOSTERÍA DE SANTO DOMINGO ♣
Map 15C7. Domínguez 72, Colonia Centro
☎(5) 510 1434 ▯▢
Still going strong after 100 years of good traditional Mexican food.

LOMA LINDA
Reforma 1105, Lomas de Chapultepec
☎(5) 520 0024 ▯▢
Situated in the fashionable Lomas residential area, w of the center. Recommended for its large Argentinian-style steaks and relaxed atmosphere.

LA MARINERA ♣
Map 14D4. Liverpool 183, Zona Rosa
☎(5) 511 3568 ▯▢
This pleasant and unpretentious Zona Rosa restaurant produces some of the best seafood to be found in Mexico City. Yet astonishingly, prices are modest.

MESÓN DEL CABALLO BAYO 🏛
Conscripto 360, Colonia Lomas Hipódromo
☎(5) 589 3000 ▥
Mexican specialties are served in this old colonial hacienda. Its proximity to the race-track attracts a lively, horsey crowd. For the popular Sunday lunch, reserve by Friday.

MESÓN DEL PERRO ANDALUZ
Map 14D4. Copenhague 20, Zona Rosa
☎(5) 533 5306 ▯▢
For sidewalk-café atmosphere, sample the well-prepared Spanish food in this establishment in the Zona Rosa.

LA PETITE FRANCE
Map 13C1. Presidente Masaryk 360, Polanco ☎(5) 250 4470 ▥
Well-presented French dishes complement the breezy Mediterranean decor in this fashionable area.

PRENDES
Map 15C6. Av. 16 de Septiembre, Colonia Centro ☎(5) 521 1878 ▯▢

A popular and almost historic venue for lunch, equally famous for its seafood dishes and for its murals.

SAN ANGEL INN ⌂ 🏛

Palmas 50, San Angel ☎*(5) 548 4514* ▨ ♪

Delicious, gourmet Mexican food, smooth and professional service in an elegant 18thC colonial building with furnishings from the same period. Combine a visit here with an excursion to the s of the city.

SPAGLIA

Map 13C1. Homero 704, Polanco ☎*(5) 203 0306/250 6932*

This Italian restaurant, near the hotel zone, has the best and most original menu of any in the city. The choice is contemporary, with unusual pastas and an exciting range of antipasti.

SUNTORY ⌂

Torres Adalid 14, Colonia del Valle ☎*(5) 536 9432* ▨ ♈ ♪ ♨

This elegant restaurant from the international chain offers an extensive range of delicious Japanese food combined with very efficient service.

TANDOOR ♦

Map 13C2. Lope de Vega 341A, Polanco ☎*(5) 203 0045* ▨

Excellent and surprisingly authentic Indian food is served here; prices are reasonable, especially for Polanco.

TRATTORIA ROMANA ♦

Map 13C3. Mariano Escobedo 543D, Polanco ☎*(5) 545 9803* ▨

The most genuine trattoria in Mexico City, with good, wholesome food, courteous service and a wide selection of desserts and sorbets.

Vegetarian restaurants

The austere-sounding **Restaurant Vegetariano y Dietetico** *(Madero 56, near Zócalo, map 15C6* ☎*(5) 321 6880* ▨*)* is excellent, as is its sister branch *(Filomata 13, 5 blocks w of Zócalo, map 15C6).*

In the Zona Rosa, try **Restaurant Vegetariano Yug** *(Varsovia 3 at Reforma, map 14D4* ☎*(5) 533 3296* ▨*)* for elegant and filling vegetarian cuisine.

Hotel restaurants

Also worth noting are the following hotel restaurants. Names given in brackets refer to the respective hotels, which can be found in WHERE TO STAY IN MEXICO CITY, on pages 75-80.

Fouquets *(*⌂ *Camino Real* ☎*(5) 545 6960* ▨*)* serves both international and French cuisine. However, for truly authentic French flavor, **Maxim's** *(El Presidente Chapultepec* ☎*(5) 250 7700* ▨*)* tries with some success to live up to its Parisian namesake. Within the same hotel is the **Arrecife** *(*☎*(5) 250 7700* ▨*)*, noted for excellent seafood.

If you seek entertainment with your dinner, the **Veranda** *(María Isabel Sheraton* ☎*(5) 525 9060* ▨*)* is the answer; it also offers a daily buffet lunch. For colonial atmosphere, try the restaurant in the **De Cortés** *(*♦ *De Cortés* ☎*(5) 585 0322* ▨ 🚍 ♪*)*. Also popular is the **Marco Polo** *(Hotel Marco Polo* ☎*(5) 207 1893* ▨*)*, with Mexican-influenced Italian cuisine. **La Fiesta** *(Holiday Inn Crowne Plaza* ☎*(5) 705 1515* ▨ ♪*)* comes to life for the Sunday afternoon barbecue brunch.

Mexico City by night

PERFORMANCES

Two essential experiences are the **Ballet Folklórico** and a visit to the **Plaza Garibaldi.** Some performances of the ballet take place at the PALACIO DE BELLAS ARTES (see page 36); most, however, are in the **Auditorio Nacional** outside the Alameda on Wednesday, Friday and Sunday. Pick up tickets beforehand at the Bellas Artes, or ask your hotel to arrange tickets and transport. The 2-hour performance features dances from all over the country, with superb costumes and choreography, and the interior of the Bellas Artes itself is well worth a visit.

The **Plaza Garibaldi** *(on Eje Lázaro Cárdenas, map 15 B6, 5 blocks N of the Bellas Artes)* is the home of Mexico's renowned *mariachi* musicians. Plan to arrive after dinner, then drift around listening to the competing bands. Later, head for one of the café-bars around the square to sip tequila and be entertained by the bar's own band. Best is the **Tlaquepaque**, which is untroubled by the drunken brawls that occasionally erupt in less salubrious establishments. The area is well patrolled by police, but it is unwise to carry much money.

Another recommended spectacle is the **son-et-lumière show** at the pyramids of TEOTIHUACÁN. Hotels will either arrange a tour to these or will put you in touch with an agency.

Times and places of concerts, ballets and Spanish-language plays are given in *The News* and the weekly *Tiempo Libre* (Free Time) magazine.

BARS AND DISCOS

For nonstop nightlife, it must be admitted that Mexico City is the equal of neither Acapulco nor New York, yet there is plenty to beguile and amuse the visitor into the small hours. Offices close around 7pm and business moves to the bars: luxury hotel lobby bars are a favorite meeting place, the most glamorous being those at the CAMINO REAL, the STOUFFER PRESIDENTE and the GALERIA PLAZA, with live music every night.

For details of the various entertainments and spectacles laid on by the luxury hotels, check in the free information sheet available at all hotel desks. The MARÍA ISABEL SHERATON and the STOUFFER PRESIDENTE usually have a big foreign name performing at one of their clubs or restaurants. The Saturday night fiesta at the DE CORTÉS hotel is always fun, with guitar music and Mexican food.

The hotel discotheques rank among the best. The **CeroCero** at the CAMINO REAL and the **Club 84** at the STOUFFER PRESIDENTE both offer loud rock music and more flashing lights than a fairground; also popular are **Lipstick** at the ARISTOS and **Le Chic** at the GALERIA PLAZA. In the s of the city, the REAL DEL SUR has a lively tropical-style **lobby bar** and the even livelier **Snobissimo** disco.

Also worth a visit after dinner is **Bar el Opera** *(map 15 C6, 5 de Mayo 10, near the Palacio de Bellas Artes* ☎ *(5) 512 8959* ▥▯*)*, a downtown lunch and drinking spot with ornate mirrors and mahogany paneling, light Mexican snacks and heavy Mexican drinking. **Catacumbas** *(map 15 C6, Dolores 16B just s of Alameda* ☎ *(5) 518 4027* ▥▯*)* is an old tourist favorite, with its subdued B-horror-movie feel and plenty of lively salsa and reggae music.

There is more live salsa music at **Tropicoso** *(map 14 D4, corner of Reforma and Niza, Zona Rosa* ▥*)* and at **Bar León** *(Brasil 5, N of cathedral* ☎*(5) 510 2979* ▥*)*; the **Carrousel** *(map 14 D4, corner of Hamburgo and Niza, Zona Rosa* ▢*)* is known for its nightly jazz performances; and **Gitanerías** *(map 14 D4, Oaxaca 15, near Zona Rosa* ▥*)* offers a flamenco floor-show and good Spanish food.

Down in the s of the city, there are several good nightspots with live music. The **Hijo del Cuevo** *(Jardín Centenario 17, Coyoacán* ☎*(5) 658 5306),* has a lively, bohemian ambience; across the square the **Mesón del Buen Tunar** *(Jardín Centenario 4, Coyoacán* ☎*(5) 554 2635)* has less conventional entertainments.

In San Angel, **El Condor Pasa** *(Rafael Checa 1* ☎*(5) 548 2050)* puts on authentic Latin American folk music.

Shopping

Anything from other parts of the country and, indeed, almost anything from other parts of the world, can be bought in Mexico City. Those with their wits about them can avoid expensive worthless rubbish and enjoy a bargainer's paradise, even in the most surprising places: the trick is to look doubtful and see what happens. It is important, however, to examine all goods thoroughly before purchase. For example, check hinges when looking at silver, and examine the stitching in leatherwork.

The best place to start is the central **Zona Rosa**, between **Chapultepec Park**, **Reforma** and **Insurgentes**, where, among the vast number of restaurants, cafés, nightclubs and hotels, there are hundreds of small shops selling silver, jewelry, leather, clothes, paintings and antiques. There are similar shops in the downtown area along **Reforma** and **Insurgentes**, and around the **Zócalo** and **Alameda Park**. Luxury hotels also have their own boutiques, which, although expensive, are useful for those in a hurry.

A new center of fashion has developed in **Polanco** along **Presidente Masaryk** and in nearby streets, where the many shops cater more to Mexico's own rich and privileged than to the tourist trade.

Department stores and shopping centers provide a helpful starting point for newcomers, and the capital's markets and craft centers should be on every visitor's list of places to visit. A selection of these follows.

DEPARTMENT STORES AND SHOPPING MALLS
Centro Comercial Perisur *(Insurgentes Sur and Periférico; closed Mon)* has three large department stores plus many boutiques and shops. The **Centro Comercial Ciudad Satelite**, w of the center on the road to Querétaro, is similar. **El Palacio de Hierro** *(map 15 C7, Av. 20 de Noviembre)* is a large downtown department store, good for inter-

national fashions. There is another branch at Durango and Salamanca *(map 14D4)*. The **Polanco** shopping mall *(map 13C2, Horacio)* comprises three large stores in one block: **El Puerto de Liverpool**, **Paris Londres** and **Woolworth's**, all close to the STOUFFER PRESIDENTE hotel.

Sanborn's has some 20 branches in strategic locations, all good for silver souvenirs and aimed at foreign visitors. The most notable one is in the **House of Tiles** *(map 15C6, Madero 4 ▣ open 7.30am-10pm)*, a 16thC building covered in blue tiles from China and nearby Puebla.

MARKETS AND CRAFT CENTERS

BAZAR SÁBADO
Plaza San Jacinto, San Angel.
Jewelry, painting, and folk art. Open Saturday 10am–8pm.

CASA DE LAS ARTESANÍAS DE MICHOACÁN
Map 13D2. Campos Eliseos and Temistocles, Polanco.
Ceramics, lacquer, copperware and jewelry from the villages of Michoacán.

CENTRO DE ARTESANÍAS BUENAVISTA
Map 14B5. Aldama 187.
A huge arts and crafts warehouse near the railroad station, which boasts of its enormous stock of 100,000 items.

CENTRO DE ARTESANÍAS CARRETA
Insurgentes 2105, San Angel.
In the basement under SANBORN'S; native art from all over Mexico is straightforwardly displayed.

CIUDADELA
Map 14C5. Av. Balderas at Plaza de la Ciudadela.
Hundreds of little stalls in a custom-built development, with glassblowers, metalworkers and weavers at work.

FONART
Patriotismo 691 (near Plaza Mexico bullring); Juárez 70, 89 and 92 (near Alameda, map 15C6); Av. de la Paz 37 (San Angel); Londres 136A (Zona Rosa, map 14D4); Insurgentes Sur 1630; and at Plaza Satelite.
Good value and a wide choice are to be found at these government-run shops, which buy direct from native artisans working all over Mexico. The **FONART Exposición Nacional de Arte Popular** *(map 15C6, Juárez 89)* is particularly good.

INDIOS VERDES
1km (½ mile) to the N of the Basilica de Guadalupe.
Large open-air tourist market; a good place to stop *en route* to Teotihuacán.

LAGUNILLA
Map 15B7. Two blocks E of the Cuitlahuac monument on Reforma Norte.
This is a large covered market, open daily. However, it is only worth visiting on Sunday, when the streets to the N (especially Comonfort) fill with the stalls of what is known as the **"thieves' market."** Crafts, antiques and general bric-a-brac are sold for prices that vary according to the apparent wealth of the purchaser. Three blocks E is the **Tepito market** *(map 15B7)*, where much of what is on sale is smuggled or stolen. It used to be easy to buy such things as illegal guns, drugs and brass-knuckles here, but recently controls on this have become tighter. Keep a tight hold on your wallet.

MUSEO NACIONAL DE ARTES Y INDUSTRIAS POPULARES
Map 15C6. Juárez 44 on the Alameda. Open standard hours.
An enormous variety of weaving, ceramics and other craft products is to be found in this collection; unlike most museums, the exhibits here are on sale.

SAN JUAN CURIO MARKET
Map 15C6. Aranda and Ayuntamiento, 4 blocks S of the Alameda.
A large modern building, with stalls on three floors.

Around Mexico City

While modern Mexico City has obliterated superb archeological sites, drained jewel-like lakes, darkened the air with smog and destroyed the magnificent landscapes beheld by the conquistadors, the region around the city remains rich with glimpses of the old Mexico. Industrialism, pollution and urban growth are indeed pressing all around, but oases of calm survive, and the twin snowy peaks of the volcanoes, Popocatépetl and Ixtaccihuatl, rise sublimely above it all.

This region comprises the **Estado de México**, which engirdles Mexico City and into which the urban zone is rapidly overflowing; the state of **Hidalgo**, to the north; and to the south, the small but highly concentrated state of **Morelos**, centered on the colonial town of Cuernavaca.

ESTADO DE MÉXICO
As befits this cradle of civilization, the region is full of major monuments of ancient peoples and fascinating archeological remains. The

most important of these are the great pyramids of the Sun and Moon at **TEOTIHUACÁN**, which even the Aztecs believed to have been built by gods. Other places to visit in this state include the impressive monastery nearby at **Acolmán**, and the extraordinary church at **TEPOTZOTLÁN**.

TOLUCA, capital of Estado de México, is a busy industrial town with little to attract the casual visitor, only becoming a tourist destination on Fridays, when it holds its famous market. This offers an excellent opportunity to buy craft products from the surrounding villages, such as the outstanding ceramic sculptures of **Metepec**.

In this area there are also highly worthwhile if little-visited Aztec sites, such as **Calixtlahuaca** and **Teotenango**. And, if training for an ascent of the daunting **POPOCATÉPETL**, you can practice on the gentler slopes of the **Nevado de Toluca** volcano. Afterwards, relax in the hot mineral waters of **Ixtapan de la Sal**, or make for the chic resort of **VALLE DE BRAVO**, where the rich and powerful of Mexico City have their weekend retreats.

HIDALGO

Hidalgo tends to be visited not for its capital, the old mining town of **PACHUCA**, nor for the nearby 16th-century monasteries, but for the imposing ruins at **TULA**, the ancient capital of the Toltecs. This militaristic people of Post-Classic times emerged in the wake of the collapse of Teotihuacán and ultimately came to abandon Tula and widen their influence to the Maya regions of Yucatán and beyond.

The environs of Tula today — the busy industrial town, concrete factories, open-cast mines and barren landscape — are man-made. When the Spanish arrived, Tula was surrounded by dense forest, which was soon burned away to provide pasture for sheep and cattle, whose over-grazing since that time has left the area near-desert. Fortunately, lovely landscapes of lakes, mountain ravines and forests survive in the little-visited north of the state.

MORELOS

While the Tula ruins are impressive, their beauty falls well short of that of the much later sites to the south of Mexico City. Many can be explored from the colonial town of **CUERNAVACA**, capital of Morelos, which retains some of its charm despite growing from a population of under 100,000 to well over a million in a few decades.

The best sites are at **MALINALCO**, at **XOCHICALCO**, in the foothills of Mount Ajusco, and at nearby **TEPOZTLÁN** (named after Tepoztecatl, the Aztec god of mild inebriation), where the rock temple soars above the colonial village on high volcanic crags. The village also contains a substantial monastery, one of many in the area that warrants a visit.

AMECAMECA and more especially **CUAUTLA**, which are both nearby, are places from which to explore other monasteries in the countryside, most of them dating from the 16th century and long ago abandoned by their monks. The ruins and ancient carvings at **Chalcatzingo**, also near Cuautla, are particularly worth seeing.

Despite its small size, the state of Morelos played a pivotal role during the Mexican revolution of 1910–1920. The haciendas of this wealthy sugar-producing state had long expanded their lands over those of the local peasantry, who were then forced to work in the cane fields and mills. The man who gave expression to the resulting protests was Emiliano Zapata, Morelos's most famous son.

Zapata's vast if motley army of peasants regularly defeated the federal forces, at least on home soil, while he refused to compromise with moderate revolutionaries on the restoration of hacienda land to the peasants. Eventually, in 1919, he was betrayed by President Venustiano Carranza and shot, and it was only under President Lázaro Cárdenas in the late 1930s that the land reforms he was fighting for were implemented.

To this day Zapata remains a national hero, if one that Mexico's modern rulers would prefer to forget. His relevance is unlikely to diminish, however, as the government's reforms of Article 27 of the constitution lead to the dismantling of Cárdenas's land reform policies and the communal lands (*ejidos*) they created.

Towns, cities and cultural sites

Starting in **TOLUCA**, this chapter gives essential information on the following destinations, arranged to follow a roughly clockwise route through the region: **VALLE DE BRAVO**, **TEPOTZOTLÁN**, **TULA**, **PACHUCA**, **TEO-TIHUACÁN**, **TEXCOCO**, **POPOCATÉPETL AND IXTACCIHUATL**, **AMECAMECA**, **CUAUTLA**, **TEPOZTLÁN**, **CUERNAVACA**, **XOCHICALCO** and **MALINALCO**.

See USING THIS GUIDE on page 50 for details on how to use this section. On the following pages, helpful pointers are given on how to get to each of the destinations covered. Along with the MEXICO map on pages 46–7, and the 4-color maps at the back of this book, they should give all the information necessary for planning your trip to this part of Mexico.

TOLUCA

Map 11E6. Capital of Estado de México. 65km (40 miles) w of Mexico City on RF15; 82km (51 miles) E of Valle de Bravo; 105km (65 miles) NW of Cuernavaca; 148km (92 miles) N of Taxco on RF55 i Lerdo Pte 101 ☎(72) 132142. Altitude: 2,680m (8,790ft). Population:1 million. Served by train (on Mexico City–Guadalajara line) and bus.

Toluca is a large industrial city, with traffic nearly as bad as the capital's, few buildings of merit to compensate and a population swollen by refugees from Mexico City's 1985 earthquake. However, it is within reach of many interesting places; they are all within a day of Mexico City, but some people prefer to stay in Toluca, saving time on the road.

WHAT TO SEE

Toluca's **Friday market** is a lively and colorful place to buy Mexican crafts, and almost anything else as well. Weaving and pottery are good value, and also on offer are leather, wood-carving and basket-work.

For examples of the entire range of local crafts, go to the **Casa de las Artesanías**, a government-run museum and shop *(Paseo Tollocán, near the market, open 10am-8pm)*, or try **Mercado Juárez** *(by the bus terminal)*, an ugly concrete building overflowing with vegetables, inexpensive clothing and local craftwork.

Also of interest is the ambitious **Centro Cultural Mexiquense** *(SE of center, open Tues-Sun 10am-6pm; closed Mon ═╡)*, formerly the Hacienda de la Pila, which houses Museums of Modern Art, Popular Culture, and Anthropology and History. The **Museo de Bellas Artes** *(Santos Degollado 102 Pte, open Mon-Sat 10am-8pm, Sun 5.30pm)*, in an 18thC Carmelite monastery, is a large museum with a collection of Mexican Art through the colonial and modern periods.

☜ **Del Rey Inn** *(Paseo Tollocán* ☎ *(72) 122122* ⓕⓧ *(72) 122567* ▥ *258 rms* ═╡ ☿ ⋙)* is a large neocolonial motel 2.5km (1½ miles) from the center toward Mexico City; **San Francisco** *(❀ Rayon 104 Sur* ☎ *(72) 133114* ▥ ═╡ ☿)* is a spacious modern hotel; **Plaza Morelos** *(❀ Aquiles Serdán 115* ☎ *(72) 159200* ▥ ═╡)* has a good restaurant.

Castel Plaza las Fuentes *(Carr. México-Toluca, Km 57* ☎ *(72) 164666, or Mexico City* ☎ *(5) 207 6876* ▥ ═╡ ⋙ ♐ ☿ ●)* is a plush country-club-style hotel 8km (5 miles) NE of Toluca: a good place for a rest before pressing on into Mexico City.

═ The best places are around the Zócalo: for Mexican food, try **Hostería de los Ramblas** *(❀ Portal 20 de Noviembre 107* ☎ *(724) 42308* ▥)* or **Fonda Rosita** *(Belisario Dominguez 101* ☎ *(724) 51394* ▢)*.

WITHIN EASY DISTANCE

Calixtlahuaca ✰
11km (6 miles) NW, then turn W off RF55 N to San Juan del Río after 8km (5 miles).
A large and interesting archeological zone, with remains of a Matlazinca town and of its Aztec ceremonial center. The Aztecs won a great military victory here in 1475, in the course of which they took more than 10,000 prisoners for sacrifice.

The most important building on the site is the circular **Temple of Quetzalcóatl-Ehecatl**, constructed on four levels, with a wide stair on the E side. A short walk to the SE is the **Temple of Tlaloc**, built in pink and gray volcanic stone. The small adjacent structure is the **Altar of Skulls**, used for human sacrifice. From the hill to the S the other important structures can be surveyed.

Nevado de Toluca ✰
43km (26 miles) SW; turn S off RF130 to Ciudad Altamirano after 18km (11 miles).
The rough mountain track from the main road finishes only about 1km (½ mile) from the summit of the 4,690m (15,383-foot) extinct volcano of **Xinantecatl**. Struggle on up the wall of the crater, with the two smooth lakes beneath you. Just as your lungs are bursting in the thin mountain air, you will suddenly find yourself on the roof of the world, with the Valley of Mexico and all its teeming millions spread out at your feet.

RF55 south to Teotenango and Taxco
148km (92 miles) from Toluca to Taxco.

After 6km (3 miles), turn E on a road for **Metepec**, 2km (1 mile) farther, a small town nearly absorbed by Toluca, whose brightly colored ornamental ceramics can be seen in shops all over the country. A specialty is the "Tree of Life," but there are also Noah's Arks and many other themes. Mondays, there is an excellent market near the church.

Near the village of **Tenango** *(on W of road after Km 26)* is the recently excavated ruined city of **Teotenango**, once a large Matlazinca center crowning some craggy uplands. The entrance is at the foot of the hill, where there is a small, well-laid-out museum (**☎** *open 9am-6pm)*. The best exhibit is a large and unique wooden drum from the nearby ruins of **Calixtlahuaca**. Drive or walk up to the ruins, imposingly grouped around a wide, grassy esplanade, and watch the archeologists at work. Tenango's **market** is on Sunday, a good opportunity to buy local *serapes*.

The road continues to the subtropical flower-filled town of **Tenancingo** *(54km/33 miles)*. Buy intricately woven *rebozos* (shawls) here, especially at the Sunday market. From here a poor road branches off to the E for MALINALCO.

Ixtapán de la Sal *(82km/51 miles)* is a charming spa town with warm mineral-rich waters said to be good for arthritis, rheumatism and circulatory diseases. There are good hotels and public pools, where you can enjoy Roman baths, massages and beautifully landscaped grounds. However, it is best avoided on weekends and holidays, when an amusement-park atmosphere can take over. From here 66km (41 miles) remain to Taxco, going by way of the **Grutas De Cacahuamilpa** (see SOUTH OF MEXICO CITY, page 132).

☞   **Ixtapán** *(Plaza San Gaspar* **☎** *(724) 30021, or in Mexico City* **☎** *(5) 264 2613* **Fx** *(5) 264 2529* ▥ *650 rms* ⊒ 𝖸 ⚘ ⋩ ♨ ⅋ ✒ 🐾 *)* is a large spa hotel next to the public baths with its own excellent facilities, in extensive gardens; **Kiss Vergel** *(San Román and Juárez* **☎** *(724) 30901* ▥ ⊒ 𝖸 *)* is a clean motel, also near the public baths.

VALLE DE BRAVO

Map 11E6. Estado de México. 82km (51 miles) w of Toluca; 147km (91 miles) w of Mexico City. Altitude: 1,870m (6,133ft). Population: 20,000. Served by bus.

Hang-gliding, sailing, riding, fishing and golf are the order of the day at this weekend resort, set high in a steep, pine-forested valley W of Toluca. The town is on the E end of the man-made Lake Avándaro, and is popular with foreigners living in Mexico. The main architectural attraction is the remarkable circular **yacht-club**, which rises and falls with the water level of the lake.

Access to sports for visitors can be a problem — it is best to arrange it through your hotel. One attraction that is open to all comers is the Sunday morning **market** in the Zócalo, with a good selection of locally made pottery on sale.

☞   **Hotel Avandaro Golf and Spa Resort** *(Fracc. Avándaro, on lakeside* **☎** *(726) 20626* **Fx** *(726) 20627, or in Mexico City* **☎** *(5) 536 7388* ▥ *108 rms*

=≡ ⬇ ◁≣ ≈≋ ♪⁰ ⁙/ ⚓ ⛾ ⚖) is an extensive residential country club with many sporting facilities, for which fees may be charged; **Los Arcos** *(Bocanegro 310* ☎ *(726) 20042* ⊞ *24 rms* =≡ ⬇ ≈≋ ⛾) is a smaller and less luxurious version, near the Zócalo; **Mary** *(on Zócalo, no* ☎ ⊞ *15 rms)* offers basic lodgings.

=≡ **Taberna del León** *(La Costera s/n* ☎ *(726) 20507* ⊞ *)* and other good restaurants line the lake; the local trout is a specialty. **El Vegetariano** *(on the Zócalo* ⊞ *)* has a pleasant garden and a far-from-purist menu. For a jolly evening, try the **Bar de los Artistas** *(* ⛾ *Bocanegra 303),* by the lake.

TEPOTZOTLÁN ☆

Map 11D6. Estado de México. 45km (28 miles) N of Mexico City on RF57. Altitude: 1,660m (5,444ft). Population: 30,000. Served by bus.

This small colonial town has one of the three finest churches in Mexico, as well as an important monastery containing a large museum of colonial art. It makes a good detour on the way to QUERÉTARO from Mexico City, or combined with the ruins at TULA to make a day's excursion from the capital.

WHAT TO SEE

Church and monastery of San Francisco Xavier, and Museo Nacional de Arte Virreinal (Viceroy's Museum) ▥
On the Zócalo ▨ *for museum. Museum open 10am–6pm; closed Mon, Tues.*
The profusely Churrigueresque facade of the church, completed in 1762, represents one of the peaks of this architectural style in Mexico. Five years after its completion, the Jesuit seminary, of which the church was part, was closed down, and it became the parish church. Inside, amid cascades of gold-leaf, is a superb painting of the *Virgin of Guadalupe* in the N transept, by Miguel Cabrera. A small door leads from the nave through a chapel to a remarkable **eight-sided chamber**, the Camarín del Virgen, so heavily ornamented that you will get a stiff neck while counting the cherubs on the ceiling.

The **Viceroy's Museum**, occupying the old seminary buildings, is reached through some cloisters on the right just inside the church. It has an extensive collection of holy relics and religious paintings, rather haphazardly distributed on several floors. Highlights are the bone relics of St Peter and St Paul in their silver cases, and the room full of pictures composed entirely of inlays of different-colored precious woods.

=≡ There are two good eating places on the Zócalo: try **Virreyes** (⊞) for inexpensive local food, or **Hostería del Convento** (⊞) for excellent Mexican and international dishes in a courtyard of the monastery.

TULA ★

Map 11D6. Hidalgo. 98km (61 miles) N of Mexico City on RF57; 88km (55 miles) w of Pachuca. Served by bus from Mexico City and Pachuca; trains from Mexico City not recommended. The ruins are just outside the modern industrial town of Tula de Allende.

One of the more interesting archeological sites, although not as grand as TEOTIHUACÁN or as beautifully sited as MALINALCO. It was founded in the 8th–9thC by the Toltecs, one of the seminomadic tribes forced s from NW Mexico by the deteriorating climate. Thus Tula became the Toltec capital, reaching its height in the 10th–11thC with a population of some 50,000.

The Toltecs achieved influence reaching as far as Costa Rica and the sw United States, although whether this was by means of military conquest or trading remains unclear; their economy was based on their control over the trade in obsidian, used to make razor-sharp weapons, and utensils. The Aztecs claimed the Toltecs as their ancestors, and they may have exaggerated their warlike qualities.

The reasons for the collapse of the Toltecs remain unclear, but it is known that Tula was ravaged by huge fires and that the population

Atlantes statues, Tula

dispersed all over Mesoamerica, many migrating to the Yucatán, where they were an important influence on the development of Maya culture. Tula was occupied right into Aztec times, its population much reduced.

One of the legendary rulers of Tula was the gentle god-king Quetzalcóatl, who was known for his dislike of human sacrifice and violence. His second coming was awaited by later cultures, including the Aztecs, and when Cortés arrived, the emperor Moctezuma fatally mistook him for the gentle god.

THE RUINS ☠

Pyramid of the Morning Star (Templo de Tlahuizcalpantecuhtli)
At the center of the site is the Pyramid of the Morning Star, bearing four giant statues of warriors *(atlantes)* who gaze out impassively across the valley. They are probably representations of Quetzalcóatl, for one of the versions of the legend has him rising into the sky like a burning bird to become the Morning Star.

Around the pyramid are various subsidiary structures of which the walls and pillars remain; they contain richly carved reliefs, some bearing traces of the bright colors in which they were painted. On the walls of the pyramid itself are remains of a frieze showing eagles and jaguars bearing human heads. To the N, on a flanking wall, there are intricate geometric patterns and a relief.

The last building of this central group is the **Burned Palace** (Palacio Quemado), on the w side. Two reclining statues stand in the main court, similar to others found all over Mesoamerica; these *chac-mools,* which were used to receive heads from human sacrifice, show the extent of Toltec influence on other cultures.

Other ruins

The other buildings at Tula have not been substantially restored, although there are plans for the **Templo Mayor**, facing the main terrace. There are also two **ball-courts** for the playing of the sacred game. Myth has it that the captain of the winning team was sacrificed, although it is hard to see how this could have been an incentive to win.

By the entrance to the site is a small **museum** (▨ *open 9am-6pm),* with a collection of pottery and sculptures from the site and some fine stone reliefs taken there for protection. A quick look around here should make it clear that the individuals outside selling "genuine" relics are up to no good.

PACHUCA

Map 11D7. Capital of Hidalgo. 91km (56 miles) NE *of Mexico City on RF85 and RF45; 88km (55 miles)* E *of Tula; 380km (237 miles)* S *of Tampico on RF105; 384km (240 miles)* S *of Ciudad Valles on RF85. Altitude: 2,430m (7,970ft). Population: 160,000. Served by train (line from Mexico City) and bus.*

An unremarkable and little-visited old mining town that is nonetheless surrounded by places of interest, including two of the finest colonial monasteries in Mexico, and the ruins of TULA. Next to the 17thC church of **La Asuncion** *(Arista and Hidalgo on Jardin Colón),* the old San Francisco monastery has been converted into the **Centro Cultural de Hidalgo** (▣ *open 10am-2pm, 4-7pm; Sun 11am-5pm; closed Mon),* with theaters, a cinema, an exhibition gallery and two museums: the **National Museum of Photography**, with 1.8 million fascinating pictures of Mexico's past and present; and the **Museo Regional de Hidalgo**, with good historical and archeological displays and relics.

Although the old part of town around the Zócalo retains some of its colonial flavor, Pachuca is only worth a longer stay if you wish to explore some lesser-known places. Otherwise, if you are passing through, just take your pick of the nearby sights that interest you and set off into the beautiful hill country around the town. In the central part of the state to the N are astonishing landscapes of bare rocks, forest, winding canyons and lakes. The best places to stop over in and explore from are SAN MIGUEL REGLA and HUASCA DE OCAMPO (see page 95).

Pachuca and some nearby villages are also known for a unique delicacy — the "pastee," a meat and vegetable pie that bears a remarkable resemblance to the British Cornish pasty, apart from the addition of chili. These are the only legacy of 250 Cornish tin-mining families who emigrated here from England in the 18thC; sadly, all other trace of them has long since disappeared.

Quality Inn Pachuca Calinda *(Camelinas 3466, a short drive s of town*
☎ *(771) 39911* 🎞 ➡️ 🐌 ⚡ ♨️ ✓ ☕ 🍴 *)* will be a first choice for many visitors;
Plaza El Dorado *(Guerrero 721* ☎ *(771) 20082* 🎞 *to* 🎞 ➡️ *)* is a spacious
modern hotel; **Grenfell** *(Plaza Independencia 116* ☎ *(771) 20277* 🔲 ➡️ *)* was
originally a 19thC stagecoach stop; **Noriega** *(♣ Matamoros 305, 2 blocks s of Plaza
Independencia* ☎ *(771) 25000* 🔲 🍴 *)* is full of colonial character and has a
good restaurant.

WITHIN EASY DISTANCE

Actopán ☆
36km (22 miles) NW on RF85, 56km (35 miles) E of Tula.
This town has a large and beautifully restored complex of fortified
16thC ecclesiastical buildings that now serves as a **museum of colonial art** (🖼 *open 10am-6pm);* there are also exhibits of native
Otomi art and crafts. Beside the dignified Plateresque **church** is a large
open chapel, with **murals** showing graphically the sufferings of the
damned. The hall of the monastery has contrasting murals showing the
tranquil benefits of the monastic life.

After another 48km (30 miles) is the smaller sister-establishment at
Ixmiquilpán *(84km/52 miles),* where enormous church-shaped bird
cages are on offer. Every Monday, there is a colorful Otomi market in the
village, and on August 14 the local fiesta is celebrated with a procession
over a carpet of flowers. Some 30km (18 miles) NE, the **Tolantango
canyon** is a truly extraordinary spectacle.

RF105 northeast to Tampico
The road winds up into the wooded hills of the state of Hidalgo, and
past the **Parque Nacional El Chico**, with its lakes, pine forests and
strange rock formations. A good center to explore it from is **Mineral El
Chico** *(turn left 29km/18 miles N of Pachuca),* with basic food and
lodging around the Zócalo. After 10km (6 miles) the attractive 18thC
mining village of **Mineral del Monte** is reached. This is one of the
villages settled by Cornish miners, so the spicy local version of the
Cornish pasty is easily available.

A turning E after 25km (15 miles) leads to **Huasca de Ocampo** *(2km/1
mile)* and **San Miguel Regla** *(5km/3 miles).* Huasca is a particularly
attractive village, known for its ceramic pots and Monday market, while
San Miguel has an interesting disused **silver works** nearby, and a major
resort hotel (see below).

On the main road beyond here there are interesting 16thC monasteries
at **Atotonilco** *(40km/25 miles),* **Molango** *(137km/85 miles)* and **Hue-
jutla** *(204km/127 miles).* The cliffs and mountains along this road are
spectacular, with amazingly twisted rock formations.

In San Miguel, the **Hacienda San Miguel Regla** *(♣ 🏛 ☎ (5) 379 4668,
in Mexico City* 🎞 *53 rms* ➡️ 🍴 ➡️ 🐌 🍷 🌿 🏌 ☕ *)* is a colonial hacienda
located near some abandoned silver mines and ore-extraction water-works. Standards have fallen somewhat at this once luxurious weekend spot, but then so have
the prices.

In Huasca, the **Las Palmas** *(on Zócalo, no* ☎ 🔲 *)* is inexpensive and primitive.

TEOTIHUACÁN ★

Map 11D7. Estado de México. 49km (30 miles) NE of Mexico City on RF85 and RF45. Served by bus.

For centuries, the great pyramids of Teotihuacán have dominated the surrounding plains, and are dwarfed only by the encircling mountains. Grouped along a monumental avenue, as long, wide and straight as an airport runway, they are the best-known and most imposing of Mexico's Pre-Hispanic ruins.

When the Aztecs came upon the vast ruined city, already abandoned for centuries, they could not believe that it had been built by mere mortals — the name in their language means "City of the Gods." It is still hard for us to believe it was the work of a civilization that did not even know the wheel. The original name of the city is not known, and little is known of the people who built it and lived there for nearly 1,000 years, until its mysterious fall around AD700.

What we do know is that the city covered 20sq.km ($7\frac{1}{2}$ sq. miles), laid out on a centrally planned grid pattern with more than 2,000 apartment compounds housing a population as high as 200,000. We also know that Teotihuacán was the center of a vast trading empire, through which it dominated most of central Mexico, and as far S as Kaminaljuyu in the Maya highlands and Tikal in the Maya lowlands.

The builders of Teotihuacán were evidently highly advanced in the fields of geometry, architecture, astronomy and the arts. We surmise, too, that they were not a militaristic race, at least until their decline set in, partly from the subject matter of their murals, partly because the buildings are laid out along astronomical rather than defensive lines.

EVENT • From October to May, there are regular **son-et-lumière** shows, with historical narrative. The performance in English takes place at 7pm; hotels will arrange tickets and transport. There are only six shows per week; currently Mondays are off, but check first. Make sure you bring warm clothing, as evenings can be chilly.

THE RUINS

The main entrance to the ruins (▓ *but* ▣ *on Sun* 𝄖 ▜ ➤ *open 8am-5pm)* is through a group of modern buildings, including shops, a cafeteria and a well-laid-out little museum. You should expect to spend at least half a day at the ruins, and may find your visit enhanced by engaging an official guide from the museum.

Avenue of the Dead (Calle de los Muertos)

Running the entire length of the site is this broad avenue, stretching away through the unexcavated areas to the S and N to the **Pyramid of the Moon**, nearly 2km (1 mile) from the museum. Opposite the museum is a large construction, about 0.5km ($\frac{1}{4}$ mile) square, wrongly known as the **Citadel** (Ciudadela). In the large central court is the **Temple of Quetzalcóatl**, where there are some remarkable stuccoed statues and reliefs of plumed serpents and other deities.

On the way N to the great pyramids, the road passes the **Superimposed Buildings** (Edificios Superpuestos) and the **Viking Group**. In

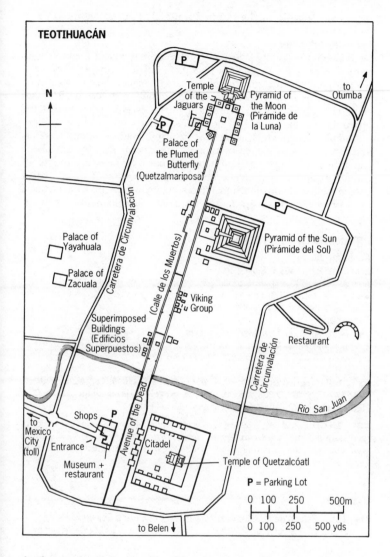

TEOTIHUACÁN

N

Temple of the Jaguars

Pyramid of the Moon (Pirámide de la Luna)

to Otumba

Palace of the Plumed Butterfly (Quetzalmariposa)

Carretera de Circunvalación

(Calle de los Muertos)

Palace of Yayahuala

Palace of Zacuala

Pyramid of the Sun (Pirámide del Sol)

Viking Group

Superimposed Buildings (Edificios Superpuestos)

Restaurant

Carretera de Circunvalación

Río San Juan

Shops

Avenue of the Dead

to Mexico City (toll)

Entrance

Citadel

Museum + restaurant

Temple of Quetzalcóatl

P = Parking Lot

| 0 | 100 | 250 | 500m |
| 0 | 100 | 250 | 500 yds |

to Belen ↓

the former there are remains of frescoes and, in the latter, a courtyard covered in two layers of loose, shiny mica. Its use is unknown, and it is difficult even to dream up a convincing one.

Pyramid of the Moon

The Avenue of the Dead ends at the **courtyard** in front of the Pyramid of the Moon (only a little smaller than the **Pyramid of the Sun**), which is now being restored and explored internally for chambers or caves. Around the court are several temples of interest. See especially the ornate **Temple of the Plumed Butterfly** (Quetzalmariposa), W of the pyramid.

Pyramid of the Sun

Dominating the countryside in every direction, the great pyramid compares in size to the Pyramid of Cheops in Egypt, although, because of the stepped construction, the actual mass is smaller. Five levels can be seen, but it is now known that it was wrongly restored in 1910, and should only have four. The view from the top is excellent, taking in the entire site and the plains and mountains around.

Deep under your feet, at the heart of the pyramid, are some chambers and a natural cave, joined by tunnels *(not open)*. The exact symbolic significance of the pyramid probably will never be worked out, although its careful astronomical orientation has been worked out. It was probably central to the religion of the inhabitants, and may even mark the mythical place of creation, for deep chambers are often prominent in contemporary religious paintings.

ENVIRONS OF TEOTIHUACÁN

Acolmán ▥ ☆
8km (5 miles) SW ▩ ✗ *Closed Fri.*
A large, fortress-like Spanish monastery, with a serenely beautiful church (1560) with a fine 17thC Churrigueresque altarpiece. The carved cross in front of the Plateresque facade carries native motifs.

Tepexpán
7km (4 miles) SW, just E of Mexico City road.
The small museum *(* ▩ *open standard hours)* contains remains of mammoths that roamed the Valley of Mexico some 10,000 years ago.

☞ **Villa Arqueológica** *(at ruins* ☎ *(595) 60244* Ⓕⓧ *(595) 60928, or reserve in Mexico City* ☎ *(5) 203 3153* ▥ *49 rms* ≋ ⴻ ⥤ *)* is one of the reliable Club Med-run chain, with an interesting archeological library.

⥤ **La Gruta** *(* ☎ *(595) 60104* ▥ *)* is in a natural grotto, 10 minutes' walk E of the Pyramid of the Sun. **Gran Tecali** *(near entrance* ☎ *(595) 60155* ▥ *)* offers an unlimited buffet to marimba music and Aztec dances. Or take a packed lunch.

TEXCOCO
Map 11E7. Estado de México. 41km (25 miles) E of Mexico City on RF190, RF150 and RF136. Altitude: 2,280m (7,478ft). Population: 500,000. Served by bus.

Now a fast-growing Mexico City overfill settlement and rising industrial center, this dusty lake-bed conurbation was, before the Conquest, a great and beautiful city of pyramids and temples towering over the lake. With a population of 20,000 to 30,000, Texcoco was the largest city in the basin of Mexico after Tenochtitlán, with which it allied in 1428 to assert Aztec dominance in the area.

Part of the lake actually survives today in Texcoco, making a valuable habitat for migrating wildfowl; but even this is now threatened by continued dessication and plans for a toxic waste dump, fiercely resisted by residents, who already have to cope with raw sewage in the dust blowing up off the lake bed. There is little to see in the town itself, but nearby are enough places of interest to make this a good day's excursion from Mexico City.

WITHIN EASY DISTANCE

Chapingo and Huexotla
N on Tlalpán road.
The **University** at **Chapingo** *(3km/1½ miles)* is a place of pilgrimage for devotees of Diego Rivera, as the many striking, visionary murals here *(open Mon-Sat 9am-1pm, 3-5pm; closed Sun),* constitute some of his finest work. At **Huexotla** *(4km/2 miles W after 8km/5 miles),* Pre-Hispanic fortifications surround a small Franciscan monastery, flanked by a Churrigueresque church. The stone carvings are clearly by native craftsmen — just look at the faces of the saints.

Chiconcuac and Papalotla
N on Tepexpán road.
Most people come to the small village of **Chiconcuac** not for the fine Baroque church but to shop for woolen clothing. It is a center for the production of thick knitted jackets, and they are less expensive here than anywhere. The nearby village of **Papalotla** *(10km/6 miles by small unnumbered road)* has a church in front of an especially fine arcaded atrium, with Baroque decoration, and, inside, fine 18thC carved wooden altarpieces.

Molino de Flores and Tepetlaotzoc
E on Calpulalpan road.
In the pleasant gardens around the old disused hacienda of **Molino de Flores** *(8km/5 miles)* stand a ruined mill and several Baroque chapels. Nearby are the remains of Aztec gardens, with irrigation channels carved into the rocks. There are more Pre-Hispanic remains at **Tepetlaotzoc** *(6km/3 miles S at 12km/7 miles),* where the wide stairway leading up to the monastery was once part of a pyramid. The buildings, although very old, are well preserved.

POPOCATÉPETL AND IXTACCIHUATL

*Map **11E7**. Estado de México. 89km (55 miles) SE of Mexico City by RF190 and RF115. Altitude: 5,452m (3,407ft) and 5,286m (3,303ft).*

Popocatépetl, the "Smoking Mountain," dominates the skylines of MEXICO CITY (smog permitting), PUEBLA and CUERNAVACA, with its tapering cone of rocks and snow often showing above a layer of clouds. The last major eruption was in 1802, so it is fairly safe to climb "Popo"; a path leads all the way to the summit from the **mountain hostel** at **Tlamacas**, not far from the **Paso de Cortés**, where Cortés first caught sight of the Aztec capital laid out in the valley below him.

Those intending to go all the way are advised to spend the night here and set out at dawn. The climbing gets slower as the oxygen diminishes (anyone showing signs of altitude sickness should immediately be escorted back to the hostel). Do not start the climb unless the weather looks good (ask advice locally), and take warm clothing and supplies. At the crater, stop and spare a thought for the poor souls whom Cortés caused to be lowered down there, while it was still active, to scrape out sulfur for gunpowder.

On the other side of the pass is the "Sleeping Lady," **Ixtaccihuatl**, a more difficult peak to climb, only to be undertaken by experienced, fully equipped mountaineers.

Albergue Vincente Guerrero (✿ *3,950m/12,956ft high at Tlamacas* ⬤ ☐ ◁≡ ⇶ ♈) is a modern lodge offering dormitory accommodation; bring a padlock for your locker.

AMECAMECA

Map 11E7. Estado de México. 59km (36 miles) s of Mexico City on RF115 and RF90. Altitude: 2,470m (8,100ft). Population: 40,000. Served by train (on Mexico City–Cuautla line) and bus.

A small market town which, together with a visit to nearby villages and a stroll on the lower slopes of POPOCATÉPETL, makes a fine day trip from Mexico City. There is a Sunday **market**, with a local crafts section.

The town

After a brief visit to the 16thC monastery by the main square, climb the hill to the church of **Nuestro Señor del Sacromonte**, overlooking the town. Here stands an ancient **statue of Christ**, venerated by pilgrims at the lively fiesta on Ash Wednesday. The views of the valley and of the great volcano behind are magnificent.

WITHIN EASY DISTANCE
Monasteries to the north

The town of **Tlalmanalco**, 10km (6 miles) N, has a 16thC monastery with an interesting Plateresque open chapel. Another 27km (16 miles) brings you to **Chalco**, an important Pre-Columbian town, not yet archeologically explored. The monastery and church here are again worth a quick visit, and it is then only 7km (4 miles) to the Mexico City–Puebla free road.

Monasteries to the south

Stop first at **Ozumba**, 10km (6 miles) to the S, to see the 16thC murals in the monastery. They show Cortés humbly welcoming the first missionaries to arrive in New Spain. See also CUAUTLA, pages 101-2.

CUAUTLA

Map 11E7. Morelos. 47km (29 miles) E of Cuernavaca on RF138; 102km (63 miles) s of Mexico City on RF90 and RF15. Population: 175,000. Served by train (on Mexico City–Izúcar line) and bus **i** *at scenic railroad station, across from Plaza Galeana* ☎*(735) 25221.*

Some years ago, Cuautla was being promoted as an alternative to Cuernavaca for weekenders and tourists. It never caught on, and there is little here apart from a few hotels and some sulfur baths. But it is at the center of one of the most fascinating areas of Mexico, and makes an ideal base for excursions, less tiring than from Cuernavaca or Mexico City. One way to view the country is on the **scenic railroad**; a steam train runs three times a week on the three-hour round trip to **Yecapixtla**, a good place to celebrate the **Day of the Dead**, November 1.

Monasteries to the north

Leave Cuautla by the road N to Amecameca, and after 12km (7 miles) turn E toward POPOCATÉPETL for **Yecapixtla** *(15km/9 miles)*, where there is a fine 16thC fortified monastery with a Gothic vaulted church and a carved stone pulpit. The same road continues to **Ocuituco** *(16km/10 miles)* and **Tetela del Volcán** *(23km/14 miles)*, both with small monasteries. The one at Tetela, now used as a convent, is less interesting, but Ocuituco's monastery has an imposing arcaded bell tower and a pretty cloister. There is a government-run **Posada Turistica** (☜) in Tetela, for which reservations can be made in the Cuernavaca tourist office.

From here, return to the Amecameca road. Turn N, then, after 4km (2 miles), turn W, which brings you shortly to **Atlatlahuacán**. Here again, a monastery dominates the village, as at **Totolapán**, some 5km (3 miles) beyond. From here, the road passes through magnificent countryside, with soaring craggy rocks rising steeply over the plains, and joins the new Mexico City–Oaxtepec highway at the pottery village of **Tlayacapan**. The large monastery here is usually closed and is falling into disrepair, but the splendid church is open.

It is then another 9km (5 miles) to **Oaxtepec**, a small, pretty town that has become a vacation center for the Mexican Social Security Institute; it is very crowded on weekends, when up to 5,000 swimmers may come to enjoy the pools filled from natural hot springs. Then, 4km (2 miles) from here, rejoin the Cuautla–Cuernavaca road at **Cocoyoc** (see page 102). Cuautla is 7km (4 miles) E, while 10km (6 miles) W lies a fortress-like monastery, with some well-preserved open chapels, at **Yautepec**.

Monasteries to the south

Leave Cuautla on RF190 for Izúcar de Matamoros, and after 21km (13 miles) turn N at the Amayuca intersection to **Zacualpan**, a further 8km (5 miles). The monastery church here is noteworthy for its ornately carved and gilded 19thC altar and for the earlier murals in the cloister. Returning to Amayuca, cross straight over RF190, heading S.

After 2km (1 mile), turn E for **Chalcatzingo** (✮), where there is a monastery and, more importantly, some fascinating and little-known ruins; ask in the Zócalo for a guide to lead you the final 1km ($\frac{1}{2}$ mile) along a track. The guardian of the site will give you a rough map, locating the various relief paintings and carvings spread about the steep hillside. The oldest may have been here for more than 2,500 years; one masterpiece depicts graphically the horror on the faces of a sea monster's victims.

Beyond the Chalcatzingo turning, the road continues s to **Jonacatepec** *(2km/1 mile)*, with a 16thC monastery, and, after 12km (7 miles), **Tepalcingo**, with a fine Churrigueresque church.

✃ **Hacienda Cocoyoc** *(*🏨 ♣ 🏛 *7km/4 miles NW of Cuautla on RF138 to Cuernavaca* ☎ *(735) 22000* 🅵ₓ *(735) 33390, or in Mexico City* ☎ *(5) 550 4422* 🛏 *325 rms* 🔚 ⇌ 🖾 📼 ⚓ ⟨⟨ ≈ ♒ ♿ ♨ ▽ *)* is a magnificent former sugar hacienda built by Cortés in 1520, allegedly for an Aztec princess. It was burned down during the revolution, but restored in the 1950s as a luxury hotel; just avoid holiday weekends and big conferences.

In Cuautla itself, prices are much lower than in Cuernavaca, but the atmosphere is rather run-down; however, the **Cuautla** *(Batalla 19 de Fevrero 114* ☎ *(735) 27277* 🛏 ⇌ ≈ *)* is clean, modern and comfortable.

TEPOZTLÁN

*Map **11**E7. Morelos. 84km (52 miles) s of Mexico City on RF95 and RF115; 27km (16 miles) E of Cuernavaca on RF115. Population: 30,000. Served by bus from Mexico City and Cuernavaca.*

Some years ago, Tepoztlán was a remote village surrounded by majestic volcanic crags, its narrow streets dominated by a massive 16thC monastery. The only inhabitants were Nahuatl-speaking Indians and a large number of anthropologists studying their customs and frequent fiestas. New roads and weekend homes have broken this isolation, and it is now both easy and worthwhile to come here for the day from Mexico City or Cuernavaca.

The great **monastery** on the Zócalo not only looks like a fortress, but was used as one by Emiliano Zapata during the 1910 Revolution. It is now in use as a local museum, containing a collection of Pre-Hispanic objects found at the **temples** high in the hills above the town. The most interesting of these is at the top of the **Cerro del Tepozteco** *(* ✿ *open 9am-4.30pm* 🎟 *free on Sun)*, about an hour's energetic climb up a well-marked path and steps from the edge of town, passing through steep gullies and ascending an alarming iron ladder. It is best avoided on weekends and holidays as the path can get quite congested.

The pyramid here was dedicated to **Tepoztecatl**, the god of mild drunkenness, who is represented symbolically by 400 rabbits — the Aztec equivalent of pink elephants. When the Spaniards arrived, they righteously hurled the idol over the cliffs, but legend has it that he landed unharmed, which only encouraged his followers.

EVENT • On the night of **September 7**, Tepoztecatl is still venerated, with dances and scenes of universal drunkenness, both in town and up at the temple. • The **carnival**, in the first week of Lent, features colorful dances. • **Holy Week** here is also a lively occasion, with dancing and a large market. • At the weekly **Sunday market**, local handicrafts are sold: gaze at the bright costumes and beads of the foreign hippies who live here.

☜ **Hotel Tepoztlán** *(Industrias 6* ☎*(738) 50522* ▥ to ▥ ⇌ ☿ ⚶ ⚓*)* is a good, modern hotel offering magnificent views; **Posada del Tepozteco** *(Paraíso 3* ☎*(738) 50323* ▥ ⚶ ⇌*)* is an elegant modern resort built in the Spanish mission style.

CUERNAVACA

Map 11E6. Capital of Morelos. 85km (53 miles) s of Mexico City on RF95; 47km (29 miles) w of Cuautla on RF138; 27km (16 miles) w of Tepoztlán on RF115; 88km (55 miles) N of Taxco on old RF95 i Morelos Sur 802 ☎(73) 143860 Altitude: 1,532m (9,575ft). Population: 1.2 million. Served by train (on Mexico City–Balsas line) and bus.

Renowned for its perfect climate and flower-filled gardens, Cuernavaca has attracted foreigners and weekenders ever since the Aztec lords sought retreat here. Cortés himself started building a retirement home here in 1532 after receiving Cuernavaca as a fief from Charles II, but died before he could occupy it.

For all that, it can prove a disappointment. Modern Cuernavaca is an industrial center of growing importance, its charm nearly smothered under massive urban growth, greatly stimulated by the 1985 earthquake in Mexico City. Its famous gardens are mostly hidden behind high walls, and the sights are too spread out to stroll around.

To enjoy Cuernavaca, it is best to stay in one of the hotels with a large and pleasant garden and to set aside plenty of time for leisurely excursions. Better still, stay with friends or relatives — it is surprising how many visitors can think of somebody they know in this city of expatriates.

The name Cuernavaca means "cow-horn" in Spanish, but that is only because the Conquistadors were unable to get their tongue round the Aztec name *Cuaunahuac*. Throughout the colonial period it remained a peaceful and prosperous town, based on a slave-and-sugarcane economy introduced by Cortés; in the 1910 Revolution it became the scene of savage massacres and lootings, when local rebel and revolutionary hero Emiliano Zapata and his peasant army sought to reconquer the land monopolized by wealthy Creoles; in 1919, before achieving his objective, Zapata was betrayed and assassinated by another hero of the revolution, President Venustiano Carranza.

In those poor villages of Morelos where he lived, he is now a popular hero, and the name Zapata can sometimes be seen newly scrawled on a wall in protest at the one-sided prosperity of Cuernavaca.

WHAT TO SEE

The Zócalo

The twin laurel-shaded plazas at the heart of the city are exceptional in Mexico for having no church. They are fun to stroll around, but if you stop for a cold drink in a sidewalk café, perhaps to the accompaniment of live *mariachi* music, expect an exhausting barrage of needy crafts sellers. The crafts — paintings and carvings from Guerrero, local pottery and weavings — are well worth buying, but shop around in the stalls across from Cortés's palace before parting with your money.

Another good place to shop around in is the **city market**, 5 blocks N, a vast network of streets and halls with everything from counterfeit watches to mountain honey; only the crafts are best bought elsewhere.

Palacio de Cortés ☰ ☆

Zócalo ☎ *Open 10am–7pm. Closed Mon.*

This impressive, fortress-like building on the SE corner of the Zócalo was built over the ruins of a small Tlahuica temple, still visible in the courtyard. Originally the headquarters of Cortés' large estates, it is now the **state museum**. The most important exhibits are Diego Rivera's huge **murals**, which show nothing less than the history of Mexico, with the emphasis on the exploitation of Indians by conquistadors.

The other displays, of antique weapons, armor, instruments of torture and pre-revolution sugar haciendas, may help one to see Rivera's point. From the rear of the first-floor loggia can be seen the peak of POPOCATÉPETL, shining white in the sun.

Borda Gardens

5mins w of the Zócalo ☎ *Open 10am–6pm.*

These quiet gardens were laid out in the 18thC by a rich Taxco mine-owner, after whom they are named. Its usually tawdry air is dispelled in the first week of May, when it is enlivened by a flower festival. At the entrance is a small **museum of contemporary art**.

Cathedral

Opposite the Borda Gardens, on Morelos and Hidalgo.

The sober and massive cathedral of Cuernavaca was founded in 1529 by Cortés, and was originally conceived as part of a Franciscan monastery. This was a staging-post for Japan-bound missionaries, and inside the cathedral are the remains of **murals** depicting 16thC mission life in the Far East. Also of note are some striking new abstract **stained-glass windows**. Every Sunday morning, there is a *mariachi* Mass with guitar accompaniment; check the time at the tourist office and arrive early; it is always crowded.

Hotel Casino de la Selva

Leandro Valle 1001 ☎*(73) 124705.*

This is known less as a hotel than as the home of some vast **murals** painted by David Siqueiros in the 1920s, mainly concerned with social injustice and as artistically bold as they are politically aggressive.

The hotel is also the starting point for **guided tours** *(* ☎ *times irregular)* of some of Cuernavaca's more beautiful houses and gardens.

Casa de Siqueiros

Venus 7 ☎ *Open 9am–2pm. Closed Mon.*

David Siqueiros, the muralist, lived and worked in this modest Cuernavaca house and workshop, with its small permanent exhibition.

Museo Brady

Casa de la Torre, Netzahualcóyotl 4 ☎ *Open by appointment* ☎*(73) 121136.*

After restoring this minor 16thC palace as his home, American artist Robert Brady filled it up with an eclectic collection of indigenous, colonial and contemporary art, much of the latter by his better-known friends and admirers. His charming house remains just as he left it at the time of his death in 1986.

Pyramid of Teopanzolco
Calle Río Balsas, 3km (1 mile) from center ☎ *Open 10am–6pm.*

It was not until 1910, when heavy shelling shook off the topsoil, that these remains of a small Aztec ceremonial center were discovered. On examination it was found that the main pyramid was built over an earlier structure, and the main staircase of the first construction has been exposed and restored. Parts of the old temple walls remain on top of the pyramid.

Salto de San Antonio
1.5km (1 mile) NW of the Zócalo, at end of Calzada.

This impressive waterfall has been tidied up and landscaped, and there is a small market nearby. A popular picnic spot.

WHERE TO STAY

CUERNAVACA HOTEL AND TENNIS CLUB ♣ ▥
Francisco Villa 100 ☎*(73) 112400*
▣*(73) 175483* ▥ *33 rms* ≈ ♨ ◁
≈F87P7MI ♫ ✔ ❤ ❂ ♪

This romantic and luxurious hotel has superb sports facilities and exotic 23-acre gardens. It is popular with the jet-set. There are 250 members of the club, who make a great show of elitism.

LAS MAÑANITAS ▥
Ricardo Linares 107 ☎*(73) 124646*
▣*(73) 183672* ▥ *No cards. 22 rms*
≈ ≈ ▦ ✔ ♈

A beautiful restored colonial hacienda, full of flowers, flamingoes, peacocks and monkeys. It usually needs reservations well in advance, and houses Mexico's most famous restaurant (of the same name).

LAS QUINTAS ▥
Av. las Quintas 107 ☎*(73) 183949*
▣*(73) 183895* ▥ *49 rms* ≈ ♨ ≈ ♈

Of the city hotels, this Spanish count's downtown mansion comes in second-best only to LAS MAÑANITAS.

POSADA DE XOCHIQUETZAL ▥
Leyva 200 ☎*(73) 120220* ▥ *16 rms*
≈ ♨ ≈ ♈

A friendly atmosphere prevails behind the grim walls of this flower-filled colonial building. Beware of a surcharge on charge/credit card transactions.

Budget hotels

Less expensive hotels near the center include **Posada Jacarandas** *(Cuauhtémoc 805* ☎*(73) 57777* ▥ ≈ ♈ *)* and **Papagayo** *(Motolina at Netzahualcoyótl* ☎*(73) 141924* ▥ ≈ ♈ ≈*)*, both pleasant and good value.

Haciendas nearby

There are three 16thC haciendas within easy reach of Cuernavaca, built on Hernán Cortés's extensive sugar estates, which have been converted into hotels as luxurious as they are historic. All were damaged during the revolution, indeed one was burned to the ground, as symbols of a system that robbed and exploited the peasantry. But today, as the stone walls bask in the hot sunshine, surrounded by gardens and swimming pools, it is hard to imagine the harsh realities of their past.

The closest of these is the **Hacienda de Cortés** *(*▥ *Plan de Ayala 410, Atlacomulco* ☎ *(73)158844* ▥ *21 rms* ≈ ♨ ≈ ♈ ⚓ ✈ *)*, with its lovely gardens. Just N of Lake Tequesquitengo is **Hacienda Vistahermosa** *(*▥ *20km/12 miles s in San José village* ☎ *(73) 120300,*

102 rms ▦ ⇶ ▣ ⚓ ⤳ ♨ ♣ ♉ ●), near the XOCHICALCO ruins; the arches of the aqueduct pass through the swimming pool, and one room has its own Roman marble bath. Parachuting is just one of the many sports on offer. Even if you don't stay here, consider coming for Sunday lunch.

Also excellent is **Hacienda Cocoyoc**, 30km (18 miles) E of Cuernavaca, which is described under CUAUTLA.

EATING AND DRINKING

Many of Cuernavaca's best restaurants are in the hotels already listed. Pride of place goes to the former haciendas, in particular to **Las Mañanitas** (▦ ⇶ ⊕ ⚓ ♉ ♪) — a restaurant so good that Mexico City businessmen used to drive out here for lunch, until the traffic made this impractical; the menu is French–Mexican, with changing exotic specialties (see WHERE TO STAY, page 105).

Moby Dick's *(Plan de Ayala 383* ☎ *(731) 57431* ▦ *)* serves good meat and seafood dishes. **Marco Polo** *(Hidalgo 26)* has delicious pizza and homemade pasta.

WITHIN EASY DISTANCE

AMECAMECA, CUAUTLA, MALINALCO, POPOCATÉPETL, TAXCO, TEPOZTLÁN, XOCHICALCO and **Ixtapán de la Sal** (see TOLUCA) can all be visited in a day.

Tequesquitengo
22km (13 miles) by RF95.

Heading S out of Cuernavaca, the parallel free and toll roads descend quickly to the tropical lowlands. After 19km (11 miles) from town, a turning to the E leads to **Lake Tequesquitengo**, where many rich Mexicans have second homes. The town is on the E of the lake, a natural volcanic crater, where boats can be rented for sailing, waterskiing, or diving in the sunken villages. Another 6km (3 miles) S of here are the exotic sulfur baths at **Tehuixtla**, a popular weekend resort.

74km (46 miles) SW toward Taxco are the famous **Grutas de Cacahuamilpa** (see SOUTH OF MEXICO CITY, page 132), stretching 69km (43 miles) into the mountains (▨ *guided tours hourly).* The **Parque Nacional Lagunas de Zempoala** *(30km/18 miles W on road to Malinalco)* (see also MEXICO CITY, page 75) preserves a lovely area of high-altitude lakes and pine forest.

XOCHICALCO ☆

Map 11E6. Morelos. From Cuernavaca, 32km (20 miles) on old RF95 to Taxco, then 4km (2 miles) SE; from Taxco, 52km (32 miles) N on old RF95, then 4km (2 miles) SE. Served by infrequent bus.

Like so many of the great ruined ceremonial centers of Mexico, little is known of the history of Xochicalco. Archeologically, it does provide important clues to the history of the whole region; artifacts and inscriptions link it not only with TEOTIHUACÁN and TULA, but with the Mixtecs, the Aztecs, and the Maya and Zapotec cultures far to the E.

It was abandoned in the 10thC, perhaps because of plague, invasions or famine, and the inhabitants literally disappeared from history. The ruins are in a commanding position on the artificially flattened summit of a foothill of Mount Ajusco.

The ruins 𝕀𝕀𝕀

☒ *Open 10am–6pm.*

The entrance to the site is from the s, into the **Plaza Inferior**, where a tall stele carved with calendrical symbols stands between two pyramids. When the site was abandoned, the stele was overturned and painted red — the color of death throughout Mesoamerica. From here a wide avenue leads past a ball-court for the sacred game, to some unrestored buildings on an artificial mound.

To the N of the Plaza Inferior is the site's finest monument, the **Pyramid of the Plumed Serpents** (Pirámide de las Serpientes Emplumadas). It is built on two levels, and around the walls of the lower stage are reliefs of numerous plumed serpents twisting around the seated figures of priests.

Across to the N and down the hill is the entrance to a network of chambers and tunnels beneath the site, some of which have been opened. In one of the chambers, an opening to the roof is oriented to admit direct sunlight only on the days of equinox. Some archeologists believe that this was used to correct the calendar between 52-year calendar cycles. It is possible, with the help of a flashlight, to make out the remains of murals.

MALINALCO ★

Map 11E6. Estado de México. 49km (30 miles) w of Cuernavaca via Ocuilán; 100km (62 miles) s of Mexico City via Cuernavaca.

A small Aztec ceremonial center carved out of volcanic crags high above the plains to the w of Cuernavaca. Although easy to reach and of great beauty and interest, it is inexplicably ignored by tourists. Leave your car at the end of the track signposted from the Zócalo in Malinalco village. If you need a place to stay, take your pick of several basic hotels around the Zócalo.

The ruins 𝕀𝕀𝕀

15mins' walk up a stone stairway **☒**

The main group of ruins lies about half way up a mountain above a village, strategically placed for the Aztec knights who controlled the local Matlazinca population here after conquering them in 1476. Begun in 1501, the buildings had not been finished when the Spaniards arrived 20 years later — such large structures were a lifetime's work for craftsmen who had no metal tools.

In the main **temple**, hewn out of the living rock, are sculptures of a jaguar and two eagles around the walls, and another eagle, in the middle of the floor in front of a round hole used for the hearts of sacrificial victims. The other nearby structures were partly hewn from the rock and partly made of stone blocks, most of which the Spaniards hauled back down to build the church and monastery in the village. Thus only the main temple has survived intact. Cut into the cliffs are the remains of a drainage system.

WITHIN EASY DISTANCE

See also CUERNAVACA, page 106 and TOLUCA, pages 90-1.

Chalma ☆

11km (6 miles) E.

A small village in the pit of a dramatic valley of cliffs riddled with caves, where religious fervor enters into full swing every Sunday. Leave your car on the main road, push down through the crowds of pilgrims and hawkers of garish religious items, and eventually you will reach the church, which contains a miraculous **statue of Christ**.

This "Christ" is probably a Pre-Columbian idol — perhaps Oxtoctéotl, the god of the caves beneath the church. A **spring** flows from them into the river, and there are extraordinary Dante-esque scenes as all pilgrims try to bathe in the sacred waters. At times of special fiestas, there are fireworks and dancing, and it is a lucky person who can even get near the church at such times.

East of Mexico City

This diverse region covers the states of **Puebla**, **Tlaxcala** and **Veracruz**, incorporating Mexico's highest mountain and the Gulf Coast at its steamiest. It has a particular claim on Mexican history, as the scene of the initial stages of the conquest of the Aztec empire by the Spanish invaders under Hernán Cortés.

IN THE FOOTSTEPS OF CORTÉS

In 1519, Cortés landed on the shores of the Gulf of Mexico and founded VERACRUZ, Mexico's premier port ever since, now known for its relaxed, Afro-Caribbean ambience. The nearby ruins of **Zempoala**, the capital of the Totonac Indians, which fell to Cortés's diplomatic cunning, are well worth seeing, but the resorts along the steamy Gulf coast near Veracruz are distinctly lackluster.

JALAPA, now the capital of Veracruz state, was the next destination of the Spanish expedition, lying inland just north of the volcano **Pico de Orizaba** (also known as Citlaltépetl). Cortés was peacefully received in

Jalapa, and enjoyed the mild and pleasant climate, but the modern city is only worth visiting for its excellent museum of the ancient cultures of the region.

Where Cortés went north of the volcano, the main modern route runs to its south through **CÓRDOBA** and **ORIZABA**, and the small town of **FORTÍN DE LAS FLORES**, which is the most pleasant place to stop, and the closest to Citlaltépetl. There are lovely walks on the lower slopes of the volcano, but the icy 5,714m (18,284-foot) summit is well beyond the reach of ordinary mortals.

From Jalapa, Cortés's route led through the mountains to **TLAXCALA**, which had long maintained its independence against the Aztecs. After several bloody battles, the fierce Tlaxcalans allied with the Spanish for their subsequent attacks on Tenochtitlán, capital of the Aztecs. Tlaxcala today is a pleasant city at the center of its small but fertile state. Mysteriously, it is off the tourist trail, despite the presence of the finest ancient murals in Mexico, at **Cacaxtla**.

Cortés's next target was neighboring **CHOLULA**, dominated by the Aztecs. This gruesome holy city and its vast pyramid claimed some 6,000 human victims a year, sacrificed at its hundreds of blood-soaked temples. At first Cholula welcomed the Spanish, but the mood changed when orders came from Moctezuma, emperor of the Aztecs, to entrap and kill them. Getting wind of this, Cortés launched a pre-emptive strike that massacred much of Cholula's population.

The grim temples were later replaced with churches, including that on the peak of the great pyramid. In a break with the usual practice, however, the Spanish founded their city on a new site, laying out the plan of **PUEBLA** on the open plain. Cholula is now a small, uneventful town, while Puebla, capital of the state, is a major city with a fine colonial center and sprawling industrial hinterland.

The state of Puebla extends well beyond the high plains around its capital, for example to the **Sierra Norte de Puebla**, the mountain range to the north of the state that divides the Valley of Mexico from the Gulf. Its high ridge catches the warm, moist air that blows off the sea, cooling it to form a near-constant blanket of fog.

The result is a dense forest that constantly drips with water, the profuse growth of mosses, lichens and epiphytes trapping the condensation. Unfortunately, the forest is fast being cleared to make way for agriculture, but the indigenous culture of the area's Nahua and Totonac peoples remains strong, especially around **CUETZALAN**, a small colonial town in the Sierra Norte.

The pyramid of **Yohuallichán**, near Cuetzalan, resembles its better-known big brother at **EL TAJÍN**, due north across unroaded foothills in the tropical heat of Veracruz. El Tajín's **Pyramid of the Niches**, surrounded by lush jungle, is one of the most impressive monuments in Mexico, built by the ancestors of the Totonac Indians of the area. To the northwest lie the lands of the Huastec Indians, while the Gulf coast leads southwest to the city of Veracruz.

The banana-shaped state of Veracruz continues to follow the Gulf coast to the southwest, eventually reaching **Coatzacoalcos**, a grimy oil town at the northern end of the **Isthmus of Tehuantepec**. The highly scenic road from Veracruz runs along the coast and into the Tuxtla mountains, and those with the time to make a short diversion away from its busy traffic will be rewarded with splendid landscapes of volcanoes, lakes and waterfalls.

Towns, cities and cultural sites

Starting in the pleasant colonial city of PUEBLA, this chapter gives information on the following destinations, arranged to follow a clockwise route: CHOLULA, TLAXCALA, TEHUACÁN, CUETZALAN, ORIZABA, FORTÍN DE LAS FLORES, CÓRDOBA, VERACRUZ, JALAPA, EL TAJÍN and COATZACOALCOS.

See USING THIS GUIDE on page 50 for details on how to use this section. On the following pages, helpful pointers are given on how to get to each of the destinations covered. Along with the MEXICO map on pages 46–7, and the 4-color maps at the back of this book, they should give all the information necessary for planning your trip to this part of Mexico.

PUEBLA ☆

Map 11E7. Capital of Puebla. 132km (82 miles) SE of Mexico City on RF150 and RF190 ℹ 5 Ote 3 ☎(22) 463563. Altitude: 2,160m (6,480ft). Population: 3 million. Served by train (line from Mexico City) and bus (the vast CAPU terminal has services across Mexico). American Express: Plaza Dorada 1, Blvd. 5 de Mayo ☎(22) 375552.

A city full of colonial mansions and churches, with walls, facades and domes covered in brightly colored *faïence* tiles, Puebla is now surrounded by a vast and growing urban-industrial sprawl. The original colonists came from an area of Spain that was famous for its intricately patterned ceramics. Unlike most Spaniards, they came to stay, not to amass a fortune for retirement to Spain, so they tried to make Puebla as much like their home as possible. The Spanish atmosphere is all the stronger because, unlike most cities of New Spain, Puebla was not built over the ruins of pyramids. Nearby CHOLULA would have been the obvious site: perhaps the blood-encrusted temples and piles of skulls proved too much for the early settlers.

The first Bishop of Tlaxcala supposedly dreamed of Puebla's fertile valley in the shadow of snow-covered volcanoes, and ordered the city to be founded there in 1531. Puebla remained strongly royalist during the War of Independence, but established more patriotic credentials during the war with the French. General Ignacio Zaragoza's citizen army heavily defeated the French army here in 1862. Although the French were not finally defeated for another five years, the day of the battle, May 5, is now a national holiday, celebrating the rejection of all foreign interventions.

The *poblanos* have always been proud of their separate character, and this is reflected as much in their architecture as in their cooking and in the women's costumes. The famous *mole* sauce, of spices, chili and chocolate, was first prepared by the nuns of Santa Rosa as a special saint's day treat for their bishop. Another specialty is *chiles en nogada,* also first prepared as a saint's day treat, this time for General Iturbide. His admirers decided to fête him with a patriotic dish of green chili, white sauce and red topping, representing the Mexican flag; it is now served all over the country during Independence celebrations in September.

Alas, the traditional costume is harder to find than the traditional food, and you are unlikely to see a *poblana* in full rig, although some smart Mexican ladies do wear it as formal dress. Known as *china poblana* after a Chinese girl who originally designed it, it is also red, white and green, covered with rich embroidery and sequins.

Industry and the ravages of the internal combustion engine have not passed Puebla by, but it makes a worthwhile day trip from Mexico City, and a good base for further explorations.

WHAT TO SEE

Most of Puebla's colonial monuments are within a few minutes' of the shady **Zócalo**, now closed to traffic. The streets are numbered in a semilogical but confusing way. Those to the N or E of the Zócalo are even-numbered, and those to the S and W odd-numbered, while each street has the name of the direction in which it points from the Zócalo. Once you have mastered it, if you ever do, it is impossible to get lost.

Cathedral 🏛

The huge Renaissance cathedral is the country's largest outside the capital, and dominates the Zócalo from the S. Begun in 1575, it was not consecrated until 1649, and only completed in the following century. The great W **doors** are wonderfully Baroque. Also notable on the exterior are the **statues of Spanish kings**, on the N doorway.

Inside, the Neoclassical **high altar** is made from the **onyx** for which Puebla is famous; the intricately carved doors and choir stalls are inlaid with onyx and mother-of-pearl. One of several ornate side chapels, the **Capilla Real**, houses 17thC paintings by Martínez Montañes.

Biblioteca Palafoxiana 🏛
7 Oriente, behind cathedral 🔳 *Open 9.30am–1pm.*

An old, tiled palace containing thousands of books on dark, carved shelves under a fine vaulted ceiling. There is a 15thC *Nuremberg Chronicle,* and a 16thC Bible printed in Greek, Latin, Aramaic and Hebrew. Sitting quietly at one of the tables, you can hardly avoid absorbing some of the ancient wisdom, although access to the books is limited to accredited researchers.

Casa del Alfeñique (Puebla Regional Museum)
4 Oriente 🔳 *Open 10am–5pm. Closed Mon.*

The excellent local museum is housed in a typical 18thC residence whose name means "Barley Sugar House." There is a fine collection of Puebla ceramics and costumes, and up on the second floor some paintings of the Battle of Puebla.

La Compañía 🏛
4 Norte.

Inside the fine Churrigueresque facade and the typical blue-and-white tiled **cupola** is the resting place, according to legend, of the original *china poblana*. If she did exist, she may have been a Mogul princess captured by pirates in the Philippines and sold into slavery.

Guadalupe and Loreto Forts and Museo del Estado (State Museum) 🏛
3km (2 miles) NE of center 🚌 *Open standard hours.*

The two 19thC forts that look across the city center mark the site of the Battle of Puebla in 1862; inside the Loreto fort there is a small **military museum** commemorating the occasion, and the four-year French occupation that followed.

The fine, modern building that stands between the forts is the Puebla **State Museum**, with archeological remains and native artifacts from the state. The centerpiece is a **jade statuette** of Olmec origin.

Santo Domingo 🏛
4 Poniente.

A 17thC Baroque church with one of the most breathtakingly opulent chapels in Mexico, the **Capilla del Rosario**. The central **statue of the Virgin** is festooned with more jewels than Cleopatra. Every surface, wall, ceiling and altar is lavishly embellished with gilded cherubs and intricate carvings.

Santa Monica Convent
5 de Mayo (1 Norte) at 18 Poniente 📷 *Open 10am–5pm. Closed Mon.*

When the Mexican state expropriated all church property in 1857, the nuns here literally went underground, into the honeycomb of secret passages, hidden doors and hollow walls. They lived there, with local cooperation, until their discovery by the authorities in 1934. The building became a museum and now has a large collection of religious sculpture and painting.

Santa Rosa Convent
3 Norte and 14 Poniente 📷 *Open 10am–5pm. Closed Mon.*

The historical kitchen where *mole* was invented has been fully restored, and there is even a small restaurant where it may be sampled. The building also houses a small museum of popular arts.

IF TIME ALLOWS . . .

Worth a quick visit are the small colonial **Museo Bello** *(3 Sur* 🚌 *open 10am-2pm; closed Sun)*, containing Puebla furniture and glassware, and the **Museo Amparo** *(2 Sur* 🚌 *open 9am-5pm; closed Tues)*, a fine mansion housing the Pre-Hispanic and colonial collections of Amparo Espinoza Iglesias.

As you make your way across the Zócalo, do not be surprised to see a bus with zebra stripes — it is picking up passengers for the **Safari Park**, 21km (13 miles) s of town toward the Valsequillo dam *(*🚌 💷 *open 10am-6pm)*. Private cars (but not convertibles) are also admitted to the park, which makes an amusing trip for those who really wanted Africa.

WITHIN EASY DISTANCE

Puebla Churches to the south
Follow road for Izúcar de Matamoros.

Two of the most perfect Puebla-style churches are on this road at

Tlaxcalancingo (8km/5 miles) and **Acatepec** (✿ 10km/6 miles). The church of **San Francisco** at Acatepec has a fine, intricately tiled and ornamented facade and a heavily carved and gilded Baroque wooden altarpiece.

The Cholula road out of Acatepec leads to the village of **Tonantzintla** (✿ 2km/1 mile), where the Churrigueresque church is a good example of the way in which this lavish style was so enthusiastically developed by native craftsmen.

34km (21 miles) along the main road is the pleasant small town of **Atlixco**, with a leafy Zócalo surrounded by tiled Puebla buildings. Visit the **parish church** and the **Hospital de San Juan**, built around a galleried court. Up on the hill overlooking the town is an austere fortified **monastery** with a commanding view of the valley.

WHERE TO STAY

COLONIAL
Calle 4 Sur 105 and 3 Ote ☎*(22) 464612* ☒*(22) 460818* ▭ *70 rms* ▭ ≡
A good, modernized colonial-style hotel in the central zone.

GRAN ALBA
Hermanos Serdán 141 ☎*(22) 460 555* ▭ *200 rms* ≡ ≋ ℘ ✓ Ⳇ ♔
Built around a modern courtyard, this excellent out-of-town hotel has superb views toward the volcanoes; it is located right next to Chalupas pyramid and church.

LASTRA
Calzada de los Fuertes 2633 ☎*(22) 359722* ▭ *51 rms* ≡ ♨ ♔
A taxi-ride from the center, this hotel is set in semitropical gardens, and has an excellent restaurant, popular for Sunday lunch.

MESÓN DEL ANGEL
Hermanos Serdán 807 ☎*(22) 482 100* ☒*(22) 487935* ▭ *200 rms* ≡ ♨ ◁ᐧ ≋ ℘ ♔ ❂ ♫
Puebla's best-known hotel is located in a southern suburb. A popular weekend spot, with colonial decor.

MISÍON DE PUEBLA
Calle 5 Pte, between Calles 25 and 27 Sur ☎*(22) 489 600* ▭ *190 rms* ≡ ≋ ▢ ♔ ♔
A new luxury hotel in the center of the commercial area, with every facility, including a swim-up bar in the pool.

POSADA SAN PEDRO
2 Oriente 202 ☎*(22) 465 077* ▭ *80 rms* ≡ ♔
A good new downtown hotel with heavy colonial decor, 5 minutes from the Zócalo.

EATING AND DRINKING

Fonda Santa Clara (✿ *3 Pte 307 in front of the Museo Bello* ☎*(22) 422 659 and 3 Pte 920* ☎*(22) 461 919* ▭ *to* ▭) serves the best *mole poblano* in town; they grind their own spices, and take hours to prepare it. **Bola Roja** *(17 Sur 1305* ☎*(22) 437 500; Plaza Dorada* ☎*(22) 407 582; Plaza Loreto* ☎*(22) 361422; all* ▭*)* has three branches serving good Mexican and regional cuisine.

Charlie's China Poblana *(Juárez 1918* ☎ *(22) 463 159* ▭*)* is a cheerful place to go for Mexican and international dishes. A more economical alternative is **Del Parian** *(Av. 2 Ote 415 at Calle 6 Nte* ☎*(22) 464 798* ▭*)*, which has a rustic decor.

For wholesome, meat-free food, make for **Zanahoria Esmeralda** *(Av. Juárez in Zona Esmeralda)*.

Hostería de los Angeles *(Camacho and Portal Morelos* ☎*(22)* *460211* ▥*)* is a favorite lunch spot on the Zócalo. Next door, **Vittorio's Pizza** *(Portal Morelos 106* ☎ *(22) 417900* ▥*)* is open all day for cheesy pizzas and pasta, served on the plaza or indoors.

CHOLULA

Map 11E7. Puebla. 12km (7 miles) w of Puebla on RF150. Altitude: 2,150m (6,450ft). Population: 45,000. Served by train (on Puebla–Izúcar line) and bus.

Formerly one of the greatest Pre-Columbian cities, the small town of Cholula boasts, in the **Great Pyramid**, the world's largest structure. It is also famed for its many churches. Recently, it became the host town to the **University of the Americas**, which offers courses to foreign students. *(For details, write to University of the Americas, PO Box 507, Puebla.)*

WHAT TO SEE

The churches

Most of the 39 churches are sited on small hills that were once pyramids. Start with the 18thC **Nuestra Señora de los Remedios**, on the **Great Pyramid**, from where the myriad tiled domes and towers of the other churches can be seen rising above the houses of the town.

Down on the main square, visit the **Capilla Real**, built in 1540; its 49 small domes and *mudéjar* timberwork give it the air of a mosque. Also here is the monastery of **San Gabriel**, with a large 16thC Gothic-vaulted church. You could carry on visiting churches until the sun goes down.

The Great Pyramid ▥ ☆

Museum ▨ Open 10am–5pm.

The 18-hectare (44-acre) pyramid of Tepanapa is now just a huge mound crowned with an 18thC church (see above), riddled with archeologists' tunnels; some 10km (6 miles) of them were dug to examine all the superimposed structures. In the Pre-Columbian era a new layer was added every 52 years, and models of all the different stages are on display at the small **museum** behind the pyramid.

There is some dispute over the origins of the ancient Cholulans, for Olmec, Toltec and Mixtec influences are all discernible. What in any event is certain is that the city's long history came to an abrupt end in 1519, when the advancing Cortés, fearing an ambush, ordered its destruction and massacred 6,000 of its 200,000 inhabitants.

✑ **Villa Arqueológica** *(*✿ *2 Pte #601* ☎*(22) 471 960* ☒*(22) 471 508, or in Mexico City* ☎*(5) 203 3153* ▥ *40 rms* ▤ ☛ ⬱ ☙ ⛩ ♒ ♈ *)*, next to the Great Pyramid, is a colonial-style inn managed by Club Med, with an archeological library and sporting facilities. **Calli Quetzalcóatl** *(on the Zócalo* ☎ *(22) 471555* ▥*)* is plain but pleasant.

WITHIN EASY DISTANCE

Huejotzingo

26km (16 miles) NW on road to San Martin Texmelucan.

A good detour on the road to Mexico City. Passing Cholula on your left, you come to the town of Huejotzingo, built around one of the best 16thC monasteries in Mexico. The town is known also for its refusal to submit to the Aztecs in Pre-Hispanic times; for its (lapsed) tradition of banditry; for the Lent Carnival; and for the Saturday market.

Start your visit to the monastery with the finely carved stone cross in the atrium; all around the atrium are the open chapels used by pilgrims and unbaptized converts. From here, enter the grim-looking church of **San Francisco**, with its great Gothic vault soaring over the Plateresque high altar. In the cloisters of the monastery itself, see the **murals** of the *Immaculate Conception*.

TLAXCALA

Map 11E7. Capital of Tlaxcala. 115km (72 miles) E of Mexico City on RF150, RF190 and RF119; 30km (19 miles) N of Puebla. Population: 75,000. Altitude: 2,250m (6,750ft). Served by train (on Mexico City–Puebla line) and bus
i Juárez 8 ☎(246) 20027 and Del Vecino 6 ☎(246) 23606.

The capital city of Mexico's smallest state is an attractive but little-visited spot, which, together with the places of interest nearby, makes a fascinating excursion.

Historically, Tlaxcala has the unique distinction of remaining unconquered by the Aztecs, despite frequent attempts to bring it under their control. When Cortés arrived, he fought several savage battles with the Tlaxcalans before they surrendered and joined him to attack the Aztecs. One of the reasons for the subsequent Aztec defeat was simple demoralization: the knowledge that the Spaniards had succeeded where for so many years they had failed.

Throughout the colonial period, Tlaxcala enjoyed special privileges. This led to its supporting the wrong side during the War of Independence; as a result, it seems to have been starved of federal funds ever since. In spite of this, Tlaxcala has just completed a tasteful restoration of the colonial section of town.

WHAT TO SEE

On the **Zócalo**, two 16thC palaces now house the local government. The modern murals on the main stair of the **Palacio de Gobierno** are both vibrantly colorful and historically informative. From here, it is 5 minutes' walk to the smaller Plaza Xicoténcatl, and up a wide, cobbled stairway to the **monastery of San Francisco** (✮). The square is named after the first Tlaxcalan king to be baptized, in a large font in a side chapel. The church's **Mudéjar timber roof**, reconstructed in the 17thC, is the finest in the Americas.

On the outskirts of town, 2km (1 mile) SE of the center, is the pueblo of **Ocotlán** (✮), where red pottery figures of animals are on sale. The 18thC **Sanctuary of the Virgin of Ocotlán**, with its Churrigueresque facade, bell towers decorated in typical Puebla tilework, and its extravagantly gilded wooden figures within, should certainly be visited. The

Virgin of Ocotlán **procession** takes place on the third Monday in May. Another 2km (1 mile) farther s is the weaving village of **Santa Ana Chiautempán**, which holds its **fiesta** on July 26.

✍ **Misión Tlaxcala** *(Km 10 Carretera Tlaxcala Apizaco* ☎ *(246) 201 78* ▥ ⇥ ≈ ⁇ *)* and **Chalets Tlaxcala** *(Revolucion 3* ☎ *(246) 20300* ▥ ⇥ ⚲ ≈ *)* are the best hotels.

WITHIN EASY DISTANCE

Cacaxtla ★
26km (16 miles) SE on unnumbered road ▨ *Open 10am–5pm.*

These are the remains of a large city that flourished here some 2,000 years ago and was abandoned around the 9thC. There are several low temple bases, some restored, but the main interest lies in the remarkable **murals** dating from 750AD, probably the best-preserved and finest Pre-Columbian paintings in the country, excelling those of BONAMPAK. They are painted on stucco in eight colors, some showing vivid and gory scenes of war, and are of especial interest to archeologists because of the Mayan style of painting, in particular the faces of the warriors, some of whom are being dismembered by patently Mexican adversaries in jaguar skins.

Some of the **date-glyphs** show resemblances to those of the Olmec culture; one can only wonder why.

La Malinche
33km (21 miles) E on RF136 (between Apizaco and Huamantla), then 15km (9 miles) S to Centro Recreacional.

This 4,461m (14,275-foot) volcano is named after Cortés's Indian mistress, whose linguistic skills were vital to the success of the conquest. From the **recreational center**, a track leads the remaining 10km (6 miles) to the summit. Check on weather conditions before climbing, and allow 6 hours for the round trip. The center has cabins with log fires and cooking facilities; bring your own food and bedding.

TEHUACÁN

Map **12***F8. Puebla. 283km (176 miles) SE of Mexico City on RF150; 236km (147 miles) NW of Oaxaca on RF131; 67km (42 miles) SW of Orizaba on RF150. Altitude: 1,640m (4,920ft). Population: 100,000. Served by air, train (on Mexico City–Oaxaca line) and bus.*

"Tehuacán" is a household word in Mexico, meaning any kind of sparkling mineral water, for this town is by far the largest producer in the country. It is also a fairly pleasant resort for liverish and infirm Mexicans, who come to take the waters. Travelers often stop for a night on the way from Mexico City to OAXACA.

The health-giving waters can be sampled free of charge at a fake **Aladdin's cave** by the Peñafiel bottling plant. Other worthwhile sights in town include the church of **El Carmen** *(Reforma Norte),* with its dazzling faïence dome, and the **Museo del Valle de Tehuacán** *(Calle 1 Norte).* Exhibits indicate that it was in this valley that the cultivation of corn began 7,000 years ago, a vital stage in the development of Mesoamerican civilizations from hunter-gatherers to settled villagers.

EVENT • On night of November 1, Day of the Dead. Fascinating and macabre ceremony at **San Gabriel Chilac** *(20km/12 miles SE; turn W off RF131 after 10km/6 miles).*

✑   **Hacienda Spa Peñafiel** *(Carretera Estación Peñafiel* ☎ *(238) 20190* ▢ *146 rms* ═ ⚹ ✍ *)*, a slightly dilapidated grand 19thC resort hotel, has enormous spring-fed swimming pools. **Mexico** *(* ♣ *Reforma Nte and Independencia Pte* ☎ *(238) 22319* ▢ ═ ⚹ *)* is another hotel with its own mineral water spring. **Iberia** *(* ♣ *Independencia s/n near Parque Juárez* ☎ *(238) 31500* ▢ *)* has been recently renovated and has an excellent Spanish/Mexican restaurant.

CUETZALAN ☆

Map 12D8. Puebla. 175km (109 miles) NW of Puebla, 316km (197 miles) E of Mexico City. Altitude: 1,200m (3,840ft). Population: 18,000. Served by bus from Puebla and Mexico City.

In the heart of Puebla's Sierra Norte, Cuetzalan is a well-preserved colonial town and an important center for the indigenous Nahua and Totonac communities in the hills around. It makes a good base for exploring the surrounding area, and is increasingly visited as a destination in its own right. Despite the continuous clearance of woodland for cultivation, there are still patches remaining of the subtropical **cloud-forest** that once covered the area. The name of Cuetzalan is derived from the locally extinct Quetzal bird of the cloud-forest, remembered in the traditional Quetzal dance.

WHAT TO SEE

The **Zócalo**, planted with trees and flowers, is of fine stone construction, with the surprisingly large **Church of San Francisco** its most conspicuous feature, closely followed by its **Palacio Municipal**. Despite the colonial appearance, the latter are both of early 20thC construction. Cuetzalan is perhaps best known for its lively Sunday market, when hundreds of Indians, most of them wearing traditional dress, congregate from the surrounding villages to trade in fruit, flowers, coffee, embroidered blouses and other craft products.

Yohuallichan

8km (5 miles) N along a poor dirt road.

The niched pyramid here is the only one to resemble that of EL TAJÍN, *(50km/31 miles N on foot),* and is clearly a product of the same civilization. Built of seven tiers, Yohuallichan's pyramid is less impressive, but the surrounding forest creates a powerful atmosphere. The additional pyramids around the 65m by 40m (208 feet by 128 feet) site are only part-excavated.

Las Hamacas waterfalls

15km (9 miles) E down a rough track.

In a much warmer zone than Cuetzalan, these lovely pools and waterfalls are refreshingly cold. The track can be negotiated by 4-wheel-drive vehicles, but the 3- to 4-hour walk is recommended, preferably accompanied by a local guide.

✏ **Posada Cuetzalan** *(Zaragoza 12* ☎ *(233) 10295* 🏢 *)* and **Posada Jackelin** *(on Zócalo* 🏢 *)* both offer rooms with private bath.

ORIZABA

Map 12E8. Veracruz. 132km (82 miles) E of Puebla on RF150 and RF190; 22km (14 miles) w of Fortín de las Flores on RF150; 67km (42 miles) E of Tehuacán on RF125 and RF150. Population: 175,000. Altitude: 1,284m (4,108ft). Served by train (lines to Mexico City and Veracruz) and bus i *Casa Consistorial, behind town hall* ☎ *(272) 43677.*

Not only does Orizaba lie at the foot of Mexico's tallest mountain, but it also possesses the country's largest brewery, the **Cervecería Moctezuma** *(* ☎ *(272) 51150)* to the w of town. Go there during working hours, or ring and arrange a guided tour — both interesting and refreshing. Another unusual sight is the all-steel-and-iron **Palacio Municipal** *(Parque del Castillo),* formerly the Belgian pavilion at the 19thC Paris International Exhibition.

The 5,714m (18,284-foot) **Pico de Orizaba**, also known as Citlaltépetl, is much more demanding to explore. There is always a cone of snow on the summit of the extinct volcano, and an experienced guide is needed. Only those in perfect condition can hope to reach the top without experiencing oxygen starvation. You might care to petition for success at the **colonial church** on the Zócalo.

✏ **Fiesta Cascada** *(Km 290 on road to Mexico City* ☎ *(272) 41596* 🏢 *⚫ ⇉ ▽)* is a pleasant out-of-town motel; **Trueba** *(Calle 6 Oriente 485 and 11 Sur* ☎ *(272) 42930* 📠 *(272) 52773* 🏢 *60 rms ⇉)* is a downtown commercial establishment; **Pluviosilla** *(7 Pte 163* ☎ *(272) 55300* 🏢 *⇐ 🏢 ⚫ ⇉ ▽)* has 43 rooms around a central courtyard.

FORTÍN DE LAS FLORES ☆

Map 12E9. Veracruz. 135km (84 miles) w of Veracruz on RF150; 166km (104 miles) E of Puebla on RF150; 110km (69 miles) s of Jalapa on scenic backroads. Population: 20,000. Served by rail (branch line from Veracruz) and bus.

The profusion of flowers and tropical plants, after which the town is named, partly smothers the colonial buildings of this very pretty small town. By contrast, the skyline falls away from the airy snow-capped peak of Mexico's highest mountain, the **Pico de Orizaba**.

The **Fortín de las Flores** hotel (see overleaf) welcomes nonresidents to its large gardens, which contain the buildings of an old hacienda and an 18thC church, as well as a large population of wild orchids and humming birds. The same hotel can arrange for visitors to play golf at a small course nearby; but be sure to take plenty of balls to replace those lost in the dense growth of bougainvillea. Less expensive hotels and eating places are to be found around the Zócalo.

Fortín de las Flores *(Calle 7 #210 at Avenida 2* ☎ *(271) 30055* 🅵🆇 *(271) 31031* 🎞 *75 rms* ⊷ ⇌ 🖴 🖢 ⇜ ♒ 🖢 🍸 *)* is a pleasant mountain resort, famous for its gardenia-filled swimming pool (new flowers daily) and large, beautiful garden.

CÓRDOBA

Map 12E9. Veracruz. 129km (81 miles) sw of Veracruz on RF150; 7km E of Fortín de las Flores on RF150. Population: 155,000. Served by train (on Puebla– Veracruz line) and bus **i** *Calle #5 308* ☎*(271) 21147.*

Here the last Spanish Viceroy signed a treaty acknowledging Mexican independence on August 24, 1821, thus furnishing this attractive colonial town with what is still its main claim to fame. On the main square, opposite the **Hotel Zevallos**, where the treaty was signed, there is a **monument to General Iturbide**, who signed for the new nation. Córdoba is now a major commercial and industrial center, but it is not a bad place to break a journey and has ample bus services in every direction.

Hotel Zevallos *(Av. 1 #111* ☎ *(271) 22722* 🎞*)*, overlooking the Zócalo, is the former home of the Counts of Zevallos, built in 1687; also on the Zócalo, **Mansur** *(Av. 1 and Calle 3* ☎*(271) 26000* 🎞 🖽*)* is clean and modern; **Palacio** *(Av. 3 and Calle 2* ☎*(271) 22188* 🎞 ⇌ 🖽*)*, recently remodeled, also has a central location and provides free car-maintenance for guests. **Real Villa Florida** *(Avenida 1 3002* ☎*(271) 43333* 🅵🆇*(271) 43336* 🎞 *75 rms* ⇌ 🍸*)* is located in a quiet suburb.

⇌ Try the restaurants in the arcade under the **Hotel Zevallos** (see above), especially the **Parroquía** (🎞).

VERACRUZ

Map 12E9. Capital of Veracruz. 431km (269 miles) E of Mexico City on RF190 and RF150. Population: 750,000. Served by air (international airport 12km/ 7 miles NW); train (on line to Mexico City) and bus **i** *Palacio Municipal, on Zócalo* ☎*(29) 327026. US Consul: Juárez 110* ☎*(29) 310142. American Express: Blvd. Manuel Camacho 2221* ☎*(29) 314411.*

The people of Mexico's oldest and busiest port are renowned throughout the country for the warmth of their welcome. Yet, although visitors can fit happily into the bustling life of the city, it does not revolve around them, and they can enjoy the blissful relief of being out of the focus of economic attention.

Unlike any other city in Mexico, there is a strong Afro-Caribbean influence on the people and culture of Veracruz, and this can be seen every day in the faces in the streets. But it is at carnival time that Veracruz becomes a Caribbean city. Fireworks light up the sky from dusk to dawn, while dancers, musicians and costumed revelers throng the streets. The lilt of the calypso and the African rhythms of the local dances fill the air, and everyone has a wonderful time.

The Spanish influence is more apparent in the buildings and especially in the area around the Zócalo, where the street life is even more active than it is in other Mexican towns. At numerous small sidewalk cafés, *Veracruzanos* sit out talking, drinking and eating delicious seafood snacks. On most evenings in the square there are bandstand concerts, and the ritual evening stroll, the *paseo,* keeps the streets busy and the atmosphere relaxed.

It was near Veracruz, on Good Friday 1519, that the Conquistadors first landed, and founded the city a short distance from the modern town. For a long time it was the only port allowed to trade with the Old World, and therefore offered rich pickings for the buccaneers who infested the sea; the town was sacked and plundered on several occasions between the 16th and 18thC.

Nor did the eventual disappearance of the pirates end the troubles of Veracruz. Long after Mexico had achieved independence, Spanish troops on the island fortress of San Juan de Ulúa kept the city under sporadic shell fire. The French invaded in 1838, followed by an American occupation in 1847 and a further French invasion in 1862, this time with English and American help. Finally, in 1914, there was yet another American occupation, preceded by a bombardment.

None of this will be held against you, however, so long as your own foreign intervention is restricted to such peaceable activities as eating seafood, strolling around the lively docks, and buying hammocks and cigars from the vendors in the Zócalo.

EVENT • There is a large and exciting **Easter carnival**, the best in Mexico, with Mardi Gras celebrations beginning the Friday before Ash Wednesday; reserve hotel rooms well in advance.

• **Mini-fiestas** are also staged several times a week — Friday night in the Zócalo, Sunday afternoon on Villa del Mar beach, and Sunday evening at Parque Ciriaco Vasques, when citizens gather for public dancing.

WHAT TO SEE

The center

The Zócalo, the **Plaza de Armas**, said to be the oldest in Mexico, is arcaded on two sides and overlooked by a small and well-worn 18thC **cathedral** and a Moorish-inspired **Palacio Municipal**. Six blocks NE is the waterfront *(malecón).* While there to take a boat to the islands, take a look at the **Biblioteca Juárez**, a library housed in an old bell tower overlooking the port, and the nearby monastic buildings, now a hotel.

On 16 de Septiembre and Canal *(8 blocks sw of the Zócalo)* is the massive 17thC **Baluarte de Santiago**, the only survivor of nine forts that once defended the city. It now houses a small regional **museum** *(■ open 10am–2pm, 4–6pm).* The **Museo Cultural de la Ciudad** *(■ Zaragoza and Morales, open standard hours)* has a collection of local Pre-Hispanic remains.

Six blocks s of Plaza de Armas is the pleasant **Parque Zamora**, by the trolley-bus terminal, and E of the park is the church of **Santo Cristo del Buen Viaje** (Christ of the Safe Voyage), where Spanish sailors would pray for deliverance from English pirates on the way back to Spain.

Isla de Sacrificios
A short distance into the gulf; take a boat from the main quay ◁€

The Spaniards discovered a **shrine** on this small island, where many human sacrifices had evidently been performed (some of the offerings found can be seen at the small museum in town). Today, there is not much specifically to see here, but the view of the town from the sea is excellent.

San Juan de Úlua
🔲 *Open 10am–5pm. Closed Mon.*

This massive, dismal fortress, on a small island opposite the port, was originally built to defend Veracruz; it became notorious as a dungeon for criminals and, especially under the long dictatorship of Porfirio Díaz, political dissidents. The prisoners existed in conditions of indescribable filth, immersed in sea water every high tide, and few emerged alive from their incarceration; exceptions included Presidents Juárez and Santa Ana. Construction began in 1528 and eventually finished in 1771, at a cost of some 40 million gold pesos to the treasury of Charles V. From 1916–60 the fortress served as an ammunition factory. It is now connected to the mainland by a causeway.

The beaches

The nearest beaches to the town center are s of the harbor at **Villa del Mar** and **Hornos**. Six blocks N of the Villa del Mar beach is an **aquarium** (🔲 *open 10am-6pm*), with a large collection of marine life from the Gulf. **Mocambo** *(6km/4 miles s of the center)* is a public beach resort area with a swimming pool.

At **Boca del Río** *(10km/6 miles s of center)* there are some deserted beaches, but development is now taking place here, so to get away from it all, take the road beyond Boca del Río as far as the jungle lagoon of **Mandinga**, 20km (12 miles) s.

WITHIN EASY DISTANCE

Zempoala 🏛 ☆
34km (18 miles) NW on RF180, then 4km (2½ miles) W 🔲 *Open 9am–6pm.*

When Cortés came across this 30,000-strong Totonac city in 1519, it was his first encounter with Mesoamerican civilization. By this time, Zempoala had fallen to the Aztecs, and the wily Cortés trapped the city into supporting his war against their rulers. By way of reward, Zempoala was the field of a fierce battle between Cortés and rival Spanish forces a year later, an experience it failed to survive.

The ruins, on the right before the village, have become somewhat run-down, but deserve far more visitors than they get. At the center of the main group is the **Great Temple**, atop a 13-tier pyramid, and nearby a 4-tier **Great Pyramid**, finished just in time for the Spaniards to ransack. Next to it is the **circular temple** to the wind god. There are other buildings nearby, including the **Templo de las Caritas** ("the small faces"), decorated with rows of grinning skulls.

The village has a few cafés around the Zócalo, and its Hotel Principal *(Hidalgo 48 🔲).*

WHERE TO STAY

Most of the luxury hotels *(all with* ▥ ≡ ⅋ ↝ *)* are along the seafront between the harbor and Mocambo. Heading s, **Emporio** *(Malecón and Xicoténcatl* ☎ *(29) 323410* Fx *(29) 312261* ▥ *202 rms* ⚓ ◉ ⚑ *)* is a lavish downtown hotel by the harbor; **Hostal de Cortés** *(Avila Camacho and Bartolomé de las Casas* ☎ *(29) 320065* Fx *(29) 315744* ▥ *108 rms* ☏ ✍ *)* is a good beachfront hotel.

On Mocambo beach itself, Veracruz's unspectacular best, **Mocambo** *(Ruíz Cortínes s/n* ☎ *(29) 371 531* Fx *(29) 371660* ▥ *125 rms* ☏ ✍ *)*, **Torremar** *(Ruíz Cortines 4300* ☎ *(29) 213 466* Fx *(29) 210291* ▥ *180 rms* ☏ ✍ *) and* **Playa Paraíso** *(* ▦ *Mocambo Highway Km 3.5* ☎ *(29) 378399* ☏ ▥ *)* are good resort-style hotels.

There are also some worthwhile hotels on the Zócalo, offering better value: **Prendes** *(* ✿ *Independencia 1064* ☎ *(29) 312041* ▥ ≡ ≡ ⅋ *)* is a traditional downtown establishment with the best seafood restaurant in Veracruz; nearby *(Independencia s/n* ☎ *(29) 312233* Fx *(29) 315135* ▥ ↜ ↝ *)* is modern and well-managed; the **Colonial** *(Lerdo 117* ☎ *(29) 320 193* ▥ ≡ ≡ ↝ ⅋ *)* is a modernized colonial-style hotel; the **Diligencias** *(Independencia 1115* ☎ *(29) 312116* ▥ ≡ ⅋ *)* occupies a fine but not very well modernized old building. Near the port, **Baluarte** *(Canal 265 at 16 de Septiembre* ☎ *(29) 322 967* ▥ *)* is also clean and economical.

DINING OUT

Veracruz is famous for its food. Inspired by influences from Spain, Africa and the Caribbean, it is rich in seafood, tropical fruits and delicious sauces. **Pardiños** *(Boca del Río, no* ☎ ▥ *) and* **El Pescador** *(Zaragoza 335* ☎ *(29) 325 252* ▥ *)* are both seafood restaurants; but the best is the one at the **Prendes** hotel. For a lively evening, try **Tilingo Charlie's** *(Malecón and Xicoténcatl* ☎ *(29) 320 020* ▥ *)*, which offers Mexican and international seafood dishes.

If you want a change from seafood, **La Parroquía** *(Independencia 105-7* ☎ *(29) 322 584* ▥ *)* serves traditional Mexican meals, snacks and excellent coffee all day long, and has opened a new branch by the pier *(Insurgentes 340* ☎ *(29) 322584)*. Another good spot is **Café la Rueda** *(Zócalo, under Hotel Diligencias* ☎ *(29) 322967* ▥ *)*.

EXCURSIONS

The Gulf road *(SE on RF180):* The first stop along the steamy Gulf of Mexico road is at the fishing port of **Alvarado** *(72km/45 miles);* try to be here at a meal time, since the unpretentious Port Authority canteen on the waterfront offers top-quality seafood at low prices. The men of Alvarado have a reputation for brawling and foul language, however, so before getting into a fight, press on to **Tlacotalpán** *(16km/10 miles s after 89km/55 miles),* a small, pretty town of thatched cottages, where you can buy local handicrafts and take a boat trip up the river.

The road then leads into the **Tuxtla mountains**, a scenic range of extinct volcanoes. The first stop is **Santiago Tuxtla** *(140km/87 miles),* founded by Cortés as a center for his sugar estates. The Zócalo is dominated by a 3m (9-foot) Olmec head, and there is another in the interesting **archeological museum** *(▩ open Mon-Sun 9am-3pm, 4-7pm except Sun; closed Mon).*

After another 14km (9 miles), **San Andrés Tuxtla** is the commercial and transport hub of the area. Just 12km (7 miles) beyond is **Lake Catemaco**, a tranquil lagoon where many *Veracruzanos* have weekend houses, and a pleasant place to break a journey. There is a lovely waterfall to explore w of the lake, the **Salto de Eyipantla**. It is reached by following a track 6km (4 miles) s off RF180, signposted 4km (2 miles) out of San Andrés toward Catemaco. At the village of **Catemaco**, there is a lively **fiesta** on July 16 in honor of the Virgen del Carmen.

≈ In Santiago Tuxtla, the **Castellanos** *(on Zócalo ☎(294) 70200 ▥▢ ▤▤ ≈≈ ⇛ ✠)* is the best place to stay. In San Andrés, there are several places around the Zócalo, including the **Del Parque** *(Madero 5 ☎(294) 20198 ▢ ⇛).*

On Lake Catemaco, **La Finca** *(2km/1 mile s of the village on RF180 ☎(294) 30322 ▥▢ ▤▤ ⚓ ◁≈ ≈≈ ⇛ ✠)* is a first-class modern motel; in the village itself, try the **Julieta** *(on the lake, no ☎ ▢ ⇛),* which is clean and peaceful. There are also numerous eating places around the Zócalo.

JALAPA (Xalapa) ☆

Map 12D9. Capital of Veracruz. 330km (206 miles) E of Mexico City on RF136 and RF140; 119km (74 miles) NW of Veracruz on RF140 and RF180; 110km (19 miles) N of Fortín de las Flores on scenic backroads. Population 300,000. Altitude: 1,406m (4,500ft) Served by train (on Mexico City–Veracruz line) and bus
i *Zaragoza s/n behind cathedral ☎(281) 87075. American Express: Carrillo Puerto 24 ☎(281) 76535.*

This state capital, like Rome, is built on seven hills. The site was chosen by the Totonac Indians of the area, whose city of Xalapa was among the first visited by Cortés. The Spanish settlers who followed him, finding the steamy climate of Veracruz unhealthy, preferred the cooler heights of Jalapa's fertile, well-watered hills as a place to establish their homes and do business.

Despite modern development, some of the town's colonial character has survived, with some fine, red-tiled mansions and churches. Jalapa has also become an important cultural center: it hosts a theater, an orchestra, a ballet company, an opera company, a large university and a fine archeological museum.

For a stroll around the old town, start at the central **Parque Juárez** and walk s; on the E side of the park are the government buildings, where some interesting modern murals can be seen. If you are feeling energetic, the highest of the hills, **Macuiltepec**, has good views of the city and, on a clear day, of the Gulf.

Although a pleasant town, Jalapa is not on the main tourist track. However, the outstanding **Museo de Antropología** attracts a regular flow of visitors.

Museo de Antropología (Anthropological Museum) ☆ ▥
w outskirts of town, on RF140 ▩ Open standard hours.
Containing the world's finest collection of Olmec, Totonac and Huastec

art, the approach to this museum is through lovely tropical gardens. Among the trees stand giant Olmec carved stone heads, with typical negroid lips and jaguar-like smiles. The building is of rose-colored volcanic stone, a grand feat of modern architecture. Inside, the 3,000 exhibits are well laid out in spacious rooms, with natural lighting.

The Olmec sculptures show their mastery at all levels, from the colossal to the miniature. Especially fine is a green stone statue of a priest or noble, holding the jaguar-child that seemingly was the most important Olmec god.

Although of later date, Totonac art is less advanced. Its most typical products are objects of polished stone incised with intricate designs. The various forms are known as "yokes," "palms" and "votive axes," but their actual function is a mystery.

☜ **María Victoria** *(Zaragoza 6* ☎ *(281) 80268* ▯ ⇌ ≋*)* has a pleasant central location; **Xalapa** *(*▥ *Victoria and Bustamante 1* ☎ *(281) 82222* ▯ ⇌ ≋*)* is the best hotel in town, with great views; nearby, **Casa de Mar** *(Victoria s/n* ☎ *(281) 73144* ▯*)* is also recommended.

⇌   There is a good selection of eating places along Zaragoza: **La Parroquía** *(Zaragoza 18* ☎ *(281) 80268* ▯*)*, as well as the **Casona del Beaterio** *(* ☎ *(281) 82119* ▯*)* and **Gondolesas** *(*▯*)*, both nearby. Of the hotel restaurants, the **Xalapa** stands out.

EL TAJÍN ☆

Map 12C8. Veracruz. 280km (175 miles) NE of Mexico City on RF130 and unnumbered road; 260km (162 miles) N of Veracruz on RF180. Served by local bus from Papantla.

Rearing up from dense tropical jungle, El Tajín is one of Mexico's most striking and important Pre-Hispanic temples. Yet it is one of the least visited of the major restored sites, being off the main tourist routes and difficult to reach without a car. Those who make the effort will be well rewarded, although the 60-hectare (150-acre) site amounts only to about a tenth of what still lies hidden beneath the undergrowth.

The site was rediscovered in 1785 by a Spanish official searching for illegal tobacco plantations. Little is known of its builders, but they are presumed to be the ancestors of the local Totonac Indians. It is thought that the city was flourishing during the Classic Period (300–900AD), that it was largely complete by 600, and that it had been long abandoned by the time of the Conquest. The site is named after the Totonac god of thunder, lightning and rain, the equivalent of the Aztec Tlaloc.

On Saturday and Sunday mornings at about 11am–noon, there is often a performance of the Huastec **flying pole-dance** (see PAPANTLA on page 126) in front of the main pyramid.

The ruins ▥

▧ *Open 10am–6pm.*

Entering from the road, you will face the Great **Pyramid of the Niches**, the masterpiece of the art and architecture of the Totonac culture. At the summit of its 6-tiered construction stand the remains of a temple. Each tier has an overhanging cornice, under which there are numerous niches adding up to the magic number of 365.

Pyramid of the Niches, El Tajín

Close your eyes and try to imagine all of the niches painted in the original dark blood-red, with the cornices in aquamarine; suddenly the dignified, crumbling structure acquires a fierce, barbaric splendor. The frieze depicts gods and sacred animals in heaven.

There are ten **ball-courts**, of which just two have been excavated, one just by the pyramid, the other a few hundred meters to the N, by which is the **Building of the Columns** with its low-reliefs of human sacrifice. Back by the entrance, there is a small **museum**, where carved stone slabs show in fine detail the playing of the sacred ball-game.

When further funds are available, the site will be fully explored, but this is unlikely to be until the 21stC, according to the provisional schedule. Until then, the amateur explorer can have a field day wandering around the hundreds of unrestored structures in the jungle.

WITHIN EASY DISTANCE
Papantla
13km (8 miles) E.
This is an agricultural center in the middle of Totonac Indian country, and the self-styled "vanilla capital of the world." Certainly the air is sometimes thick with its sweet smell, as vanilla is the area's favorite cash crop.

Papantla is also famous for the "**Danza de los Voladores**" (flying pole-dance) which takes place every year on Corpus Christi, and on some Sundays throughout the year. Four costumed dancers, ropes around their waist, climb up a 30m (100-foot) pole, then launch themselves into space, spiraling down to the ground in dizzying loops. This is an ancient religious ceremony in honor of Tunatiuh, the Totonac sun god; but the missionaries, who thought it just a dangerous game, failed to stamp it out.

While in Papantla, take a look at the murals in the **Palacio Municipal** *(on the Zócalo),* in honor of the Totonac people.

30km (19 miles) E on RF180 is the growing beach resort of **Tecolutla**, near a Totonac township known for its hats of woven palm-fiber.

Poza Rica

15km (9 miles) N of Papantla.

This is a busy industrial town, full of heavy traffic, oil refineries and oil workers. As it is also a major crossroads and bus terminus, it may be difficult to shun entirely.

☞ In Papantla, **Totonocapán** *(Olivo and 20 de Noviembre* ☎ *(784) 21220* ▥ ⇥ *)* is a little charmless, on the main road, making **Tajín** *(Nuñez 104* ☎ *(784) 20121* ▥ *),* with its fine views, the better choice. In Tecolutla there are several beach hotels, including the **Hotel Balneario Tecolutla** *(Matamoros s/n* ☎ *(232) 50901* ▥ ⇥ ≈≈ *).*

COATZACOALCOS AND MINATITLÁN

Map 7H10. Veracruz. 172km (107 miles) w of Villahermosa on RF180; 311km (194 miles) SE of Veracruz on RF180; 284km (177 miles) N of Tehuantepec on RF185. Population: 400,000. Served by air, train (on Veracruz–Mérida line) and bus.

Important twin regional centers that form unavoidable staging posts on many journeys. The port of Coatzacoalcos has plenty of sleazy low life, but its large red-light districts, beloved of sailors and oilmen, are not recommended for tourists.

☞ **Club Terranova** *(*🚗 *7.5km/4½ miles toward Minatitlán* ☎ *(921) 25100* ▥ *200 rms* ⇥ ▦ ≈≈ ⌁ ⬤ ♈ ⊙ ♌ *)* is an exclusive luxury resort, especially favored by tired oil executives.

There are many ordinary commercial hotels, but two reasonable ones are **Margón** *(Zaragoza 302* ☎ *(921) 20572* ▥ ▦ ⇥ *)* and **Valgrande** *(Hidalgo 207* ☎ *(921) 21624* 𝐅𝐱 *(921) 23139* ▥ *62 rms* ▦ ⇥ *),* which serves excellent seafood. More luxurious choices include the **Brisa Motor** *(Zaragoza 2001* ☎ *(921) 20490* ▥ ⇥ ≈≈ ▦ ♈ *)* and the **Terranova Travelodge** *(Km 7.5 on road to Minatitlán* ☎ *(921) 45100* 𝐅𝐱 *(921) 45482* ▥ ⇥ ♈ ≈≈ ▦ *).*

Those wishing to avoid Coatzacoalcos could stop at Acayucan, 90km (56 miles) W on RF180 and RF185, where the **Kikadu** *(Ocampo Sur 7* ☎ *(924) 50410* ▥ ⇥ ▦ ⬅ *)* offers reasonable accommodation.

South of Mexico City

This region comprises the states of **Guerrero** and **Oaxaca**. Despite Guerrero's proximity to Mexico City and its highly developed coast, which includes such resorts as Acapulco, its interior is surprisingly remote, its mountains inhospitable and its approach to law enforcement idiosyncratic. This anomalous state is named after Vicente Guerrero, the 19th-century general of the War of Independence, who fought a brilliant guerrilla campaign from its Sierra Madre Sur until he was betrayed and shot in 1831.

Indeed, the tradition of guerrilla activity in this region never quite died, and underwent a revival in the 1970s in both Guerrero and Oaxaca. This happened in response to political corruption and the theft of land from local farming communities, most of them made up of indigenous people. However, the guerrillas were soon eliminated, and a strong-arm style of government has persisted in the region ever since, while unresolved land disputes proliferate.

GUERRERO

Of course, the great majority of visitors to Guerrero will never experience any problems, limiting their attentions to the Pacific resorts and to TAXCO, a charming colonial silver-mining city in the north of the state, near Mexico City. Taxco is famous for its silverware, and its hundreds of craftspeople produce a significant proportion of Mexico's jewelry.

The name of ACAPULCO still conjures up glamorous images straight out of travel brochures, but the resort may have become too much of a big, dirty city for some people, despite its lovely bay. One alternative is to travel west to ZIHUATANEJO, once a small fishing village but now the better half of IXTAPA, the nearby luxury resort.

Traveling east from Acapulco, the coastal road winds between impressive mountains and coastal swamps and lagoons, and through the village of **Coajinicuilapa**. Founded in 1562 for the African slaves who were brought over to work on sugar plantations, it is still inhabited by their descendants.

To ease tourists' unhindered passage to the coast, a brand-new divided highway will soon link Mexico City to Acapulco, reducing the journey time to about four hours. The road passes high above the **valley of the Río Balsas**, where Nahua villagers carve superb masks and mythical beasts of wood. Farther south, the state capital of CHILPANCINGO is really only worth stopping at to explore the nearby villages, each with its own craft product, and the nearby **caves of Juxtlahuaca**.

OAXACA

Across the border in the state of Oaxaca, the town of **Pinotepa Nacional** has an interesting market that serves the local Amusgo Indians, and the beach resorts that follow are generally modest and relaxed. PUERTO ESCONDIDO has grown gently out of a fishing village, while PUERTO ANGEL remains one still. The nearby beach at **Zipolite**, which is known for its nudism and laid-back living, is the Xanadu of gringo hippies.

A little farther along the coast, there is a sharp stylistic discontinuity at HUATULCO, a new mega-resort in construction, spread along a series of lovely beaches, with half a dozen or so luxury hotels already in operation. One of its extravagances is a reconstruction of the Zócalo in Oaxaca, capital of the state.

Situated on a high inland plain on the far side of the Sierra Madre Sur, OAXACA itself is one of Mexico's most popular tourist destinations, with a lovely colonial center and markets overflowing with Indian crafts. Adventurous visitors should consider going to some of the nearby craft-producing villages, such as **Coyotepec**, known for its burnished black ceramics. There are also some colonial monasteries within easy reach, such as the vast complex at **Culiapán**, where General Guerrero was shot.

The area also holds several of Mexico's most important Pre-Hispanic sites, including MONTE ALBÁN. Built by the Zapotec people of the area but later taken over by the Mixtecs, it covers an entire mountain top with its monuments. By contrast, MITLA, a much later site nearby, was apparently built by the Mixtecs. It is exceptional both for its fine geometrical carvings and for its excellent state of preservation.

At the eastern extremity of the state lie the hot lowlands of the **Isthmus of Tehuantepec**, with its unattractive commercial ports and oil refining cities. This would be an undistinguished end to Oaxaca, were it not for the presence of Mexico's largest surviving rainforest, the **Selva Chimalapa**, homeland of the Zoque Indians.

The government recently published plans for a major road right through the heart of the forest, but these were dropped after a national uproar. The future of the forest is still not assured, however, as it continues to be encroached upon by illegal loggers and cattle ranchers, many of them from the neighboring state of Chiapas.

Even more than in other parts of Mexico, the police forces of this region are reputed to operate like the private armies of state governors. The remoter parts of both states are also centers of drugs production, a violent, corrupt business said to bring huge profits to some people in very high places — so take local advice before heading off into faraway mountains. And as for Guerrero's reputation for banditry, which is still a problem in remote areas, off-duty state police are often held responsible by local people. Whatever the truth of this, one sensible precaution is to avoid driving late at night.

Towns, cities and cultural sites

The main urban centers and places of interest in this part of Mexico are covered here, starting with TAXCO, in the N of Guerrero, proceeding via CHILPANCINGO to the coast at ACAPULCO, then NW up the coast to ZIHUATANEJO AND IXTAPA. The route then veers SE along the coast of the state of Oaxaca, covering PUERTO ESCONDIDO and PUERTO ANGEL, HUATULCO and finally TEHUANTEPEC, before traveling inland to the state capital, OAXACA and the nearby archeological sites of MITLA and MONTE ALBÁN.

See USING THIS GUIDE on page 50 for full details on how to use this section. On the following pages, helpful pointers are given on how to get to each of the destinations covered. Along with the MEXICO map on pages 46–7, and the 4-color maps at the back of this book, they should give all the information necessary for planning your trip to this part of Mexico.

TAXCO ★

*Map **6**H8. Guerrero. 185km (116 miles) sw of Mexico City, 122km sw of Cuernavaca on old RF95; 146km (91 miles) s of Toluca on RF55. Altitude: 1,662m (5,484ft). Population: 100,000. Served by air taxi and bus* **i** *Calle Florida s/n (N of town)* ☎*(762) 22279.*

Even those who prefer to stay off the tourist circuit would make a mistake by staying away from Taxco. It is a colonial mining town of irresistible charm, with narrow cobbled streets winding up, down and around the hills, and domed and spired churches rising above terracotta roofs. The town should be explored on foot; just walking around the streets is such a pleasure that it should keep you busy for a morning or so, as you glimpse a succession of arresting sights.

You may end your walk rather poorer than when you started — for this is a city of silver. There are about a hundred silver stores, glittering and beckoning the visitor. Although designs are generally of a high standard, quality and prices are far from uniform, so do shop around before making a purchase. Many shops sell silver items by weight, so the price per gram makes a good standard of comparison.

Cortés himself ordered the initial explorations for silver in the locality, and these met with some success, although Taxco's prosperity really dates from the 18thC, when French nobleman José de la Borda struck the fabulously rich San Ignacio vein.

After his death in 1778, the town's fortunes waned, not to be revived again until an American, William Spratling, came to Taxco in 1929. He was a writer and university lecturer, but gave all this up to throw himself into designing, producing and marketing silver jewelry. Now, more than 2,000 people work in the silver industry, and many more in the tourist business. William Spratling, who died in 1967, is now revered in the same way as a patron saint of Taxco.

Taxco is also a good place to find other characteristic crafts of Guerrero, such as the wooden masks and fish of the Balsas valley. Explore the extensive **market**, just down from the Zócalo, and take a look at **Arnoldo's** mask store *(Plazuela de los Gallos 2)*.

EVENTS • At **Easter**, there are processions throughout Holy Week, the most exciting time of year in Taxco. Maundy Thursday sees the Zócalo transformed into a Garden of Gethsemane for the arrest of Christ; events culminate in a gruesome re-enactment of the Passion on Good Friday.

• Visitors at the end of November can witness the **silver festival**, when jewelers submit their latest designs to a prize-giving committee.

• On January 18, February 24, March 8 and May 3, there are other important **religious festivals**.

WHAT TO SEE

For a good view of the town, leave the Zócalo on Calle Guadalupe and climb the narrow lane up to the church of the **Virgin of Guadalupe**. Those who are inspired (and energetic) can continue for another 2km (1 mile) up a mountain path to the summit of the **Cerro de Atachi** (◀€), from where the entire Valley of Taxco and the surrounding villages can be surveyed.

The principal sights are in and around the Zócalo.

Santa Prisca 𝕸

The great Baroque facade of Santa Prisca dominates the laurel trees of the charming little Zócalo, and is thought by many to be the finest church in Mexico. It was built in the 1750s by Count de la Borda as a special thanksgiving for his good fortune. Over the doorway, exquisitely carved in the local pink stone, is a relief of *St John the Baptist and the Infant Christ*. Inside, the altars form a profusion of carved and gilded decoration.

Over the doorway to the **Chapel of the Indians** hangs an oil painting of *The Martyrdom of St Prisca in Rome,* the most important of 56 paintings that hang here by Miguel Cabrera (died 1768), a Zapotec Indian who became a great (Christian) religious painter. There are more of his works in the sacristy.

Museo Guillermo Spratling (Spratling Museum)

Behind Santa Prisca 🕿 *Open 10am–5pm. Closed Mon.*

The museum occupying the old home of William Spratling contains a history of the local silver industry, which he is largely responsible for founding, as well as prize pieces of work. Also on display is Spratling's collection of Pre-Columbiana.

Casa Figueroa

🕿 *Guadalupe 2. Open 10am–1pm, 3–7pm. Closed Mon.*

Now an art gallery and museum, the house is named after the Mexican artist who restored it in the 1940s to serve as his own studio and home. Also known as the House of Tears, it was originally built in the 18thC by a local magistrate, using the forced labor of Indians who were unable to pay their debts.

IF TIME ALLOWS . . .

The home of Taxco's original silver king, José de la Borda, is now occupied by a **silver store**, which bears his name, in Calle Muñoz s/n.

On the other side of the Zócalo, in Plaza San Juan, is the **Casa Grande** (🔲 *open 10am-1pm; closed Sat, Sun),* the house of the mayors of Taxco, with various exhibits commemorating the revolutionary José Morelos' short stay here in 1815. Dedicated sightseers should also visit the **Casa Humboldt** (*N of Zócalo, on Ruíz de Alarcón),* which is named after the famous explorer who stayed here for one night in 1803. The facade is adorned in the moorish Mudéjar style, with a series of complex interlocking geometric designs; it is usually possible to walk into the lovely little courtyard.

Five minutes' walk from here, past the Palacio Municipal, is the large old monastery of **San Bernadino**, rebuilt after a fire in 1805. About 1km ($\frac{1}{2}$ mile) from here, up Morelos and along the Cuernavaca road, is the interesting old **Hacienda del Chorillo**, close to the ruins of a silver-ore-refining works. A taxi may be the best way to get here, but, beyond, a **cable car** runs up to the MONTE TAXCO hotel (see next page). It is worth going up for a drink and the view, even if you are not a guest there.

EXCURSION

Grutas de Cacahuamilpa ★

49km (31 miles) N; w off Cuernavaca road after Km 39.

The vast network of caves at Cacahuamilpa (🕿 *✗ compulsory but at irregular intervals, open 10am-3pm)* are well lit and safe. The 2km (1-mile) tour passes through forests of stalagmites into chambers the size of concert halls, and past historical graffiti by such distinguished folk as Maximilian's empress, Carlota (for those not of royal blood, the adding of new graffiti is forbidden). If you can, stop at **Las Granadas waterfalls** on the way.

WHERE TO STAY

DE LA BORDA
Cerro del Pedregal 2 ☎*(762) 20025*
▥ *146 rms* ⇌ ❤ ◖⟨ ⇗ ♈ ♫

This is an older but well-restored hotel, 15 minutes' walk up from the Zócalo.

HACIENDA DEL SOLAR ☗
Calle del Solar, Taxco Viejo ☎*(762) 20323*
▥ *21 rms* ⇌ ▱ ❤ ◖⟨ ⇗ ♒ ✔ ⚔ ♈
Set in vast grounds 3km (1½ miles) s, this beautiful resort hotel boasts the best restaurant in Taxco, with panoramic views across the town.

LOS ARCOS ✿ ▥
Juan Ruíz de Alarcón 2 ☎*(762) 21836*
▥ *26 rms* ⇌ ⇗ ♈
Near the Zócalo, this 17thC former monastery has rooms full of character and a cloister filled with flowers.

MONTE TAXCO
Londres 117, Fracc. Lomas de Taxco, N *off RF95* ☎*(762) 21300* ▥ *160 rms* ⇌
❤ ◖⟨ ⇗ ♒ ✔ ⚔ ♈
A former Holiday Inn on a hill overlooking the town, with a **cable-car** link to the **Hacienda del Chorillo** (see page 132). Sadly, it lacks atmosphere.

POSADA DE LA MISIÓN
John F. Kennedy 32 ☎*(762) 20063*
▣*(762) 22198* ▥ *160 rms* ⇌ ❤ ⇗
♈ ♫

This substantial Spanish mission-style hotel has a **Juan O'Gorman mural** beside its heated pool, as well as a good restaurant.

POSADA LOS CASTILLO ✿ ▥
Juan Ruíz de Alarcón 7 ☎*(762) 21396* ▥
15 rms ⇌ ♈
This pleasant, small inn is housed in a well-restored 17thC courtyard building.

RANCHO TAXCO VICTORIA
Carlos J. Nibbi 5 and 7 ☎*(762) 40280*
▣*(762) 20617* ▥ *to* ▥ *64 rms* ⇌ ❤
⇗ ♈
Representing the union of the Rancho Taxco and Victoria hotels, this is a large establishment with considerable variation among the rooms. It has pleasant gardens and a central location.

EATING AND DRINKING

Taxco's hotel restaurants rank among the best in Mexico, and there are some good places around the Zócalo, including **Los Balcones** (*Los Gallos 5* ☎*(762) 20680* ▥*)* and **El Alarcon** (*Juárez 26* ☎*(762) 20344* ▥*)*, both for Mexican specialties. **Sr Costilla's** (*Plaza Borda 1* ☎*(762) 23215* ▥*)* is a typically riotous member of the Carlos'n'Charlie's chain.

Of the hotel restaurants, the best is at the **Hacienda del Solar** (▥), serving gourmet Italian food, while filling meals and excellent value are on offer at **La Hacienda** (*✿ Calle Bailar* ☎*(762) 20633* ▥*)*, part of the Agua Escondida hotel.

CHILPANCINGO

Map **6***H8. Capital of Guerrero. 280km (174 miles)* s *of Mexico City on RF95; 133km (83 miles)* N *of Acapulco on RF95. Population: 90,000. Served by bus.*

A busy, fast-expanding town that is growing rich on the state's agriculture and on the lumbering industry in the Sierra Madre. There is little to detain the tourist, but you may find interesting crafts in the **market** near the bus station. If you stop here for a snack, see the **murals** in the **Palacio de Gobierno** on the Zócalo, commemorating, among other things, the first-ever Mexican Congress, held in the town in 1813.

EXCURSIONS

The countryside around Chilpancingo offers two rewarding trips for the energetic and independent traveler. There is no commercial organization of these excursions, and until recently the area had a reputation for minor banditry. This is now under control, but you are advised to keep to the routes suggested.

Juxtlahuaca caves ☆
49km (31 miles) SE via RF95, then turn E toward Colotlipa.

In the Zócalo of **Colotlipa**, a small but charming colonial town, you can engage a guide who will accompany you on the final 8km (5 miles) to the caves, open them up and give you a guided tour. Besides stalactites and waterfalls, there are **Olmec cave paintings** dating from around 1000BC, possibly the oldest on the continent, as well as some petrified skulls.

Bring swimsuits and sneakers for the last stretch through an **underground river**, from where the adventurous can squeeze through a narrow passage to a wonderful garden of crystalline calcite. You should also bring a flashlight to supplement the hurricane lamps. An overnight stop may be necessary in **Colotlipa**, which has several small hotels near the Zócalo (🗔).

Mexcala and river Balsas
50km (31 miles) N on old RF95.

Once the starting point for an exhilarating raft trip through gorges and white water to Ciudad Altamirano, Mexcala is now at the top of a vast muddy reservoir serving a hydroelectric dam. There are plans for a second dam just upstream, which would flood the entire upper Balsas valley; however, the scheme has been fiercely resisted by the Nahua Indians of the valley.

A trip up the valley is still possible from **Xalitla** *(5km/3 miles N of Mexcala)* to the village of **San Agustín**, famous for its paintings, and under the new road bridge to the village of **San Francisco**, where many of the valley's wooden masks and mythical beasts are carved.

☚   **Parador del Marques** *(on RF95 just s of town* ☎ *(747) 26773* 🗔 ━ ⇌ *)* also features a trailer park; **Posada Meléndez** *(Juárez 50* ☎ *(747) 23087* 🗔 ⇌ ⇪ ⫙ ━ *)* and **Jacarandas** *(Rufo Figueroa s/n* ☎ *(747) 24444* 🗔 ⇌ ⫙ ⫙ ━ *)* are other recommendations.

ACAPULCO ★

Map 6I8. Guerrero. 400km (250 miles) s of Mexico City on new RF95 (open end 1993). Population: 2 million. Served by air (international airport 30km/19 miles E) and bus ℹ *Costera Miguel Alemán 187* ☎ *(74) 851249/51304. US Consul: Club del Sol Hotel* ☎ *(74) 857207. UK Consul: Hotel Las Brisas* ☎ *(74) 846605. American Express Travel Service: Costera Miguel Alemán 709–4* ☎ *(74) 845550; Hotel Continental Hyatt* ☎ *(74) 840909; Hotel Regency Hyatt* ☎ *(74) 842888. See map on page 136.*

The very name of Acapulco conjures up an image of sun, sand, sea, sex and the international jet-set — all available in abundance except the latter, who are a little thin on the ground these days. Its reputation was formed in the 1950s, when exotic vacations were available only to the jewel-studded few, but nowadays, with 4 million visitors a year, Acapulco is no longer so exclusive. Since the less you wear, the better your disguise, anyone you meet nowadays on Acapulco's beaches may be a celebrity; but the real stars mostly prefer to stay in their private villas up in the hills, or have made for other, more discreet pleasure spots.

In the wake of this explosion in popularity, the Mexican government has launched a million-dollar "Aca-limpia" facelift to reglamorize the resort, cleaning up around its edges, enforcing planning controls, picking up rubbish off the streets and seeking to improve the bay's dubious water quality — and about time, too. However, the increasingly busy traffic that clogs and pollutes the city has so far escaped attention, and an ever-growing population of hopeful immigrant workers threatens to overwhelm even the best of efforts. But despite these problems, there can be no doubting that Acapulco remains one of the world's premier resorts.

Deep-sea fishing, paragliding, surfing or golf provide ways to fill the days while waiting for night-time. Like no other place in the world, Acapulco comes alive at dusk. Around the bay, the mountains become dark shadows before the starry tropical sky. The lights of high-rise hotels and cars along the Costera gleam and wink, reflecting in the calm ocean like a giant fairground. Suddenly, there are people everywhere, strolling, strutting, preening, sitting and tapping their feet to the disco beat that wafts along on the breeze.

It is even rumored that there are some visitors who have never seen Acapulco in daylight, when it is both beautiful and dramatic. For even the most determinedly blasé, the blue sky, green mountains plunging down to the sea, tropical flowers and palm trees, and the sheltered bay with its perfect beaches and great crescent of white towers, will prove irresistible. But be warned that many visitors will no longer swim in the sea, because of the pollution of the once pristine bay.

EVENTS • For details of events, see the **free information sheets** distributed at all hotels. The large hotels all organize various entertainments and fiestas.

• There are also frequent performances of the **Ballet Folklórico** at the **Centro Acapulco** (see ACAPULCO BY NIGHT, page 140).

WHAT TO SEE

The town

Acapulco has an interesting history, but one of which little evidence survives. It was one of the first Spanish ports, rapidly becoming the main entry point for precious cargoes on their way from the Far East and South America to Spain. These made the overland journey to Veracruz via Mexico City on horses and mules. The only relic of those days is the pentagonal **Fuerte San Diego** *(500m/550yds E of the Zócalo on the waterfront; closed Tues),* built in the 18thC to protect the port.

The **Zócalo** itself is surrounded by small shops and cafés, with a bizarre **Neo-Byzantine cathedral**. But the real focus of interest in Acapulco is the **Costera Miguel Alemán**, the waterfront boulevard,

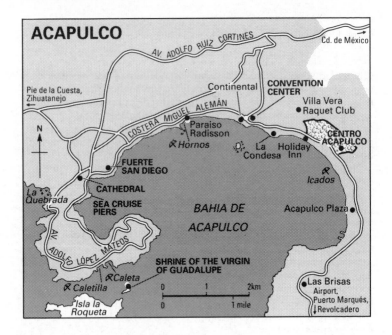

where nearly all the smart hotels, restaurants and shops are located. It is usually known just as the "Costera," and, quite simply, the Costera *is* Acapulco.

La Quebrada

Due w of the Zócalo, by the Plaza las Glorias El Mirador Hotel, there are some jagged **cliffs** around a narrow inlet. Every day and night, the most daring *acapulqueños* dive into the shallow and turbulent waters from a height of 40m (130 feet). It needs split-second judgment and nerves of steel, and is especially dramatic after dark when they dive holding flaming torches.

Divers and spectators alike can get their breath back at the bar of the nearby **hotel**, although a more dramatic view of the action is to be had from the steps below.

ACTIVITIES

Take the children to the new multilevel **Aquarium** (✿ *Playa Caleta pier* ☎), with swimming and fish pools, to the **CICI children's theme park** (*Costera and Colón on Playa Icacos*) complete with wave-making pool, and to **Parque Papagayo** (*Playa Hornos*), with its full-sized galleon and space shuttle replica.

The cultural center, the **Centro Acapulco** (☎ (74) 823828, *see page 140*), contains the **Museo de Acapulco** (☎ *open standard hours*), which has two rooms of Pre-Columbian finds, and one of local crafts that are also for sale.

136

BEACHES AND WATER-SPORTS

Acapulco today may be challenged by the new, custom-built resorts at Ixtapa and Cancún, which offer a different, perhaps less worldly range of pleasures. But for sheer variety of outdoor activities, it has no rival. Every conceivable water-sport may be sampled in Acapulco, from deep-sea fishing to the exhilarating experience of paragliding.

The 50 or so beaches around Acapulco fall in and out of fashion with bewildering rapidity, so if you want to keep up with the jet-set, be prepared to move fast. A variety of water-sports is available at all beaches in the bay, and chairs, parasols and thatched huts can be rented. Many of the larger hotels extend right down onto the beaches; with reasonable discretion, anyone willing to tip the attendants can use the pools and terraces. Anything from a Cuba Libre to a 3-course meal can be purchased at the beachside restaurants.

All beaches are public and free, but the price of services varies with what the vendor can get away with. Beach vendors can be a nuisance, although, for the idle, they take the walking out of souvenir-hunting. One painless way to explore is on a half-day yacht cruise, with a good party atmosphere (tickets from hotels).

Swimming in the sea is not generally recommended, due to side currents and strong surf. Pollution is another hazard: the debris is most visible, but sewage poses a greater risk to health. If in doubt, stick to swimming pools. Surfing is discouraged on beaches near the center.

La Condesa, in the center of the bay, near the Condesa del Mar hotel, is currently the most crowded and expensive of the beaches, and probably the most fun. Avoid the gay section if your preferences lie elsewhere. East from the Condesa del Mar, **Hornos** is a good beach for the late afternoon and a game of mini-golf.

Caleta and **Caletilla** face **La Roqueta Island** on the western peninsula. Both are small, well-protected bays, especially popular in the mornings and good for those on a budget. Boats leave every few minutes for the island, optimistically billed as a safari park, where a pleasant beach is inhabited by some notoriously alcoholic donkeys. Take a glass-bottomed boat and see the underwater **shrine of the Virgin of Guadalupe (✫)**.

12km ($7\frac{1}{2}$ miles) NW of town is **Pie de la Cuesta**, a village on a sandbar backed by the enormous **Laguna de Coyuca (✫)**, a brackish jungle lagoon, full of birds and water-hyacinths, with facilities for boating and swimming. Come here to catch a spectacular sunset and to drink a long cocktail, or join Mexican tourists for grilled fish and *mariachis*. But don't be tempted to swim in the ocean: the waters are infested with sharks and stingrays, and the surf is dangerous.

Heading w from the Condesa del Mar, along the airport road lie several beaches. **Icacos**, long, uncrowded, with usually calm waters, stretches out toward the Las Brisas peninsula. Above **Pichilingue**, round to the E of the peninsula in Puerto Marqués Bay, are the villas of the rich. **Puerto Marqués**, in a miniature version of Acapulco bay, is one of the high-fashion beaches, with good swimming and innumerable diversions.

After the deep inlet at Pichilingue, the site of the new Diamond Point development, comes **Revolcadero Beach (✫)**, overlooked by two of the most exclusive hotels, but suffering from large waves, a strong undertow and occasional shark-scares. A few miles farther on, **Barra Vieja** has some pleasant beach cafés, although, once again, swimming is rough. Out past the airport is the **Laguna Tres Palos**, larger and wilder than Laguna de Coyuca.

WHERE TO STAY

ACAPULCO PLAZA 📖
Costera 123 ☎(74) 859050 ☒(74) *855285* ▦ *1,585 rms* ▤ ⬤ ⬟ ☒ ⬦ ⟨⟨ ⤳ ⬢ ℘ 📖 ♈ ○ ♪
Location: On the beach at the center of the bay, due s of the center on the road to the airport. Operated by Holiday Inn, this is the largest, most central of the luxury hotels, with attractive split-level rooms and six restaurants. Tuesday and Thursday are fiesta nights.

LAS BRISAS 📖 ♨
Carretera Escénica 5255 ☎(74) 841664 ☒(74) 842269; *in US* ☎(800) 228 3000 ▦ *300 rms* ▤ ⬤ ⬟ ☒ ⬦ ⟨⟨ ⤳ ⬢ ℘ ♈ ○ ♪
Location: 13km (8 miles) s on the airport road. An all-pink dream village covering 300 hectares (750 acres), hewn out of the cliffs overlooking the bay. At the center is a 17thC fortress, surrounded by clusters of pink villas and blue swimming pools. Even the fleet of jeeps (at guests' disposal) is pink.

CALINDA ACAPULCO QUALITY INN ♣
Costera 1260 ☎(74) 840410 ☒(74) 844676 ▦ *357 rms* ▤ ⬤ ⬟ ⬡ ⬠ ☒ ⬦ ⟨⟨ ⤳ ⬢ ℘ ♈ ○ ♪
Location: On Playa Condesa. A tall cylindrical tower on a busy part of the beach, with the advantage of good package deals.

CAMINO REAL ACAPULCO DIAMANTE 📖
Baja Catita 18 ☎(5) 203 3113 ☒(5) 250 6935; *in US* ☎(800) 228 3000 ▦ *192 rms* ▤ ⬤ ⬟ ⬦ ⟨⟨ ⤳ ⬢ ℘ ♈ ○ ♪
Location: On Puerto Marqués bay, toward the airport. This is one of Acapulco's newest luxury hotels, the first major development in the new Diamond Point mega-resort with its own fast-developing sports and shopping facilities, including two new golf courses.

FIESTA AMERICANA CONDESA ACAPULCO 📖
Costera, at Playa Condesa ☎(74) 842858 ☒(74) 841828 ▦ *500 rms* ▤ ⬤ ⬟ ⬡ ℘ ⬦ ⟨⟨ ⤳ ⬢ ℘ ♈ ○ ♪
Location: Near the center of the bay. In the evening, bands play in the lively, bustling lobby, which is a riot of flowers and fountains. There are wonderful views of the bay, even from the swimming pool.

HYATT CONTINENTAL ACAPULCO
Costera s/n ☎(74) 840909 ☒(74) 842120 ▦ *448 rms* ▤ ⬤ ⬟ ☒ ⬦ ⟨⟨ ⤳ ⬢ ℘ ⬤ ♈ ○ ♪
Location: At the center of the bay. This Hyatt hotel is less expensive, but nearly as luxurious, as the ACAPULCO PLAZA (see above). A vast pool surrounds a tropical island with a restaurant and bar.

HYATT REGENCY ACAPULCO 📖
Costera 1 ☎(74) 842888 ☒(74) 843087 ▦ *694 rms* ▤ ⬤ ⬟ ⬡ ☒ ⬦ ⟨⟨ ⤳ ℘ ⬤ ⬢ ♈ ○ ♪
Location: To the e of the bay on Icacos beach, near the naval base. Good value in summer, when meals are not obligatory. Extensive pools create a lovely ambience, and sports and excursions are well organized.

PARAÍSO RADISSON ACAPULCO
Costera 163 at Playa Hornos ☎(74) 855596 ☒(74) 855543 ▦ *422 rms* ▤ ⬤ ⬟ ⬡ ☒ ⬦ ⤳ ⬢ ℘ ♈ ○ ♪
Location: Near the center of the bay. The social program and water-sports are good here, but the pool and beach are small. Delicious seafood dishes are served at the **Supper Club**.

PIERRE MARQUÉS 📖
Playa Revolcadero ☎(74) 842000, *in US* ☎(800) 223 1818 ▦ *344 rms* ▤ ⬤ ⬟ ☒ ⬦ ⟨⟨ ⤳ ℘ ⬢ ⨯ ♈ ○ ♪

Location: 16km (10 miles) s on the airport road. This elegant family hotel is a favorite with golfers and tennis players. Facilities are shared with the adjacent, even more luxurious PRINCESS (see below), under the same management. Two 18-hole golf courses are available .

PRINCESS 🏨 ♣

Playa Revolcadero ☎(74) 843100 🅵🆇(74) 843664, in US ☎(800) 223 1818 🎞 1019 rms 🍽 ➡ ⇌ 🖼 🎿 ☂ ⇎ ≋ ⚲ 🦐 :/ 🏋 ☿ ☯ ♪

Location: 18km (11 miles) s on the airport road. This dramatic structure, built in the style of an Aztec pyramid, is smothered in tropical blooms and set among 192 hectares (480 acres) of gardens. Attractions include four swimming pools complete with waterfalls, palm trees and a swim-up bar. (See PIERRE MARQUÉS, above.)

VILLA VERA RACQUET CLUB 🏨

Lomas del Mar 35 ☎(74) 840333 🅵🆇(74) 847479 🎞 80 rms 🍽 ➡ ⇌ 🖼 🎿 ☂ ⇎ 🦐 ⚲ ☿ ☯ ♪

Location: Near the center of the bay. The restaurant and poolside bar are among the best, and the tennis courts are of sunbaked clay, all providing glamorous luxury for affluent sophisticates at exclusive prices. The under-16s are excluded.

Budget hotels

For travelers whose budgets do not extend to the dizzy extremes of the jet-set, Acapulco also has a number of more inexpensive hotels to offer. Some recommendations follow.

- **Casablanca**   Cerro de la Pinzoha s/n ☎(74) 821212 🅵🆇(74) 8212517 🎞 106 rms ⇌ ☿ ≋ On the hilltop.
- **Embassy**   Costera 50, one block from the beach ☎(74) 840273 ▢ ⇌ ☿ 🍽
- **Fiesta**   Azueta 10 near Zócalo ☎(74) 820019 🎞 Basic but pleasant.
- **Los Flamingos**   López Mateos s/n ☎(74) 820690 🅵🆇(74) 839806 🎞 ⇌ ☿ ≋ In La Caleta district, with an authentic Hollywood past.
- **La Palapa**   Fragata Yucatán 210 ☎(74) 845363 🅵🆇(74) 848399 🎞 376 rms ⇌ ☿ ≋ 🍽

EATING AND DRINKING

In addition to the many hotel restaurants, there is a wide choice of independents. **Blackbeard's** *(Costera 101 on Playa Condesa* ☎*(74) 842549* 🎞 *♪ ☙)* has a piratical atmosphere: fun for lunch, romantic for dinner. Next door, **Mimi's Chili Saloon** *(* ☎*(74) 842549)* is good for Tex-Mex. **Bohio** *(Roca Sola 17* ☎*(74) 843454* 🎞*)* is a quiet retreat from Acapulco's high-speed hustle, with good seafood, what's more. Similarly peaceful is the Japanese **Suntory** *(Costera 36* ☎*(74) 848088* 🎞*)*, with its manicured garden.

The typically wacky branch of the **Carlos'n'Charlie's** chain *(Costera 999* ☎*(74) 840039* 🎞 *♪ closed Tues)* is the original version from the 1970s; arrive early for its good seafood and hamburgers, as reservations are not accepted. **Embarcadero** *(Costera 25* ☎*(74) 848787* 🎞*)* has a strange mixture of Polynesian fantasy and "elegant dockside decor" — waiters dressed as stevedores, desert island monkeys and parrots; try one of the Mexican-Chinese inventions.

Las Madeiras *(Carretera Escénica 39 above Las Brisas* ☎*(74)*

844378 ▥*)* has a luxurious decor of glinting silver, dark polished wood and leather, as well as fine views, not to mention superb international and Mexican cuisine. Nearby, **Los Rancheros** *(Carretera Escénica 38* ☎*(74) 841908* ▥*)* offers fine Mexican food and views to match.

Picalagua *(Juárez 19* ☎*(74) 822142* ▢ ✿ ♥*)* has a simple decor but outstanding seafood, including shark, crab, turtle, or a delicious *ceviche de pulpo* (raw octopus in lime marinade); one rival is **Pipo's** *(Almiral Breton 3* ☎*(74) 822452* ▢*)*, one of the oldest restaurants in Acapulco, with the highest-quality seafood, prepared in Mexican style.

Villa Demo *(Av. del Prado 6* ☎*(74) 842040* ▥*)* is the best Italian restaurant in town, with fine gardens and shaded terraces. On Playa del Moro, **Yes** *(* ☎*(74) 848873* ▢ *to* ▥*)* offers inexpensive beachside lunches, candlelit dinners and cocktails. Vegetarians should look out for the distinctive green signs of **100% Natural** *(* ☎*(74) 853982)*, which has branches scattered around town, including several on the Costera.

ACAPULCO BY NIGHT

In truth, many beaches can rival those here; but it is after dark that Acapulco becomes the queen of Mexican resorts.

The hotels offer a variety of shows, discos, *dîners dansants* and nightclubs. But the real fun lies away from the hotels, and each year, a different and new place becomes the top spot, where everyone has to be seen. This can only be discovered via the grapevine, as the news will only reach the guidebooks a year later. But nights can be spent in adequate style at the older favorites.

Discos open around 10pm (but never really get going until midnight) and stay open for as long as the dancers can stand the pace, which is often until dawn. Many have pure oxygen added to the atmosphere, which has the result of reducing the effects of tiredness and alcohol — but only until you step outside.

Dress is outrageous and elegant, so leave the jeans at home. Long lines often form outside the popular establishments, in which case your best chance of getting in is to look wilder and more glamorous than the opposition.

More adventurous visitors may enjoy a visit to Acapulco's **Zona Roja**, with its transvestite shows, strip clubs and other seedy nightlife. But watch out for taxi drivers trying to chalk up a commission by taking you to **La Huerta** *(Malpaso s/n* ☎*(74) 820118)*, which has a disco but is also the town's most famous brothel.

The **Centro Acapulco** *(Plaza Mexicana* ☎*(74) 847050* ▥ ▽ ●
♪ ▤*)*, should be a feature, for at least one evening, on every visit to Acapulco. The complex, which houses theaters, movie theaters, restaurants and bars, is always busy, with activities ranging from serious cultural events, such as the **Ballet Folklórico**, to the **Disco Centro**, where there is enough space-age technology to reach the moon, and a distinctive atmosphere created by a strange mixture of lasers and mock-Aztec deities.

Call the center at the number above for information in English on plays and movies.

Bars

A large part of Acapulco's nightlife caters to the gay community, so prepare to be broad-minded on your nocturnal adventures. The most welcoming and entertaining gay bar, for non-gays also, is **Disco 9** *(Desportes 110)*. **Boccaccio's** *(Costera 5040* ☎ *(740) 41900)* has an organized party atmosphere, with beauty contests and other such entertainments, while **Gallery** *(opposite Acapulco Plaza at Desportes 11* ☎ *(74) 843497)* is famous for its transvestite floorshow and **Peacock Alley** gay disco.

More in the mainstream are the **Hard Rock Café** *(Costera 37* ☎ *(74) 846680)*; the **Restaurant-Bar Tropicana** *(Playa Hornos)*, for live salsa dancing; **El Fuerte** *(Costera 239 at Las Hamacas Hotel* ☎ *(74) 826161)*, for flamenco enthusiasts; and **Beto's Safari Club** *(Costera, next to Blackbeard's)*.

Dedicated disco dancers should make their debut at **UBQ** (The Ultimate in Beauty and Quality), at Costera 115 *(* ☎ *(74) 844777)*, where the music is loud and the drinks very cold.

The best lightshow is at **Magic** *(Costera and Yucatán* ☎ *(74) 848815)*, but other contenders are **Baby'O** *(Costera 22* ☎ *(74) 847474 couples only)*, with its own Jacuzzi, barbershop and breakfast room, and **News** *(Costera 12* ☎ *(74) 845902)*.

If it's the views that turn you on, **Fantasy** *(La Vista Centre* ☎ *(74) 846727)* used to have the best, until it was surpassed by **Extravaganza** *(Carretera Escénica s/n* ☎ *(74) 847164)*, built into a cliff above the bay.

Other popular bars are **Eve** *(Costera 115* ☎ *(74) 844777)*, **Jackie O** *(facing the Hyatt Continental* ☎ *(74) 840843)* and **Le Jardin** *(Yanez Pinzón 10* ☎ *(74) 848295)*, owned by the VILLA VERA RACQUET CLUB (see WHERE TO STAY).

SHOPPING

Specialties include Taxco silver, leatherware and fashionable resort gear. The easiest way to shop in Acapulco is simply to lie on the beach, where anything from stuffed parrots (best avoided) to Rolex watches (probably fake) can be bought from enterprising hustlers. In the hotel shops, prices are fixed and the selection is greater. The best hotels for shopping in are the **Princess** and **Las Brisas** (see WHERE TO STAY).

More dedicated shoppers will not miss a visit to the gleaming new shopping mall at the **Centro Acapulco**. Silver is a good buy here. Near the HYATT REGENCY hotel, similar but smaller malls are the **Flamboyant** and **El Patio**.

In the streets around the **Zócalo** are the smaller, older shops where there are bargains to be had, while **Av. Hidalgo** has its share of smarter establishments. But for real bargains, visit the markets and crafts centers. Start at the government-run FONART store *(Costera 267)* for crafts from all over Mexico.

More local specialties can be seen and bought at the **Museo de Acapulco** *(Costera 4834, by the Centro Acapulco)*. Try also the small crafts section at the **Acapulco market** *(two blocks back from the waterfront Customs House)* and the **Pueblito** *(Costera, at Reyes Católicos)*.

EXCURSIONS

The coastal road SE toward PUERTO ESCONDIDO is usually in fair condition, but bridges occasionally disappear during the rainy season, so it is wise to inquire. The coast is known as the "Costa Chica" (Little Coast), as opposed to the "Costa Grande" (Big Coast), NW toward Zihuatanejo.

Shortly after the airport, faces denoting descent from escaped African slaves become noticeable; at the largest of the coastal villages, **Cuajinicuilapa** *(240km/150 miles)*, African customs have survived almost unchanged. Farther on, at **Pinotepa Nacional** *(286km/179 miles)*, African blood has mixed with the local strains. The fiestas of the religious calendar are a fascinating medley of cultures.

From Pinotepa, either head N for OAXACA or continue toward PUERTO ESCONDIDO and PUERTO ANGEL. Hotels along the route are rudimentary, but beautiful **deserted beaches** all the way more than compensate. Those with scuba gear who are prepared to sleep under the stars should take the track from Cuajinicuilapa to **Punta Maldonaldo**, famous for its countless species of brightly colored tropical fish.

ZIHUATANEJO AND IXTAPA ☆

*Map **5**H7. Guerrero. 241km (151 miles) NW of Acapulco on RF200. Population: 50,000. Served by air (international airport 24km/15 miles N) and bus **i** Paseo del Pescador 20, Zihuatanejo ☎(753) 42207, and opposite Stouffer Presidente, Ixtapa ☎(753) 31967.*

Some years ago, Zihuatanejo was a small, isolated fishing port, exporting bananas and attracting a few intrepid seekers after the unspoiled beaches of its sheltered bay. Mexico's Tourist Ministry changed all that when, in the early 1970s, it selected the deserted beaches of **Ixtapa**, 8km (5 miles) NW up the coast on the broad Bahía del Palmar, as the site for an entirely new luxury resort.

Ixtapa has a futuristic image, with gleaming high-rise pleasure machines sitting like a row of interstellar cruisers along the beach. Unlike CANCÚN, founded at the same time, it has not rocketed immediately to commercial global status and, despite offering the very latest in glamor and luxury, it is a more relaxed place, walkable and far better value. But Ixtapa is still expanding: the massive **Marina Ixtapa** complex (at the time of writing, still under construction) will bring 7,000 new accommodation units, and another 2,000 are on stream from smaller projects.

Some might find Ixtapa sterile and characterless, but Zihuatanejo, with the feel of a sleepy fishing village, is popular with budget-conscious travelers who prefer atmosphere to comfort. The particular advantage of a vacation at either of these two resorts is that a quick escape to a completely different style of entertainment is always possible.

WHAT TO SEE
The beaches

The beaches near Zihua are separated by rocky promontories, and are best reached by taxi from the town center or by boat from the quayside. There is no regular service to the more remote beaches, so make sure that the taxi driver or boatman has clear instructions on when to pick you up. The four main beaches are described below, from SE to NW along the coast.

Las Gatas　　Perhaps the best of all is this isolated beach, out on Punta Gorrobo, on the E side of Zihuatanejo bay. It has an excellent pedigree, having once been the exclusive preserve of the Purepecha (Tarascan) rulers in Pre-Columbian times. The name of Las Gatas (The Cats) is thought to have been given by the Conquistadors; they chose it because of a high wall built around the beach to protect sunbathing monarchs from the fierce jungle wildcats.

The wall is no more, but, luckily (for the tourists, that is), the cats have also disappeared. According to some authorities, the cats in question were actually cat-sharks, and the wall was built underwater. In any case, there are no sharks here today either, and scuba and snorkel equipment can be rented on the beach.

Playa La Ropa　　This highly agreeable beach is long, wide, uncrowded, open to the Pacific surf and easily reached from Zihua. It is also the best for water-sports, with windsurfing, waterskiing and paragliding. The name of La Ropa (The Clothes) comes from a time when a Chinese ship carrying a cargo of shirts was wrecked and the contents washed up on the beach.

Overlooking the beach is an amazing, vast Greek temple surrounded by marble statues and manicured lawns. This is the vacation home of a former chief of police, said to have become fabulously rich in an inexplicable way . . . .

Playa Madera　　A small and secluded beach at the deepest part of the bay, 15 minutes' walk from Playa Principal. It is good for children, as no motorboats come in close to the shore, although the surf can be quite strong.

Playa Principal　　The main town beach under the shops and cafés of the waterfront is crowded on weekends. It is good for children as it is protected from the open ocean.

Playa El Palmar　　This lovely 3km (2-mile) stretch of sand is open to the full force of the Pacific surf; swimming is thus only possible on calm days. Despite being lined along much of its length with the hotels of Ixtapa, it is seldom crowded.

Isla Ixtapa

This is a small island about 15km (9 miles) off the coast from Punta Ixtapa at the NW end of Bahía del Palmar, with an irregular boat service from Zihua and Ixtapa. Regular boats run to and from a spot near the Club Med on the mainland opposite, the last boat leaving at about 5pm. There are three **beaches** with restaurants serving fresh seafood, and the **woods** of the interior are a wildlife reserve, with semi-tame deer and noisily squawking parrots of all colors.

Bird-watchers should consider renting a boat to **Morro de los Pericos**, a small, rocky island with an amazing variety and abundance of nesting seabirds.

WHERE TO STAY

Ixtapa

CLUB MED ♣
Playa Quieta ☎*(753) 43380* ℻*(753) 43164* 🚷 *375 rms* ⇌ ⚭ ☎ ≈ ✓ ➤ ♒ ♈ ☉ ♪
Attractive villas, clustered on a secluded beachfront, form this exclusive club. It has all the expected, impeccably organized sports and social life for children and their adults.

HOLIDAY INN IXTAPA
Blvd. Ixtapa on Playa Palmar ☎*(753) 31066* ℻*(753) 31991* 🚷 *to* 🚷 *237 rms* ⇌ ⚭ ≈ ☎ ♒ ➤ ♙ ♈ ☉ ♪
One of the best of this reliable chain, with all the usual facilities, and well-landscaped pools and gardens.

KRYSTAL IXTAPA
Blvd. Ixtapa on Playa Palmar ☎*(753) 30333* ℻*(753) 30216* 🚷 *254 rms* ⇌ ⚭ ☎ ≈ ♒ ♈ ☉
A beautiful, ultramodern beachfront hotel, with a lively disco and every amenity.

POSADA REAL IXTAPA ♣
Paseo del las Palmas s/n ☎*(753) 31625* ℻*(753) 31865; in US* ☎*(800) 228 3000* 🚷 *to* 🚷 *110 rms* ⇌ ☎ ≈ ♒ ♈ ☉
This well-appointed representative of the Best Western chain offers some of the best value in Ixtapa, especially in high season.

SHERATON IXTAPA RESORT 🏨
Paseo de Ixtapa s/n ☎*(753) 31858* ℻*(753) 32438* 🚷 *332 rms* ⇌ ⚭ ⚜ ≈ ✓ ☎ ♒ ♙ ♈ ☉ ♪
The Sheraton is among the newest luxury hotels in Ixtapa, with every facility you could wish. Try the **Mexican fiesta** on Friday nights.

STOUFFER PRESIDENTE IXTAPA 🏨
Blvd. Ixtapa s/n ☎*(753) 30018* ℻*(753) 32312* 🚷 *to* 🚷 *304 rms* ⇌ ⚭ ≈ ♒ ☎ ♙ ✓ ♈ ☉ ♪
An attractively designed, low building with an extraordinary multilevel swimming pool. There is plenty of entertainment for adults and children.

WESTIN RESORT IXTAPA 🏨
Playa Vistahermosa ☎*(753) 43300* ℻*(753) 30751* 🚷 *428 rms* ⇌ ⚭ ≈ ♒ ☎ ✓ ♙ ♈ ☉ ♪
Every conceivable facility is on offer at this highly luxurious hotel. For a start, there are six restaurants, four bars, and vast acres of swimming pools to lounge in or beside, and a secluded beach.

Zihuatanejo

On Playa La Ropa, **Villa del Sol** *(* ☎*(753) 42239* ℻*(753) 42758* 🚷 *46 rms* ⇌ ≈ ☎ ♈ ▤ ♒*)* is a sophisticated family-run village, consisting of 21 cottages with terraces, hammocks and South Sea Island decor. **Catalina-Sotovento** *(* ☎*(753) 42032* ℻*(753) 42975* 🚷 *to* 🚷 ⇌ ♈ ▤ ≈*)* is the union of two older, colonial-style hotels, on a cliff above the beach. **Villas Las Urracas** *(* ☎*(753) 42049* 🚷*)* has few facilities, but a pleasant ambience surrounds the 16 bungalows.

On Playa Madera, **Palacios** *(* ♣ ☎*(753) 42055* 🚷 ⇌ ≈ ☎*)* is an economical beachfront hotel; nearby, **Villas Miramar** *(* ☎*(753) 42106* 🚷 ▤ ⇌ ≈ ♈ ☎*)* is more upmarket, and some of its rooms have ocean balconies; **Irma** *(* ☎*(753) 42025* 🚷 *to* 🚷 *77 rms* ≈ ⇌ ♈*)* is a pleasant hotel on a hill above the beach, with a good restaurant and access to water-sports.

Most of the least expensive hotels are in the village itself; one of the best is **Raúl Tres Marías** *(Juan Alvárez 52* ☎*(753) 42977* 🚷 ⇌*)*, basic but clean, just a block from the beach.

EATING AND DRINKING

Hotels in Ixtapa, and especially the KRYSTAL, all have good restaurants, with an emphasis on international dishes. But the more interesting independent restaurants are almost all in Zihuatanejo.

In Zihuatanejo, **Coconuts** (⌂ *Guerrero 4 at Alvarez* ☎ *(753) 42518* ▥ ⊜ ℣ *)* is an elegant restaurant with an international menu; **Kontiki** (✿ *Playa la Ropa* ☎ *(753) 42471* ▥ ☙ ◐ *)* is a lively place on the beach, with enormous pizzas and cheesecake; **La Mesa del Capitán** *(Bravo 18* ☎ *(753) 42027* ▥ ☙ *)* serves fresh seafood and steaks amid a cheerful atmosphere; and **La Bocana** *(Juan Alvarez 13* ☎ *(753) 43545* ▱ *)* is one of the best seafood restaurants.

Also in Zihua, **Club de Playa** *(Playa Madera* ☎ *(753) 42935* ▱ *)* is a pleasant beach restaurant serving fresh seafood and tortillas; the remoter **La Perla** *(at far end of Playa la Ropa* ☎ *(753) 42700* ▱ *)* is one of the best of the *palapa* restaurants that line the beach; and the **Fish Market** *(Punta de Morro, in Mio Villas and Condos* ☎ *(753) 42828* ▥ *)* is worth a visit for its dramatic location alone. The **Garrobos**, at the Raúl Tres Marías (see opposite), is probably the best of the hotel restaurants.

In Ixtapa, **Carlos'n'Charlie's** *(next to the Posada Real hotel* ☎ *(753) 43325* ▥ *)* is a lively spot.

NIGHTLIFE

Something is always happening at one of Ixtapa's big hotels; the KRYSTAL's **Christine** club is the most popular at the time of writing. Most have their own disco or nightclub, and each will provide a free entertainment schedule. A popular non-hotel nightspot is the **Joy Disco and Concert Club** (☎ *(753) 42256),* in the Galerias Ixtapa shopping mall.

The two fashionable discos in Zihuatanejo are at the **Posada Caracol** hotel and **Kontiki** restaurant. Beach discos come and go, but the **Ibiza** (☎ *(753) 42309),* above Playa La Ropa, is a current favorite. Opposite, the **Bay Club** (☎ *(753) 44844)* is a sophisticated restaurant/bar with live jazz nightly. The seafront Mariano's is one popular bar, as is **La Cabaña del Capitán**, above La Mesa del Capitán (see above) restaurant.

SHOPPING

The only places to shop in Ixtapa are the boutiques in the luxury hotels, or the **Galerias Ixtapa** and **La Puerta** shopping malls, where there is plenty of choice, but high prices and no bargaining.

It is much more fun to shop in Zihua, at the little shops along the **Paseo del Pescador** waterfront and around the **Zócalo**. Prices are low, the selection good, and haggling is expected. The town market, on **Paseo del Cocotal**, has a small craft section.

SPORTS AND ACTIVITIES

Most water-sports are available on the main beaches, so inquire at your hotel if you need to rent any equipment, for example for **scuba-diving** around the bay's dramatic underwater landscapes. **Deep-sea fishing** can also be arranged through the hotels, or by bargaining with the entertainingly aquatic characters down at the quay in Zihua.

Golf and **tennis** are available to all at the well-designed **Palma Real Golf Club**, behind the Ixtapa hotel zone, on payment of a small fee. The **Zihuatanejo Scuba Center** *(Paseo del Pescador 4* ☎ *(753) 42147)* rents equipment, arranges trips and has a helpful bilingual staff. Developments in hand will add 350 berths to the **Marina Ixtapa**, as well as a second golf course and 3km (1 mile) of navigable canals.

EXCURSIONS

There are several good beaches heading SE along RF200 to Acapulco. **Playa Blanca** *(18km/11 miles)* and **Barra del Potosí** *(25km/15 miles)* are both low-key beach villages with lots of *palapa* restaurants and hammock space.

In the other direction, just across the Michoacán border, you can take a guided tour of the vast new steel complex at **Lázaro Cárdenas** (98km/61 miles). The small resort 22km (13 miles) up the coast, **Playa Azul**, is a favorite with steel workers and Mexican families, but its charm is a thing of the past.

PUERTO ESCONDIDO

Map 6I9. Oaxaca. 242km (151 miles) S of Oaxaca on RF175; 69km (43 miles) W of Puerto Angel intersection on RF200; 403km (251 miles) E of Acapulco on RF200. Population: 50,000. Served by air and bus **i** *Pérez Gasga s/n at 5a Poniente* ☎*(958) 20175.*

An "undiscovered" fishing village, whose beautiful beaches and relaxed atmosphere are fast being discovered by quite a crowd. Luxury hotels are arriving, but the emphasis here is definitely on beach life rather than nightlife.

The main beach is pleasant and palm-fringed but quite busy; the nicer swimming beaches to the W at **Puerto Angelito**, **Carrizalillo** and **Bacocho** (for that all-over tan) are accessible on foot or by boat. To the SE, first is **Playa Marinero**, then after the point lies the 16km (10-mile) **Zicatela** beach. Mainly used by surfers for its huge waves, it has a dangerous undertow and often more cows than people.

☞ **Paraíso Escondido** *(♣ Unión 10* ☎ *(958) 20444* ▥ ⇥ ▦ ≋ ◄) has a good location on a hill overlooking the sea. **Rancho el Pescador** *(coast road to Acapulco, Km 1.5* ☎ *(958) 20391* ▥ ⇥ ≋*)* is a small fishing and beach resort. **Posada Real** *(Benito Juárez s/n on Playa Bocacho* ☎*(958) 20446* ▣*(958) 20192* ▥ *100 rms* ⇥ ≋ ▦ ♫ ▼*)* is a modern Best Western hotel W of town, in a still rather empty new hotel zone.

1km (½ mile) E at the start of Zicatela beach, **Santa Fé** *(Del Morro 10* ☎*(958) 21070* ▥ ⇥ ≋ ▼ ▦*)* is an excellent new Spanish villa-style beach hotel. **Las Palmas** *(Gasga s/n* ☎*(858) 20230* ▥*)* has a good restaurant and pleasant gardens overlooking the beach; nearby, **El Rincón del Pacífico** *(* ☎ *(958) 20056* ▥*)* is of a similar standard.

Those wanting to stay a week or more should consider **Villas de Puerto Escondido**, four villas set in delightful gardens W of town *(reservations in Mexico City* ☎ *(5) 535 6939).*

≡ Not surprisingly, the local specialty is seafood, and there is an abundance of waterfront restaurants along the pedestrianized seafront. The best and most enduring is **Santa Fé** (at the hotel of the same name), with a choice of seafood and vegetarian dishes, superb views and ambience.

EXCURSIONS

Manialtepec Lagoon *(13km/8 miles N on RF200 and 12km/7 miles long),* surrounded by jungle swamps teeming with wildlife, makes a great expedition. Having got there *(bus service along coast),* negotiate a boat ride with a fisherman.

The lagoons at the **Parque Nacional Lagunas de Chacahua** *(70km/43 miles W on RF200)* are harder to reach, but tours are available to both places through travel agents.

PUERTO ANGEL

Map 6I9. Oaxaca. 69km (43 miles) E of Puerto Escondido on RF200 to Pochutla, or 35km (21 miles) W of Huatulco on RF200 to Pochutla, then 13km (8 miles) S. Served by bus.

This peaceful resort is a miniature version of Puerto Escondido as it used to be: an isolated fishing village with some fine beaches and basic facilities. The best beach in town is **Playa Panteón**, small and sheltered on the W side of the bay, and a few miles W is the laid-back **Zipolite Beach**, a spot much favored by the hammock-slinging crowd, where nudity is the rule. Its *palapas* and beach restaurants serve a good selection of inexpensive seafood.

By the time of your visit, the notorious San Agustinillo turtle slaughterhouse, to the W of Zipolite, should have permanently closed, now that the Mexican government has given the Olive Ridley turtles of the area, and other species of turtle, the official protection they need to prevent their extinction.

❧ **Angel del Mar** *(● Playa Panteón,* ☎ *(958) 40398* ▥ *to* ▥ ≡ ≋ ◖ *no cards)* is the best in town, on a hill above the beach. However, **Posada Cañon Devata** *(W end of Playa Panteón, no* ☎ ▥ ≋*)* wins on charm, with pleasant tree-shaded gardens, an excellent all-day vegetarian restaurant and its own artist-in-residence. Also recommended is **Soroya** *(Uribe s/n across the pier, no* ☎ ▥ ≡ ▤ *).*

There are various cheaper dives, but the economically-minded would do better to head for Playa Zipolite, with its **Casa Gloria** (▭) *palapa* village and pleasant **Shambala** vegetarian restaurant.

HUATULCO (Bahías de Huatulco)

Map 7I11. Oaxaca. 260km (162 miles) S of Oaxaca, 35km (21 miles) E of Pochutla on RF200; 158km (98 miles) W of Tehuantepec on RF200. Served by air (international airport) and bus **i** *Av. Guamichil at Bugambilias* ☎ *(958) 10326.*

Development is coming fast to the 11 lovely bays and 33 beaches near the fishing village of Santa Cruz de Huatulco, planned as the new mega-resort of the 1990s. The town's main business is now the provision of board and lodging for hotel staff and laborers working on the project. An international airport, a wide coastal boulevard, a golf course and some major hotels have arrived, and the inland village of **Santa Maria Huatulco** is being developed as the urban center, complete with a replica of the Zócalo at Oaxaca. A less formal center has also sprung up around the bus station at **La Crucecita** (the little crossroads), just off the main road.

The choice of hotels is still limited, but more will arrive over the coming years to cater to an intended 2 million visitors a year. Projects in the pipeline include **Puerto Chahue**, on Bahía Chahue E of Santa Cruz, which now sports a trailer park and cheap café. On the now empty **Bahía de Cacatla**, to the W, the construction of a 444-hectare (1,100-acre) "city resort," complete with marina and golf course, will soon be under way.

In all, some 4,400 new rooms are planned for 1994, rising to 30,000 in 2018, covering an area of 20,800 hectares (52,000 acres). Certainly Huatulco's location, with forested hills descending to sandy bays and pristine waters, is magnificent. The question, still open, is whether such natural beauty can survive the onslaught of mass tourism.

WHERE TO STAY

CASTILLO HUATULCO
Bahía Santa Cruz ☎*(958) 70051–6* ▥
56 rms ═▦ 🕭 ➼ ➼ ♨ ☥ ○
This new luxury hotel near the marina, the first on Santa Cruz bay, offers the usual impressive range of facilities, with the bonus of imaginative architecture in a fine setting.

CLUB MEDITERRANÉE ▥
Bahía de Tangolunda ☎*(958) 10033*
▣*(958) 10161* ▥ *340 rms* ═▦ ♨
▸/ ➼ 🕭 ♈ ☥ ○
A large and completely self-contained luxury resort hotel, which offers all water-sports including sea-kayaking.

ROYAL MAEVA
Bahía de Tangolunda ☎*(958) 10000*
▣*(958) 10220* ▥ *320 rms* ═▦ ₺ 🕭 🕭
➼ ♨ ♈ ☥ ○
A well-organized social life and many sporting activities, based on the Club Med program, are offered by this luxurious hotel.

SHERATON RESORT ▥
Bahía de Tangolunda ☎*(958) 10055*
▣*(958) 10113* ▥ *346 rms* ═▦ ₺ ♨
♨ ▸/ ♈ ➼ 🕭 ♟ ☥ ○
A beautifully designed luxury resort hotel next to the golf course, with water-sports and all facilities.

Budget hotels
Fortunately, the expensive resort hotels do not hold a complete monopoly. These are a couple of the less pricey options. As the resort grows, further diversity is sure to develop.

- **Posada Binniguenda** *(Benito Juárez 5, Santa Cruz Huatulco* ☎*(958) 40080* ▥ *75 rms* ▦ ═▦ ♨*)*, a well-established non-resort hotel, clean and set in colorful if untidy gardens.
- **Suites Bugambilias** *(La Crucecita, off the Zócalo* ☎*(958) 70018)*.

EATING AND DRINKING
Most visitors never leave their hotels, but those who do have a choice of several independent eating places at **La Crucecita**. It already has a

mini-**Carlos'n'Charlie's** (☎ *(958) 70005* ▨▨▢) and numerous sidewalk cafés around the plaza. There are also several informal beachside establishments, such as the one on Bahía Chahue.

TEHUANTEPEC

Map 7I10. Oaxaca. 250km (156 miles) se of Oaxaca on RF190; 158km (98 miles) e of Huatulco on RF200; 284km (177 miles) s of Coatzacoalcos on RF180, RF185 and RF200. Population: 50,000. Served by air, train (branch off lines connecting Mexico City, Veracruz and Guatemala City) and bus.

Considering the reputation and geographical importance of this town (it gives its name to the isthmus of tropical lowlands dividing North and Central America), it is a disappointing place, dusty and squalid, with indifferent hotels. But with the influx of oil wealth to the area have come plans to revitalize the isthmus rail link between here and the Gulf, to rival the Panama Canal; so there is still a chance that Tehuantepec may yet achieve a renaissance.

Until then, its main claim to fame is one that causes much concern to men all over Mexico — by popular repute, it is a town run by women, where men take the orders. The women are tall and renowned for their beauty. Unlike the men, who wear appropriately drab clothing, many women frequently wear the magnificent traditional costume of rich gold embroidery on red cloth. On fiesta days, their splendor is such that they rival European royalty, with heavy necklaces of gold coins and an extraordinary head-dress.

EVENTS • From around June 24 for a week, Tehuantepec holds its **fiesta**. This is a colorful, lively occasion; photography is tempting but risky — the Tehuanas are reputed to give rough treatment to anyone suspected of ogling.

EXCURSIONS

Juchitán *(26km/16 miles e on RF200)* is run along similar matriarchal lines as Tehuantepec, and this is a better place to buy the local costumes. The city has a long history of resisting the rule of Mexico City, dating back through the colonial era to the resistance of its Zapotec founders. Its highly effective antigovernment campaigns stimulated repressive measurès in the 1980s, but following several recent Presidential visits, a more enlightened administration is now seeking to turn the political tide with huge spending programs.

Juchitán has important **fiestas** on August 13 and September 3, when the women of the town perform graceful dances.

Avoid **Salina Cruz**, 18km (11 miles) s on RF200, but a series of lovely deserted **beaches** begins about 20km (12 miles) to its w on RF200 to Huatulco.

☜ **Calli** *(RF190 2km/1 mile e on RF190* ☎ *(971) 50085* ▨▨▢ ▤▤▤ ● ⇥ ⋙ *)* is the nicest place to stay, but **Donaji** *(Juárez 10* ☎ *(971) 50064)* has the advantage of a central location.

OAXACA

*Map **6**H9. Capital of Oaxaca. 541km (338 miles) SE of Mexico City on RF190; 249km (155 miles) N of Puerto Angel on RF175; 251km (156 miles) NW of Tehuantepec on RF190; 246km (153 miles) SE of Tehuacán on RF131 and RF190. Altitude: 1,694m (5,590ft). Population: 300,000. Served by air, train (terminus of line from Mexico City) and bus* **i** *Morelos 200 at 5 de Mayo* ☎*(951) 64828. US Consul: Alcala 201* ☎*(951) 43054. UK Consul: Hidalgo 817* ☎*(951) 65600. American Express: Dr Valdivieso 2* ☎*(951) 62700.*

If you want to see all of Mexico in a week, come to Oaxaca, a beautiful colonial city, surrounded by great archeological sites such as MITLA and MONTE ALBÁN, Indian villages, old monasteries and magnificent scenery. It is also only a half-day's drive or a short flight from here down to the Pacific beaches. The state that Oaxaca commands is poor in minerals, and, just as it escaped the ravages of the Spanish mine-owners, it is now avoiding the ravages of Pemex (Petróleos Mexicanos), which has laid waste so much of the neighboring states of Campeche, Tabasco and Chiapas. However, the ravages of poverty and environmental degradation are nevertheless taking their own terrible toll.

Unknown civilizations flourished in the Valley of Oaxaca's thick forests as much as 3,000 years ago, making it one of the oldest continuously inhabited areas in the country. When the Spaniards arrived, the two great cultures of the Valley, the Zapotecs and Mixtecs, were exhausted by their struggles and had both fallen under the sway of the Aztecs. Cortés himself fell in love with the area and intended to retire to his large estates there. Although he died too soon, his descendants still retain the title of "Marquis of the Valley of Oaxaca."

The famous sons of Oaxaca include two presidents of Mexico. One was the Zapotec Indian Benito Juárez, the first indigenous president of Mexico and hero of the bitter war against the French. The other was the rather less popular dictator, Porfirio Díaz, who ruled Mexico with an iron fist for the 35 years before the 1910 Revolution. During the *Porfiriato* period, as today, the rich got richer and the poor stayed poor, and nowhere in Mexico is this more true than in the state of Oaxaca, whose arid countryside includes some of the poorest communities in Mexico.

With the forests long since cleared, drought is a constant fear, but conflicts over land and water rights pose an even greater threat, with the Indians invariably losing out to influential landlords and businessmen.

EVENTS • **La Guelaguetza**, Oaxaca's biggest festival, is held on the last two Mondays of July on Cerro del Fortín, a nearby hill; this is a superb occasion to witness authentic Indian music and dance, and ritualized battles between Mixtec and Zapotec tribes.

• The most unusual fiesta in Oaxaca is on December 23, the **Night of the Radishes**, when superbly carved radishes are brought into town for an annual competition. The party spirit continues right through the Christmas festivities.

• Many of the native **dances** of the state are performed regularly in town — inquire for details at your hotel, or at the tourist office, which will also help you to visit a fiesta nearby. • Other regular attractions include the **Saturday market**, and music in the **bandstand** on the Zócalo, at Sunday lunchtime and at 7pm most evenings.

WHAT TO SEE
Cathedral and Zócalo
Days in Oaxaca all seem to start and end under the trees of the Zócalo. Before dawn, the Indians walk in from their villages, and sit talking until the market starts; long after midnight, the last tourist staggers back to his hotel. Nearly all round the clock, it hums with social, musical and commercial activity — although creative inactivity over a coffee or glass of beer is usual.

On the N side of the Zócalo is the **cathedral**, started in 1544 and finished some two centuries later. The facade is Baroque, with an old wooden-cogged clock presented to the city by the king of Spain. Opposite is the splendid 19thC Neoclassical **Palacio de Gobierno**, with murals of the state's history around the stair.

Museo Rufino Tamayo ☆
Morelos 503 at Díaz ☎*(951) 64750* 💳 *Open 10am–2pm, 4–7pm; Sun 10am–3pm. Closed Tues.*

In an old, carefully restored colonial mansion is a fine display of Pre-Hispanic pottery and sculpture, originally the personal collection of the artist Rufino Tamayo, who presented it to his home state. There are exhibits from all over the country, arranged geographically and chronologically. Perhaps the most delightful item is the **model** of a **ballcourt** for the sacred game, with figurines representing the participants and spectators.

Museo de Oaxaca 🏛
Macedonio Alcalá 202/4 💳 *Open 10am–2pm, 5–8pm. Closed Mon.*

This small museum occupies the house said to have belonged to Hernán Cortés; but it is most worth visiting for the paintings by Miguel Cabrera, a native artist born near Oaxaca in 1695. It lies one block E and two blocks N of the Zócalo.

Santo Domingo and Museo Regional de Oaxaca 🏛
Alcalá and Gurrión 💳 *Open 10am–6pm (5pm weekends). Closed Mon.*

A massive 16thC monastery church with an ornately carved facade between two high bell towers. The interior is an opulent profusion of white and gold, typical of the amazing energy with which Mexico seized on the Baroque style and made of it something unique. Particularly notable is the early 18thC **Capilla del Rosario**. In the anticlerical upheavals of the 1860s, the church was turned into a stable and badly damaged. All but the side chapels have now been fully restored.

The monastery lies three blocks N of the Museo de Oaxaca (not to be confused with the Museo Regional de Oaxaca), which is laid out in a series of galleries around the monastic cloister. Pride of place goes to the rich treasures of **gold** and **jade** from the tombs at MONTE ALBÁN. There is also a large collection of **ceremonial masks and costumes** from the different tribes of the valley; some of the Indian women in town for the market still wear the traditional costumes, and with a bit of study here, you will be able to identify their home villages.

Casa Juárez

García Vigil 609 ☎*(951) 61860* 🖭 *Open 10am–2pm, 4–7pm. Closed Mon.*

This is the 19thC house in which Benito Juárez, the Zapotec President of Mexico, lived from the age of 12 as a servant. It is now a museum, well stocked with Juárez memorabilia.

Basílica de la Soledad

Independencia and Galeana ☎*(951) 67566. Open 5.30am–9pm.*

This Baroque church, built in 1682, houses the **statue of the Virgin**, Oaxaca's patron saint. Today she stands in a gilded shrine, wearing a magnificent robe of jewel-studded black velvet and a 3-kilogram gold crown. The Virgin was found in the pack of an unaccounted-for stray mule that had died. A church was built to commemorate the miracle.

The statue then proved to have supernatural healing powers, and ever since has been the object of fervent piety from a devout populace.

WHERE TO STAY

MARQUÉS DEL VALLE ♣

Portal de Claviera s/n on Zócalo ☎*(951) 63474* ▥ *95 rms* ☲ ☒

This is a well-run traditional hotel. Standards are high, but the rooms are on the small side.

MISIÓN DE LOS ANGELES

Porfirio Díaz 102 ☎*(951) 51500* ▥ *155 rms* ☲ ☜ ♆ ☒ ♫ 🖭

A quiet and agreeable hotel with large gardens, about 15 minutes' walk from the Zócalo.

MISIÓN PARK INN OAXACA

Jalisco 15, San Francisco del Agua ☎*(951) 50100* ▣*(951) 50900* ▥ *160 rms* ☲ ☜ ☒

This luxurious modern hotel is set in a residential area, 15 minutes' walk from the center.

PRINCIPAL

5 de Mayo 208 ☎*(951) 62535* ▯ *23 rms* ☲ ♫

This hotel, housed in a colonial courtyard building, has become very popular, so reserve or arrive early.

SEÑORIAL ♣

Portal de los Flores 6, on Zócalo ☎*(951) 63933* ▣*(951) 63668* ▯ *127 rms* ☜ ☒ ☒

With a small swimming pool, pleasant roof garden, decent-sized rooms, parking and an excellent location, this must be Oaxaca's best-value accommodation.

STOUFFER PRESIDENTE OAXACA ▥

5 de Mayo 300 on Zócalo ☎*(951) 60611* ▣*(951) 60732* ▥ *91 rms* ☛ ☲ ☜ ☒

This is Oaxaca's most interesting hotel: the 16thC Santa Catalina convent, subsequently pressed into use as town hall, theater and jail, has now been beautifully restored, and decorated with native weaving. Its pleasant **cocktail bar** and **fiesta** on Fridays are open to non-residents.

VICTORIA ▦

Pan-American Highway, Km 545 ☎*(951) 52633* ▣*(951) 52411* ▥ *151 rms* ☲ ▭ ☙ ⟨⟨ ☜ ✓ ♆ ☒ ⊙

The Victoria has a prominent position overlooking the city, with a good restaurant and gardens.

EATING AND DRINKING

Of the hotel restaurants, the STOUFFER PRESIDENTE has its **Refectorio** in a 16thC hall; **El Tule** at the VICTORIA offers superb views across the city; and the MISIÓN DE LOS ANGELES is also recommended.

Elsewhere, **El Patio** (♣ *Hidalgo 819* ☎*(951) 61885* ▥ *to* ▥ *)* is in the colonial style; specialties include delicious regional meat dishes. **La Flor de Oaxaca** *(López 311, one block E of Zócalo* ☎ *(951) 65522*

▥) serves wholesome regional cuisine amid simple decor. For seafood, there is nowhere better than **La Morsa** *(Porfirio Díaz 240* ☎*(951) 52213)*, with its tropical garden and fountains.

There are also many good restaurants on the Zócalo. Some think **Mi Casita** *(Hidalgo 616* ☎*(951) 69256* ▥*)* the best for regional cuisine, but the upstairs **Asador Vasco** *(*☎*(951) 69719* ▥*)* is more elegant and puts on a nightly floorshow at 9pm. Down below, the economical **Restaurant-Bar del Jardin** is popular, with a wide menu.

Vegetarians should try the **Pisces** *(Hidalgo 119, w of Zócalo* ▢*)* or **Arca de Emmanuel** *(Niños Heroes 1023* ☎ *(591) 56412* ▢*)*.

SHOPPING

Each of the villages around Oaxaca has its own craft specialty and its own market day. Every day, but especially on Saturdays, the villagers pour into the **Mercado Juárez**, s of the Zócalo, making it the best place to buy weaving, embroidery, pottery, hammocks, baskets and other such items.

Alternatively, the **Mercado de Artesanías** *(2 blocks s of Mercado Juárez)* is open daily, and there are two government-run shops, FONART *(García Vigil at Bravo)*, and **Aripo** *(García Vigil 809)*. The tourist office has details of special markets and fiestas at nearby villages.

A specialty of the jewelry stores near the Zócalo are reproductions of the Monte Albán tomb finds.

EXCURSIONS

Besides its coast, and the archeological sites of MITLA and MONTE ALBÁN, both lying less than an hour from the city, the state of Oaxaca offers a generous variety of excursions.

Some nearby villages

At **Cuilapán** *(✫ 12km/7 miles sw)* the Dominicans decided to build their largest monastery in New Spain. The **ruins** are indeed vast, and although the project was never completed, they are well worth a visit. The **church**, for a long time roofless, but now restored as a working building, has a simple Renaissance facade flanked by round towers. Next to it is another, smaller church that must have been used only by the monks.

Behind the monastery, a monument marks the spot where the revolutionary hero General Vincente Guerrero was shot in 1831.

Zaachila *(6km/3 miles farther)* is on the site of the last capital of the Zapotec kingdom, which held out against Aztec and Mixtec would-be invaders until the Spanish conquest. There is one small restored structure, many **burial mounds**, and carved **monoliths** in the Zócalo.

Two of the tombs in the main court have been excavated, and their contents are in the Museo Nacional de Antropología in MEXICO CITY. During excavation, local feelings ran so high that the archeologists were kept under armed guard.

The **market** is held every Thursday; although a lively occasion, it is not aimed at tourists.

RF175 south to Puerto Angel

San Bartolo Coyotepec and **Santa Rosa Coyotepec** (★ *15km/9 miles)* are two potters' villages famous for their shiny black terracotta tableware and figures. The workshops welcome visitors, who can watch pots and plates being made without the benefit of a wheel.

On **August 23–24**, San Bartolo celebrates its patron saint's day with some unusual dancing, involving performers with wooden masks and wigs of cactus fiber.

Ocotlán *(another 20km/12 miles)* has an interesting church, and is specially worth visiting on Friday for its riotous **market**, where you can buy local ceramic figurines and other crafts.

RF190 northwest to Mexico City via Cuautla

The village of **Atzompa** *(3km/1½ miles* s at Km 6) is known for the green-glaze pots and fine figurines of its many potters, who hold their market on Tuesday. **San José Mogote** *(10km/6 miles from Oaxaca)* is a mostly unexcavated early ceremonial center, built by the ancestors of the Zapotecs beginning around 1300BC.

Nearby **San Pablo Etla** *(12km/7 miles)* has its market on Wednesday, making this the best day to visit its Plateresque church and 16thC Dominican monastery; on **April 1**, there is a larger-than-usual market and some lively celebrations.

Etla has a sister monastery at **Huitzo**, 22km (13 miles) farther on, and there is another church and monastery at **Yanhuitlán** (★ *119km/74 miles)*. The latter's monastery has a fine collection of painted wooden effigies of saints, and in the upper galleries of the church is a caissoned ceiling, a good example of a difficult technique. Under the rib-vaulted nave of the church stands an ornate altarpiece.

Take the road s to Costa Chica after Km 130, and 13km (8 miles) farther on, you will reach the 16thC monastery church of **Teposcolula** with its interesting open chapel. It has suffered some earthquake damage, but most of the fine decorative stonework is intact.

In the village of **Coixtlahuaca** *(10km/6 miles N at Km 135),* the Aztec language of Nahuatl is still spoken, rather than the local Mixtec, as it remained an Aztec trading post after the decline of the Mixtec period. The Spaniards used the stones from the temples to build the large monastery and church; the latter has a large **rose window**, uncommon in Mexico. The many sights on RF190 to Mitla are described under MITLA.

✍ A possible overnight stop is at **Huajuapán**, after 195km (121 miles), where the **García Parral** *(on the Zócalo* ☎ *(953) 20742* ▯▭ ⬱ ⚓) offers welcome respite to the weary traveler.

MONTE ALBÁN ★

Map 6H9. Oaxaca. 12km (7 miles) w of Oaxaca. Altitude: 2,113m (6,972ft).
Served by bus and numerous tour agencies.

Around the time of the fall of Rome in AD410, this breathtaking ceremonial center of the Zapotec people was a large and flourishing city.

The mountain that it crowns was terraced, right down to the plain, with houses and temples. Founded around 500BC by people culturally related to the Olmecs, the city flourished for 1,200 years, with a population reaching more than 25,000.

Then, around 700AD, the Zapotec culture went into decline, as the Mixtecs rose in power and influence through a combination of conquest, trade and intermarriage. By the 15thC, the city was reduced to a necropolis for Mixtec kings. Dating from this period are the hundreds of tombs dotted around the site, some of which yielded rich treasures that can be seen in the Museo de Oaxaca in OAXACA. By the time the Spanish arrived, the Mixtecs themselves had fallen under Aztec domination, and Monte Albán was falling into ruin. It is still a place of inspiring natural and man-made grandeur, and should be a part of any tour of Oaxaca.

The ruins ▥
▦ *Open 9am–5pm.*

The restored part of the city is a large group of buildings around the great esplanade on the artificially flattened hilltop. If at first you feel impressed by the restrained dignity of the architecture, remember that the Zapotecs painted it with all the colors of Joseph's coat.

The site is entered from the N, passing, on the left, a **court** for the **sacred ballgame**. Before you are three large structures aligned N to S

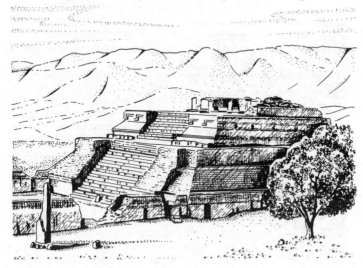

down the center of the esplanade; behind these is a smaller, older building that is out of alignment, with parts nearly 2,000 years old that were built by the Zapotecs' unknown predecessors.

The S edge of the esplanade is bordered by a large raised platform with the remains of a temple in the center. Standing here, and facing back up the esplanade, the building on the right is known as **El Palacio**. The second building on the left is the remarkable **Monumento de los Danzantes**, the sides of which are decorated with reliefs of dancers who have notably negroid features, suggesting that the Zapotecs may have been descended from the Olmecs of the Gulf. On a few of the stones are glyphs indicating the age of the carvings.

There are other structures to the s of the main groups, one of which, with remains of a typically Zapotec **temple-patio-sanctuary** on the upper level, is pictured on the previous page. Around here you may meet youths trying to sell artifacts "from the tombs." Be warned that if they are fake (99.9 percent are) they have no value; if they are genuine, it is illegal to buy one.

MITLA ★

*Map **7**H10. Oaxaca. 42km (26 miles) SE of Oaxaca on RF190. Served by bus.*

The intricate **geometric stonework** of the palaces at Mitla is unique among Mexico's major ruins, and a visit to the site is essential. Just who was responsible for this masterpiece has long been a point of academic controversy. When the Spaniards came, Mitla was inhabited by Zapotecs, but the architecture is typical of the more sophisticated Mixtecs,

Stonework, Mitla

known to have arrived in the area around the 10thC, when the Zapotec civilization was in decline.

Possibly Mitla was built during the 13thC, by Zapotecs who were heavily influenced by the Mixtec culture. Unlike many of Mexico's ruins, it was never overgrown by jungle, nor used as a stone quarry by the Spaniards, who merely contented themselves with building a church in one of the less important courtyards, at the end of the track through the site.

The ruins ▥

☒ *Open 9am–6pm.*

The most important ruins in Mitla are those in what is known as the **Columns Group**, just to the s of the Church Group, and consists of two diagonally adjacent courts surrounded by chambers. On the N side of the largest court, a stair leads up to a triple doorway through which the long and narrow **Hall of Columns** is entered. A passage from here leads to a small court, where the walls are decorated in the typical Mitla style with thousands of small interlocking pieces of stone used to make complex patterns. The number of precisely carved stones is well in excess of 100,000 — like Rome, Mitla was not built in a day.

In the smaller court of the group, there is a **cruciform tomb** decorated in the same way; the contents were lost to graverobbers. In another tomb to the N of this court, there is a large **column** that supported the roof of an adjacent tomb. Locally they say that if you embrace this column you will know the day of your death.

There are three other groups of buildings: the **Adobe** and **Arroyo** groups, over a small *barranca* to the W, and the **South** group. These smaller and less well-preserved buildings are of no great interest. Market stalls near the entrance to the ruins sell native embroidery at low prices.

Mitla Town *(bear left at fork at Km 40)* is a small settlement near the ruins. Visit the small **Frissell Museum**, which has some locally discovered Zapotec and Mixtec artifacts, sharing a restored 18thC hacienda with the **Posada la Sorpresa** *(❧ no ☎ ═ ▱)*, a simple hostelry with just six rooms and the **La Zapoteca** restaurant: you should arrive early if you want to stay.

RF190 southeast from Oaxaca to Mitla

The road to Mitla passes many places of sightseeing interest; the distances given below are from Oaxaca.

Readers of records books will know that the enormous cypress tree at **Santa María del Tule** (13km/8 miles) has the greatest circumference of any tree in the world. The girth and the height are nearly equal — 41m (135 feet) each way — and it dates from around two thousand years ago. It remains a sad reminder of the valley's once rich forests. Dancing takes place in front of the church on August 15 and February 2 (Michaelmas).

Tlacochahuaya *(turn right at Km 18, continue 2km/1 mile)* is a village on the Oaxaca–Mitla road with a fine 16thC Dominican monastery; the adjacent miniature 17thC church is well worth visiting for its profuse and colorful paintings of flowers and birds in the trees.

The fairly large Pre-Classic site of **Dainzú** *(just s of the road at Km 23)* has as its most important structure a pyramid faced with 30 carved stone slabs, most of which show players of the sacred ball-game; these are best viewed in the afternoon sun.

Teotitlán del Valle *(26km/16 miles)* is a Zapotec village of weavers, famous for its *serapes*. In Holy Week, the colorful Feather Dance is performed in front of the church. **Lambityeco** *(28km/18 miles)* is a small site dating from after the fall of Monte Albán in 700AD; two houses have been excavated, revealing some good stone friezes and sculptures. **Tlacolula** *(32km/20 miles)* is worth visiting on Sundays for its fascinating Indian market full of weavings and other crafts.

The fortified hill that dominates the archeological zone of **Yagul** *(turn left at Km 35, continue 1.5km/1 mile)* has a magnificent view of the whole Oaxaca Valley. It was occupied throughout the life of Monte Albán, but the main buildings date from the later period, when the Mixtecs had taken the site over from the Zapotecs. A large ball-court has been fully restored, and is flanked by two courts. Overlooking the area is the **Palacio**, with a series of chambers around small terraces.

West of Mexico City

This route west from the capital will lead you through a varied physical and cultural landscape of lakes and volcanoes, colonial towns and Indian villages, before reaching Mexico's second city, Guadalajara. It then continues down to a series of charming resorts on a still largely undeveloped Pacific coast. The region combines four states: **Jalisco**, **Nayarit**, **Colima** and **Michoacán**.

JALISCO

Jalisco epitomizes Mexico at its most Mexican. This single state is home to **TLAQUEPAQUE**, birthplace of *mariachi* music, to a small town called **TEQUILA**, whose eponymous product fuels the fiesta spirit across the country, and to Mexico's second city, **GUADALAJARA**.

Unfortunately Guadalajara, capital of Jalisco, is growing to compete with the federal capital in bustle and pollution as well as in culture and urban sophistication. It also managed to produce a disaster to compare with Mexico City's exploding gas tanks when, in 1990, sewers in a working class district filled with flammable hydrocarbons seeping from a nearby petrochemical plant and exploded, killing 200 people and destroying entire rows of houses.

All the more reason, then, to migrate the short distance south to the peaceful shores of LAKE CHAPALA, Mexico's largest lake. Weekend retreat for Guadalajara's businessmen, Chapala's shores also shelter colonies of expatriates, who are now increasingly worried that the city's developing industries and rising population may demand so much water as to reduce the lake to nothing but a series of muddy puddles — in another best-avoided emulation of its greater rival.

Another favorite retreat is PUERTO VALLARTA, on the Pacific coast, which in the early 1970s grew from a quiet fishing village into one of Mexico's premier resorts, as the public followed in the steps of Hollywood. Several billion dollars of investment later, it somehow remains part of real Mexico, in contrast to its computer-selected, custom-built competitors.

NAYARIT

Most visitors hardly notice the small coastal state of Nayarit, north of Jalisco, as they drive between the popular resorts of Puerto Vallarta and Mazatlán. But the discerning traveler can escape to the sleepy, seaside town of SAN BLAS, discover the reputed birthplace of the Incas at **Mexicaltitlán**, and explore the wild **Sierra de los Huicholes**, home to Indian tribes whose conquest remains far from complete.

COLIMA

South of Jalisco, also on the coast, the state of Colima is even smaller than Nayarit, but is projected into greater prominence by the presence of MANZANILLO, which doubles as busy port and luxury resort. Never destined for the hype of Acapulco or Puerto Vallarta, Manzanillo attracts a loyal following of vacationers, who prefer its more relaxed atmosphere and lower prices. The state capital, COLIMA, a pleasant town in the foothills of nearby volcanoes, remains little visited.

MICHOACÁN

But most rewarding, as well as closest to Mexico City, is the state of Michoacán, nearly as famous for its political violence as for its charming cities and splendid countryside. The state is perhaps carrying on an ancient tradition of resistance, since it was one of the hotbeds of the struggle for independence from Spain in the early 19th century. A well-established center of opposition to the dominance of the ruling PRI party, the civic buildings in its capital, MORELIA, are frequently subject to sit-ins in protest at electoral fraud. Political assassinations remain disturbingly frequent occurrences.

Not that such matters need overly concern the tourist in Morelia, who is permitted to enjoy the stately colonial architecture, visit nearby indigenous communities famous for their crafts, and relax unmolested on the tranquil shores of **Lake Patzcuaro**. Less accessible and far smaller than Lake Chapala, it is also far lovelier, with the added benefit of the ruins of **Tzintzuntzán** rising above its limpid waters — a reminder of the magnificent past of the area's still-proud Purépecha Indians.

URUAPÁN is another good place to visit. Although the town has become somewhat busy, the subtropical forests and waterfalls around are beautiful, and hikers can climb nearby **Paracutín**, Mexico's newest volcano. It rose up unexpectedly in 1943, destroying several villages, having rudely ignored the injunctions of the local priest and the holy water he sprinkled on the sulfurous fumes, as they emanated from an unfortunate peasant's cornfield.

A word of warning: Michoacán's lonely and undeveloped Pacific coast road is a favorite haunt of bandits. On no account drive along it at night.

Towns, cities and cultural sites

Starting in **MORELIA**, this chapter gives essential information on the following places, arranged to follow a roughly E–W route through the region: **PATZCUARO, URUAPAN, LAKE CHAPALA, GUADALAJARA, COLIMA, MANZANILLO, PUERTO VALLARTA, TEPIC** and **SAN BLAS**.

See USING THIS GUIDE on page 50 for details on how to use this section. On the following pages, helpful pointers are given on how to get to each of the destinations covered. Along with the MEXICO map on pages 46–7, and the 4-color maps at the back of this book, they should give all the information necessary for planning your trip to this part of Mexico.

MORELIA ☆

Map 10D5. Capital of Michoacán. 311km (194 miles) w of Mexico City on RF15 via Toluca; 363km (226 miles) SE of Guadalajara on RF15; 167km (104 miles) s of Guanajuato on RF110, RF45 and RF43; 56km (35 miles) E of Patzcuaro on RF14 and RF15. Served by air, train (on Mexico City–Guadalajara line) and bus. Altitude: 2,080m (6,822ft). Population: 300,000 **i** *Clavijero Palace, Nigromante 79 at Madero* ☎*(451) 32654.*

Founded in 1541 by de Mendoza and named Valladolid after his birthplace, Morelia retains a historic and strongly Spanish character. Travelers come to Morelia less than to the colonial cities to the N, and there is a calmer, less touristic atmosphere. In charm and interest, Morelia certainly equals its better-known rivals, and it is much more accessible now the new airport is open, and following improvements on the road to Mexico City.

In 1828, it took the present name in honor of its most famous son, José María Morelos, a revolutionary priest who led the struggle for independence against the Spanish and was eventually executed in 1813. The man who signed his death warrant was another native of Morelia, although you will see no statues to Agustín Iturbide. He was an opportunistic professional soldier who fought on several sides during the War of Independence. In 1822 he was crowned Emperor of the Catholic Kingdom of Mexico. Like Morelos, however, his luck ran out, and in 1824 he too found himself betrayed, blindfolded and up against a wall.

But Morelia's best-loved modern hero is without doubt Lázaro Cárdenas, the one-time state governor who, as President of Mexico, returned to the local Purépecha Indians their stolen lands.

Morelia is of a manageable size, but for a good orienting view, take a walk in the hills up toward **Santa María**, s of town. The spires, domes and treetops of this charming city spread out in the valley below.

WHAT TO SEE

Zócalo

Colonnaded on three sides, the Zócalo has tranquil tree-shaded gardens and is a good place to sit out at a café, drinking in coffee and atmosphere, and listening, perhaps, to one of the evening **concerts** that are often held on the central bandstand.

On the E side is the imposing mid-17thC Baroque **cathedral**, with its tall twin bell-towers added a century later. Notable are the low-reliefs on the doorways and the religious oil paintings by Miguel Cabrera, the silver baptismal font used to baptize both Morelos and Iturbide, and one of the largest and most ornate organs in the Americas.

N of the cathedral is a large colonial mansion, once the seminary for Michoacán, and now the **Palacio de Gobierno** (🔲 *usually open during office hours).* On the main staircase are fine murals by Alfredo Zalce, showing historical scenes from the Conquest to the 1917 Revolution.

On the SW corner of the Zócalo is the **Museo Michoacana** (📷 *open standard hours),* in a small 18thC palace, with collections of Pre-Columbian and colonial art, especially of the local Purépecha culture. The third floor has a large mural of *The Four Horsemen of the Apocalypse* by Cantú.

Casa de Morelos

Iturbide and Morelos, two blocks w and two blocks s of the Zócalo 📷 *Open 9am–6.30pm.*

A 1758 house, bought by Morelos in 1801 and now a museum. It preserves various documents and personal possessions, and even the blindfold that he was wearing when executed. In the courtyard are two antique carriages; Morelos used one of them to carry the Last Sacraments to the sick and dying.

Morelos fans should also see the **Casa Natal** *(Corregidora 113* 🔲 *open Mon-Sat 9.30am-7pm; Sun 9.30am-3.30pm),* the house where Morelos was born, next to the 16thC church of **San Agustín** *(Corregidora and Hidalgo, a block s of the Zócalo.)*

Palacio Clerijero

Madero and Nigromante, one block w of the Zócalo. Open 9am–6pm.

This former Jesuit school, now used as a library, has a beautiful courtyard and magnificent 18thC architecture. Built in 1660, the Jesuits used it for more than a century until they were expelled in 1767.

Collegio de San Nicolás 🏛

Madero and Nigromante, opposite Palacio Clerijero 📷 *Open standard hours.*

This college was founded in 1540 by the first Bishop of Michoacán, Vasco de Quiroga, and moved to this location in 1580. Miguel Hidalgo studied here and returned briefly as rector. Always a controversial figure, he was fired, only to launch the independence movement in 1810.

The court of the main building is arcaded in the Baroque style, and the walls are decorated with murals.

Collegio de las Rosas Teresitas ⅏
Tapía and Prieto, on Jardín de las Rosas, two blocks N of the Zócalo.

Dating from 1743, this is the oldest music college in the Americas, and still in use as a choir school by the famous *Niños Cantores de Morelia*. The church of **Santa Rosa**, part of the college, has a Baroque facade and a beautiful altarpiece. To attend a rehearsal or performance of the choir, ask at the college.

Museo del Estado
Tapía and Prieto, across from Jardín de las Rosas. Open 9am–8pm. Closed Mon.

This museum of Michoacán's history has excellent Purépecha artifacts, ancient and modern, as well as a re-created 18thC pharmacist's store.

Convento del Carmen
Benito Juárez s/n, four blocks N of the Zócalo. Open 9am–7pm. Closed Sun.

Next to the 18thC church of **El Carmen**, the charming cloisters and buildings of the former convent have become Morelia's **art center**, with frequent performances and a good café.

Convento de San Francisco
On Humboldt, three blocks E of the cathedral.

Well worth a visit is the 16thC **church of San Francisco**, with its massive bell tower and tiled dome. The adjacent monastery is now the **Casa de Artesanías** *(☎(451) 21248, open 9am-8pm)* an excellent emporium and museum of local crafts.

Bosque Cuauhtémoc
Twelve blocks E of the Zócalo.

Through this large, pleasant park runs an impressive 18thC **aqueduct**, close to the small and unremarkable **Museo de Arte Contemporáneo** *(☎ open standard hours)*.

In the center of the park is a fine **orchid garden**, which catches the tropical colonial atmosphere of the whole town, and to the E is the **Sanctuary of the Virgin of Guadalupe**, which seems dazzlingly over-decorated.

WHERE TO STAY

POSADA DE LA SOLEDAD ⅏
Zaragoza 90 ☎(451) 21888 ℻(451) 22111 ▥ 58 rms � ☿

Located in a historic 1719 building a block from the Zócalo, this hotel and its cloistered courtyard are tranquil and deeply atmospheric.

VILLA MONTAÑA ⌂ ⅏
Patzimba 201, 5km (3 miles) s of the city ☎(451) 40231 ℻(451) 51423 ▥ 55 rms �
◻ ☙ ⟨€ ⇶ ⌖ ☿ ♫

With its fine view across Morelia, the Montaña is one of Mexico's very special hotels. It comprises beautifully furnished private villas, which surround a rambling colonial hacienda. There are four things not found here — air conditioning, disco, telephones and television.

VIRREY DE MENDOZA ⅏
Portal de Matamoros 16 ☎(451) 20633/20045 ▥ 58 rms �

Traditional comfort and a good restaurant are the main features of this renovated 18thC mansion on the Zócalo.

❧ Also good are: **Alameda** *(Madero and Prieto* ☎*(451) 22405* [Fx]*(451) 38727* ▥ *114 rms);* **Quality Inn Calinda Morelia** *(Camelinas 3466* ☎*(451) 41427* ▥ *126 rms);* and the **Catedral** *(Zaragoza 37* ☎*(451) 30783* ▥*)*, a colonial mansion overlooking the Zócalo. The less expensive hotels are concentrated around the bus station, 3 blocks N and W of the Zócalo; or try **Posada Don Vasco** *(Vasco de Quiroga 232* ☎*(451) 21484* ▢*)*, set around a quiet garden courtyard.

⇌ The hotel restaurants are generally good, especially **El Jardín** at the Virrey de Mendoza; and don't miss **Posada de la Soledad**'s Sunday lunch with *mariachi* musical accompaniment. For a genuine Purépecha meal on the Zócalo, try **El Rey Tacamba** *(Portal Galeana 577, no* ☎*)*, where even the menu is bilingual, in Purépecha and Spanish.

Other good choices around the Zócalo are **Los Commensales** *(Zaragoza 148* ☎*(451) 29361* ▢*)* and the **Bar Casino Restaurant** *(Madero s/n)*. A couple of blocks NW, **Boca del Río** *(Gómez Farias 185* ☎*(451) 29974* ▥*)* is the place for seafood.

SHOPPING

Michoacán is well known for its arts and crafts, largely thanks to the efforts of the first Bishop of Michoacán, Vasco de Quiroga, who introduced new skills and products to the Purépecha Indians. In Morelia you will find pottery, wood-carving, copper and lacquerware.

A good place to start is at the government-run **Casa de Artesanías** *(in the former Convento de San Francisco, see above),* although there is more bustle and bargaining at the **Mercado Independencia** *(Lázaro Cárdenas)*.

ENVIRONS OF MORELIA

Cuitzeo
35km (21 miles) N on RF43 to Salamanca and Guanajuato.
A small fishing village on the shallow Lake Cuitzeo. Its Zócalo is also the forecourt of a 16thC monastery. The two **churches** and the **monastery cloister** are fine examples of 16th–17thC colonial architecture, embellished with superb gargoyles.

Yuriria
66km (41 miles) N; on RF43, turn E after 62km (38 miles).
A large 16thC fortified lakeside **Augustinian monastery** built over the Purépecha city of Yuririapúndaro, now a national monument. After visiting the monastery, relax by the lake, or charter a boat and go fishing. Beyond, the road passes through magnificent volcanic country.

Mil Cumbres
70km (43 miles) E on RF15.
The official viewing point for the thousand peaks of the **Sierra Madre Occidental National Park**.

San José Purua
137km (85 miles) E, 5km (3 miles) W of RF15, 15km (9 miles) S of Tuxpán.
The inhabitants of this small spa town tell visitors that they live in Mexico's Shangri-La. The claim has some justification, for it is a pretty

place, set in a small canyon and surrounded by luxuriant vegetation. It is a good place to spend a night, and perhaps wallow awhile in the health-giving geothermal waters.

☞ **Spa San José Purua** *(reservations in Mexico City* ☎ *(5) 510 4949* ▥ ⇶ ══ ⓨ ⊙ ♨ *)* is a faded palace in a superb location.

PATZCUARO ☆

Map **10**D4. *Michoacán. 56km (35 miles) w of Morelia on RF15 and RF14; 54km (33 miles) w of Uruapán on RF14. Altitude: 2,218m (7,275ft). Population: 65,000. Served by train (line to Morelia) and bus* **i** *Portal Hidalgo 9 (on Zócalo)* ☎*(454) 21888 and Casa de Las Once Patios* ☎*(454) 21214.*

As you stroll through the narrow cobbled streets of Patzcuaro, admire the calm waters of Mexico's highest lake and gaze across at the rolling hills of Michoacán, you are a good distance from the nearest international airport. This simple fact has kept away the foreign retirees and artistic communities who cluster around the less attractive shores of Lake Chapala.

Like Chapala, Patzcuaro is not truly a Mexican town, but neither is it foreign, for the Purépecha tribes have been living around the lake since time immemorial (they are also known as Tarascans, but consider this term to be derogatory). Theirs was once a great and powerful kingdom, whose ruined capital can be seen at nearby **Tzintzuntzán**. They now live a dignified but straitened existence, farming and fishing in the lake with those great sweeping nets so beloved of photographers.

The Purépechas' first colonial master was Nuño de Guzmán, whose appalling crimes shocked even his fellow Conquistadors. Eventually, in 1540, he was removed, and Bishop Vasco de Quiroga was sent to bring life back to the devastated area. One of his methods was to teach the Indians of each village a different craft. To this day his name is venerated by Purépechas, and the area remains rich in handicrafts. On Fridays there is a big **market** next to Plaza Bocanegra, and this is the day to buy weaving, copper ware or any other of "Tata Vasco's" many legacies.

EVENTS • The tourist office will advise on details, but some special dates for religious celebrations are **Good Friday** and **October 8**, both celebrated with processions and dances. • During **Holy Week** in Tzintzuntzán, locals re-enact the Passion with alarming realism. • On November 1 and 2, the **Day of the Dead** is celebrated with great enthusiasm in all the nearby villages, and especially on the island of **Janitzio** (see THE LAKE AND ISLANDS, page 165).

WHAT TO SEE

The center

The colonial buildings around the leafy **Zócalo**, Plaza Vasco de Quiroga, could well take half a day to visit before you even start on the lake. Begin on the Zócalo itself with the 17thC **Casa del Gigante** (House of the Giant), opposite the Palacio Municipal, named after the 3.5m (11-foot) painted statue of a soldier, up on the second floor.

Leave the square on Portugal, to the right of the Casa del Gigante, and turn left on Levin for the **Museo de Arte Popular** (Museum of Folk Arts), housed in the 16thC Collegio de San Nicolás *(open 9am-7pm; closed Mon)*, which was founded by Don Vasco in 1540 to teach the Purépecha Spanish. Exhibits demonstrate the range of the crafts devised by Don Vasco for his Purépecha flock, including some fine ceremonial masks.

Just a block to the N is the large **Basilica de Nuestra Señora de la Salud** (Our Lady of Health), begun by Don Vasco in 1543. The Virgin in question is a statue made from a special worm-proof vegetable erected on a frame of cane, the object of great devotion at fiesta times.

From the W door of the basilica, the narrow Calle del Conejo leads straight ahead to the Plaza Bocanegra, where the 16thC church of **San Agustín** has been converted into a library. On the walls are **murals** painted in 1942 by **Juan O'Gorman**, one of the 1930s school of Marxist muralists, showing the history of Michoacán, with plenty of evil-looking Spaniards grinding the faces of the Purépecha poor. Across the square is an extensive and lively local **market** to explore.

Finally, before going down to the lake, visit the **Casa de los Once Patios**, with its five (not eleven) patios, a thriving little crafts center in the old residence on Colimilla, SE of the Zócalo, which also houses a tourist office.

The lake and islands

It takes about 25 minutes on a small ferry to reach the largest of the seven islands, **Janitzio**. This is mostly occupied by a pretty little fishing village dominated by the **tiled dome** of the church, a rather dreadful monument to Morelos, and an increasing number of souvenir stores.

On the night of the **Day of the Dead**, on November 1, the villagers stay up till dawn in the graveyard, chanting by candlelight; all the while boats come and go with offerings for the dead, with the candles on the prows glinting over the dark waters of the lake. However, this once eerie and moving scene has now become such a tourist attraction that you will find more authentic experiences elsewhere.

You might hire a boatman at the jetty and explore the lake and islands at leisure. At sunset, the elegant geometric shapes of **butterfly nets** reflect in the shimmering water: photographers should stock up on film.

For a good view of town and lake, head W out of the Zócalo along Ponce de León, past the old Customs House and the pottery market in front of San Francisco church. It is about 5km (3 miles) to the summit of an extinct volcano called **El Estribo**. By the time you return, a supper of grilled whitefish from the lake will be more than welcome.

SIGHTS NEARBY

Tzintzuntzán ruins ☆
17km (10 miles) N by lakeside road.
Near the village of **Tzintzuntzán** on a hillside overlooking the lake are the ruins of the old Purépecha capital, which once had a population as large as Patzcuaro does today. Although only partly restored, the grandeur of the five main Post-Classic temples around the great terrace is

proof of the high level of civilization that had been reached by the time of the Conquest. Indeed, the Purépechas repeatedly repelled Aztec attacks, retaining their independence right up to the Spanish Conquest, and the Aztecs regarded them as artistically superior.

Near the site is a large 16thC **monastery**, built using stones from the pyramids. In the forecourt are some ancient olive trees that have survived since the 16thC, despite a ban on their planting in Spanish America, to protect the farmers of Spain.

From here the road around the lake leads to the village of **Quiroga**, 9km ($5\frac{1}{2}$ miles) farther on. It is known for its intricately decorated wooden boxes and furniture, one of Vasco's industries that still flourishes after four centuries.

Another of these can be seen at **Santa Clara del Cobre** (now, officially at least, called **Villa Escalante**), 15km (9 miles) s of Patzcuaro. Copper-working is the specialty here, and the sound of metal-beating echoes right through the village. The **copper fair** in early August is always an impressive sight, with great regiments of pots and kettles shining in the sun.

All around the lake and in the hills are hundreds of villages worth exploring for their churches, crafts and timeless charm. Two of the most interesting and unspoiled are **Erongaricuaro** *(w of the lake)*, known for its weavings, and **Ario de Rosales** *(25km/15 miles s of Santa Clara)*.

Zirahuén *(20km/12 miles w of Patzcuaro on RF14, then s on back-road to Santa Clara)* is a small village on a lovely lake of the same name. **Lake Zirahuén**, steeped in legend, is a perfect spot for lotus eaters who can stay in lakeside cabins, and makes a good destination for a quiet day out. One excellent restaurant, the **Troje de Ala**, is a 20-minute boat ride from the village *(open Fri, Sat, Sun, hols)*.

WHERE TO STAY

Patzcuaro has an excellent selection of hotels around the Zócalo. At the upper end of the scale are the **Misíon San Manuel** *(Portal Aldama 12* ☎*(454) 21313* ▥ *68 rms* ⧖ ☑*)* a converted colonial town-house with a typical maze of rooms and patios, and **Mansión Iturbide** *(Portal Morelos 58* ☎*(454) 20368* ▥ *12 rms* ⧖*)*, a centrally located 17thC mansion hotel replete with old-world charm and comfort.

Rather less expensive is **Los Escudos** *(* ♣ *Portal Hidalgo 5* ☎*(454) 21238* ▥ *30 rms)*, an early colonial building around a courtyard. **Mesón del Gallo** *(* ♣ *Dr Coss 20* ☎*(454) 21474* ▥ ⧖ ⋙*)* is another small, pleasant, downtown hotel. **Posada de la Basílica** *(Arciga 26* ☎*(454) 21108* ▥ *11 rms* ⧖*)* has colonial rooms with fireplaces overlooking the lake; **Fiesta Plaza** *(on Plaza Bocanegra* ☎*(454) 22515/6* ▥ *60 rms* ⧖ ⋙*)* is also pleasant, in the colonial style.

Posada de Don Vasco *(Calzada de las Americas 450* ☎*(454) 20227* 🗷*(454) 20262* ▥ *103 rms* ⧖ ❤ ◁≪ ⋙ ♪○ ⋁ ☑ ♫*)* is a Best Western out-of-center colonial-style hotel toward the lake, with Purépecha dancing in the evenings. Nearby, the **Motel Patzcuaro** *(Calzada de las Americas 506* ☎*(454) 20767* ▥ *14 rms* ⧖ ⋙ ♪○*)* is excellent value with a pleasant garden.

EATING AND DRINKING

Visit **Hostería de San Felipe** (♣ *Lazaro Cárdenas 321* ☎*(454) 21298* 🎟️*)* for local specialties and atmosphere. **El Patio** *(Plaza Vasco de Quiroga 19* ☎*(454) 20484)* serves anything from light snacks to full Mexican meals right through the day. **Las Truchas** *(on the dockside overlooking the lake, no* ☎ 🎟️*)* serves fresh fish cooked to order. Opposite the museum, **Chocolate Joaquinta** *(Enseñanza 38)* serves irresistible, steaming hot chocolate.

URUAPÁN

Map 10E4. Michoacán. 54km (33 miles) w of Patzcuaro, 110km (68 miles) w of Morelia on RF14. Population: 300,000. Altitude: 1,610m (5,280ft). Served by bus **i** *5 de Febrero 17* ☎*(452) 20633.*

A pretty, although increasingly busy town in the semitropical hills of Michoacán; its name in the language of the local Purépecha Indians means "Place of Flowers," a title still justified by the impressively luxuriant parks. At the center is **Plaza Morelos**, a large market square occupying four blocks of the town's grid plan; every Sunday it fills with Purépechas selling the crafts of their villages.

It also contains **La Guapatera**, a 16thC hospital and church for the education and care of the Purépecha Indians, which is recognizable by its fine Plateresque doorway. The buildings are now used for the **Museo Regional de Arte Popular** *(* 🎟️ *open standard hours* ☎ *(454) 22138)*, with a collection of crafts from all over Michoacán, most notably the **lacquerware**, made of lemon-scented linaloa wood, for which Uruapán is famous.

ENVIRONS OF URUAPÁN

Paracho
36km (22 miles) N on RF37.
This is a small village that attracts musicians because of the hand-made violins and guitars produced in its many workshops. It is especially worth visiting for its **fiestas**, of Santiago on July 25 and San Francisco on October 4.

Paracutín volcano
70km (43 miles) NW to Angahuán, 30km (18 miles) N on RF37, then 40km (25 miles) w.
Mexico's newest volcano started as a smoking hole in the middle of a cornfield in 1943, and blasted its way up to 700m (2,296 feet) above the land before ceasing activity as suddenly in 1951. The thick covering of volcanic ash, which made local farmers' lives a choking misery during the eruption, has repaid them by markedly improving the fertility of their land.

Angahuán, a traditional Purépecha village of traditional *"trojé"* dwellings and a fine 16thC church, is the place to engage guides (and ponies, if you ride). **Paricutín** village, half an hour's walk away, is buried under lava, except for its church spire. The volcano itself is a far longer walk, six or seven hours there and back, so it may be a good idea to rent a cabin in the village.

Eduardo Ruiz National Park

8 blocks w of Zócalo along Independencia.

Just across the Río Cupatitzio from Uruapán is the Eduardo Ruiz National Park, a small paradise of subtropical vegetation kept lush and green by the springs from which the river emerges before forming delightful pools and waterfalls as it rushes down the valley.

La Tzaráracua waterfall

11km (6 miles) s to sign on RF37, then walk 1.5km (1 mile).

A short walk through pine forest from a parking lot near the road takes you to this magnificent waterfall where the Río Cupatitzio drops 50m (164 feet) off a sheer cliff; a good stop on your way to the coast.

WHERE TO STAY

Uruapán's charm resides in the lush countryside around, so most of the best hotels are likewise out of town. At the top end is **Mansión de Cupatitzio** *(♥ 🏨 in the National Park, w of town* ☎ *(452) 32100 ▥ 53 rms ⇌ ☙ ≋ ☯)*, a popular weekend spot with a country-club atmosphere and a fine restaurant.

Hacienda Caracha *(Km 17 on RF37 heading s* ☎ *(452) 36212 ▥ ⇌ ☯ ☙ ≋ ♪)* is a well-equipped resort-style hotel catering mostly to Mexican families, busy on weekends. **Pie de la Sierra** *(♥ Km 4 on Carapan road* ☎ *(452) 42510 ▥ 73 rms ⇌ ☯ ☙ ≋)* has a lovely sylvan setting and a good restaurant. **Paraíso Uruapán** *(Km 2 on Patz-cuaro road* ☎ *(452) 21640 ▥ ⇌)* is more of a motel, but a good one.

In the downtown, the best place is the **Plaza Uruapán** *(Ocampo 64 on the Zócalo* ☎ *(452) 30333 ▣ (452) 33980 ▥ 124 rms ⇌ ☯ ☻)*, but you will get better value at the charming **Villa de Flores** *(Emiliano Carranza 15* ☎ *(452) 21650 ▥)*, or the modern **Victoria** *(Cupatitzio 11* ☎ *(452) 36700 ▣ (454) 39662 ▥ 82 rms ⇌ ☯)*.

⇌ **Emperador** *(Portal Matamoros 18* ☎ *(452) 31850 ▥ ▭)* is one of many excellent eating places on the Zócalo with good regional specialties. One very good place to try the local coffee in its many varieties is the **Café Tradicional** *(just N of the Zócalo on Carranza).*

LAKE CHAPALA

*Map **9**D3. Jalisco. 48km (30 miles) s of Guadalajara. Population: 35,000. Served by bus from Guadalajara* **i** *Auditorio Ribera de Chapala* ☎ *(376) 53136.*

The shores of Mexico's largest inland lake, which covers more than 1,000sq.km (375sq. miles), are the haunts of weekenders from Guadalajara, and havens for writers, painters and retired people, many attracted from the US by the sunshine and low cost of living. However, the water quality is threatened by industrial discharges and inadequate sewage treatment — so make sure that any local fish you eat are well cooked. Some even fear that the lake may disappear altogether — as in Mexico City — from the over-extraction of groundwater.

WHAT TO SEE

The town

Stop first at the **Chapala Society Headquarters**, in the center, where copious information is available on anything from chess partners to the best fishing spots. If your catch is poor, choose from a large number of small restaurants along the sides of the lake, which serve fresh whitefish from the lake's rather muddy waters. Here the atmosphere is lively, particularly on weekends, with numerous vendors and *mariachis* from Guadalajara.

The lake

Heading westward along the lake there are several highlights.

Ajijic *(8km/5 miles),* a colonial pueblo with a sizeable artistic community, has several art galleries and shops selling local crafts, as well as most of the hotels. Locals still speak in hushed tones of the "Night of the Long Knives" in 1965, when respectable citizens took the law into their own hands and ran out of town any excessively Bohemian or insufficiently free-spending foreign elements. In 1926, that all-time great Bohemian, D.H. Lawrence, stayed here when he wrote *The Plumed Serpent.*

Farther around the lake, **Cosala**, with its thermal baths and a periodic geyser, is followed by **Jocotepec** *(6km/3 miles from Ajijic),* worth a visit on Sunday for its market — bargain for woven *serapes* (ponchos).

✿   **Chula Vista Country Club** *(3km/1 mile w of Chapala toward Ajijic* ☎ *(376) 52213* ▥ ☱ ✔ ⚲ *)* is a pleasant country hotel with a 9-hole golf course. In Chapala itself, the **Nido** *(Madero 202* ☎ *(376) 52116* ▥ *31 rms* ☱ ⚲ *)* is a slightly run-down turn-of-century establishment, and excellent value.

In Ajijic, **Posada Ajijic** *(Domicilio Conocido* ☎ *(376) 53395* ▥ ☱ *)* has moved to a larger site near the lake, but its colonial-style cabins look like they've always been there, and it still has the best restaurant in town.

Possible rivals include the colonial-style **Danza del Sol** *(Zaragoza 165* ☎ *(376) 52505* ▣ *(376) 52836* ▥ *67 rms* ☱ ⚲ ⚶ *)* and the **Real de Chapala** *(Paseo del Prado 20* ☎ *(376) 52519* ▣ *(376) 52474* ▥ *85 rms* ☱ ⚲ ⚶ *),* with lovely lakeside gardens and restaurant.

In Jocotepec, stay at the lakeside **Paseo del Pescador** *(no* ☎ ▢ *).*

☱   Many excellent restaurants cater to the expatriate community, especially **Posada Ajijic** *(see above);* **Cazadores** *(Ramon Corona 18* ☎ *(376) 52162)* is also recommended for its Mexican specialties, as is **Meson de Ajijic** *(Hidalgo 17* ☎ *(376) 53611),* with its long list of desserts.

GUADALAJARA ☆

*Map **9**C3. Capital of Jalisco. 530km (331 miles) w of Mexico City on RF15. Altitude: 1,600m (5,248ft). Population: 6 million. Served by air (international airport 19km/11 miles s), train (station 15km/9 miles E of center) and bus*
i *at airport, and at Degollado 50* ☎ *(36) 148665 and Morelos 102* ☎ *(36) 582222, both on Plaza Tapatía. UK Consul: Gonzalez Gallo 1897* ☎ *(36) 358927. US Consul: Progreso 175* ☎ *(36) 252700. American Express: Plaza Los Arcos, Vallarta 2440 at Quevedo* ☎ *(36) 300200. See map on page 171.*

Once the most Spanish city of New Spain, Guadalajara remained for many years proudly remote from the rest of Mexico. Today it is changing rapidly, as if to live up to its position as the country's second city. However, a combination of industrial growth and ever-increasing traffic is at last bringing Guadalajara a taste of the pollution and chaos that hangs over the capital.

One working-class neighborhood experienced another sinister repercussion of industrial growth in 1990, when hydrocarbons leaked from storage tanks into sewers and blew up, plowing up entire streets and killing 200 people.

But despite the expanding urban sprawl, the town's center is attractive and easily spanned on foot. Here, where four gracious squares surround the cathedral and stately colonial buildings abound, it does not seem so long ago that haughty Spanish nobles strode out from their mansions. Even now, the locals like to be called *Tapatíos,* after the tasseled cloaks that were the height of elegance during colonial times.

The state of Jalisco was originally a part of the province of New Galicia; the area's conquest was far from easy, and only in 1560, after years of bloody fighting, was Guadalajara sufficiently established to become the provincial capital. It soon became an important center of commerce; much of the wealth generated was poured into the building of the city, and the parks and wide tree-lined boulevards constitute a triumph for Spanish town planning. Even today, modern buildings have to fit into the original master-plan.

Surprisingly, given its Spanish character, Guadalajara joined the 1810 rebellion, and for a short while was even the seat of a revolutionary government. But after this brief spell in the limelight it returned to gracious provincial isolation and conservatism, shaken only slightly by the revolution of a century later.

The more lasting revolution began when the highways and railroads eventually arrived and the city began to resume its former economic importance. The large new international airport opened up the area to tourism; many fly here to explore the colonial cities, the mountains, and the coast of western Central Mexico.

Indeed, the excellent temperate climate and relaxed atmosphere have attracted some visitors so much that they have decided to retire to Guadalajara and nearby LAKE CHAPALA. To cope with the foreign influx, many new hotels and restaurants have opened in recent years, making the city, and the state of Jalisco as a whole, one of Mexico's most attractive travel destinations.

Nowhere more than in Mexico does human life become isolated, external to its surroundings, and cut off tinily from the environment. Even as you come across the plain to a big city like Guadalajara, and see the twin towers of the cathedral peering around in loneliness like two lost birds side by side on a moor, lifting their white heads to look around in the wilderness, your heart gives a clutch, feeling the pathos, the isolated tininess of human effort.
(D.H. Lawrence, *Mornings in Mexico,* 1927)

WHAT TO SEE

The main sights are scattered in groups around the city, and are arranged accordingly in the section that follows. The central landmark and point of reference is the **cathedral**, which stands astride four important colonial plazas arranged like a cross in the center of the pedestrianized Metropolitan Plaza area.

To the s is the Zócalo, the Plaza de Armas; w at the apex of the cross is the Plaza los Laureles; n is the Plaza de Hombres Illustres; e is Plaza de la Liberación, occupying two blocks; and one block beyond is the massive Plaza Tapatía, straddling Calzada Independencia. In October, the whole area fills up with stalls, music, dancing and fireworks at night.

The city center

Cathedral ▥

The cathedral dominates the city in every respect; when you lose your sense of direction, just look for its twin bell towers, strange Byzantine creations on the skyline. They were rebuilt after an earthquake early this century, and just about complete the collection of architectural styles embodied in the cathedral, which ranges from Moorish through

171

Classical Greek to Gothic. It was consecrated in 1616 after nearly 50 years of construction.

There are several fine **oil paintings** in the side chapels: see especially the *Assumption of the Virgin,* attributed to Murillo. A good way to orient yourself is to climb the **bell tower**, for a magnificent view.

Palacio de Gobierno ▥
Plaza de Armas.

Behind its Neoclassical facade of gray volcanic stone, this is the home of huge 1930s murals by José Clemente Orozco; they show the oppression of the Mexican people by foreigners, reserving a heroic position for Hidalgo, who announced the abolition of slavery here in 1810.

Museo Regional del Estado (Jalisco State Museum) ▥
N side of Plaza Liberación ▧ ▣ Open standard hours.

An amazingly varied range of exhibits fills the maze of rooms, courts and corridors of this 17thC seminary building, opposite the Neoclassical Rotonda de los Héroes de Jalisco, beside the cathedral.

Prize exhibits include the dried-up arm of a notorious assassin and the first phonograph to reach Guadalajara, and there is any amount of Pre-Hispanic and colonial relics and art. It is easy to spend a whole day here, going around, losing oneself and finding wisdom. In the modern picture galleries, be sure to see the early works of the 1930s muralists, Orozco and Rivera. The colonial section includes a Murillo *Self-portrait* and *Life of St Francis of Assisi.*

In the same building *(but with separate entrance at Hidalgo 292)* is the **Museum of Paleontology**, worth visiting for its fossilized mammoth skeleton, still accompanied by the bones of a hunter and the stone arrowheads he used in his vain attempt to kill the mammoth.

Teatro Degollado ▥
E side of Plaza da la Liberación.

An ornate Neoclassical 19thC theater modeled on Milan's La Scala, which is now the cultural center of Guadalajara; the opulent interior is well worth a look. The theater is flanked by the colonial churches of **Santa María** and **San Augustín**; both belonged to monasteries that have now disappeared.

Hospicio Cabañas ▥
Calle Hospicio, on the bottom of Plaza Tapatía ▧ Open standard hours.

This enormous 19thC orphanage, all cloisters, courtyards and flowers, is still in use today; visitors are often invited to meet the children who live here.

The building was designed by the great Neoclassical architect Manuel Tolsa, but the main attractions are the 1930s **murals** by Clemente Orozco. They fill the chapel, and each panel has a different theme, including political, Biblical and historical pieces, all adding up to a passionately Mexican view of the world. The most famous panel is *The Four Horsemen of the Apocalypse,* a composition of stunning dynamism.

Mercado Libertad
Off Calzada Independencia.

In this enormous marketplace it is the rule to bargain fiercely over the price of any pottery or leatherwork that takes your fancy. Just s of the market is the **Plaza Mariachis**, which is blocked with café tables but nonetheless thronged with hundreds of *mariachi* musicians in silver-embroidered costumes, all cheerfully trying to outplay one another. Just N is the city's **bullring**.

South of the center

Seven blocks S of the Plaza de Armas, down Av. 16 de Septiembre, is a charming little **garden** overlooked by the 17thC church of **San Francisco de Asís**, with a fine Baroque facade. Opposite is the church of **Nuestra Señora de Aranzazu**, whose high altars drip with gold-leaf.

From here it is 12 blocks S to the leafy **Parque Agua Azul**. At its northern tip, on a large traffic circle, is the **Museo de Artesanías (** 🖾 *open standard hours)*, where a wide range of folk pottery and weaving is exhibited, most of it for sale at reasonable prices. Ten minutes' walk farther S, by the railroad station on 16 de Septiembre, is the small **Museo de Arqueología (** 🖾 *open 10am-1pm, 3-7pm; closed Mon)*, with some fine human and animal pottery figures from COLIMA.

West of the center

Proceeding along Juárez, later Av. Vallarta, from the center, the former **Convento del Carmen** (six blocks) is now a flourishing **arts center**. After another six blocks, the **University buildings** ancient and modern confront each other across the street.

The next place of note is the **Museo José Clemente Orozco** *(Av. Vallarta near Minerva fountain, 4km/2 miles W of center* 🖾 *open standard hours)*, which preserves the studio of the great 1930s muralist who made the giant political mural a cultural tradition of Mexico. On display are some of the studies Orozco made for his murals and hundreds of his paintings, although none of the murals themselves. The paintings clearly chart his development from Realism in his youth to later Symbolism and Expressionism.

WHERE TO STAY

Guadalajara's hotels fall into two main categories: expensive out-of-center deluxe establishments, and good-value hotels at the heart of the downtown action, often in restored colonial buildings.

Out of the center

CAMINO REAL 🏨
Av. Vallarta 5005 ☎(36) 478000 🖾(36) 476781 ▥ 208 rms ⬱ ⬩ ⬩ ⬩ ⬩ ⬩ ⬩ ⬩ ⬩
Location: 5km/3 miles W of center. A colonial-style resort hotel with large airy rooms in low bungalows and a wide range of shops and pools.

CROWNE PLAZA HOLIDAY INN
López Mateos 2500 ☎(36) 315566 🖾(36) 319393 ▥ 300 rms ⬱ ⬩ ⬩

⬩ ⬩ ⬩ ⬩ ⬩
Location: 6km (3½ miles) SE, near Plaza del Sol shopping mall. A reliable favorite, belonging to the ubiquitous worldwide chain, with a rooftop restaurant and reasonable location.

FIESTA AMERICANA 🏨
Aurelio Aceres 225 ☎(36) 253434 🖾(36) 303725 ▥ 391 rms ⬱ ⬩ ⬩
⬩ ⬩
Location: 4km (2½ miles) W of center at

the Minerva monument. This hotel, housed in a bold, modern building, has a multitude of bars and restaurants, as well as flamboyantly appointed rooms.

HYATT REGENCY 🏨
López Mateos Sur and Moctezuma ☎*(36)* 226688 ☒*(36)* 229877 ▥ 345 rms ═╡ ♥ ⚓ ℘ ♈ 🐎 ♈ ● ♍ ⚓

Location: SE of town toward Plaza del Sol shopping center. In addition to the usual facilities, a Jacuzzi, gym and a baby-sitting service are on offer.

QUINTA REAL 🏨
Av. México 2727 ☎*(36)* 150000 ☒*(36)*

301797 ▥ 53 rms ═╡ ♥ ⚓ ℘ ♈ ● ⚓

Location: W of center. This luxurious colonial-style hotel is a newer, smaller, more intimate and more expensive version of the CAMINO REAL, with every facility and an excellent restaurant.

EL TAPATÍO GRAN SPA RESORT 🏨
On Chapala road ☎*(36)* 356050 ☒*(36)* 356664 ▥ ═╡ 120 rms ═╡ ♥ ◁ ⚓ ℘ ♈ ⚓ ● ♍ ♟ ⚓

Location: 6.5km (4 miles) SE. This is a well-appointed multilevel country club resort, on a hilltop overlooking the town. Plenty of amusing nightlife.

Downtown hotels

The following list shows some of the best downtown hotels.

- **Aranzazú** *(Revolución 110* ☎*(36) 133232* ☒*(36) 145045* ▥ *500 rms* ═╡ ♍ ▮ ⚲*)* is a modern hotel, whose twin towers are a useful landmark.

- **Frances** *(♣ Maestranza 35, off Plaza Liberación* ☎*(36) 131190* ▥ *40 rms* ═╡ ♈ ●*)*, in a 1610 colonial building with fountains and chandeliers, home of MAXIM'S disco.

- **De Mendoza** *(Carranza 16* ☎*(36) 134646* ☒*(36) 137310* ▥ *110 rms* ═╡ ♈ ♍*)*, a comfortable colonial hotel.

- **Posada Guadalajara** *(López Mateos 1280* ☎*(36) 212022* ▥ ═╡ ♈*)*

- **Quality Inn Calinda** *(♣ Juárez 170* ☎*(36) 148 650* ▥ *172 rms* ═╡ ♥ ♍ ♈*)* has live entertainment in the lobby, and a rooftop bar.

- **San Francisco Plaza** *(Degollado 267* ☎*(36) 138954* ▥ ═╡*)* is a colonial hotel, with a busy restaurant.

EATING AND DRINKING

Restaurants at the luxury hotels all offer an international menu and nightly entertainment. Saturday night at the **El Tapatío** and Sunday buffet lunch at the **Camino Real** should not be missed, and the San Francisco Plaza is also good.

Guadalajara's most famous restaurant, **Copa de Leche** *(Juárez 414* ☎*(36) 141845* ▥ *open all day)* is really three in one, with a sidewalk café, balcony and indoor dining room, each with its own menu. Other good places include the **Café Madrid** *(Juárez and 16 de Septiembre)* and the café in the **Convento del Carmen** arts center (see page 173).

The family-run chain of **Cazadores** restaurants *(Américas 159* ☎*(36) 158878; Jalisco 606* ☎*(36) 351983; Niños Héroes 62* ☎*(36) 148235; Unión 405* ☎*(36) 159710; all* ▥*)* all serve delicious Mexican food. In Tlaquepaque, the **Restaurant sin nombre** *(Madero 80, Tlaquepaque* ☎*(36) 354520* ▥*)* offers delicious local food among peacocks and *mariachis.* Also in Tlaquepaque, **El Abajeno** *(Juárez 231* ☎*(36)*

359015 ▭*)* and **Mariscos Progreso** *(Progreso 80* ☎ *(36) 574995*▭*)* serve good regional food.

Las Margueritas *(* ♣ *López Cotilla 1477* ☎ *(36) 168906* ▭*)* serves fresh and plentiful vegetarian meals on an open terrace. In Zapopan, **Hacienda de la Flor** *(* ⬠ *A. Ortega 764* ☎*(36) 333178* ▥*)* offers great seafood and regional dishes by candlelight in an old hacienda. Every night is party night at the **Guadalajara Grill** *(López Mateos 3771* ☎ *(36) 315622* ▥*),* part of the Carlos'n'Charlie's chain.

GUADALAJARA BY NIGHT

Until recently, the conservative local authorities discouraged after-hours liveliness, and most of the action is at the hotels, with the obvious exception of the **Plaza Mariachi** (see MERCADO LIBERTAD on page 173), where you should certainly go once during your stay. Hotels will provide free English-language listings of the entertainments taking place, and of the program at the **Teatro Degollado** (see page 172), which can range from classical opera to folkloric ballet. *(For cultural information in English* ☎ *(36) 157 992).*

The luxury hotels all have bars with entertainment, and discos. Try the **Lobby Bar** at the FIESTA AMERICANA, the Hyatt's **ice-rink disco**, the **Factory** at the ARANZAZÚ, or the less glitzy **Maxim's Disco** at the FRANCES.

ENVIRONS OF GUADALAJARA

On the outskirts of the city is a spectacular ravine and two former Indian villages, now incorporated into the metropolis.

Barranca de los Oblatos
11km (6 miles) N along Independencia.
A **cable-car** makes the dizzying 700m (2,296-foot) descent into the Río Santiago ravine, or you can stand at the top and gaze down. It is crowded on weekends.

San Pedro Tlaquepaque ☆
7km (4 miles) E of center, off RF90 to Mexico City **i** *by the church* ☎*(36) 351503.*
A center for all manner of traditional Indian crafts, San Pedro Tlaquepaque is known above all for its hand-painted pottery. There are numerous shops where you can see weavers, glass-blowers and metal-beaters at work. *Mariachi* music is said to have originated here; certainly there is a lot of it played around the Zócalo, especially during the **fiesta** on June 29.

It is easy to spend an entire day wandering around the pedestrianized center. But if time allows, continue to the potters' village of **Tonalá** *(* ☆ *8km/5 miles E on RF90).* Its finely painted animal figurines are sold all over Mexico, but prices are lower here, and there is the fun of seeing them being made.

The spectacular **waterfalls** at **Juanacatlán** are about 20km (12 miles) SW from Tlaquepaque, off an unnumbered road.

Zapopán
8km (5 miles) NW of center, signposted off Avenida de las Americas at the end of Vallarta.

The second village has a basilica whose miraculous statue of the Virgin is the focal point of one of Mexico's largest fiestas in October each year (October 4 is the most important day, but it continues until October 12). The streets fill with fervent worshipers, *mariachi* bands and dancers, escorting the Virgin on a long procession around the city. The basilica hardly merits a visit at other times, although it is a good example of 17thC Baroque.

FARTHER AFIELD

San Juan de los Lagos *(150km/93 miles NE on RF80)* is renowned for its spectacular religious festivals, which attract pilgrims from all over the state and beyond. The main dates are between January 20 and February 6 (especially February 2), August 1 to 6 and November 21 to December 12, depending on the year's calendar *(ask at the Guadalajara tourist office)*.

Tequila *(60km/37 miles NW of Guadalajara on RF15 to Tepic and Puerto Vallarta)* is a small town with a big reputation, having given, to a grateful world, the ambrosial and alcoholic bliss of the drink that bears its name. A must for tipplers is a visit to one of the **distilleries**, where cactus juice is processed into firewater for worldwide consumption. **Feast days** in Tequila are May 3 and December 8, when the town's liquor flows freely.

La Magdalena *(another 18km/11 miles NW on RF15)*, a pleasant colonial town, has become a center for semiprecious stones: magpies will find irresistible the glittering arrays of opal, agate and jade.

Tapalpa *(84km/52 miles S of Guadalajara on RF80 and RF54, then turn right after 54km/33 miles)* is a pretty, highland village and a good center for hiking in the mountains. You can take your pick of hotels and restaurants on the Zócalo: try the **Posada La Fuente** or the more modest **Hotel Hacienda**.

COLIMA ☆

Map 9E2. Capital of Colima. 220km (137 miles) SW of Guadalajara on RF54; 136km (85 miles) E of Manzanillo on RF200 and RF110. Altitude: 500m (1,640ft). Population: 95,000. Served by air, train (on Guadalajara Manzanillo line) and bus
i Hidalgo 75 ☎(331) 28360.

Colima is a pleasant, semitropical city of gardens and 18thC buildings aired by fresh mountain breezes from the great Nevado de Colima, the mountain that dominates the town and the surrounding fertile plain. Although a rewarding place to spend a day or two, it is neglected by tourists, who are eager to get to the fun zones of the coast. Perhaps they are also worried by the town's very own volcanoes, the 3,960m (12,988-foot) **Fuego de Colima** and the 4,330m (14,202-foot) **Nevado de Colima**, which some volcanologists predict will produce a major eruption within 50 years.

In Pre-Hispanic times Colima was the center of the Tecus people, who maintained their independence from the Aztec empire but succumbed to

Francisco Cortés in 1524. The thousand-year-old ruins of their capital, Chanalá, survived near the modern city into the early 20thC, when all traces were destroyed.

The civilization is best known for its distinctive pot-bellied *tepescuintle* **pottery dogs**, which command a high price among collectors; note that any you are offered locally will be fakes.

EVENTS • On February 2, there is a **fiesta of the Virgin**, to whom the local peasants have a fierce devotion: celebrations begin a week ahead with dances, fireworks and long religious ceremonies. • A week or so later, amateur **bullfighters** can try their luck in the ring; participation is only for the brave (or foolish).

WHAT TO SEE

Museo de las Culturas de Occidente (Museum of Western Cultures) ☆
Galvan at Ejército National, 4 blocks E and 6 blocks N of the Zócalo ☎*(331) 23155* 🕮 *Open 9am–7.30pm. Closed Mon.*
This well-organized museum has a collection of finely detailed ceramic figurines, sculptures and everyday objects that combine to give a clear impression of life in pre-Conquest Colima. Especially charming are the figures of the small, pot-bellied dogs, once a culinary delicacy.

Museo Zaragoza (Zaragoza Vintage Car Museum) ☆
Belisario Dominguez 80, 6 blocks E of the Zócalo 🕮 *Open standard hours.*
This might seem a surprising place to find one of the best collections anywhere of antique American cars, but here are some 350 of them, all in working order. There are many more being restored at the **Zaragoza family ranch** outside town, which real enthusiasts may be allowed to visit *(ask at the museum)*.

A number of other museums are also worth a look. The **Museo de Culturas Populares** *(Museum of Popular Culture, 27 de Septiembre and Zamora, 7 blocks N of the Zócalo* 🕮 *open 9am-2pm, 4-7pm; closed Mon)* has a fascinating collection of masks and costumes from all over the country, and a FONART crafts store. The **Museo Regional** *(Portal Morelos 1, on Zócalo, open 9am-2pm)* is a small museum, currently being renovated, of folk art ancient and modern, in a fine colonial building.

PLACES OF INTEREST NEARBY

From Colima, a paved road leads 11km (6 miles) N to the village of **Comalá**, famous for its wrought-iron work and painted masks and furniture. Farther N are coffee haciendas and the lovely **Laguna la María**, set in a park that makes a popular weekend camping spot.

For the adventurous, there is magnificent walking on the foothills of the volcanoes beyond. However, the summits are a hard climb away and may involve a night spent out on the mountain.

🍴 **Los Candiles** *(Blvd. Camino Real 399* ☎*(331) 23212* 🎞 ⊨ ≈𝕩*)* is the best of three motels in a row, with a good restaurant; the **América** *(Morelos 162* ☎*(331) 20366* 🎞 ⊨ 🎏 ◆ ≈𝕩 𝕐 ⚘*)* offers all mod. cons., steam bath and Jacuzzi behind its conventional facade. On the Zócalo, try the **Casino** *(Portal Morelos 11* ☎*(331) 21406* 🎞*)*, or the **Ceballos** *(Portal Medellin 12* ☎*(331) 24444* 🎞*)*, in a fabulous old building that was once very grand.

MANZANILLO

Map 9E2. Colima. 351km (219 miles) SW of Guadalajara on RF80 and RF200; 260km (162 miles) S of Puerto Vallarta on RF200; 136km (85 miles) W of Colima on RF110 and RF200. Population: 100,000. Served by air (international airport 8km/5 miles N), train (terminus of line from Guadalajara via Colima) and bus i in Palacio Municipal, Juárez 244 ☎(333) 20000. American Express: Hotel Las Hadas lobby ☎(333) 32100.

One of the country's most important commercial ports, with a bustling downtown area of no great charm behind the cranes and wharves. Until a new airport was opened in 1974, this was a minor tourist destination, although it was always a favorite with the surfing fraternity. All that has changed: hotels, mini-resorts and marinas have sprung up along the coast, and the new **Rancho Majagua** mega-resort, based on a brand-new "typical" Mexican town, is due to extend along 17km (10 miles) of nearby beaches and cliffs.

Manzanillo is set on a wide double bay, with a sweeping backdrop of volcanic hills. Here the Spaniards built the galleons that set out to conquer the Philippines, but few buildings from that period remain, although in the narrow streets leading to the Zócalo there are some old, pretty wooden houses. Back around the Zócalo are arts and crafts stores selling (expensive) nicknacks.

More important are the shops selling equipment for fishing expeditions. Hotels or waterfront restaurants will help to arrange boat charter. You have more security if you do it this way: dealing with the owners direct may be cheaper, but the boats will probably be less reliable.

The beaches nearer town are quite crowded and occasionally polluted, although they offer a full range of water-sports. The **Playa Azul** becomes more pleasant as it curves N away from the center. Beyond the LAS HADAS hotel (see below) is the small **Playa de la Audiencia**, and then the larger **Playa de Santiago**, where the surf can be quite rough. Lovers of solitude will need to head farther out, but will not be disappointed. The beaches to the N are renowned for surfing.

WHERE TO STAY

CLUB MAEVA
Near Las Hadas hotel (see below) ☎(333) 32223 ᴇx(333) 30395 ▥ 514 rms ≈ ❧ ⌘ ⍨ ⌖ ✓ ➤ ♛ ♈ ◐ ♌

A self-contained beach resort run along Club Med lines, with 100 villas set in tropical gardens.

CLUB SANTIAGO
Playa Miramar ☎(333) 30413 ▥ 297 rms ≈ ⌘ ⍨ ⌖ ✓ ➤ ♈ ◐ ♌

Accommodation at this excellent resort hotel is in a mixture of villas, hotel rooms and condominium apartments, with facilities for all sports, a lively nightlife and a superb beach.

LAS HADAS RESORTS ⌸
Peninsula de Santiago ☎(333) 30000 ᴇx(333) 30430 ▥ 220 rms ≈ ❧ ⌘ ⍨ ⌖ ✓ ➤ ♐ ♛ ♈ ◐ ♌

This Moorish-style village festooned with flowers provides superb sporting facilities, its own private marina and an organized social program; enjoy the "Cocktail Cruise" yacht at sundown — recommended, for the views are stunningly beautiful.

PLAYA DE SANTIAGO ♣
On Playa Santiago ☎(333) 30055 ᴇx(333) 30344 ▥ 105 rms ≈ ⌖ ⍨ ⌖ ✓ ♈

Once the best in town, this is still a great-value resort hotel, with a nice little beach and its own small island.

LA POSADA
Lázaro Cárdenas 201 on Las Brisas Peninsula ☎*(333) 31899* ▥ *24 rms* ⇥ ⋙ ⛾
An intimate American-run hotel with

striking all-pink decor, a relaxed atmosphere and a great view of the port.

SIERRA RADISSON PLAZA ☗
Av. de la Audiencia 1 ☎*(333) 32000*
Fx*(333) 32272* ▥ *350 rms* ⇥ ⋙ ♒
♨ ⛾ ⋮ ⛾
A new, high-rise luxury beachside hotel with all facilities, including a nursery.

❧ Other options include **Playasol las Hadas** *(near Las Hadas hotel* ☎*(333) 30308* ▥ *220 rms* ⇥ ⛾ ⋙*)* and **Fiesta Mexicana** ☗ *(Km 8.5 Carretera Santiago* ☎*(333) 32180* ▥ *185 rms* ⇥ ⋙ ⛾ ❍ ♒ ♨ ♪*)*. Downtown, try the **Colonial** *(Mexico 100* ☎*(333) 21080*▥ ⇥*)*, claimed to be Manzanillo's only remaining historic building.

Hotels nearby

Barra de Navidad (5km/3 miles N)

Cabo Blanco *(*☎*(321) 70022* Fx*(333) 70168* ▥ *101 rms* ▦ ⇥ ♒ ♨ ⛾ ❍*)* is a good modern hotel $\frac{1}{2}$ km ($\frac{1}{4}$ mile) from the beach; **Sands** *(Morelos 24* ☎*(333) 70018* ▥ *to* ▥ *42 rms* ⇥ ⋙ ☛ ⛾ ❍*)* is a decent, plain hotel for surfers and fishermen, overlooking the lagoon; near the sea, the **Delfin** *(Morelos 23* ☎*(333) 70068* ▥ ⇥ ⋙*)* has a pleasant shaded garden; or try the **Bogavante** *(Legazpi s/n* ☎*(333) 70384* ▥*)*, overlooking the beach. In nearby **Melaque** *(3km/1 mile away)*, the best choice is the **Orientales** *(Salgado and Obregón* ☎*(333) 324028* ▥ ⇥ ⛾ ⋙*)*, an unusual Japanese-style beachside hotel.

Costa de Careyes (139km/86 miles N)

CLUB MED PLAYA BLANCA ☗
☎*(321) 20005* Fx*(333) 20008, or*
Mexico City ☎*(5) 533 4800* ▥ ⇥ ⋓
◖ ⋙ ♒ ♨ ♪ ⛾ ❍ ♪
The usual well-organized vacation fun, in a private resort village with superb sporting facilities.

COSTA DE CAREYES
Costa Careyes ☎*(333) 70050* Fx*(333) 70107* ▥ *90 rms* ⇥ ◖ ⋙ ♒ ⛾ ❍ ♣
This strangely underpopulated deluxe resort hotel provides comfortable accommodation amid an assortment of boutiques, restaurants and bars.

EATING AND DRINKING

Of Manzanillo's hotel restaurants, the expensive ones serve the usual brand of international food, but the **Colonial** (see above) stands out for its fresh homestyle cooking, while LA POSADA serves good value meals from breakfast to dinner.

The following independents along the beachfront Santiago highway are also good: **La Bamba** *(*☎*(333) 31930* ▥*)*, for Mexican food and atmosphere; **L'Récif** *(near Vida del Mar* ☎*(333) 30624* ▥*)*, with a superb French menu and views across the sea; **Osteria Bugatti** *(near Las Brisas* ☎*(333) 32999* ▥*)*, for Italian-style seafood; **Carlos'n'Charlie's** *(near Las Brisas* ☎*(333) 31150* ▥*)*, as outrageous as ever; and **Juanito's** *(*☎*(333) 31388* ▥*)*, an American-style barbecue and hamburger bar.

MANZANILLO BY NIGHT

Apart from those in hotels, discos come and go like summer rain. Current high spots are **Oui** (☎(333) 32333) and **Enjoy** (☎(333) 32839) on the Santiago road. Of the hotels, LAS HADAS has by far the best and most expensive nightlife.

ENVIRONS OF MANZANILLO

Heading s down the coast, the road passes the tropical **Laguna Cuyut-lán** after 41km (25 miles) and then arrives at a stretch of black-sand beaches. The villages along here never achieved resort status, partly because black sand becomes scorchingly hot, and also because of the vast spring waves, almost a tourist attraction in themselves, which unfortunately bring with them masses of seaweed, which subsequently decays on the beaches.

The most agreeable of the villages is **Boca de Pascuales** (60km/37 miles s), where you can sit in a thatched beach hut and eat freshly-caught fish. All have simple accommodation and offer idyllic seclusion.

Heading N, **Barra de Navidad** (56km/35 miles) is a pleasant place to spend a few days doing nothing very much, and is more peaceful than nearby **San Patricio Melaque** (3km/1 mile N). A fishing village strung out along a sandbar between the ocean and a freshwater lagoon, Barra is attracting low-key development, with plenty of lower-priced hotels. The surf is strong: not for beginners.

PUERTO VALLARTA

*Map **5**G6. Jalisco. 395km (246 miles) w of Guadalajara on RF15 and RF200; 171km (106 miles) s of Tepic on RF200; 260km (162 miles) N of Manzanillo on RF200. Population: 300,000. Served by air (international airport 11km/6 miles N), bus and ferry (21hrs to La Paz, Baja California)* **i** *Palacio Municipal, Juárez and Independencia, on Zócalo ☎(322) 20242–4. US Consul: Farian del Puente 12A ☎(322) 20069. American Express: Centro Comercial Villa Vallarta H6 ☎(322) 26876/7.*

The badly-kept secret of Puerto Vallarta's delights finally leaked out in the early 1970s, and in no time a picture-book fishing village blossomed into one of the country's top five resorts. It all began during the local filming of *Night of the Iguana,* when (offscreen) Richard Burton and Elizabeth Taylor titillated the world's voyeurs with an extravagant premarital dalliance. With such a start, an international airport was bound to follow.

All the same, the town, with its narrow streets and low red-tiled houses, has kept most of its charm. During the high season, from November to April, it is hugely popular.

Most of the old houses are on the N bank of the Río Cuale, which flows into the Bahía de Banderas under the "Gringo Gulch" cliffs, named after the wealthy foreign community that followed in the footsteps of the superstars to settle in luxury eyries above the town and bay. The island in the river, the **Isla Río Cuale**, is linked to the mainland by bridges to the N and S, and contains a pleasant **park**, an **archeological museum** and an **outdoor market**.

Across the bridge to the N is the busy **Mercado Municipal**. The older hotels and restaurants are mostly in the commercial district to the N, although some of the less expensive establishments are in the blocks to the S of the Cuale. The luxury hotels are on the beaches on both sides of town, and thus do not set the tone of the place.

The atmosphere in "P.V." (as it is known) is less hectic than that at Acapulco, although far from inhibited or unsophisticated. Further development may change this, however, with several large marina and condominium developments planned or in progress along the nearby coastline, especially to the N.

But for the time being, life in P.V. carries on at its own pace. With its 10,000 hotel rooms playing host to a million tourists a year, it is certainly no undiscovered hideaway; but it somehow avoids being an out-and-out tourist-exploitation machine.

BEACHES AND ACTIVITIES

As might be expected from a luxury resort, every imaginable watersport is available. It is also possible to arrange riding in the hills behind the town. As always, hotels are the best source of advice. There is a new **golf club**, for which hotels can arrange temporary membership.

The beaches

The main beach is the **Playa de los Muertos** (Beach of the Dead) to the S of the Río Cuale, named after an unseemly episode involving pirates during the 17thC. The name was thought unduly morbid for P.V.'s new fame, however, and was recently changed to **Playa del Sol**, although the old name has stuck.

As for the other beaches, the farther you go out of town, the more square meters of sand you get per person and the fewer services and activities are available. Among the best are **Playa de Oro**, stretching N toward the airport, and **Mismaloya** *(11km/6 miles s)*, now suffering from unplanned development, where *Night of the Iguana* was shot. The latter is best reached by boat from the *malecón* (waterfront); on the way, don't miss **Los Arcos**, the famous rock arches that rise up from the sea.

For an unspoiled coastline, drive the 40km (25 miles) N to **Playa Destiladeras** on Punta de Mita, at the N end of the bay, which has excellent coral beaches. Or take a day cruise to the fishing villages to the S, of which the most important is **Yelapa** (two hours away). Here you can either laze around in the sun, eating fresh grilled fish, or follow the river through the village to an impressive waterfall, about half an hour's walk inland, where the water drops 20m (66 feet) into a lovely pool.

Yelapa is no longer such a small place, its population boosted by some 500 emigrés from the US; and it is almost busy during the 11am–3pm high peak. To enjoy the calm that descends once the boats have departed, bring a hammock to sleep in, and consider traveling on to the smaller, quieter nearby villages of **Quimixto** and **Las Animas**, reached by boat from Yelapa.

WHERE TO STAY

CAMINO REAL 🏨
Playa las Estacas ☎*(322) 30123* Ⓕ*(322)*
30070, or in US ☎*(800) 228 3000* 🛏
337 rms ⩵ ⚲ ⬳ ⛆ ♨ ⚐ 🛎 ☕ ⚑
⊙ ♫

A luxury beach resort s of town with
lively and well-organized sports and social arrangements.

CONRAD PUERTO VALLARTA
Paseo de la Marina, Marina Vallarta
☎*(322) 11100* Ⓕ*(322) 11121* 🛏 *200*
rms ⩵ ⚲ ⬳ ⛆ ♨ ⚐ 🛎 :/ ⬤ ☕ ⚓

This huge hotel, stretching along 250m
of beach, offers all the usual palm-
shaded pools and sports facilities at two
thirds the price of some of its rivals.

FIESTA AMERICANA PLAZA
VALLARTA 🏨
Playa las Glorias ☎*(322) 24448* Ⓕ*(322)*
25236 🛏 *434 rms* ⩵ ⚲ ⬳ ⛆ ♨ 🛎
☕ ⊙

A well-appointed luxury hotel; home to
the John Newcombe Tennis Club, with
12 courts.

FIESTA AMERICANA PUERTO
VALLARTA 🏨
Playa los Tules ☎*(322) 22010* Ⓕ*(322)*
42108 🛏 *291 rms* ⩵ ⚲ ⬳ ⛆ ♨ ⚐
⚑ :/ 🛎 ☕ ♫

A spectacular modern pyramid on the
beautiful Los Tules beach, sophisticated
and luxurious.

GARZA BLANCA 🏨
Playa Palo María ☎*(322) 21083* Ⓕ*(322)*
21268 🛏 *80 rms* ⩵ ⚲ ⬳ ⛆ ♨
⚐ ☕ ⊙ ♫

This exclusive resort with beachfront
cottages comprises the main hotel on
the quiet, clean beach.

HYATT CORAL GRAND
Km 8.5 on coast road s ☎*(322) 30707*
Ⓕ*(322) 30609, or in US* ☎*(800) 223*
1234 🛏 *120 rms* ⩵ ⚲ ⬳ ⛆ ♨ ⚐
☕ ⊙ ♫ ⛵

A pink palace on the beach set in lovely
tropical gardens; suites only, some with
private whirlpool.

KRYSTAL VALLARTA 🏨
Playa Vallarta ☎*(322) 21459* Ⓕ*(322)*
40222 🛏 *432 rms* ⩵ ⚲ ⬳ ⛆ ♨ ⚐
🛎 ☕ :/ ⬤ ⊙ ♫

The Krystal has perhaps the most character of all the big deluxe hotels in
Puerto Vallarta. It occupies a rambling
complex of tennis courts, gardens,
swimming pools and villas, spread
across 32 acres.

QUINTA REAL
Pelicanos 311, Marina Vallarta ☎*(322)*
10800 Ⓕ*(322) 10801* 🛏 *466 rms*
⩵ ⚲ ⬳ ⛆ ♨ :/ ⚑ ☕ ♫

This expensive new hotel is sited away
from the beach, but right on the golf
course instead.

VILLA DEL PALMAR
Km 3, Paseo de las Palmas ☎*(322)*
40904 Ⓕ*(322) 46837* 🛏 *541 rms* ⩵
⚲ ⬳ ⛆ ♨ ⚐ 🛎 :/ ⬤ ☕

A large and well-equipped beach hotel
that offers competitive rates for its
standard, with a wide range of facilities
available.

Budget hotels

In addition to the luxury hotels listed above, there are numerous more
modest establishments, many of them on the beach. **Las Palmas** (♥
Km 2.5 on road to airport ☎*(322) 20650* 🛏 *153 rms* ⩵ ⬳ ☕ ⚐
⊙*)* offers excellent beachside quality for the price, as do the clifftop
Playa Conchas Chinas (*Km 2.5 on RF200 to Mismaloya* ☎*(322)*
20156 🛏 *55 rms* ⩵ ☕ ⬳*)*, **Playa Los Arcos** (*Olas Altas 380*
☎*(322) 21583* Ⓕ*(322) 20583* 🛏 *to* 🛏 *146 rms* ⩵ ☕ ⬳*)*,which
is fun if not quite "smart," and the **Buenaventura** (*Av. México 1301*
☎*(322) 23737* Ⓕ*(322) 46400* 🛏 *210 rms* ⩵ ☕ ⬳*)*, just five
minutes from the center.

Even lower prices prevail downtown, away from the beach. Try **Posada de Roger** *(Basilio Badillo 237* ☎ *(322) 20836* Ex *(322) 30482* ▯ *52 rms* ══ ✿✿*)*, a block from Playa Los Muertos; **Yasmin** *(Basilio Badillo 168* ☎ *(322) 20087* ▯ *27 rms)*, plain but clean, also a block from the beach; or **Posada Río Cuale** *(Serdán 242, s of the river* ☎ *(322) 20450* ▯ *22 rms* ══ ♈ ✿✿*)*.

In Yelapa (see page 181), stay at the **Lagunita** *(reservations: Venezuela 309* ☎ *(322) 21932* ▯ ══ ♈ ✿✿*)*, an easy-going village of beachside *cabañas*.

EATING AND DRINKING

The luxury hotels all have excellent (and expensive) restaurants. The **Fiesta Americana** and **Krystal** win the most acclaim, the Sunday afternoon buffet with *mariachi* music at the **Camino Real** is always fun, and **El Set** *(* ⌂ *at the Conchas Chinas* ☎ *(322) 20302* ▦ ◁€ *)*, dramatically situated on a cliff-top, is popular for sunset cocktails.

The dominant fare in P.V. is, of course, seafood, available in abundance at **Moby Dick** *(31 de Octubre 128* ☎ *(322) 21444* ▯ *)*, reckoned to have the best seafood in town; but the more Mexican **Balam** *(Basilio Badillo 425* ☎ *(322) 23451* ▯ *)* is nearly as good, and much less expensive. Also good for fresh seafood is **La Palapa** *(Pulpito and Olas Altas above Playa de Los Muertos* ☎ *(322) 25225* ▯ *)*, with its great sunset views and occasional *mariachis*.

Seafood is only one part of the joke-filled menu at the lively **Carlos O'Brian's** *(Malecón 286* ☎ *(322) 21444* ▦ *)*. Nearly as rumbustious is **La Hacienda** *(Aguacate 274* ☎ *(322) 20590* ▯ *)*, where the specialty is flaming your dinner to the sound of live music. **Andale** *(Olas Altas 425* ☎ *(322) 21054* ▯ *)* combines an elegant Italian-Mexican restaurant with a popular bar. Another good place for a night out is the **Hard Rock Café** *(Díaz Ordaz 652* ☎ *(322) 25532* ▯ *)*.

At **Chez Elena** *(* ⌂ *Hotel los Cuatro Vientos, Matamoros 520* ☎ *(322) 20161* ▦ ◁€ *)*, in the hills above the town, the adventure is as much in getting there as in the interesting food. Jazz lovers will enjoy **Le Bistro** *(on Isla Río Cuale* ☎ *(322) 20283* ▯ *)*, an elegant restaurant with a gourmet menu, with jazz quartets in the evenings; nearby, a less expensive alternative is **Franzi's** *(* ▯ *)*.

Out of town, **Chico's Paradise** *(20km/12 miles s on RF200* ▦ ✿ ◁€ *)* is a "tropical fantasy" beach restaurant in luxuriant jungle near waterfalls, serving simple, enjoyable food; on the way there, look in at **Chee Chee's** *(Boca de Tomatlán* ☎ *(322) 20920* ▯ ✿✿*)*, with its own pool and other entertainments.

P.V. BY NIGHT

Ask your hotel for details of beach parties, shows and fiestas at other hotels. Some of the best discos and nightclubs are at the main hotels: the CAMINO REAL has the loudest rock-and-roll; the FIESTA AMERICANA has its well-equipped **Friday López** disco club; another current favorite is the KRYSTAL'S **Christine**. There are piano bars with entertainment and dancing at the FIESTA AMERICANA and **Playa de Oro** *(Las Garzas 1)*.

Other discos include: **Sundance** *(Lázaro Cárdenas 329 at Insurgentes* ▥*),* for elegant decor and high decibels; the hi-tech **Cactus** *(Vallarta 399 and Dieguez* ☎*(322) 26077* ▥*);* and **The City Dump** *(Ignacio Vallarta 278* ☎*(322) 20719* ▥*),* open until very late and popular with the young and seriously trendy; outrageous elegance is the style here.

TEPIC

*Map **5**F6. Capital of Nayarit. 226km (141 miles) NW of Guadalajara on RF15; 171km (106 miles) N of Puerto Vallarta on RF200; 290km (181 miles) S of Mazatlán on RF15. Population: 200,000. Served by air, train (on Guadalajara–Nogales line) and bus* ***i*** *Av. México 32 Sur at Del Ejército* ☎*(321) 29545/6.*

Tepic was founded in 1542 on the fertile slopes of the extinct volcano Sanguangüey, but its position on the edge of the mountain territory of the marauding Huichol and Cora Indians prevented the town from prospering until after the 1910 Revolution, when the railroad arrived.

On the central square is the 18thC **cathedral**, in the Neo-Gothic style. At the W end of the main drag, Avenida México, is the church of **Santa Cruz**, built in 1744 by the site of a miraculous growth of **grass** in the shape of a cross in the middle of bare ground, which can still be seen. The more Christianized of the Huichols come here to venerate the cross.

Those who admire the Huichol beads and costumes can purchase them from shops and vendors around the Zócalo, and examples of Huichol and Cora weaving and artifacts can be seen at the **Museo Regional de Antropología e Historia** *(México 91 Nte at Zapata* ☎ *(321) 21900, open 9am-2pm, 4-6pm; closed Mon),* together with local archeological finds. The **ceramic figures** from Ixtlán del Río are highly expressive.

Visitors to the wild Huichol mountains will need an official permit *(issued from the Palacio de Gobierno),* and should bear in mind that the Huichols remain a proud and unconquered people. Visits can be arranged through the tourist office.

ENVIRONS OF TEPIC

Ahuacatlán

75km (47 miles) S on RF15.

The small 16thC **monastery** here is a good place in which to stop off briefly and enjoy the shade of the cloister. A short distance beyond the town you will encounter an extraordinary desolate moonscape of black sands and twisted rocks, left behind by the 1885 eruption of nearby **Monte Ceboruco**.

☜ **Fray Junípero Serra** *(Lerdo 124 Pte* ☎ *(321) 22525* ▣ *(321) 22051* ▥ *90 rms* ⊟ ♈ ▦*)* is a big hotel on the Zócalo; **Alta Mirano** *(Minas 19* ☎*(321) 27131* ▥*)* and **Sierra de Alicia** *(México and Lerdo, no* ☎ ▢*)* are also good and central. **La Loma** *(Paseo de la Loma 301* ☎*(321) 32222* ▥ ▦ ⊟ ♈ ⬟ ⬥*)* is a modern motel.

▄▄ Many of the town's best restaurants are lined up along Insurgentes (RF15); these include **El Farallón** *(Insurgentes 276 Pte* ☎ *(321) 31124* ▥*)* for seafood; **Roberto's** *(Insurgentes at Paseo de la Luna* ☎ *(321) 33005* ▥*)* for international cuisine; and **La Terraza** *(* ♣ *Insurgentes 98 Pte* ☎ *(321) 32180* ▥ *)*, an unpretentious wayside diner. Downtown, **Wendy's** *(México 178 Nte* ☎ *(321) 26067* ▥*)* is a good snack bar, open all day.

EXCURSIONS
Mexicaltitlán
97km (60 miles) NW; turn W off RF15 after 57km (35 miles).

As you drive N, there are several roads leading down to tropical beaches and little fishing villages, including SAN BLAS. At 57km (35 miles), a turn W leads through **Santiago Escuintla** down to the amazing village of Mexicaltitlán, built, with radiating streets, on a circular island some $\frac{1}{2}$ km ($\frac{1}{4}$ mile) across in the mangrove swamps. In Santiago Escuintla, visit the **Huichol Culture Centre** *(20 de Noviembre at Constitución* ☎ *(323) 51171).*

Mexicaltitlán is a 15-minute boat journey from the pier at **La Batanga**, served by bus from Tepic via Escuintla. Some academics believe that the Aztecs originated here, but there is little evidence one way or the other. Every June 29, there is a **canoe race** round the island, followed by cheerful celebrations to mark the feast of St Peter and St Paul.

⌖ The nearest accommodation is around the Zócalo at Escuintla, for example, the **Casino** *(Ocampo 40* ☎ *(323) 50850* ▥*)* or the **Vallarta** *(Hidalgo 2 Juárez* ☎ *(323) 50280* ▥*)*

RF15 southwest to Guadalajara
This scenic road, at its best near Tepic, weaves its way among volcanoes and passes several places of interest. One pleasant spot is **Santa María del Oro** *(after 32km/20 miles turn 11km/6 miles E),* a village near a lovely volcanic lake. Stay in a lakeside cabin among the fruit trees at the English-run **Koala** *(* ☎ *(321) 23772* ▥*).*

Ixtlán del Río *(after 87km/54 miles)* is worth stopping at to visit the remains of a large Toltec-influenced Post-Classic **ceremonial center** *(4km/2 miles S of the modern town),* most of it unexcavated. The ceramic finds are mostly in Tepic's regional Museum. For details of further places of interest along this road, see GUADALAJARA, on page 176.

SAN BLAS
Map 5F6. Nayarit. 69km (43 miles) W of Tepic: 34km (21 miles) N on RF15, then 35km (21 miles) SW. Population: 25,000. Served by bus.

When Cancún, Ixtapa and Huatulco were selected to become Mexico's space-age resorts, lovers of San Blas could breathe again. It is a sleepy place, surrounded by the palm-shaded ruins of great colonial mansions. Up on a hill overlooking the town are the remains of a **fortress**, built as a defense against the depredations of ruthless English buccaneers; San Blas was the home port for galleons arriving from the Far East with precious cargoes, and thus came under frequent attack.

Nowadays the only ships using the port are deep-sea fishing launches, the occasional yacht, and motor boats off on daily trips around the jungle lagoons and estuaries. Your hotel, or the marina, can arrange fishing trips, and boats for the jungle leave from the waterfront beneath the fort: there are more than 300 species of bird to be spotted here, so bring binoculars. One word of caution: the local wildlife includes an impressive diversity of mosquitoes; come armed with insect repellant.

Although nightlife is developing in San Blas, with a few discos open in the tourist season, the nearby beaches and their excellent surfing waves remain the main attraction. For the authentic shipwrecked experience, head for the still undeveloped **Playa de Matanchén**, 4km (2 miles) down the coast. Another good beach is **Playa del Rey**, on the spit of land across the water from the port — best reached by boat.

☜ **Las Brisas** *(Cuauhtémoc 106 Sur* ☎*(321) 50112* ▦ ≋ ▦ ⊒ ❤*)*, modern and bright, has parrots squawking in the pleasant gardens. **Posada del Rey** *(Campeche 10* ☎*(321) 50123* ▦ ≋ ⊒ ⵏ*)* is a small hotel with a lovely rooftop restaurant and bar. **Misión San Blas** *(Cuauhtémoc s/n* ☎*(321) 50023* ▦ ⊒ ≋*)* is located on the edge of a lagoon and is a useful motel for fishermen. The **Marino Inn Motel** *(Batallón and Las Islitas* ☎*(321) 50340* ▦ ≋ ▦ ◉ ⊒ ⵏ*)* has all the essential facilities, even if it is slightly deficient in charm.

For more of a sense of history, try **Los Flamingos** *(Juárez 163* ☎*(321) 50448* ▦ ⊒*)*, an older hotel built around a flower-filled courtyard, or **El Bucanero** *(Juárez 75 Pte* ☎*(321) 50101* ▦ ≋*)*, a romantically crumbling 19thC mansion.

⊒ Perhaps San Blas' most memorable restaurant is **McDonald's** *(Juárez 75 Pte* ☎*(321) 50432* ▦*)* — no relation — which serves excellent seafood, and has an upstairs bar with live music. **La Isla**, also known as **Chez Tony's** *(Mercado Sur and Paredes* ☎*(321) 50407* ▦*)*, is also known for its seafood and marine decor.

Of the hotel restaurants, **Posada del Rey** *(*▦*)* and **Las Brisas** *(*▦*)* are particularly recommended. And you need not be frightened to sample grilled fish from the little restaurants along the beach — it is all fresh, and very good value.

North of Mexico City

To the north, and slightly to the west of Mexico City, lies Mexico's colonial heartland. Rich in precious metals and graceful colonial buildings, it comprises the states of **Querétaro**, **Guanajuato**, **Aguascalientes**, **Zacatecas** and **San Luis Potosí**.

This part of the country was of great importance in colonial times, because of its mineral wealth. The primary purpose of the Viceroyalty of New Spain was to supply the mother country with silver, which was then promptly squandered on ruinous European wars and subsidies to the perpetually strained Spanish exchequer. The rich mines of this region provided the bulk of that silver, making it the biggest silver producer in the world.

One legacy of this is a wealth of colonial architecture that is unique in Mexico: vast, echoing monasteries and convents, and well-preserved silver-mining towns with sumptuous mansions, ornate public buildings, lavish churches and elegant squares.

QUERÉTARO

This area of Mexico was also pivotal in the fight for independence. By the early 19th century, the Mexican-born Spaniards of the "Bajío" states of Querétaro and Guanajuato were the leaders of the colonial revolt. **QUERÉTARO**, in 1810, was Mexico's first city to declare independence, the cry spreading across the Bajío and to the rest of the country.

Today, the proximity of Querétaro to Mexico City has made it a focus for industrial development, with factories spreading fast over the productive agricultural land that surrounds it. But the wealth generated in this way has at least meant that its colonial center is well looked after, and the city is well worth a visit.

GUANAJUATO

The neighboring state of Guanajuato is larger than Querétaro, and much of its industry is concentrated around **LEÓN**. Its finest cities, **SAN MIGUEL DE ALLENDE** and the state capital, **GUANAJUATO**, have thus been left relatively intact.

Out of the way and squeezed into a steep valley, Guanajuato is a lovely place in which to spend a few days exploring the historic sites. But its peaceful, civilized ambience belies its past. Its mines once produced a third of the world's silver, worked by the forced labor of the local Otomí and other Indians, and many of its finest buildings ran with blood during the war of independence.

Pride of place in the state goes to San Miguel de Allende, with its expatriate community of artists, writers and retired people living among its narrow cobbled streets, gracious colonial buildings and shaded gardens. There can be few more pleasant places to learn Spanish than at one of San Miguel's many language schools, but you might have little cause to break out of English once outside the classroom.

AGUASCALIENTES

The climate gets drier to the north, but the tiny state of Aguascalientes still enjoys productive agriculture and some splendid landscapes. The city of **AGUASCALIENTES** itself is attractive but hardly special, except for its hot springs and the labyrinth of tunnels below, unfortunately closed.

ZACATECAS

Marking the division between the fertile lands to the south, and the windswept high plains of northern Mexico, is **ZACATECAS**, the attractive capital of its state at the north of the region. In colonial times this was the outer extremity of civilization, and the only reason for going this far was for the fabulous seams of silver ore in the surrounding mountains.

Spanish prospectors discovered silver here in 1546, after noting the silver ornaments of the local Zacateco Indians. Mining began two years later, once the Indians were defeated and enrolled for service in the mines. Unable to take the pace of endless underground toil, they rapidly perished and had to be replaced by others from farther afield. To get an idea of the conditions they endured, visit the gruesome **El Eden** mine, which is open to visitors.

SAN LUIS POTOSÍ

Across to the east, San Luis Potosí is an extensive state, once again dominated by mining, except for the eastern area, which makes up the **Huasteca** (see CIUDAD VALLES, pages 212-3). It has only one city of importance; its capital, **SAN LUIS POTOSÍ**.

Silver was discovered here in 1592, an event that led rapidly to the subjugation and enslavement of the Guachichil Indians of the area. Subsequently the capital of northern Mexico, and indeed of the entire republic for part of the 19th century, San Luis Potosí remains an important commercial center, even if its national significance has diminished. This attractive city is a good place to break your journey for a few days.

But the state's most fascinating destination is **REAL DE CATORCE**, a not-quite-abandoned mining town in the high, desert north. It is now enjoying a modest resurgence as discerning visitors come to experience the faded charm of its intact 18th and 19th-century buildings, and stay at its friendly hotels.

Towns, cities and cultural sites

Starting in **SAN JUAN DEL RÍO**, this chapter gives essential information on the following places, which are arranged to follow a roughly S–N route through the region: **QUERÉTARO, CELAYA, SAN MIGUEL DE ALLENDE, GUANA-JUATO, DOLORES HIDALGO, LEÓN, AGUASCALIENTES, ZACATECAS, SAN LUIS POTOSÍ** and **REAL DE CATORCE**.

See USING THIS GUIDE on page 50 for details on how to use this section. On the following pages, helpful pointers are given on how to get to each of the destinations covered. Along with the MEXICO map on pages 46–7, and the 4-color maps at the back of this book, they should give all the information necessary for planning your trip to this part of Mexico.

SAN JUAN DEL RÍO

Map 11D6. Querétaro. 168km (105 miles) NW of Mexico City on RF57 and RF45; 52km (32 miles) SE of Querétaro on RF57. Population: 50,000. Served by train (on Mexico City–Querétaro line) and bus i Niños Heroes and Morelos, Tequisquiapán ☎(467) 30757.

Until the new toll road to Querétaro was opened, the country's main N to S road passed through the center of this colonial town. This made it an important center for handicrafts, but it was noisy, dusty and crowded. Now returned to a more tranquil existence, it remains the best place in Mexico to buy semiprecious stones.

Around the Zócalo and on the main street are innumerable shops selling opals, amethysts, aquamarines and other stones from all over Latin America. It is known also for the local basket-work, cheese and wine: inexpensive wine can be bought by the case at the **Cavas de San Juan**, about 1km ($\frac{1}{2}$ mile) out of town toward the spa town of Tequisquiapán.

EVENTS • 24 June is the festival of **San Juan Bautista**, when the saint is taken on a joyous procession from church to river for his annual bath.

WITHIN EASY DISTANCE

Tequisquiapán
20km (12 miles) from San Juan del Río on RF120.

RF120 leads NE through the land of the Otomí Indians and up into the wild mountains of the Sierra Gorda toward Ciudad Valles. The Otomí village of **Tequisquiapán** is the official center of Mexico, but since becoming a fashionable weekend resort it has lost much of its charm.

Every weekend thousands of people arrive to bathe in the hot volcanic springs, said to cure everything from arthritis to insomnia. The best advice is to visit during the week, when it is less crowded. At the latest count there were 22 hotels. Inquire at the tourist office for details and directions.

The Five Churches of the Sierra Gorda
N on RF120 from Tequisquiapán.

To the N of Tequisquiapán is the **Sierra Gorda**, once inhabited by wild and rebellious Jonace Indians, who were never conquered by the Aztecs, and submitted to the Spanish only in the mid-18thC. The missionaries who took on the dangerous task of evangelizing the area built five churches, known as "The Five Churches of the Sierra Gorda," all within a day's walk of each other.

The two finest are on the main road at **Jalpán de Serra** *(181km/113 miles from Tequesquiapán, at the junction with RF62 to Río Verde)*, named after Fray Junipero Serra, who led the area's evangelization before moving on to Baja California, and at **Landa** *(20km/12 miles E)*. Both churches have profusely decorated Baroque facades. The other three are at **Tancoyol** *(17km/10 miles E of Jalpán on RF62, then 16km/10 miles N)*, **Concá** *(34km/21 miles W of Jalpán, then 1km/$\frac{1}{2}$ mile S)* and **Tilaco** *(10km/6 miles E of Jalpán on RF120, then 16km/10 miles S)*.

The side roads are rough, and there are few really good places to stay until Ciudad Valles.

❧ **Mansión Galindo** *(8km/5 miles N of San Juan on RF57, turn left (S) toward Amealco for 5km/3 miles* ☎*(467) 20050* Ⓕⓧ*(467) 21486, or in Mexico City* ☎*(5) 533 3350* ▥ *177 rms* ☲ ▥ ❤ ⚘ ♨ ✦ ⬆ ✦ ● ♪ ▲*)* is a former luxury weekend resort in a beautifully restored hacienda, once owned by Cortés, and subsequently a monastery; it now has modern wings.

Even grander, the **Estancia de San Juan** *(8km/5 miles N of San Juan on RF57* ☎*(467) 20120* Ⓕⓧ*(467) 23235, or in Mexico City* ☎*(5) 514 5721* ▥ *108 rms* ▥ ❤ ⚘ ✦ ⬆ ♨ ⬆ ▲*)* has fine old buildings and beautiful gardens.

At Tequisquiapán *(20km/12 miles NE of San Juan del Río)*, **Las Cavas** *(Media Luna 8* ☎*(467) 30804* ▥ *90 rms)* is the best hotel. **Balneario el Relox** *(Morelos 8 Nte, near Zócalo* ☎*(467) 30066* ▥*)*, **Las Delicias** *(Prol. 5 de Mayo s/n* ☎*(467) 30180* ▥*)* and **La Querencia** *(Juarez Ote s/n* ☎*(467) 30111* ▥*)* are all good spa hotels *(all have* ☲ ⚘ ▼ ❤ ▲*)*.

At Jalpán, **Posada Junipero Serra** is a pleasant place to stay the night, but go to the **Hacienda San Nicolas** *(⚘)* in Concá if you are planning a longer stay. There are no phones at either, but the Querétaro tourist office may be able to obtain reservations.

QUERÉTARO

Map 10C5. Capital of Querétaro. 215km (134 miles) NW of Mexico City on RF57 and RF45, 63km (39 miles) SE of San Miguel de Allende on RF111 and RF57, 202km (126 miles) S of San Luis Potosí on RF57, 150km (93 miles) SE of Guanajuato on RF110 and RF45. Altitude: 1,970m (6,461ft). Population: 800,000. Served by air, train (on Mexico City line to San Luis Potosí, Guadalajara and Zacatecas, tracks diverging after Querétaro) and bus i on Zocaló at 5 de Mayo 62 ☎(42) 140179. American Express: Av. Technologico 118–1 ☎(42) 161500.

Although set in an unattractive industrial hinterland that threatens to spread far into the Bajío, Querétaro is one of Mexico's most handsome colonial cities. Required to house some of the capital's overflowing multitudes, it is paying a high price for its rapid growth. But the historic center has been turned into a pedestrian zone, and some of the revenues from industry have been used to restore older buildings.

Querétaro has been at the center of events in Mexican history ever since the conspiracy to overthrow the Spanish was hatched here in the years leading up to the Proclamation of Independence on September 16, 1810. The plotters were warned of their impending arrest by the sympathetic wife of the local provost, and fled to nearby DOLORES HIDALGO to start the struggle. By the time independence was achieved in 1821, they were nearly all dead, although the *Corregidora,* as she was known, lived on to a ripe old age.

Later, in 1848, it was in Querétaro that the treaty handing over Texas and New Mexico to the US was signed. Also here, the would-be Emperor Maximilian was executed in 1867 after his defeat nearby by Benito Juárez. In 1917, after the Revolution, the new Constitution was drawn up in the town's **Teatro de la Republica**, then the seat of Congress. Finally, in 1927, Mexico's dominant political party was founded here; it has ruled ever since, now known as the Party of Institutional Revolution (PRI).

WHAT TO SEE

The center

The main square, with its pretty little **Jardín Obregón**, is about four blocks N of the large **Alameda Park**. At its center is an ornate cast-iron bandstand where concerts are given on Thursday and Sunday evenings *(7.30-9pm).* Just S of here, along Juárez, is the small **Plaza de la Constitución**, ringed by stone posts each bearing the name of a state of Mexico, and commemorating the writing of the 1917 Constitution.

The square is dominated by the church of **San Francisco**, with its fertility-inducing statue of Christ, and in the large adjacent 17thC monastery is the **Museo Regional** (▨ *open 10am-3.30pm, 4-6pm; closed Mon).* It has a collection of bizarre historical memorabilia, such as the actual keyhole through which the *Corregidora* whispered her warning to the plotters, and also collections of colonial paintings and other assorted relics.

Leave the square along 5 de Mayo; on the arcaded Plaza Independencia can be seen the actual **Casa de la Corregidora**, now the

Palacio Municipal. Unless some function is taking place, you can view the room in which the *Corregidor* imprisoned his wife in a vain attempt to prevent her warning the plotters of their danger.

Plaza de Santa Clara
One block w of the Plaza de la Constitución, along Madero.

Once the forecourt of Mexico's wealthiest convent, Plaza de Santa Clara is now a small garden. The **church** of Santa Clara has a facade that is almost austere, but inside is a riot of Churrigueresque gold archangels and cherubs. In the center of the square is the beautiful Neoclassical **Fountain of Neptune**, designed in 1797 by the Bajío's own architect, Eduardo Tresguerras.

For two blocks around the plaza, there is a heavy concentration of churches, monasteries and mansions. Stroll around and visit a few; of particular interest is the **Palacio Federal**, *(Allende 14 Sur, open 11am-6pm; closed Mon)* in an Augustinian monastery of 1731 a block to the s. Now used as the Museo de Arte, it contains much colonial religious art and other contemporary works, but the building itself, with its heavy Baroque ornamentations, is the greater attraction.

The mansion **Casa de los Perros**, behind the Palacio, is decorated with some delightfully ugly gargoyles. One block s and three blocks w along Arteaga, the 18thC church of **Santa Rosa** is extravagantly Baroque, with a strong Moorish influence.

Convento de la Cruz (Monastery of the Cross)
Independencia, 6 blocks E of center. Open 9am–2pm, 4–6pm.

This fine working monastery is named after the miraculous cross that appeared in the sky during an early encounter between the Spaniards and the local Chichimeca Indians in 1531. A chapel and a stone cross were immediately erected, but the monastery was not completed until the late 17thC.

Around the Baroque **cloister** are rooms containing a collection of rare antique books, testifying to the monastery's position as a great center of learning. You can also admire the **miraculous tree** with its cross-shaped thorns, and the **cell** in which the emperor Maximilian was imprisoned before his execution.

A lively religious festival is held at the monastery on September 14.

IF TIME ALLOWS . . .

The spot where the Emperor Maximilian was executed, atop the **Cerro de las Campañas**, 1.5km (1 mile) w of the center, is marked by a statue of his victor, President Benito Juárez, glaring down on the small chapel commemorating Maximilian. Along Ejército Republicano, on the E edge of the town, is the impressive 76-arch **aqueduct**, finished in 1735 and still in use.

꙳ **Casa Blanca** *(Constituyentes 69 Pte* ☎ *(42) 160100* ▥ *62 rms* ⫢ ⩗*)* is a fine choice for one night. The **Holiday Inn** *(*▨ *Constitución 13 Sur* ☎*(42) 160202* [Fx] *(42) 168902* ▥ ⫢ ⩗*)* offers all the modern comforts on the outskirts of town; **Mesón de Santa Rosa** *(Plaza Independencia at Pasteur Sur 17* ☎*(42) 145623* ▥ ⩗ ⫢ ⵏ *)*, a charming conversion of a 16thC townhouse, has a good international restaurant.

Real de Minas *(Constituyentes 124 Pte* ☎*(42) 160444* [Fx]*(42) 160662* ▥ *200 rms* ⊏ ≈) is reliable, with a good restaurant; **Amberes** *(Corregidora Sur 188* ☎*(42) 128604* ▥ ⊏) is a modern high-rise on the Alameda. A less expensive option on the Zócalo is the **Plaza** *(Juárez 23,* ☎*(42) 121138* ▯), or try the more modern **Hidalgo** *(Hidalgo 14, (42) 120081* ▯), a block N.

4km (2 miles) N on the San Luis Potosí road, **Hacienda Jurica** *(* ▥ *Km 229 on RF57* ☎*(42) 180022* [Fx]*(42) 180136* ▥ *to* ▥ *178 rms* ⊏ ⌂ ❣ ⊀ ≈ ♨ ☘ ⚑ ◉ *)* is a beautiful country club hotel in a colonial hacienda.

⊏ **Fonda del Refugio** *(Jardín Corregidora 26* ☎*(42) 120755* ▥*)* serves excellent Mexican cuisine; the nearby **El Cortijo de San Juan** *(Jardín Corregidora 14* ☎*(42) 129708* ▯*)* is less formal and enjoyed by hearty eaters; **La Corregidora** *(near the Zócalo at Corregidora 1* ☎*(42) 141313* ▥*)* specializes in seafood; the **Comedor Vegetariano** *(Vergara 7* ☎*(42) 141088* ▯*)* has excellent Mexican and international vegetarian dishes.

SHOPPING

Querétaro is famous for its **semiprecious stones**. Items of onyx, amethyst and opal are widely sold: chess sets, ashtrays, imitation Pre-Columbiana, and so on. Basket-work is another good buy here.

CELAYA

Map 10C5. Guanajuato. 45km (28 miles) w of Querétaro on RF45 and RF57. Altitude: 1,800m (5,900ft). Population: 180,000. Served by train (on Mexico City–San Luis Potosí line) and bus.

Celaya is a typical town of the Bajío, clean and agreeable, with well-kept parks. At the center of town is the **Jardín Municipal** (Municipal Garden), with the modern colonnaded local government building to one side.

Behind it is the old **Plaza de Armas**, with a famous **Independence monument** designed by Celaya's best-known son, the architect, poet, sculptor and painter Francisco Tresguerras (1759–1833), whose work can be seen all over the town.

Celaya is famous for its *cajeta,* a dish made from caramel, milk and cinnamon. Make sure you try the delicious *crepas con cajeta* at one of the local restaurants.

WHAT TO SEE

Convent and Church of San Francisco ▥
Guadalupe Victoria and Doblado.

Francisco Tresguerras is buried here in the small chapel. The buildings were started in the 17thC, but Tresguerras was responsible for their reconstruction, and the ornate high altar and entire facade of the church are attributed to him.

Templo De Carmen ▥
Obregón and Madero.

This elegant and very un-Mexican Neoclassical church is Tresguerras' most famous work. The *Last Judgment* and other murals in the chapel are his too.

☜ **Mary** *(López Mateos and Zaragoza* ☎*(461) 20629* ▥ ⇌*)* has a locked garage for guests' cars; **Motel Campestre** *(Pan-American Highway Km 264* ☎*(461) 20079* ▥ ⇌ ≋*)* is a convenient stopover; for a more luxurious stay, try the **Celaya Plaza** *(Mateos 1023* ☎*(461) 32052* ▥ ⇌ ≋ ☕ ➤*)*.

SAN MIGUEL DE ALLENDE

Map 10C5. Guanajuato. 63km (39 miles) NW of Querétaro on RF57 and RF111, 40km (25 miles) SE of Dolores Hidalgo on RF51. Altitude: 1,970m (6,463ft). Population: 110,000. Served by train (on Mexico City–Querétaro–San Luis Potosí line) and bus **i** *Plaza Allende near church* ☎*(465) 21747. American Express: Hidalgo 1 Centro* ☎*(465) 21695.*

Not only is San Miguel one of the finest colonial cities of the Bajío, but within that category it also has a unique atmosphere, resulting from the presence of a large number of foreign residents. Unlike other Mexican towns, it offers dog-training classes, Scrabble competitions, a large branch of the American Legion, and a host of other unlikely activities. In the bars or around **El Jardín** (as Plaza Allende is often called), you are bound to run into some of the many artists, writers or retirees who have chosen to make their home in the land of cheap tequila and servants. And who knows . . . You may even be convinced enough to stay and start writing that novel.

In 1938, a Mr Sterling Dickinson founded an art school. Success came after World War II, as returning GIs found that their education grants went farther, s of the border, and the school now offers courses in almost every art medium imaginable. The town was declared a national monument in 1926 and, despite some uncontrolled development on the outskirts, the center has been excellently preserved, thanks largely to the efforts of the foreign community.

The best way to discover the town is to ramble at leisure through the narrow streets — punctuated by frequent stops at the abundant cafés, bars, restaurants, art galleries and craft stores — past enchanting little street-corner fountains, churches great and small, ornately carved facades of colonial mansions, and innumerable flower-filled courtyards glimpsed through open doorways. Finish by sitting under the trees at the Plaza Allende — the central meeting place for everyone.

The square is named in honor of the local hero of the War of Independence, Don Ignacio Allende. He was a creole — a Mexican-born Spaniard — who, along with his fellow conspirators, resented being treated as a second-class citizen by native Spaniards. His career began in the royalist army, but he deserted to become the leader of the peasant army that stormed the towns of DOLORES HIDALGO and GUANAJUATO. After a defeat at CHIHUAHUA in 1811, Allende was executed. He rapidly became a popular martyr, and his memory inspired further revolts until final success was achieved in 1821.

Some useful addresses in San Miguel are: **Academía Hispano Americana** *(Insurgentes 21* ☎*(465) 20349)*, the language school; **Centro Cultural Ignacio Ramirez** *(Calle Canal* ☎*(465) 20289)*, the gallery, museum and art school; **Centro Internacional** *(H. Macias 101 ☎ (465) 20435)*, the school of writing; **Instituto Allende** *(San Antonio 20 ☎ (465) 20190)*; and the **public library** *(Insurgentes 25)*, for both Spanish and English books.

EVENTS • September 29, night before and subsequent weekend, **Day of St Michael the Archangel**. One of Mexico's most riotous, colorful fiestas, celebrated on a Friday. Festivities last all weekend; hotels are full of fun-seekers from Mexico City, so reserve well ahead.

• Other local festivals include **17 January**, when animals are taken to church to be blessed, and **21 January**, Allende's birthday. **Easter week**, **Good Friday** and **Independence Day** (16 September) are also important occasions.

WHAT TO SEE

Plaza Allende (El Jardín)

On the s side of this central square stands the **Parroquía**, a bizarre and towering late 19thC Gothic structure of pink stone, which serves as a good landmark. It is said to

have been designed by an illiterate stonemason, inspired by postcards of the great European churches. Although the interior is quite ordinary, there is an alleged piece of the **True Cross**, and the much revered **Señor de la Conquista**, made of corn paste, to add interest.

On the left of the church is an arcade housing a café and the tourist office. To the right, just to the s of the square, is the **Museo Casa de Allende** *(🖸 open 10am-4pm, Sun 2pm; closed Mon)*, the house where Ignacio Allende was born, with a plaque over the door reading *Hic natus, ubique notus* (Born here, famous everywhere).

Also on the square, on the NW corner, is the most opulent of San Miguel's mansions, the **Casa del Mayorazgo de Canal**, which was built during the

Parroquía, San Miguel de Allende

18thC by the mining dynasty of Canal. One block away to the w, down Calle Canal, is the old convent that houses the **Bellas Artes Cultural Institute**, which has some interesting murals.

The great 12-sided dome of the **church** is said to have been designed by the mason who was responsible for the Parroquía; the postcard, this time, was doubtless of the Duomo in Florence.

195

Plaza de San Francisco

A group of churches embellishes this open square a block N of the Zócalo down the Calle de San Francisco. In the middle of the square is a **statue** of Allende on horseback. The facade of the **church** of San Francisco, built in the late 18thC, is in the ornate Churrigueresque style, but the tower and interior are more coolly Neoclassical.

The largest of the churches is the **Oratorio de San Felipe Neri**, which houses several large **murals** showing the life of San Felipe, attributed to Miguel Cabrera (died 1768), an Indian painter whose work far outclassed that of his Spanish mentors. To the W, facing the vegetable market, lies the small but perfectly formed **Iglesia del Salud**.

Leave the square by Insurgentes, passing a number of churches, each worth a visit, until after five blocks you reach the church of **San Juan de Díos**, facing a large courtyard with a bronze head of *Miguel Hidalgo*.

Instituto Allende

Calzada Ancha de San Antonio 20 ☎*(465) 20190. Open 10am–1pm, 4–7pm. Closed Sun.*

An old hacienda, on the outskirts of town toward Celaya, which is the powerhouse of San Miguel's cultural revolution. It is well worth a visit to find out about cultural events taking place during your stay, and to see its collection of 18thC art. While you are in this area, take a stroll in the **Juárez Park** and up to the **Cerro de los Chorros** (Hill of the Springs), for excellent views of the city.

WITHIN EASY DISTANCE

Atotonilco

16km (10 miles) N*, just* W *of RF51.*

The 18thC monastery, completed in 1740, is a religious shrine that attracts pilgrims from all over Mexico. The profuse and varied decoration of the chapels contains examples of every kind of Mexican popular religious art. This was the first stopping point of the independence army after it left Dolores in 1810, Allende and Hidalgo taking the religious banner of the Virgin of Guadalupe for their battle colors.

On the road to Atotonilco ("place of hot waters" in Nahuatl) are some public hot springs at **Manatiales de Grutas**, where hot springs emerge in a cave *(12km/7 miles)*, and **Tamboada** *(8km/5 miles)*. Visitors may either use these, or use the private facilities of the nearby hotels **Parador del Cortijo** (☎ *(465) 21700)* and **Hacienda Tamboada** (see page 197), which opens its facilities to those who attend its afternoon buffet.

See also DOLORES HIDALGO and GUANAJUATO.

WHERE TO STAY

ARISTOS

San Antonio 30 by Instituto Allende ☎*(465) 20149* ⓕ*(465) 21631, or in Mexico City* ☎*(5) 211 0112* ▥ *85 rms* 🍴 ❧ ⛶ ♈

Homesick Americans will find plenty of company at this colonial-style hotel set in pleasant gardens.

CASA DE SIERRA NEVADA Ⅲ

Hospicio 35 ☎*(465) 20415* ⓕ*(465) 22337* ▥ *22 rms* 🍴 *No cards* ♈

This is a beautiful but excessively formal inn, just one block from the plaza. Reservations are vital; this is where the then US Vice-President George Bush stayed in 1981.

HACIENDA DE LOS FLORES
Hospicio 16 ☎*(465) 21808* ▥ *11 rms*
⇌ *No cards* ⌦ ☘
An intimate hotel with charmingly decorated rooms.

HACIENDA TAMBOADA
8km (5 miles) toward Dolores Hidalgo
☎*(465) 20888* ☒*(465) 21798* ▥ *70 rms* ⇌ ⌂ ⌦ ❦ ♉ ⁂ ✦ ☘ ⚓
A pleasant resort hotel with its own mineral waters and volcanically heated pool. Sunday lunch is a social event *(☎ to inquire about free bus service).*

POSADA LA ERMITA
Calle Real 64 ☎*(465) 20777* ▥ *25 rms* ⇌ ⌦ ☘
Once the home of Mexico's biggest movie star, Cantínflas, this is now a luxurious colonial-style inn.

POSADA SAN FRANCISCO
Plaza Allende 2 ☎*(465) 22425* ☒*(465)*
21466 ▥ *46 rms* ⇌ ☘
This ancient-looking hotel was actually built in the 1950s. Attractions include fireplaces in the larger rooms, and a busy cocktail bar.

RANCHO EL ATASCADERO ♣ ▥
1.5km (1 mile) toward Querétaro ☎*(465) 20206* ☒*(465) 21541* ▥ *51 rms* ⌦ ⁂ ✦ ☘
Expert riding instruction is one of the sporting opportunities provided at this 17thC colonial hacienda. The rooms are large and pleasant, and the hotel runs a minibus service to town.

VILLA JACARANDA ▥
Aldama 53 ☎*(465) 20811* ☒*(465) 20121* ▥ *16 rms* ⇌ ⌦ ☘ ⚓
This 19thC former town house of a Spanish nobleman retains its original furniture, a pleasing touch of style. Most of the rooms come with a private terrace or balcony.

Budget hotels

Decent lower-budget hotels in San Miguel include the **Central** *(Canal 19* ☎*(465) 20851* ▥*)* near the Jardín, the **Casa Carmen** *(Correo 31* ☎*(465) 20844* ▥*)*, and the **Posada Carmina** *(Cuna de Allende s/n,* ☎*(465) 20458* ▥*)*.

EATING AND DRINKING

The best hotel restaurants are at POSADA LA ERMITA, CASA DE SIERRA NEVADA, VILLA JACARANDA and HACIENDA DE LOS FLORES. On weekends, head out for lunch at the HACÍENDA TAMBOADA (see above), and don't forget your swimsuit.

El Patio *(▥ Correo 10* ☎*(465) 20017* ▥*)* is good for both Mexican and continental cuisine. **Mamá Mía** *(Umarán 8* ☎*(465) 22063* ▥*)*, as its name implies, has a delicious selection of pizzas and pasta. It sometimes features live folk music.

Pancho's y Lefty's *(Mesones 99* ☎*(465) 21857* ▥*)* and **La Fragua** *(Cuna de Allende 3* ☎*(465) 21114* ▥*)*, with a lovely old courtyard, both serve Mexican food accompanied by live music until the early hours.

NIGHTLIFE

San Miguel has plenty of discos, bars and restaurants with entertainment (see EATING AND DRINKING), as well as some more earthy dives. A few examples are: the **Laberintos Disco** *(San Antonio 7* ☎*(465) 21706* ▣*)*; **El Jardín** *(San Francisco 4* ☎*(465) 21706* ♪*)*, a sophisticated piano bar; and the loud **El Ring Disco Club** *(Hidalgo 25* ☎*(465) 21998* ▣*)*.

GUANAJUATO ★

Map 10C5. Capital of Guanajuato. 366km (228 miles) NW of Mexico City on RF57, 56km (35 miles) E of León on RF45 and RF110, 150km (93 miles) NW Querétaro on RF45 and RF110, 54km (33 miles) SW of Dolores Hidalgo on RF110. Altitude: 2,050m (6,724ft). Population: 100,000. Served by train (off the main Querétaro–Aguascalientes line) and bus i Juárez and 5 de Mayo ☎(473) 21574 and Plaza de la Paz 14 ☎(473) 20086.

This is a labyrinthine city of narrow streets and small tree-shaded squares, and underneath it all, a strange subterranean road, winding along the bottom of the steep valley in the town's old main sewer. For 250 years, it was the richest city in New Spain, producing a third of the world's silver, and the wealthy mine owners have left their mark in the mansions and richly endowed churches that hide around every corner.

It has also been a seat of learning since the Jesuits opened a university in 1732; this is now housed in a modern building near the Plaza de la Paz, carefully designed to complement the predominant colonial style.

Even when there are no festivals, Guanajuato is a wonderful place to spend a few days, taking in the sights at a leisurely pace, and sitting on the ornate cast-iron benches under the trees in the **Jardín de la Unión** drinking coffee and chatting to the students, who are often keen to practice their English. Explore the town on foot, but only after you have driven around the **Carretera Panorámica**, the road that makes almost a full circuit of the city high in the surrounding mountains.

The best view is from the statue of *El Pípila,* a local hero from the War of Independence, which can also be reached by 10 minutes' energetic climbing up a steep lane signposted off Juárez.

Getting around Guanajuato can be confusing, especially if encumbered with a car. There is no Zócalo as such, but a series of charming gardens and *plazuelas*. These run E–W along the main street, Avenida Juárez, in the order Jardín Reforma, Plaza de la Paz, and Jardín Unión.

EVENTS • Every year, in spring, costumed students put on a series of weekend performances of **Spanish one-act plays** *(entremeses)* by writers such as Lope de Vega or Cervantes. The Plaza de San Roque is candlelit for the outdoor performances. Not to be missed, even by non-Spanish speakers; tickets in advance from the Teatro Juárez.

• In October and early November, the more serious **International Cervantes Festival** is held. Theater groups and orchestras from all over the world perform in the squares and the two theaters. The festival lasts for three weeks, and hotel rooms must be reserved months in advance.

• An alternative is to catch the free student performances in the Plazuela San Roque, held at 8pm on Sunday nights in term-time.

• There are also many religious fiestas of interest, usually featuring processions, dances and fireworks. Dates include: Last Friday of Lent, **Fiesta de las Flores**, held in the morning in the Jardín Unión; **Easter**; May 21–31, **Feast of the Virgin of Guanajuato**; July 4, **Feast of the Virgen del Refugio**; November 7–14, the colorful **Fiesta de las Illuminaciones**; at **Christmas**, candlelit processions through the streets. For details of all of these, check at the tourist office.

WHAT TO SEE

Plaza de la Paz

The wealth of the town is amply displayed in the 18thC and 19thC palaces around the square, but most of all in **La Parroquía** (𝗺), a 17thC church with a magnificent yellow facade. Inside is a highly venerated wooden **statue of the Virgin** sent as a gift by Philip II of Spain in 1557, and known to have been in existence since the 8thC, making her the oldest Christian statue in Mexico. She stands on a pedestal of solid silver, and her robes are liberally studded with precious stones.

Jardín de la Union

This is Guanajuato's most popular square, always full of life. Its main building is the **Teatro Juárez** (𝗺), an extraordinary Neoclassical building finished in 1903. Even if you are not attending a performance, it is worth persuading the doorman to let you look inside at the plush extravaganza of red velvet, brass lamps, ornate carving and intricate cast-iron railings. In the interests of symmetry, the roof-line statues of the *Muses* are supplemented by a tenth member.

The church of **San Diego**, next to the Teatro Juárez, has a fine Churrigueresque doorway.

To the N on Pocitos is the church of **La Compañía**, built in 1747–65 by the Jesuits who ran the university. Its great dome dominates the city, and its Baroque facade, with three ornate doorways, is one of the best in the country.

NW along Pocitos, past the modern University, is the **Museo del Pueblo** *(open 10am-2pm, 4-7pm; closed Mon),* a small museum of ancient and contemporary art created by the muralist Chavez Morado. After another kilometer you reach the **Museo Rivera** *(Pocitos 47 𝗺 open Tues-Sat 10am-1pm, 4-6pm, Sun 10am-2.30pm; closed Mon),* where the muralist Diego Rivera was born in 1886. It retains its family furniture, and a permanent exhibition of his smaller works.

Alhóndiga de Granaditas

Pocitos at Calle 5 de Mayo 𝗺 Open 9am–2pm, 4–6pm; Sun 10am–4pm. Closed Mon.

A massive, grim stone structure with horizontal slit windows, built by the Spanish as a grain warehouse, which dominates the hill above the market and tourist office.

During the War of Independence, the royalists were besieged here by Hidalgo's revolutionary mob. It seemed that they could manage to hold out indefinitely, when a young miner, nicknamed *El Pípila,* blasted open the heavy wooden doors on a suicide run. Some 2,500 defenders were massacred and the city pillaged, making Guanajuato the insurgents' first major victory.

It was recaptured some months later in 1811, and subsequently Allende's and Hidalgo's heads were among those displayed on a hook high on the Alhóndiga, being removed only in 1821 with the final defeat of Spain. The building now houses a local museum containing much historical memorabilia, Pre-Hispanic remains, and colorful murals depicting Guanajuato's violent past.

Mercado Hidalgo 🏛

Av. Juárez. Open daily: best in morning.

Built in the late 19thC, during the period of dictatorship known as the *Porfiriato,* this huge and impressive cast-iron-and-glass market is very like contemporary English Victorian stations and markets. Energetic bargaining may secure handicrafts, such as tin-work, leather, weaving or pottery, at good prices.

Just outside the town on the Guadalajara road is the **cemetery** *(Panteón Civil),* where guides enthuse about the collection of 100 disinterred corpses, amazingly preserved in the mineral-rich soil, in the **Museo de Momias** (🏛 *standard hours),* boasting that it is Mexico's most popular museum.

EXCURSIONS

Cerro del Cubilete

30km (18 miles) w; take Silao road and turn N at 10km (6 miles).

Well before you get there, the vast 1922 **statue of Christ** comes into view, standing on a bizarre domed structure. A popular picnic spot, some claim that this, not **Tequisquiapán** (page 190), is the true geographical center of the Republic. The views of the Bajío are excellent.

La Valenciana 🏛 ★

3km (1½ miles) from center, on road for Dolores Hidalgo.

Dominating this small village is one of Mexico's most magnificent **Baroque churches**, built from 1765–88 by the Count of Valenciana, who owned the nearby 600m-deep (1,968-foot) silver-mines. Steps lead from the village square up to the Churrigueresque facade, of which only one bell tower was completed (construction of the second was blocked by the jealous ecclesiastics of Guanajuato).

Before entering, walk around to the side of the tower to see the **statue of St Joseph** above the door. The church is vaulted in somber volcanic stone, and contains three ornate, gilded altars adorned with religious statues and oil paintings, and a notable carved pulpit.

On the other side of the road, it is a short walk to the **Valenciana mine shafts.** Some are long abandoned, and others still in use. It is said that silver-ore dust from these mines was mixed into the church mortar.

WHERE TO STAY

CASTILLO DE SANTA CECILIA 🏛

1km (½ mile) N on RF110 ☎*(473) 20485* 🖳*(473) 20153* 🎢 *88 rms* 🍽 🛥 ◀€ 🚣 🍷 ●

Converted from a 17thC gold and silver mine, this fantastical medieval castle offers all modern comforts and a romantic vaulted restaurant. Highly entertaining.

HACIENDA DE COBOS ♣ 🏛

Hidalgo 3 at Juárez ☎*(473) 20350* 🎢 *40 rms* 🍽 🍷

A romantic small inn, housed in colonial silver-ore-processing buildings in the center of town. Simple rooms and courtyard dining.

HOSTERÍA DEL FRAILE ♣ 🏛

Sopeña 3 ☎*(473) 21179* 🎢 *37 rms* 🍽 🍷

Formerly a 17thC coin mint, this hotel is centrally located opposite the TEATRO JUÁREZ (see page 199). It offers excellent rooms in a building that is full of character, but parking can be a problem in this part of town.

PARADOR SAN JAVIER 🏨 🏛
Plaza Aldama 92 ☎*(473) 20626* 📠*(473)*
23114 🖮☐ *115 rms* 🛏 🏊 ≋ ☯ ⊙ ♪
A colonial inn located 2km (1 mile) N on
RF110, with a large, modern extension.
The older rooms have fireplaces.

POSADA SANTA FE 🏛
Jardín de la Unión 12 ☎*(473) 20084* 🖮☐
50 rms 🛏 ☯ ⚓
This masterpiece of 19thC ornament is
worth having a look around, even if you
don't stay here.

REAL DE MINAS
Nejayote 17 ☎*(473) 21460* 📠*(473)*
21508 🖮☐ *180 rms* 🛏 🏊 ◁€ ≋ ⤴
☯ ⊙
This is a large modern hotel on the

outskirts of town, N on RF110. Guests
can rent motorcycles.

SAN DIEGO 🏛
Jardín de la Unión 1 ☎*(473) 21300* 🖮☐
60 rms ◁€ 🛏 ☯ ⊙
Housed in a 17thC convent building on
the Zócalo. Ask for a room with a balcony; the views are superb.

SAN GABRIEL DE BARRERA 🏨 🏛
Km 2.5 on Marfil road ☎*(473) 23980* 🖮🖮
139 rms 🛏 ▱ 🏊 ◁€ ≋ ⤴ ☯
This beautifully converted 18thC hacienda, set in ornamental gardens, offers the best accommodation in town.
The hotel is a visitor attraction in its own
right, for its superb Spanish chapel and
12thC altarpiece.

EATING AND DRINKING

There are excellent hotel restaurants at the CASTILLO DE SANTA CECILIA,
HACIENDA DE COBOS, PARADOR SAN JAVIER, and SAN GABRIEL DE BARRERA hotels (see above), which are all open to nonresidents.

For a less formal meal, there are many good places to choose from on
and near Jardín Unión and along Juárez. Some recommendations:

- **Cafetería Nieva** *(Allende 3 on Jardín Unión),* busy and very
  Mexican.
- **Casa Valadez** *(Sopeña 3 on Jardín Unión* ☎ *(473) 21157* 🖮☐ *),* for
  delicious Mexican food in a spacious paneled gallery.
- **Nutricional Vegetariano** (🖮☐), near the TASCA DE LOS SANTOS,
  serves filling *comida corridas*.
- **Pizza Piazza** *(Plaza San Fernando* ☎*(473) 23094* 🖮☐ *),* a popular
  place for students.
- **Tasca de los Santos** *(Plaza de la Paz 28* ☎*(473) 22320* 🖮☐ *),*
  open all day for Spanish food.

DOLORES HIDALGO

*Map **10**C5. Guanajuato. 54km (33 miles)* NE *of Guanajuato on RF110; 265km
(165 miles)* NW *of Mexico City on RF57 and RF110; 40km (25 miles)* N *of San
Miguel de Allende on RF51. Altitude: 1,990m (6,527ft). Population: 120,000.
Served by train (on San Luis Potosí–Querétaro line) and bus* **i** *on Zócalo left of
church* ☎*(468) 20801.*

One important event guaranteed this small town in the Bajío a place in
history, without which it would have remained eternally obscure. On
September 16, 1810, the revolutionary priest Father Miguel Hidalgo
rang the church bells to summon his flock, and then proclaimed the
famous *Grito de Dolores* (*grito* means shout) to launch an uprising
against Spanish rule. After a decade of bloodshed (which included
Hidalgo's own death at Spanish hands), the rebellion was successful.

Every year on September 16, the *grito* is proclaimed all over Mexico. The President himself comes to Dolores to perform this function at least once during his term of office.

Another reason to come here is to buy the pretty glazed **tiles** of the town, whose manufacture, according to local tradition, was introduced by Hidalgo.

WHAT TO SEE

The **Casa de Hidalgo** *(Morelos 1* ☎ *open 9am-1pm, 4-6pm; closed Mon* ☎ *(468) 20171),* where Hidalgo lived from 1804–10, is now a museum, containing his possessions and assorted bric-a-brac from the War of Independence. The 18thC **church** is on the Zócalo, and although the bell that Hidalgo rang was melted down for bullets, it is worth a visit for the Churrigueresque facade and altarpiece. Opposite the church is a fine Baroque building, now a government office.

The **Museo de la Independencia** *(Zacatecas 6,* $\frac{1}{2}$ *block* w of Zócalo, open Mon-Fri 9am-2pm, 4-7pm; Sat, Sun 9am-3pm) is short on relics, but long on information about the independence movement and its historical roots.

✎ There are plans to build two large new hotels here, but until then try **Del Caudillo** *(Querétaro 8* ☎ *(468) 20198* ▢ ➔ *)* or **Posada Cocomacán** *(on the Zócalo* ☎ *(468) 20018* ▢ *),* an unrestored colonial building.

LEÓN

*Map **10**C4. Guanajuato. 228km (142 miles)* E *of Guadalajara on RF80 and RF45; 47km (29 miles)* w *of Guanajuato on RF110 and RF45; 112km (70 miles)* SE *of Aguascalientes on RF45. Altitude: 2,052m (6,730ft). Population: 1.2 million. Served by air, train (on Mexico City–Aguascalientes line) and bus. American Express: Blvd. Mateos at Saavedra* ☎ *(471) 41866.*

The largest, most industrialized of the Bajío cities. It has the only major airport in the region, and you may need to spend a night here. It is not a tourist destination in its own right.

WHAT TO SEE

There are several agreeable parks near the center, and on the Zócalo is the pleasant church of **Nuestra Señora de la Luz** (1746). Behind the square is the church of **Nuestra Señora de los Angeles**, where there is a collection of religious wood-carvings.

However, to the E along Madero is the magnificent 18thC church of **Templo Expiatorio**, with ornate marble carving, plenty of gold-leaf and a fascinating catacomb underneath. León is the leather capital of Mexico, and all around the center are shops selling footwear and riding gear.

✎ **La Estancia** *(López Mateos 1311* ☎ *(47) 163939* Fx *(47) 163940* ▥ *151 rms* ➔ ☒ ⌂ *)* is an agreeable motel; another large motel with a pleasant garden is **Real de Minas** *(López Mateos s/n* ☎ *(47) 143677* Fx *(47) 133570* ▥ *175 rms* ➔ ☒ ⌂ *);* the **Balneario Comanjilla** *(Km 45-387 Carretera Panamericana*

☎*(47) 120091* 🎬 ⇌ ⌙ ⌁) is a colonial-style out-of-town spa hotel, known for its sulfurous waters.

In the downtown, **Fiesta Americana** *(López Mateos 1102* ☎*(47) 136040* Fx*(47) 164430* 🎬 *211 rms* ⇌ ⌙ ⌁) is a modern hotel with all facilities, favored by executives on expense-accounts.

AGUASCALIENTES

Map **10**B4. *Capital of Aguascalientes. 252km (157 miles)* NE *of Guadalajara on RF70 and RF54; 112km (70 miles)* NW *of León on RF45; 135km (84 miles)* S *of Zacatecas on RF45. Altitude: 1,890m (6,200ft). Population: 405,000. Served by air, train on Querétaro–Torreón and Mexico City–Zacatecas lines) and bus* **i** *Plaza Patria 141 by cathedral* ☎*(491) 51155 and Avenida de las Americas 502* ☎*(491) 60123. American Express: Centro Comercial El Dorado* ☎*(491) 33323.*

A colonial silver city, surrounded by the thermal springs after which it is named. Aguascalientes is the capital of Mexico's smallest state, formerly part of Zacatecas, but created in 1823 by President Santa Ana in exchange for a kiss from the Mayor's wife.

Few colonial buildings remain, but the fine climate and tree-shaded parks make it a pleasant stopover. Local embroidery is reasonably priced. The city, founded in 1575, was built over a labyrinth of ancient tunnels and chambers built by the Chichimec Indians *(not open to the public)*.

WHAT TO SEE
Zócalo
The 18thC Baroque **cathedral** on the main square has interesting colonial paintings in the nave. Opposite is the 17thC **Palacio de Gobierno**, built of red sandstone, with 1960s murals in the courtyard by Oswaldo Cunningham, a student of Diego Rivera's. Four blocks N and four blocks E of the Zócalo, at Zaragoza 505, is the small **Museo de la Ciudad** *(Museum of the City, open 10am–2pm, 2.30-8pm; closed Mon)*, with its interesting collection of 20thC paintings.

The **Cultural Center** *(behind the cathedral on Carranza)* and the nearby **Museo Regional** *(open 9am-2pm, 4-8pm; closed Mon)* provide additional attractions.

But not to be missed is the **Museo Posada** *(six blocks s of the Zócalo on Jardín Encino, open 10am-2pm, 4.30-8pm)*, with its superb collection of the works of José Guadalupe Posada, Mexico's best-loved artist. Born in the city in 1852, he is famous for his *calaveras* — skeletal figures in situations of everyday life — and his biting political caricatures.

The most accessible of the spas is **Ojo Caliente**, near the sports center in the eastern outskirts *(7am-7pm)*, but those at **Jesús María** *(14km/8 miles* NW, *served by frequent buses)* are better. Relax there after walking in the wooded mountains of the **Bosque Fria National Park**, 50km (31 miles) NW in the state of Zacatecas.

EVENTS • The most exciting time to visit Aguascalientes is the week of the **Fería San Marcos**, which begins on April 25. The streets are taken over by bullfights and cockfights, heavily gambled over, and other Saturnalian pursuits, in a tradition continued since 1640.

EXCURSION

Hotels will arrange visits to the nearby **Peñelas Hacienda**, said to produce the fiercest fighting bulls in Mexico. Impromptu visitors are not encouraged.

❧ **Francia** *(Plaza Principal 113* ☎*(491) 56080* ▥ 🅵🆇*(491) 70140* ➡) has 101 large, pleasant rooms. The **Hotel Las Trojes** *(Blvd. Norte and Blvd. Campestre* ☎*(491) 61620* 🅵🆇*(491) 41183* ▥ *160 rms* ➡ 🍽 ⋙ ⥁ ♈*)* and **Río Grande** *(Chavez 101* ☎*(491) 61666* ▥ *75 rms*➡ ☐ ⟿ ♈*)* are agreeable modern hotels.

Also recommended is the **Medrano** motel *(José Maria Chavez Sur 904* ☎*(491) 55500* 🅵🆇*(491) 68076* ▥ ➡ ⋙*)*. There are several inexpensive places around the Zócalo, such as the **Señorial** *(* ☎*(491) 51630* ▥*)*.

ZACATECAS

Map 9A3. Capital of Zacatecas. 318km (198 miles) N of Guadalajara on RF54; 135km (84 miles) N of Aguascalientes on RF45; 190km (118 miles) W of San Luis Potosí on RF49; 296km (185 miles) SE of Durango on RF45 and RF49; 402km (251 miles) S of Torreón on RF49; 379km (236 miles) SW of Saltillo on RF54. Altitude: 2,440m (8,005ft). Population: 300,000. Served by air, train (on Mexico City–Chihuahua line) and bus ℹ Hidalgo 61, on the Zócalo opposite the cathedral ☎*(492) 26683. American Express: Enlace 313* ☎*(492) 20859.*

Wedged into a narrow gorge on the frontier between fertile central Mexico and the arid north, Zacatecas is one of the old mining towns of Central Mexico, still unsullied by modernity. It has some fine, well-preserved colonial architecture including Mexico's finest cathedral, and outstanding collections of colonial art.

The skyline is dominated by the ragged rocks of the **Cerro de La Bufa**, from which the chapel of **La Virgen del Patrocinio** commands a bird's-eye view of town. The pink-stone mansions and churches are eloquent testimony to the wealth that silver once brought to the town, but the run-down and sprawling outskirts, of more modern origin, suggest that the good times have passed.

The town was founded in 1546 when Juan de Tolsa struck a rich vein of silver ore. Mining began two years later, reaching a peak in the next century, when the city grew to be the third richest in the country, with more than 2,000 mines. In the 1910 Revolution, Zacatecas was the scene of the final defeat by Pancho Villa of General Huerta, Mexico's short-lived drunken dictator.

WHAT TO SEE

For a good orienting view of the city, the best place is the chapel of **La Virgen del Patrocinio**, which can be reached either by car *(turning signposted off the Durango road)* or by the **scenic cable-car** *(* 🚡 *12.30-7.30pm; closed Mon)*.

Cathedral ⛪ ★
Plaza Hidalgo.

On the S side of the main square, this cathedral is probably the finest example of the amazing flowering of the Churrigueresque style in 18thC Mexico. Every part of the facade is profusely ornamented, with the extravagant fantasies of the rich mine owners frozen in pink sandstone. Work was started in 1612, but the building was not completed until 1760, and the dome is a later 19thC addition.

Santo Domingo 血
Callejón de Veyna.
Just w of the Zócalo, past the 18thC Palacio de Gobierno, the facade of this Jesuit church has a restraint and elegance that offers a sharp contrast to the excesses of the cathedral. The main door is at the top of a wide, curved stair, and inside is a fine Churrigueresque altarpiece.

About 1km ($\frac{1}{2}$ mile) N of the cathedral up Hidalgo is the **Pedro Coronel Mask Museum** *(▣ open 10am-2pm, 4-7pm; closed Thurs)*, in the former Convento de San Francisco, restored to house an outstanding collection of 6,000 Mexican Indian ritual masks, Oriental artwork, and paintings by artists including Picasso, Chagall and Goya, all bequeathed by the Zacatecan artist Pedro Coronel. The part of town to the w of here is known as **Old Zacatecas** (Viejo Zacatecas), with pretty little squares and their 18thC palaces.

One kilometer s down Hidalgo lies the attractive **Parque Estrada**, overlooked by the **Museo de Francisco Goitia** *(Enrique Estrada 102, open 10am-2pm, 5-8pm; closed Mon)*, housed in a former governor's palace. The museum has collections of 19th and 20thC work by Zacatecan artists, including that of Pedro Coronel.

El Eden Mine
3km (1$\frac{1}{2}$ miles) w of center on Calle de la Loma. Open noon–7.30pm; closed Mon
✗ compulsory. Or come Thurs-Sun, 10pm–2am, for a rave-up disco.
The source of Zacatecas' colonial riches was in mines such as these, where Indian slaves worked under appalling conditions; many were just children, and your guide will tell you that at least eight died each day. A **miniature train** now goes through dark tunnels and across flooded mine shafts. At the exit is a gift store, with silver jewelry and mineral samples from the mine. The mine is the home of Mexico's most unusual disco.

EXCURSIONS

La Quemada (Chicomóztoc) 血
56km (35 miles) s on RF54 ▣ Open 9am–5pm. Closed Mon.
One theory is that these well-defended 12thC buildings, on a natural terrace high above the plain, were built by the Nahuatlacas tribe, relatives of the Aztecs; another is that the Aztecs themselves lived here during their migration to the Valley of Mexico from their unknown home. However, the architecture suggests links with the Toltecs.

Halfway up the wide causeway is the group known as **The Cathedral**, because of a line of large columns, and at the summit are the sturdy bulwarks and a votive **pyramid**.

Guadalupe Monastery 血
5km (3 miles) E on RF45/49.
The small town of **Guadalupe**, now merging with Zacatecas, is domi-

nated by this large and elaborate Franciscan monastery. Founded in 1707, it still has some monks in residence.

The complex houses several museums: the **Museum of Vice-Regal Art** *(open 10am-2pm, 5-8pm)*, with its fine collection of 17th and 18thC painting, mostly religious; and the **Museum of Regional History** *(open 10am-4.30pm; closed Mon)*, with an odd mixture of exhibits ranging from vintage cars to Huichol Indian art.

☜ **Quinta Real** *(González Ortega s/n* ☎*(492) 29104-7* Ⓕ*(492) 28440* ▥ *49 rms* ▬▬ ⍦ �*)* is an excellent modern hotel in the colonial style, incorporating an old aqueduct and bullring. **Aristos** *(Loma de la Soledad s/n* ☎*(492) 21788* Ⓕ*(492) 26908* ▥ *100 rms* ▬▬ ⍦ � ☞*)* is a good modern hotel, offering great views. **Best Western Gallery** *(López Mateos and Callejón del Barro* ☎*(492) 23311* ▥ *141 rms* ▬▬ �*)* is a modern, central hotel.

Located by the scenic cable-car station is **Del Bosque** *(Periférico Díaz Ordaz s/n* ☎*(492) 20745* ▥*)*, a motel with bungalows. **Paraíso Radisson** *(*▥ *Hidalgo 703 on Zócalo* ☎*(492) 26183* Ⓕ*(492) 26245* ▥ *115 rms* ▬▬ ⍦*)* is an excellent hotel in a historic colonial building. **Posada de los Condes** *(*♣ ▥ *Juárez 107 at Hidalgo* ☎*(492) 21073* ▥ ▬▬*)* is a reasonable downtown hotel in a 17thC building, with an inexpensive restaurant; or try the similar **Posada de la Moneda** *(Hidalgo 413* ☎*(492) 20881)*.

▬▬ **Mesón de la Mina** *(Juárez 15* ☎*(492) 22773* ▥*)* serves ample portions of Mexican food; if it is full, try **El Jacalito** *(Juárez 18* ☎*(492) 20771* ▥*)*, another wholesome Mexican restaurant on the same block; the QUINTA REAL hotel has the finest dining in Zacatecas, but for atmosphere go to the restored **market** opposite the cathedral, with its fashionable cafés and bars, and **La Cuija** *(* ☎*(492) 28275* ▥*)* with its well-prepared local dishes.

SAN LUIS POTOSÍ

Map **10**B5. Capital of San Luis Potosí. 202km (126 miles) N of Querétaro on RF57; 264km (165 miles) W of Ciudad Valles on RF70; 190km (118 miles) E of Zacatecas on RF49; 535km (334 miles) S of Monterrey on RF57. Altitude: 1,965m (6,445ft). Population: 750,000. Served by air, train (on Mexico City–Monterrey line and on Aguascalientes–Tampico line) and bus **i** Oltón 130 ☎(48) 123143. American Express: Venustiano Carranza 1077 ☎(48) 176056.

The small Franciscan settlement of San Luis gained the name "Potosí" after the discovery of gold and silver ores nearby in 1592. In this way it was hoped the mines would reproduce the glories of the great silvermines at Potosí in Bolivia, the name meaning "of great wealth" in the South American tongue of Quechua.

As was the case with its namesake, the local Indians, here the Guachichil, were not equal to the Spaniards' appetite for precious metals, and as they died out further Indians were drafted in from around the country. The town grew rapidly over its arid plain to become Mexico's third city, and although it is now an important center, it retains much charm.

For a while, San Luis was the provisional capital of Mexico, after President Juárez, evading the French armies, set up his government here in 1863. Later it became the capital of northeastern Mexico, and has always had strong links with Texas. Texans still come here to consult the land registry in cases of dispute. If you are driving N to S, San Luis is a natural place to break your journey, and a destination in its own right.

WHAT TO SEE

The **Jardín Hidalgo** in the Plaza de Armas is the center of life in San Luis. On its E side is the 17thC **cathedral**, which provides examples of every architectural style from Gothic to Byzantine via Baroque. It faces the **Palacio de Gobierno** where, in office hours, you can visit a Hall of Mirrors and a patriotic gallery of Mexican heroes in wax.

Two blocks E, on Calle de Villerías at Plaza del Carmen, is an 18thC Baroque jewel, the **Templo del Carmen**, adorned with shells and colored tiles, whose Neoclassical high altar was designed by the famous Bajío architect, Eduardo Tresguerras. Also on Villerías, opposite the Neoclassical **Teatro de la Paz**, is the famous **Museo Nacional de las Máscaras** *(open 10am-2pm, 4-6pm; closed Mon* 🖼 *)*, with its spectacular collection of masks from all over Mexico. A block E lies the **Alameda**, an extensive garden, once the monastic orchard.

Much smaller, although also pleasant, is the **Jardín Guerrero**, with its trees and fountains in the Plaza San Francisco, SW of the Plaza de Armas. On its W side is the **Casa de Artesanías** *(open standard hours)*, devoted to the sale of local crafts. Just S is the church of **San Francisco**, then the fine Churrigueresque facade of the **Aranzazu Chapel**, with its oil paintings within.

Next door, the **regional museum** *(on Galeana 450* 🖼 *open Tues-Fri 10am-1pm, 3-6pm, Sat-Sun 10am-noon; closed Mon)* has an interesting collection of Huastec antiquities and local crafts, housed in the original Franciscan monastery. Another good place for crafts, especially locally made silk shawls *(rebózos)*, is the **Mercado Hidalgo** *(Calle Hidalgo)*.

EVENTS • The **festival of San Luis** is on 25 August, with a grand procession and flying eggs filled with confetti, and coinciding with a large agricultural fair. • **Easter** is another lively time, and much of May is occupied with an **arts festival**.

EXCURSIONS
RF57 east to Ciudad Valles

This road travels the 264km (165 miles) to Ciudad Valles through the magnificent landscape of the Sierra Madre Oriental, before it drops sharply into the lush, tropical Huasteca country. After 128km (80 miles), **Río Verde** is a good place in which to stop, with the pleasant **Plaza** *(* 🕿 *(487) 20100* 🍽 🛏 *)* on the Zócalo. The nearby **Laguna Media Luna** *(3km/1 mile W, then 10km/6 miles S)* makes a lovely day-trip.

There are some lovely **waterfalls** along the remainder of the route — see CIUDAD VALLES, page 213.

WHERE TO STAY

Downtown, the best hotel is the **Panorama** *(Carranza 315* 🕿 *(48) 121777* ▥ *127 rms* 🍽 🛏 *)*. Other good choices are the **María**

Christina *(Sarabia 110* ☎*(48) 129408* ▥ ⇥*)* and the **Concordia** *(Othón and Morelos* ▥ ⇥*)*. The **Ring** *(San Luis 12* ☎*(48) 126174)* is small and traditional.

The grander hotels are mostly out of town, such as the large and modern **Hostal del Quijote** *(Km 420 on RF57* ☎*(48) 181312* Ⅸ*(48) 180651* ▥ *211 rms* ⇥ Ⓨ ⚭*)* and the **Real de Minas** *(Km 426.5 on RF57* ☎*(48) 182616* ▥ ⇥ Ⓨ ⚭*)*.

If you want a motel, try the **Cactus** *(* ❦ *Glorieta and Juárez, on RF57 to Mexico City* ☎*(48) 121871* ▥ ⇥ ⚭ ⛊*)*.

EATING AND DRINKING

La Lonja *(Aldama 300* ☎*(48) 128119* ▥*)* is a good choice for authentic Mexican dishes, at a price. **La Cabaña Huasteca** *(Cuauhté- moc and Mariel* ☎*(48) 122990* ▥*)* serves local Huasteca specialties. **Posada la Virreina** *(Jardin Hidalgo 3* ☎*(48) 127150* ▥*)* is an exclusive gourmet establishment in a turn-of-the-century mansion. At the other end of the scale, **El Bocalito** *(Plaza San Francisco* ▢*)* is famous for its *comida corridas.*

REAL DE CATORCE ☆

Map 7F8. San Luis Potosí. 191km (119 miles) N of San Luis Potosí on RF57 or 344km (215 miles) S of Monterrey on RF57 then W 30km (18 miles) W at Matehuala. Population 100. Served by bus ⓲ *from Casa de la Moneda, no* ☎

This well-preserved mining outpost is named after the 14 *(catorce)* bandits who made their headquarters here. Sparsely inhabited, it is almost a ghost town, except for the fact that some life still goes on in its largely empty streets and buildings.

Emphasizing the town's other-worldliness, the only access is via 3km $(1\frac{1}{2}$ miles) of dark **tunnel**. It is also known for the hallucinogenic cacti growing in the hills all around, the goal of the long pilgrimages made by the Huichol Indians of Nayarit, who collect them every April for their religious rites. The one time the town is full is for its **fiesta**, which begins on 4 October and lasts for a week.

WHAT TO SEE

The **church** dedicated to the Virgin Mary is surprisingly well main- tained, supported by hopeful pilgrims whose offerings decorate the walls. Opposite is the imposing mint, the **Casa de la Moneda**, now a gallery for arts and crafts, and housing the volunteer-staffed informa- tion office. Beyond it lies the **museum**, with a chaotic but intriguing collection of memorabilia from the town's history.

❧ The **Real** *(* ☎*(488) 22593* ▥ ⇥*)* is a nicely renovated old house, which also offers the best restaurant in town.

The North-East

This large and disparate region of Mexico, comprising the states of **Nuevo León**, **Coahuila** and **Tamaulipas**, is mostly ignored by tourists, although it is receiving increasing attention from US businesses. The most recent economic stimulant has been the negotiation of the North American Free Trade Agreement. Already many US corporations have relocated their manufacturing capacity in Mexico to take advantage of the cheap labor and relaxed environmental controls.

Add to this the substantial oil fields of the area (which is contiguous with the oil-rich US state of Texas), the presence of **MONTERREY**, Mexico's most dynamic industrial city, the fertile agricultural lands of the Gulf coast, and the proximity of the timber and mineral resources of the northwest region, and this part of Mexico has all the ingredients necessary for an economic miracle.

But there is a downside to this dynamism. The influx of US dollars has led to a high-priced hybrid economy, and a parallel cultural hybridization has brought out some of the least attractive features of both countries. And while the low wages that attract the multinational corporations to relocate here may be a lifeline for many Mexican workers, wealth still remains the preserve of the few, and grisly slums and exposure to toxic wastes the fate of the many. As a visitor, you would be well advised to avoid the area closest to the border, or at least to travel through it as fast as possible.

NUEVO LEÓN

The foremost destination in this state is MONTERREY, state capital and a thoroughly Mexican city, with lovely places to explore in the nearby mountains of the **Sierra Madre Oriental**, running from north to south of the state. However, industrial pollution in Monterrey is starting to rival that of the capital, and few visitors stay longer than they need to.

COAHUILA

West from Monterrey lies the state of Coahuila, whose vast, arid expanse is broken by two important industrial towns. Closest to the frontier is SALTILLO, a growing car-building center that retains sufficient charm to make it a good alternative to spending the night in Monterrey. The other, TORREÓN, forms part of an industrial complex with Gómez Palacio, in Durango state (see THE NORTH-WEST, page 238).

TAMAULIPAS

MATAMOROS, near the Gulf coast in the state of Tamaulipas, is the one border town that suggests itself as a destination in its own right, but even here there is little reason to linger. As you make the long trek south across the steamy, low-lying plains of the Gulf, CIUDAD VICTORIA, the state capital, provides a resting place. Sports fishermen can find enormous bass and catfish in the nearby rivers and reservoirs.

As for the coast, the beaches are of hard-packed, muddy sand, sometimes polluted with oil, fringed with salt marshes and mosquito-rich lagoons that are better suited to wildfowl than tourism. There are only two accessible stretches of beach, both developed strictly for local tourism, at **Lauro Villar**, near Matamoros, and at **La Pesca**, due east of Ciudad Victoria.

The first serious destination in this state is TAMPICO, whose rough, salty character befits such a flourishing port and oil town. It is great fun, as long as you manage to avoid arguments with drunken sailors on shoreleave. It also marks the beginning of the **Huasteca**, the homeland of the Huastec Indians, which spreads into the neighboring states of San Luis Potosí and Veracruz.

THE HUASTECA

For geographical reasons this section includes the eastern, Huastec part of San Luis Potosí, centered on CIUDAD VALLES. While the city itself is of little tourist interest, it lies in the heart of some beautiful country, with waterfalls, tropical jungles clinging to steep mountain slopes, volcanic hot springs, and fascinating Indian villages.

Towns, cities and cultural sites

Starting in **TAMPICO**, this chapter gives essential information on the following places, which are arranged to follow a s-n route through the region: **CIUDAD VALLES, CIUDAD VICTORIA, MONTERREY, SALTILLO, MATAMOROS, REYNOSA** and **NUEVO LAREDO**.

See USING THIS GUIDE on page 50 for details on how to use this section. On the following pages, helpful pointers are given on how to get to each of the destinations covered. Along with the MEXICO map on pages 46–7, and the 4-color maps at the back of this book, they should give all the information necessary for planning your trip to this part of Mexico.

TAMPICO

Map 12B8. Tamaulipas. 468km (292 miles) n of Mexico City on RF70 and RF105; 138km (86 miles) ε of Ciudad Valles on RF70; 242km (151 miles) se of Ciudad Victoria on RF85, RF81 and RF180; 502km (313 miles) nw of Veracruz on RF180. Population: 600,000. Served by air (airport 8km/5 miles nw), train (on lines from Monterrey, Ciudad Victoria, San Luis Potosí and Ciudad Valles) and bus
i Palacio Municipal ☎(12) 122668. UK Consul: 2 de Enero 102 ☎(12) 129817. American Express: Hidalgo 5004 ☎(12) 139888.

Surrounded by grim marshes, Tampico, together with its sister cities of **Ciudad Madero** to the s and **Altamira** to the n, is a busy port and oil town, which aims to overtake VERACRUZ in importance. The oil boom began in 1880, and Tampico fast became a haven for foreign oil companies, until their assets were nationalized in 1938 by President Lázaro Cárdenas. Although the city was founded in 1533 on a Huastec Indian site, occasional floods, hurricanes and French attacks have ensured that no early colonial buildings survive. Nonetheless, Tampico is a pleasant place to stop for the night.

The central **Plaza de Armas**, the focus of the town, comes to life in the evening, when there are often bandstand **concerts**. You may be surprised by the swastika pattern on the floor of the strange 1930s **cathedral**. But, architecturally, the cathedral is quite outclassed by the **bandstand**, which might be best described as a psychedelic Moorish wedding cake of cast-iron. A block s and ε is **Plaza Libertad**, whose Parisian-inspired architecture contrasts with the very Mexican **Mercado Hidalgo** below, which spills over toward the port.

Culture-seekers should not miss the **Museo de la Huasteca** (🖾 *open 10am-1pm; closed Mon)* in **Ciudad Madero** *(1km/½ mile w)*, where they can learn about the local Huastec people, and see their 3,000-year-old ceramic pots and sculptures. The 50,000 or so modern Huastec Indians inhabit a large area from VERACRUZ to SAN LUIS POTOSÍ. Today, they live mainly on agriculture, while also producing a wide variety of handicrafts.

The wildlife in the area around Tampico has suffered under the onslaught of industrial pollution, although **deep-sea fishing** is still a possibility that can be arranged through your hotel. The beaches near town are generally polluted; even **Playa Miramar** *(15km/9 miles n* *beyond Ciudad Madero),* often surprisingly tar-free, has an untidy air, but the water is pleasant for swimming, and there is a beautiful unspoiled **island** off the coast, which can be reached by boat from the harbor *(no organized service).*

EXCURSION

Laguna de Tamiahua

105km (65 miles) s on RF180 to Naranjos, then 40km (25 miles) e to Tamiahua.
This enormous sea lagoon has the small resort village of **Tamiahua** on its w shore, where you can swim, eat, drink and relax. It is often crowded on weekends, when it is best to rent a skiff and go fishing.

WHERE TO STAY

Tampico has two good resort hotels: **Camino Real** *(▥ Hidalgo 2000* ☎*(12) 138811* ℻*(12) 139226* ▥ *103 rms* ☂ ≈ ▤ ⇒ ☑ ☒ ●*),* and **Posada de Tampico** *(▥ Prolongación Hidalgo Km 2.2 (RF80)* ☎*(12) 133050* ℻*(12) 280855* ▥ *130 rms* ⇒ ☑ ☒ ≈ ☺*).*

In the downtown area, **Colonial** *(Madero 210 Ote* ☎*(12) 127777* ▥ ⇒ ☒ ≈ ●*)* is modern and attractive, as is **Inglaterra** *(Salvador Díaz Mirón 116* ☎*(12) 125678* ℻*(12) 140566* ▥ *126 rms* ← ≈ ⇒*).* **Impala** *(Díaz Mirón 220 Pte* ☎*(12) 120990* ▥ ← ≈ ☒*),* also central, is a less expensive alternative.

EATING AND DRINKING

The main hotels all have good restaurants, especially **Posada del Rey** *(Madero 118* ☎*(12) 124464* ▥ *not recommended as hotel),* with its choice of three eating venues.

There are various cafés around the Zócalo, and several good seafood stops. These include **Mariscos Diligencias** *(Tampico 415 Ote* ☎*(12) 141279* ▥*),* **Del Mar** *(Aduana 309 Sur* ☎*(12) 125035* ▥*)* and the upmarket **Jardín Corona** *(Hidalgo 1915* ☎*(12) 139383* ▥*).* The local **crabs** are renowned for their size and flavor.

CIUDAD VALLES

Map 11B7. San Luis Potosí. 475km (296 miles) n of Mexico City on RF45 and RF85; 138km (86 miles) w of Tampico on RF70; 264km (165 miles) e of San Luis Potosí on RF70; 232km (145 miles) s of Ciudad Victoria on RF85. Population: 150,000. Served by train (on San Luis Potosí–Tampico line) and bus.

This hot, lowland town may be of little intrinsic interest, but it has some pleasant hotels, making it a useful stopping-point for drivers, and a good center for exploring nearby villages in the mountains. The roads s to Mexico City and w to San Luis Potosí are unusually scenic.

On the outskirts there is a small **Museo Regional Huasteco** *(s on RF85, open Mon-Fri 9am-1pm, 4-6pm)* with a collection of Huastec antiquities from nearby sites. It is sometimes possible to see the extraordinary **Huastec flying pole-dance** (✪) in one of the villages to the s of Ciudad Valles; your hotel will advise.

EXCURSIONS

El Consuelo
28km (17 miles) E on RF70 to Tamuín, then 6km (3 miles) on foot with guide.
This an extensive classic Huastec site, dating from about AD900. It consists mostly of low **ceremonial platforms**, which have lost their painted stucco over recent decades.

Tamazunchale
107km (66 miles) s on RF85.
Known as "Thomas and Charlie" to the thousands of Americans who passed through when it was on the main N–S road. On Sundays, Huastec Indians pour in from all around to the **market**, an animated and attractive scene, with native embroidery at bargain prices.

Tancanhuitz de Santos
51km (31 miles) s on RF85, then 20km (12 miles) w.
This small Huastec village comes to life for its Sunday market.

Waterfalls east off RF70
Cascadas de Micos *(9km/5 miles E to sign, then 11km/6 miles N)* is an 80m (260-foot) series of five falls, ending in a clear, shady pool. 2km (1 mile) N from the village of **Tamasopo** *(73km/45 miles E of Ciudad Valles, then 3km/1 mile N)* is a splendid **triple cascade**, and there are many other lovely spots to explore along the valley; a guide will gladly lead you to **El Arco**, a rock arch spanning a deep pool in the river.

Xilitla
88km (55 miles) s; turn w after 72km (45 miles) on RF85.
This large and interesting Huastec village, set in richly tropical country, was built around the remains of a 16thC Augustinian monastery. Xilitla is most worth visiting for the **follies** of British sculptor Edward James, who lived here from 1949, building weird constructions in the jungle below the village until his death in 1980.

The village is at its liveliest on **fiesta** day, on August 27, but the lodgings around the Zócalo are likely to be full at this time.

Posada don Antonio *(Carretera Mexico-Laredo (RF85) at Km 15* ☎*(138) 20066* ▥ ⇄ ⋙ ✔ ▤*)* is a quiet hotel, with vast grounds providing many sporting facilities, including a golf course. The **Taninul** *(15km/9 miles w, then s to the river Tampaón* ☎*(138) 20000* ▥ ⇄ ⋙ ⚓ 🏇*)* is a faded spa hotel in the country, offering hot sulfur baths, horseback riding and generous home cooking.

Valles *(Carretera Mexico-Laredo 36 Nte* ☎*(138) 20050* ⟨Fx⟩*(138) 20022* ▥ to ▥ 93 rms ⇄ ⋙ ⬤*)* is a good hacienda-style motel closer to town, while **Rex** *(Hidalgo 418* ☎*(138) 20345* ▥*)* is basic but central.

CIUDAD VICTORIA

*Map **4**E8. Capital of Tamaulipas. 270km (168 miles) SE of Monterrey on RF85; 242km (151 miles) NW of Tampico on RF80 and RF85; 312km (195 miles) s of Matamoros on RF101; 232km (145 miles) N of Ciudad Valles on RF85. Population: 210,000. Served by air, train (on Monterrey–Tampico line) and bus i Rosales 272 at 5 de Mayo* ☎*(131) 21057.*

The first major city on the way s from MATAMOROS, Ciudad Victoria offers more to anglers and buyers of leather clothing than to culture-seekers. However, the **cathedral** and **Palacio de Gobierno** on the Zócalo are worth a glance, as is the cluttered **Museo de Historia e Antropología** (*Matamoros s/n, open 10am-4pm; closed Mon*), full of local Pre-Hispanic artifacts and other historic junk.

Around 80km (50 miles) s of the city, the **El Cielo Biosphere Reserve** is a unique 143-hectare (357,000-acre) expanse of cloud-forest, part of which is open to tourists. An hour's drive to the w of Ciudad Victoria, the **Balcones de Moctezuma**, a Huastec site that has recently been exca-vated, will soon be open to the public.

FISHING

Anglers can warm up on catfish in the nearby rivers, and graduate to bass in the large reservoirs nearby. The best known of these is **Lago Vicente Guerrero** (*54km/33 miles NE on RF101*), which was stocked with 500,000 black bass in 1970. The fish have now grown to a huge size as they swim among the flooded ruins of **Padilla**, the village in which the self-styled Emperor Iturbide was executed in 1824. Travel agents in town can book you into sporting cabins around the lake.

At **Soto la Marina,** 120km (75 miles) E, there is good river fishing, and 30km (18 miles) farther at **La Pesca,** on the coast, excellent sea fishing; this peaceful, run-down village is now due for a 24,000-hectare (60,000-acre), 9,000-unit tourism mega-project.

The **Everest** (*Morelos 126 at Hidalgo* ☎(131) 24050 ☒(131) 21443 ▥ 102 rms ⊨ ▦ ⋘ ⵙ) is one well-equipped downtown option. There are also a number of good hotels on the Zócalo itself, for example, the faintly upmarket **Sierra Gorda** (*Hidalgo Oriente 990* ☎(131) 222010 ☒(131) 29799 ▥ 87 rms ▦ ⊨) and the pleasant but modest **Los Monteros** (*Hidalgo 962 Ote* ☎(131) 20300▢).

Those in search of a taste of luxury should make for **Hacienda Santa Engracia** (*40km/25 miles N on RF85* ☎(131) 24356 ▥ ⊨ ⵙ ⛷ ⵜ ⋘), set amid peaceful orange groves.

MONTERREY

*Map **4E8**. Capital of Nuevo León. 228km (142 miles) s of Nuevo Laredo on RF85; 270km (168 miles) N of Ciudad Victoria on RF85; 83km (51 miles) E of Saltillo on RF40. Population: 4.5 million. Served by air (international airport 22km/13 miles NW), train (on lines from Mexico City, Matamoros, Nuevo Laredo, Tampico, Torreón) and bus **i** Matamoros and Zaragoza on the Gran Plaza ☎(83) 450 870 and ☎(800) 235 2438. US Consul: Constitución 411 Poniente ☎(83) 430 650. UK Consul: Privada de Tamazunchale 104 ☎(83) 782 565. American Express Travel Service: Av. San Pedro 400-103 ☎(83) 566035.*

As befits one of Mexico's great industrial cities, Monterrey is rapidly catching up with the capital in terms of pollution, congestion, over-population and expense. It is now the source of about 25 percent of Mexico's industrial production, with its major steel, concrete, glass, textiles and beer factories, as well as the fast-growing *"maquiladora"* cross-border assembly plants.

Like Mexico City, Monterrey is ringed by mountains that trap and concentrate the smog produced by factories in or near the city center. Despite all this, Monterrey has enough compensations to reward the unhurried visitor for a day or two, including some spectacular areas of natural beauty nearby.

WHAT TO SEE

Monterrey's town center has been thoroughly revitalized by the addition of the **Gran Plaza**, 100 hectares (40 acres) of gardens, fountains, monuments and imaginative modern buildings. Although built at the cost of demolishing several entire blocks, the Gran Plaza has created an open space that stretches from the bold, new **Palacio Municipal**, across the old Zócalo, **Plaza Zaragoza**, to the **Palacio de Gobierno** on the old Plaza 5 de Mayo, which is now known as the **Esplanada de los Héroes**.

The space between the two plazas, which was formerly a downtown area full of shops, hotels and restaurants, is now occupied by two magnificent **fountains** and a giant **statue** of the *Workers of Nuevo Leon*, with the **City Theater** and **State Congress** buildings facing each other on either side.

Plaza Zaragoza is dominated by the Baroque **cathedral** and the 70m (224-foot) **Faro de Comercio**, from the summit of which a green laser slices the night sky. The old **municipal palace**, built in the mid-19thC around a 16thC courtyard, is now a cultural center, where occasional **concerts** are held on the patio. Just s are the twin avenues, Constitución and Independencia, that flank the dry bed of the river Catarina.

The **Palacio de Gobierno**, built in 1908 of pink stone, has an uninterrupted view along the length of the Gran Plaza. In its small **museum room** (☑ *usually open during office hours)* are the actual guns used for the execution of Emperor Maximilian in 1867. Also worth a visit is the **Museo de Arte Contemporaneo** *(Gran Plaza at Zuazua and Ocampo* ☎ *(83) 424820, open 11am-7pm; closed Mon),* with its exhibitions of Latin American art.

Padre Mier leads w past Enrique de la Mora's beautiful modern church of **La Purísima** to Chepe Vara hill, overlooking the town, and the 1789 **Palacio del Obispo** (Bishop's Palace). Because of its dominant position, the palace was a center of action during the Mexican–American War of 1846, the French intervention and the Revolution, and now contains a small **museum** (☒ *open standard hours)* telling the story of this turbulent period. A noted exhibit of the museum is a **printing press** that was used to print revolutionary pamphlets.

Firmly rooted in the 20thC, if aspiring to the 21st, is the shiny new cylinder of the **Centro Cultural** ALFA *(Roberto Sada 1000 at Gómez Marín, open 3pm-9.30pm; closed Mon* ☎ *(83) 783510).* Despite its name, this is really a museum of science and technology, incorporating a planetarium, a 180-degree IMAX movie show and hands-on exhibits. About 5km (3 miles) SW of the center, it is served by buses from La Alameda.

After all this intellectual refreshment, head N for the huge **Cuauhtémoc brewery** *(Universidad 2022* ☎*(83) 724 894* 🔲 *tours at 11am, noon and 3pm; closed Sat, Sun)*, where the visit ends with free beer and a tour of the **Baseball Hall of Fame**.

EXCURSIONS

Cola de Caballo
40km (25 miles) sw; turn w off RF85 after 35km (21 miles).
The impressive triple waterfall is a popular weekend picnic spot, and horses are available for hire. The name means "Horse-tail."

Grutas García and the Huasteca Canyon
w on RF54 to Saltillo.
The dizzying **Huasteca Canyon** is a favorite outing, 3km (2 miles) S of the main road after 16km (10 miles). After 25km (15 miles) on the main road, turn N and drive 21km (13 miles) farther to the **Grutas García**, the best of the sights around Monterrey. Access to the caves is by **cable-car**, and the visit includes an **underground lake** and forests of stalactites and stalagmites; it is safe and well lit.

Mesa Chipinque
18km (11 miles) w; leave city by Colonia del Valle.
Monterrey's favorite weekend resort is at the end of a steep, winding road on a mountain plateau with fine views across the city. Hire horses at the MOTEL CHIPINQUE for rides through the quiet pine forests. Combine this with a visit to the Huasteca Canyon (see above).

WHERE TO STAY

CAMINO REAL 🏨
Hidalgo 310 Ote at Carranza ☎*(83) 406 390* 💵*(83) 451 984* 🛏 *240 rms* 🍽 ♿ ♨ ⇗ 🎾 ⓨ ⚓
Part of the Camino Real chain, this is a large, comfortable downtown commercial hotel with a pleasant garden. Sporting facilities include a jogging track and squash courts.

FIESTA AMÉRICANA 🏨
José Vasconce 300 Ote ☎*(83) 633 030* 💵*(83) 634 207* 🛏 *307 rms* 🍽 ♨ ⇗ ⓨ ⊙ ⌂
Monterrey's largest, newest and most expensive luxury hotel, the Fiesta Américana is also a dramatic feat of modern architecture.

HOLIDAY INN CROWNE PLAZA 🏨
Constitución 300 Ote ☎*(83) 196 000* 💵*(83)443 007* 🛏 *408 rms* 🍽 ♨ ⇗ ♒ ⓨ ⊙ ◼ ⌂
This new 14-floor downtown luxury hotel has every facility you could wish.

HOLIDAY INN MONTERREY 🏨
Universidad 101 Nte ☎*(83) 762 530* 💵*(83) 320 565* 🛏 *200 rms* 🍽 ♨ ⇗ ♒ ⓨ ⊙ ⌂
This luxurious colonial-style hotel is located 13km (8 miles) N of the center in the industrial district, and has good sports facilities.

MONTERREY CLARION
Morelos 574 Ote ☎*(83) 435 120* 💵*(83) 447 378* 🛏 *to* 🛏 *200 rms* 🍽 ⇗ ♒ ⓨ ▣
This substantial downtown hotel is on the Gran Plaza, near the cathedral.

RADISSON PLAZA GRAN HOTEL ANCIRA 🏨
Hidalgo 498 and Escobedo ☎*(83) 457 575* 💵*(83) 450 057* 🛏 ⇗ ♙ ⓨ
Plenty of turn-of-the-century atmosphere and elegance can be found in this well-maintained 1912 luxury hotel, in addition to spacious, tastefully furnished rooms.

Budget hotels

Less expensive hotels include the **Colonial** (♣ *Hidalgo 475 Ote* ☎ *(83) 436 791* ▢ *67 rms* ⇌), two blocks from the Gran Plaza in one of the city's oldest buildings. Most of the lower-priced hotels are around the bus station, where the **Soles** *(Jiménez 1120 Nte* ☎*(83) 770776)* and the **Patricia** *(Madero 123 Nte* ☎*(83) 750775)* are the pick of the bunch *(both* ▢*)*.

Hotels nearby

HACIENDA COLA DE CABALLO
On RF85, 40km (25 miles) s of Monterrey
☎*(828) 50660 or (83) 437 730* ▢ *to* ▥
75 rms ⇌ ❧ ⦑ ≋ ➡ ♉
For a good range of sports facilities and great views, this motel in the country should fill the bill.

MOTEL CHIPINQUE
On RF40 18km (11 miles) sw of Monterrey
☎*(83) 781 100* ▥ *60 rms* ⇌ ⌂ ❧ ⦑ ≋ ♂ ♉
This is a pleasant mountain resort on the Mesa Chipinque, but crowded on weekends. Some rooms have fireplaces.

EATING AND DRINKING

As usual, the best hotels have good restaurants offering international cuisine. However, a number of independent restaurants are well worth trying. **Rey de los Cazadores** *(Hidalgo 215 Ote* ☎*(83) 427 313* ▥*)* serves traditional Mexican food in the pleasant surroundings of a restored older house and its sunny courtyard. **Mérida** *(Zaragoza 522 Nte* ☎*(83) 751 310* ▥*)* specializes in distinctive Yucatán cuisine.

Santa Rosa *(Plaza Hidalgo* ☎*(83) 427 111* ▥ *to* ▥ ♉*)* offers regional dishes in the flower-filled garden of an 18thC mansion. The specialty at **El Tío** *(Hidalgo and Mexico* ☎*(83) 460 291* ▥ ❧ ⌦ ♉*)* is spit-roasted kid. **Luisiana** *(Plaza Hidalgo* ☎*(83) 431 561* ▥ ♉*)* has good steak and seafood dishes.

Mana *(*▢ *Vasconcelos 143 Ote, Colonia del Valle)* caters to vegetarians, and is open all day. The **Blue Shell** *(Gómez Morin 313, Colonia del Valle* ☎*(83) 785 097* ▥*)* is a dedicated seafood restaurant.

EXCURSION

Monclova
194km (121 miles) NW on RF53.
The first major city on the road s from PIEDRAS NEGRAS, Monclova was the capital of Texas in the 19thC, when that state was part of Mexico. Hotels can arrange a visit to the fascinating **steelworks** on the edge of town, where you will see scenes straight from Dante's *Inferno*.

❧ **Kalionchis** *(Harold R Pape s/n* ☎*(863) 32511* ▥ ▦ ≋ ⇌ ♉ ➡*)* is the best hotel in town. If it is full, try **Gil Cantú** *(Carranza 410* ☎*(863) 31333* ▥ ⇌ ♉ ▦*)*.

SALTILLO

Map **4**E8. *Capital of Coahuila. 83km (51 miles) w of Monterrey on RF40; 427km (266 miles) N of San Luis Potosí on RF57; 277km (173 miles) E of Torreón on*

RF40; 445km (278 miles) s of Piedras Negras (US border) on RF57. Altitude: 1,650m (5,280ft). Population: 500,000. Served by air, train (on line from Piedras Negras or Nuevo Laredo and Monterrey to Mexico City via San Luis Potosí) and bus **i** *Venustiano Carranza 2454, 3rd floor* ☎*(841) 55811, and at Convention Center* ☎*(841) 54444.*

Most tourists just pass through Saltillo, although the city fathers would like them to stay longer and enjoy the dry, sunny climate, and shop in the pleasant colonial center, now engirdled with the industrial sprawl of relocating US car builders.

Saltillo's two plazas make an interesting contrast. The **Plaza de Armas** is very formal, with the 1920s neo-colonial **government palace**, the enormous Churrigueresque 18thC **cathedral** and an almost complete absence of street life. Just a few blocks away, the **Plaza Acuña** is a true people's park, full of street vendors, stalls, children at play, families and families-in-the-making, a fascinating microcosm of Mexican life.

For shoppers, Saltillo is famous for its brightly colored *serapes* (ponchos). The best shops are on **Plaza Acuña**, **Calle Victoria** and **Mercado Juárez**, and they may be able to arrange a visit to a weaving workshop. Other local products include silver, leather, and grotesque masks hammered out of sheet-tin.

If you're heading s to SAN LUIS POTOSÍ, be sure to visit **Real de Catorce**, 253km (158 miles) farther (see NORTH OF MEXICO CITY, page 208).

Camino Real *(* **■** *Blvd. los Fundadores 2000, 5km/3 miles s on RF57* ☎*(841) 52525* **Fx***(841) 53813* **▥** *117 rms* ≕ ≋ ▤ ❣ ♨ ☕ ☂ ❒ ♪ ✦ *)* is set in 4 hectares (10 acres) of gardens, and has an Olympic pool. **Motel la Fuente** *(Blvd. los Fundadores Km 3* ☎*(841) 52599* **▥** *52 rms* ▤ ▢ ▨ ≕ ≋ ☂ *)*, closer to town on the same road, is less luxurious but also recommended.

In the downtown area, **San Jorge** *(Manuel Acuña 240 Nte at Aldama* ☎*(841) 22222* **Fx***(841) 30600* **▥** *to* **▥** *120 rms* ≋ ≕ *)* is a good hotel, near Plaza Acuña. Another attractive option is **Urdiñola** *(Victoria 207 Pte* ☎*(841) 40940* **▥** ≕ *)*, a block from the Plaza de Armas, or you could try the **Huizache** *(Venustiano Carranza 1746* ☎*(841) 61000* **Fx***(841) 62662* **▥** ≕ ☂ ▤ *)*, a well-equipped motel.

MATAMOROS

Map **4E9**. *Tamaulipas. 323km (201 miles) E of Monterrey on RF40 and RF2; 312km (195 miles) N of Ciudad Victoria on RF101. Population: 475,000. Served by air (international airport 11km/6 miles NE), train (terminus of line from Monterrey) and bus* **i** *"Gateway to Mexico" tourist area* ☎*(891) 23630. US Consul: Primera 2002 at Azaleas* ☎*(891) 67270. American Express: Morelos 94–107 at 5a* ☎*(891) 33311.*

So turbulent has been the history of this border town that it has a story to tell from almost every regional conflict since its foundation in 1765. Raids by pirates, Apaches and Comanches were only the start. Matamoros was then occupied by the US Army during the 1846 war, and Maximilian's troops were besieged here at the end of the French intervention. In the American Civil War, it became an arms supply point for the Confederates.

Today, Matamoros is a peaceful border city that welcomes thousands of visitors every month. They find little in the way of Mexican atmosphere, but plenty of oil industry grime and dockyard sleaze. Few stay for long, but if you are here overnight, take a stroll near the Zócalo, Plaza Allende, to see the French-built **theater**, **cathedral** and **Casa Mata fort**. A small local museum is located in the fort *(Degollado Ote and Guatemala* ☎ *open standard hours)*, but the historical bric-a-brac is of less interest than the building in which it is housed.

Also nearby, on Calle 9, are three markets selling a variety of folk art and crafts from all over Mexico; but the best bargains are to be had at the **Mercado Juárez** *(Calle 10a and Matamoros)*. On the outskirts of town, toward the **International Bridge** and the soaring arches of the **Gateway to Mexico**, is a large **tourist area** with recreational facilities and a helpful tourist office.

Those in search of a bit of beach fun can head to **Playa Lauro Villar** *(38km/23 miles E on RF2)*, a low-key resort on a wide open expanse of hard-packed sand.

☜ **Del Prado** *(Obregón 249* ☎ *(891) 39440* Ⓕ*(891) 32777* ▥ *120 rms* ⇋▤ ♈ ♨ ⋙*)* is the best in town, a small colonial-style resort. **Nieto** *(10a Bravo and Bustamante 140* ☎ *(891) 30997* ▥ ▦ ⇋*)*, recently remodeled, has a restaurant that caters to the famished. **Gran Ritz** *(Matamoros and Septima 612* ☎ *(891) 21190* ▥ *100 rms* ▦⇋*)* is an established hotel in the downtown area. **Plaza Matamoros** *(Bravo and 9a* ☎ *(891) 61602* ▥ ⇋*)* is modern and, for the price, surprisingly snazzy.

REYNOSA

*Map **4**D9. Tamaulipas. 225km (140 miles) E of Monterrey on RF40; 98km (61 miles) W of Matamoros on RF2. Population: 500,000. Served by air, train (on Monterrey–Matamoros line) and bus* **i** *Immigration building on Mexican side of Río Bravo/Grande bridge* ☎*(892) 21189. American Express: Avila Camacho 1325* ☎*(892) 26016.*

A border town of no great charm with rapidly developing oil and gas industries, Reynosa has little to offer the tourist except reasonable accommodation and the usual seedy nightlife, although the center does retain some of its character. Sports fishermen stay here for the nearby **Presa del Azúcar**, 80km (50 miles) NW on RF2. The name means "Sugar Dam," and it is certainly sweet to anglers, as the lake teems with black bass and other species.

☜ **Astromundo** *(Juárez and Guerrero* ☎ *(892) 25625* ▥ ⋙ ⇋ ➤*)* is the top downtown establishment, while **Posada los Virreyes** *(Ortega and Madero* ☎ *(892) 21985* ▥ ⋙ ⇋ ➤*)* is a good modern motel. **Virrey** *(Hidalgo and Balboa* ☎ *(892) 31050* ▥ ⇋ ⋙ ➤*)* is another modern motel, 3km (2 miles) from the town center, on the Monterrey road.

NUEVO LAREDO

*Map **4**D8. Tamaulipas. 223km (139 miles) N of Monterrey on RF85. Served by air (international airport 10km/6 miles SW), train (line to Monterrey) and bus.*

Population: 300,000. US Consul: Allende 3330 ☎*(871) 40512. American Express: Reforma 3311* ☎*(871) 54455.*

An ordinary border town on the Río Grande (known in Mexico as the Río Bravo), founded in the aftermath of the Mexican–American war, Nuevo Laredo has some decent hotels and a huge variety of souvenir stores. The former big attraction of the post-prohibition era, the **race-track** on the s side of town, has shut down, to be replaced by booming *"maquiladora"* industries.

✍ Nuevo Laredo is well provided with hotels and motels. The following are recommended: **Hacienda Motor** *(* 🏨 *Reforma 5530* ☎*(871) 44666* ▯ ▦ ➼*),* a motel s of town toward the airport; **Reforma** *(Guerrero 882* ☎*(871) 26250* ▥ ➼*),* the best downtown hotel; **Motor Hotel El Río** *(Reforma 4402* ☎*(871) 43666* Ⓕⓧ*(871) 51232* ▥ *to* ▦ *149 rms* ≋ ➼ ☡*);* and **Villa del Monte** *(Guerrero 2001* ☎*(871) 45535* ▦ ≋ ➼ ☡*).*

The North-West

This is a truly vast region, most of which consists of desert, sparsely watered rangelands and impassable mountains. The four states that comprise it are **Sinaloa** and **Sonora** on the Sea of Cortés and, across the continental divide of the Sierra Madre Occidental, **Durango** and **Chihuahua**, the latter being the largest state in Mexico.

But for all the size of the northwestern region, not to mention the Houdini-like escapades of the notorious revolutionary Pancho Villa, which are its main claims to fame, this part of Mexico contains relatively few tourist destinations. Cities are limited to narrow corridors along the roads to the east and west of the Sierra Madre, along the Sea of Cortés and across the high inland plains.

CROSSING THE SIERRA MADRE
Between the east–west road near the US border and another road level with the southern tip of Baja California, the only routes across the Sierra Madre are a number of unmapped logging tracks and the spectacular **CHIHUAHUA–PACIFIC RAILROAD**.

Although the railroad, completed in 1961, has failed to meet the hopes of its financiers, the dramatic scenery it passes through makes it a delight for many thousands of visitors a year; it is one of the region's top attractions. Linking CHIHUAHUA, capital of its state, with the port of LOS MOCHIS in Sinaloa, it passes through the famous **Copper Canyon**, which dwarfs its northerly rival, the Grand Canyon. There are numerous opportunities to stop along the route, with hotels that organize hikes into the mountains and visits to Tarahumara Indian communities.

Chihuahua itself is a busy town, long established as a center for the cattle-ranching that occupies the surrounding expanse of semi-arid pasture, and for the logging of the Sierra Madre's much abused, if still extensive, pine forest. The state's second city is CIUDAD JUÁREZ, an increasingly industrialized border town, famous for its cut-price dentistry.

PARRAL, in the south of the state, is a former colonial mining town that has also found new importance as a lumbering center, most of its timber coming from the forests of the Tarahumara Indians in the nearby Sierra. The logging, from which the Indian communities derive little or no benefit, is a growing cause of friction.

Farther southeast, straddling the border between Durango and Coahuila, is the best-avoided industrial complex of TORREÓN and **Gómez Palacio**. DURANGO, capital of its state, is a much nicer place to stop, smaller, cleaner and with some fine colonial buildings. Founded as a mining town, it now lies in the center of a cattle-ranching area, while the nearby landscapes of dried-out mountains, cliffs and canyons have made it a popular location for low-budget Westerns.

THE PACIFIC COAST

The road between Durango and MAZATLÁN, on the Pacific coast in the state of Sinaloa, plunges through the rugged mountains to make one of the most spectacular journeys in Mexico. Mazatlán itself has a curiously split personality, as it combines the roles of modern luxury resort and run-down commercial port. But most visitors, except those who travel on the ferry to **La Paz** in BAJA CALIFORNIA, see only its white-sand beaches and deluxe hotels.

North along the coast lies CULIACÁN, the unexciting capital of Sinaloa, and the center for a flourishing agricultural area. As one of its major crops is marijuana, trips into the countryside cannot safely be recommended. LOS MOCHIS, to the north, has a similarly low charm factor, but is hard to avoid, as the terminus of the Chihuahua–Pacific railroad and the principal port for ferries to LA PAZ in Baja California.

Beyond the border, in the state of Sonora, lies the homeland of the Yaqui and Mayo Indians, but the towns of **Navojoa** and **Ciudad Obregón** have few attractions. Only the old mining town of ALAMOS, inland from Navojoa, is a tourist destination, with its colony of foreign artists and retired people living in restored Moorish-inspired palaces.

Sonora's most important tourist asset lies close to the fishing port of GUAYMAS, where there are plans to turn the lovely bay of SAN CARLOS into a resort to rival CANCÚN. With its proximity to the US, a stunning backdrop of arid mountains, the clear waters of the Sea of Cortés and perfect white-sand beaches, it has all the ingredients of success. But, for the present, San Carlos is a pleasant, low-key spot with just a handful of hotels.

Even less developed is the resort of **Bahía Kino**, which lies farther up the coast and due west of **HERMOSILLO**, the capital of Sonora. Between here and the US border, there is little to attract tourists. A number of minor resorts line the desert coast of the northern end of the Sea of Cortés, a godsend to the residents of Phoenix, Arizona, but hardly significant otherwise. As for **Nogales** and **Agua Prieta**, the principal border towns, there is little reason to linger in either.

Towns, cities and cultural sites

Starting in **MAZATLÁN**, this chapter gives essential information on the main destinations in northwestern Mexico, traveling N to **CULIACÁN**, **LOS MOCHIS**, **ALAMOS**, **GUAYMAS AND SAN CARLOS** and **HERMOSILLO**, then NE inland to **CIUDAD JUÁREZ** and S to **CHIHUAHUA**, **PARRAL**, **TORREÓN** and finally **DURANGO**. Following **CHIHUAHUA** is a section on the **CHIHUAHUA-PACIFIC RAILROAD**, a tourist attraction in its own right.

See USING THIS GUIDE on page 50 for details on how to use this section. On the following pages, helpful pointers are given on how to get to each of the destinations covered. Along with the MEXICO map on pages 46–7, and the 4-color maps at the back of this book, they should give all the information necessary for planning your trip to this part of Mexico.

MAZATLÁN ☆

Map 5F6. Sinaloa. 522km (326 miles) NW of Guadalajara on RF15; 432km (270 miles) S of Los Mochis, 222km (138 miles) S of Culiacán on RF15. Population: 700,000. Served by air (international airport 13km/8 miles SW), ferry (to La Paz in Baja California ☎(69) 117020), train (on Guadalajara–Nogales line) and bus i Loaiza 100, Los Sabalos ☎(69) 140222. US Consul: Circunvalación 120 Centro ☎(69) 152205. American Express Travel Service: Plaza Balboa 4 & 16, Camarón Sábalo ☎(69) 130600.

The Nahuatl name of this thriving resort and shrimping port means "Place of Deer," but it should now perhaps be rechristened "Place of Fish," so numerous are the sportsmen who congregate here all year round to try their luck in the Sea of Cortés. Set on a peninsula, Mazat-lán has two waterfronts: to the W, gleaming luxury hotels and long white-sand beaches look out across the Pacific; facing inland, across a natural harbor, are the commercial docks, always busy with luxury cruisers, freighters and trawlers. The new **Zona Dorada** area, NW from the peninsula along the bay, is home to all the glitziest hotels.

The frivolous elegance of Acapulco or Puerto Vallarta would not appeal to the Mazatlán regulars, who are not jet-setters, but arrive for the most part by car. There are said to be more camper parks here than in all the rest of Mexico. They come to get value for money, a suntan and, if all their dreams come true, a 600lb marlin. However, the complexion of Mazatlán may be in for a change, as there are plans for a $100 million 600-berth marina complex with associated hotels and golf course, covering 360 hectares (144 acres) of an unspoiled offshore island.

EVENTS • Mazatlán is famous for its **carnival**, on Ash Wednesday and the preceding week; it claims to be the world's third biggest, after those in Rio de Janeiro and New Orleans.

WHAT TO SEE

After a hard day's fun, a stroll along the waterfront downtown area, the **Olas Altas**, is best punctuated with frequent refreshment stops. If you still feel energetic, it is a short climb up to the **lighthouse** on the southern tip of the peninsula, from where the views of the city are excellent. On the way, pause at **El Mirador**, where the young bloods of Mazatlán perform a perilous dive off a high rock into shallow water.

Behind the Mirador is the **Cerro de la Nevería**, or Icebox Hill. Before the days of refrigerated ships, ice was stored here for shipping shrimps up to the US. The lighthouse is said to be second in height only to that at Gibraltar, and can be seen from far out to sea. At sunset, you can see the ships in the distance, reflected in the shimmering red-and-gold waters.

Going the other way from Olas Altas up Playa Norte, an excellent **aquarium** lies about half way along, and up Desportes (☎ *(69) 117 815, open 10am-5pm)*. It shows the rich marine life and complex ecology of the Sea of Cortés, which is now, unfortunately, under threat from the shrimp trawlers that are plowing up the fragile seabed.

Most visitors never get to see the scruffy town behind the port, which is a pity. It has an authentic Mexican atmosphere, and contains some good colonial buildings that are at last being restored, such as the **Teatro Angela Peralta** on Calle Carnaval. The best time to visit is on Sunday evenings, when the **bandstand** in the Zócalo comes alive to the sound of oompah-band music, which is a cultural legacy of Mazatlán's German immigrants.

Beaches

The sea off the downtown **Playa Olas Altas** (Big Wave Beach) is as vigorous as its name suggests, more for surfers than ordinary swimmers. Heading N, the next beach is **Playa Norte**, which extends for about 4km (2 miles) along Avenida del Mar; however, its quality is patchy, and the better beaches are farther N in the **Zona Dorada**, where the coastal road is known as Camarón Sábalo.

The Zona Dorada's first beach, **Playa Las Gaviotas**, is sheltered by Isla de los Venados (see below) and usually calm enough for children. The next, **Playa Sábalo**, is sheltered by Isla de los Pajaros, but the waves can get quite strong all the same. Farther N still, across the mouth of Laguna El Sábalo, a saltwater lagoon, **Playa Los Cerritos** remains undeveloped, its white sands open to the full ocean surf.

There are several small islands out at sea. The most accessible is the **Isla de los Venados**, which has a popular beach just a 10-minute boat ride from the hotel zone. It is a rather longer journey to **Isla de la Piedra**, with its 16km (10 miles) of palm-fringed beaches; this is a popular weekend destination for Mexican families, but more than big enough to absorb the crowds.

Plans for the island's large-scale development have been delayed, so for the time being it retains its unspoiled charm — but who knows for how much longer?

EXCURSION
RF40 to Durango

This spectacular road is the first to cross the Sierra Madre s of the US border. As well as offering fantastic views, there are also several good places to stop along the route. **Concordia** *(45km/28 miles E)* is a pretty former mining town known for its ceramic productions. **Copala** *(88km/55 miles E)* is another historic mining village, and a pleasant place to break a journey.

Stay at the **Posada San José** (🔲 🍽), small and friendly with a good restaurant, or carry on to **Loberas** *(another 10km/6 miles E)*, where the **Villa Real** (🔲 🍽) is a Bavarian-inspired lodge with an authentic German menu. More distant spots are described under DURANGO (page 239).

WHERE TO STAY

CAMINO REAL 🏨
Punta del Sábalo ☎*(69) 131111* 🆑*(69) 140311* 🔲 *169 rms* 🍽 ❧ ⟨⟨ ≋ ⌘
♨ ✒ 🏊 ⚓ 🕭
Mazatlán's most glamorous resort hotel boasts glittering nightlife and a choice of two excellent restaurants. Guests are transported down the cliffside to the beach in the panoramic comfort of the hotel's own funicular railroad.

EL CID MEGA RESORT 🏨
Playa Sábalo ☎*(69) 133333* 🆑*(69) 141311* 🔲 *to* 🔲 *1,100 rms* 🍽 ❧ ⟨⟨
≋ ⌘ ♨ ⚓ 🍷 ✒ ⊸ 🔴 🕭
This self-contained vacation town may not win any beauty contests, but it can offer a choice of 15 restaurants and bars, six swimming pools, a squash club, sauna and health center, and an active social program.

HOLIDAY INN ❀ 🏨
Camarón Sábalo 696 ☎*(69) 132222* 🆑*(69) 141287* 🔲 *to* 🔲 *204 rms*
🍽 ≋ ⌘ 🍷 🍷 ♨ ✒ ⊸ ⚓ 🍷 🔴 🕭
Much favored by families, this hotel delivers the efficiency expected from the Holiday Inn chain. Paragliding is available for guests.

OCEANO PALACE
Playa Sábalo ☎*(69) 130666* 🆑*(69) 139666* 🔲 *205 rms* 🍽 ≋ ⌘ 🍷 🔴 🕭
The young jet-setters' disco-hotel has a cheerful restaurant, and the bars are open until all hours.

PUEBLO BONITO 🏨
Camarón Sábalo 2121 ☎*(69) 143700* 🔲 *135 rms* 🍽 ≋ ♨ ⌘ 🍷 🔴 🕭
This is a beautifully designed luxury hotel in the Mexican style.

Budget hotels

Mazatlán has an excellent selection of lower-priced hotels, many of them with good seafront positions. Downtown, **La Siesta** (❀ *Olas Altas 11* ☎*(69) 112640* 🆑*(69) 137476* 🔲 *58 rms* 🍽 🍷 🔴 🕭) is a seafront hotel at the heart of the downtown area, with its own disco and the **El Shrimp Bucket** restaurant. Also downtown, the **Belmar** *(Olas Altas 166* ☎*(69) 151111* 🔲 🍽 🍷 ≋ 🎴)*, once the number-one spot, is now showing its age. Other central choices are **Freeman** *(Olas Altas 79 Sur* ☎*(69) 112114* ▢ *97 rms* ⇌ Ⴗ ▦ *)* and **Sands** *(Av. del Mar 1910* ☎*(69) 153104* [Fx]*(69) 121025* ☞ ⇌ Ⴗ ▦ *)*, on Playa Norte.

Reasonably-priced hotels on the better beaches to the N include the **Caravelle Beach Club** *(Camarón Sábalo s/n* ☎*(69) 130200* ▥ *118 rms* ⇌ Ⴗ ☞ ▦ *)*, the **Riviera** *(Camarón Sábalo 51* ☎*(69) 134822* ▢ *to* ▥ *244 rms* ⇌ Ⴗ ☞ ▦ *)* and the **Plaza Gaviotas** *(Loaiza s/n by Playa Gaviotas* ☎*(69) 134322* [Fx]*(69) 136685* ▥ *66 rms* ⇌ Ⴗ ☞ ▦ *)*.

EATING AND DRINKING

Be sure to try Mazatlán's local specialty, the *parillada* (mixed seafood grill). Of the hotels, the **Camino Real**, **La Siesta** and **Oceano Palace** have the best restaurants, but they have serious competition from **Casa Loma** *(* ▥ *Gaviotas 104* ☎*(69) 135398* ▥ 🖐 *)*, in a beautiful colonial townhouse, which serves international and local cuisine.

Rather less formal eating-places are **Tres Islas** *(Camarón Sábalo s/n* ☎*(69) 135932* ▥ *)*, a *palapa* complete with *mariachis,* views across to the islands, and an excellent *parillada,* and **Señor Frog** *(Av. del Mar s/n* ☎*(69) 121925* ▥ 🎵 *)*, part of the Carlos'n'Charlie's chain, specializing in seafood with silly names.

Good downtown choices include **El Marinero** *(5 de Mayo and Clausen* ☎*(69) 117682* ▥ *)*, the top seafood spot, **Casa de Tony** *(Mariano Escobedo 111* ☎*(69) 151262* ▥ *)*, a gourmet colonial-style restaurant and **Copa de Leche** *(Olas Altas 33* ☎*(69) 125753* ▥ *)*, a seafront café and restaurant.

The economically challenged will enjoy the huge choice of places along **Avenida del Mar**, serving a wholesome diet of *tacos,* fruit juice and coconut milk.

MAZATLÁN BY NIGHT

Now that the serious sportsmen are being joined by more relaxed pleasure-seekers, the nightlife of Mazatlán has become more exciting. Discos abound and are so popular that, in the smart hotels, it is sometimes necessary to reserve. The **Camino Real** has a wild, space-age light-and-sound show, but the **El Caracol Tango Palace** *(next to El Cid Resort* ☎*(69) 133333)* is the most modern and extravagant.

Smaller, short-lived places spring up along the beach; some that seem set to last are the **Valentino Disco Club** *(Punta Camarón* ☎*(69) 136212)* and **Frankie-Oh** *(Av. del Mar 1300* ☎*(69) 125800)* and the popular, low-tech, open-air **Sunset** disco-bar *(N end of Camarón Sábalo).*

CULIACÁN

Map **2E5**. *Capital of Sinaloa. 222km (138 miles)* NW *of Mazatlán on RF15; 210km (131 miles)* S *of Los Mochis on RF15. Population: 600,000. Served by air, train (on Guadalajara–Nogales line) and bus. American Express: Guerra 235 Sur* ☎*(671) 61494.*

At the center of an unpleasant urban-industrial sprawl and with no features of real touristic interest, Culiacán might best be avoided. If you decide to overnight here, be warned that the rich agricultural land around grows more than just tomatoes; drugs, primarily cannabis, are among the abundant crops. This leads to occasional disturbances in remote parts of the countryside, and tedious vehicle checks.

To the w, the remote mountains of the Sierra Madre are penetrated only by logging trails leading through into the state of Durango. The vast vacation camp on the outskirts is for the employees of the Mexican Social Security Institute.

San Luis Lindavista *(Av. las Palmas 1* ☎ *(67) 131500* ▥ ➤ ☒ ᾳ ▦ ◪ *)* has good views over town from its hilltop. **Ejecutivo** *(* ♣ *Obregón and Madero* ☎ *(67) 139300* ▥ ➤ ᾳ *)* is located downtown. **Los Tros Ríos** *(on RF15 5km/3 miles N* ☎ *(67) 124040* ▥ ➤ ᾳ *)* is an ordinary motel.

LOS MOCHIS

Map 2E5. Sinaloa. 206km (128 miles) NW of Culiacán on RF15; 225km (140 miles) S of Ciudad Obregón on RF15. Population: 300,000. Served by air, train (on Guadalajara–Nogales and Chihuahua–Pacific lines), bus, and ferry (from Topolobampo, 24km (15 miles) SW, to La Paz in Baja California ☎ *(681) 20141, tickets from Juárez 125* ☎ *(681) 25642) ℹ Allende 2 Cuauhtémoc* ☎ *(681) 27610. American Express: Alvaro Obregón 471–A Poniente* ☎ *(681) 22084.*

This busy agricultural town doubles as a major transport terminus, chiefly distinguished for its position at the head of the spectacular railroad line across the Sierra Madre from Chihuahua, the CHIHUAHUA–PACIFIC RAILROAD. Your hotel will be able to reserve your rail tickets — ask when you make your reservation. The **Santa Anita** hotel (see overleaf) can make reservations at Balderrama hotels along the route.

The main port for LA PAZ is nearby at **Topolobampo** *(24km/15 miles s)*, with daily morning departures for the 8-hour crossing. There is now a "**Baja Express**" speedboat service as well — half the time, but four times the price. Topolobampo is also the place to charter a boat for a day's **deep-sea fishing**.

While out at sea, pass by the **Isla Farallón** to enjoy the noisy spectacle of the sea-lions fighting for space in which to sun themselves, or drop in on **Isla Santa María**, a deserted island of beaches and sand dunes.

EXCURSIONS

Guasave
60km (37 miles) SE on RF15.
Just to the w of the main road is this small town, where on October 7 the **feast of the Rosary** is celebrated in pagan style. The highlight is the performance of Mayo Indian dances, including the **stag** dance and the **coyote** dance.

Mochicahui
24km (15 miles) NE; turn NE off RF15 after 16km (10 miles).

Follow the road alongside the railroad to this Mayo pueblo, where the fiesta on June 24 involves the "baptism" of a sacred statue in the river Fuerte, accompanied by fireworks, processions and dancing.

70km (43 miles) farther, the road reaches the colonial mining town of **El Fuerte** (also on the railroad), near a large **reservoir** with good fishing.

Santa Anita (♣ *Hidalgo and Gabriel Leyva* ☎ *(681) 57046* Fx *(681) 20046* ▥ *133 rms* ☰ ☒ ▦ *)* is a central hotel that serves as a clearing house for hotel reservations along the railroad line to Chihuahua; several of the hotels are under the same (Balderrama) management. The Santa Anita also runs its own bus service to the station.

Other hotels include the plain but clean **Los Arcos** *(Allende Sur 534, near bus station* ▥ *).* The **Plaza Inn** *(Gabriel Leyva 701* ☎ *(681) 20075* ▥ ≈ ☰ *)* and **Las Colinas** *(s of town, on International Highway* ☎ *(681) 20101* ▥ *116 rms* ☰ ≈ ☒ ♨ *)* are both convenient motels.

ALAMOS ☆

*Map **2**D5. Sonora. 247km (154 miles) SE of Guaymas: 194km (121 miles) S on RF15 to Navojoa, then 53km (33 miles) E; 210km (131 miles) N of Los Mochis: 158km (98 miles) N on RF15, then 53km (33 miles) E. Altitude: 450m (1,440ft). Population: 25,000. Served by bus* **i** *Hotel Los Portales, on Zócalo* ☎ *(642) 80053.*

Alamos was formerly the capital of western Mexico and rivaled Taxco in silver production, but stricken by droughts, Indian uprisings, failing silver reserves and the 1910 Revolution, its population dwindled. Now it is only a tenth of what it was in the days when the town gloried in the name of Pueblo Real de la Limpia Concepción de Los Alamos.

But it is starting to regain some of its past splendor: back in the 1940s, Alamos was discovered by foreign artists and retired people, most of them from Arizona. The incomers restored the magnificent 18thC Baroque and Moorish-style houses on the outskirts, where they made their homes. Thanks to their efforts, the town has been designated a national monument, and the newest building is more than a century old.

The area is renowned as the home of the Mexican Jumping Bean, which can be bought in the Zócalo. It makes an unrewarding pet; disappointingly, the movement is caused by an insect inside the bean.

WHAT TO SEE

Casa de los Tesoros (House of the Treasures) ▥
Obregón 10.
The best known of the restored residences, about two blocks from the square, is a low building with a colonnaded courtyard, which now houses a hotel. Stop here for a meal, to enjoy the colonial interior.

Zócalo (Plaza de Armas)
This small, charming, cobbled square is arcaded on three sides. On the fourth is the church of **Nuestra Señora de la Concepción** (1784), which replaced an earlier Jesuit Mission, burned by rebellious Mayo Indians.

The narrow streets around the square are full of impressive mansions built during the prosperous 18thC. Worth a special look is the **Museo**

Costumbrista de Sonora *(Zócalo, open 10am-1pm, 4-8pm)*, a small but interesting museum of local history.

➴   **Casa de los Tesoros** *(* 🏛 *Obregón 10* ☎ *(642) 80010* ▥ � ᪣ *)* is a fine colonial inn (see page opposite); if it's full, try the nearby **Mansión de la Condesa Magdalena** *(* 🏛 *Obregón 2* ☎ *(642) 80221* ▥ ➤né *)*, another well-restored colonial building.

➤né   Both hotels have excellent restaurants. Alternatively, for wholesome local food go to **Las Palmeras** *(Cárdenas 9 on the Zócalo* ☎ *(642) 80065* ▢ *)*.

EXCURSIONS
Ciudad Obregón
67km (41 miles) N of Navojoa on RF15.
A dusty, modern city with a population of about 300,000, on the Guadalajara–Nogales railroad, Ciudad Obregón has an airport, but little else to offer the tourist. There are reasonable hotels and restaurants for passing travelers, some of whom use it as a base for trips into the Sierra Madre.

Motel Costa de Oro *(* ✿ *Miguel Alemán and Allende* ☎ *(641) 41765* ▥ ➤né ᪣ *)* and **Valle Grande Obregón** *(* ✿ *Miguel Alemán and Tetabiate* ☎ *(641) 40940* ▥ ➤né ᪣ *)* are good places to stay.

Indian Villages
Around Navojoa, 53km (33 miles) W on RF15.
Villages in this area are the homes of the Yaqui and Mayo Indians. Wild and rebellious until recently, they now live more or less at peace with Spanish-speaking society. Indeed, their culture and customs are slowly disappearing under the assault of the Coca-Cola civilization.

The villages have been much visited recently by travelers searching fruitlessly for the Yaqui sorcerer Don Juan, the subject of Carlos Castaneda's series of books. Remarkable works though they are, they have little to do with the harsh realities of life in a subsistence economy in the bleak deserts and mountains of Sonora.

EVENTS   • You can sometimes visit native **festivals**, but they are of more significance to anthropologists than to tourists. One of the more accessible takes place between May 10 and 20 at **Etchojoa**, 20km (12 miles) SW of Navojoa, when men in deer masks perform the "stag dance."

GUAYMAS AND SAN CARLOS
*Map **2**D4. Sonora. 413km (258 miles) S of Nogales on RF15; 247km (154 miles) NW of Alamos on side-road and RF15; 136km (85 miles) S of Hermosillo on RF15; 780km (487 miles) N of Mazatlán on RF15. Population: 250,000. Served by air, boat (3 ferries per week to and from Santa Rosalia in Baja California), train (on Guadalajara–Nogales line) and bus **i** Av. Serdán, behind the Palacio Municipal* ☎ *(622) 22932.*

The working port of Guaymas, or more particularly the nearby tourist development of **San Carlos** *(12km/7 miles NW)*, has long been tipped as a future Acapulco. The qualifications are all there: it is near the US, and has a perfect climate, excellent fishing and natural beauty. On three sides are the desolate mountains and deserts of Sonora and, on the fourth, palm-shaded beaches face the clear waters of the Sea of Cortés, which offer wonderful scuba diving.

Some resort hotels have opened, and others will follow, but the main attraction for the time being is the **deep-sea fishing**. There is a good, secure **marina** for boat owners, with a multitude of small-time charter-operators: remember to check the radio and safety equipment. Hotels can help, and can also arrange **horseback riding** up in the hills.

In the future, the "**Soldado de Cortés**" project is due to develop 3.5km (2 miles) of beach into a new mini-city with marina, golf courses, shopping malls and hotels.

There are few reminders of Guaymas' disturbed history. During the 19thC it was attacked from all sides. The best place to enjoy the contemporary peace is on Guaymas' premier beach, **Playa Miramar** at Bacochibampo. However, there is little reason to stop in Guaymas; best head over to San Carlos, unless you are taking the ferry to La Paz.

WHERE TO STAY

San Carlos' newest hotel is the bright pink **Howard Johnson's** *(Playa de los Algodones* ☎ *(622) 60777* ▥ *176 rms* ⇌ ☿ ⋙ ≋ ⤴ ❍*)*, with every facility. The nearby **Club Mediterranée** *(*🏨 *Playa de los Algodones* ☎ *(622) 60076* ☒ *(622) 60070* ▥ *430 rms* ⇌ ⋙ ⛱ ⤴ ⌂ ▦ ✓ ☿*)* is a classic Club Med resort with a well-organized sports and social scene, and an excellent diving program.

Playa de Cortés *(Playa de Bacochibampo* ☎ *(622) 20121* ☒ *(622) 20135* ▥ *to* ▥ *122 rms* ⇌ ⧊ ⋙ ⛱ ⤴ ⤴ ❍*)* is a pleasant traditional hotel, popular with water-sports enthusiasts. **Posada de San Carlos** *(12km/7 miles* N ☎ *(622) 60122* ☒ *(622) 60451* ▥ *120 rms* ⇌ ⋙ ⛱ ⤴ ✓ 🐟 ♨ ☿ ♪*)* has a good seafood restaurant and is pleasantly relaxing. Comfortable if undistinguished, **Fiesta San Carlos** *(*♣ *Km 8, San Carlos Bay* ☎ *(622) 60229* ▥ *33 rms* ⇌ ⋙ ⤴ ☿*)* is less expensive than its rivals. Near the ferry, the **Rubi** *(Serdán and Calle 30* ☎ *(622) 21069* ▥ ⇌*)* is clean and convenient.

EXCURSIONS

Yaqui Indian reservation

Begins 25km (15 miles) E *of Guaymas.*

Under the dictator Porfirio Díaz, the Yaqui lands were sold off to landlords and speculators. The Indians themselves were sold as slaves to work on henequen plantations in the Yucatán, or simply hanged. These injustices were only rectified in 1930, many years after the revolution, when President Lázaro Cárdenas created this reservation.

Even now, disputes continue: at issue are the rights to water for irrigation, which is vital to make the land produce. And, with the government's constitutional reforms on land tenure, the integrity of the reservation itself may now be at risk. (See ALAMOS, page 229, for further information on the Yaqui Indians.)

HERMOSILLO

Map 2C4. Capital of Sonora. 277km (173 miles) s of Nogales on RF15; 136km (85 miles) N of Guaymas on RF15; 623km (389 miles) sw of Mexicali on RF2 and RF15. Population: 600,000. Served by air, train (on Guadalajara–Nogales line) and bus ℹ Palacio Administrativo, at Tehuantepec and Comonfort ☎(621) 72392. US Consul: Monterrey 141 ☎(621) 72613/72375. American Express: Edificio Lupita, Rosales and Monterrey ☎(621) 71718.

Named after a leader of Mexico's war of independence, Hermosillo is the first major town on RF15 heading s from MEXICALI and Nogales. It has no real tourist attractions, but the town is well-provided with hotels, making it a convenient stopover.

EXCURSIONS

Bahía Kino
107km (66 miles) w on a good road.
A small fishing village with 15km (9 miles) of continuous beach, Bahía Kino is gaining in importance as a resort, and is now especially popular with the camper crowd. The sea fishing and scuba diving are good, and all equipment can be rented on the spot.

Across the alarmingly named **Estrecho del Infiernillo** (Straits of Hell) is the **Isla del Tiburón** (Shark Island) nature reserve; it is also inhabited by Seri Indians, who now make a living selling woodcarvings and ceremonial baskets to tourists. However, most of the 500-strong tribe now lives on the mainland, to the N of the resort.

There is a small Seri **museum** in town *(main street, open 9am-1pm, 4-7pm)*, which records the history of the tribe, with artifacts and many old photographs.

WHERE TO STAY

The **Comfort Inn Calinda** *(Rosales 87 and Morelia ☎(621) 72396 Fx(621) 72424 ▥ 111 rms ⇌ ≋ ☿ ○ ⋔ 🍽)* is a large high-rise hotel in the downtown area with three restaurants; it is part of the Quality Inn/Calinda chain.

Some 5km (3 miles) from the center, the **Holiday Inn** *(🏨 Eusebio Kino 369 ☎(621) 51112 Fx(621) 55721 ▥ 255 rms ⇌ ≋ ☿ ○ ⋔ ⚲ ⚓)* is all you would expect; if it's full, try the **Bugambilia Valle Grande** *(across the road at Kino 712 ☎(621) 45050 Fx(621) 66443 ▥ 108 rms ⇌ ☿ ≋ 🍽)*.

Also good is **Pitic Valle Grande** *(Kino at Ramón Corral ☎(621) 44570 Fx(621) 66473 ▥ 144 rms ⇌ a/c] ☿ ≋ ◨)*. One lower-priced option is **San Alberto** *(Serdán and Rosales ☎(621) 31840 Fx(621) 25216 ▯ 164 rms ⇌ ☿ 🍽)*.

At **Kino Bay** *(104km/65 miles w of Hermosillo)*, the mission-style **Posada del Mar** *(Fracc. Bahía de Kino ☎(624) 81205▯ 48 rms ⇌ ≋ ☿ 🍽 ○)*, by the beach, has charming poolside gardens: this is still the best hotel in town, if a little past its best. **Posada de Santa Gemma** *(Mar de Cortés ☎(624) 45576/20026 ▥ 28 rms ⇌ ≋ 🍽 ☿ ○)* is a beachside motel with 14 pleasant, two-roomed bungalows.

CIUDAD JUÁREZ

Map 3B6. Chihuahua. 375km (234 miles) N of Chihuahua on RF45; 1,866km (1,166 miles) N of Mexico City. Population: $1\frac{1}{4}$ million. Served by air (international airport 17km/10 miles S), train (terminus of lines from Chihuahua and Los Mochis) and bus **i** *Palacio Municipal, Benito Juárez* ☎*(16) 140837. US Consul: Av. López Mateos Nte 924* ☎*(16) 134048; UK Consul: Fresno 185* ☎*(16) 175791. American Express: Prol. Mejía and Pronaf 369* ☎*(16) 160066.*

For many people arriving across the Río Grande from El Paso, this is the first taste of Mexico. Although certainly more Americanized than other Mexican cities, Ciudad Juárez is the largest and most interesting of the border towns. It has some good hotels and Mexican restaurants, as well as two bullrings and several markets for Mexican crafts, which survive although the recession has hit hard.

One of the town's more curious boasts is a population of dentists sufficient for a city three times the size, catering to the one-day visitors who come across for a bullfight and cut-price dental work.

WHAT TO SEE

The oldest building, dating like the town from 1659, is the shrine of **Nuestra Señora de Guadalupe** on the Zócalo, with massive adobe walls and hand-carved wooden beams.

From 1864–66, while the French troops of Emperor Maximilian were occupying Mexico City, President Benito Juárez governed Mexico from the house at Av. 16 de Septiembre #527, which is open to visitors *(standard hours)*. Like the city, the **Cultural Center** on the Zócalo is named after President Juárez. It has examples of folk arts, archeological remains from Casas Grandes (see page 234), and historical items including mementos of the 1910 Revolution, when the city was stormed twice by the bandit revolutionary Pancho Villa.

EXCURSION

See **Casas Grandes** (under CHIHUAHUA, page 234).

☞ Ciudad Juárez is well stocked with moderately-priced hotels that cater to passing travelers. Near the PRONAF commercial and shopping mall on the NW edge of town is **Del Prado** *(Centro PRONAF* ☎*(16) 168800* ▥ *150 rms* ▬ ☒ ▦ ⋙*)*. The **De Luxe** *(Lerdo Sur 300* ☎*(16) 150082* ▥ *71 rms* ▦ ⋙ ▬*)* has a downtown location, and the **Quality Inn Calinda Juárez** *(Hermanos Escobar 3515 Ote* ☎*(16) 163260* ℻*(16) 137250* ▥ ▬ ⋙ ☒ ▦*)* is a reliable member of the chain.

CHIHUAHUA

Map 3C6. Capital of Chihuahua. 376km (235 miles) S of Ciudad Juárez on RF45; 462km (288 miles) NW of Torreón on RF45 and RF49. Altitude: 1,430m (4,690ft). Population: 1 million. Served by air (international airport 16km (10 miles) NE), rail (on Ciudad Juárez–Mexico City line, and terminal of Los Mochis line) and bus **i** *Libertad and Calle 13 2nd floor* ☎*(14) 160000. American Express: Guerrero 1207* ☎*(14) 126030.*

Although usually associated with miniature dogs, Chihuahua is also the name of Mexico's largest state (at 244,938 sq.km/95,679 sq. miles, it is larger than the British Isles), and of that state's capital city. The latter, pleasant and prosperous, is situated on a wide plain to the E of the Sierra Madre, surrounded by forests in the mountains and cattle ranches on the plain.

Chihuahua was founded in 1709, its original wealth coming from nearby silver mines, few of which are now in operation. Now it makes its money from timber, irrigated agriculture, cattle-ranching and relocated US industries. Although the city is not, in itself, a major tourist attraction, many visitors pass through and spend a night or two here, for it is located on a main N–S highway, and is, of course, a terminus of the breathtaking CHIHUAHUA–PACIFIC RAILROAD (see pages 234-6).

WHAT TO SEE
The city center
Downtown Chihuahua is spread around three main plazas, **Constitución**, **Zaragoza** and **Hidalgo**, all within a few blocks of each other. Start at Constitución, with a visit to the richly decorated 18thC Baroque **cathedral**, financed by profits from the local silver-mines. The **carvings** of the twelve Apostles on the facade are especially fine, and a **museum** of religious art lurks in the crypt *(open 9am-3pm; closed weekends)*.

Leaving the plaza and keeping the 20thC municipal palace to the right, Plaza Hidalgo is reached in about 5 minutes. In the middle stands a large **monument to Father Miguel Hidalgo**, executed near here in 1811 after the initial failure of his rebellion against Spanish rule. On one side of the square is the building, now the **Palacio Federal**, where Hidalgo and his fellow conspirator Ignacio Allende were imprisoned. Opposite is the **Palacio de Gobierno**, partly built as a Jesuit college in 1711. The rebels were shot on the patio here; the scene is shown in vivid 20thC **murals** by Aaron Mora.

Two blocks to the N, on the Plaza Zaragoza, is the church of **San Francisco**, where Hidalgo's headless body was kept until 1823. Only then, following the success of the revolution he had launched, could the body be buried together with the missing head, which had been taken for public display in Guanajuato.

Museo Regional
Paseo Bolivar 401 ☎*(14) 123834* 🎫 *Open standard hours.*
Formerly Quinta Gameros, this restored French Neoclassical-style mansion now houses interesting displays of local history and archeology.

Pancho Villa's House (Casa Pancho Villa)
Calle 10 and Mendez 🎫 *Open standard hours, but closed on Sun, not Mon.*
During the uprising of 1910, the notorious bandit and revolutionary, Pancho Villa, was based in Chihuahua. It was here that he raised the *División del Norte* army, whose victories helped to secure the downfall of the dictator Porfirio Díaz.

One of Villa's several widows has turned this house into a shrine to his memory. Exhibits include Villa's clothing and guns, and even the bullet-riddled car in which he was assassinated in 1923.

EXCURSIONS

Aquiles Serdán
45km (28 miles) SE off RF45.

This pretty mining village is best visited on Friday or Sunday evening for the music and dancing that fills the Zócalo, or for its **fiesta** on September 16.

Casas Grandes 🏛
Map 2C5. 353km (220 miles) NW of Chihuahua on RF45 and RF10, or 271km (169 miles) SW of Ciudad Juárez on RF2 and CH10, to Nuevo Casas Grandes (also on Los Mochis–Ciudad Juárez railroad), then 6km (3 miles) SW on CH18. Open 9am–5pm. Closed Mon.

This is an important archeological site, which makes the long detour worthwhile. The city covers 6 sq.km ($2\frac{1}{2}$ sq. miles), and was built by the people of the North American Pueblo–Oasis Culture around AD1000, at the meeting-point with the Toltec empire. It remained an important center until destroyed by the Apaches in 1340. The site is only partially restored, but the ruins and landscape are impressive.

The road to the ruins continues to **Colonia Juárez** *(21km/13 miles farther SW)*, since 1844 home to a several-thousand-strong, all-American Mormon community.

◆ In Nuevo Casas Grandes, stay at the convenient **Motel Hacienda** *(☎ (168) 41048 ▥ ⊒ ▨)*, which can arrange trips into the Sierra Madre.

At the luxury end of the market are: **Palacio del Sol** *(▥ Independencia 500 ☎ (14) 166000 ▣ (14) 159947 ▥ 200 rms ⊒ ♈ ●)*; **Castel Sicomoro** *(Periférico s/n ☎ (14) 135445 ▣ (14) 131411 ▥ 131 rms ⊒ ♈ ▨ ▤)*; **El Presidente** *(▥ Libertad 9 ☎ (14) 160606 ▥ to ▥ ▨)*, conveniently central; and **Chihuahua Park Plaza** *(Victoria 409 ☎ (14) 167770 ▣ (14) 153538 ▥ 132 rms ⊒ ➡ ▨)*, right in the center.

Better for those on a budget are the **Victoria** *(♥ Juárez and Colón ☎ (14) 128893 □ ⊒ ▨)*, which offers good value just 15 minutes' walk from the center, and **San Juan** *(Victoria 823 ☎ (14) 128491 ▥)*, in a run-down prewar mansion.

⊒ Chihuahua is renowned for its steaks. The juiciest are at **La Calesa** *(Juárez 3300 at Colón ☎ (14) 128555 ▥)* and the **El Presidente** hotel (see above). Other good restaurants within a taxi ride from the center are **El Bandido** *(Av. de Las Américas 1303 ☎ (14) 1394492 ▥ to ▥)*, with Wild West decor, and **Los Paradores de Tony Vega** *(Juárez 3316 ☎ (14) 151333 ▥)*, for steaks and international cuisine.

Downtown, **La Parilla** *(Victoria 420 ☎ (14) 505856 ▥)* has good food and low prices, but for an alternative to endless animal protein, try **El Vegetariano** *(Libertad and Calle 13 ▥)*.

CHIHUAHUA–PACIFIC RAILROAD ★
Map 3C6. 650km (406 miles) between Chihuahua and Los Mochis. First-class trains depart from either end at 7am for the 12hr journey, followed by slower second-class trains at 7.20am and noon, which take 14hrs.

Between Chihuahua and the Sea of Cortés lies the **Sierra Tarahumara**, a wild and grandiose section of the **Sierra Madre** mountain range. While it is possible to penetrate this region in a rugged vehicle, there are no reliable maps, and the roads are poor even when they exist as shown. By far the best way to get into the Sierra is on the 650km-long (406-mile) Chihuahua–Pacific railroad, which links CHIHUA-HUA with LOS MOCHIS on the coast. This miracle of engineering took 90 years to build at a cost of $100 million, and was only completed in 1961, creating a direct rail link from Kansas City in the US to the Mexican Pacific shores.

The journey provides endless breathtaking views of soaring, jagged mountains, vertiginous canyons and exuberant tropical vegetation, transected by the line's 39 bridges and 86 tunnels. On the w side of the high point at El Divisadero (2,465m/8,085 feet), the train passes through the 1,500m-deep (4,920-foot) **Copper Canyon** (Barranca del Cobre), a series of linked canyons, deeper and up to four times wider than the Grand Canyon in the US.

The entire journey takes about 14 hours, with frequent stops at which you can break your journey and venture forth into the mountains.

An estimated 50,000 Tarahumara Indians inhabit the region, many of whom cling to a traditional way of life, subsisting on corn, wild plants and small rodents, and sheltering in caves. Others have become more integrated into mainstream society, and will sell you their crafts at every opportunity. It is worth bearing in mind that this is one of the few ways for them to earn money. Meanwhile, the predatory logging of their high-altitude pine forests continues to cause friction between the Tarahumara and the state authorities.

There are several places to stop near the railroad, with reasonable hotels but only average food. Each hotel organizes its own expeditions to canyons, waterfalls and Tarahumara Indian villages. Most exciting is the demanding 4-day expedition by mule down the **Copper Canyon** from **El Divisadero**. All the major stops are listed below, ordered from Chihuahua to Los Mochis. The main booking agent, **Balderrama**, has two offices: in Los Mochis, at the **Hotel Santa Anita** (*Hidalgo and Gabriel Leyva* ☎(*681*) *57046* Ⓕ(*681*) *20046; in Chihuahua, Reforma 1600–2* ☎(*14*) *165950*).

RAILROAD STOPS

Ciudad Cuauhtémoc
1½ hrs from Chihuahua, 10½ hrs from Los Mochis.
This first stop, still on the plain, serves a community of 30,000 German-speaking Mennonites, who survive rather well on 100,000 hectares (250,000 acres) of reclaimed scrubland.

Estación Creel
2,238m (7,341ft). 4hrs 40mins from Chihuahua, 7hrs 20mins from Los Mochis.
Creel is a small town in the heart of excellent walking country, with old missions, waterfalls and hot springs to be discovered in the mountains. Although the town is not particularly attractive, this is the most popular stop, being particularly well-stocked with hotels.

A comfortable place to stay is the **Parador de la Montaña** (*near the station* Ⅲ *35 rms* ⚏ ☎(*145*) *60075* ◖● ⛷ ♈ *)*, a good center for expeditions, which the hotel will arrange. If good value and hikers' camaraderie come higher on your list of priorities, you should make for the **Casa Margerita** *(opposite the station at López Mateos and Parroquía 11* ☎*(145) 60045* ☐ *21 rms, no cards)*.

Otherwise, board one of the buses that meet the trains for the 28km (17-mile) journey to **Cabañas Cañon del Cobre** *(*▥ *23 rms* ⇶ ⌂ ◁€ ⌂ ♈ *reservations: Balderrama)*. This simple hotel, with no electricity or telephone, set in beautiful country, is the best place to stay; it organises daily expeditions and occasional performances of Tarahumara music.

A possible side journey is to **Batopilas**, 118km (73 miles) s of Estación Creel at the end of a magnificent road, an old silver-mining village in a warm river-valley, with several basic hotels. Nearby, explore the **La Bufa** goldmine *(6km/4 miles N)* and the deserted mission of **Satero** *(4km/2 $\frac{1}{2}$ miles S)*.

El Divisadero

2,465m (8,085ft). 6hrs from Chihuahua and Los Mochis.

This is the highest point of the trip, with panoramic views over the Copper Canyon. The train stops here for 20 minutes, so that passengers can take in the scenery.

If a short stop is not long enough, get off and stay at **Cabañas Divisadero Barrancas** *(*▥ *52 rms* ⇶ *reservations: Calle 71 #2116, Apdo Postal 661, Chihuahua* ☎*(14) 151199* ☒*(14) 156575)*, a few minutes from the station, with breathtaking views of the Copper Canyon, its own Tarahumara guides and regular cheerful sing-songs.

Rather less special is the **Hotel Posada Barrancas** *(*▥ *39 rms; reservations: Balderrama)*. After 10 minutes W, there is a brief stop at Posadas for the **Mansión Tarahumara** *(*▥ *46 rms; reservations:* ☎*(14) 154721* ☒*(14) 165444)*, a brand-new medieval castle offering all modern comforts and good food.

Cuiteco and Bahuichivo

1752m (5,747ft). 7hrs 20mins from Chihuahua, 4hrs 40mins from Los Mochis.

These two stops lie just a few km apart. Cuiteco is a very small affair, with rustic accommodation on offer at **Cabañas Pinar** (☐ ⇶). Bahuichivo is the station for **Cerocahui**, an old mission village 12km (7 miles) s in a valley of apple orchards, now a minor center of exploration. The best place to stay is **Misión Cerocahui** *(buses meet all trains* ▥ *28 rms* ⇶ ⌂ ◁€ ⌂ ♈ *reservations: Balderrama)*, in a fine colonial building with no frills, electricity or telephone; it organises daily hikes to little-known **canyons** that are even deeper than the Copper Canyon.

El Fuerte

10hrs 40mins from Chihuahua, 1hr 20mins from Los Mochis; 78km (48 miles) E of Los Mochis by road.

In the warm foothills of the Sierra Madre, this old colonial defense outpost has grown into a small town, and is a far nicer place to spend the night than LOS MOCHIS. The best hotel is the **Posada Hidalgo** *(Hidalgo 101* ☎*(681) 30242* ▥ *30 rms* ⇶ ♈ ● ≋), a lovely 19thC hacienda set among tropical gardens. This is a popular spot for fishermen, who try their luck in the nearby reservoirs.

PARRAL (Hidalgo del Parral)

Map 3D6. Chihuahua. 286km (178 miles) s of Chihuahua on RF45 or 212km (132 miles) s of Chihuahua on improved back-road; 410km (256 miles) N of Durango on RF45. Altitude: 1,660m (5,444ft). Population: 100,000. Served by train (branch line from Jiménez on Torreón–Chihuahua line) and bus.

Parral is a small colonial mining town, in the dry and dusty mountains of the Sierra Madre, which makes an interesting diversion and is only an hour's drive from the main N to s highway. Its greatest claim to historical fame is the fact that Pancho Villa, the famous bandit-cum-hero of the revolution, was shot here by eight assassins as he visited a well-loved mistress.

WHAT TO SEE

In the Zócalo is the colonial **Palacio Municipal**, with its own pleasant gardens, and the parish church, completed in 1710, with a fine Churrigueresque altar. Two blocks away, toward the river, is the **Palacio Pedro Alvarado**. The building is only irregularly open, but is worth visiting for its ornate interior, all marble and onyx, with crystal chandeliers. It was built by a humble silver miner who struck so lucky that at one point he offered to pay Mexico's national debt.

Another miner who struck lucky was an Indian who financed the building of the 17thC church of **La Virgen del Rayo** (Our Lady of the Thunderbolt), on the other side of the river. The colonial state governor had the Indian tortured to reveal the location of his gold-mine; but he died silent. Today, the church, colorfully decorated with Indian motifs, is still used with pride by local Indians.

Parral's most famous son was the notorious revolutionary, Pancho Villa. His house is now a grocery store, and the place of his assassination in 1923, in **Calle Barreda**, is marked by a plaque.

✎   Although there are no luxury hotels here, two reasonable choices are **Camino Real** *(Prolongación Av. Independencia* ☎*(152) 22050* ▥ ⇌ ≈�), a motel s of town, and the central **Turista** *(Plazuela Independencia 12* ☎*(152) 24447* ▥ ⇌).

EXCURSIONS

Up into the mountains to the sw are two small mining villages, about 5km (3 miles) apart: **San Francisco del Oro** *(24km/15 miles)* and **Santa Barbara** *(28km/17 miles)*. The scenery en route is impressive, and the villages have an atmosphere evocative of colonial mining times. Some maps show a road from here to the Pacific coast, but for the time being there are only logging roads into the mountains. The main road peters out at **Guadalupe y Calvo** *(200km/125 miles sw)*, a small town with a very big sawmill.

TORREÓN

Map 3E7. Coahuila. 375km (234 miles) w of Monterrey on RF40; 462km (288 miles) se of Chihuahua on RF49 and RF45; 229km (143 miles) nw of Durango on

RF40 and RF49; 277km (173 miles) E of Saltillo on RF40. Population: 900,000.
Served by air, train (on Mexico City–Ciudad Juarez line, and link line to Monterrey)
and bus.

Mexico's youngest city was founded in 1875 and therefore has few
colonial buildings. Together with the linked cities of **Gómez Palacio**
and **Ciudad Lerdo**, it is an important part of the country's industrial
base but, if you are passing, not a disagreeable place to spend the
night. If you do so, take a look at the **Museo Regional de la Laguna**
(Cuauhtémoc and Juárez; open 9am-5pm), in the **Bosque Carranza**
park, with displays about the local Indian tribes.

Del Prado *(Paseo de la Rosita 910 and Fuentes* ☎ *(17) 212424* Fx *(17)*
212958 ▥ *146 rms* ⬛ ♈ ≋*)* is the best hotel, in a residential zone. **Palacio**
Real *(Morelos 1280 Pte* ☎ *(17) 160000* Fx *(17) 168608* ▥ *to* ▥ *139 rms* ⬛
♈ ≋*)* is also good, in the business district, and **Paraíso del Desierto** *(Inde-*
pendencia 101 Ote and Jiménez ☎ *(17) 161122* ▥ ⬛ ♈ ≋*)* is a plush motel.

DURANGO

*Map **3**E6. Capital of Durango. 411km (256 miles) S of Parral on RF45; 229km*
(143 miles) SE of Torreón on RF49 and RF40; 319km (199 miles) E of Mazatlán
on RF40; 598km (373 miles) N of Guadalajara by RF54 and RF45. Altitude:
1,890m (6,199ft). Population: 350,000. Served by air, rail (on lines from Mexico
City and Monterrey) and bus **i** *Hidalgo 408 Sur and 5 de Febrero* ☎*(181)*
12139. American Express: 20 de Noviembre 810 Ote ☎*(181) 70023.*

Like many of the colonial cities, Durango began life as a mining town,
with the forcible baptism of the local Chalchihuita and Tepehuano
Indians who were then marched off in chain-gangs to the mines. The
mines are still active, supplying the industries of MONTERREY with copper, mercury, gold, lead, silver and iron. Indeed, there is so much iron
under the hills that compasses are useless in the area. A busy, fast-
growing town, Durango is also the commercial center for a rich cattle-
ranching area.

Many visitors will have seen Durango's bare Sierra Madre peaks and
canyons before without realizing it, for they have starred in more Westerns than John Wayne. Ask at the tourist office for details of which movie
sets around town can be visited during your stay — with luck, guns may
be blazing and cameras rolling at one of them. Watch for the sets 14km
(8 miles) N, near the RF45 to PARRAL.

WHAT TO SEE

In the center of town, on the N of the Zócalo, is the 18thC **cathedral**,
built in a mixture of Baroque and Churrigueresque styles. The tower is
supposedly haunted by the ghost of a young girl who died of a broken
heart there. The nearby **Palacio de Gobierno** *(Zaragoza and 5 de*
Febrero) has some fine 20thC **murals**.

The town's theater, the **Teatro Victoria**, is another colonial building
next door, and the **Casa del Conde de Suchil**, a former office of the

Inquisition, lies just up the street. This has been restored and converted into shops, with an open-air café in the incongruously pleasant (given its sinister past), highly ornate courtyard. The **Regional Museum** *(Victoria and Serdán, open 10am-5pm; closed Mon)* tells the sad story of the local Indians, who perished by the thousand in the mines.

≈ﾗ   **Campo México Courts** *(♣ 20 de Noviembre Oriente* ☎*(181) 87744* 🅵🆇*(181) 83015* ▥ *80 ṛms* ≕ ⅋ ▦ ≋)* is a good motel E of the center. Centrally located is the **Gobernador** *(20 de Noviembre 257* ☎*(181) 31919* 🅵🆇*(181) 11422* ▥ *98 rms* ≕ ▦ ≋)*, much favored by film crews. The **Plaza Catedral** *(Constitución 216 Sur* ☎*(181) 32480* ▥ ≕)* is an attractive colonial building downtown. Next to the cathedral, the **Posada Duran** *(Febrero 20* ☎*(181) 12412* ▥ ≕)* has a faded colonial splendor.

≕   **Café Nevería La Bohemia** *(20 de Noviembre 907* ☎*(181) 15422* ▥)* has vegetarian meals, German dishes and regional specialties. **La Majada** *(20 de Noviembre Oriente* ☎*(181) 19344)* is a good choice for the more carnivorous. **Casa de la Monga** *(Negrete 308 Pte* ☎*(181) 17162* ▥)* has a good range of regional specialties.

SHOPPING

Durango blown-glass can be bought either at the **Escuela de Artesanías** *(on the Mazatlán road)* or in the shops and market back in the center. Look for the local specialty: ashtrays with a scorpion cast in the glass (the Durango *alacranes* have a deadlier sting than any other Mexican scorpion). **Semiprecious stones** are also a good buy.

EXCURSIONS

RF40 west to Mazatlán
319km/199 miles.
This is the first proper road across the Sierra Madre s of the Mexican border, and is both spectacular and slow. After 100km (62 miles), in the **Puerto de los Angeles National Park**, is the village of **El Salto**, with basic hotels and guides to escort you into the mountains. There are more villages and stopping points farther w (see MAZATLÁN, page 225).

Thermal springs
Take RF26 NW from Durango toward Tepehuanes.
The road out of town soon climbs up into the mountains, where the Tepehuano Indians live. On the way are thermal springs, reputed to cure almost every illness; these include **Valparaiso** on the outskirts of town, and, farther on, **Canatlán** *(69km/43 miles)* and **Tepehuanes** *(172km/107 miles)*.

Baja California

This 1,300-kilometer (812-mile) spit of land is a vast, inhospitable region of wild mountains and barren plains, the arid monotony of the landscape broken only by occasional oases and rare, high-altitude forests and pastures. Paradoxically, it is its very emptiness and isolation that are propelling the peninsula into stardom as a vast playground for North Americans, who are attracted to its wonderful beaches and the luminous waters of the surrounding seas.

Baja California consists of two states, **Baja California Norte**, which runs from the US border to Guerrero Negro, roughly halfway down, and **Baja California Sur**, in the south. The peninsula's geography and climate are similar to those of Mexico's northwestern mainland, from which it began to detach itself 20 million years ago.

The resulting **Sea of Cortés**, also known as the Gulf of California, which separates Baja California from the mainland, contains one of the world's richest concentrations of marine life, teeming with huge fish, whales and dolphins.

HISTORY

This was among the first regions of Mexico to encounter Spanish con-quistadors. The first naval expedition reached the site of modern La Paz in 1533, and Cortés himself followed, in search of pearls, in 1535. He was driven out after a few years by the poverty of the land and the ferocity of the Pericué and Guaicura Indians, but a legend of limitless wealth somehow stuck. The peninsula, then thought to be an island, was named California, possibly after the earthly paradise of a popular romance, or as the "hot oven" *(callida fornax)* it remains.

Baja California was then left in relative peace until the arrival of Jesuit missionaries in the late 17th century, serving, in the interim, as a haunt of pearl-fishers and pirates. Thomas Cavendish and Francis Drake were among those who hid away in its coves, between their devastating attacks on Spanish treasure ships heading across the Pacific.

The first successful missions arrived in 1683, led by the formidable Eusebio Francisco Kino, later joined by Juan de Salvatierra. When the Jesuits were expelled from the Americas in 1768, the Franciscans moved in, followed by the Dominicans five years later.

While there is every reason to admire the missionaries' faith, endur-ance and resilience, their effect was to disrupt complex indigenous societies living in a fine balance with the earth, to introduce fatal new diseases such as smallpox and even the common cold — to which the natives had no resistance — and to lay the way for colonists to take over the richest lands, rivers and springs. Of the estimated 50,000 people of nine major tribes that inhabited the peninsula, less than a tenth survived into the 19th century, and their numbers are now reduced to a handful of Kilawa Indians in the high Sierras of the north.

In the Mexican–American War, Baja was occupied by US troops, who were eventually expelled. Two more US attempts at colonization fol-lowed, both under the guise of creating an independent state. One Richard Walker, seeking to create a utopian state based on slavery, went so far as to invade La Paz in 1853 with a few of his friends. But he was soon repelled, and later met his death trying a similar gambit in Nicaragua.

In 1910, a certain Richard Perris kindly offered to name his proposed new republic *Porfiria,* in return for the gift of the peninsula from the Mexican dictator, Porfirio Díaz. This scheme also came to nothing.

ORIENTATION

Baja falls into three parts: the north, the middle and the south. The north is dominated by the US and by the border towns of TIJUANA and MEXICALI, capital of Baja California Norte, and contains the bulk of the peninsula's 2 million people. Unless your visit is limited to a day-trip from the US, you should go at least as far as ENSENADA, a lively port and resort on the Pacific coast, or to **San Felipe**, on the Sea of Cortés.

Until recently, human impact farther south was limited to a few fishing villages at coastal oases, and abandoned mission churches amid drifting sands. The pleasures of Baja were primarily for the adventurous, particu-larly those equipped with small planes. In 1973, a highway was opened that meanders down the peninsula, passing through some of the most desolate and beautiful landscapes on earth. Although no longer a major adventure, it is demanding on car and driver and should not be under-taken at night. Fill your tank at any opportunity, and carry food, water and spares.

In the wake of the road, occasional agricultural oases have sprung up, nourished by age-old groundwater. And a number of resorts have also become established, the finest of them on the Sea of Cortés. One such, **LORETO**, has been selected for mega-resort status, but there are many far finer spots. **GUERRERO NEGRO**, on the west coast, is a famous place for whale-watchers. And Indian **cave paintings** have been discovered nearby, high in the central mountains; the hardy can hire mules and guides at **San Ignacio** to visit them.

The road eventually reaches the fast-developing tourist zone to the south of the peninsula, between **LA PAZ**, the capital of Baja California Sur, and the cape at its southern extremity. The entire southern zone is experiencing the paroxysms of development, as some 30,000 hotel and condominium units — and associated golf courses and marinas — are constructed, most of them in the **LOS CABOS** region, around **Cabo San Lucas** and **San José del Cabo**.

With its perfect beaches, natural beauty and rainless climate, the location is well chosen, but there is a danger that the sheer scale and pace of development will create a hyper-expensive but anonymous paradise, lacking charm or character. Mass tourism also poses a threat to the delicate ecology of land and ocean. For example, shrimp trawlers in the Sea of Cortés scoop up and kill some fifty pounds of diverse and beautiful marine life for every pound of shrimp harvested.

Towns, cities and cultural sites

This chapter gives essential information on the main centers in Baja California, starting in **TIJUANA**, crossing E to **MEXICALI**, then traveling N–S to **ENSENADA, SAN QUINTÍN, BAHÍA DE LOS ANGELES, GUERRERO NEGRO, SAN IGNACIO, SANTA ROSALIA, LORETO, LA PAZ** and ultimately **LOS CABOS**.

See USING THIS GUIDE on page 50 for details on how to use this section. On the following pages, pointers are given on how to get to each of the destinations covered. Along with the MEXICO map on pages 46–7, and the 4-color maps at the back of this book, they should give all the information necessary for planning your trip to this part of Mexico.

FACTS AND FIGURES

- Distance from Tijuana to Cabo San Lucas: 1,678km (1048 miles).
- **Airports**: Cabo San Lucas, Ensenada, Mexicali, La Paz, Tijuana.
  Aerocalifornia (☎ *(682) 21113)* offers an air taxi service on the peninsula.
- **Car ferries**: La Paz–Los Mochis, La Paz–Mazatlán, Santa Rosalia–Guaymas.
- Maps **1**&**2**.

TIJUANA

Map 1A2. Baja California Norte. 763km (476 miles) NW of Hermosillo on RF2 and RF15; 116km (72 miles) N of Ensenada on RF1; 189km (118 miles) W of Mexicali on RF2; 32km (20 miles) S of San Diego, US. Population: 1.6 million. Served by air (international airport 16km/10 miles SE), train (terminus of line from Mexico City) and bus ℹ Revolución 2 Calle 1a ☎(66) 881685. US Consul: Tapachula 96 ☎(66) 817400. UK Consul: German Gedovias 5–201 ☎(66) 840585. American Express: Edificio Husa A, Taboada and Orozco ☎(66) 840456.

For countless Americans, "TJ" is all they have ever seen of Mexico. With its slums, beggars and seedy sex-joints, it is hardly the greatest advertisement. All the same, it is visited by nearly twice its own population each month, and the border, crossed by 30 million people a year (and that's only the official figure), is the world's busiest.

The attractions are many: cheap false teeth and auto repairs, bullfights, *jai-alai* (see below) and simple curiosity to see another country. Sex is no longer a big draw; the permissive society across the border was bad news for the porn barons of TJ. The notorious **Zona Norte**, however, is still in business, and could be a nostalgic stroll if you were last here as a lonely young serviceman during World War II; but vice here just isn't what it was.

Until the 1920s, TJ was no more than a dusty frontier village. The meteoric urban and industrial growth began with Prohibition in the US, when suddenly every humble liquor-vendor became rich beyond the dreams of avarice. Today much of the town's action takes place along **Avenida Revolución** — restaurants, bars, discos and more besides.

For those here just for the day, formalities are minimal. The problems are encountered on the way back, on those days when the US Customs are meticulously searching vehicles for drugs and contraband.

WHAT TO SEE

Time may be saved by leaving your car in the US and taking taxis in TJ. A good way to pass time while waiting for a backlog of cars to get through Customs is at the **Palacio de Jai-Alai** *(on Revolución, between Calles 7a and 8a ☎(66) 851612)*. Here the amazingly fast hand-ball game of *jai-alai* is played every evening except Thursday, and the betting is fast and furious.

Bullfights are usually on Sundays, but the tourist office will advise. The largest bullrings are **El Toreo de Tijuana** *(on Agua Caliente, S of town)*, and the **Plaza Monumental** *(beside the port)*. Another attraction is the **Hipódromo de Agua Caliente** racetrack *(SE of town on Agua Caliente, toward the Country Club)*; here, dogs race on weekday evenings, while it is reserved for horses on weekends *(for information ☎(66) 817811, or in San Diego ☎(619) 260 0600)*.

Tijuana's **Cultural Center** *(Independencia and Paseo de los Héroes ☎(66) 841111, open 11am-7pm)* is a good introduction to Mexico and Mexican culture, with a panoramic **Omnimax movie theater (▨)** housed in the modernistic structure.

Beach-lovers should make for **Playa Rosarito** *(29km/18 miles S on* *the Ensenada toll-road),* a fast-developing resort area with a long beach and plenty of bars, *taco* stands and restaurants and nightspots, especially along Blvd. Benito Juárez. The hotels, most of them expensive, stretch out along the coast to the s.

WHERE TO STAY

The twin-towered **Fiesta Inn** *(Agua Caliente 4558* ☎*(66) 817 000* Ⓕ*(66) 817016, or in US (800) 343 7825* ▥ *422 rms* ⇥ ☒ ﹏ ﹪ ●*)* is Tijuana's biggest luxury hotel. **Lucerna** *(Paseo de los Héroes 10902 at Rodríguez* ☎*(66) 841000* Ⓕ*(66) 840417* ▥ *170 rms* ﹌ ﹏ ▰*)* is a smaller rival with greater charm. **Corona Plaza** *(Agua Caliente 1426* ☎*(66) 862345* ▥ ⇥ ☒ ﹏ ≈ ●*)* is a large, modern hotel. **El Conquistador** *(Agua Caliente Sur 1777* ☎*(66) 864801* Ⓕ*(66) 861340* ▥ *110 rms* ⇥ ☒ ﹏*)* offers colonial-style accommodation in a pleasant southern suburb.

More central are **Palacio Azteca** *(16 de Septiembre 213* ☎*(66) 865 301* ▥ ⇥ ☒ ﹏*)* and **Villa de Zaragoza** *(♥ Madero 1120* ☎*(66) 851 832* ▥*)*, a good motel near the Palacio de Jai-Alai. There are some good Best Western hotels: the **Country Club Motor** *(Tapachula 1* ☎*(66) 811333* Ⓕ*(66) 817066* ▥ *130 rms* ⇥ ☒ ﹏ ﹪ ≈*)*, near the racetrack; **Hacienda del Río** *(Blvd. Gran Taboada 10606* ☎*(66) 848 644* Ⓕ*(66) 848620* ▥ ⇥ ☒ ﹏*)*, in the new financial center; and the **La Mesa Inn** *(Díaz Ordaz 50* ☎*(66) 816522* Ⓕ*(66) 812871* ▥ *122 rms* ▰ ☒ ﹏*)*. One less expensive hotel is the downtown **Hotel Caesar** *(Revolución 827 and Calle 5a* ☎*(66) 880550* ▥ ⇥*)*, whose restaurant claims to have invented the Caesar salad.

In nearby Playa Rosarito, the **Quinta del Mar** *(Km 255 on Tijuana-Ensenada road* ☎*(661) 21145* ▥ ⇥ ☒ ﹏*)* is a recently-completed resort hotel. Another good choice, on the beachfront, is the **Rosarito Beach** *(☎(661) 21300* Ⓕ*(661) 21176 or (800) 343 8382* ▥ *141 rms* ⇥ ♣ ☒ ﹏*)*, an extravagant 1920s resort hotel in the hacienda style, with fine ocean views.

SHOPPING

Tijuana has a large selection of Mexican handicrafts and souvenirs, and it is also a duty-free zone. There *are* bargains to be had, but be sure of the prices at home before you buy. In the shopping district around and along **Constitución** and **Revolución**, anything from Taxco silver to Japanese cameras can be bought.

There are also a number of shopping complexes scattered around town, of which the largest is **Plaza Río Tijuana**, on the landscaped stretch of Paseo de los Héroes, beside the Cultural Center. Here you will find restaurants, department stores, a multitude of shops and, with a bit of luck, a **fiesta** in full swing.

MEXICALI

Map 1A2. Capital of Baja California Norte. 189km (118 miles) E of Tijuana on RF2; 623km (389 miles) NW of Hermosillo on RF15 and RF2. Population:

850,000. Served by air (international airport 10km/6 miles SW), train (end of line from Mexico City and Guadalajara) and bus. American Express: Holiday Inn ☎65) 660609.

This is a popular border crossing-point at the head of the Pacific Highway. Traditionally an agricultural center, Mexicali now sees growing conflicts between farmers, who rely on intensive irrigation, and the demands for water of the industries and inhabitants of this fast-expanding *maquiladora* city. It is certainly a prosperous town, with an authentic "Amexican" atmosphere. But there are only souvenir stores and the occasional bullfight to contribute a truly Mexican element. To see the real Mexico, press on.

EXCURSIONS

To get to the main highway that bisects the peninsula, either head W to TIJUANA on RF2, or turn left onto RF3 after 133km (83 miles) at Tecate for the last 112km (70 miles) to ENSENADA. A small road leads 149km (93 miles) S along the Colorado river estuary to the fishing village of **San Felipe**. It has excellent beaches to the N and S, and boats can be chartered for **deep-sea fishing**, but it sometimes attracts a slightly boisterous crowd. The roads beyond cannot be recommended for cars.

In Mexicali: the **Holiday Inn** *(Av. de los Héroes 201 at López Mateos ☎(65) 573600 Fx(65) 570555 ▥ 220 rms ⬱ ⅄ ≋)* is in the civic center. A few kilometers SE of town, **La Lucerna** *(Benito Juárez 2151 ☎(65) 661000 Fx(65) 664706 ▥ 200 rms ⬱ ⅄ ≋)* has a charming small tropical garden.

In San Felipe: **La Trucha Vagabunda** *(Av. de los Cedros Sur ☎(657) 71333 ▥ ⬱ ⅄ ◐ ≋)* has an excellent hillside position; on the beachfront, **Las Misiones** *(Misión de Loreto 148 ☎(657) 71280 Fx(657) 71283, or in US (800) 336 5454 ▥ 241 rms ⬱ ⅄ ≋ ⤴)* is popular, but large and lacking in character; **El Cortés** *(Mar de Cortés ☎(657) 71055/6 ▥ ⬱ ⅄ ⤙ ≋)* is a more interesting choice, with spacious *cabañas*.

Aquamarina San Felipe *(Camino del Sur ☎(65) 640393 ▥ 140 rms)* is a Best Western resort 16km (10 miles) SE of San Felipe on an isolated beach, complete with marina.

ENSENADA

Map 1B2. Baja California Norte. 116km (72 miles) S of Tijuana on RF1 or the divided RF1D; 191km (119 miles) N of San Quintín on RF1. Population: 200,000. Served by air and bus ℹ López Mateos 1350b ☎(667) 62222.

This resort town is growing in popularity, for it is only a 1½-hour drive from the US border and enjoys a fine setting on the beautiful white-sand bay of **Todos Santos**. Ensenada is also the last proper town on the way S before LA PAZ, at the S of the peninsula.

Although Ensenada is an active fishing and shipping port, the central area around the waterfront has the feeling of a much smaller place, and compared to Tijuana it is positively peaceful. For a good view of the city, stroll out along Av. Segunda to the lookout point on **Chapultepec Hill**, or take a boat-trip out into the bay from the quayside.

Founded in 1602, Ensenada first became important during the Gold Rush in 1870, and during Prohibition it became a center for smuggling liquor into the US. When the drinkers departed, it turned to shipping cotton and to fishing, augmented today by tourism. Good wines are also produced in the area, and your hotel can arrange a visit to the **Bodegas de Santo Tomás** *(Miramar 666* ☎*(667) 82509)* to sample some champagne-style varieties. However, the main attraction of Ensenada is the **deep-sea fishing**: all hotels can arrange boat charters — or simply walk down to the harbor and ask around.

EVENTS There is always something happening here, but these are some of the highlights of Ensenada's calendar: • March: **Mardi Gras Carnival**, and a **bicycle race** from Tecate. • May: **Newport–Ensenada yacht race**. • June: an 800km (500-mile) **off-road race** departs. • August: **San Diego–Ensenada motorboat race**. • October: **Ensenada small-plane rally**. • November: a 1,600km (1,000-mile) **off-road race** departs.

WHAT TO SEE

The **Riviera del Pacifico** *(Lázaro Cárdenas and Riviera)* is a magnificent former casino dating from 1930. However, gambling was banned eight years later, and after decades of deterioration the building has now been restored as a cultural center.

WHERE TO STAY

Forte Travelodge *(López Mateos and Blancarte 130* ☎*(667) 81601-5* Ⓕⓧ*(667) 40005* 🔲 *52 rms* ⚊ ⚊ ☺ ♈*)* is a pleasant Mexican-style hotel, with the **El Rey Sol** restaurant *(see below)*. **Corona** *(Lázaro Cárdenas s/n* ☎*(667) 64023* 🔲 ⚊ ⚆ ⚊*)* is a new, beachfront hotel, built in an interesting Mexican style. **La Pinta** *(Av. Florencia and Blvd. Los Bucaneros* ☎*(667) 40044* 🔲 ⚊ ⚊*)* is a comfortable courtyard hotel. **Misión Santa Isabel** *(López Mateos and Castillo 1100* ☎*(667) 83616* 🔲 ⚊ ♈ ⚊*)* is modern, in a colonial-style building.

Out of town, **Estero Beach** *(♣ 11km (6 miles)* S ☎*(667) 66225* Ⓕⓧ*(667) 66925* 🔲 *to* 🔲 *109 rms* ⚊ ⚘ ⚊ ⚆ ☺ ⚡ ⚒ ⚑ ♈ ⚉*)* is a complete vacation resort, providing water-sports and duty-free stores. **Las Rosas** *(RF1* N *of town* ☎*(667) 44310* 🔲 *to* 🔲 *32 rms* ⚊ ⚆ ⚊ ⚓*)* is a modern pink marble palace whose rooms all look out across the ocean. **Quintas Papagayo** *(on the beach, 1½ km/1 mile* N *of Las Rosas* ☎*(667) 83675* 🔲 *51 rms* ⚊ ♈ ⚆ ⚊*)* is a self-contained resort village. Near the tourist office, **America** *(Mateos 1309* ☎*(667) 61333* 🔲*)* is basic, but clean.

EATING AND DRINKING

For a special treat, **El Rey Sol** *(⚱ López Mateos 100* ☎*(667) 81733* 🔲*)* has superb French and Mexican cuisine, while **Casamar** *(Lázaro Cárdenas 987* ☎*(667) 40417* 🔲*)* offers upmarket seafood. However, **Bahía de Ensenada** *(Riveroll and Mateos 109* ☎*(667) 81015* 🔲*)* is nearly as good, and much less expensive. Vegetarians will appreciate **Señor Salud** *(Calle 9 and Espinoza* 🔲*)*.

EXCURSIONS
La Bufadora
16km (10 miles) s, then 19km (11 miles) w.
An energetic ocean geyser, La Bufadora can either be approached by road or viewed from one of the boats that leave from the harbor.
Parque Nacional San Pedro Mártir
120km (75 miles) s on RF1, then 98km (61 miles) e to government observatory.
The **Sierra San Pedro Mártir**, the snowy peaks of which reach a height of 3,078m (10,095 feet), is the highest land on the peninsula. In contrast to the arid lowlands, it offers verdant, pristine landscapes of pine woods and alpine meadows, rich in wildlife that includes horned sheep. The clear skies also make it perfect for the astronomical observatory, at the end of the road into the park.

☜ 50km (31 miles) off RF1, the 25,000-hectare (62,500-acre) **Meling Ranch** *(PO Box 1326, Ensenada, no ☎ ▥ ⇌ ⚓ ⇌)* is a wonderful place to stay, and organizes trips into the Sierra.

SAN QUINTÍN

Map 1B2. Baja California Norte. 189km (118 miles) s of Ensenada on RF1.
Population: 15,000. Served by bus.

This town lies in the center of a rich agricultural oasis producing irrigated vegetable crops. Although it is near the sea, its potential as a resort is limited by the dusty gray sand of its beaches. The nearby **Bahía San Quintín** is the site of an abandoned 19thC British settlement, reached by rough tracks from Lázaro Cárdenas, 5km (3 miles) s of San Quintín.

The RF1 beyond San Quintín skirts the Pacific for 58km (36 miles), then veers inland through a boulder-strewn cactus desert, dotted with peculiar cirio ("boojum") trees. To the s of Cataviña, the road passes through the **Parque Nacional Las Virgenes**, which protects some of the most extraordinary landscapes in Mexico.

EXCURSION
El Mármol
154km (96 miles) se just past San Agustín on RF1, then follow the track e.
In this onyx-mine, now disused, the stone was deposited by active mineral-rich volcanic springs. If you are planning to visit, it is best to hire a guide and horses in San Agustín.

☜ **La Pinta** *(14km/8 miles s and 4km/2 miles w ☎ (800) 262 2656 ▥ ⇌ ☆ ⇌)* occupies a remote spot above Playa Santa María. There are several motels above the bay, including **Molino Viejo** *(no ☎ ▥)* and **Ernesto's** *(no ☎ ▥)*.

BAHÍA DE LOS ANGELES

Map 1C2. Baja California Norte. 465km (290 miles) s of Ensenada on RF1, then 70km (43 miles) e.

This out-of-the-way spot on the Sea of Cortés is one of the finest on the peninsula. There are superb beaches, and the dusty hills and dry mountainous islands across the straits contrast dramatically with the vivid blue of a sea that teems with marine life — turtles, fish, dolphins, seals, finback whales and seabirds.

The largest of the islands, the 76km (47-mile) **Isla Angel de la Guardia**, reaches a height of 1,250m (4,100 feet). Development is limited, but there are boats for rent and basic accommodation. 19km (11 miles) s, in the hills, is the ghost town of **Las Flores**, the site of silver-mines that were active between 1890 and 1910, under several US and British companies. 13km (8 miles) N along the coast is the **Punta la Gringa** beach, the best in the area.

✎ **Villa Vitta** *(reservations in US* ☎ *(619) 298 4958* ▥ ═▤ ♈ ♠ ≈▥ *)* is the best place to stay; if it is full, **Casa Díaz** (▥ ═▤) is the alternative.

GUERRERO NEGRO

Map 1C3. Baja California Sur. 574km (358 miles) s of Ensenada on RF1.

This small town is named, according to local legend, after a British treasure ship called the *Black Warrior* that sank nearby, the wreckage of which lies undiscovered on the seabed. Guerrero Negro lies near the Pacific coast, just s of the border into Baja California Sur. The frontier is marked by a vast steel **eagle sculpture** of monumental ugliness.

The main tourist attraction is **Scammon's Lagoon**, an enclosed sea lake on the Pacific, just W of town, where gray whales congregate to mate after their 10,000km (6,250-mile) migration from the Bering Sea. This "whale paradise" was discovered in 1846 by the British whaler Charles Scammon, who estimated its population at 25,000 whales at the height of the spring mating season.

By 1874, some 10,000 of them had been slaughtered, and the whales were commercially extinct by 1900. The local seals were then similarly reduced in numbers, until they were given the protection of the Mexican government in 1922.

Fortunately, both species have since recovered somewhat, and the entire area has been designated the **Parque Natural de Ballena Gris**. Hordes of nature-lovers arrive every year to watch the mating whales, renting boats and planes to get close to the action. It is a fascinating occasion, although not without hazards in a boat. Out of season, tourist numbers are likely to remain small, as there are no local beaches.

EXCURSIONS

The salt flats s of town have been converted into the world's biggest **salt-works**, covering 80sq.km (50sq. miles) and worth a visit.

The **Vizcaino peninsula**, on the far side of the lagoons and the Vizcaino desert, has excellent beaches, but they are accessible only by boat, airplane or 4-wheel-drive. **Playa Malarrimo**, on the N of the peninsula, is a famous haunt of beachcombers.

After 25km (16 miles) N on RF1 and 25km (15 miles) E on a dirt road to **El Monte**, there are a number of little-visited **Indian paintings** along mountain canyons.

The **Misión Santa Gertrudis** *(32km/20 miles SE on RF1, then 42km/26 miles E to El Arco on RF18, then 40km/25 miles E on a dirt road)* is a well-preserved early mission settlement in the Sierra Santa Agueda. After its foundation in 1697, it became a center for the local Cochimí Indians, perhaps because it took over a vital spring to irrigate its crops and vineyards.

✧ **La Pinta** *(Paralelo 28, near the eagle monument; reservations via Mexico City* ☎ *(5) 395 0333,* ▥ *29 rms* ⬥ ⥱ ⚓ ☀ ♈ ♈ *)* is one of Baja's reliable chain. Less pricey are **El Morro** *(* ☎ *(685) 70414* ▥ *32 rms* ⥱ *)* and the **San Ignacio** *(* ☎ *(685) 70270* ▥ *14 rms)*, both unpretentious motels on Zapata, s/n.

SAN IGNACIO

Map 1D3. Baja California Sur. 717km (448 miles) s of Ensenada on RF1.

This 1728 mission village is built around an oasis, created by a dam on the Río Santa Martha, and is famed for its groves of nearly 100,000 date-palms. The massive 5km (3-mile) embankment to the E was built with Indian labor as a protection against the flash floods that periodically devastate the steep-sided valley.

Among the canyons of the Sierra San Francisco, the volcanic range to the N, lurk Indian cave paintings estimated to be 1,000 years or more old. Many of them depict deer, wild pig and wolves, while others portray the Indians themselves, sometimes in hunting scenes. Some of the best-known paintings are in the delightfully named Salsipuedes ("Get out if you can") canyon. Expeditions can be arranged, for example at the Posada San Ignacio. Various tracks lead w to rudimentary fishing establishments.

✧ **La Pinta San Ignacio** *(reservations: Mexico City* ☎ *(5) 395 0333* ▥ *28 rms* ⬥ ⥱ ⚓ ♈ ☀ *)* is a haven for weary travelers. A less expensive, friendly alternative is **Posada San Ignacio** *(Carranza 22, SE of the Zócalo).*

SANTA ROSALÍA

Map 1D3. Baja California Sur. 790km (493 miles) s of Ensenada on RF1.
Population 14,000. Ferry three days a week (currently Sun, Tues, Fri) to Guaymas (information and reservations ☎ *(685) 20013).*

This late 19thC mining town on the Sea of Cortés was founded by the now-defunct El Boleo Copper Company, under joint French and German ownership. Even importing Seri and Yaqui Indians from the mainland as cheap labor failed to save the company when the ore was worked out, but new deposits have now been found and the mine has been started up again under Mexican ownership. Santa Rosalía's buildings have given the town a peculiarly French character, and its famous

1898 prefabricated **iron church**, designed by Gustave Eiffel (of Eiffel Tower fame), is still going strong.

The main town **beach** has been the victim of mine-spoil and is now less than alluring, so the best local beach is s of town, beyond the **El Morro** hotel (see below). Be warned that the town gets intolerably hot and dusty outside the winter season.

ENVIRONS OF SANTA ROSALÍA

There are good beaches south from Santa Rosalía, for example at **San Bruno** *(25km/15 miles s on RF1),* but the best are around **Punta Chivato** *(40km/25 miles s on RF1, then 19km/11 miles E on dirt road).*

Mulegé, 63km (39 miles) s on RF1 *(853km/533 miles s of Ensenada)* is a pretty Jesuit mission town of the early 18thC, now a small resort, on a palm-shaded oasis at the N end of the lovely Bahía Concepción. Farther s are many lovely sheltered beaches the length of the enclosed 50km-long (31-mile) bay, easily accessible from RF1.

🗨 **Frances** *(11 de Julio 30, Santa Rosalia* ☎ *(685) 20829, map 1 D3* ▥ ⇛ ⋈ ⅄ *)* and **El Morro** *(1.5km/1 mile s of town on main highway* ☎ *(685) 20414,* ▥ ⇛ ⋈ ⅄ *)* are the best hotels in town.

At Punta Chivata, the **Hotel Punta Chivita** *(* ☎ *(685) 30188* ▥ ⇛ ⅄ ⋈ *)* is a little earthly paradise.

In Mulegé, **Vista Hermosa** *(on the lighthouse road* ☎ *(685) 30222* ▥ ⇛ ⋈ *)* is a well-run colonial style hotel on a hilltop just out of town; **Serenidad** *(off RF1 3km/2 miles s* ☎ *(685) 30111* ▥ *52 rms* ⇌ ⇛ ⋈ ⬟ � icons⬤ ⅄ ◉ *)* is an established hotel set in the shade of riverside palms and mangroves, with an excellent restaurant and its own airstrip. You can rent equipment and receive instruction in underwater sports, and there is organized social life. One inexpensive alternative is the **Terrazas** *(* ♣ *(667) 857 0414* ▥ *Zaragoza s/n* ☎ *(685) 30009* ▥ *).*

LORETO

Map **2D4**. *987km (616 miles) s of Ensenada on RF1. Population 15,000. Served by bus and air, via new international airport 7km (4 miles) sw* **i** *Kiosk by Bancomer on Zócalo* ☎*(683) 30609* ▥.

Founded in 1697, this was the first European settlement in the Californias, and subsequently the capital of Baja until devastated by a hurricane in 1829. Loreto today is a small port built around a large old **mission building**, with a revamped seaside boardwalk. But it is again rising to prominence with FONATUR's development of **Nopoló**, 6km (3 miles) s, into a huge new resort.

The first hotel, the **Stouffer Presidente**, is already in place, while a large marina and golf course have opened at **Puerto Escondido**, 16km (10 miles) s, the first steps of a major satellite project. The less-than-fantastic setting and beach quality leaves cynics wondering if FONATUR's famous computer might have developed a bug.

For an insight into the original mission life, visit the **Museo de los Misiones** *(by the church on the Zócalo, open 9am-4pm; closed Mon and Tues),* packed with displays and artifacts.

EXCURSIONS

There are two offshore islands, both with reefs that are excellent for diving and easily reached by boat. The smaller, **Isla Coronados**, is a **sea-lion sanctuary**, and the much larger **Isla del Carmen** is a major salt-producer, yielding some 10,000 tonnes a year.

Misión San Javier *(3km/2 miles s on RF1 and 37km/23 miles sw on a dirt road)* is a well-preserved 1758 mission, still used as a church by a handful of residents of the surrounding valley.

RF1 takes you the 337km (210 miles) s to LA PAZ across a fertile, irrigated plain, where centers of population include **Villa Insurgentes**, 90km (56 miles) s, and the 50,000-strong **Ciudad Constitución**, after another 30km (18 miles). From there, tracks lead E to whale-spotting points on **Bahía Magdalena**.

In Loreto, **La Pinta** *(Madero s/n ☎(683) 30025* Fx *(683) 30026, 50 rms* ▥ ⊐≡ ⵣ ⋙*)* has a good beachside location. **Misión de Loreto** *(López Mateos 1* ☎*(683) 30048* Fx *(683) 30648, 54 rms* ▥ ⊐≡ ⵣ ⋙ ⛟*)* is also recommended, and has fishing boats for rent.

To the s, in the new resort area, the **Stouffer Presidente** *(Blvd. Misíon de Loreto, Playa Nopoló* ☎*(683) 30700* Fx *(683) 30377, reservations: (5) 395 0333 or (800) 325 6000* ▥ *235 rms* ⬌ ⊐≡ ⌂ ⌖ ⋙ ⵥ ⛱ ✔ ⛵ ⛟ ⵣ ❂*)* is an extensive, self-contained resort, with all facilities, including a strange, underground discotheque.

LA PAZ

Map 2E4. Baja California Sur. 1,350km (844 miles) s of Ensenada on RF1. Population: 180,000. Served by bus, by air (international airport 10km/6 miles sw), by ferry (from Pichilingue, 18km/11 miles N on RF11) ☎*(682) 53833 to Los Mochis–Topolobampo (8 hours) and Mazatlán (16hrs), and by Baja Express hydrofoil (Malecón at 16 de Septiembre* ☎*(682) 56311, or in US* ☎*(800) 828 3242) to Los Mochis–Topolobampo (3$\frac{1}{2}$ hours)* i *Alvaro Obregón 2130* ☎*(682) 25939. American Express: Alvaro Obregón 1570* ☎*(682) 27676.*

La Paz occupies a sheltered position that makes it a natural harbor — one that attracted the Spanish as long ago as 1533, with Hernán Cortés following soon after in search of pearls from the bay's rich oysterbeds. Pearl-fishing continued until the oysters mysteriously died out in 1940, making La Paz even more of a backwater than it already was. But that changed with the arrival of the road in 1973, since when La Paz has boomed to become a sizeable modern city and resort. More recently, the focus of commercial tourism has begun to shift s to **Cabo San Lucas** and **San José del Cabo**, the two resorts that make up LOS CABOS.

Fishing is the main tourist attraction, and boats and gear can be rented through any hotel or directly from the new 260-berth marina. For the less predatory, other sports are available, such as golf on the city's 18-hole course. The maze of streets between the sea and Plaza Constitución (the Zócalo) is attractive, with many old buildings.

But the real center of life is the **seafront**, so be sure to join the locals for an evening stroll up and down Paseo Alvaro Obregón, where the best seafood restaurants are to be found. Over a fish steak and an ice-cold beer, watch the **Sea of Cortés** pass through all shades of red and orange to inky black.

At some point during your stay, consider a visit to the **Anthropology Museum** *(5 de Mayo and Altamirano* ☎*(682) 20162, open Mon-Sat 9am-1pm, 4-7pm)* to find out about the long-extinct aboriginal inhabitants of the region.

Beaches

The beaches around La Paz are among the finest to be found anywhere. There are some wonderful examples N of the **Pichilingue ferry terminal** *(18km/11 miles N on RF11)*. Basically, the rule is that the farther you go, the better the beaches get, and the fewer facilities you will find.

Playa Balandra *(after 3km/1 mile)* is sheltered among the rocks, while **Playa Tecolote** *(after 4km/2 miles)* is a lovely broad expanse of sand, open to the wind and sea, toward Punta Coyote. Farther N is **Isla Espiritú Santo**, with its excellent beaches and rock pools: negotiate your passage with a fisherman.

To explore the beaches E of La Paz, follow the BC286 road from La Paz across the Sierra la Gata, via the village of San Juan de los Planes, to **Ensenada de los Muertos** *(63km/39 miles)*, a settlement on **Bahía los Muertos**, which has many lovely beaches.

About 5km (3 miles) back, a road turns off left to **Punta Arena de la Ventana**, another lovely beach with its own hotel. Alternatively, you can turn left at the intersection on BC286, after about 45km (28 miles), to the **Centro Turistico Las Cruces**, nestled between the Sierra and the sea and sheltered by **Isla Cerralvo**.

🛏 **Cabañas Los Arcos** *(A. Obregón 498 Sur* ☎*(682) 22744* Ⓕ*(682) 54313* ▥ ⚏ ⋙ *)* has 28 waterfront *cabañas.* The **Gran Baja** *(Calle Rangel s/n* ☎*(682) 23900* Ⓕ*(682) 20755* ▥ *250 rms* ⚏ ⋙ *)* is the largest hotel in town. **La Concha Beach Resort** *(at Playa Caimancito, 5km/3 miles N on Pichilingue road* ☎*(682) 26544* Ⓕ*(682) 26218* ▥ *111 rms* ⌇ ⚏ ⋙ *)* offers every facility, including water-sports.

Decent budget choices include **Gardenias** *(Aquiles Serdán 520 Norte* ☎*(682) 23088* ▥ ⚏ ⋙ 𝍷 *)*, **La Perla** *(Alvaro Obregón 1570* ☎*(682) 20777* Ⓕ*(682) 55363* ▥ *100 rms* ⚏ ♈ ▰ ⋙ *)*, on the seafront, and **Lori** *(Nicolas Bravo 110* ☎*(682) 26726* ▥ *)*, all of which are clean and pleasant. **La Posada** *(* ♣ *3km/1 mile s on RF1 to Playa Sur at Reforma* ☎*(682) 24011* ▥ ⚏ ⋙ *)* is a small inn with a fine restaurant.

Out of town, **Hotel Las Arenas** *(Punta Arena de la Ventana, no* ☎ *reserve through travel agent, or in US* ☎*(800) 423 4785* ▥ *)* is a beautiful, self-contained resort with its own airstrip (see BEACHES, above); **Club El Morro** *(3km/1 mile N on RF11 to Pichilingue* ☎*(682) 24084* ▥ ⚏ ⋙ *)* is a Moorish-inspired hotel on Palmira beach.

⚏ Enjoy the sunset at the seafront **Yate** *(Malecón and 16 de Septiembre* ▥ *)*, or even sunrise, as it's a good place for breakfast, too. **Las Brisas** *(Malecón at Colegio Militár* ▥ *)* is more upmarket, with good seafood and steaks under a *palapa* roof; the Carlos'n'Charlie's chain has also arrived, in the shape of **La Paz–Lapa** *(Obregón and Marqués de León* ☎*(682) 26025* ▥ *)*, on the beach.

Vegetarians and wholefooders will love **El Quinto Sol** *(Belisario Domínguez and Independencia* 🏠*)*. For nightlife with your dinner, try the **La Terraza** *(La Perla Hotel, on Malecón* ☎ *(682) 20777),* with its lively restaurant and upstairs nightclub, **La Cabaña**.

LA PAZ TO LOS CABOS

This stunning stretch of coastline has some of Mexico's most breathtaking beaches. Most of the coast remains undeveloped, but luxury hotels are springing up, often in surprisingly remote places. RF1 *(on the E coast)* and RF19 *(on the W coast),* which begins 27km (16 miles) s of La Paz, form a loop around this southern tip of the peninsula. Dominating the landscape is the forested **Sierra la Laguna**, with its impressive 2,164m (7,097-foot) peak, the **Picacho de Zacatosa**.

Buenavista *(103km/64 miles SE of La Paz on RF1)* and the adjacent **Los Barriles** make a windsurfing center of international importance on the broad Bahía Palmas. A rough road runs N from here along the coast to the remote beaches of **Punta Pescadores** and **Boca de Alamo**. To reach the more developed area to the s, turn right off RF1 after another 20km (12 miles) to **La Ribera**. The unpaved road then continues s and w along about 80km (50 miles) of magnificent coastline, with many lovely beaches, before reaching **San José del Cabo**, 183km (114 miles) s of La Paz on RF1.

Going the other way, RF19 meets the coast at the attractive small town of **Todos Santos** *(77km/48 miles s of La Paz),* surrounded by mango trees. The beaches to the s, facing the open Pacific, are famous among surfers, but usually too wild for ordinary swimming. Todos Santos is also the place to arrange expeditions into the Sierra: ask at the Todos Santos Inn. RF19 continues s along the coast to Cabo San Lucas, the southernmost point of Baja California.

🐎 **Rancho Buenavista** *(Km 103.5 Carretera al Sur* 🎦 *62 rms* 🍴 *reservations through Baja High Wind Center, US* ☎ *(415) 332 0110)* is only recommended for those participating in the center's program. Otherwise, try the nearby **Club Spa Buenavista** *(1.5km/1 mile farther down the road),* **Playa Hermosa** or **Palmas de Cortés,** *(all* 🎦 *with* 🍴 ⛱ 🍹 *but no* ☎ *)* A little farther s, **Rancho Leonero** *(in US* ☎ *(619) 274 2454,* 🎦 🍴 🍸 ⛱ 🎣 🍹 🏄*)* is a luxurious beachside ranch.

In Todos Santos: **Misíon de Todos Santos** *(* ☎ *(682) 27173* 🏠*)* is basic but clean; **California** *(Juárez s/n* ☎ *(682) 40002* 🏠 🍴 🍸 ⛱*)* is a neo-colonial oasis; the **Todos Santos Inn** *(Obregón 17, no* ☎ 🏠 🍴*)* is an old hotel in the town center.

LOS CABOS

*Map **2**F4. Baja California Sur. 1,550km (969 miles) s of Ensenada on RF1. Population: 25,000. Served by air (international airport 11km (6 miles) N of San José), sea (cruise lines) and bus. American Express: c/o Tourcabos, Playa de Los Cabos* ☎ *(684) 20982* **i** *Palacio Municipal, Mijares s/n* ☎ *(684) 21560. American Express: Plaza Los Cabos B2, San José del Cabo* ☎ *(684) 21982.*

Arch of Cortés, Cabo San Lucas

The dramatic cape region, at the s tip of Baja California, is already the fourth tourist destination in Mexico, and is set for sustained growth. It is now the focus of a massive development effort, which will add some 20,000 accommodation units, 3,000 marina berths and several thousand hectares of golf-course by the year 2000.

For much of its recorded history, the cape was a haunt of whalers and pirates. It was here, in 1587, that Thomas Cavendish lay in wait to capture the *Santa Ana,* a Spanish treasure-ship loaded with gold, spices and silks. Similar attacks continued well into the 18thC. Partly in response to such attacks, and partly to subdue the fierce Pericué Indians of the region, the Spanish founded a mission at San José del Cabo in 1730 and, later, another at Cabo San Lucas, on a protected inlet near the southern tip.

Tourism was pioneered in the 1940s by North Americans in pursuit of marlin, swordfish and sailfish, but only took off with the arrival of the RF1 highway in 1973. A further attraction is provided by gray whales from Alaska, which congregate off the cape between December and March to mate, closely watched by whale-lovers in "panga" skiffs. The waters of the cape are claimed to offer the best diving outside the Caribbean.

Of the two resorts, **Cabo San Lucas** is the most developed, with gleaming white luxury hotels springing up like dragon's teeth. **San José del Cabo** *(33km/20 miles NE),* built in the Spanish style around a tree-shaded plaza, retains the atmosphere of a small fishing port. Much recent development has also taken place between the two, along the divided RF1 (Los Cabos) highway.

Beaches

The beaches of the area are lovely, but the accessible ones mostly have hotels looming up behind, or soon will — not that this has diminished the popularity of **Playa Médano**, just E of Cabo San Lucas. To get away from the crowds, set off for the little coves out by the cliffs, which can only be reached by boat. The glass-bottomed launches that tour the cliffs will take you there and pick you up later.

These tours cruise out, past pelicans and basking seals, to the natural **Arch of Cortés** (☆) where the waters of the Pacific and the Sea of Cortés meet in a churning witches' cauldron under the ragged rocks. Make sure you take one of the evening cruises, leaving the dock at 4.30-5pm, with entertainment included in the price.

Two wild and rugged beaches are **Playa Vista de los Arcos** *(5km/3 miles E of Cabo San Lucas)*, with views of the Arch, and **Playa Barco Varado** *(8km/5 miles E of Cabo San Lucas)*, with the remains of a wrecked freighter. Safer for swimming are **Playa Palmilla** *(7km/4 miles W of San José del Cabo)*, **Playa Bledito** *(13km/8 miles W of San José del Cabo)*, and **Playa Santa María** *(8km/5 miles W of San José del Cabo)*.

EVENT • San José del Cabo celebrates its **fiesta** on March 19.

HOTELS AND RESTAURANTS

South of La Paz, hotels tend to be very expensive, but they are often less so if booked as a package abroad. Many of them insist on "American Plan," meaning that you have to pay for meals, whether you want them or not. However, this may be negotiable, especially out of season. A number of independent restaurants have recently opened, so there is no shortage of alternatives.

Cabo San Lucas

CALINDA BEACH 🏨
Km 4.5, Carretera Transpeninsular, on the beach toward the promontory ☎(684) 30044/5 🖷(684) 30077 ▨ 125 rms ▬ ⇌ ⌂ ◁ ⚲ ⌕ ✈ ⛛ ❂ ⚓
This luxurious, adobe-built terraced village can also offer a magnificent view of the whales in winter.

FINISTERRA 🏨
Blvd. Marina, at the end of the promontory ☎(684) 30000/30100 🖷(684) 30590 ▨ 110 rms ⇌ ⌂ ◁ ⚲ ⌕ ➤ ⛛ ⚓
This hotel is built into a beachside cliff, with spectacular views over the swirling waters. The minimalist, no-frills architecture has its admirers.

HACIENDA BEACH RESORT 🏨
Playa Médano, opposite the marina ☎(684) 30122/3, or in US (800) 733 2226 ▨ 114 rms ▬ ⇌ ⌂ ⚲ ⌕ ➤ ⛛ ⚓ ✈
A modern hotel in the colonial style, and set amidst luxuriant gardens, the Hacienda Beach Resort has safe swimming on the beach, as well as a range of other water-sports.

MARINA ♣
Blvd. Marina and Guerrero ☎(684) 30030 ▨ 31 rms ⇌ ⌕ ⛛ ⚓
Plain but pleasant, this hotel in the downtown area offers good value for money.

⇌ **El Galeón** *(Marina s/n, near pier* ☎ *(684) 30443* ▨*)* has fine Italian food, as does **Romeo y Juliete** *(Marina s/n, a short distance N* ☎*(684) 30225* ▨*)*, but without the view. For entertainment with your dinner, head for **Squid Roe** *(Cárdenas s/n* ☎*(684) 30655* ▨*)*, a typically over-the-top Carlos'n'Charlie's eatery; or try **El Marlin Sonriente** *(Marina and Matamoros* ☎*(684) 30606* ▨*)*. It has an impressive Tex-Mex menu, but many customers are there strictly for the festive ambience, and of course the tequila.

Other options include the *palapa* restaurants on **Playa Médano**, which are also good places to escape from the midday sun on the beach.

San José del Cabo

BEST WESTERN POSADA REAL
Mijares s/n, in the hotel zone ☎(684) *20155* 🆔(684) 20460 ▦ *150 rms* ⇶ ☿ ☊ ♨ ➤ ♨ ♨ 🎵

This new hotel, convenient for the golf course, offers a high standard of comfort, in an intimate atmosphere.

COLLI
Hidalgo s/n in downtown ☎(684) 20756 ▦ *12 rms* ⇶

A small courtyard inn with roof terrace, clean and friendly but with no frills.

STOUFFER PRESIDENTE
Blvd. Mijares s/n, 1km (½ mile) e of San José

☎(684) 20238 🆔(684) 20232 ▦ *to* ▦ *240 rms* ⇶ ➤ ☿ ☊ ♨ ☊ ♨ ➤ ☿

This beach resort hotel is set on an enchanting lagoon, which has 200 species of wildfowl. The best hotel in San José, it has shops, a baby-sitting service and every other facility you could wish for.

TROPICANA INN ♣
Mijares 30, toward the beach ☎(684) 20907 ▦ *40 rms* ⇶ ☿ ☊

Opened in 1991, and gracefully designed in the neo-colonial style around a courtyard, this hotel offers good value in its price category.

⇶ Many of the best places to eat are along Mijares. Try **Damiana** *(Mijares 8* ☎ *(684) 20499* ▦*)* for mouthwatering dinners near the Zócalo. Less fancy, but highly appetizing, is the menu at **André Mar** *(Mijares 34* ☎*(684) 20374* ▦*)*, which has an attractive garden. For drinks and snacks in the open air, there is no better place than the nearby **Café Europa**.

Of the hotel restaurants, the PALMILLA (see below) truly stands out, for food as well as location.

Between the Cabos

CABO SAN LUCAS 🏨
Chileno bay, half way between the Cabos. No ☎ *(in US* ☎*(800) 421 0777)* ▦ *125 rms* ⇶ ☊ ☿ ♨ ♨ ☊ ♨ ➤ ☿

This deluxe, modern beachside hotel in the "Spanish mission" style has beautiful 7-room villas and its own private airstrip, tucked away in a 1,000-hectare (2,500-acre) estate covered in palm trees.

MELÍA CABO REAL 🏨
Km 19.5 on Los Cabos highway above Bledito Beach ☎(684) 30754 🆔(684) 31003, or in US ☎(800) 336 3542 ▦ *300 rms* ⇶ ☿ ♨ ☊ ♨ ♨ ➤ ⮑

This extravagant new resort hotel sprawls across the hillside, shimmering with acres of pools and waterfalls like a desert mirage.

MELÍA SAN LUCAS 🏨
Paseo del Pescador s/n on Playa Médano, 5km (3 miles) w of Cabo San Lucas ☎(684) 31000 🆔(684) 30420 ▦ *187 rms* ⇶ ☿ ♨ ☊ ♨ ♨

This is a new, and very expensive, luxury hotel in the hacienda style. Sited on a sheltered beach, it offers a wide range of watersports.

PALMILLA
Playa Palmilla, 8km (5 miles) w of San José ☎(684) 20583, or in US ☎(800) 854 2608) ▦ *72 rms* ⇶ ♨ ☊ ♨ ♨ ➤ ☿

This exclusive, neo-Moorish, hacienda-style fishing resort has its own airstrip and two detached villas, all in the middle of a 360-hectare (900-acre) Jack Nicklaus-designed golf course.

TWIN DOLPHIN 🏨
Km 11 on Los Cabos Highway ☎(684) 30496/30140 🆔(684) 30256, or in US ☎(800) 421 8925 ▦ *50 rms* ⇶ ☿ ☊ ♨ ♨ ➤

The contemporary, Japanese-inspired design of this deluxe hotel and its ultra-modern *casitas* has given it an almost austere atmosphere. Ideally suited to to the ultra-wealthy who really do want to get away from it all.

The South-East

This region, comprising the states of **Chiapas** and **Tabasco**, is one of the most rewarding in Mexico, for its archeological wealth, its Maya cultural heritage, and its verdant landscapes of mountains and forests.

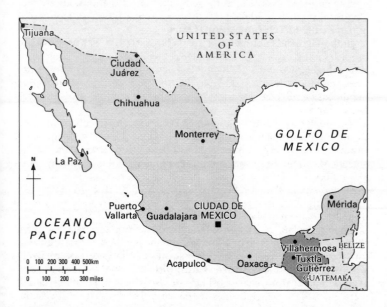

CHIAPAS

Officially part of Mexico, Chiapas is really a geographical and cultural offshoot of Central America. Its high volcanic ridges are extensions of the highlands of Guatemala, and its indigenous Maya inhabitants form a continuum with their neighbors to the south and west, cut off from the main body of Mexico by the **Isthmus of Tehuantepec**, the true geographical divide.

As in Guatemala, the Maya peoples retain their ancient culture and identity in the face of many threats. But whereas, in Guatemala, entire Indian villages are routinely bombed out of existence, the Indians of Chiapas face more subtle dangers — those of cultural erosion, the breakup and theft of their lands, high-handed officialdom, and political corruption that has penetrated right to the heart of indigenous society.

It is worth remembering that, but for an accident of history, Chiapas, the size of Costa Rica, could have become a country in its own right, instead of being annexed into the Mexican Federation on the breakup of the colonial Viceroyalty of Guatemala, in 1821. However, to judge by the state of Central America, Chiapas is better off where it is.

TUXTLA GUTIÉRREZ, capital of Chiapas since 1892, is hot, busy and unpleasant, but difficult to avoid as the state's transport hub. On the other hand, it has an excellent safari-style zoo with a strong conservation ethic, and the nearby **Sumidero Canyon**, now easily visited by speedboat, is a memorable sight.

To its south rise up the cloud-shrouded peaks of the **Sierra Madre Sur**, with its lower slopes planted with coffee, which gives way to sugar, cocoa and bananas on the fertile, muddy reaches of the Pacific coast. Its remote and inaccessible upper reaches are home to enormous areas of cloud-forest of extraordinary beauty and biological diversity, protected in part by the **El Triunfo National Park**.

In the highlands northwest of Tuxtla lies SAN CRISTÓBAL DE LAS CASAS, the old colonial capital. This is the main center for the strongly indigenous central highlands, and a growing focus of tourist interest. Further northwest, the mountains drop down to the tropical lowlands, where forests of pine and scrub oak give way to the exuberant rainforests of the **Selva Lacandona**.

This region of mountain and forest is named after its inhabitants, the Lacandon Indians, of whom only a few hundred remain. The long-haired Lacandones are frequently revered as the last true descendants of the ancient Maya, but this claim is no truer of them than of the many other Maya peoples of Chiapas, who pursue a less romantic, agricultural existence. Unlike their forebears, who fiercely resisted the 16thC Spanish invaders, the Lacandones are now a gentle people, worlds apart even from their Maya neighbors.

Their homeland and its surroundings contain numerous Classic Maya sites of great beauty. The best known, and most visited, is PALENQUE, but trips to out-of-the-way sites such as BONAMPAK and YAXCHILÁN are highly worthwhile. Lesser sites such as **Chinkultic**, near the LAGUNAS DE MON-TEBELLO, and **Toniná**, near Ocosingo, are also well worth visiting. Natural wonders of the area include massive **caves** and potholes in the limestone rock, and the amazing waterfalls at **Agua Azul**, south of Palenque.

As for the rainforest, it is still being destroyed by colonizers, land speculators, cattle-ranchers and timber-cutters, for whom national park designations appear to serve as an open invitation to come in and help themselves, allegedly with the backing of local politicians. The **Lagunas de Montebello National Park**, east of San Cristóbal near the Guatemalan border, is just one example of the phenomenon.

TABASCO

Tabasco is a far smaller and, with reason, less-visited state. Its rainforests have nearly all fallen to the chainsaws of lumbermen, or the flames of cattle-ranchers, while exploration for oil has left large areas contaminated with toxic residues.

But those passing across the plains of Tabasco to the Yucatán peninsula should stop at the ugly state capital, the curiously named **VILLAHERMOSA**, to see its excellent **museum** and **park** dedicated to the Olmec people. The Olmecs, whose ancient heartland this is, predated the flowering of Maya civilization by centuries, laying the foundation for all subsequent Meso-American civilization. The newly-excavated nearby Maya site of **Comalcalco** is also well worth a visit.

Towns, cities and cultural sites

The main cities and archeological sites in this part of Mexico are covered in the following pages, starting with the capital of Chiapas, **TUXTLA GUTIÉRREZ**, following a counterclockwise course through **TAPACHULA AND THE CHIAPAS COAST**, NE to **SAN CRISTÓBAL DE LAS CASAS**, SW to the **LAGUNAS DE MONTEBELLO**, then NW to the Maya site of **PALENQUE**. This is the most likely spot from which to make the trek (or take a plane) to the ruins of **BONAMPAK AND YAXCHILÁN**. The route ends in **VILLAHERMOSA**, state capital of Tabasco.

See USING THIS GUIDE on page 50 for details on how to use this section. On the following pages, pointers are given on how to get to each of the destinations covered. Along with the MEXICO map on pages 46–7, and the 4-color maps at the back of this book, they should give all the information necessary for planning your trip to this part of Mexico.

TUXTLA GUTIÉRREZ

Map **7**H11. *Capital of Chiapas. 294km (183 miles) s of Villahermosa on RF190 and RF195; 85km (53 miles) w of San Cristóbal on RF190. Altitude: 574m (1,838ft). Population: 500,000. Served by air and bus* **i** *Belisario Dominguez 950 at Central Poniente* ☎*(961) 24535. American Express: Plaza Bonampak 14* ☎*(961) 26998.*

A fast-growing modern city with a hot subtropical climate, Tuxtla is emphatically *not* a tourist destination — except for its **zoo**, reputed to be the best in Latin America. It is, however, an important transport hub, and may prove hard to avoid. If you have to stay, enjoy a cool night in one of the air-conditioned hotels, a welcome break after the steamy heat of the isthmus or the rigors of traveling in Chiapas. Tuxtla can be a good base from which to make the most of the nearby sights.

WHAT TO SEE

Tuxtla's main attraction is the excellent **Zoomat** *(Cerro Hueco, in SE outskirts* 🖸 *open Tues-Sun 8am-5pm; closed Mon),* certainly the best zoo in Mexico, where you can see animals native to Chiapas in a semiwild forest environment containing some of the last of the huge trees that once covered the area. You are unlikely to see most of the animals it houses elsewhere during your stay: most are elusive and shy, and the continuing destruction of Chiapas' forests is fast removing their habitat. The zoo works hard to promote conservation in Chiapas, and to postpone the day when its animals may be the last survivors of their kind.

The **Museo Regional de Chiapas** *(Calz. de los Hombres s/n* ☎ *open Tues-Sun 9am-4pm; closed Mon)* contains Olmec sculptures from the N of the state, Maya objects from nearby sites, some colonial artifacts and local indigenous weaving. It is located in the new **Parque Madero** complex, with its 1,200-seat theater, public swimming pool and shady **Botanical Garden** *(* ☒ *open Tues-Sun 9am-2pm, 4-6pm; closed Mon)*.

EXCURSIONS

Chiapa de Corzo
14km (8 miles) E on RF190.
At the center of this small town's Zócalo is a bizarre 16thC **fountain**, built in the Moorish style to resemble the crown of the kings of Spain. Near the Zócalo is a small **museum** of regional handicrafts and Maya artifacts, from the ceremonial center that made the colonial town's foundations. One *stele*, dating from 36BC, is the oldest known example. But Chiapa is most often visited for the nearby **Sumidero Canyon** (see below), accessible by boat from the dock.

El Sumidero Canyon ☆
The gorge cut by the river Grijalva, 15km (9 miles) long and 1,200m (3,936 feet) deep, is one of the most spectacular natural sights in Mexico. Legend has it that in 1528 a whole tribe of Indians threw themselves to their deaths here, rather than submit to the Conquistadors. The once-churning waters have now been smoothed by a **hydroelectric dam**, so the boatmen of Chiapa de Corzo do good business, taking tourists down the gorge by power-boat. Boats run until mid-afternoon, and the trip takes around 2–3 hours. It is also possible to see the gorge from above, from a number of lookout points signposted along the roads SE of Tuxtla.

Simojovel de Allende
78km (48 miles) NE; turn N onto RF195 after 34km (21 miles) on RF190.
Since Pre-Columbian times, this fascinating hillside village has been a source of **amber**. In the village can be bought small pieces of jewelry, cigarette holders and so on. Rarer, and more expensive, are the pieces containing fossilized insects.

Ocozocoautla
36km (22 miles) W on RF190.
This is a *pueblo* of the tall and graceful Zoque Indians, an agricultural people who have more or less adopted the Catholic faith, with a few pagan improvisations. At fiestas, they wear beautiful embroidered tunics to perform the traditional dances. If you buy one, do not wear it until you have left the area, out of respect. 26km (16 miles) farther W is the **Aguacero waterfall** on the Río La Venta, with an 800-step path down to the river.

☞ There are some good places to spoil yourself after a hard journey. **Bonampak** *(Belisario Domínguez 180* ☎ *(961) 32050* ☒ *(961) 27737* ▥ *100 rms* ⍔ *)* is a comfortable modern hotel. **Humberto** *(* ♣ *Central Pte 180* ☎ *(961)*

22044 □ ⇥ ⟶) offers good value near the Zócalo. The **Flamboyant** (🏨 *Belisario Domínguez, Km 1,081* ☎*(961) 50888/50999* [Fx]*(961) 50087* ▥ *118 rms* ⇥ ⛄ ⚘ ≈ ☀ ○) is a new resort. This hotel, and the **Real de Tuxtla** (🏨 *Pan-American Highway, Km 1,088* ☎*(961) 25958* ▥ ⇥ ⛄ ⚘ ≈), are the two most luxurious in the state.

⇥ **La Selva** *(Belisario Domínguez 1,360* ☎*(961) 26251* ▥), has good, regional specialties to the sound of *marimbas,* while **Las Pichanchas** *(Central Ote 837* ☎*(961) 25351* ▥) offers an accompaniment of live *mariachi* music. Near the zoo, **La Palapa de Amado** *(Libramiento Sur Ote 3125* ☎*(961) 37670* □) is famous for its fresh seafood.

In Chiapa de Corzo, one place to try is **Los Angeles** *(on the Zócalo* □).

TAPACHULA AND THE CHIAPAS COAST

Map 7I11. Chiapas. 256km (160 miles) SE of Tuxtla Gutiérrez on RF190; 243km (151 miles) S of Comitán on RF190. Population: 150,000. Served by air, train (on line to Mexico City) and bus. Guatemalan consulate: Calle 1 Ote 3 ☎*(962) 61252* **i** *Palacio Municipal, on Zócalo* ☎*(962) 63543.*

Much of the wealth of Chiapas comes from this fertile, well-watered Pacific coastal plain. It is rich with fruit orchards, cacao- and sugar-plantations, worked by indebted Indians who are brought down from the highlands in cattle trucks. Between TUXTLA and the coast is the high ridge of the **Sierra Madre Sur**. There are a number of small resorts along the coast, although the area does not appear set for star status, as the sand all too often degenerates into mud.

The biggest city on the plain is **Tapachula**, a steamy, tropical place near the Guatemalan border, at the foot of a towering extinct volcano, **Tacaná** (4,064m/13,329 feet). Its numbers have been swollen by refugees from Guatemala, with some adverse consequences. Nevertheless, Tapachula makes a good overnight stop on the way to Central America. The atmosphere is lively, especially around the large Zócalo, **Parque Hidalgo**, with its shaded gardens and open-air cafés.

The **Museo de Antropología** *(Mexico 225, in Parque de los Exposiciones)* has a fascinating but little-visited collection of local Maya finds, including some from Izapa (see page 262), as does the small **Museo Regional** *(Palacio Municipal, on the Zócalo)*.

Tonalá *(220km/137 miles NW of Tapachula on RF200; 174km/109 miles S of Tuxtla Gutiérrez on RF190 and RF200)* is a small town with few attractions. It does, however, have one decent hotel (see overleaf), should you need to break your journey here.

ALONG THE COAST
Tonalá resorts

A road runs S off RF200, SE of Tonalá, to **Cabeza de Toro** *(17km/10 miles)* on the coast, and nearby **Puerto Arista**, a small fishing-village-cum-resort just NW, with a lovely beach. Beware of the undertow, if you swim in the sea. A rough road leads some 15km (9 miles) SE along the coast to **Boca del Cielo**, a smaller and nicer version of Puerto Arista, on a sandbar between the Pacific and **Laguna la Joya**.

There is one decent hotel in Puerto Arista (see below); or take your choice of *palapas* under which to sling a hammock. Excellent fresh **seafood** is available almost everywhere.

Izapa

11km (6 miles) E of Tapachula on RF200.

The last ruin before the border, dating from 1000BC to AD1000, should not be missed by addicts. At its height, from 300–50BC, the site covered 3,500 hectares (8,645 acres), but only a small part has been excavated. The chief attractions are the **relief sculptures** on the *stelae,* showing the sacred ball-game, the execution of prisoners and other cheerful scenes of everyday Maya life.

There is a second area of ruins, containing the **Esculturas Escondidas** (Hidden Sculptures), concealed, as their title implies, in the depths of banana and cacao plantations about 1km ($\frac{1}{2}$ mile) to the S. It is best to engage a guide.

Puerta Madero

27km (16 miles) SW of Tapachula.

Tapachula's black-sand beach resort is not set up for luxury tourism. Freshly grilled fish is available from palm-thatched beach restaurants, but swimming is dangerous, due to the undertow, except for a small area to the S, and there is nowhere decent to stay.

In Tapachula, **Loma Real** *(Coastal Highway 200 at Km 244* ☎ *(962) 61440* Ⓕˣ *(962) 64817* ▥ ⇶ ⩘ ◑ ⵏ *)* sits on its own hilltop, and is popular with business travelers. Toward the border, **Kamico** *(Prol. Central Ote s/n* ☎ *(962) 62640* ▥ ⇶ ⩘ ⵏ ▦ *)* is also good, set in pleasant gardens. The **Fénix** *(4a Norte 19, near the Zócalo* ☎ *(962) 50755* ▱ *)* is a decent, low-budget hotel.

In Tonalá, try the **Galilea** *(on Zócalo* ☎ *(36) 30239* ▥ *)*. In Puerto Arista, **Bugambilias** *(on seafront* ☎ *(36) 30675* ▱ *)* is the best place to stay.

SAN CRISTÓBAL DE LAS CASAS ★

Map 7H11. Chiapas. 85km (53 miles) E of Tuxtla Gutiérrez on RF190; 88km (55 miles) NW of Comitán on RF190; 200km (125 miles) S of Palenque. Altitude: 2,050m (6,720ft). Population: 125,000. Served by bus and air taxi ℹ On NW corner of Zócalo in Palacio Municipal ☎ *(967) 80414.*

San Cristóbal is an attractive colonial city, high in the mountains of the Sierra Madre Sur. It is also an island of Spanish-speaking culture in a great and diverse sea of Indian tribes, each with its own language, costumes and culture. The city provides a refuge for other tribes, notably the anthropologists and missionaries, although the vacation-package tribe is not heavily in evidence. One attraction is the cool highland climate, a welcome break from the surrounding steamy lowlands.

The houses are low and stuccoed, with a few larger colonial mansions around the Zócalo, and the town is dominated by two strategically placed **churches**, up on the hills on the outskirts. But architecture is only the second of San Cristóbal's attractions: pride of place must go to the local population, who are always in evidence at the daily (except Sunday)

market *(6 blocks N of Zócalo),* one of the most colorful in Mexico. Almost all of the women, and most of the men, wear traditional costumes; but to see them in full splendor you will have to go out to the **villages** on market day (usually Sunday), or to one of the frequent **fiestas**.

San Cristóbal was founded in 1528 after savage battles between the Chamula Indians and a Spanish army led by the soldier and chronicler Bernal Díaz del Castillo, who is famous for his eye-witness account of the Conquest. St Christopher was designated as the patron saint of the town, which was named accordingly. However, it was soon more widely known as *Villaviciosa* (Wicked City) because of the appalling exploitation of the Indians by Spanish landowners.

This was at its height when Fray Bartolomé de las Casas (1474–1566) arrived in 1544 as Bishop of Chiapas, and began to fight for their rights, much to the displeasure of his compatriots. He returned to the Spanish Court and wrote a long report on the situation, which finally had some effect in 1565, when the King of Spain decreed that improvements should take place. As a result, de las Casas is to this day an (uncanonized) patron saint of the Indians.

Conflicts continue to this day within the Indian communities and between the Indians and the State, based on political, economic and religious divisions under a frequently corrupt hard-line leadership. As a result, some 50,000 people have been illegally expelled from their villages, and have been forced to build new communities around San Cristóbal, or in cleared forest in the lowlands. Most of the Indians selling craft goods in the town are the victims of such expulsions, and their income from tourists is a vital support to them and their families.

EVENTS   All the usual religious feasts are celebrated, with particular gusto. • Particular to San Cristóbal is the **day of the patron saint**, on July 25. Festivities start as early as July 18, and culminate in a candlelit procession and vigil on the night of July 24. • The **day of the Virgin**, December 12, is celebrated with horseback processions, *marimba* music and dancing.

• In addition, there are frequent small fiestas in different areas of town, marked by the detonation of huge bangers and rockets echoing through the valley, and the more melodious sound of *marimba* music.

See also INDIAN VILLAGES NEARBY, pages 265–6.

WHAT TO SEE
The town

The 16thC Plateresque **cathedral** on the Zócalo is outwardly unremarkable, but it contains some fine **Baroque altars** and an ornately carved and gilded pulpit. Across the Zócalo is a fine, unnamed **mansion** of similar age, with a statue of a mermaid on the facade.

Leave the Zócalo on 20 de Noviembre and walk six blocks N to the church of **Santo Domingo**, where rose-colored statues of the Apostles guard the Baroque facade. Inside, kneeling before the gilded altars, will be Indians making their devotions, prostrating themselves with loud protestations, making small offerings and lighting a multitude of candles. Outside, and reaching down to the adjacent church of **La Caridad**, is a pleasant tree-shaded **plaza**, with a multitude of colorful stalls selling locally-made weaving and other crafts.

Next door, the **Centro Cultural de los Altos de Chiapas** *(open 10am-2pm; closed Mon)*, the former Convento de Santo Domingo, houses the **Pellizzi Collection** of Chiapan textiles. The most complete collection of textiles from any Indian area in the Americas, it forms a unique historical and cultural record, with more than 700 pieces documenting every aspect of ceremonial and utilitarian weaving.

Na-Bolom Centro de Estudios Científicos (Na-Bolom Center) ☆
Vicente Guerrero 33, on outskirts of town along Real de Guadalupe ☎*(967) 81418. Open, by appointment, noon–5pm.*

Museum, library, photographic archive and home-away-from-home for archeologists, anthropologists and Lacandon Indians, the Center is housed in a colonial seminary, with the buildings grouped around an elegant, plant-filled courtyard. Exhibits include Lacandon artifacts and artworks, as well as local Maya finds.

The center was founded by the Danish explorer Frans Blom and his wife Gertrude, who settled here in 1950 and devoted their lives to studying and helping the people of Chiapas, under pressure from the evangelizing, industrializing 20thC, and to the research of Maya sites.

The Bloms are credited, in particular, with saving the Lacandon Indians from literal extinction, by assuring their rights to 600,000 hectares (1,482,000 acres) of rainforest. Although Lacandon numbers have increased from 200 to 500, their culture is still under threat, and the rainforest is still suffering from unchecked invasion and exploitation.

The center also functions as a hotel (see below), thereby raising much-needed funds; hotel guests dine with staff and the other visitors.

WHERE TO STAY

Santa Clara *(♣ 1 Insurgentes* ☎*(967) 81140* Fx*(967) 81041* Ⅲ ⇗ ⇌ ☂ ⬤ ⬥*)* is the 16thC former home of conquistador Diego de Mazariegos, right on the Zócalo. The **Posada Diego de Mazariegos** *(5 de Febrero 1* ☎*(967) 81825* Ⅲ ⇌*)* is an elegant colonial hotel, popular with tour groups. The **Na-Bolom Center** *(Vicente Guerrero 33* ☎*(967) 81418* Ⅲ ☙*)* is in a class of its own, with 13 rooms full of character and decorated with local crafts (see above).

Fray Bartolomé de las Casas *(Insurgentes 2 and Niños Héroes* ☎*(967) 80932* Ⅲ ⇗*)*, one block from the Zócalo, has an authentic colonial atmosphere, as do the **Flamboyant** *(1 de Marzo 15* ☎*(967) 80045* Fx*(967) 80514* Ⅲ *52 rms* ⇗ ⬤*)* and **Ciudad Real** *(Plaza 31 de Marzo 10* ☎*(967) 80464* Fx*(967) 80187* Ⅲ *33 rms* ⇗*)*.

Mansión del Valle *(Diego de Mazariegos 39* ☎*(967) 82581-3* Fx*(967) 82581* Ⅲ *45 rms* ⬤ ⇗*)* is a pleasant motel w of the center, but not as good as **Molino de la Alborada** *(Periférico Sur s/n* ☎*(967) 80935* Ⅲ ⇌ ☙*)* or **Parador Ciudad Real** *(Diagonal Centenario 32* ☎*(967) 81886* Ⅲ ⇌*)*.

Of the less expensive hotels along Real de Guadalupe, **Casa Margarita** *(♣ Real de Guadalupe 34* ☎*(967) 80957* ▭*)* is the best, with a pleasant sunny courtyard.

EATING AND DRINKING

El Teatro *(1 de Marzo 8* ☎ *(967) 83149* Ⅲ*)* is a French and Italian gourmet establishment. **Madre Tierra** *(* ✿ *Insurgentes 19* Ⅱ*)* offers a wide range of wholesome dishes, refreshing drinks and cold beers, as well as delicious homebaked bread. From breakfast to teatime only, you could try its other branch *(General Utrillo 33),* in a beautiful colonial courtyard with fountain.

La Galería *(Hidalgo 3* ☎ *(967) 83149* Ⅲ*)* is an upmarket restaurant, bar and nightspot, with live piano music. **Casa de las Imagines** *(* ✿ *Belisario Dominguez 11* ☎ *(967) 80370* Ⅱ*)* has a wide menu of Mexican food, as well as a bar, bookstore and movie theater on the beautifully restored colonial premises.

Sadly, the cafés that once graced the portals of the Zócalo have all been taken over by hardware stores, but there are plenty of inexpensive places to breakfast, as you watch the world go by in the market.

SHOPPING

San Cristóbal is one of the best places in Mexico to buy native weaving and other handmade goods; most of the shops are on **Calle Real de Guadalupe**, off the Zócalo. The **plaza** outside the church of Santo Domingo is full of stalls.

Among the best buys are intricately woven belts, bracelets, hair-ribbons, ponchos, string bags, leatherware and *huipils* (embroidered blouses). Quite a lot of what you see, particularly in the shops, may have been imported from Guatemala.

INDIAN VILLAGES NEARBY

Many fascinating Indian villages lie within a short distance of San Cristóbal. The following Tzotzil villages are the two nearest and most important; both are served by *colectivo* from the market zone, and are best visited on Sunday (market day).

San Juan Chamula
11km (6 miles) N.

This large village of thatched adobe homes is clustered around a 16thC Dominican church. This is the spiritual center for the entire Chamula people, who are spread out across 50 villages to the N. The religion that is practiced here bears only small resemblance to orthodox Catholicism, and is dominated by the worship of saints, who substitute for pre-Christian gods. The rituals carried out in the church are conducted by traditional healers.

The village administers itself with a minimum of interference, and is one of the few accessible places in Mexico where traditional costumes are still widely worn. The women wear *huipils* (embroidered blouses) and heavy dark-blue skirts with thin, embroidered bands. The men wear rough, white cotton shirts and pants, covered by a black woolen tunic. The village officials have ribbons on their hats. San Juan Chamula is the village that has suffered most from the expulsion of religious and political dissenters (see page 263).

Admission to the church is by ticket (▨), which also acts as a permit

16thC Dominican Church,
San Juan Chamula

for photography in the village. But be prepared to pay the subject of a picture a sum negotiated in advance, and on no account attempt to take a picture in the church.

FIESTAS   Some of the most important fiestas in San Juan Chamula's calendar: • the **Easter Carnival**, with fascinating dances; • May 3, the **Day of the Cross**; • June 24, the **patron saint's day**; • December 31 to January 4 (civil ceremonies).

Zinacantán
10km (6 miles) NW of San Juan Chamula.

Zinacantán is run along similar lines to SAN JUAN CHAMULA, and is the center for the 18,000 Zinacantecs to the W of San Cristóbal. There have been expulsions here, but on a far smaller scale than in Chamula.

The costumes here are the finest in Chiapas, with the women in elaborately embroidered *huipils,* and the men wearing distinctive pink ponchos, short pants and flat straw hats trailing colorful ribbons. If they are blowing free, this means that the wearer is a bachelor. The Zinacantecs have recently taken to large-scale flower-growing.

FIESTAS   Worth attending: • January 20 (**San Sebastián**); • August 10 (**San Lorenzo**).

OTHER EXCURSIONS

Estación Biológica Huitepec
Km 3.5 on the road to Chamula and Zinacantán. Open daily 9am-5pm.

This is an important 135-hectare (333-acre) reserve on the 2,750m (9,020-foot) **Huitepec** volcano, run by ProNatura-Chiapas. The reserve is preserving the last remaining species-rich forest of the region, which elsewhere has been destroyed by woodcutting and cultivation.

The wooded hills around San Cristóbal are deceptive in appearance, as the forest has become scrubby and species-poor, due to over-exploitation. In the beautiful Huitepec reserve, trees soar to more than 30m (98 feet), festooned with ferns and bromeliads, which receive their water from the cloud that descends each night. Among the 600-plus plant species here, there are endemic shrubs and bamboos that exist nowhere else. Visitors can take a 2km (1-mile) **guided walk** through the forest.

Grutas de San Cristóbal
In the recreational park, 11km/6 miles SE of San Cristóbal de las Casas on RF190 🔊 ✗ *compulsory.*

These impressive caves extend many kilometers into the limestone mountains. They are illuminated for the first kilometer, showing the huge stalactites and stalagmites in the dark caverns.

FARTHER AFIELD

Comitán
88km (55 miles) SE on RF190.
The last town before LAGUNAS DE MONTEBELLO and the Guatemalan frontier, Comitán is bisected by a dusty expanse on each side of the Pan-American Highway, but has a pleasant hill-town climate. The small **museum** (🔊 *open standard hours; closed lunch)* has artifacts from nearby **Chincultic**, including a fine *stele*.

The **airport** at Comitán (☎ *(933) 20390)* is said to offer the least expensive air tours to the ruins at BONAMPAK and YAXCHILÁN (**i** *by the church on the Zócalo* ☎ *(933) 20532);* for travelers who are planning to venture farther into Central America, the **Guatemalan consulate** is nearby (☎ *(933) 22669).*

Those traveling to PALENQUE should consider a visit to the Maya ruins of **Toniná** near Ocosingo *(84km/52 miles N),* and the waterfalls at **Agua Azul**: see under PALENQUE, page 270.

🍴 The **Internacional** *(B. Dominguez 22 Sur* ☎ *(933) 20110/1* 💳*),* **Los Lagos de Montebello** *(3km/1½ mile s of center* ☎ *(933) 21092* 💳*)* and **Real Balun Canan** *(Primera Poniente 5 Sur* ☎ *(933) 21094* 💳*)* are full during February, because of prolonged religious celebrations.

LAGUNAS DE MONTEBELLO
Map 8I12. Chiapas. 142km (88 miles) SE of San Cristóbal de las Casas, turning E off RF190 after 102km (63 miles). Served by bus from Comitán.

There are about 60 lakes, large and small, in the **National Park of Montebello**, a once-remote area of forests and mountains near the Guatemalan border. Sadly, it has been ravaged by the impact of refugee camps and settlers from Guatemala and Mexico. Behind a facade of trees, much of the forest has been destroyed for cultivation.

After the park entrance, the paved road comes first to the group known as the **Lagunas de Colores**, where each lake is a different color, caused by minerals reflected in their waters. On a good day, they range from turquoise to emerald green.

The unpaved road to the right has a series of tracks leading down to some beautiful lakes, including **Lago Montebello** and **Lago Pojoj**, before passing **Lago Tsiscao** on the right. The track to the right leads down to the village of **Tsiscao**, with its friendly, basic hostel overlooking the lake. The main road goes on to **Las Dos Lagunas** and the severely deforested slopes that surround them, then continues along the border.

The Lagunas are best visited by car, due to the long distances involved; and the weather is unpredictable, although sunshine is reasonably certain at the height of the dry season. On good days, **swimming** can be superb.

NEARBY

Chincultic ☆
2km (1 mile) N of the road, 5km (3 miles) before the park entrance.
Climb the central acropolis of these Maya ruins for a superb view of the lakes and farmland around, not to mention the **pyramids** and **ball-courts** of the old city and the remnants of forest clinging to the cliffs.

PALENQUE 🏛 ★

*Map 7H11. Chiapas. 150km (93 miles) SE of Villahermosa on RF186. Population: 25,000. Served by air (air taxi from San Cristóbal de las Casas, Tuxtla and Villahermosa), train (on Coatzacoalcos–Mérida line) and bus **i** at Palacio Municipal, E of Zócalo ☎(934) 50114.*

Of all Mexico's Maya cities, it is usually Palenque that enchants and fascinates visitors the most. The buildings are on low hills, surrounded by the exuberant tropical jungle that concealed them for nearly a millennium. Although they are smaller than the great monuments of the Yucatán, their delicate proportions and intricately modeled stucco decoration are unrivaled. Some observers have seen similarities to the temples of Cambodia, and the burial chamber at the heart of the **Temple of the Inscriptions** (illustrated on page 30) is paralleled only in the Middle East. This all adds to the mystery of the Maya.

> *. . . if you like wild nature, the setting of Palenque is a finer one — on a great circular plateau half-way up the mountainside, with the jungle falling precipitously below into the plain and rising straight up behind . . . temples or palaces open up, emerging obscurely from the jungle . . . they have looked out for a minute, old wrinkled faces, and will soon withdraw.*
> (Graham Greene, *The Lawless Roads;* US title *Another Mexico;* 1939)

Palenque was inhabited long before the Christian era, and rose to become a powerful independent city. Its zenith was reached, however, between AD600 and 800, during which time it dominated much of the Usumacinta watershed. The city was abandoned as the Dark Ages waned in Europe. Restoration work began in 1940, but much remains to be done on the myriad green-covered mounds that spread out far into the jungle.

A **National Park** has been created at Palenque, encompassing 2,000 hectares (4,940 acres) of forest. Howler monkeys, jaguars, peccaries and other wild animals are still found, but their future is bleak. The park is too small to maintain viable populations, and the forest around is being rapidly stripped by ranchers and settlers from the highlands.

There is little to recommend the fast-growing modern town of Palenque itself, and visitors are advised to leave it off their itineraries, as far as the logistics of travel permit.

THE RUINS 🔲 Open 8am–5pm.

The Palace

Entering the site, directly ahead is a striking 4-story **tower**, rising over a group of buildings known as the Palace. The tower may have been used for astronomical observation, but it is unique in Mexico and its purpose is unknown. In the small **temples** around the courts of the Palace are many examples of the finely detailed **stucco reliefs** for which Palenque is famous, and leading down to the E court is a beautifully ornamented **stairway**. On leaving the Palace, walk around the exterior walls, decorated with large **carved panels** of deities.

Temple of the Inscriptions

Near the Palace is a steep pyramid crowned by the **Temple of the Inscriptions** (see illustration on page 30), in which are numerous carved hieroglyphs relating to the Maya calendar. The most remarkable feature of this pyramid is **Pacal's Tomb**, the burial chamber at its center, which was discovered only in 1952; it is reached down a deep, narrow stairwell from the top of the pyramid, originally filled with rubble that took three years to clear. The richly carved 5-ton **sarcophagus**, which contained the remains of Palen-

Mayan **relief**, Palenque

que's greatest ruler, Pacal, depicts his descent into to the Underworld.

Pacal (AD603–684) acceded to power on July 29, AD615. His reign saw Palenque become the dominant power of the SW Maya lowlands. Such information was translated from Maya writings at Palenque by various scholars including Wolfgang Gockel, giving a picture of a highly structured society obsessed by power struggles, war, court intrigue and natural disasters. Most of the funerary offerings are now in the **Museo Nacional de Antropología** in MEXICO CITY (see pages 69–70), from whence the famous jade **Mask of Pacal** was stolen in a much publicized robbery in 1985. Fortunately it has since been recovered.

Other buildings

Across the stream are several smaller, widely-spaced buildings. From the great pyramid, you arrive first at the **Temple of the Sun**; to its N is a building known as **Edifice XIV**, which has a fine **low-relief** of a prince accepting offerings from a humbly genuflecting woman.

Behind are the carved **Temple of the Cross** and, to the s, the **Temple of the Foliated Cross**. On the hillside 500m (1,640 feet) s up the course of the stream stands the **Temple of the Jaguar**, which is still surrounded by jungle. From there, it is possible to walk up the steeply climbing path for a few miles into the jungle, before it reaches an *ejido* (communal farm). Alternatively, you can follow the stream down toward the temples and **ball-court** of the **North Group**.

Nearby is a small **museum**, containing stucco masks and sculptures from the ruins. Behind the museum, a path to the road travels alongside the stream, which forms pools and waterfalls as it goes, making this a pleasant place to cool off on a hot day.

❋ In a superb jungle setting, 4km (2 miles) from the ruins, the 14 bungalows of **Chan Kah** *(Carretera Ruinas, Km 3* ☎*(934) 50318* ℻*(934) 50489* ▥ *30 rms* ➡ *no cards* ⇴ ⅋*)* are placed around a lagoon-like stone-lined pool. **La Cañada** *(Cañada 18* ☎*(934) 50102* ▥ *20 rms* ➡ ⅋*)*, on the outskirts of town, heading toward the ruins, has a good restaurant and accommodation in thatched bungalows.

To the e of town, with good views across surrounding hills and countryside, **Misíon Palenque Park Inn** *(Rancho San Martin de Porres* ☎*(934) 50300* ℻*(934) 50499, in US* ☎*(800) 648 7818* ▥ *144 rms* ➡ ▱ ⇴ ⅋ ⅋*)* is a modern hotel, with a swimming pool fed by a natural spring.

Nututun Palenque *(Km 3.5 Carretera Ocosingo* ☎*(934) 50100* ℻*(934) 50161* ▥ *42 rms* ➡ ⅋*)* is beside a tributary of the Usumacinta river, which is good for swimming. With its large, modern rooms, this is one of the best hotels.

For budget travelers, the **Palenque** *(5 de Mayo 15, on Zócalo* ☎*(934) 50188* ▱ ➡*)* is one option, but the best suggestion is to sling a hammock under a *palapa* at the **Mayabel trailer park** *(in the National Park, below the ruins).*

➡ Good restaurants are to be found in the hotels **La Cañada** and **Misíon Palenque** *(see above).* **La Selva** *(Km 5, on road to ruins* ☎*(934) 50363* ▱*)* serves excellent local dishes.

EXCURSIONS

A reasonable all-weather road leads across the mountains to SAN CRISTÓBAL DE LAS CASAS *(210km/131 miles)* via the small town of **Ocosingo** *(110km/68 miles)*. After 25km (15 miles), watch for the sign for the **Misol-Ha waterfall**, which drops into a deep pool that is marvellous for swimming. You can stay in the **cabins**, but bring your own food and blankets.

60km (37 miles) from Palenque, a turning leads 3km (2 miles) w to the beauty spot of **Agua Azul**, where clear, blue water falls in immense cascades down the steep hills. The swimming in the limestone pools is superb, but the currents are powerful. There are a number of restaurants but no accommodation that could be called respectable. Agua Azul is at its best in dry weather, as rain washes a lot of mud into the water from the increasingly deforested slopes.

From Ocosingo a track leads 14km (8 miles) E to the ruins of **Toniná** (✎), a little-visited Classic Maya center, accessible by bus or 4-wheel-drive vehicle. Toniná is best known for its unusual **stone monuments** dating from AD495–909, but it also preserves some interesting and unusual architectural features. From the top of the pyramids are fine views across the valley, once forested but now given over to cattle-ranching.

Tenosique *(92km/57 miles E by road or 71km/44 miles by train)* is a small trading outpost on the banks of the river Usumacinta, which flows through the rainforest along the Mexico–Guatemala border. From here, the enterprising can venture into the jungle in canoes, or on mules, to see nearby Maya ruins such as those of **Pomoná**, a Classic site now undergoing excavation and restoration.

Tenosique is also the departure point for the increasingly well-traveled short-cut to **Flores** in Guatemala, which involves a boat-ride to **El Naranjo**, across the border, then a long, hard bus journey.

BONAMPAK AND YAXCHILÁN ★

Map 8H12. Chiapas. Both 130km (81 miles) SE of Palenque by air, served by air taxi from Palenque, Ocosingo, San Cristóbal de las Casas (40mins, 15mins between Bonampak and Yaxchilán), Comitán and Villahermosa.

The ruins at Yaxchilán and Bonampak can both be visited on an amazing day's excursion by light plane. But those with explorer's blood may prefer to make an arduous overland journey lasting several days, equipped with hammocks and mosquito-repellant.

The bumpy dirt road from Palenque runs to **San Javier** (6 hours by bus), a roadside Lacandon settlement where Lacandon families will, for a small fee, make space for your hammock and share their food. From here, it is a tough 16km (10-mile) hike through the forest to **Bonampak**, and it is also possible to visit other Lacandon villages, such as **Najá** and nearby **Lacanjá**. A guide, easily recruited in **San Javier**, is recommended for all such journeys.

The Lacandones, a gentle and beautiful people, continue to live a semitraditional life in the forest, and can easily be distinguished by their uncut black hair and simple, white cotton smocks.

The main road continues to **Frontera Echeverría** (2 hours by bus), a village on the banks of the Río Usumacinta, served by one or two buses a day from Palenque. Here you can rent a boat to **Yaxchilán**, about half an hour's journey downstream. Yaxchilán is a very pleasant place in which to spend a few days: it has a resident caretaker, a caretaker's wife who prepares ample meals of beans and tortillas, and hammock space under mosquito-free *palapas*. Remember that if you fly in, you will be whisked away after a few brief hours.

Another option is to come from or continue into Guatemala, which lies on the far bank of the Usumacinta. The quickest and least expensive route is via the Guatemalan frontier-post, just upstream from Frontera Echeverría, which is served by a daily bus to Flores.

However, a more interesting journey is up the Usumacinta to **Sayaxché**, then E up its tributary, the Río de la Pasión. Sayaxché is a good center from which to explore further Maya ruins such as **Seibal**, before continuing by road to **Flores** and **Tikal**, the greatest of all the ancient Maya cities.

The Painted Temple of Bonampak ★

The plane will land beside the ruins, which stand on high ground near the river Lacanjá. From the strip, walk straight into a large, open space, surrounded by palaces and temples, with a large *stele* in the middle, showing a priest-king, and, to the N, a monumental **stairway**.

At the top of this stairway, on the right, is the famous three-chambered **Painted Temple**, in which flash photography has been banned in order to limit the deterioration of the murals. More than any other Maya work of art, these vivid, natural paintings give an idea of the way of life of this mysterious civilization. Those unable to make the journey can see a full-sized replica at MEXICO CITY's **Museo de Antropología** (page 70).

The **left-hand chamber** shows a religious ceremony; richly dressed priests perform dances, and may well be praying for the victory that follows in the **central chamber**. Here are scenes of war, with warriors wearing leopard-skins sacrificing their prisoners. In the **right-hand chamber**, the victory banquet is in progress, with musicians, acrobats and dancers, anxious servants tending to their masters' every need, and prisoners being tortured. Up on the hill, behind the main group of buildings, are other **temples**, half-smothered by green tendrils.

Yaxchilán ★

This important Classic Maya center stands on its own loop on the mighty Río Usumacinta as it winds through the forest. The buildings, a blend of Maya styles, rival in beauty and interest any other site in Mesoamerica. Of special note is the carving on the limestone lintels of the **temple doorways**, miraculously preserved through the centuries.

The site remains only partly excavated and restored, with piles of upturned masonry undisturbed under the snaking forest roots, echoing to the boom of howler monkeys. Unlike the more manicured sites, Yaxchilán seems alive with whispering ghosts. A proposed hydroelectric dam on the Usumacinta would leave the site permanently underwater, however, so make this worthwhile and memorable trip while you can.

VILLAHERMOSA

Map 7H11. Capital of Tabasco. 169km (105 miles) E of Coatzacoalcos on RF180; 150km (93 miles) NW of Palenque on unnumbered road and RF186; 423km (264 miles) SW of Campeche on RF180 and RF186; 193km (120 miles) N of Tuxtla Gutiérrez, 310km (193 miles) N of San Cristóbal, on RF190 and RF195. Population: 500,000. Served by air and bus i Lerdo 101 ☎(93) 123171, and Paseo Tabasco 1504 in Tabasco 2000 center ☎(93) 150693. American Express: Sarlat 202 and Fidencia ☎(93) 141818.

The name Villahermosa means "beautiful town," but sadly, any charm it may have had has been swept away by oil wealth. It is a hot, crowded, congested and polluted city, but most travelers in this part of Mexico end up spending a night here (consider staying in an expensive hotel). However, the two **museums** are excellent, and you should stop to see the **Parque la Venta**, even if you are just passing.

WHAT TO SEE

CICOM Anthropology Museum ☆
Carlos Pellicer 511 on Grijalva river ☎*(931) 218033* 🔳 *Open 9am–8pm.*

This huge cultural complex, containing Maya and Olmec artifacts from all over Tabasco, provides an enjoyable way to familiarize yourself with the art of these vanished cultures, before a visit to the major sites. The museum is dedicated to Carlos Pellicer Cámara (see below).

Exhibits include **Olmec sculptures** of warriors, monkeys and semihuman jaguars and a fine colossal head of a warrior with a jaguar-like smile or snarl, copies of Pre-Hispanic *códices* (painted scrolls), reproductions of the **murals** from BONAMPAK, and **pottery figurines** from the island of Jaina. The first two floors are devoted to the Maya and Olmec cultures, and the top floor gives an introduction to Mexico's ancient peoples.

Parque la Venta ★
Adolfo Ruíz Cortines s/n (road to Coatzacoalcos), 1.5km (1 mile) w of center, N of Paseo Tabasco ☎*(93) 152228* 🔳 *Open 8am–4.30pm.*

This lakeside garden and open-air museum painstakingly re-creates part of the ruins found at **La Venta**, in the swamps of w Tabasco, dating from 1500BC and 500BC. It was a major center of the mysterious **Olmec** people, who were the first urban civilization of Mesoamerica.

The extent of the site only came to light following drainage for oil drilling; its contents were saved from destruction by local historian and archeologist Carlos Pellicer Cámara, who campaigned for their transfer to this specially created park. There is little to see at La Venta itself but the wreckage of oil extraction.

The highlights are four of the giant **monolithic heads** that are a typical product of Olmec sculpture. They weigh up to 20 tons apiece, and facially they are both negroid and jaguar-like, for the Olmecs were a negroid people who worshiped a jaguar god. Other pieces include the famous *Madonna and Child,* probably showing a goddess holding a jaguar-featured baby. There are also low-relief *stelae* (stone tablets), depicting gods, animals and richly caparisoned nobles.

Part of the effort at realism in the park is a small **zoo**, containing animals that roam the swamps around La Venta; often these escape from their cages and are pursued by staff and visitors. The Olmecs may also have kept a zoo: a construction of thin stone cylinders in the park was almost certainly a **cage** for captured jaguars.

Monolithic **Olmec head**

The nearby **Natural History Museum** *(open 9am-8pm; closed Mon)* has interesting displays on the region's fast-disappearing ecological heritage.

WHERE TO STAY

The **Hyatt Villahermosa** *(Juárez 106* ☎ *(93) 134444* ⌷Fx⌷ *(93) 151235* ▥ *to* ▥ *209 rms* ⫤ ⴲ ⵘ ⵗ *)* is the top downtown choice. **Holiday Inn Tabasco Plaza** *(Tabasco 1407* ☎ *(93) 164400* ▥ *145 rms* ⫤ ⴲ ⵙ ⵘ *)* is a typical member of the well-known chain; **Plaza Independencia** *(♦ Independencia 123 off Zócalo* ☎ *(93) 121299* ▥ ⫤ ⵘ *)* is pleasant, and good value.

Cencali *(▨ Juárez at Tabasco, near Laguna de las Ilusiones* ☎ *(93) 151999* ⌷Fx⌷ *(93) 121862* ▥ *116 rms* ⫤ ⵚ ⵘ *)* is a colonial-style hotel in lush gardens near the airport. Near the bus station, try the **Maya Tabasco Best Western** *(Ruíz Cortines 907* ☎ *(93) 121111* ⌷Fx⌷ *(93) 121097* ▥ *153 rms* ⫤ ⵘ ● *)*, which has a good restaurant. **Villahermosa Viva** *(▨ Paseo Tabasco 1201 and Ruíz Cortines* ☎ *(93) 150000* ⌷Fx⌷ *(93) 153073* ▥ *260 rms* ⫤ ⵘ ● *)* is oriented mainly toward the business traveler.

EATING AND DRINKING

The aptly-named **Club de Pesca** *(27 de Febrero 812* ☎ *(93) 122197* ▥ *)* specializes in seafood. **Los Guayacanes** *(at CICOM Museum* ☎ *(93) 121530* ▥ *)* can offer a wide menu and fine views across the river. **Los Pepes** *(Madero 610* ☎ *(93) 120154* ▥ *)* is good for Mexican meals and snacks.

After visiting CICOM, pop into **Los Tulipanes** *(Carlos Pellicer 511* ☎ *(93) 129209)* for excellent seafood.

EXCURSIONS

Comalcalco

☆ *55km (34 miles) NW. Open 8am-5pm.*

This is a recently restored Classic Maya site of great beauty, yet few people have heard of it. Comalcalco was a major center of cocoa cultivation during the 6th–12thC, which made it of great value: cocoa beans served as currency. Its Chontal Maya inhabitants, allied with the Toltecs in the 9thC, appear to have played a critical role in undermining the Classic Maya centers to the SE in Chiapas and Guatemala.

Although built in the same style as PALENQUE, Comalcalco is unique in being built of brick rather than stone. **Oyster shells** were an important building material here: they were burned to produce both the mortar and the stucco with which the buildings were faced, and were mixed with clay and sand to make the bricks.

Near the large pyramid is a **burial chamber** decorated with stucco **reliefs** of Maya princes and gods. The **Building of the Masks** (Edificio de los Mascarones), also in the main group, is heavily decorated with stucco masks.

Paraíso *(25km/15 miles N of Comalcalco)* is a quiet resort and fishing village between the sea and Laguna Mecoaca, worth a lunchtime visit for its excellent seafood restaurants.

The Yucatán Peninsula

The Yucatán's package of gorgeous beaches, coral reefs, Maya ruins, rich forests and colonial cities, along with its friendly, tropical ambience, provides a combination of attractions that few places can equal.

Long inaccessible from the main body of Mexico, the peninsula remains curiously detached from it to this day. Despite the arrival of roads and airports, this massive lump of low-lying limestone, seared by tropical heat, patched with thick forest and dotted with the ruins of ancient Maya civilizations, runs, or rather strolls, at a pace all of its own. It comprises three states: **Quintana Roo** in the east, **Yucatán** in the north, and **Campeche** in the southwest.

The region proved one of the most resistant to Spanish conquest, succumbing only in the mid-16th century to the cruelties of Bishop de Landa and his Franciscan monks, who burned dissidents alive for heresy. But having conquered, the Spanish were unable to find the gold they expected, and for centuries the peninsula remained a colonial backwater, growing sugar-cane where the water-supply permitted.

It was only in the 19th century that hacienda owners realized the economic potential of the fiber-rich henequen cactus, used in rope-making, which was then planted across vast areas by enslaved Maya Indians. The wealth that resulted was responsible for the colonial elegance of **MÉRIDA** today. Meanwhile, the appalling conditions and land grabs endured by the Indians stimulated bloody rebellions and even bloodier reprisals, culminating in the War of the Castes in 1847–49.

Today, the peninsula is instead dominated by international tourism. For just as the central and northeastern US sinks into its bitter winter, the clouds of the Yucatán peninsula's rainy season are swept away by cool breezes that relieve the oppressive summer heat, making this the perfect time to visit.

QUINTANA ROO

CANCÚN, at the north of the state of Quintana Roo, is one of the world's top resorts, glittering with Miami-style luxury hotels, its wide beaches washed by the blue waters of the Caribbean. And for those who find the experience un-Mexican or just plain expensive, there are many lower-key resorts along the state's eastern coast, all sharing the same crystal sea and shimmering white sand.

Nearby **ISLA MUJERES** — the fateful first landing point in Mexico of Hernán Cortés, in 1517 — is something of a backpackers' haven, while the coral reefs of **COZUMEL**, another island to the south, are famous among scuba divers, who also make for the less renowned but no less lovely shores of **AKUMAL**.

Farther south, **TULUM** is best known for its Post-Classic Maya ruins, perched on seaside clifftops. It is also a favorite haunt of budget travelers, who sling their hammocks in the *palapas*— palm-roofed shelters — that fringe the beach. The extensive ruins of **COBÁ**, an important Classic Maya site inland from Tulum, remain largely unexcavated and off the beaten tourist track.

Just beyond Tulum lies the vast **Sian Ka'an Biosphere Reserve**, a region of pristine swamps and jungles, where Indians continue to live a traditional way of life. The next city is **CHETUMAL**, the unremarkable state capital near the Belizean border. The east–west road from Chetumal skirts a number of fascinating Post-Classic Maya ruins, well worth the trouble of exploring.

YUCATÁN

The best-known Maya ruins on the peninsula are those at **CHICHÉN ITZÁ** in the state of Yucatán, a major site whose later buildings show the influence of the Toltecs of the Valley of Mexico. Easily accessible from the mega-resort of **CANCÚN**, the ruins are among the busiest in Mexico, best avoided at the equinoxes when the famous optical illusion known as the "shadow-snake" brings hordes of extra visitors.

On the western side of the peninsula lies **MÉRIDA**, a large, well-preserved colonial town, capital of the state of Yucatán, and an important tourist destination that prides itself on its Parisian architecture. But be warned — at the height of summer Mérida can be one of the hottest places in the world. If the heat gets really unbearable, however, the cooling waters of the Caribbean are never far away, for example at the minor resort of **Puerto Progreso** on the north coast.

Mérida is an excellent base from which to explore the nearby Maya ruins. The ruins at UXMAL are the jewel in a cluster of ruins and 16th century monasteries, most of which receive only a few visitors.

CAMPECHE

The state of Campeche lies farther south, with its interesting colonial capital of the same name. The state has escaped becoming a major focus of tourism, perhaps because its coast abuts the soupy waters of the Gulf, not the clear Caribbean. Also, the Maya ruins scattered across the state are mostly unexcavated and hidden in the deep forest. In any case, they are less spectacular than the larger ruins to the north.

Towns, cities and cultural sites

Starting in CAMPECHE, this chapter gives information on the following destinations, arranged to follow a broadly clockwise route: UXMAL, MÉRIDA, VALLADOLID, CHICHÉN ITZÁ, CANCÚN, ISLA MUJERES, ISLA DE COZUMEL, AKUMAL, TULUM, COBÁ, CHETUMAL and CIUDAD DEL CARMEN.

See USING THIS GUIDE on page 50 for details on how to use this section. On the following pages, helpful pointers are given on how to get to each of the destinations covered. Along with the MEXICO map on pages 46–7, and the 4-color maps at the back of this book, they should give all the information necessary for planning your trip to this part of Mexico.

CAMPECHE ☆

Map 8G12. Capital of Campeche. 219km (136 miles) sw of Mérida on RF180; 211km (131 miles) NE of Ciudad del Carmen on RF180; 423km (264 miles) NE of Villahermosa on RF180 and 186. Population: 250,000. Served by air, train (on Coatzacoalcos–Mérida line) and bus i Plaza Moch-Couoh, between Ruíz Cortines and 16 de Septiembre ☎(981) 62815/66767.

This fascinating old city is built over the Maya city of Ah Kin Pech. Although Campeche was officially founded by conquistador Francisco de Córdoba in 1517, the Itzá and Cocome tribes put up fierce resistance, and were only defeated 23 years later, in 1540. Any sense of peace was short-lived.

Wealthy Campeche, a glittering target for the pirates of the Caribbean, many of them based on the island that is now Ciudad del Carmen, was frequently looted and burned. Indeed, it is surprising that the massive fortifications were not erected until the end of the 17thC, following a devastating attack in 1623 that saw most of the population massacred. The maritime attacks then ceased, but up until the 19thC the walls remained a useful defense against rebellious Maya peasants.

The fortified port is bounded on three sides by **forests**, the historical source of its wealth, where the Conquistadors discovered precious woods. Logwood was the most important; a costly red dye made from it was exported as far as England, where it was used for soldiers' coats.

Despite its fine heritage of colonial architecture, Campeche does not look only to the past, but is a thriving industrial and agricultural center. Oil is the predominant industry. Fishing for shrimps is also important; they form the basis of Campeche's distinctive seafood recipes.

WHAT TO SEE

Los Baluartes (The Forts) ☆

All but one of the eight forts remain, as do the two main gates to the city, the **Puerta del Mar** and the **Puerta de Tierra**, and some of the walls. Originally there were 2km ($1\frac{1}{4}$ miles) of walls, which took two years to build, using slave labor from nearby villages.

An official guide may be hired at the **Baluarte San Carlos** *(Calle 8 and Calle 65)*, which houses the **Museo de la Ciudad** *(open Tues-Sat 8am-8pm, Sun 9am-1pm)*, dedicated to the city's colorful history, with pirate relics and arms, portraits of the more villainous raiders and a model of the city as it used to be. This is the most important and oldest of the forts, dating from 1676. On its roof are ancient cannons, while underneath is a warren of passages linking it to other forts. The remaining forts are mostly lined along Calle 8.

At the smaller **Baluarte de la Soledad** is a collection of Maya *stelae*. The **Baluarte San Pedro** is home to an exhibition of local arts; and the **Baluarte de Santiago** *(Calle 8 and Calle 9 ☎(981) 66829)* is surrounded by the city's botanical gardens.

Away from the center, to the s, the **Baluarte San Miguel** is now a **museum of archeology** *(▧ open Mon-Sat 9am-2pm, 3-8pm, Sun 9am-1pm)*, with pottery from the island of Jaina, just along the coast. The **moat** is said to have been full of crocodiles — but then it was also said to have been filled with quicklime . . . .

Downtown

On the Zócalo, the **Catedral de San Bartolomé** (1546) is the oldest church on the peninsula, and lacks the distinctive Mexican flavor of later churches. The *Stations of the Cross* were painted by native craftsmen under Spanish direction, which explains the Mayan look of the faces.

The **Museo Regional** *(Calle 59 #36 and Calle 14 ☎(981) 69111, open Mon-Sat 9am-8pm, Sun 9am-1pm; closed Mon ▧)* is a colonial mansion, dating from 1790, with displays on the history of the state, and Maya artifacts from nearby sites. **Mansión Carabajal** *(Calle 10 #584 at Calle 51 ☎(981) 67560, open Mon-Sat 9am-2pm, 5-8pm)* is an excellent example of a grand, Moorish-style colonial building.

EXCURSIONS

Edzna ☆ ▥
42km (26 miles) E on RF261, then 19km (11 miles) s on RF188 ▧
This Maya city dates from the 3rdC, reaching a population of 70,000 by

the 5thC. Decline set in during the 7thC, however, and by 800 Edzna had fallen to more powerful Chenes centers to the SE. The site features an unusual 5-level decorated pyramid, a ball court, a pyramid emblazoned with stucco masks of the sun god, and across the surrounding land, a huge canal and irrigation system, recently excavated.

RF180 to Mérida

This is the quick, direct route between Campeche and Mérida. **Hecelchakán** *(36km/22 miles)* is home to an interesting but little-visited **Museo Arqueológico** *(on the Zócalo, opening hours variable)* with some lovely clay figures from nearby Jaina island, and Puuc *stelae.*

In the village of **Becal** *(99km/61 miles)* are the damp caves in which the renowned Campechano hats are manufactured from palm leaves; ask in the Zócalo for Don Pastor Chuc, who opens his family cave to visitors.

RF261 to Mérida

This is the slow route, which begins by heading E from Campeche before swinging N through a region rich in Maya ruins, including UXMAL (see also EDZNA, above).

The first place to stop at is **Bolonchén de Rejon** *(110km/68 miles),* which means "Nine Wells" in Maya. This small village does indeed have nine wells, and lies close to the **Xtacumbilxunaan** network of caverns *(3km/2 miles s),* which can be explored with the help of a local guide. These are typical of the peninsula, which is honeycombed with similar geological formations. The enormous *cenotes* (wells) near almost all the major ruins are formed by the collapse of caves near the surface.

 Ramada Inn *(Ruíz Cortinez 51* ☎ *(981) 62233* Fx *(981) 11618 or* ☎ *(5) 535 8583* ⅢⅢ *119 rms* ⊑ ≋ ● *)* is the town's most luxurious hotel. **Baluartes** *(Ruíz Cortines s/n* ☎ *(981) 63911* Fx *(981) 65765* ⅢⅢ *102 rms* ⊑ ≋ ♈ ▤ *)* is recommended. **América** *(Calle 10 #252* ☎ *(981) 64588* ⅢⅢ ⊑ *)* is a simple but clean family hotel, and **López** *(Calle 12 #189* ☎ *(981) 63344* ⅢⅢ *39 rms* ⊑ ▤ *)* is of a similar standard.

 Si Ho Playa *(* ⛾ *35km/21 miles s on RF180* ☎ *(981) 64044* Fx *(981) 66154* ⅢⅢ *78 rms* ⊑ ⚘ ⟨⟨ ≋ ℞ ⁒ ✓ ➤ ♈ *)* is an neo-colonial resort that offers such distractions as fishing, water-sports and tours of archeological zones.

⊑ The colonial **Miramar** *(Calle 8 and Calle 61* ☎ *(981) 62883* ⅢⅢ *)* has excellent seafood, and more. Of Campeche's hotel restaurants (see above), the **Ramada**'s (ⅢⅢ) is predictably good, but hardly interesting; the **Baluartes** has its pleasant **Le Jardin** café (ⅢⅢ); the **López** serves filling meals and snacks (ⅢⅢ).

For vegetarian delights, make for **Natura 2000** *(Calle 12 and Calle 59).*

UXMAL ★

*Map **8**G12. Yucatán. 78km (48 miles) s of Mérida on RF261 and RF180. Served by bus and tour operators.*

When Uxmal was built, it was surrounded by a rich, if seasonally dry, tropical forest, but the fires that devastated the Yucatán in the 16thC have left no more than thorny scrub. This detracts little from the glory of some of the finest remaining Maya buildings and one of the world's great archeological sites, which rivals Ephesus, Luxor and Macchu Pichu in splendor if not in setting.

Along with CHICHÉN ITZÁ, Uxmal is the central part of any visit to the Yucatán. Its very name, Maya for "thrice built," embodies its past. However, indications are that Uxmal represents at least *five* phases of abandonment and reconstruction. Its inhabitants may have been forced to leave their city in times of drought, as it had no *cenote* (well), instead relying entirely on rainwater.

The earliest buildings date from the Classic period of the 6thC, and the city reached its apogee in the 9th–10thC, ascending in power as the cities of the southern lowlands declined. As the site has never been properly surveyed, its extent and population remain uncertain. In the 10thC, Uxmal came under Toltec influence, becoming part of the Mayapan League. It was deserted for the last time in the 14thC as the League broke up.

Many of the buildings are unrestored, and archeologists will be working here for many years to come. To have the latest discoveries pointed out, it is necessary to engage an official guide. The tour lasts up to four hours, but most people like to stroll around on their own afterwards. Uxmal and the nearby ruins (☎) are open 8am–5pm.

EVENT • **Son-et-lumière**, in English. One (varying) day a week.

THE RUINS ▥

The Magician's Pyramid (Pirámide del Adivino)
As you enter the site, this steep, elliptically-based pyramid is immediately opposite. It is said to have been built in a single night by a magician, an unlikely story since it shows evidence of various architectural styles from the 6th–10thC. It is a stiff climb, and a harder descent.

The Great Pyramid
In the same group of buildings, on the sw corner of the Palace, is the Great Pyramid, from the summit of which there is a good view of the city. Over to the w can be seen the **Dovecote** (El Palomar), incorrectly named by the Spaniards. Looking N, the small **House of the Turtles** (Casa de las Tortugas) is near the Palace: walk over here to see the turtles carved in relief over a simple frieze.

In the opposite direction is the oldest building on the site, the small **Pyramid of the Old Woman** (Pirámide de la Vieja).

The Nunnery (Cuadrángulo de las Monjas)
Just behind the pyramid is the entrance to "The Nunnery," which consists of four buildings standing around a large, nearly square court. The monumental entrance to the s building is especially fine, while the most important building of the group is on the N side, raised on a terrace, and with a heavily ornamented frieze; note especially the masks of the rain god Chac, of vital importance in a city that depended entirely on rainfall for its water.

Far from being a nunnery, as the Spaniards supposed, there is evidence that these buildings were used to house young women who were passing a final, debauched year before being sacrificed to Chac.

The Palace of the Governor
Due s of the Nunnery is this magnificent long building, thought by many authorities to be the finest achievement of Maya architecture. It was probably the administrative center of the city, so, for once, the

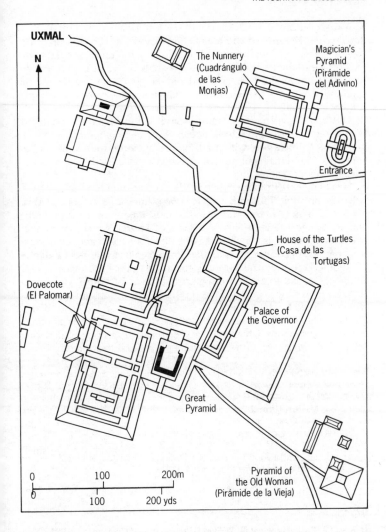

Spaniards guessed more or less right. The contrast between the elegant simplicity of its proportions and the geometric complexity of the frieze provides an entirely satisfying artistic tension.

EXCURSIONS

The country between Uxmal and MÉRIDA is one great archeological zone, sliced across by the RF184. Places to the N of the road are described under MÉRIDA; those to its S are described here. The three sites of importance in this area can easily be included in a visit to Uxmal. Most hotels in Uxmal or Mérida will arrange tours and guides for their guests.

Kabah is 22km (13 miles) s on RF261. Just to the E of the road stands the amazing **Temple of the Masks** (also known as "Codz Poop"). The facade is decorated with hundreds of masks of the rain god Chac, from the cornice to the base. Other buildings are less restored, but there are plans to renovate the main pyramid and the large arch that formed the ceremonial entrance to the 18km (11-mile) limestone causeway or *sacbe* leading to Uxmal.

The jungle is still master of most of **Sayil**, 27km (16 miles) s on RF261, but the large 3-story **Palacio** has been partly restored. Another temple, known as **El Mirador**, with a tall open-stonework roof-comb, is $\frac{1}{2}$km ($\frac{1}{4}$-mile) s. The remains of numerous cisterns, once used to store water, have been found here.

7km (4 miles) E from Sayil toward Labna on an unnumbered road, you will pass the ruins of **Xlapak**, with its solitary unrestored building. **Labna** is reached 4km (2 miles) farther E. The most important structure in this jungle-covered site is the massive **Arch of Labna**, which once linked two courts. Nearby is a high pyramid with a roof-comb and, over to the N, a complex of courts and chambers known collectively as **El Palacio**.

Another 25km (15 miles) NE from Labna toward the junction with RF184 at Oxcutzcab are the unsignposted **Caves of Loltún** (flowers of stone), entered by a gravel drive on the left. These magnificent caves were occupied by the ancient Maya and again during the Caste War of the late 19thC, when they served as a refuge. There remain cave paintings, cisterns and carvings, which may be seen on the hour-long guided tours *(open 9am-3pm; for tour times, inquire at Uxmal ticket office).*

All these hotels have good restaurants, and can arrange trips to nearby sights. **Hacienda Uxmal** *(Km 78 on Mérida-Campeche road* ☎*(99) 247142* **Fx***(99) 252397* ▥ *80 rms* ▤ *is an elegantly restored hacienda. Slightly farther from the ruins is **Misión Uxmal Park Inn** *(Nuna 4* ☎*(99) 247308* **Fx***(99) 247308* ▥ *50 rms* ▤ *), on a hill-top.

Villa Arqueológica *(Carretera Muna Santa Elena s/n* ☎*(99) 247 053, or in Mexico City* ☎*(5) 203 3153* ▥ *49 rms* ▤ *) is one of the Club-Med operated chain, with a good archeological library. For something more modest, try **Rancho Uxmal** *(4km/2 miles N, no* ☎ ▭ *).

MÉRIDA ☆

*Map **8**G12. Capital of Yucatán. 206km (128 miles) NE of Campeche on RF180; 116km (72 miles) w of Chichén Itzá. Population: 700,000. Served by air (international airport 6km/3 miles SE), train (on line from Mexico City) and bus* ℹ *Peon Contreras Theater, Calles 60 and 57* ☎*(99) 249389. US Consul: Paseo Montejo 453* ☎*(99) 255011; UK Consul: Calle 58 #450* ☎*(99) 216799. American Express Travel Service: Paseo Montejo 494 (between Calles 43 and 45)* ☎*(99) 284222.*

If you stroll down the **Paseo Montejo**, Mérida's wide boulevard with its elegant buildings, you could almost be on the Champs Élysées. The local passer-by, on the other hand, might be straight off the Maya murals at Bonampak. Nothing is quite like the rest of Mexico here —

the food, dress, manner of speech, music, or even the sense of humor. Nowhere else in the country, for instance, do you hear so many men giggling. It all adds up to a lively, distinctive and attractive city, and a good base for day trips to the nearby Maya ruins.

Mérida was founded in 1542 by Don Francisco Montejo the younger, on the site of the Maya city of Ichkansiho — a useful source of building stone. An army of 60,000 Maya Indians laid siege to the new city, but were routed (according to Spanish historians) by a force of 250. The subsequent upheavals of Mexican history more or less passed remote Mérida by; but in the mid-19thC, Yucatán was racked by its own peculiarly vicious Caste War. The Maya tribes rebelled against their enslavement on plantations, and killed most of the whites and *mestizos* on the peninsula, only Mérida and Campeche holding out. Not until 1901, after 50 years of fighting, did the Mexican army drive the last rebels into the forests of Quintana Roo and exact their own appalling vengeance.

Until modern highways and railroads linked Mérida with the rest of the Republic in the 1960s, it took almost as long to get from there to Mexico City as to get to Europe. The wealthy owners of the sisal plantations looked to Europe for their culture, and liked to refer to the city as "The Paris of the West" — although the steamy heat they endured was, and still is, unmistakably tropical.

Mérida also liked to be known as "The White City," for the white shirts or *guayaberas* of the inhabitants, the white buildings, the white sails of the artesian windmills pumping up water, and its general cleanliness. Nowadays, both shirts and houses can be in any color, the windmills have disappeared, and the city is no cleaner than any other.

WHAT TO SEE

Mérida has streets with numbers, not names, and the point of reference is the Zócalo, **Plaza de la Independencia**, at the intersection of Calles 60 and 61. The odd-numbered streets run E–W, with higher numbers at the s, and even-numbered streets run N–S with higher numbers at the w. Paseo Montejo, the main drag, runs along the line of Calle 56, beginning seven blocks N and two blocks E of the Zócalo.

The Zócalo

The **Cathedral** is an oddly proportioned 16thC construction, notable only for the widely venerated *Christ of the Blisters*. This statue was carved in the 16thC from the wood of a tree said to have remained miraculously undamaged despite burning all night. The blisters came from another fire, from which the statue was rescued later on, although it was thought miraculous that the damage was no worse. The miracles are celebrated in early October with an orgy of popular devotion.

Palacio Montejo (**Ⅲ 🔀** *open 10am-noon, 4-6pm; closed Sat, Sun)* is a fine example of colonial architecture. Until 1980 it belonged to the Montejo family, for whose ancestors, a father and son who subdued the Yucatán, it was built in 1549. It now belongs to a bank, which has restored it and opened most of it to the public. The magnificent Plateresque **doorway** has carvings of Conquistadors trampling Indians underfoot.

While in the Zócalo, take a look at the modern **murals** in the **Palacio de Gobierno**, illustrating the dark side of Yucatán's history, painted by Fernando Castro Pacheco.

North of the Zócalo

Following Calle 60 N from the Zócalo toward the **Museo Regional de Antropología** leads you to a pretty little plaza on the right, the **Parque Cepeda Peraza** (also known as Plaza Hidalgo), facing a large **library** of the same name and the 17thC Jesuit **Iglesia de Jésus**.

A block farther on is the grand Italianate **Teatro Peón Contreras**, built in 1900–8 and, opposite, the **university**, founded in 1618 but recently modernized. Farther N, a detour down Calle 50 leads to some gates from the old city fortifications.

Museo Regional de Antropología (Regional Museum of Anthropology) ★
Palacio Cantón, Paseo Montejo and Calle 43 ☎*(99) 23055* 🖭 *Open Tues–Sat 8am–8pm; Sun 8am–2pm. Closed Mon.*

A more informative introduction to the ruins of the Yucatán than any amount of reading, this excellent museum is housed in an elegant mansion that was once used by the governors of the state, but is due to move to a former prison on Calle 59. The emphasis is, of course, on the Maya culture, but exhibits from the Valleys of Oaxaca and Mexico help to place the Maya in their general context.

The museum contains a collection of architectural fragments from a number of sites: ornamental masks, *stelae,* large sculptures of gods, and a finely carved altar from CHICHÉN ITZÁ. Most striking is a collection of **elongated skulls**, showing how the Maya distorted the heads of their children.

Smaller pieces include musical instruments and beautifully worked jade jewelry. The various masks of the gods, still with traces of paint, are impressive, and there are rare collections of shell ornaments and copper work. The collection of pottery figurines from the island of Jaina shows how the skill of the Maya craftsmen could transcend the religious symbolism of their culture.

Museo de Arte Popular (Museum of Folk Art)
Calle 59 between 48 and 50 🖭 *Open 8am–8pm; Sun 9am–2pm. Closed Mon.*
This museum, W of the Zócalo, has an extensive and fascinating collection of local crafts, as well as a well-stocked government-run shop.

WHERE TO STAY

CALINDA MÉRIDA
Calle 59 #455 at Calle 52 ☎*(99) 239444* 🖾*(99) 248090* 🎬 *120 rms* � ✿ ◁€ ♨ ☡ **O**
This modern hotel, built into a colonial structure, has large, airy rooms. Ask for one on an upper floor, all of which have fine vistas over the rooftops of the city.

CARIBE
Calle 59 #500 at Calle 60 ☎*(99) 249022*

🖾*(99) 249733* 🎬 *56 rms* � ☡ ♨
Near Parque Hidalgo, this pleasant hotel is built around an airy courtyard, with a small rooftop pool.

CASA DEL BALAM
Calle 60 #488 ☎*(99) 248844* 🖾*(99) 245011* 🎬 *54 rms* � ♨ ☡
Built around a leafy courtyard, close to the Zócalo, this is a traditional hotel, with colorful tapestries in the rooms.

EL CASTELLANO
Calle 57 #513 ☎*(99) 230100* Fx*(99) 263389* ▥ *170 rms* ⇌ ≋ ¥ ● 𝅘

This centrally-placed modern hotel has its own nightclub and shops.

D'CHAMPS ✿ 血
Calle 70 #543 ☎*(99) 248655* Fx*(99) 236024* ▥ *100 rms* ⇌ ❦ ≋ ¥

This is a comfortable hotel near the Zócalo, in a splendid colonial palace with modern extensions.

FIESTA INN YUCALPETÉN
Calle 19 #19, Yucalpetén, 42km (26 miles) N of town ☎*(993) 50300* Fx*(99) 350699* ▥ *88 rms* ⇌ ≋ ⚓ ♒ ↯ ♨ ¥ ● ❦ ⚓

This luxury resort hotel, which occupies an enviable site on Mérida's nearest beach, offers every facility.

HOLIDAY INN 血
Av. Colon 498 at Calle 60 ☎*(99) 256877* Fx*(99) 257755* ▥ *208 rms* ⇌ ≋ ¥ ● ♒ ↯

Neo-Mayan in design, this member of the well-known chain has a good and popular disco.

MONTEJO PALACE ✿
Paseo de Montejo 483 ☎*(99) 247644* Fx*(99) 280388* ▥ *90 rms* ⇌ ≋ ¥ ● 𝅘

A modern hotel, tastefully built in the colonial style.

Worth considering . . .

The following hotels in Mérida can also be recommended:

- **Colon** *(Calle 62 #483* ☎ *(99) 234355* Fx *(99) 244919* ▥ *53 rms).*
- **Gran Hotel** *(Calle 60 #496 near Parque Hidalgo* ☎ *(99) 247622* ▥*)*, a fascinating, if faded, reminder of Mérida's former opulence.
- **María del Carmen** *(Calle 63 #555* ☎ *(99) 239133* Fx *(99) 239290* ▥*)*, part of the Best Western chain.
- **Mérida Misión Park Inn** *(Calle 60 #491* ☎ *(99) 239500/239800* Fx *(99) 237665* ▥*)*, another reliable chain hotel.
- **Paseo de Montejo** *(Paseo de Montejo 482* ☎ *(99) 239033* Fx *(99) 280388* ▥ *92 rms)*, with a good restaurant.

EATING AND DRINKING

Mérida's culinary specialty is traditionally prepared game from the nearby forests — surely a better alternative to turning the forests into cattle ranches. The best place to eat it is **Alberto's Continental Patio** *(*血 *Calle 64 #482* ☎ *(99) 212 298* ▥ ❦ ⚓ 𝅘*)*, one of Mexico's best restaurants, which also has a good range of Arab delicacies to offer. **Los Almendros** *(*◉ *Calle 50A #493* ☎ *(99) 212 851* ▥*)* is good for regional dishes including "poc chuc," a Mayan pork stew. **El Faisán y el Venado** *(two branches: Calle 59 #617* ☎ *(99) 218 352 and Calle 86 #526* ☎ *(99) 219 955* ▥*)* cooks its game with all the customary spices.

For lighter fare, **Express** *(Calles 59 and 60* ☎ *(99) 281691* ▥*)* is the most popular of a number of places on Parque Hidalgo, with a vast and inexpensive menu, open from early in the morning. **Café Pop** *(Calle 57 #50 at Calle 60)* is another good place for all-day snacks and drinks. **La Guaya** *(Calle 60 #472* ☎ *(99) 232144* ▥*)* is a courtyard restaurant specializing in fresh vegetarian fare. Reliable **Soberani's** *(*◉ ✿ *Calle 56A #504* ☎ *(99) 210288* ▥*)* is the place for freshly caught seafood, although the decor is best ignored. Of the hotel restaurants, the CASA DEL BALAM's stands out for its local cuisine.

MÉRIDA BY NIGHT

Much of Mérida's nightlife takes place at the hotels, with **folkloric shows** every night at the PANAMERICANA, the **Aloha** rooftop nightclub at the MONTEJO PALACE, wild **discos** at the HOLIDAY INN, and "human sacrifice" every day except Sunday at the MISIÓN MÉRIDA. Another lively place is **Tulipanes** *(Calle 42, between Calles 43 and 45 ▥)*, an otherwise indifferent restaurant that offers a sacrifice routine and other entertainments.

For something more authentic, try the **Trovador Bohemio** *(Calle 55, on Plaza Santa Lucia 23* ☎ *(99) 230385)*, while the action moves to the Plaza itself on Thursday evenings. Other plazas feature their own entertainments on different nights of the week — inquire at your hotel, or in the tourist office.

Frequent dance, concert and theater performances are held at the **Teatro Peón Contreras** (see page 284) and the nearby **Teatro Daniel Ayala**. For information in English on cultural events ☎(99) 230 123.

SHOPPING

Most visitors to Mérida cannot resist one of the **hammocks** for which it is famous. You can even buy a "familial" sized hammock (200 strings), but it takes years of practice for a family to sleep in one. The keenest prices are to be found at the **market** on **Calles 56** and **65**. Make sure that you go for cotton, not nylon; and be sure that the weave is "doble," or preferably "triple," a reference to the density of weaving.

Hat stalls are also abundant — the best hats can be rolled up and passed through a ring; these are the true **Panama hats**, which, curiously, have always been manufactured in Yucatán for export to Panama. Another good buy are the pleated *guayabera* shirts that have caught on all over Mexico as elegant semiformal wear: originally always white, they can now be any color. If you want to keep the Yucatán's coral, seashells and turtles where they belong — in the sea — avoid buying anything made out of them.

EXCURSIONS

Celestún *(90km/56 miles W, on RFs 180 and 261)* is a Mexican resort with a sandy beach, and cheap cafés and hotels. It lies on the edge of a **national park** designed, not altogether successfully, to provide a secure home for flamingoes: unfortunately, the birds suffer from frequent harassment by insensitive tourists.

Dzibilchaltún *(✩ 25km/15 miles NE: turn E off RF261 to Progreso after 15km/9 miles)*: a Maya ceremonial center in continuous use from 500BC until the Spaniards arrived. It was a large city, but only a small part near the central *cenote* (well) has been restored. Human remains, jewelry and 6,000 items of sculpture have been found at the bottom of the *cenote* (in which swimming is allowed . . .).

Progreso *(another 18km/11 miles N)* is the closest beach to Mérida. Formerly a major port, it is now visited mostly by cruise ships taking advantage of its 6km (3-mile) pier, and survives as a minor resort. **Yucalpetén** *(9km/5 miles W of Progreso)* is a newer resort, home to the

FIESTA INN hotel (see WHERE TO STAY). A road stretches 80km (50 miles) E along wide expanses of mostly undeveloped white-sand beach.

Izamal *(67km/41 miles E on RF180, then 18km/11 miles N)* is a fascinating if little-visited historic center, with the immense church and monastery of **St Anthony of Padua** — an inflated creation of Bishop de Landa, which history has passed by — standing on the foundations of the Popul Chac pyramid. The many unexcavated mounds may be seen covered in jungle from the top of the **Kinich Kakmo** (the Maya sun god) **pyramid** opposite.

Beyond, RF180 travels toward VALLADOLID *(160km/100 miles E)* and CHICHÉN ITZA *(204km/127 miles E)*.

RF18 SE winds its way through a region rich in Maya ruins and monasteries. **Acanceh** *(27km/16 miles)* has both a 16thC church and a Maya pyramid set about the Zócalo. **Tecoh** *(a further 8km/5 miles S on RF18)* has an enormous mission church, worth a quick look.

The next place of interest, just past Telchaquillo, is **Mayapan** *(another 14km/8 miles, 49km/30 miles SE of Mérida on RF18)*, the region's leading Post-Classic Maya city. The ruins are unimpressive compared to the great Classic sites, indicative of the decline of Maya civilization, but Mayapan effectively ruled the lowland Maya world from 1200 until shortly before the Spanish conquest. Most of its 3,600 buildings remain covered in jungle.

Tekit *(another 19km/11 miles SE)* has a fine Moorish-influenced church, while the important church and monastery at **Mama** *(8km/5 miles S)* is notable for its fine carvings and decorations by Maya craftsmen. The 17thC church at **Teabo** *(16km/10 miles SE of Tekit on RF18)* is worth a visit.

The small town of **Mani** *(14km/8 miles W of Teabo on RF18)* is best known as the place where the Maya *códices* (painted manuscripts) were burned in 1562, destroying our chances of ever really understanding Maya civilization. Mani was the biggest Maya city at the time of the Spanish Conquest, and the first to convert to Christianity: the Zócalo is dominated by a huge Franciscan church and monastery built in 1549, one of the earliest in the Yucatán.

It was only when the people failed to abandon their former ways that Fray Diego de Landa consigned thousands of *códices* to the flames, believing them to be works of the devil. Just four escaped incineration.

Oxkutzab *(another 11km/6 miles S)*, on the junction of RF18 with RF184, is famous for its **market**, with every variety of tropical fruit. Eat here, or at **Ticul** *(16km/10 miles NW on RF184)*, with its branch of **Los Almendros** on the Zócalo, before going on to UXMAL *(30km/18 miles W)*.

VALLADOLID

Map 8G13. Yucatán. 44km (27 miles) E of Chichén Itzá on RF180; 160km (100 miles) E of Mérida on RF180. Population 50,000. Served by bus.

Founded by Francisco de Montejo in 1543 on top of the Maya town of Zací, Valladolid today is an attractive and well-preserved colonial town, the second largest in the state. The city is too far from the beach for the average tourist, so few stay here, but it is a good place to stop for lunch while traveling across the peninsula. There are several places of interest to visit, including the 16thC **monastery of St Bernard** and the lovely *cenote* at **Dzitnup** *(5km/3 miles W of town)*.

From Valladolid, RF295 leads N to the Gulf Coast at the unattractive village of **Río Lagartos** *(85km/53 miles)*, which has beautiful deserted beaches and lagoons nearby. "Alligator River" is now free of hungry carnivores, but the wetlands provide valuable breeding grounds for flamingos and other wildlife.

Drive on through the large and ugly town of **Tizimín** *(51km/31 miles)*, except during the **fiesta** of the **Tres Reyes** (Three Kings) on January 1–6, which attracts pilgrims from the whole peninsula. At **Kikil** *(57km/35 miles)*, a large Franciscan church is slowly going the way of the Maya cities; see it while you can.

☞ The **Mesón del Marques** *(Calle 39 #203, on Zócalo* ☎ *(985) 62073* ▥▢
〓 ⋈ ▦ *)* has a touch of old-time splendor. The nearby **Zací** *(Calles 44 and 39* ☎ *(985) 62127* 〓 ⋈ *)* is a spacious and modern alternative.

〓 **Cenote Zací** *(* ♣ *Calle 36* ☎ *(985) 62107* ▢ *)*, near a *cenote* (well), and **Casa de los Arcos** *(Calle 39 between Calles 38 and 40* ☎ *(99) 62467)* both serve regional specialties. There are also several good restaurants around the Zócalo, such as the **María de la Luz** café.

CHICHÉN ITZÁ ★

*Map **8**G13. Yucatán. 119km (74 miles) E of Mérida, 44km (27 miles) E of Valladolid on RF180; 205km (128 miles) E of Cancún on RF180. Served by air taxi (from Cancún and Mérida) and bus.*

This is the best-known of the ruined Maya cities, forming the high point of any visit to the Yucatán Peninsula. Founded in the 5thC AD, it reached its peak in the 9th–12thC, falling under Toltec influence around AD1000. It thus became the center of the new, flourishing Maya–Toltec civilization, and grew into a vast ceremonial complex covering some 10sq.km (4sq. miles).

Then, 100 years before the arrival of the Spaniards, the great city was suddenly abandoned, and the inhabitants returned to the simple rural life their descendants still lead today.

About 30 of the structures have now been uncovered and restored. As well as the main ruins, there are hundreds of jungle-bound temples and pyramids for the energetic explorer; it should be easy to find a small boy who will act as guide for a small fee.

Those with time to spend the night at a hotel in Chichén will find the **Caracol Observatory** impressive and eerie under starlight. It is worth rising at dawn for the view of the ceremonial complex from the **Castillo Pyramid** in the mellow light, evocative of the far-off days, when the sun rose over a great bustling metropolis.

VALLADOLID *(44km/27 miles E)* has inexpensive hotels and a number of good eating-places.

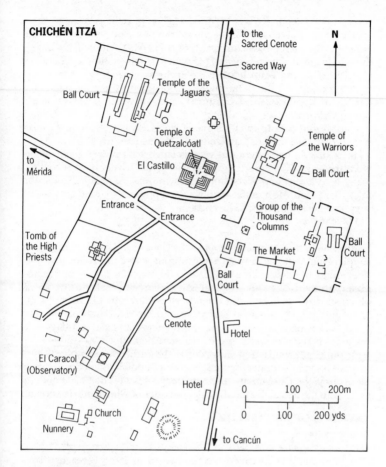

THE RUINS 🏛

El Castillo and environs

N of the highway 🚌 ✗ *Open 8am–5pm.*

The most important and impressive ruin is the great terraced pyramid known as **El Castillo** (The Castle), which provides striking evidence of Maya skill in engineering and arithmetic. On the equinoxes, the great carved heads of serpents at the foot of the stair look as if they have shadow bodies, undulating up the side of the balustrade to the summit, but you will be lucky to see the phenomenon through the crowds.

The pyramid has 365 steps, one for each day of the year, leading to the **Temple of Quetzalcóatl** (The Plumed Serpent) at the summit. Similarly, the terrace sections correspond to the 18 months of the Maya "year," and the side panels to the 52 years of the Maya "century."

Inside this temple is a **stone throne**, carved in the shape of a jaguar, before which is a *chac-mool,* a reclining figure upon which offerings were

289

placed (illustrated in ART AND ARCHITECTURE, on page 32).

The other buildings of the central complex can be seen from the pyramid. The sacred **ball-court**, at 146m (467 feet) in length, the largest in Mesoamerica, has walls decorated with low-reliefs showing sacrificial rites. Nearby is the **Temple of the Warriors**, where frescoes show the Toltec conquest of the peninsula. Immediately to the right stands the **Group of the Thousand Columns**, each of which is carved like a plumed serpent.

The **sacred** *cenote* (well), some 300m (327 yards) N along a causeway, is 60m (192 feet) in diameter and 20m (64 feet) deep.

In troubled times, sacrificial victims laden with precious ornaments were thrown down here to appease the gods. Divers have recovered many gold and jade objects, but unknown treasure remains under the thick, dark mud. Most of the victims were apparently young girls, and it was considered an honor to be chosen.

Old Chichén ☆
s of the highway.

First on the left is a smaller *cenote,* which was used only for the water supply. One of the older ruins, it dates from before the Toltec invasion. The round building at the center of Old Chichén is a sophisticated **observatory** used by the original Maya people to make astronomical observations for their complex calendar. It is known as **El Caracol** (The Snail) because of its **spiral staircase**, rare in Maya architecture. The windows are placed so as to record the longest and shortest days, and openings in the roof were used for accurate nighttime observations.

In the same group is a small version of the Castillo, used by the Toltecs to store bones. Other nearby buildings were known to the Spaniards as the **Abbey**, the **Church** and the **Nunnery** — names that have nothing to do with the actual uses of the buildings, about which little is known.

ENVIRONS OF CHICHÉN ITZÁ

Balancanché ☆
4km (2 miles) E of the ruins ▨ 𝒦 *(erratic, every hour or so during daylight).*

This huge network of caverns, rediscovered in 1959, is reached by a well-signposted track. Some of the caves were used by both the Maya and the Toltecs as sanctuaries, and offerings and incense burners have lain undisturbed for more than 1,000 years. In one shrine, a Maya god stands guard over a lake of blind fishes. The caves are cold and slippery, and in places claustrophobic.

Hacienda Chichén *(near the ruins; reservations* ☎ *(99) 248844* ▥ ▰ ▱*)* consists of cottages set around an old hacienda, itself constructed from Maya ruins. **Mayaland** *(by the ruins* ☎ *(985) 62777 or* ☎ *(99) 252122* ▣ *(99) 252397* ▥ *to* ▥ *64 rms* ▰ ▱*)* is a colonial-style hotel in rambling gardens. **Misión Chichén Itzá Park Inn** *(2km/1 mile from the ruins* ☎ *and* ▣ *(985) 62671* ▥ ▰ ▱*)* is a spacious modern hacienda-style hotel. **Villa Arqueológica** *(near the ruins* ☎ *(985) 62830 or Mexico City: (5) 203 3153* ▥ ▰ ⁓ ▱*)* is a pleasant Club Med-operated inn with a good archeological library.

Low-priced food and accommodation is available in **Pisté** *(2km/1 mile w),* an unsophisticated village, with the **Posada El Paso** among other inexpensive hotels and restaurants. Any of the hotels near the archeological site are normally happy to serve meals to nonresident visitors.

CANCÚN ★

Map 8F13. Quintana Roo. 319km (199 miles) E of Mérida on RF180. Population: 200,000. Served by air (international airport 26km/16 miles S) and bus
i Avenida Tulum 26 ☎(988) 48073; and at airport. US Consul ☎(988) 42411. American Express Travel Service: Av. Tulum and Brisas, Suite A ☎(988) 41999; and at Intercontinental Hotel ☎(988) 50755.

The name means "crock of gold" in the Maya tongue, apt enough for the place that generates a quarter of Mexico's entire tourism income. It is hard to believe that, only a few decades ago, there was nothing here but a 20km-long (12-mile) golden-white sandbar, stretching out through coral reefs into the luminous blue sea. Tourist gold seemed a long way off when the spot was selected for development into a 21stC super-resort, and there was widespread criticism as construction began during the 1970s — criticism that resurfaced after the devastation of Hurricane Gilbert in 1988 and the forest fires of 1989.

But that has mostly been forgotten now, as nearly three million sun-worshipers from all over the world jet in every year to sample a unique blend of underwater, beachside and nighttime delights. Cancún has even hosted international summits, at the gleaming **Convention Center**, where the island curves sharply to the S.

In spite of the already high level of development, new projects are under way or being planned. These include the **Malecón Cancún**, an 80-hectare (200-acre) development along a walkway between city and island, and the **Puerto Cancún** mega-project, which will see two golf courses, a polo field, hotels, condominiums, shops and a 1,850-berth marina taking shape over 360 hectares (900 acres) of coastline. From the air, the curving sweep of great hotels is a surreal sculpture of white concrete, palm trees and limpid blue pools.

Cancún is serviced entirely by the custom-built **Ciudad Cancún**, on the mainland, linked to the resort by a causeway. The city is not attractive, and remains a place in which to conduct business, or to lodge, eat and drink at lower prices than in the tourist zone. Still, the main streets, such as Avenida Tulum, are quite lively, with many shops, hotels and restaurants along their length and in the side-streets. Frequent local buses run the entire length of the island from Ciudad Cancún, taking in **Puerto Juárez**, from where ferries depart for ISLA MUJERES.

As for the beaches, the island heads off E from the city along **Playa Tortugas**, followed by **Playa Caracol**, both facing N toward ISLA MUJERES. Around **Punta Cancún**, (marked by the CAMINO REAL hotel) the island swings S, enclosing **Laguna Bojorquez**, a section of the far larger **Laguna Nichupté** salt-water lagoon.

The first beach on this southerly stretch is the popular 8km-long (5-mile) **Playa Chac-mool**, which gives way to the long unspoiled **Playa del Rey**, now the site of a major Japanese-financed development project.

This beach is named after the Ruinas del Rey, a minor Maya temple on a peninsula that juts into the lagoon.

At **Punta Nizuc**, the s end of the island, the coast swings back inland and the road joins back up with RF307. Most of the hotel beaches face the lagoon, not the open sea, which means that they are far safer, but not much good for surfing.

SPORTS AND ACTIVITIES

GOLF   Cancún has an excellent if occasionally gusty golf course, the **Pok-ta-Pok** (☎(988) 30871), designed by Robert Trent Jones on a 1km-long ($\frac{1}{2}$-mile) island in Laguna Nichupté. Watch out for the small Maya ruin at the 12th hole. Equipment can be rented at the club, near the Convention Center.

WATER-SPORTS   The large hotels all make their own arrangements for guests. Waterskiing, deep-sea fishing, boat rental and other facilities are also available at the **Cancún Yacht Club**, on the left after leaving the mainland. The best snorkeling and scuba-diving are at the s end of the island; arrangements can be handled through your hotel, or try the **Lagoon Club** (☎(988) 31111), **Scuba Cancún** (☎(988) 31011) or **Aqua Tours** (☎(988) 30400).

Punta Cancún, the promontory past the CAMINO REAL hotel, is worth exploring, although the water can be rough. Real enthusiasts should head s to AKUMAL and COZUMEL.

WHERE TO STAY

Most of Cancún's hotels are in the hyper-expensive class, indeed the whole Cancún experience seems to take place in dollars rather than pesos. If the no-holds-barred luxury adventure is your objective, this selection of some of the most palatial hotels should help you choose.

Throwing caution to the winds is not totally obligatory, however, even in Cancún. A few of the less costly options are listed under CANCÚN ON A BUDGET. Some are on the beach, but most of them are in the downtown area, where they cater mostly to commercial travelers.

CAMINO REAL 🏨
Punta Cancún, the N tip of the island
☎(988) 30100 ⓕ(988) 31730 ▥ 381
rms ➘ ⊟ ⟨⟨ ♨ ⍟ ♒ ✓ ⛵ ♈ ● ♪
This beautifully designed low-rise pleasure resort has its own beach and lagoon. All water-sports are available, and boats can also be rented.

CLUB MEDITERRANÉE 🏨
Punta Nizus, 19km (11 miles) SE of the city
☎(988) 42409 ⓕ(988) 42090 ▥ 410
rms ➘ ⊟ ⟨⟨ ♨ ♒ ⍟ ➙ ♈ ● ♪ ✓
Situated on a secluded peninsula at the SE tip of the island, this well-designed, Mayan-style village offers all water-

sports, in addition to an organized social scene.

KRYSTAL CANCÚN 🏨
Kukulcán s/n ☎(988) 31133 ⓕ(988) 31790 ▥ 344 rms ➘ ⊟ ⟨⟨ ♨ ♒ ✓ ♈ ●
A high-class beachside hotel with a difference, the Krystal Cancún includes Jacuzzi, sauna and a full range of watersports, as well as all the other delights of a hotel in this class.

MARRIOTT CASA MAGNA 🏨
Kukulcán Retorno s/n, 2km (1 mile) s of downtown ☎(988) 52000 ⓕ(988)

51385 ▦ *488 rms* ⇀ ⊒ ⫷ ⩙ ⏰
✓ ⚑

One of the newer additions to Cancún, this huge, Moorish-inspired palace has every comfort and its own wide stretch of beach.

PLAYA DE ORO

Kukulcán s/n, on the central ε shore
☎*(988) 51366* ℻*(988) 51363* ▦ *174 rms* ⇀ ⊒ ⫷ ⩙ ⏰ ✓ ⚑

Considerably smaller and more intimate than most of the deluxe hotels, the Playa de Oro is also less expensive than most of its rivals.

RITZ-CARLTON ⏰

Retorno del Rey #36 ☎*(988) 51212* ℻*(988) 51015* ▦ *370 rms* ⊒ ▤ ⩙

⏰ ⚑ ⛺ ⩙ ⛴
Opened in 1993, the Yucatecan representative of the opulent Ritz-Carlton chain has a stained-glass atrium, a 360m (1,200-foot) stretch of beach and every facility for pampering its guests, including a nanny service.

SHERATON CANCÚN RESORT ⏰

16km (10 miles) s of downtown ☎*(988) 31988* ℻*(988) 50083* ☎*73339* ▦ *622 rms* ⇀ ⊒ ⫷ ⩙ ⏰ ♨ ✓ ⛺ ⚑
● ⏰

This is a major four-building complex, on a wide, flat stretch of sand to the s of the island, with a choice of bars, restaurants and entertainments. Famous for its pyramidal design, it has some genuine archeological remains nearby.

Worth considering . . .

A number of other beach hotels *(all with* ⊒ ⩙ ✓ ⏰ ⚑ ● ⏰ *as well as water-sports and shopping)* are also worth looking at. They include the hacienda-style **Fiesta Américana Cancún** *(* ⏰ *Cancún Blvd. s/n* ☎*(988) 31400* ℻*(988) 32502* ▦ *281 rms)*, which features waterfalls in the lobby; the nearby **Holiday Inn Crowne Plaza** *(* ⏰ *Kukulcán Km 18.5* ☎*(988) 51022* ℻*(988) 50313)* ▦ *363 rms);* and the **Meliá Cancún** *(Kukulcán 23* ☎*(988) 51114* ℻*(988) 51263* ▦ *450 rms)*, an ultramodern hotel with its own golf course.

Otherwise, you could consider **Villas Tacul** *(* ⏰ *Kukulcán Km 5.5* ☎*(988) 30000* ℻*(988) 30349* ▦ *)*, 23 attractively decorated private villas, just as luxurious but quieter than the resort hotels.

Cancún on a budget

Beachside bargains, relatively speaking, include the pyramidal **Calinda Quality Beach** *(* ⏰ ⚘ ☎*(988) 31600* ℻*(988) 31857* ▦ *470 rms)*, the **Maya Caribe** *(Kukulcán Km 6* ☎*(988) 30602* ℻*(988) 30605* ▦ *128 rms)*, the **Girasol Norte** *(Kukulcán Km 9* ☎*(988) 30624* ℻*(988) 32246)* ▦ *67 rms)* and **Dos Playas** *(Kukulcán Km 6.5* ☎*(988) 30500* ℻*(988) 32037* ▦ *105 rms)*, near the golf course.

Downtown, affordable options include **Plaza de Sol** *(* ⚘ *Yaxchilán 31* ☎*(988) 43888* ℻*(988) 44393* ▦ *86 rms* ⊒ ⩙ *)*, **María de Lourdes** *(Yaxchilán 80* ☎*(988) 44744* ℻*(988) 41242* ▦ *51 rms* ⊒ ⩙ ♫ *)*, **Novotel** *(Tulum 2* ☎*(988) 42999* ▦ *40 rms* ⊒ ⩙ *)* and **Soberanis** *(Coba 5, near Tulum* ☎*(988) 41858* ℻*(988) 43400* ▦ ⊒ *)*.

EATING AND DRINKING

Most of the hotel restaurants are good, which is just as well, as many charge for meals whether you eat them or not. But this has not prevented a good number of independent restaurants from running successfully; and hotels are only too happy to serve their rivals' guests.

Of the hotel restaurants, the **Calypso** at the CAMINO REAL is perhaps the finest, but the SOBERANIS' famous seafood is at least as popular, and comes at a fraction of the price; for amusement as well as gastronomy, try dining in a reconstructed set from the movie *Casablanca* at the KRYSTAL'S **Bogart's** restaurant.

In the welter of international cuisine, genuine Mexican food can be hard to find in Cancún. Fortunately, there is a branch of **Los Almendros** *(Bonampak and Sayil* ☎ *(988) 40807* ▥ *)*, with its authentic Yucatec dishes. More expensive, **El Mexicano** *(Costa Blanca Center* ☎ *(988) 44873* ▦ *)* has good regional cuisine, and musical accompaniment.

For a choice of Mexican and international styles, try **El Pescador** *(Tulipanes 5 at Supermanzana* ☎ *(988) 42673)*, with its excellent seafood, and **La Habichuela** *(Margaritas 25* ☎ *(988) 43158* ▥ *)*, a huge *palapa* restaurant with a pleasant garden.

Looking out across Laguna Nichupté, perfect for enjoying the sunset, are **Lorenzillo's** *(Kukulcán Km 10.5* ☎ *(988) 31254* ▥ *)*, perched on its own sandbank, and **Carlos'n'Charlie's** *(Kukulcán Km 5.5* ☎ *(988) 30846* ▥ 🍸 *)*, with its usual high-spirited waiters and clientele.

Also with a lovely setting is the **Chac-Mool** *(on Chac-Mool beach* ☎ *(988) 31107* ▦ *)*. A good bolt-hole in the downtown area is **Cafetería Pop** *(Tulum 26* ☎ *(988) 41991* ▢ *)*, for snacks and meals all day long.

CANCÚN BY NIGHT

Helpful young men in the airport, and hotel receptionists, distribute *Cancún Tips,* a free entertainment guide to the resort, including details of **Mexican fiesta nights** and **beach parties**. These are usually open to all, but drinks and food can be expensive. Much of the nightlife is still centered on the major hotels, but they have had to work hard to maintain their position. The **Aquarius** disco at the CAMINO REAL and **Christine's** at the KRYSTAL are both popular hi-tech discos, while the disco at the MARRIOTT specializes in hits from the '60s.

The best of the independents include **La Boom** *(Kukulcán Km 3.5* ☎ *(988) 31372)*, and **Daddy'O** *(Kukulcán Km 9.5, near the Convention Center* ☎ *(988) 33333)*, based on Acapulco's Baby'O. The scene in the city is rather more rough and ready, with some amusing bars along Avenida Tulum, such as the **Alexander** *(at the corner with Uxmal)* and **Bananas** *(Tulum 11)*. But compared to ACAPULCO, Cancún's nightlife is still fairly tame, and closes down early.

SHOPPING

Although Cancún is a duty-free zone, prices are high. Not that this stops tourists from spending their money in the shopping malls springing up along Paseo Kukulcán. Among the best are **Plaza Caracol** *(near Convention Center)* and **Plaza Nautilus**, both with a good selection of elegant resort wear, souvenirs, jewelry and Mexican craft items.

Be prepared to bargain at the **Plaza Garibaldi** market *(corner of Tulum and Uxmal)* and the **Centro de Artesanías** *(Av. Tulum, downtown)*. Most hotels have their own craft stores, but there you can expect to pay extra.

ISLA MUJERES

Map 8F13. Quintana Roo. 8km (5 miles) E of Puerto Juárez. Island 8km (5 miles) at longest and 4km (2 miles) at widest. Population: 15,000. Served by air and frequent all-day ferry services from Puerto Juárez (just NE of Cancún, passengers only) and Punta Sam (5km/3 miles N of Puerto Juárez, for vehicles) i Hidalgo 6 ☎(988) 20316.

Mexico's third Caribbean island paradise (see CANCÚN and ISLA DE COZU-MEL), this used to be where the friendly, scruffy crowd relaxed after an exhausting second-class bus-tour of the Yucatán. Unfortunately, it now plays host to hordes of day-trippers from Cancún, and has lost much of its charm. Since Hurricane Gilbert in 1988, new development has taken place, along with extensive renovations, and prices have risen. But while the island is no longer exactly cheap, money still goes much further here than in Cancún or Cozumel.

Its name, meaning Island of Women, was given to the island by Hernán Cortés and his sailors in 1517 when they made it their first landing point in Mexico. History relates that the name resulted from the numerous female statues they encountered in the Maya temples, but other interpretations have also been put forward.

The island

"Isla Muj" is a long, low strip of jungle, fringed by coconut groves, white sand, luminous blue waters and coral reefs. The town, little more than a village, is on a spit of land to the NW, with the open sea to the N and E, and the Bahía de Mujeres to the S and W. The whole island can easily be explored on foot; even the airfield is only 15 minutes' walk from the town. Otherwise, taxis (always arrange the round trip in advance) and rented motorcycles are the best way of getting around.

To see everything in comfort, take one of the daily **boat-trips** around the island, which also go to the **bird sanctuary** on nearby **Isla Contoy**, $2\frac{1}{2}$ hours away in a slow boat. On the way, the boat pauses over the skeleton of a **sunken galleon**, where lurid-looking fish glide in and out of its shattered ribs. Take along snorkel gear and join them. Another stop is at the **Maya temple**, near the lighthouse on the southern tip of the island, but not much remains of it after Hurricane Gilbert.

The best beach near town is the NW-facing **Playa Cocos**, which has unfortunately lost most of its coconut trees, and its shade, to a mysterious blight. The other main beach, **Playa Lancheros** *(8km/5 miles SE, toward the southern tip of the island)* is away from most day-trippers, and has a lovely sweep of white sand. A little farther SE, the stony **Playa Garrafón** was famous for the richness of its underwater life, which caused the area to be designated a national park. However, much of the coral has since died. On the way back, stop at the **Mundaca pirate fortress** *(near Playa Lancheros)*, a center for the white-slave trade during the 19thC.

Another possible excursion is to the **turtle park** on the W coast, on the long point at the S end of Bahía de Mujeres. Large crowds gather to try and ride on the hapless animals — an unpleasant experience for them, and for any watching animal-lovers.

Sleeping on the beach is not recommended, but there are some beachside *palapas* under which you can safely sling a hammock for a small fee. Finally, if you have an important travel connection to make on the mainland, it is advisable to take a ferry in good time, for a happy-go-lucky attitude to punctuality prevails among the locals.

☜　Isla Mujeres' best hotel is the **Costa Club Resort** *(🏨 Punta Norte* ☎ *(988) 20153* 🖾 *(988) 20187* 🎞 *160 rms* ⊒ ◁⤢ ⋘ ⤧ ⅋ ● ♪*)*, on its own island at the N tip of the island; it is also close to the village and Playa Cocos, and overlooks the **Zazil-ha** (Luminous Waters) **lagoon**. Nearby, the **Na Balam** *(Zazil-Ha 118* ☎ *(988) 20279* 🎞 *12 rms* ⊒*)* is a small village of beachside *palapas*.

The **Cabañas María del Mar** *(Av. Carlos Lazos 1* ☎ *(988) 20179* 🎞 *66 rms* ⋘ ⊒ ●*)*, round the coast on Playa Cocos, offers rooms of varying price and quality; nearby, a short walk from the beach, **Poc-Na** *(Matamoros 91* ☎ *(988) 20090* ▭*)* is a basic, cheap and friendly hostel.

Other hotels in town include the modern **Posada del Mar** *(Av. Rueda Medina 15A* ☎ *(988) 70300* 🖾 *(988) 70266* 🎞 to 🎞 *46 rms* ⊒ ⋘ ⅋ ●*)*, across from the village beach, once the best on the island; **Perla del Caribe** *(♿ Av. Madero 2* ☎ *(988) 70444* 🖾 *(988) 20011* 🎞 *90 rms* ⋘*)*, a new hotel right on Playa Norte, plain but pleasant; and the **Rocamar** *(Av. Nicolas Bravo at Guerrero* ☎ *(988) 20101* 🎞 *35 rms* ⊒ ⅋*)*, a beachside bargain near the Zócalo.

At the far S of the island, on a hill near Playa Garrafón, is **María's Kin-Kin** *(El Garrafón* ☎ *(988) 31420/20015* 🎞 *9 rms* ⊒*)*, a delightful spot, which is much visited for its excellent restaurant. Be sure to reserve, as accommodation is limited.

⊒　For an elegantly served seafood meal, go to **María's** restaurant at the **El Garrafón** hotel. Elsewhere, the prices are lower, the service more relaxed, but the seafood is delicious. To start with try **Miramar** *(Rueda Medina Sur, next to the pier on the Malecón* ▭*)*, with a good view of dockside activity; or **Gomar** *(Hidalgo and Madero, near the Zócalo* ▭*)*, for good local dishes.

When the going gets hot, slip into the air-conditioned **Villa del Mar** *(Rueda Medina Sur, near the pier* ▭*)* for wholesome Mexican food. Those inclined toward wholefoods will love **The Roof** *(Hidalgo 12* 🎞*)*, with a range of exotic vegetarian fare. And if you're after a lively night out, try **La Peña** *(Guerrero 5* 🎞*)*.

ISLA DE COZUMEL ☆

Map 8G13. Quintana Roo. Island 45km (28 miles) at longest, 18km (11 miles) at widest. 2½ hrs S of Puerto Morelos and Cancún; 1hr E of Playa del Carmen (66km/41 miles S of Cancún, 63km/39 miles N of Tulum on RF307) — check ferry times at Chetumal or Mérida. Population: 32,000. Served by air (international airport 3km/1½ miles S of San Miguel), and passenger ferry from Puerto Morelos and Playa del Carmen ℹ Malecón, near the pier ☎*(987) 20218. American Express: Calle 11 Sur at Av. Pedro Coldwell* ☎*(987) 20433.*

Island resorts have always had a special mystique and appeal, but it took more than four centuries for Isla de Cozumel to take off as a resort after its first foreign visitor, Hernán Cortés, arrived from Cuba in 1519. It became a useful base for pirates, most of them English, before sinking into a long tropical torpor. But World War II changed all that — US servicemen who had been stationed here came back on vacation, spending their days under the crystal-clear waters around the reefs, and their nights in hammocks on the beach.

Thereafter the resort, with a fine airfield left by the Americans, grew rapidly, and its astonishingly clear sea gave it a continuing reputation as the skindiving capital of the world. Unfortunately, a large Maya city has disappeared, bulldozed under the runway. There are still dozens of small overgrown ruins dotted around the interior and E coast, which can be visited with a guide and a rented jeep.

The island is nearly flat, far larger than its northerly neighbor, ISLA MUJERES, and covered by thick and thorny scrub inhabited by stinging insects. The beaches, by contrast, are idyllic, and the 25 or so **coral reefs** around the coastal waters are so abundant in marine life and dramatic underwater landscapes that they have been designated a national park. Inspired by Jacques Cousteau, who declared Cozumel "one of the finest diving areas in the world," the diving fraternity sets the tone and the atmosphere; yet there are many others who just come to relax and bake in the sun.

The new super-resort, up the coast at CANCÚN has creamed off the most frenetic pleasure-seekers, but Cozumel is certainly catching its share of investment. Still, the pace remains casual and friendly, even if the prices are higher than they used to be.

WHAT TO SEE

The island's only town is **San Miguel**, where life is concentrated along the seafront and around the Zócalo. This a pleasant place in which to spend the evening; you can sit at a café and discuss your day, which will probably have been spent chasing multicolored fish in and out of sunken shipwrecks. All around the plaza and pier are the diving stores, which also arrange lessons and guides for novices. After a three-day course, you should be eligible for a certificate of competence.

The major resort hotels are all fringed by the excellent white-sand beaches along the coast either way out of town. To the N are **Playa San Juan** (*4km/2 miles, beyond the marina* ⇌) and **Playa Santa Pilar** (*5km/3 miles* ⇌), both pleasant and sheltered from the open ocean. SW from town, **Laguna Chankanaab** (*9km/5 miles; swimming prohibited*), forms part of the botanical and underwater gardens of the **Parque Chankanaab**, which also contains a lovely beach open to the sea (no restrictions on swimming).

A little farther S, there is a succession of fine beaches, beginning with the shell-strewn **Playa Maya** (*another 4km/2 miles* ⇌). The popular beach of **San Francisco** (*6km/3 miles from Chankanaab* ⇌ ♛) is not only excellent for swimming; it is also the setting-off point for the Colombia reef and the 5km-long (3-mile) **Palancar reef**. Snorkel equipment is available for rent, and there are plenty of *palapas* for snacks, drinks and shade. Don't eat too many locally-caught fish, or there'll soon be none left.

Playa Escondida (*8km/5 miles from Chankanaab* ⇌) is sheltered and peaceful, the perfect place to get away from everything.

At this point the road cuts deeper inland, reaching the E shore some 18km (11 miles) from Chankanaab. A sandy track off to the right leads past a minor Maya ruin, the **Tumba del Caracol**, to the island's southerly point, **Punta Celerain** *(4km/2 miles)*, which is marked by a lighthouse. But the main road heads NW along the wild, undeveloped coast, which is open to the full force of the ocean surf. The long, unspoiled beach at **Punta Chiquero** *(8km/5 miles from the junction ═)* is held by some to be the finest on the island.

Punta Morena *(7km/4 miles N of Punta Chiquero, 16km/10 miles SE of San Miguel ═)* is more easily reached from San Miguel on the Carretera Transversal, which cuts the island in half, but the rocky beach and high surf are not conducive to safe swimming. About 2km (1$\frac{1}{4}$ miles) N of here, the main road swings NW inland to **San Miguel** *(14km/8 miles)*, leaving a sandy track to run the remaining 21km (13 miles) to **Punta Molas**, on the island's N tip.

On its way, it passes **El Castillo** *(14km/8 miles)*, a small Maya temple, reaching a lighthouse and further Maya remains on the point. On the way back to San Miguel, a diagonal short-cut goes past the extensive, recently restored Maya ruins of **San Gervasio**.

To get to the places outside town, either take a taxi — numerous and cheap — or rent a car or motorcycle; there are now about 100km (62 miles) of paved road, so a day's exploring can be fun. Another good way to see the island is to take one of the day **cruises** organized by the hotels.

Those who tire of the sea and the sun may be interested in a visit to the new **Museo de Cozumel** *(Av. Norte between Calles 4 and 6* ☎ *(987) 20838* ═ ■ *open 10am-1pm, 4-7pm; closed Fri),* with a collection that specializes in the island's ecology. Its upstairs restaurant can be heartily recommended.

WHERE TO STAY

LA CEIBA BEACH
Punta Paraíso, s Zone ☎*(987) 20844* Ⓕ*(987) 20065* ▥ *to* ▥ *114 rms* ═ ♨ ⁌ ⋈ ☏ ℘ ⬤ ♈ ⬤

Oriented toward the diving community, this hotel provides tuition and a scuba "adventure trail" out onto the reef, starting from the beach.

EL COZUMELEÑO ⌂
Playa Santa Pilar, N Zone ☎*(987) 20050* ▥ *84 rms* ⋈ ☏ ♈ ⬤ ↻

This comfortable beach hotel provides a sophisticated, if incongruous, Parisian atmosphere, with enough facilities to keep guests occupied day and night.

FIESTA AMERICANA SOL CARIBE ⌂
Playa Paraíso, s Zone ☎*(987) 20700* Ⓕ*(987) 21301* ▥ *220 rms* ═ ⁌ ⋈ ☏ ℘ ⬤ ♈ ⬤ ↻

This vast, Mayan-style pleasure-pyramid has its own diving instructor and diving store, as well as a popular disco.

GALÁPAGO INN DIVE RESORT ♣
Km 1.5 on Chankanaab road ☎*(987) 21133* ▥ *54 rms* ═ ⋈ ☏ ⬤ ♈

Very much geared toward diving, the Galapago Inn has an excellent seafood restaurant, which is lively in the evening.

MELIA MAYAN COZUMEL
Playa Santa Pilar, N Zone ☎*(987) 20411* Ⓕ*(987) 21599* ▥ *180 rms* ═ ♨ ⁌ ⋈ ℘ ♈

An attractive beachside hotel that offers a wide range of water-sports, including a full diving program.

STOUFFER PRESIDENTE ⌂ ♣
Km 6.5 on the Chankanaab road s ☎*(987) 20322* Ⓕ*(987) 21360* ▥ *259 rms* ═ ♨ ⁌ ⋈ ☏ ℘ ⬤ ♈ ⬤ ↻

The first luxury hotel on Cozumel, the Stouffer Presidente is still the most expensive, but its diving and entertainment facilities are excellent.

Budget hotels

There are some less expensive hotels in good locations, such as the **Mara** *(Playa San Juan* ☎*(987) 20300* ▨ ⇌ ⋙*)*, with many of the features of hotels double the price: the motel-like **Villablanca** *(Km 3.5 on the Chankanaab road* ☎*(987) 20730* ▣*(987) 20865* ▨ *43 rms* ⇌ ℘ ⋙ ⛾*)*, well-placed for diving around the nearby reefs; **Playa Azul** *(Playa San Juan* ☎*(987) 20033* ▣*(987) 20110* ▨ *72 rms)*; and **La Perla** *(♣ s Zone* ☎*(987) 20188* ▣*(987) 20819* ▨ *to* ▨ *22 rms* ⇌ ⋙)*.

Another option is to stay in town, where the best bargains are to be had, and travel out daily to the beaches. Good deals here include the **Vista del Mar** *(Rafael Melgar 45* ☎*(987) 20545* ▨ *26 rms)*, on the seafront; the **Misión San Miguel** *(Juárez 2, on the Zócalo* ☎*(987) 20068* ▣*(987) 21820* ▨ *97 rms* ⋙ ⇌ ℉*)*, right at the heart of the action; the **Flores** *(Salas 72* ☎*(987) 21842* ▨ *30 rms)*, basic but clean; and the **Maya Cozumel** *(Calle 5 Sur # 4* ☎*(987) 20011* ▣*(987) 20781* ▨ *to* ▨ *38 rms* ⇌)*, half a block from the beach.

EATING AND DRINKING

Before dinner, take a sunset stroll along the seafront, known as the **Malecón** but officially named Avenida Rafael Melgar, perusing the menus of the restaurants that line it and stopping for an occasional drink to check the quality of service.

Las Palmeras *(Malecón 27, across from the pier* ☎*(987) 20532* ▨)* is efficient and popular, open from early till late; **Carlos'n'Charlie's and Jimmy's Kitchen** *(Malecón at Calle 2* ☎*(987) 20191* ▨)* serves excellent food to the usual fun-loving crowd. The sophisticated **Rolandi's** *(Malecón 23* ☎*(987) 20946* ▨)* has crispy wood-oven-baked pizzas. If the waiters let you in, you can be sure of an elegant gastronomic night out at **Pepe's Grill** *(Malecón at Salas* ☎*(987) 20213* ▨)*.

Oddly, some of the best seafood is to be had away from the seafront, for example at the nautical **El Capi Navegante** *(Av. 10 Sur at Calle 3* ☎*(987) 21730* ▨)* and at the simply-decorated **Soberanis** *(♣ Calle 1 and Sur 5, near the Zócalo* ☎*(987) 20246* ▨)*, a no-frills restaurant with a good and varied menu.

Other options are the hotel restaurants, good but generally expensive, or the seafood *palapas* that fringe the beaches, ideal for lunch, drinks and shade in the heat of the day.

COZUMEL BY NIGHT

No longer do the resort hotels have a monopoly on Cozumel's after-hours entertainment, although the major hotels each have a **Mexican fiesta night** that is open to everyone (free magazines give details). The FIESTA AMÉRICANA SOL CARIBE has live Mexican music every night among the fountains of the **lobby bar**. Next door, **Ernesto's** *palapa* bar is also fun, with live music in the evenings, but there is no need to look smart.

Nightspots in San Miguel include **Disco Neptuno** *(s end of Av. Melgar, the waterfront)*, a popular spot, and **Scaramouche** *(Av. Melgar at Salas*

▩ ❧). For a more cultural experience, try the **Museo de Cozumel** (see page 298), which puts on musical and theatrical performances.

EXCURSION

Playa del Carmen

66km (41 miles) s of Cancún, 63km (39 miles) n of Tulum on RF307.

This minor resort village is best known as the port for the ferry to Cozumel. As a result, it remains rather quieter, and much less expensive, than the island itself, especially once you have wandered a short way along the palm-fringed beach that fronts a becalmed Caribbean sea. If you decide to go no farther, there are plenty of good places to stay here.

At **Xcaret**, 7km (4 miles) s, there is a lovely *cenote* to explore, complete with its own small Maya ruin.

❧ The best hotel in town is the neo-colonial **Molcas** *(by the ferry terminal* ☎ *(987) 21100* ▥ *36 rms* ⁂ ◗ *)*, closely followed by the **Blue Parrot Inn** *(n of center on the beach, no* ☎ ▥ *31 rms* ◗ *)*. In the same area, there are a number of pleasant beachside *cabañas;* the best equipped are at the **Yax-Ha** *(no* ☎ ▥ *)*, but those at **Cabañas Bananas** and the **Nuevo Amanecer** *(no* ☎ ▥ *)* are not far behind.

Punta Bete *(8km/5 miles n)* is a more secluded beachside hangout for snorkelers, turtle-watchers and lotus-eaters, with several upmarket *cabaña* establishments: the **Kai-Luun**, the **Posada del Capitán Lafitte** and the **Shangri-La Caribe** *(no* ☎ ❧ ◗ ▥ *)*.

AKUMAL ☆

Map 8G13. Quintana Roo. 102km (63 miles) s of Cancún, 36km (22 miles) s of Playa del Carmen, 30km (18 miles) n of Tulum on RF307.

This peaceful, exclusive luxury resort lies on a Caribbean bay protected by offshore reefs — the main focus of interest among the diving fraternity that comes here. The coconut palms, replanted after being killed off by blight, are now growing well, so you may also be able to enjoy their welcome shade.

In addition to the luxury hotels, there are some good beach restaurants (especially the **Lol-Ha**), and a small village nearby with a few shops. The coast s to TULUM and n to **Playa del Carmen** (see above) is littered with lovely beaches and sea lagoons, too numerous to list.

WHAT TO SEE

Puerto Aventuras

This is a new self-contained resort in construction on a 200-hectare (500-acre) site a few kilometers n of Akumal, soon to include several luxury hotels, a 200-slip **marina** and a **golf course**.

Underwater Museum

On shore ▩ *if entered from land. Usually open, no regular hours.*

An interest in skin-diving is indispensable, as most of the museum is underwater. On dry land you can see the smaller and more perishable relics retrieved from wrecked galleons far out at sea; the most famous of these is the *Mantanceros,* a Spanish vessel that lay undiscovered on the seabed from 1741 to 1926. Larger pieces, such as great cannons and anchors covered in barnacles and coral, have been towed in under the lee of the shore. Visits to the wrecks, and to submerged Maya ruins, can be arranged at any hotel. There are facilities for scuba novices, but of course it takes a few days for the uninitiated to get to that stage.

Xel-há ☆
10km (6 miles) s. Open 8am-5pm.
This natural aquarium of interconnected coastal lagoons and under-water caves is now a national park. The water is crystal clear; the fish are numerous, diverse, unafraid and psychedelic, somehow surviving the daily slick of sun oil; and there is even an **underwater Maya shrine** to discover. Diving gear can be rented here; just arrive early, before the Cancún tour buses.

☙　**Club Akumal Caribe Villas Maya** *(N end of beach; reservations:* ☎ *(800) 351 1622, or 800 351 1622 in US* ▥ ⥱ ⇙*)* was the first of the luxury hotels. **Las Casitas Akumal** *(reservations:* ☎ *(988) 22554* ▥ ⥱ ⇙*)* has 14 luxurious villas overlooking the bay. **Hotel Club Aventuras Akumal** *(* ☎ *(988) 22887* ▥ ⥱ ⇙ ✿ ℘*),* a few miles s, is a diving-oriented resort with all facilities.

The only budget accommodation is at the **Restaurant Zacil**, which has a few *cabañas* to rent (▤).

TULUM ★
Map 8G13. Quintana Roo. Tulum: 132km (82 miles) SE of Cancún on RF307; 39km (24 miles) SE of Coba.

Perhaps the most beautiful of the Yucatán's ruins, Tulum is a small city walled on three sides and, on the fourth, looking out across the clear blue waters of the Caribbean. Architecturally it is less important than the great cities of the peninsula, which precede it by centuries, but when you sit in the sun, idly watching the giant basking lizards and listening to the surf and the rustle of the palm trees, such academic matters will be far from your mind.

Tulum was a Late Post-Classic center, occupied from around AD1200, and one of the few cities still inhabited when the Spaniards arrived; it was seen by explorers as early as 1518, who described it in glowing terms, comparing it favorably with the Spanish city of Seville.

The ruins are reached by turning 3km (1½ miles) E off RF307 at the modern **Tulum village**, with shops, inexpensive restaurants, bus stops and other conveniences lined up along the road. A road from the ruins skirts s along the coast, behind a perfect beach lined with *palapa* restaurants and *cabaña* accommodation.

WHAT TO SEE

Tulum ruins ▥
▧ *Open 9am–6pm.*
At the center of the city's coastline, over some cliffs, stands the **Castillo**

301

(Castle). This is in fact a temple, with a pyramidal base and a wide ceremonial stair leading to an upper sanctuary. To the N of the court-yard, behind the Castillo, is the small **Temple of the Diving God**, where a stucco relief shows just that.

Just w of here, the **Temple of the Frescoes** has one of the rare surviving examples of Maya painting, showing divinities, serpents and sacred offerings, all in blue-green on a black wall. Outside, on the main facade, the Diving God appears again on a stucco relief; he is to be found at several places in Tulum.

An unusual feature is the **wall** defending the inland borders of the site, the only one of its kind. It was originally 6m (19 feet) thick and 3–5m (10–16 feet) high, with a walkway and parapet, and some 700m (763 yards) long. On the seaward side, cliffs rise some 12m (38 feet) from the water, sheltering a few small **beaches**, safe for swimming on a calm day.

There is a succession of *cabaña* establishments along the coast s from Tulum on the road to Boca Paila. The ones close to the ruins are dirty and charmless, but the **Aldea Dzib-Ak-Tum** *(3km/1½ miles s, no* ☎ ☐ ☶ ☰), on the rocks at the end of the beach, manages a touch of elegance under the shade of coconut palms. Also good and inexpensive are the **Cabañas Chac-Mool** *(4.5km/3 miles)* and **Cabañas los Arrecifes** *(10km/6 miles, no* ☎ *both* ☐ ☰ ☶ *)*.

EXCURSION

Sian Ka'an Biosphere Reserve

This 5,000sq.km (2,000sq.-mile) reserve of tropical swamps, lagoons and rainforest begins just s of Tulum, extending down the coast for about 160km (100 miles). Within its boundaries live 1,200 species of plant, 366 bird species, 320 land vertebrates including jaguars, while manatees reside in its waters and four species of turtle lay their eggs on its beaches.

The reserve also contains 30 known Maya sites, and many more that have yet to be discovered. Today's Maya communities continue to pursue a largely traditional existence, their economy supplemented by the small-scale, carefully controlled cutting and milling of forest hardwoods. In the Maya tongue, Sian Ka'an means "where the sky was born."

Tourist facilities are few and access limited. The easiest way to get into the reserve is on the rough paved road s from Tulum ruins, which runs along a wide, forested sandbar between the open sea and a series of sea lagoons, reaching down to the fishing village of **Boca Paila** *(24km/15 miles),* where *cabaña* accommodation is available. The road deteriorates on its way to **Punta Allen**, an even smaller village with few facilities.

For information about the reserve, call **Amigos de Sian Ka'an** in Cancún *(Plaza America, Av. Cobá 5, Suite 48-50* ☎ *(988) 42201/ 49583),* who also run day-trips from Cozumel.

COBÁ ★

*Map **8**G13. Quintana Roo. 42km (26 miles) NW of Tulum; 129km (80 miles) SW of Cancún, turning S off RF180 at Nuevo X-Can; 57km (35 miles) E of Valladolid, turning E off RF180 at Chemax.*

With a dramatic location, deep in the rainforest alongside five lakes, the extensive and largely unexcavated Maya ruins of Cobá make one of the peninsula's most majestic and mysterious sights.

The city was founded by AD623 and became one of the main centers of Maya civilization, lasting from the 7thC right up until the Conquest, with an estimated 6,500 structures over 45sq.km (18sq. miles), and a population of some 40,000. Further restoration seems certain to reveal Cobá as one of the wonders of the world.

The ruins ▥

▧ *Open 8am–5pm.*

The site is huge, consisting of groups of ruins several kilometers apart. The main group stands in the jungle between lakes Cobá and Macan-xoc, dominated by the 24m (77-foot) **Castillo**, similar in height to the Castillo at CHICHÉN ITZÁ.

From here it is a 2.5km (1½-mile) walk through the forest, along a limestone causeway or *sacbe,* to the **Nohuch-Mul** pyramid, at 42m (134 feet) the highest on the peninsula. Although of Late Classic construction, the temple on its summit is Late Post-Classic and similar to those of TULUM, apparently honoring the same **Diving God** (see page 302). It was at the base of this pyramid that the best preserved of the 23 sculptured *stelae* found in Cobá was discovered.

The ruins are remarkable for the network of *sacbes*, 4.5m-wide (14-foot) causeways of limestone, which connect the various centers of Cobá and also connect Cobá with other cities. Sixteen have been identified, some revealed by satellite photography. The longest runs about 100km (62 miles) w to **Yaxuna**, just s of CHICHÉN ITZÁ. Although apparently ideal for wheeled traffic, the paths were actually used by human bearers, the Maya using neither the wheel nor beasts of burden. The pictures also reveal the existence of an extensive network of irrigation canals.

✧ The top hotel is the **Villa Arqueológica Cobá** *(2 Pte # 501, no ☎ for reservations via Mexico City ☎ (5) 203 3153 ▥ 40 rms ☰ ▢ ◁ ≈ ♨),* a Club-Med operated inn with a good library for serious study of the Maya. There is also a less expensive hotel in the village, **El Bocadito** *(no ☎),* with a surprisingly good restaurant.

CHETUMAL

Map 8H13. Capital of Quintana Roo. On the border of Belize, 571km (356 miles) E of Villahermosa on RF186; 379km (236 miles) s of Cancún, 233km (145 miles) s of Tulum on RF307, turning E on RF186. Population: 100,000. Served by air (from Mexico City and Mérida) and bus ℹ Palacio de Gobierno 2nd floor, Blvd. Bahía s/n ☎(983) 23663.

Chetumal is a small, dusty, modern town baking under a tropical blazing sun, surrounded on three sides by thick jungle, and on the other by the limpid Caribbean sea in the sheltered Bahía de Chetumal. What makes it bizarre is that every other shop seems to sell cameras, videos, hi-fi and jewelry, or Dutch cheese, English tea and other incongruous delicacies — the state of Quintana Roo is a duty-free zone, until 1996 at any rate, although prices are far from low.

Chetumal's **seafront** has recently been upgraded, making a pleasant *malecón,* or pedestrian walkway. But the city is mainly one that travelers pass through on their way to somewhere else. And it makes a good base for bird-watching or archeological expeditions into the jungle.

Ask at the tourist office for advice on the condition of forest tracks leading to the countless Maya ruins, or on where to hire a guide. Visits can also be made to neighboring **Belize**, with frequent direct services running from the huge modern bus station w of the center.

EXCURSIONS

Bacalar
40km (25 miles) NW off RF307.
A village just off the main road, on the shores of **Laguna Bacalar**, a 55km-long (34-mile) freshwater lagoon. The village's ruined 18thC **Fuerte de San Felipe**, built in 1729 as a defense against buccaneers, changed hands several times during the Maya revolt of the 19thC, finally falling to the Mexicans in 1901. Just s of the lake is the large **Cenote Azul**, its fish sharply defined in the clear dark waters, with adjacent restaurant.

Kohunlich ☆
56km (35 miles) w on RF186, then 9km (5 miles) s on a track.
Excavations progress at this recently uncovered Pre- and Early Classic Maya site on the road to Francisco Escarcega. Near the entrance is a large **pyramid**, from the top of which the whole site can be seen — so far, just five of some 200 buildings have been uncovered.

The most interesting buildings are grouped around the central terrace. The **Temple of the Masks** is especially notable, the features of the stucco masks suggesting a strong Olmec influence. The **ball court**, dating from AD100, is among the oldest known.

Laguna Milagros
14km (8 miles) w on RF186, then 100m (109 yards) down signed track.
Another lovely turquoise lake, far smaller than Laguna Bacalar, but rich in wildlife, including parrots, toucans, herons and orioles.

Xpujil, Becán and Chicanná
120, 126 and 128km (80 miles) w along RF186. Open 7am–5pm ▨
thatched ⟁ *at Xpujil.*
These three sites can all be visited on a day trip from Chetumal, and make a good introduction to the Río Bec style in which pyramids are shaped into steep facades. The ruins are mostly unexcavated and surrounded by jungle.

Xpujil lies 100m (109 yards) to the N of the road, from which it is easily spotted, as its three tower-pyramids rise above the trees. One of these pyramids can be climbed, by a very steep stairway. Visitors to **Becán** *(6km/3 miles w)* must watch for the sign, as the site lies 500m (545 yards) N of the road; its pyramids and palaces cover a huge, largely unexcavated area, surrounded by a wide ditch, which is presumed to be defensive in purpose.

Chicanná *(2km/1 mile w)* lies some 750m (817 yards) s of the road; here the excitement is not in its grand constructions, but in the **masks** of

Chac, the rain god, and other stucco work in the **temple** presiding over the grassy plaza.

❖   The best hotels are the **Continental Caribe** *(Héroes 171* ☎ *(983) 21100* ⊞ *to* ⊞ *64 rms* ≣ x ∾*)* and the modern **Del Prado** *(Chapultepec and Héroes 138* ☎*(983) 20544* xx *(983) 20920* ⊞ *80 rms* ≣ ∾*)*. Budget travelers are also catered to, at the **Caribe Princess** *(Obregón 162* ☎ *(983) 20520* ⊞ ≣ ≡*)*. The best choice, if you don't need to be in town, is the **Hotel Laguna** *(Bugambilias 316, Bacalar* ☎ *(983) 23517* ⊞ ∾ ≣*)*; its wide terraces front onto Laguna Bacalar and, although it is slightly worn, the price compensates.

CIUDAD DEL CARMEN

Map 7H11. Campeche. 191km (119 miles) NE of Villahermosa on RF180; 246km (153 miles) SW of Campeche on RF180. Population: 80,000. Served by air, 6km (3-mile) car ferry from the W (irregular sailings 7am–7pm to Isla Aguada, linking the coast road) and bus.

An adventurous, leisurely alternative to the inland road from VILLAHER-MOSA to CAMPECHE is the coast road, via Ciudad del Carmen. The route passes deserted white-sand beaches bordered by coconut groves, with occasional glimpses of Maya Indians paddling their tree-trunk canoes. In fact, the route is not all road: three of the four ferries along the way have been replaced with bridges, but there is still one 6km (3-mile) stretch of water to the W of town, linking **Isla del Carmen** and **Isla Aguada**.

Ciudad del Carmen is hardly the high point of the trip, but it is a good place to stop for a night, and in any case impossible to avoid. It lies on the W end of the Isla del Carmen, a thin ribbon of sand across the mouth of the **Laguna de Terminos**. Once a haunt of pirates, the lagoon later became a shrimp-fishing center, and now its main business is oil exploration. Despite the oil spills, the lagoon still contains shark, barracuda, tarpon and other fish: ask at your hotel for information on boats and guides for hire. Some are based at **Isla Aguada**, on the far side of the ferry.

The city and environs

Start with a walk along the **waterfront**, passing fishermen mending their nets, small shipyards, a naval station, and much photogenic quay-side bustle. Out to sea, bobbing at anchor, are hundreds of shrimpers, although many are now disused because of the oil boom. To the N of the city are **beaches**, now rather oil-covered, and to the S is the **fishermen's district** where fresh shrimps, octopus and cold local beer can be enjoyed at waterfront cafés.

❖   The substantial **Eurohotel** *(Calle 22 #208* ☎*(938) 20130* ⊞ ≣ ∾ x ●*)* is the best in town, a good place to meet tired oil executives. Also good is **Isla del Carmen** *(Calle 20 #11* ☎*(938) 22212* ⊞ ≣ ≡*)*, near the airport. Budget options include the **Lli-re** *(Calle 32 #25 at Calle 29* ☎ *(938) 20588/9* ⊞ ≣ ≡*)*, clean but faded, and the **Internacional** *(Calle 20 at Calle 33, #39* ☎ *(938) 21344* ⊞*)*, near the Zócalo.

Practical information

Practical information

Before you go

DOCUMENTS REQUIRED

Foreigners entering Mexico as tourists must hold a **passport**. Unless they are on a trip of not more than three days, limited to the border area, they are also required to obtain a **tourist card** (valid for a single entry). These are issued free at Mexican embassies, consulates and tourist offices, and on most incoming flights. They can also be obtained at frontiers, but it saves time to get them in advance. Valid for 90 or 180 days, they can be extended at any immigration office.

Children under 18 traveling with only one parent will also need a document, signed and sworn in front of a lawyer, giving consent for that parent and the child to travel in the other parent's absence.

Tourists from many countries, including the US, UK, Canada and the Republic of Ireland, do not require a **visa**. Note that non-US citizens, touching down in the US on their way to Mexico, may need a **US visa**.

Foreigners entering Mexico for business purposes should obtain a **business visa** from an embassy or consulate; there are four categories of business visa, depending on the nature and duration of the business in question, and a charge is levied for most of these. However, business visas valid for under 30 days are generally free.

Although tourist office personnel are uniformly friendly and helpful, the same cannot be said of all consular staff: make sure you apply for any business visa well in advance, and be prepared for bureaucratic complications. **Vaccination certificates** are not needed.

If you intend to drive in Mexico, any valid national or international **driver's license** is acceptable; insurance and other formalities will be dealt with by your car-rental company. If you are driving across the US border, there are further requirements. See GETTING THERE on page 311.

INSURANCE

Travelers are advised to insure their possessions against loss, damage or theft. Medical insurance is indispensable; be sure that your policy covers repatriation. Cancellation insurance may be worth considering. See GETTING THERE on page 311 for motor insurance requirements.

CURRENCY

The unit of currency is the **new peso** (N$), which in January 1993 replaced the old, devalued peso ($) at a rate of $1,000 = N$1. It is divided into 100 **centavos** (¢). Old coins and notes will continue to circulate alongside the new until the end of 1993.

New peso coins have been issued to the value of 5¢, 10¢, 20¢, 50¢, N$1, N$2, N$5 and N$10; these are far smaller than their equivalents in the old coinage. The N$10 is roughly the same size as the old $200. Carefully watch your change while you get used to the coinage.

New notes have been issued to the value of N$10, N$20, N$50, N$50 and N$100; these are similar in appearance to the old notes of equal value, issued in denominations of $2,000, $5,000, $10,000, $20,000, $50,000 and $100,000, minimizing the chance of confusion.

As you travel, bear in mind that the larger notes are difficult to change in remote areas, and embarrassing to produce among poor people. So before you venture off the well-trodden tourist path, stock up with plenty of low-value notes and coins. Even if you are relying mostly on travelers' checks or credit cards, always carry at least N$100, in mixed denominations, to cover all eventualities. For small purchases and tips, and in remote areas, there is no substitute for cash.

At the time of writing, there are no **currency controls** on tourists: any amount of cash or travelers checks can be taken in and out of Mexico, and any amount of Mexican currency can be reconverted when leaving.

TRAVELERS CHECKS

Travelers checks in dollars issued by American Express, Thomas Cook, Barclays and Citibank can be changed at **banks** and at **Exchange Offices** *(Casas de Cambio)*. They are often accepted in payment by shops, hotels, and so on, but it is best to check before running up a large bill.

Make sure you read the instructions included with your travelers checks. **It is important to keep a separate note of the serial numbers of your checks, and the telephone number to call in case of loss**. Each check company has its own network of offices and agents, through which refunds may be obtained in the case of loss or theft. The **American Express** network (offices are listed under individual cities) is the most extensive and its service the quickest.

PERSONAL CHECKS

American Express offers various check-cashing facilities to cardholders, or by prior arrangement. Otherwise, personal checks can be cashed at some banks and hotels, but are not generally accepted. Under Mexican law, issuing a check without having the funds to back it is an act of fraud that may put the perpetrator in prison.

CHARGE AND CREDIT CARDS

American Express cards, and to a lesser extent **Diners Club**, are accepted in the more expensive hotels, restaurants and shops, and by airlines, car-rental agencies and travel agents. **MasterCard** and **Visa** are far more widely accepted, as they are offered by Mexican banks to their customers. Any hotel, restaurant or shop with any pretensions to respectability will happily accept them.

The words "**No cards**" appear in this book, where places that might be expected to take cards in fact do not.

In tourist areas, some charge and credit cards can be used to obtain Mexican currency from wall **cash dispensers**. Charge/credit cards may also be used to obtain cash from banks or foreign exchanges; expect to pay a commission for this service.

The **exchange rate** on charge and credit card purchases is entirely up to the company: when inflation is high in Mexico this is usually (but not always) to your advantage. At some lesser establishments, attempts are made to impose a surcharge on charge and credit card users; if possible, refuse to pay, and make sure that charge and credit card bills cannot subsequently be altered.

Always keep an independent record of your **card numbers** and **expiry dates**, as a precaution in case of theft. Also, try to take a card that is obviously foreign, limiting the ability of a Mexican thief to make use of it. Emergency telephone numbers are listed under EMERGENCY INFORMATION (see page 339).

American Express has a **MoneyGram®** money transfer service that makes it possible to wire money worldwide in just minutes, from any American Express Travel Service Office. This service is available to all customers and is not limited to American Express Card members. See USEFUL ADDRESSES on page 337.

TOURIST OFFICES

The **Mexican National Tourist Council** *(main office: Mariano Escobedo #726, Mexico 5, DF* ☎*(5)533 0540)* is a useful source of information. Before they depart, North American visitors may wish to contact the regional office for the US and Canada *(405 Park Ave., Suite 1002, New York, NY 10022* ☎*(212) 755 7261)*.

Visitors from the UK can get in touch with the **Mexican Ministry of Tourism** *(60–61 Trafalgar Sq., London WC2N 5DS* ☎*(071) 734 1058* [Fx]*(071) 930 9202)*.

Two Mexican Tourist Offices near the US–Mexican border are in **San Antonio** *(* ☎*(512) 366 3242)* and in **Los Angeles** *(* ☎*(213) 659 8730)*.

GETTING THERE
By air

Mexico City is served by numerous international airlines. There are 49 other international airports, including those at Acapulco, Bahías de Huatulco, Cancún, Cozumel, Guadalajara, La Paz, Manzanillo, Mazatlán, Mérida, Monterrey, Puerto Vallarta and Zihuatanejo, which receive regular flights from US cities and some charter or vacation package flights.

Bargain-hunters will find it well worth their while to shop around for discounted fares, while residents of the southern US can save money by bussing to a major Mexican border city and picking up an internal flight to their final destination.

At long last, **British Airways** runs a nonstop service, three times a week, from London Heathrow to Mexico City. Otherwise, the UK traveler has a choice of daily services using US gateways, offered by **Continental**, **American** and **United Airlines**. A number of European airlines, including **KLM**, **IBERIA** and **Air France**, also run direct scheduled flights to Mexico City from Europe.

Reservations out of Mexico should be confirmed 72 hours in advance; failure to do this can result in the loss of seats. Those leaving Mexico by air should always retain $US12 in cash to pay the international airport departure tax: check that this sum has not gone up.

By train

Mexico City is served by trains from the border cities of Mexicali, Nogales, Ciudad Juárez, Piedras Negras, Nuevo Laredo and Matamoros. There is no direct link with the US rail network. The trip is even less expensive than going by bus, but is also slower and less punctual. Accommodation is reasonable on **express trains**, especially on the Nuevo Laredo *Regiomontaño*. A **sleeping compartment** costs surprisingly little more than the ordinary fare; early reservations can be made through a travel agent, or at MEXICO CITY's **Buenavista** station.

By bus

Buses are more reliable than trains, with frequent and inexpensive deluxe services from all frontier cities to the capital. The longest such journey is from **Tijuana** (42 hours), the shortest from **Matamoros** (14 hours). Reservations can be made at **Greyhound-Trailways** offices in the US or through travel agents. There are no round-trip tickets, and return reservations are best made on arrival at Mexico City.

By car

The major routes from the US border to Mexico City have all been improved recently, and further upgrading is constantly taking place, so there are long stretches of 4- and 6-lane divided highways. Since night-driving in Mexico is not advisable, at least one overnight stop will be necessary on the way to Mexico City.

The 3,000 PEMEX gas stations are all claimed to offer **unleaded gasoline**, but availability cannot always be guaranteed, especially in remoter areas. If your car is fitted with a **catalytic converter**, consider having it removed on the Mexican side of the border and replaced on return to the US, in order to avoid poisoning the catalyst with lead.

Note that those entering the country by car will face a certain amount of tedious bureaucracy, and that precise regulations are subject to change on short notice. At the time of writing, you will be required either to pay $US10 by charge/credit card or to post a bond for $US100 (or 2 percent of the car's value, whichever is greater) at the border. You will need to show the car's **registration certificate** and either **proof of ownership** or signed authorization from the owner.

If you have no charge or credit card, you must leave your registration certificate at the border post, and reclaim it on you way out. All drivers must also take out Mexican **insurance**, either beforehand or at the border; the policies offered by the **AAA** (American Automobile Association) and **Sanborn's** *(in US ☎ (512) 686 0711)* are both fine.

The more expensive **juridical insurance** also acts as a kind of bail bond, and can save the holder from prison after an accident or other incident. You are advised to check the precise position with the **Mexican Tourist Office** before departure (see TOURIST OFFICES, page 310).

See also GETTING AROUND, page 315-6, and CAR BREAKDOWNS, page 338.

By ship

From ports on both US seaboards, a variety of **cruises** leave for Mexican resorts. On the Pacific side, Cabo San Lucas, Mazatlán, Puerto Vallarta, Zihuatanejo and Acapulco are the most popular destinations; Veracruz and Mérida are also ports of call for cruise liners heading to the Caribbean.

Prices are high but fair, bearing in mind the quality of accommodation, food and entertainment offered. Special packages are the best deal, including air fares from Europe or inland US cities.

From Europe, there are no regular sailings to Mexico, although some around-the-world cruises stop at Veracruz.

DISABLED TRAVELERS

Mexico has not become disability-conscious, and only the adventurous should consider a trip here. They are certain to experience discomfort, inconvenience and incomprehension.

CHILDREN

Mexicans are renowned for their indulgent love of children, and will make every effort to ensure that your children enjoy Mexico at its best. Most obviously enjoyable for children are resort vacations, with plenty of sunshine, sand, sea and paddling pools. Many hotels have special entertainment programs for children, cable TV direct from the US and supervised beach areas.

However, long sightseeing tours are less suitable, at least for younger children. While older children may well be fascinated by colonial monasteries and Maya ruins, youngsters may suffer from heat, insect bites, stomach upsets and exhausting journeys.

Mexico City is not a healthy environment for children, as the combination of high altitude and pollution can make breathing uncomfortable; the same applies to a lesser extent to other cities, including **Guadalajara** and **Monterrey**.

CLOTHES

In most of the country, informality is the rule, so feel free to dress however you feel comfortable. But it is as well to note that women may cause offense or attract unwelcome interest by wearing very short shorts or dresses, or figure-hugging clothes, away from tourist areas. Mexicans do not generally wear shorts, except at beach resorts, but visitors should not let that deter them where comfort or the demands of a suntan are at stake.

It can be useful to have at least one smart outfit: a lightweight suit for men, and a short evening dress for women, are the correct attire for visiting the smarter clubs and restaurants.

In the hotter regions, avoid artificial fabrics, which quickly become unpleasant to wear, especially in areas of high humidity. Remember that parts of Mexico can get quite cold, with night frosts at high altitude common in winter from N to S. A **warm jacket** or **sweater** (easily purchased when needed) is well worth packing; even in the tropical areas, nights can be surprisingly cool.

In the **rainy season**, be sure to carry some kind of waterproof clothing, or an umbrella. At all times of year a **hat** (best bought in Mexico) is advisable, to keep the direct sun off your head and face. It is also important to have a good pair of high-sided **walking shoes** with non-slip soles, for clambering over ruins.

CUSTOMS

Tourists are allowed to import reasonable quantities of anything clearly intended for personal use, including one camera *plus* one 8mm movie camera *or* one video camera, each with 12 rolls of film/tape, a television, a boat without motor, a surf board and five used toys per child.

In addition, travelers over the age of 18 may import duty-free: 50 cigars plus 200 cigarettes plus 250gm of tobacco; 3 liters of wine or liquors; and gifts to the value of $US120. Illegal drugs, weapons, pornography and perishable goods including canned food, chocolate, plants, flowers and seeds are prohibited. It is inadvisable to bring pets.

In Mexico City, and some other international airports, there is a "traffic light" system, which randomly stops about one in ten people, whose luggage is laboriously searched. If you get a **green** light, you're through; if it's a **red** light, stop and be patient.

When returning home, regulations for nationals vary with each country. Make sure you have **receipts** for purchases made in Mexico, and for any expensive or new items you took with you. The export from Mexico of **archeological remains** and certain **antiques** is forbidden.

Getting around

BY AIR

Mexico has two major internal airlines, **Mexicana** and **AeroMexico**, linking all major cities and resorts to Mexico City, and with a nation-wide network of offices. Several other internal airlines with a more restricted national coverage have also recently grown up from a regional base, including **Taesa**, **Saro** and **AeroLitoral**. The major lines have modern, well-maintained airplanes, although time-keeping is often lax. In addition, there are numerous regional airlines, some using excitingly antique planes.

If you are traveling between minor destinations, you will probably have to change planes in Mexico City or one of the larger regional centers. Schedules, fares and routes are all subject to change: major hotels and travel agents have up-to-date information. Bear in mind that there is an airport **departure charge** on internal flights, currently US$3.

In general, it will cost less to buy an all-in ticket outside Mexico that includes internal flights, than to buy the internal tickets separately, especially if you are using the international arms of **AeroMexico** or **Mexicana**. Excursion fares and package deals are available on some routes. Distance for distance, fares generally cost slightly less than they do in the US, and far less than European flights.

There is invariably a **bus** or **taxi service**, with a fixed tariff, between airports and the city they serve.

The following **central reservation numbers** for internal flights may be useful; remember that you should confirm all flights 72 hours before departure.

AIRLINE	PHONE	BASED IN	SERVES
AeroCalifornia	(682) 26655	La Paz	Baja California
AeroGuadalajara	(3) 647 2791	Guadalajara	Central N
AeroMar	(5) 207 7566	Mexico City	Central N and W
AeroMexico	(5) 207 8233	Mexico City	Nationwide
Aviación Noroeste	(62) 175007	Hermosillo	The N
Mexicana	(5) 325 0990	Mexico City	Nationwide
Saro	(5) 592 0787	Mexico City	Nationwide
Taesa	(5) 705 6164	Mexico City	Nationwide

BUSES

A bus passes along every main road in Mexico every few minutes or so, and even on the humblest dirt track at least twice a day. All except express buses will stop more or less anywhere to pick up or set down — just stand by the side of the road and wave.

The routes are operated by hundreds of rival companies operating every category of bus, from brand-new super-deluxe air-conditioned down to shambling third-class country buses from the 1940s. Tourists may as well travel in the highest category available, as the price difference is usually minimal. All prices are very low compared to those in the US or Europe.

Most cities have a central bus station, usually close to the center, from which the bus companies operate, although there may be several stations each serving different companies or destinations. If in doubt as to where to go, ask your taxi driver for the *central camionera* and tell him your destination. Tickets are sold at the station and should be obtained as far in advance as possible to assure good seats; there are no **round-trip** fares. Some hotels will send out a messenger to collect tickets.

Buses within major towns cost very little, but can be dirty and crowded, and may also follow unpredictable routes. Some knowledge of Spanish and local geography is necessary before using them.

RAILROAD SERVICES

Trains are even cheaper than buses, but are slower and less reliable. They rarely arrive on time, and such details as water supplies and air conditioning tend to be neglected. The new luxury services available to some destinations, such as Guadalajara and San Luis Potosí, are exceptions to the rule. Trains from the US border to Mexico City are better than those s of the capital, which, for all but the most dedicated railroad enthusiasts, are best avoided.

One trip definitely best made by train is the breathtaking ride across the mountains from LOS MOCHIS on the Pacific coast to CHIHUAHUA (see **CHIHUAHUA–PACIFIC RAILROAD**, pages 234–6). Always travel first class (**primera**) and if possible reserve a seat (**primera especial**) — preferably next to a window, but away from the direct sun.

Those intending to travel extensively by rail should inquire about the **Pase Estrella** (Star Pass), available in the US and valid for 30 or 60 days, which can save you 50 percent on 1st-class fares.

TAXIS

Taxis are a convenient way to get around in cities and towns. Prices are low, especially when the driver uses the meter; if there is one in the taxi, its use is compulsory, the only exception being the special **tourist cabs** (which, incidentally, have bilingual drivers). If no taxi appears when needed, ask for the nearest *sitio* (cab stand), and either telephone or go there.

In towns where taxis have no meters, there is usually a fixed system of tariffs, and only if you are actually going outside the town limits is it necessary to bargain in advance over the price.

Many **taxi drivers** (as all over the world) are dishonest and truculent. Do not let yourself be intimidated, and do complain to the local tourist office about any abuses. One surprising detail is that many taxi drivers have only the most elementary knowledge of their city, and, what's more, are unable to read maps. If in doubt, wait for a more helpful and knowledgeable driver to come along.

In the capital and other large cities, collective minibus taxis (*peseros* or *colectivos*) operate up and down main avenues, charging a fee set by the authorities. Like buses, they have their destination written on the front. See also MEXICO CITY, pages 56-7.

GETTING AROUND BY CAR

Driving in Mexico is undoubtedly more dangerous than in the US or Europe, and accidents are frequent. However, it is the most convenient way to see much of the country, and if you are frankly forewarned of the hazards, it is easier to avoid them.

Some roads are well maintained, but even on highways, potholes and rocks can be a nasty surprise. An additional hazard on minor roads are the *topes* (speed-bumps, or "sleeping policemen"), which are poorly marked and can easily destroy a car's suspension.

The real danger, however, comes from the other road users: many drivers are irresponsible and undisciplined, changing lanes and stopping without looking or indicating.

A particular hazard is the ambiguous **left signal**, which may either indicate that the driver is about to turn left, or that it is safe for you to pass. Be especially careful if you are turning left and have an impatient driver close up behind. Kamikaze cyclists and wandering drunks, children and livestock present further hazards.

Many cars and trucks have faulty lights (if any), and Mexicans in any case often drive unlit at night, in the erroneous belief that this is saving their batteries. In general, **driving at night** is especially hazardous, with the added danger of banditry on remote stretches of road. In the cities, traffic jams are bad and traffic lights often disregarded. Priority goes to the largest or fastest car on traffic circles and at intersections, and to the first car to flash its lights on minor roads.

Parking is always a problem, solved by the Mexican upper classes by the simple expedient of having a chauffeur to sit in the car and drive around in circles if trouble approaches. As you park, anywhere in the country, you will often be approached by a young boy, offering to look after your car. It is always worth accepting the offer: the peso or two you shell out will do wonders for international relations and the redistribution of wealth, not to mention the security of your vehicle.

Mexican **road signs** more or less follow the international pattern, but are often hard to see, being set high on the walls of corner buildings. A large **E** indicates that parking is available. If the **E** has a line through it, parking is illegal. The sign *caseta de cobro* means **toll-booth**; it is invariably worth taking the **toll-roads** *(cuota)* in preference to the older, free *(libre)* roads, for they are faster and better maintained.

Mexican **automobile laws** are randomly enforced, often, regrettably, with the aim of securing a small bribe for the policeman involved. It is usually advisable to pay even if you are entirely innocent, especially if the alternative is a trip to the police station; but do not be afraid to bargain.

Speed limits are not observed, but foreigners are advised to comply, if only for safety's sake. Cars that have been illegally (or in some cases legally) parked are sometimes towed away, or have their license-plates removed by the police. In either case, it is a nightmare to recover them and involves considerable time and expense. It is necessary to take a taxi to the nearest **police station** *(delegación)*, and hope that the car has not been lost or sold. See also EMERGENCY INFORMATION on page 338 and BEFORE YOU GO on page 311-2.

AUTOMOBILE CLUB

The **AMA (Asociación Mexicana Automovilista)** *(Orizaba 7, CP07000 Mexico DF* ☎ *(5) 511 5940)* offers maps and touring information, and has reciprocal arrangements with some foreign automobile clubs. Check with yours before you go.

RENTING A CAR

There are numerous **car-rental companies** in Mexico, but most of these are strictly local and their vehicles may not always be reliable. For safety and security, you are probably better off sticking to the larger chains, although these will be more expensive than their cut-price rivals. The cost, unfortunately, differs little from current rates in Europe and the US.

Another advantage of the larger firms is that you can usually return your car to a different location, although there will be an extra charge ranging from the excessive to the outrageous.

WHERE TO RENT A CAR IN MEXICO

	AVIS	BUDGET	DOLLAR	HERTZ	NATIONAL	PAYLESS
Acapulco	✔	✔	✔	✔	✔	✔
Aguascalientes	✔	✔	✔			
Cabo San Lucas	✔	✔				
Campeche	✔					
Cancún	✔	✔	✔	✔	✔	
Celaya	✔					
Chihuahua	✔	✔	✔	✔		
Ciudad del Carmen	✔	✔				
Ciudad Juárez	✔	✔	✔	✔		
Ciudad Obregón	✔	✔	✔			
Ciudad Victoria	✔	✔				
Coatzacoalcos	✔	✔	✔	✔	✔	
Colima	✔	(✔)				
Cozumel	✔	✔	✔	✔	✔	
Cuernavaca	✔	✔				
Durango	✔					
Ensenada	✔					
Guadalajara	✔	✔	✔	✔	✔	✔
Guaymas	✔	✔				
Hermosillo	✔	✔	✔			
Huatulco	✔	✔	✔	(✔)		
Ixtapa/Zihua	✔	✔	✔	✔	✔	✔
La Paz	✔	✔	✔			
León	✔	✔	✔	✔		
Manzanillo	✔	✔	✔	(✔)		
Matamoros	✔	✔	✔	✔	(✔)	
Mazatlán	✔	✔	✔			
Mérida	✔	✔	✔	✔	✔	
Mexicali	✔	✔	✔	✔		
Mexico City	✔	✔	✔	✔	✔	✔
Los Mochis	✔	✔	✔			
Monterrey	✔	✔	✔	✔	✔	(✔)
Morelia	✔	✔				
Nogales	✔					
Nuevo Laredo	✔	✔	✔			
Oaxaca	✔	✔	✔	(✔)		
Pachuca	✔					
Palenque	✔					
Puebla	✔	✔	✔			
Puerto Escondido	✔	(✔)				
Puerto Vallarta	✔	✔	✔	✔	✔	✔
Querétaro	✔	✔	✔			
Reynosa	✔	✔	✔	✔	(✔)	
Saltillo	✔	✔	(✔)			
San Cristóbal LC	✔					
San José del Cabo	✔	✔	✔	✔		
San Luis Potosí	✔	✔	✔			
Tampico	✔	✔	✔	✔	✔	(✔)
Tapachula	✔					
Tijuana	✔	✔	✔	✔	✔	
Toluca	✔	✔	✔			
Torreón	✔	✔				
Tuxtla Gutiérrez	✔	✔	✔			
Uruapán	✔					
Veracruz	✔	✔	✔	✔	✔	
Villahermosa	✔	✔	✔	✔		
Zacatecas	✔					

(✔) Opening expected during 1993.

The agency will want to see your driver's license, and may impose a minimum age limit of 25. Insurance is arranged through the rental company, and should be regarded as compulsory even if it may seem optional. To avoid complications, a charge/credit card is the best method of payment. Reservations can be made from home through any branch of the international agencies.

Do not be too surprised if the car you reserved is not the one you get, but do refuse to pay extra for an upgrade. Always check such details as lights, brakes, tire wear and pressure, steering, oil, water, spare tire, wipers and so on. And check the car for dents, in case you are charged for them on your return.

All the major car-rental companies now have toll-free numbers that are valid anywhere in the country except Mexico City, and locations can change with a bewildering rapidity. In this edition, therefore, the Mexico City and toll-free numbers are given below, and a table of rental companies and their locations is given on the previous page, while details of rental companies in individual cities have been removed.

Typically, car-rental companies operate from the local airport, and/or from one or more hotels in town, possibly with an out-of-center main office.

Toll-free and Mexico City numbers

	MEXICO CITY	FAX	TOLL-FREE
Avis	(5) 588 8888	(5) 588 3227	(800) 70777
Budget	(5) 271 4322	(5) 277 3056	(800) 70017
Dollar	(5) 207 3838	(5) 207 0774	(800) 90010
Hertz	(5) 566 0099	(5) 592 2967	(800) 70016
National	(5) 533 0375	(5) 208 7667	(800) 90186
Payless	(5) 208 7221	(5) 208 0246	(800) 90283

MEXICO ON TWO WHEELS

Two-wheelers should watch out in city traffic and on busy roads, as some macho drivers regard 2-wheel transport as fair game. In general, **motorcyclists** and their machines are vulnerable in Mexico, lacking the security of a lockable steel box around them.

The same applies to cyclists, although cycling can be a good option in places, especially on the Yucatán Peninsula, with its broad, flat roads and light traffic. **Mopeds** and **bicycles** can often be rented at resorts; on ISLA DE COZUMEL in particular, this is a good way to get around.

BOAT SERVICES

Apart from various ferry services across river estuaries and to inshore islands, the only useful boat services within Mexico are from the mainland to Baja California. Schedules and frequencies vary and should be checked at a travel agent. Routes are Los Mochis–La Paz, Mazatlán–La Paz and Guaymas–Santa Rosalia.

Reservations for cars, or for a cabin, should be made as far ahead as possible. The service provided is generally basic but inexpensive, at least for foot passengers.

WALKING

A visit to Mexico inevitably entails a good deal of walking. Just bear in mind that city **sidewalks** often contain unexpected holes where service covers have gone missing, piles of rubble, and other hazards, so watch where you are putting your feet.

When walking in the **country**, it is inadvisable to venture out alone, because of the risk (however remote) of falls, robbers, scorpions, mad dogs, vipers and other dangers. Always carry a **water bottle**, as dehydration can take place rapidly on a hot day, and local water supplies may be contaminated; otherwise, you will have to rely on soft drinks, which can be found in the remotest of villages.

ADDRESSES

The prefixes *Avenida* (Avenue) and *Calle* (street) are usually omitted, and streets are known simply by their name. Common suffixes are *Nte* or *Norte* (N), *Sur* (S), *Pte* or *Poniente* (W) and *Ote* or *Oriente* (E). The road along a seafront is usually referred to as the *Malecón* (waterside), whatever its real name, and the same applies to the main square, always called the *Zócalo,* for a reason explained in MEXICO CITY (see page 57).

Addresses without numbers often have the suffix *s/n (sin número).* An address may also be given as *Domicilio conocido,* meaning that the establishment or individual in question is so well known in the given village/street that further information is superfluous.

MAPS

Lack of accurate base information makes all Mexican maps to some extent unreliable. Some road-building programs, for example, are shown as having been completed long before the event, while others that have been finished years ago are mysteriously omitted. The **full-color maps** at the end of this book compare favorably with most.

Free maps distributed by tourist offices are accurate only for main roads, and the only reliable street guide to the whole of Mexico City is published by ROJI and sold on newsstands. Another widely available map is the PEMEX **road atlas**, found in bookstores and large gas stations.

A series of 1:50,000 and 1:250,000 maps is published by INEGI, the National Institute of Statistics, Geography and Information. They have a small office at Mexico City airport, a head office at Balderas 71, Mexico City *(map 14 C5; all maps available for sale here),* and regional offices in Durango, Guadalajara, Hermosillo, Mérida, Monterrey, Oaxaca, Puebla, San Luis Potosí and Toluca.

On-the-spot information

HEALTH

Few visitors to Mexico suffer any severe health problems, many even escaping the stomach upsets known collectively as Moctezuma's Revenge. For those who are stricken, however, most cases are mild, resulting simply from a change of diet, in which case the symptoms disappear after a few days.

However, there are more severe infections that can be acquired in food and drink, such as **hepatitis A**. Precautions should therefore be taken, in a country where sanitary provisions fall well below US or European standards:

* At high altitudes, where the digestion works slowly, avoid excesses of food or alcohol.
* Avoid tap water or anything that may have been washed in it. Water purification tablets are of only limited use, but iodine treatment (5 drops of standard iodine tincture to 1 liter of clear water, left for at least half an hour) is more effective.
* Peel all fruit, or wash it in an antiseptic solution.
* All meat, especially pork, should be well cooked.
* Buy roadside snacks only from those stalls that are visibly clean and are cooking all food thoroughly at high temperature, thus killing any bacteria. These can be safer places to eat than some restaurants, where there is no way of knowing if the kitchen is filthy.
* Avoid unpasteurized milk.
* Always wash your hands before eating or handling food.

A further possible hazard is **malaria**, which, according to the World Health Organization, exists in Mexico throughout the year in some areas **not** commonly visited by tourists. Malaria tablets are therefore recommended for travelers in rural and tropical areas; take medical advice on which tablets to take and in what dosages, and bear in mind that you should begin to take the tablet before entering an affected area.

TIME-KEEPING

Mexican time-keeping is both art and science: it is always difficult for foreigners to get used to Mexicans' idea of time, which is imprecise and elastic. It is socially disastrous, for example, to arrive punctually at a function or party, and meetings generally start about one hour after the stated time. Lateness is not a mark of discourtesy.

To make it clear that you are going to arrive at a certain hour, or that someone else should do so, a useful phrase is *hora inglesa* (English time). The Mexican counter to this is the word *ahorita* (a diminutive of "now"), which can mean anything from ten minutes later to infinity. "Right now" translates as *"ahorita mismo"*. If you should ever hear the phrase *"un poquito mas al rato,"* be prepared to wait a good few hours.

Mexico uses a 24-hour timetable for public transport schedules. Remember that time zones vary: if you want to make sure about your local time, ring the **speaking clock**, on ☎03.

TIME ZONES
Most of Mexico remains on Central Time all year round, does not observe Daylight Saving Time and is therefore 6 hours behind Greenwich Mean Time (GMT). The western coastal states of Baja California Sur, Sonora, Nayarit and Sinaloa, in the NW, are on Mountain Time, 7 hours behind GMT. Baja California Norte is on Pacific Time, 8 hours behind GMT: this is the only state to operate Daylight Saving Time, from April to late October.

BUSINESS HOURS
Shops and offices generally open by 10am, and offices close down for lunch from 2–4pm or even longer. Evening closing can be as late as 7.30pm.

MUSEUM OPENING HOURS
The opening hours of Mexican museums, or at least the smaller or regional ones, are erratic by any standards; late opening, early closing and unscheduled lunch breaks should never come as a surprise. As a general rule, Monday is the closing day, and opening hours are from 10am–6pm; this is referred to in this book as "standard hours," and significant variations, where appropriate, are noted.

RUSH HOURS
Rush hours affect all major cities and towns and, as a rule, coincide with the start and finish of shopping and business hours. But they are getting longer all the time. Public transport becomes unpleasantly crowded, and traffic grinds to a halt.

OUTGOING MAIL AND TELEGRAMS
Mexican mail is inexpensive, but slow and somewhat erratic. It is advisable to mail letters at **post offices** *(oficina de correos)* or at **hotel desks**. Post offices open Monday to Friday 9am–7pm, Saturday 9am–1pm. **Sending packages abroad** is reasonably secure, but do not send objects of value (sending a package from abroad *into* Mexico invites loss or at least damage).

International and national **telegrams** are best sent via a hotel desk.

GENERAL DELIVERY/POSTE RESTANTE
Correspondence sent to a named individual at *Lista de Correos, Correo Principal, CITY NAME* will be held for a month at the city's main post office for collection; proof of identity is required to pick it up. An alternative is to have mail sent to hotels where you will be staying, marked with the approximate date of arrival. American Express also accept mail for their clients.

Formalities such as "Miss" or "Esq" added to a name can cause confusion; the surname should be written in capitals. When picking up mail, note that it may be held under your first name and/or your surname; be persistent. Note that packages sent to Mexico from abroad are virtually guaranteed to be lost or damaged.

MAIN POST OFFICE (OFICINA DE CORREOS)
Correo Mayor   Eje Central, Lázaro Cárdenas and Tacuba, Mexico City (map **15**C6). ☎(5) 521 7394. Open Monday to Friday 8am to midnight; Saturday to Sunday 8am–8pm.
International telegrams   Telecomm, Tacuba 8, Mexico City ☎(5) 521 2679, near the post office (map **15**C6). Open 8am to midnight.

BANKS AND CURRENCY EXCHANGE
Money and travelers checks may be exchanged at banks, open Monday to Friday 9am to 1.30pm, or at **Exchange Offices** *(Casas de Cambio)* at international airports and elsewhere, which offer a quicker service and remain open for longer hours. US dollars in small bills are almost universally accepted at varying rates of exchange. Most **hotels** will change money at the official rate, although some may try to make a profit. In general, the more expensive the hotel, the worse the rate.

TELEPHONE SERVICES
The Mexican telephone system is notoriously inefficient. Its recent privatization may change this, as much-needed investment floods in, but for the time being the main gain has been to investors, who have seen the value of their stock multiply while Mexicans put up with business, or lack of it, as usual. Years-long waits for installation, months-long waits for repairs, and phone bills inflated by fictitious calls are all regrettably common.

Still, tourists will find numerous **telephone booths** in all the cities, from which **local calls** can be made for the minute sum of **10¢** (insert the coin before dialing). Local calls from public booths in **Mexico City** are, at the time of writing, **free**.

Long-distance calls are often most easily made through the **operator** *(☎02)*, transferring the charge *(por cobrar)*. All towns and cities also have long-distance call offices *(cabina de larga distancia)*, but you may have to wait in line for some time, and it is quicker, although more expensive, to make calls through hotel switchboards.

Direct dialing throughout Mexico and to much of the world is now also usually possible. For calls outside the local area or toll-free (beginning in **800**), first dial the national access code (**91**) followed by the exchange code (given in brackets throughout this book).

Because of high taxes, international calls from Mexico are far more expensive than the other way round. You should either call collect through the **international operator** *(☎09)*, who speaks English, or arrange to be called back. Direct dialing is easy, especially to the US: dial **95**, followed by the 10-digit US number.

When you answer the telephone in Mexico, the most authentic utterance is the word *"bueno,"* with a strongly emphasized, drawn out final syllable.

CUSTOMS AND ETIQUETTE
Greetings
Most visitors will be surprised by the open friendliness shown by Mexi-

cans. Men frequently greet one another with great bear-like hugs *(abrazos)* and vigorous back-slaps. Indiscriminate kissing of women and general handshaking is *de rigueur* at social gatherings, at least in the higher ranks of society. Courtesy breaks down when it comes to standing in line, when the principle of survival of the fittest rules.

Status of women

Although there are some signs of change, Mexican society is strongly male-dominated. Foreign women accustomed to more equal treatment would do better to be amused, rather than irritated, at the courteous but patronizing behavior of men. In crowds, women will occasionally be pestered, but although this is irritating, there is seldom malicious intent; if this is a recurrent problem, try to eliminate all possible provocation in your manner of dress (see CLOTHES, page 312–3).

PHOTOGRAPHY

Mexico is a paradise and a challenge for the shutter-happy visitor. Lighting conditions are harsh, and the use of a "haze" (UV) filter will ensure better results. It is advisable to bring plenty of film with you.

A **permit** is required for 16mm movie-cameras and above; video-cameras and 8mm filming are legal for tourists. In some **museums** there is an extra charge for photography. The only other restrictions are on photographing military installations. In remote areas, cameras may be regarded with great suspicion. Never take pictures of people without permission, and be prepared to part with the odd peso from time to time.

LOCAL PUBLICATIONS

In Mexico City, a daily English-language newspaper, *The News,* is published; it is sold in all resorts and major cities. In addition to this, various free magazines and handouts are available at the desks of good hotels. Also in the capital, the weekly *Tiempo Libre* is a worthwhile guide to everything going on, and little knowledge of Spanish is needed to understand the listings.

PUBLIC LAVATORIES/BATHROOMS

Away from airports and railroad and bus stations, public lavatories are few and far between, and decidedly unsavory. Hotels and restaurants will usually oblige passers-by in need, but, in even the smartest establishments, standards of hygiene can be astonishingly low. Men's toilets are signposted *hombres, caballeros* or *señores:* women's *damas, mujeres* or *señoras.* It is advisable to carry your own tissues.

ELECTRIC CURRENT

Electricity is supplied at 110V 60 cycles AC — the same as in the US. European travelers may need transformers and socket adaptors for the flat, 2-prong plugs in general use.

TIPS

The general rule for tourists is to leave a tip *(propina)* if in doubt. Taxi drivers are the only exception, although it is usual to leave any small change. At restaurants, a tip of 10–15 percent is expected, although if there is a service charge, leave less. Tipping at hotels is less common: make sure that any tips you leave actually get to the people who made your stay pleasant. It is also customary to tip car-watchers, porters, gas station attendants, theater ushers and so on; the current price of a beer will be sufficiently generous. Somewhat larger sums are given to hairdressers, manicurists and tourist guides.

BRIBES

The line between a tip *(propina)* and a bribe *(mordida)* can easily become blurred. Customs officials, bureaucrats, traffic police and reservations clerks can all become more helpful when primed.

But be careful: many people will happily accept the equivalent of a few dollars in recompense for doing their job more swiftly than they otherwise might, but will take offense at the idea that they can be paid to actually break the rules, especially by foreigners. In order to overcome these understandable scruples, larger sums may be required.

THE LAW

The first point to emphasize is that **few tourists ever get into trouble with the Mexican law**, and those that do are often treated leniently. However, if you are arrested for an alleged crime, you may be detained for **up to 72 hours** without being charged. During this time, you can request a government-appointed lawyer; but you would be better advised to contact your **consulate** (addresses are given on page 337).

Mexican law is based on the Napoleonic system, whereby suspects are considered guilty until proved innocent.

One obvious way to get into trouble is by committing a **driving offense**. For minor infractions, an on-the-spot fine *(multa)* or bribe *(mordida)* will settle matters. In the case of a major accident, everyone involved is normally **jailed** while the police sort things out. Tourists with **juridical insurance** (see GETTING THERE, page 311) will be released more quickly.

In the case of **drug offenses**, tourists are treated, if anything, more harshly than Mexicans. Consular officials are unable to help, and long sentences are routinely handed out. The drugs world is full of violent, ruthless criminals and covert police agents. If you are searched by the police, insist on turning out your own pockets, for cases of "planting" are not unknown.

One area where trouble is possible is **nude swimming and sunbathing**, which is illegal on public beaches — see SPORTS, page 336.

ASSISTANCE FOR TOURISTS

The personnel on the 24-hour English-language tourist assistance numbers listed in USEFUL ADDRESSES (page 337) can also provide legal and other emergency advice. There is also a special-purpose tourist-protection agency, the **Procaduría de Protección al Turista**. It has representatives in every state capital, as well as a **24-hour hotline** in Mexico City (☎ *(5) 250 0151).*

POLICE

In Mexico City and some resorts, special **tourist police** are on patrol in central areas. They are helpful and friendly, and many speak various foreign languages.

Otherwise, on the whole, it is wise to steer clear of encounters with the Mexican police, in particular the state police forces. While many officers are certainly beyond reproach, stories of bribery and extortion are commonplace in Mexico.

If you do find yourself in trouble of any kind, the best advice is to maintain a respectful reserve, and to cooperate, but not always too readily. For example, if invited to the police station to sort things out, you should always insist on settling matters on the spot.

Likewise, show important documents, such as your passport or driver's license, when asked to do so, but do not let them out of your grasp. If things look serious, contact your embassy; and try the **Tourist Assistance** collect-call number under EMERGENCY SERVICES, page 338.

NATIONAL HOLIDAYS

Official national holidays are listed below. On these days, banks and offices close, but most restaurants and some shops remain open. Banks and offices may also close unpredictably to celebrate local holidays. Days marked (•) may also be observed. For details of holidays and events throughout the Mexican calendar, see EVENTS IN MEXICO on pages 48–50.

January 1; Constitution Day, February 5; March 21, birthday of Benito Juárez; Easter Thursday; Good Friday; May 1; May 5 (•); September 1 (•); September 15–16, Independence Day; October 4–12, Virgin of Zapopán fiesta; October 12 (•); November 1–2, Day of the Dead; November 20, Anniversary of the 1910 Revolution; December 12, Virgen de Guadalupe; Christmas Day.

FIESTAS

Every Mexican town has four or five annual fiestas, and sometimes more, typically celebrated with fireworks, processions, dancing, bull-fights, religious services and a heavy intake of alcohol. Some of the better known and nationally celebrated fiestas are listed in EVENTS IN MEXICO, pages 48-50. See also EVENTS under individual destinations.

Where to stay

Mexican hotels provide a very pleasant surprise for those revisiting the country after a long absence. Massive financial investment, and a new generation of professional managers, have largely eliminated the comically dreadful establishments of popular tourist lore.

PRICES

The high-class city and resort hotels are as expensive as those in Europe or the US, with prices for a double room sometimes reaching from $80 or so to well above $200 per night. Budget hotels, however, are cheaper than their US or European equivalents: $10 will secure a basic but clean room in most of the country, but $20 may be needed in Mexico City and the resorts. In the mid-range, decent accommodation with air conditioning where the climate demands it, en suite bathroom, gardens and swimming pool, may be found for around $30–60, depending on location.

Tariffs are fixed by the **Tourism Secretariat**, which also publishes erratic 1-to-5-star ratings, based on lists of facilities rather than charm. Tax at 15 percent is added to all hotel bills, but tips are at your discretion. A single traveler usually pays 80 percent, or even 100 percent, of the double room rate.

* For an explanation of price categories used in hotel listings in this book, see HOW TO USE THIS BOOK on page 7.

RESERVATIONS

The resorts and popular inland vacation spots fill up to capacity during holiday weekends and around the times of well-known fiestas or other events. It is advisable to make reservations at least two weeks ahead, and, in some popular destinations, you should allow months rather than weeks to secure the hotel of your choice. Some hotels will accept telephone reservations, but this gives the traveler little security.

It is safer to reserve through a travel agent, who can wire a deposit. Always carry your hotel confirmation: if the hotel has overbooked, they are legally obliged to find you suitable alternative accommodation. Unless hotels are advised of a late arrival, rooms will not be held beyond 6pm.

CATEGORIES OF ACCOMMODATION

Most **luxury hotels** in Mexico are controlled by international hotel chains. In addition to the standard high-quality rooms and service, they usually offer cable-TV from the US, personal telephone, air conditioning, shops, travel agents, sports facilities, social programs and organized excursions. Staff often speak good English.

In the resorts, some hotels try to insist on the "**American Meal Plan**" (full board). In theory this is not allowed, but sometimes the only recourse is to change hotels.

Medium-priced hotels usually offer restaurants, en-suite shower rooms, television, air conditioning where necessary, and at least one staff member who speaks English. Cities such as Cuernavaca, Guanajuato, Morelia, San Miguel de Allende and Taxco boast old **colonial inns** in 16th–17thC town houses. In a similar price range are the American-style **motels** that line the main highways around most Mexican cities, especially in the N.

A word of caution: the seedier-looking motels often function to some extent as brothels.

All Mexican cities have amazingly **cheap places** to stay in, usually found around the main square and near the bus station. In these, telephone reservations are unheard of, English is rarely spoken, and anything but cash is greeted with a puzzled stare. Always check the room before signing in, for some are quite unacceptable. If staying in such places, consider carrying your own sleeping bag to keep out the bedbugs.

In the S, especially in coastal areas, a preferable budget option is to carry a hammock, which may be slung under *palapas* (palm-roofed shelters) for just a dollar or two. Nights can be surprisingly cold, so take a blanket or sleeping bag; and consider a mosquito net in jungle areas. When equipped with walls, a *palapa* becomes a *cabaña,* warmer, more secure and roughly double the cost.

Finally, in the main coastal resorts, **self-contained apartments** and **bungalows** are available on condominium-rental or time-share arrangements. They are moderate to expensive in price. Make arrangements before leaving for Mexico.

Food and drink

As you launch into your breakfast, lunch or dinner in any corner of the globe, consider that many of the foods you are eating may have originated in Mexico. Among the well-known foods from Mexico are Indian corn (maize), vanilla, chocolate, squash, marrows, pumpkins, capsicums, chili, avocados, tomatoes, peanuts, papaya and turkey. Mexican cuisine, based on these indigenous ingredients and supplemented with Spanish additions and culinary traditions, is delicious, and has evolved into a wide range of regional variations.

Many people have preconceptions about Mexican food, often based on the Tex-Mex dishes popular in the US. But good although Tex-Mex cooking can be, it bears little resemblance to the real taste of Mexico, where sour cream is not seen from one year to the next, guacamole comes with hot green chilies in it, and meat is a rarity, often of dubious origin.

The food most people eat is both far plainer and more wholesome than the popular image. And while it does sometimes live up to its reputation for red-hot chili spice, the latter is usually provided in a separate sauce, a "salsa," which you are at liberty to ignore. You are more likely to encounter the exquisitely subtle use of spices and flavors characteristic of genuine Mexican cooking.

One recent phenomenon is the arrival of the *"nueva cocina Mexicana,"* the Mexican answer to *nouvelle cuisine,* a subtle combination of indigenous and French influences. It is certainly delicious, but perhaps not for the hungry.

RESTAURANTS
Recommendations in this book concentrate, although not exclusively, on restaurants offering authentic Mexican cuisine. There are usually plenty of inexpensive restaurants around a town's Zócalo or waterfront *(malecón),* but their standards can vary from day to day. The best idea is to walk around and see where the locals eat. With a few creditable exceptions (mostly in MEXICO CITY, see page 83), hotel restaurants are pricier and less interesting.

It is always a good idea to telephone beforehand to see if reservations are advisable; reservations by phone are usually accepted, and the table is held for about 10 minutes after the stated time. Adequate notice for most places would be the morning of the same day.

Restaurant prices are always considerably lower than they are in the US or Europe. Even luxury restaurants are up to 50 percent cheaper, although imported wines can erode that advantage. A tax, currently 15 percent, is added to all bills, and a 10-15 percent tip is customary. Fixed-price menus are rare in the evening, but excellent-value fixed-price *"comida corrida"* lunches are more common.

Most restaurants open around 12.30pm and close when the last diner is persuaded to leave, usually around midnight, but often earlier in provincial establishments. Mexicans eat their lunch between 2 and 4pm, but it often goes on for hours and overlaps with early evening diners. The most popular hour for dinner is 9.30–10.30pm. Hotel restaurants have more rigid hours, usually 12.30–2.30pm and 7.30–10.30pm.

* For an explanation of price categories used in our restaurant listings, see HOW TO USE THIS BOOK on page 7.

MEXICAN CUISINE
Some of Mexico's regional dishes have become so famous that they are now served all over the country. No vacation would be complete without sampling, for example, *guajalote con mole* (turkey in *mole* sauce).

The sauce, first invented in Puebla, is often known as *mole poblano;* it is very complicated, made from up to 40 different ingredients, including unsweetened raw chocolate. Also from Puebla is the stuffed chili dish called *chiles en nogada,* with a topping in the national colors, served only around the time of the independence celebrations (September).

Tortillas
For thousands of years, the main staple of Mexican cooking has been the *tortilla:* a highly nutritious pancake of Indian corn (maize), soaked in water, softened with lime, ground into a paste and formed into shape. The cultivation of corn is still, for many, a religious activity, reflecting the native creation myth that God had several unsuccessful attempts at making man out of earth, wood and stone, before finally choosing corn as the ideal material.

To this day corn is the foundation of the indigenous diet and culture. One of the most characteristic sounds of the countryside is the fast hand-clapping of housewives beating out the day's *tortillas,* although the laborious grinding of the corn kernels on a stone *metate* is now a rarity in all but the remotest areas.

Tortillas are served with every meal and are the basis of numerous snacks and dishes, the two most famous being *tacos* and *enchiladas,* both consisting of rolled *tortillas* filled with whatever takes the chef's fancy and served with a spicy sauce. The ubiquitous *enchiladas Suizas,* filled with chicken in a rich cream-and-cheese sauce, are hardly Swiss.

The most authentic way to eat *tortillas* is with *frijoles refritos.* These are beans refried with onion, garlic and spices, with a good dollop of *salsa verde, roja* or *cruda* — green, red or raw salsa, respectively made from simmered-down chili and green tomatoes *(tomates);* chili and ordinary red tomatoes *(jitomates);* and a fresh, vitamin-rich mixture of chopped tomato, green chili, onion, salt, lemon juice and coriander leaves.

Other *tortilla* snacks include *tostadas, gorditas, flautas* and *chilaquiles.* There are many others. If you buy from street stalls, be sure to choose a clean-looking vendor and stall and make sure that everything is thoroughly cooked. The other well-known Mexican snacks, *tamales,* also use the same corn dough as *tortillas,* but are made with only a handful of it, stuffed with meat or jam and then steamed in corn leaves.

There are enormous differences in quality. Most *tortillas* are now machine-processed out of bulk-grade grain, still a healthy food, but flat and tasteless compared to the authentic hand-ground, hand-formed *tortillas* made from locally-grown corn. These are now found only in remote areas, away from machinery and power supplies, and in the very best restaurants. Be sure to eat some before you leave.

Meat dishes

The best meat dishes come from the N of Mexico, which practices the style of cooking known as *norteño.* Large, juicy steaks are the specialty of the cattle-ranching state of Chihuahua, but the drier and more barren states of the NW concentrate on kid *(cabrito)* dishes, usually served with wheat *tortillas.* A favorite now found all over the country is *carne asada a la Tampiqueña,* well-beaten strips of steak served grilled with a selection of beans, vegetables and *guacamole* (avocado paste with chili, garlic, lemon, salt and tomato).

Mexican barbecued meat *(barbacoa)* is cooked for many hours in an underground pit. If meat is unnamed, simply described as "carne," it will often be pork. While it should be perfectly safe if well cooked, bear in mind that pigs often serve as village sewage-disposal systems.

Seafood

It is advisable to eat seafood only at coastal cities, and in the smarter inland restaurants. The freshest and best seafood is often served at the humble beachside huts that line all popular beaches.

For starters, a good choice is the deliciously chewy *ceviche* fish cocktail, made from uncooked fish pickled in lime juice; a variation on this is *ceviche de pulpo* (squid). To follow, the most famous of Mexican fish dishes is the *huachinango a la veracruzana* (red snapper Veracruz-style), a delicately flavored fish served in an aromatic red sauce of garlic, spices and mild chilies.

Lobster, giant shrimps and crawfish (crayfish) are the basis of other interesting dishes, but shrimp fisheries in particular are often highly damaging to marine ecosystems. More exotic are game-fish steaks, while *tortuga* (turtle) should no longer be seen on Mexico's menus, since the animals have now won official protection.

Desserts

Puddings are the only disappointment of Mexican cooking. Most are excessively sweet, sticky concoctions of milk, eggs and sugar. It is best to choose one of the tropical fruits, such as *papaya* (paw-paw), *plátano* (banana), *grenadillas* (passion fruit), *piña* (pineapple), *zapote* (a sweet, tropical fruit), mango or pomegranate. In smarter restaurants, ice creams *(nieves* or *helados)* are delicious.

WHAT TO DRINK

Mexico's most famous alcoholic offering to a grateful world is, of course, **tequila**, the ambrosial firewater made from distilled cactus juice. Many prefer it straight with salt and lemon, but the Cointreau-laced **margarita** cocktail is a less dramatic assault on the taste buds. For a smooth-tasting, well-aged tequila, ask for "**Conmemorativo**."

Also made from cactus, and similar to tequila, is **mescal**, famous (or infamous) for the dead worm at the bottom of the bottle. The poor relation of these two is *pulque*, a stronger-tasting version of tequila originating from a different cactus, which is a popular route to oblivion among *campesinos* and low-paid workers. Most foreigners find it unpalatable.

Like many other countries, Mexico claims to have the best **beer** in the world. The claim may not be entirely justified, but Mexican beer is so much better than the US version that it is causing deep concern among US brewers, as their customers desert them in droves. There are two varieties, dark *(oscura),* and light *(clara).* Good *oscuras* are Negra Modelo and Tres Equis, and among the *claras* are Bohemia, Dos Equis and Carta Blanca.

Local **wines** are less reliable, but producers have been learning from the dramatic recent improvement in both quality and quantity of Californian wines. **Brandy** — of sorts — and excellent **rum** are also produced in Mexico, together with a plethora of strange and sticky regional liqueurs. Before trying them, remember that, at the altitude of Mexico City, alcohol can have up to three times its normal intoxicating effect.

Coffee, tea and nonalcoholic drinks

The most typically Mexican way to drink coffee is as a **café de olla**, brewed for hours, with cinnamon and sugar added. If you want coffee with milk, ask for it *con crema* (with cream), and not *con leche,* which will summon a concoction of warm milk and instant coffee. Ordinary breakfast coffee is called **café américano**, and is served black. *Espresso* and *cappuccino* are often available.

For a cup of tea, ask for **té negro** (black tea) to distinguish from the (more interesting) local herbal teas. These are normally served with a heavy dose of sugar, so be careful to specify *sin azúcar* if you want to avoid this. Good for morning tea is *yerba buena* (mint). After a large dinner, try some *té de manzanilla* (camomile).

Mexico has the highest per-capita consumption of soft drinks in the world. This means that Coke and Pepsi-Cola are almost universally available, as well as a variety of alarmingly colored local *refrescos* (soft drinks). The reason for their popularity in even the poorest, most remote villages is simple: priced at N$1 or less, they are the one and only luxury that can be afforded.

While some may decry the long reach of the multinational corporations, at least the *refrescos* are safe to drink, and the drinks trucks provide a vital lifeline into far-off regions. Mysteriously, the farther you get from civilization, the more the drinks go down in price.

Healthier and infinitely more delicious are Mexico's **fresh fruit juices** *(jugos)*, widely available from restaurants, street vendors and market stalls. Those accustomed to prepacked orange juice will be amazed at the flavor and vitality of the freshly squeezed variety, which may then be liquidized with banana, pineapple or papaya, to make a *licuado*. Don't miss the experience.

•   See the MENU GUIDE in MEXICAN SPANISH.

Shopping

They are restrained visitors indeed who can leave this nirvana of shopping without at least doubling the weight of their luggage.

SHOPPING AND BUSINESS HOURS
Hours are not always as advertised, and are subject to long and irregular breaks. Shops are generally open Monday to Saturday between 10am or so and 7pm or later, closing for lunch for an hour or two in early afternoon only in smaller towns.

In commercial districts, shops often close on Saturday afternoon and Sunday, but in tourist centers, shopping hours are frequently extended into the evening and over Sunday. Large suburban shopping malls often close on Monday instead of Sunday.

BUYER BEWARE . . .
The most important rule is to watch out for inferior, shoddy goods; this applies to almost anything you might wish to buy. The other rule (except in department stores) is to **bargain**: a little simulated lack of interest, or a willingness to pay in cash, can work wonders.

Where there are no marked prices, and in all markets, aim for at least 25 percent off the asking price, and don't be surprised if the price drops even further.

As a sadly general rule, the more English a trader speaks, the higher, inevitably, are his prices.

WHAT TO LOOK FOR
Folk arts and crafts
Regional specialties from all over Mexico are often available in major

tourist centers, with no price increase from the place of origin; the state-run **FONART** shops provide a good starting-point. It is illegal to export genuine Pre-Columbian items, and even some colonial artifacts.

Old traditions live on in hand-woven **textiles**, often using Pre-Columbian patterns and techniques. Beware of garish imitations, in the N especially, although SALTILLO is known for *serapes* (ponchos), rugs and *rebozos* (shawls). Traditions are stronger w of the capital around CHAPALA, MORELIA and PATZCUARO. The states of Chiapas and Oaxaca in the SE produce fine weaving and embroidery; the heavily decorated *huipils* (blouses) are particularly eye-catching.

As a general rule, do not wear native costume in the areas of origin, both out of respect, and to avoid being made fun of.

The native gifts for proportion and decoration also live on in **ceramics**. Best-known are the towns of Metepec (see TOLUCA), PUEBLA and Tlaquepaque (see GUADALAJARA). In Metepec are produced the brightly colored "Trees of Life" that adorn homes all over Mexico. Tableware can chip easily with heavy use, an exception being the striking black pottery (which is slightly radioactive) from the villages near OAXACA.

Other good purchases are **leather goods**, from all over Mexico; **hammocks** from the Yucatán and Oaxaca; **native paintings** on **tree bark** *(amate)* from the state of Mexico; **lacquerware** from URUAPÁN and guitars from nearby Paracho; semiprecious stones from SAN JUAN DEL RÍO and La Magdalena (see GUADALAJARA); and copper from Santa Clara del Cobre (see PATZCUARO).

Silver and jewelry

The main center for the production of silver jewelry in Mexico is the pretty colonial town of TAXCO, in the mountains of Guerrero. It is a good idea to check the hallmark (it should read **925**) and the strength of any moving parts, such as hinges. Silver is also sold in Mexico City and other major tourist centers; the **Tane** chain of shops is known for its exquisite designs and high prices, and branches can be found in some luxury hotels and in MEXICO CITY's Zona Rosa.

In the state of Oaxaca, look out for interesting **gold jewelry**, based on the Pre-Columbian treasures found in the tombs of MONTE ALBÁN.

Watches

Convincing-looking imitations of expensive watches, complete with prestige brand names, are sold at bargain prices in every street market under no pretense of being genuine. They may even fool your friends, until they pick them up and find they are made of aluminum rather than stainless steel. Other, less prestigious, but genuine brand-named watches are also sold at about half the US or European price.

Casual clothing

Big resorts have a plethora of boutiques offering casual but elegant clothing, often of famous multinational sports brands; prices are generally competitive with those in Europe or the US. If you are after a more Mexican look, the embroidered patterns on women's clothing are mostly based on original native costumes. *Guayabera* pleated shirts, originating from the Yucatán Peninsula, are a must for men. Acceptable as semiformal wear throughout Mexico, they are cool and comfortable.

In Mexico City, fashions are sophisticated and cosmopolitan, and prices are relatively low. However, the quality of the goods is not always of the highest: watch out for poor stitching, and for non-color-fast dyes in the brighter hues.

The same is true of shoes, which initially seem an excellent bargain but can cause disappointment. For both clothes and shoes, however, you can rely on the well-known international brands, which maintain high standards.

Nightlife

After an exhausting day of traveling and sightseeing, many visitors to Mexico are entirely content with a quiet evening in a restaurant, a meal washed down with a couple of beers and perhaps accompanied by some music, and followed by an early night and well-deserved sleep. But the more nocturnally ambitious will find, at least in the resorts and big cities, that plenty of more exciting options are available.

Much of the nightlife, especially for tourists, revolves around the big luxury hotels. These often have nightclubs, discotheques, sophisticated lobby bars with live musicians, and a selection of restaurants; there may also be regular "Mexican fiesta" nights. In the larger resorts, some such entertainment will be on offer every night.

But while this hotel-based nightlife may be fun for a few evenings, it is hardly the authentic Mexican experience. Fortunately, there are alternatives. At all the big resorts, for example, there are numerous independent beachside discos (which come and go with alarming rapidity) and dimly-lit clubs full of shady characters wearing sun-glasses, not to mention all the usual bars and restaurants.

Some restaurants double as entertainment spots; members of the **Carlos'n'Charlie's** chain tend to be particularly exuberant.

ACAPULCO is almost synonymous with nightlife; some visitors never see the resort in daylight. However, most resorts keep more modest hours, winding up the action at 2–3am. To keep up to date with what is happening and where to go, find one of the free English information sheets, available in all the big resorts, detailing the various events and entertainments on offer.

There are also rather more authentically Mexican bars, known as *cantinas*. However, some of these can be a little rough, and may leave tourists feeling less than entirely welcome; you'll have a better time if you speak some Spanish. *Cantinas* that do not admit women are likely to be the sort of macho, heavy-drinking places that are best avoided anyway.

Perhaps the most Mexican evening of the lot is to be spent getting blasted by *mariachis* in MEXICO CITY's **Plaza Garibaldi**, or in GUADALAJARA's original **Plaza Mariachi**. Remember that the music will get progressively louder, and the trumpets perilously closer to your ears, until you pay the *mariachis,* at which point they will redirect their attentions to their next victim.

Sports and activities

CAMPING

At all major resorts, there are organized campgrounds and trailer parks with reasonable facilities. Because of the risk of small-time banditry, avoid camping in isolated places. Camping is legal on most out-of-town beaches, on common land and in national parks.

The best specialist guide, the *Rand McNally Campground and Trailer Park Guide*, has a section on Mexico. The **American Automobile Association** (**AAA**) issues a list of campgrounds.

FISHING

Good **deep-sea fishing** is available at all the major resorts and ports; hotels will arrange permits and the charter of boats. Better bargains (but less reliable boats) are to be found by asking around waterfront bars. Check safety equipment before taking a charter. The **Mexican Department of Fisheries** has an office at 1010 2nd Ave. #1605, San Diego, CA 92101 (☎ *(619) 233 6956)*, for information on fishing and boating fees, licenses and regulations.

If fishing is the main purpose of your vacation, the best waters are in the **Sea of Cortés**, which acts as a kind of fish trap between the mainland and Baja California. The best resorts include MAZATLÁN, GUAYMAS, ENSENADA and CABO SAN LUCAS. The most commonly found large fish include tuna, shark and swordfish.

Inland fishing, in lakes, reservoirs and rivers, is also possible; but equipment rental is not always easy, so it is best to bring your own. In Central Mexico, anglers try their luck on the lakes at PATZCUARO, CHAPALA and VALLE DE BRAVO. In the N and NW, there are numerous large lakes formed by **irrigation dams** — for examples, see MATAMOROS, where the **Presa Vincente Guerrero** is famous, and LOS MOCHIS.

GOLF

Mexicans are taking to golf with a vengeance, which is both good and bad news for the visitor. Most of the inland courses are private, and visitors will only be admitted as the guests of a member, or if they have reciprocal membership arranged in advance through their home club.

On the other hand, new golf-courses are now being built at a fantastic rate at all the main resorts, many of them as part of integrated "mega-project" developments. Access provides no problem, as most such courses are hotel-owned and guests are given preference; clubs can be rented.

The best resort courses include those at the **Pierre Marqués** at ACAPULCO, the **Palma Real** at IXTAPA, the **El Palmar** at MANZANILLO and the **Avándaro** at VALLE DE BRAVO.

HORSEBACK RIDING

Most resort hotels have horses for hire, and guides. One good long trek is into the spectacular **Copper Canyon** in Chihuahua state (see page 235). Near Mexico City, good hotels for riding include **Hacienda San Miguel Regla** near PACHUCA (see page 95); the **Hotel Jurica** near

QUERÉTARO (see page 193); and the **Rancho el Atascadero** near SAN MIGUEL DE ALLENDE (see page 197).

HUNTING
Under military pressure, there has recently been a dramatic clamp-down on hunting in Mexico. Those caught hunting without licenses or breaking regulations face arrest by the military police, and mandatory jail sentences. There are also great difficulties involved with the import of guns, and illegally imported guns will invariably be confiscated, and their owners jailed.

The only practical option for determined hunters is to use the services of a specialist agency, which can arrange licenses, guns and registered guides. Remember that many wildlife species are becoming increasingly rare and endangered and enjoy protected status; those found killing them will be liable to arrest.

MOUNTAINEERING
In recent years, Mexicans have suddenly begun to take an interest in mountain climbing. The volcanoes near the capital make an interesting climb, the easiest being POPOCATÉPETL.

More dangerous and challenging is the 5,714m (18,746-foot) **Pico de Orizaba** (see page 119), Mexico's highest peak. Good maps do not exist, and expeditions without registered guides are foolhardy. Have good, modern survival equipment.

SAILING
Small yachts are widely available for charter at the major seaside resorts, and by the large inland lakes. The fast pace of coastal development is bringing a rash of new marinas, especially on the **Pacific Coast**, but there are still long stretches with no facilities, on which self-sufficiency will be required.

A boat will get you to many lovely and otherwise inaccessible parts: remote beaches, offshore islands and fishing villages. Be careful around the border areas; zealous officials may suppose you to be involved in drug-running.

SPECTATOR SPORTS
Baseball, **soccer**, **American football** and **horse-racing** are all popular; hotel desks and tourist offices have details. Less familiar are the *charreadas* (Mexican rodeos), *jai-alai* (a very fast ball-game, resembling squash, often accompanied by lively betting) and bullfighting.

SURFING
The best surfing waters in Mexico are down the **Pacific coast** of the mainland, and off BAJA CALIFORNIA. There are few rental facilities or shops, and the sport is prohibited on many easily accessible beaches, because of the dangers to other swimmers. **Sharks** are, of course, a hazard, so inquire locally about their favorite feeding grounds and meal times.

Areas with the best reputation for surfing are s of ACAPULCO, N of ENSENADA, N of MANZANILLO, N of MAZATLÁN, around PUERTO ESCONDIDO, and the W coast of BAJA CALIFORNIA, particularly the stretch N of CABO SAN LUCAS.

SWIMMING

Take local advice on swimming, as vigorous surf and currents, not to mention sewage pollution, may make swimming dangerous. Bear in mind too that most Mexican resort beaches are smart, fashion-conscious places, where nude swimming and sunbathing are distinctly frowned upon, not to mention illegal.

Fortunately for committed naturists, there are many places in Mexico where the practice is well established and semi-officially tolerated. These include the quieter stretches of the **Yucatán coast**, to the s of CANCÚN (see page 291–2); parts of the **Pacific coast**, notably **Playa Zipolite**, near PUERTO ESCONDIDO (see page 146); and much of BAJA CALIFORNIA (pages 240–56).

TENNIS

Tennis is now a popular sport in Mexico, and courts have sprung up all over the country. Almost all resort-type hotels have courts for the use of guests, with rackets and balls for rent; but serious players should take their own, as those provided by hotels are of variable quality.

Useful addresses

TOURIST INFORMATION

The **Secretariat of Tourism** *(Presidente Masaryk 172, Mexico City* ☎ *(5) 250 8555),* also known as SECTUR, offers a prompt and efficient desk and telephone service.

Telephone information can also be obtained from special **tourist numbers**. SECTUR operates a 24-hour toll-free service *(* ☎ *(5) 250 0123/8601/8419)* covering the entire country. INFOTUR has a telephone service *(* ☎ *(5) 525 9380– 7),* covering Mexico City, from 9am to 9pm.

American Express Travel Service *(main office in Mexico City: Reforma 234 at Havre, 06600 DF, Mexico City, map 14 D4* ☎ *(5) 207 7204/7049/6950* Ⓕ*(5) 207 3507)* is a valuable source of information for travelers in need of help or advice, with branches all over the country.

Details of tourist offices and American Express Travel Service branches in other major cities are given under individual destinations.

TOUR OPERATORS

There are numerous tour companies in Mexico, of which **American Express** *(Reforma 234, Mexico City, map 14 D4* ☎ *(5) 207 7204/7049/6950* Ⓕ*(5) 207 3507)* and **Grey Line Tours** *(Londres 166, Mexico City* ☎ *(5) 533 1665/1540)* are reliable. Tours can also be arranged through travel agencies and major hotels.

MAJOR PLACES OF WORSHIP

Details of services in English are given daily in *The News*.

EMBASSIES AND CONSULATES IN MEXICO CITY

Australia   Plaza Polanco Torre B (10th floor), Jaime Balmes 11, Colonia de los Morales, 11510 Mexico DF ☎(5) 395 9988 Ⓕ(5) 395 7870/7153
Belize   Thiers 152b, Colonia Anzures, 11590 Mexico DF ☎(5) 203 5642/5960, map 13D3
Canada   Schiller 529, 11560 Mexico DF ☎(5) 254 3288/33 Ⓕ(5) 724 7982, map 13C2
Guatemala   Esplanada 1025, Lomas de Chapultepec, 11000 Mexico DF ☎(5) 540 7520/520 9249
New Zealand   Homero 229, 8th floor, 11570 Mexico DF ☎(5) 250 5999, map 13C2
UK   Río Lerma 71, 06500 Mexico DF ☎(5) 207 2449/2569 Ⓕ(5) 207 7672, map 14C4; consular section at Rio Usumacinta 30, 06500 Mexico DF ☎(5) 207 2089, map 14C4
US   Reforma 305, 06500 Mexico DF ☎(5) 211 0042 Ⓕ(5) 511 9980, map 14C4

Emergency information

EMERGENCY SERVICES
- **Police** ☎06
- **Fire** ☎(5) 736 3700 (Mexico City)
- **Ambulance** ☎(5) 557 5758/59/60 (Mexico City Red Cross)
- **Tourist Assistance** ☎(5) 658 1111 (Mexico City; toll-free nationwide)
- **Green Angels** ☎(5) 250 0123 (national hotline)

HOSPITALS WITH EMERGENCY DEPARTMENTS
- **American British Cowdray**, Calle Sur and Observatorio, Colonia Las Americas, Mexico City ☎(5) 277 5000; emergencies ☎(5) 515 8359
- Elsewhere, ask at hotels, or see Yellow Pages under *Sanatorios.*

OTHER MEDICAL EMERGENCIES
Look in the telephone directory Yellow Pages for *Médicos* (doctors) or *Dentistas* (dentists). Hotel desks will help.

LATE-NIGHT PHARMACIES
These are rare. See Yellow Pages: *Farmacias – Servicio de 24 Horas.*

AUTOMOBILE ACCIDENTS
- **Do not** call the police, unless strictly necessary.
- **Do not stop** if you see an accident. Witnesses of accidents are sometimes jailed to prevent them from disappearing. If questioned by the police, deny any involvement.
- ☎ the number in your car rental agreement.
- **Do not admit any liability**, or incriminate yourself.
- Try to **persuade witnesses** to stay and give evidence.
- If the other driver is insured, **exchange details**.
- **Contact your insurance company** as soon as possible. There are no roadside phones on the open road; if in need of help, it is necessary to stop a passing driver.

CAR BREAKDOWNS
A 700-strong fleet of special repair trucks, known as the "**Green Angels**," patrols main roads and tourist routes. The service is free, except for mechanical parts. Pull off the road and raise the hood.

The Green Angels have a national 24-hour hotline (see above). Otherwise, call the number in your car rental agreement, or ask a passing driver to alert the nearest garage with towing service: see telephone directory Yellow Pages under *Automóviles – talleres de reparación.*

LOST PASSPORT
Your consulate will issue emergency documents.

LOST TRAVELERS CHECKS
Follow the instructions provided with your travelers checks, or contact the nearest office of the issuing company. Contact your consulate or **American Express** in emergencies.

LOST CHARGE/CREDIT CARD
These 24-hour emergency hotlines should be called immediately upon loss or theft of the following cards:
* **American Express**, ☎(5) 598 7500/8133, or you can either call the nearest branch office, or call collect, via international operator to any main Amex office worldwide
* **Diners Club** ☎(5) 580 0122
* **Visa** ☎(5) 559 0323, or call collect via international operator to any main office worldwide
* **MasterCard** ☎(5) 588 4422, or call the MasterCard International Service Center in the US, collect, via the international operator, at ☎(314) 275 6690

EMERGENCY PHRASES
Help!   *¡Ayúdame!*
There has been an accident.   *Ha sucedido un accidente.*
Where is the nearest telephone/hospital?   *¿Dónde está el teléfono/hospital el mas cercano?*
Call a doctor/ambulance!   *¡Llame a un médico/ambulancia!*
Call the police!   *¡Llame a la policía!*
Watch out!   *¡Cuidado!* or *¡Cuidate!* (informal)

A guide to Mexican Spanish

This glossary covers the basic language needs of the traveler: for pronunciation, essential vocabulary and simple conversation, finding accommodation, visiting the bank, shopping, and for eating out.

It takes longer to say things in Spanish, which has only about 20 percent of the words available in English. For example, "chaleco salvavidas debajo de su asiento" means "Life vest under your seat." When uncertain of the appropriate word, try English. Help comes in unexpected places. "Perpendicular" in English is exactly the same in Spanish.

PRONUNCIATION
Spanish is a phonetic language in which the spelling matches the pronunciation. One letter whose pronunciation is not obvious is the *h*, which is always silent. While *z* and, in certain circumstances, *c* are lisped in central Spain, this would be considered highly affected in Mexico, or anywhere else in Latin America.

Stress is on the next-to-last syllable in words ending in a vowel, *n* or *s*. Other words are stressed on the last syllable. Exceptions are indicated by a written accent indicating where the emphasis lies, e.g., inglés.

Gender
Gender is indicated below where appropriate. Adjectives are given in the masculine form, with the alternative ending used when it accompanies a feminine noun.

REFERENCE WORDS

Monday	lunes	Friday	viernes
Tuesday	martes	Saturday	sábado
Wednesday	miércoles	Sunday	domingo
Thursday	jueves		

January	enero	July	julio
February	febrero	August	agosto
March	marzo	September	septiembre
April	abril	October	octubre
May	mayo	November	noviembre
June	junio	December	diciembre

First	primero, -a	Third	tercero, -a
Second	segundo, -a	Fourth	cuarto, -a

... o'clock	las ... (la una)	Quarter to ...	... menos cuarto
Quarter-past ...	... y cuarto	Quarter to six	las seis menos cuarto
Half-past ...	... y media		

Mr	señor/Sr	Ladies	señoras, damas, mujeres
Mrs	señora/Sra		
Miss	señorita/ Srta	Gents	caballeros, señores, hombres

Red	rojo, -a	Blue	azul
Yellow	amarillo, -a	Black	negro, -a
Green	verde	White	blanco, -a

BASIC COMMUNICATION

Yes/no   *sí/no*
Please   *por favor*
Thank you (very much)
   (muchas) gracias
You're welcome   *de nada*
I'm very sorry   *lo siento mucho/perdón*
Excuse me   *perdone/perdóneme/con permiso/disculpe*
Hello   *hola, bueno* (answering telephone)
Now/just now/right now
   ahora/ahorita/ahorita mismo
Good morning/good day
   buenos días
Good afternoon   *buenas tardes*
Good night   *buenas noches*
Goodbye   *adiós*
Morning   *mañana* (f)
Afternoon   *tarde* (f)
Evening   *tarde* (early), *noche* (after dark), *madrugada* (early hours after midnight)
Night   *noche* (f)
Yesterday   *ayer*
Today   *hoy*
Tomorrow   *mañana*
Next week   *la semana próxima*
Last week   *la semana pasada*
. . . days ago   *hace . . . días*
Month   *mes* (m)
Year   *año* (m)
Here   *aquí*
There   *ahí, allí*
Over there   *allá*
Big   *gran(de)*
Small   *pequeño, -a*
Hot   *caliente*
Cold   *frío, -a*
Good   *buen(o), -a*
Bad   *mal(o), -a*
Beautiful   *bonito, -a/ hermoso, -a*
Beautiful   *bello, -a*
Well   *bien*
With   *con*
And   *y*
But   *pero*
Very   *mucho*
All   *todo(s), toda(s)*
Open   *abierto, -a*
Closed   *cerrado, -a*
Entrance   *entrada* (f)
Exit   *salida* (f)
Free (unoccupied or free of charge)   *libre*
Left   *izquierda*

Right   *derecha*
Straight ahead   *derecho*
Near   *cerca (de)*
Far   *lejos (de)*
Above   *encima*
Below   *abajo*
Front   *delante (de)*
Behind   *detrás (de)*
Early   *temprano, -a*
Late   *tarde*
Quickly   *rápido*
Pleased to meet you.   *Mucho gusto/ Encantado, -a.*
How are you?   *¿Cómo está (usted)?* (formal); *¿Qué tal?* (informal)
Very well, thank you.   *Muy bien, gracias.*
Do you speak English?   *¿Habla (usted) inglés?*
I don't understand.   *No entiendo.*
What did you say?   *¿Mande?/ ¿Como dice?*
Please explain.   *¿Puede usted explicarme, por favor?*
Please speak more slowly (slow down, please).   *Más despacio, por favor.*
My name is . . .   *Me llamo . . .*
I am American/English.   *Soy americano, -a/inglés, -esa*
Where is/are . . . ?   *¿Dónde está/ están . . . ?*
Is there . . . /Do you have?   *¿Hay . . . / Tiene usted?*
What?   *¿Qué?*
When   *¿Cuándo?*
To pay   *Pagar*
To charge   *Cobrar*
How much?   *¿Cuanto?*
Expensive   *caro, -a*
Cheap   *barato, -a*
That's too much/It costs too much.
   Es demasiado/Cuerta demasiada.
Too expensive   *Demasiado.*
I would like . . .   *quisiera . . . / querría . . .*
Where is the bathroom/WC?   *¿Dónde está el baño?*
Where is the telephone?   *¿Dónde está el teléfono?*
I don't know.   *No sé.*
Just a minute.   *Un momento/ momentito* or *Espera un rato (ratito).*
That's fine/OK.   *Está bien.*
What time is it?   *¿Qué hora es?*
I don't feel well.   *Me siento mal/no me encuentro bien.*

ACCOMMODATION

Arriving at the hotel

I have a reservation. My name is . . .   *Tengo una reservación. Me llamo . . .*
A quiet room with bath/shower . . .   *Un cuarto tranquilo con baño/ducha . . .*
 . . . overlooking the sea/park/street/back.   *. . . con vista al mar/al parque/*
a la calle/atrás.
Does the price include breakfast/service/tax?   *¿El precio incluye desayuno/*
servicio/impuestos?
This room is too large/small/cold/hot/noisy.   *Este cuarto es demasiado*
grande/pequeño/frío/caliente/ruidos.
That's too expensive. Have you anything cheaper?   *Eso es demasiado caro. ¿Tiene*
usted algo más barato?
Where can I park my car?   *¿Dónde puedo estacionar?*
Is it safe to leave the car on the street?   *¿Se puede dejar el coche en la calle?*
Do you have a room?   *¿Tiene usted un cuarto?*

Floor *piso* (m)	Lounge *salón* (m)
Dining room/restaurant	Manager *gerente/*
comedor/restaurante (m)	*director* (m)

What time is breakfast/dinner?   *¿A qué hora se sirve el desayuno/la cena?*
Is there a laundry service?   *¿Hay servicio de lavado?*
What time does the hotel close?   *¿A qué hora cierra el hotel?*
I'll be leaving tomorrow morning.   *Me voy mañana por la mañana.*
Please give me a call at . . .   *¿Puede usted despertarme a . . . por favor?*
Come in!   *¡Adelante!/¡Pase usted!*

SHOPPING

Where is the nearest . . . ?   *¿Dónde está . . . más cercano, -a?*
Where is there a good . . . ?   *¿Dónde hay un buen/una buena . . . ?*
Can you help me/show me some . . . ?   *¿Puede usted ayudarme/enseñarme . . . ?*
I'm just looking.   *Sólo estoy mirando.*
Do you accept charge/credit cards/travelers checks?   *¿Acepta usted tarjetas de*
crédito/cheques de viaje?
Can you deliver/ship to . . . ?   *¿Puede usted enviar a . . . ?*
I'll take it.   *Lo llevo.*
I'll leave it.   *Lo dejo.*
Can I have it tax-free for export?   *¿Puedo comprarlo libre de impuestos para*
exportación?
This is faulty. Can I have a replacement/refund?   *Este tiene una falta. ¿Puede*
cambiármelo/devolverme el dinero?
I don't want to spend more than . . .   *No quiero gastar más de . . .*
I'll give you . . . pesos for it.   *Le daré . . . pesos.*
Can I have a stamp for . . . ?   *Quiero un timbre para . . . ?*

Shops

Antique store *tienda de antigüedades* (f)	*ropa/moda* (f)
Art gallery *galería de arte* (f)	Department store *grandes*
Bakery *panadería* (f)	*almacenes* (m)
Bank *banco* (m)	Delicatessen *mantequería* (f)
Beauty parlor *salón de belleza* (m)	Fish store *pescadería* (f)
Bookstore *librería* (f)	Florist *florería* (f)
Butcher *carnicería* (f)	Greengrocer *tienda de verduras y*
Cake shop *pastelería* (f)	*frutas* (f)
Chemist/pharmacy *farmacia* (f)	Grocer *tienda de comestibles* (f)
Clothes/fashion store *tienda de*	*alimentación* (f)

Hairdresser   barbería (men's),
  peluquería (women's)
Jeweler   joyería (f)
Market   mercado (m)
Newsstand   quiosco de periódicos (m)
Optician   óptico (m)
Photographic store   tienda de
  fotografía (f)
Post office   oficina de correos (f)

Shoe store   zapatería (f)
Souvenir store   tienda de recuerdos (f)
Stationer   papelería (f)
Supermarket   supermercado (m)
Tobacconist   tabaquería (f)
Tourist office   oficina de turismo (f)
Toy store   juguetería (f)
Travel agency   agencia de
  viajes (f)

At the bank

I would like to change some dollars/pounds/travelers checks   Quisiera cambiar
  unos dólares/unas libras esterlinas/unos cheques de viajero.
What is the exchange rate?   ¿A cuánto está el (tipo de) cambio?
Can you cash a personal check?   ¿Puede usted cobrarme un cheque personal?
Can I obtain cash with this charge/credit card?   ¿Puedo sacar dinero con esta
  tarjeta de crédito.
Do you need to see my passport?   ¿Quiere usted ver mi pasaporte?

SOME USEFUL GOODS

From the pharmacy:

Adhesive bandage   esparadrapo (m)
Antiseptic   antiséptica (f)
Antiseptic cream   crema antiséptica (f)
Aspirin   aspirina (f)
Bandages   vendas (f)
Band-Aid   curitas (f)
Cotton   algodón (m)
Diarrhea/upset stomach pills   píldoras
  para diarrea/el estómago trastornado (f)
Indigestion tablets   pastillas para
  indigestión (f)
Insect repellant   repelente para
  insectos (m)
Razor blades   hojas de afeitar (f)

Sanitary napkins   compresas (f)
Shampoo   champú (m)
Shaving cream   crema de afeitar (f)
Soap   jabón (m)
Sunburn cream   crema para
  quemaduras del sol (f)
Sunglasses   gafas de sol (f)
Suntan cream/oil   crema (f)/aceite (m)
  bronceador, -a
Tampons   tampones (m)
Toothbrush   cepillo de dientes (m)
Toothpaste   oasta de dientes (f)
Travel sickness pills   píldoras para
  mareo (f)

Clothing

Bra   sostén (m)
Coat   abrigo (m)
Dress   vestido (m)
Jacket   chaqueta (f)
Pants (trousers)   pantalones (m)
Shirt   camisa (f)
Shoes   zapatos (m)
Skirt   falda (f)

Socks   calcetines (m)
Stockings/tights   medias (f)/
  leotardos (m)
Sweater   suéter (m)
Swimsuit   traje de
  baño (m)
Underpants for women   bragas (f),
  for men   calzoncillos (m)

Miscellaneous

Film   película (f)
Letter   carta (f)
Money order   giro postal (m)

Postcard   tarjeta postal (f)
Stamp   timbre (m)/estampilla (f)
Telegram   telegrama (f)

DRIVING

Gas/service station   estación de PEMEX (f)/gasolinera (f)
Fill it up, please.   Lleno (Llénelo), por favor.
Give me . . . pesos worth.   Déme . . . pesos por favor.
I'd like . . . liters of gas/petrol.   Quiero . . . litros de gasolina.
Can you check the . . . ?   ¿Puede usted mirar el/la . . . ?
There is something wrong with the . . .   Hay algo que no va bien en el/la . . .

Battery	*batería* (f)	Lights	*luces* (f)
Brakes	*frenos* (m)	Oil	*aceite* (m)
Engine	*motor* (m)	Radiator	*radiator* (f)
Exhaust	*tubo de*	Tires	*llantas* (f)
	escape (m)	Water	*agua* (f)
Fan belt	*correa* (f) *de ventilador*	Windshield	*parabrisas* (m)

My car won't start.   *Mi coche no arranca*
My car has broken down/had a flat tire.   *Se me descompuso el coche/una llanta ponchada.*
The engine is overheating.   *El motor se calienta.*
How long will it take to repair?   *¿Cuánto tardará en repararlo?*

Car rental
Where can I rent a car?   *¿Dónde puedo alquilar un coche?*
Is full insurance included?   *¿Está incluido un seguro a todo riesgo?*
Is it insured for another driver?   *¿Es asegurado para un otro conductor?*
Unlimited mileage   *kilometraje ilimitado*
Deposit   *un depósito* (m)
By what time must I return it?   *¿A qué hora tengo que devolverlo?*
Can I return it to another depot?   *¿Puedo devolverlo a otra agencia?*
Is the gas tank full?   *¿Está lleno el tanque de gasolina?*

Road signs

¡ Alto!   stop
Calle bloqueada   road blocked
Calle sin salida   no exit
Calzada deteriorada   bad road surface
Caseta de cobro   toll booth
Ceda el paso   yield/give way
Centro ciudad   town center
Cruce de ferrocarril   level crossing
Cuidado/con precaución   caution
Cuota   toll
Deslizamientos   slippery surface
Despacio   slow
Desviación   detour

Dirección única   one way
Estacionamiento permitido   parking permitted
Obras   road works
Otras direcciones   other directions
Peaje   toll
Peligro   danger
Prohibido estacionar   no parking
Salida de emergencia   emergency exit
Senso único   one way
Todas direcciones   all directions

Other methods of transport

Aircraft	*avión* (m)	
Airport	*aeropuerto* (m)	
Bus	*autobús, camión* (m)	
Bus stop	*parada de autobús* (f)	
Ferry/boat	*transbordador, embarcadero, ferry, barco* (m)	
Port	*puerto* (m)	
Rail station	*estación ferrocarril* (f)	
Train	*tren* (m)	
Ticket	*boleto* (m)	

Ticket office   *taquilla* (f)
One-way/single   *de ida*
Round trip/return   *de ida y vuelta*
Is there a reduction for children, students?   *¿Hay discuerto para (niños, estudiates)?*
First/second class   *primera/segunda clase*
Sleeper/couchette   *coche-cama, carro dormitorio* (m)

When is the next . . . for . . . ?   *¿A qué hora sale el próximo . . . para . . . ?*
What time does it arrive?   *¿A qué hora llega?*
What time does the last . . . for . . . leave?   *¿A qué hora sale el último . . . para . . . ?*
Which platform/quay/gate?   *¿Qué andén/muelle/puerta?*
Is this the . . . for . . . ?   *¿Es éste el . . . para . . . ?*
Is it direct? Where does it stop?   *¿Es directo? ¿Dónde para?*
Do I need to change anywhere?   *¿Tengo que hacer transbordo?*
Please tell me where to get off.   *¿Me diría usted cuándo tengo que bajar?*
Is there a buffet car?   *¿Hay un coche-comedor?*

Food and drink

Have you a table for . . . ? ¿Tiene usted una mesa para . . . ?
I want to reserve a table for . . . at . . . Quisiera reservar una mesa para . . .
  personas a las . . . .
A quiet table. Una mesa tranquila.
A table near the window. Una mesa cerca de la ventana.
Could we have another table? ¿Nos puede dar otra mesa?
The menu, please. El menú, por favor.
I'll have . . . Tomaré . . .
Can I see the wine list? ¿Puedo ver la lista de vinos?
I would like . . . Quisiera . . .
What do you recommend? ¿Qué recomienda usted?
I did not order this. No he pedido esto.
Lunch/dinner comida/cena (f)
Bring me another. Otro/a, por favor.
The check/bill, please. La cuenta, por favor.
Is service included? ¿Está incluído el servicio?

Some essential words

Breakfast desayuno (m)
Lunch almuerzo (m)
Dinner cena (f)
Restaurant restaurante (m)
Hot caliente
Cold frío, -a
Glass vaso (m)/copa (f)
Bottle botella (f)
Half-bottle media botella (f)
Orangeade/lemonade
  naranjada/limonada (f)
Water agua (f)
Ice hielo
Iced . . . fría/ . . . con hielo
Mineral water agua mineral/
  Tehuacán (m)
Carbonated con gas
Noncarbonated sin gas
Beer/lager cerveza (f)
Draft beer cerveza de barril
Orange/apple/grapefruit juice
  jugo de naranja/manzana/
  toronja (m)
Carafe jarra (f)
Red wine vino tinto (m)
White wine vino blanco (m)
Rosé wine vino rosado
Dry seco

Sweet dulce (m)
Salt sal (f)
Pepper pimienta (f)
Mustard mostaza (f)
Oil aceite (m)
Vinegar vinagre (m)
Bread pan (m)
Butter mantequilla (f)
Cheese queso (m)
Egg huevo (m)
Milk leche (f)
Coffee café (m)
  white con crema/leche
  (without) sugar (sin) azúcar
(Brewed) decaffinated coffee
  café descafinado en máquina
Ice cream helado (m)
Chocolate chocolate (m)
Honey miel (m)
Sugar azúcar (m)
Tea té negro (m)
Camomile tea té de manzanillo (m)
Mint tea té de yerba buena (m)
Steak filet (m)
well done muy hecho/bien cocido
  medium regular
  (very) rare (muy) poco hecho/poco
  cocido

MENU GUIDE

Cover charge cubierto
Bread pan
Appetizers entremeses
Soups sopas
Pasta pastas
Fish pescados
Seafood mariscos

Vegetables verduras
Minced meat carne
  picada
Salads ensaladas
Cheeses quesos
Fruit frutas
Sweets postres

White/red/rosé wines
 vinos blanco/tinto/rosado
Beers   *cervezas*
Aceite (de oliva)   olive oil
Aceitunas   olives
(en) Adobo, adobado   marinated,
 pickled
Aguacate   avocado
Agua de fruta   fresh fruit drink
Ahumado, -a   smoked
Ajillo, ajo   garlic
Albaricoques   apricots
Albóndigas   spiced meatballs
Al(l)ioli   garlic mayonnaise
Almejas   clams
Almendras   almonds
(en) Almibar   (in) syrup
Anchoas   anchovies
Anguila   eel
Angulas   baby eels
Arenque   herring
Arrachera   tripe
Arroz   rice
Asado   grilled/broiled
Atole   corn-meal gruel
Atún   tuna
Aves   poultry
Azafrán   saffron
Barbacoa   Mexican barbecued meat
Berenjena   aubergine, eggplant
Berros   watercress
Besugo   sea bream
Biftec, bistec   steak, beefsteak
Birria   mutton stew
Bocadillos   sandwiches
Bonito   bonito (striped tuna)
Boquerones   a kind of anchovy
Buey   beef, ox
Buñuelitos, buñuelos   fritters with a
 wide variety of fillings
Butifarra   seasoned pork sausage
Caballa   mackerel
Cabeza   head
Cabrito   kid
Cacerola   casserole
Calabaza   squash, pumpkin
Calamares (en su tinta)   squid (in their
 own ink)
Caldeirada   poached fish in garlic and
 paprika sauce/fish and seafood stew
Caldereta   lamb or fish stew
Caldo   broth or soup-stew of meat and
 vegetables
Callos   tripe
Camarones   shrimps
Camotes   sweet potatoes
Cangrejo   crab, crayfish
Caracoles   snails

Carne (de res)   meat (beef)
(a la) Brasa   charcoal broiled
Braseado, -a   braised
(en) Brochetas   skewered
Carnero   mutton
Carnitas   cubes of roast meat
(de la) Casa   of the restaurant
Caza   game
Cazador   hunter's style
Cazuela, cazuelita   casserole
Cebolla   onion
Cecina   salty dried meat
Centolla   (large) crab
Cerdo   pork
Cerezas   cherries
Cerveza   beer
Ceviche   fish marinated in lime
 juice
Chabacano   apricot
Chamorro   knuckle
Champiñones   mushrooms
Chicharrón   pork crackling
Chicharros   peas
Chilaquiles   tortilla strips in sauce
Chile   chili, red pepper
Chilindrón   thick tomato sauce made
 with ham and red peppers
Chipirones   small squid
Chipotle   a type of spicy pepper
Chongos   sticky milk pudding
Chorizo   spiced pork sausage
Chuleta   chop, usually veal
Chuletón   large beef or veal rib
 steak
Cigalas   crayfish
Cilantro   coriander
Ciruela   plum/prune
Cochinillo   suckling pig
Cochinita   suckling pig meat
Cocido, -a   cooked, boiled
Col   cabbage
Cola   tail
Coliflor   cauliflower
Conejo   rabbit
Cordero   lamb
Coquinas   small clams
Corazón   heart
Corb(v)ina   sea bass or perch
Costilla   rib
Crema   cream
Crepa   crepe
Criadillas   bull's testicles ("prairie
 oysters")
Crudo, -a   raw
Cuajada de leche   similar to yogurt
Dulces   sweets, desserts
Durazno   peach
Duro   hard (-boiled)

Ejote   stringbean
Empanada   meat, fish or seafood pie
Empanado, -a   fried in breadcrumbs
Enchilada   filled tortilla roll in sauce
Ensalada   salad
Entremeses   hors d'oeuvres
(en) Escabeche, escabechado   pickled, marinated
Escalfado   poached
Escarola   endive
Escudella catalana   thick soup with meats and vegetables
Espárragos   asparagus
Espinacas   spinach
Estofado   stew (ed)
Faisán   pheasant
Fiambres   cold cuts
Fideos   pasta, noodles
Filete   fillet, usually steak
Flameado   flambé
Flan   caramel dessert
Flor de calabaza   squash (pumpkin) flowers
Frambuesas   raspberries
Fresas, fresones   strawberries
Fresco, -a   fresh, cold
Frijoles   beans
Frío, -a   cold
Frito, -a   fried
Fritura   fried dish/fritter
Fruta   fruit
Galletas   biscuits
Gallina   fowl
Gallo   cockerel
Gambas   large prawns
Ganzo   goose
Garbanzos   chickpeas
Gazpacho   chilled vegetable soup
Gorditas   mini tortilla snack
Granada   pomegranate
Gratinado, -a   browned, with cheese or breadcrumbs
Guacamole   avocado purée (usually with chili)
Guajolote   turkey
Guanabana   apple-like tropical fruit
Guayaba   guava
Guisado   stew/stewed
Guisantes   peas
Habas   broad beans
Hamburguesa   hamburger
Helado   ice cream
Hervido, -a   boiled, poached
Hígado   liver
Higos   figs
Hinojo   fennel
Hongos   mushrooms

(al) Horno   baked
Huachinango   red snapper
Huevas   fish roe
Huevos   eggs
   cocidos   boiled
   al plato   fried or baked
   a la mexicana   scrambled with chili
   rancheros   in red sauce on a tortilla
   revueltos   scrambled
Huitlacoche   corn fungus
Jabalí   wild boar
Jaiba   crab
Jamón   ham
Jicame   sweet parsnip
Jitomate   tomato
Judías   beans
(en su) Jugo   (in its own) juice
Jugo   juice
Lacón   pork shoulder
Langosta   spiny lobster
Langostino   large prawn
Lechazo   young lamb
Lechón   suckling pig
Lechuga   lettuce
Lengua   tongue
Lenguado   sole
Lentejas   lentils
Licuado (de plátano, papaya)   liquidized fruit drink (with banana, papaya)
Liebre   hare
Limón   lemon
Lombarda   red cabbage
Lomo, Lomita   loin (prime cut)
Longaniza   spicy sausage
Lubina   sea bass
Macedonia   fruit salad
Machacas   dried donkey meat
Maiz   corn, maize
Mamey   sweet tropical fruit
Mango   mango
Manitas de puerco   pork trotters
Mantequilla   butter
Manzana   apple
Mariscada   mixed grill of seafoods
Mariscos   shellfish
Mejillones   mussels
Melocotón   peach
Melón   melon
Membrillo   quince, quince jelly
Menestra de legumbres/verduras   mixed sautéed vegetables flavoured with ham
Merengue   meringue
Merluza   cod
Migas   fried bread croutons
Mojarra   perch
Mole   spicy chocolate sauce

Moluscos   mussels
Naranja   orange
Nécoras   small crabs
Nieve   water ice
(en) Nogada   walnut sauce
Nopal(ito)   cactus fruit
Nueces   nuts, walnuts
Ostiones/ostras   oysters
Paella   saffron rice dish with meat, fish
  or seafood
País (del)   Mexican/local
Pan dulce   sweet rolls
Papas   potatoes
Papaya   papaya (paw-paw)
(a la) Parrilla   grilled, broiled
Parrillada (de mariscos, de pescados)
  grilled or broiled seafoods or fish
Pastel   pâté/pie, pastry, cake
Patatas   potatoes
Pato   duck
Pavo   turkey
Pechuga   breast (usually chicken)
Pepinos   cucumber
Perca   perch
Pescadilla   small fish (like whitebait)
Pescado   fish
Pez espada   swordfish
Pibil   spicy roast
Picante   hot (spicy)
Pierna   leg
Pimientos   sweet peppers
Piña   pineapple
Pinchitos   kebab
Pipián   spicy stew
Plancha   grilled
Plátano   banana
Plátano macho   plantain
Platija   plaice
Pollo   chicken
Potaje   soup
Pozole   meat and hominy soup
Pulpo   octopus
Pulque   cactus beer
Quesadilla   tortilla snack
Queso   cheese
Rábanos   radishes
Rabo de toro/buev   oxtail
Rape   anglerfish, monkfish
Rebozado, -a   fried in batter or
  breadcrumbs
Refresco   soft drink
Refritos   re-fried beans
Relleno -a   stuffed
Repollo   cabbage
Res   beef
Riñones   kidneys
Róbalo   sea-perch, sea-bass
(a la) Romana   deep-fried

Salado, -a   salted
(en) Salazón   cured
Salchicha   sausage
Salchichón   salami
Salmonete   red mullet
Salsa   sauce
  borracha   Pulque sauce
  mexicana   chili sauce
  roja/verde/cruda   red/green/raw
  veracruzana   a spicy red sauce
Salteado, -a   Sautéed
Sandía   watermelon
Sangrita   drink of tomato juice, chili
  and orange
Sardinas   sardines
Setas   wild mushrooms
Sincronizadas   ham, cheese and tortilla
  snack
Solomillo   tenderloin
Sopa   soup
  de Mariscos   seafood soup
  de Arroz   spicy boiled rice (not soup)
Sope   mini-tortilla with beans, chicken
  and cheese
Surtido   assortment
Taco   a tortilla snack
Tamale   meat-filled roll of maize dough,
  steamed
Tarta   savory tart or pie
Tartaleta   savory or sweet tart
Tehuacán   soda water
Ternasco   baby lamb
Tiburón   shark
Tocino   bacon
Toro (de lidia)   beef (from the bullring)
Toronja   grapefruit
Torta   sandwich
Tortilla   corn crepe
Tortillas de trigo   wheat crepe
Tortilla española   potato omelet
Tortuga   turtle (avoid!)
Tostado, -a (adj)   toasted
Tostada (noun)   a tortilla snack
Tronco   slice
Tripa   tripe
Trucha   trout
Trufas   truffles
Tuna   cactus fruit
Uvas   grapes
(al) Vapor   steamed
Venado   venison
Venera   scallops
Verduras   vegetables
Vieiras   scallops
Vino blanco/tinto/rosado
  white/red/rosé wine
Zanahorias   carrots
Zapote   sweet tropical fruit

Index

- **Bold** page numbers indicate main entries.
- *Italic* page numbers indicate illustrations and maps.
- Map references refer to the maps at the end of the book.
- See also the LIST OF STREET NAMES IN MEXICO CITY on page 361.

INDEX OF PLACES

GENERAL INDEX

List of street names in Mexico City

- All streets mentioned in the MEXICO CITY section of this book (pages 51-86) that fall within the area covered by our Mexico City maps **13** to **15** are listed below.
- Map numbers are printed in **bold** type. Some smaller streets are not named on the maps, but the map reference given below will help you locate the correct neighborhood.

CONVERSION FORMULAE

To convert	Multiply by
Inches to Centimeters	2.540
Centimeters to Inches	0.39370
Feet to Meters	0.3048
Meters to feet	3.2808
Yards to Meters	0.9144
Meters to Yards	1.09361
Miles to Kilometers	1.60934
Kilometers to Miles	0.621371
Sq Meters to Sq Feet	10.7638
Sq Feet to Sq Meters	0.092903
Sq Yards to Sq Meters	0.83612
Sq Meters to Sq Yards	1.19599
Sq Miles to Sq Kilometers	2.5899
Sq Kilometers to Sq Miles	0.386103
Acres to Hectares	0.40468
Hectares to Acres	2.47105
Gallons to Liters	4.545
Liters to Gallons	0.22
Ounces to Grams	28.3495
Grams to Ounces	0.03528
Pounds to Grams	453.592
Grams to Pounds	0.00220
Pounds to Kilograms	0.4536
Kilograms to Pounds	2.2046
Tons (UK) to Kilograms	1016.05
Kilograms to Tons (UK)	0.0009842
Tons (US) to Kilograms	746.483
Kilograms to Tons (US)	0.0013396

Quick conversions

Kilometers to Miles	Divide by 8, multiply by 5
Miles to Kilometers	Divide by 5, multiply by 8
1 meter =	Approximately 3 feet 3 inches
2 centimeters =	Approximately 1 inch
1 pound (weight) =	475 grams (nearly $\frac{1}{2}$ kilogram)
Celsius to Fahrenheit	Divide by 5, multiply by 9, add 32
Fahrenheit to Celsius	Subtract 32, divide by 9, multiply by 5

KEY TO MAP PAGES

1-8 MEXICO
9-12 CENTRAL MEXICO
13-15 CENTRAL MEXICO CITY

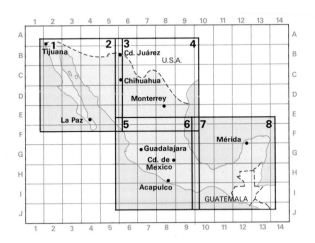

KEY TO MAP SYMBOLS

Area Maps

===== Highway
▬▬▬ Main Through Route
───── Other Main Road
───── Secondary Road
‒ ‒ ‒ Minor Road, Track
(40) Mexican Road No.
(10) US Road No.
══ Railway
‒ ‒ ‒ Ferry
✈ Airport
✦ Airfield
‒ . ‒ International Boundary
∴ Ancient Site, Ruin
⋔ Monastery, Church
☒ Good Beach
• 3703 Height in Meters

City Maps

▨ Major Place of Interest
▢ Other Important Building
▢ Built-up Area
† † Cemetery
▨ Park
✚ Hospital
i Information Office
✉ Post Office
† Church
Ⓜ Metro Station
15 Adjoining Page No.

0   100   200km
├─────────┴─────────┤
0   50   100 miles

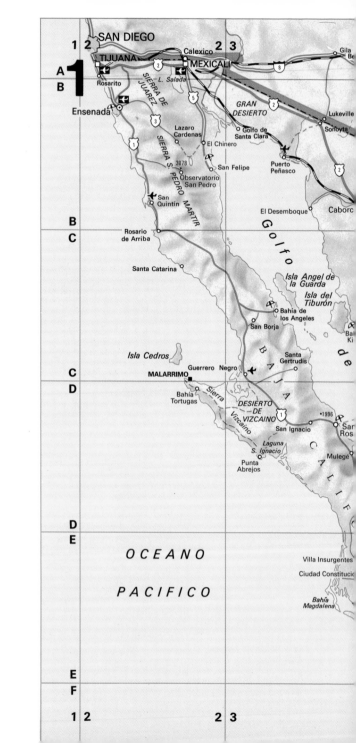

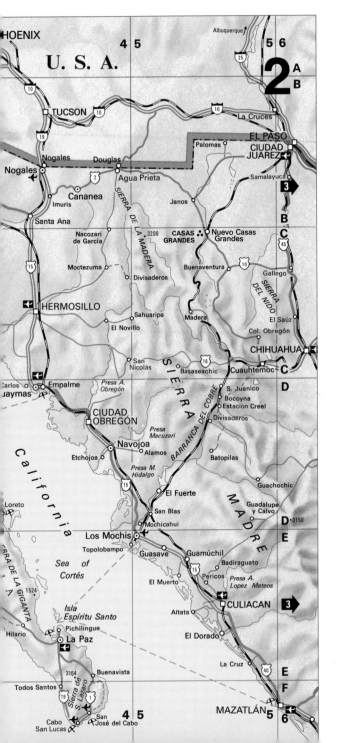

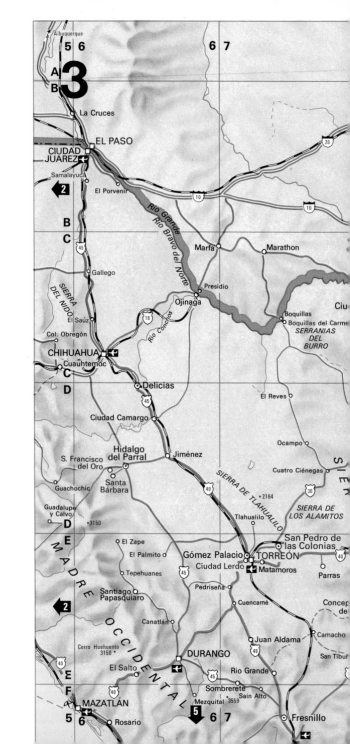

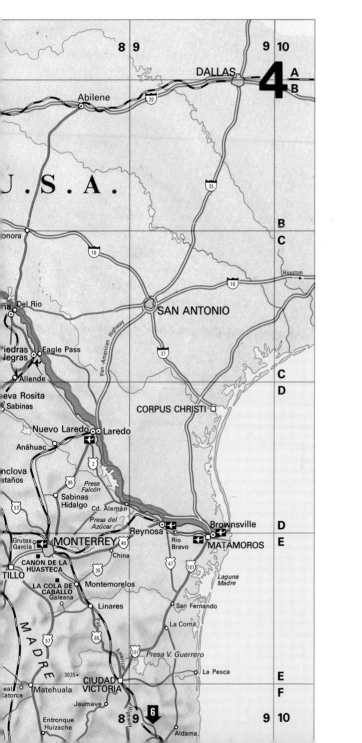

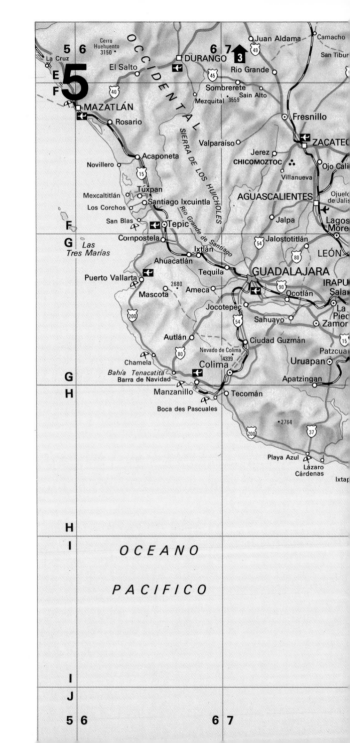

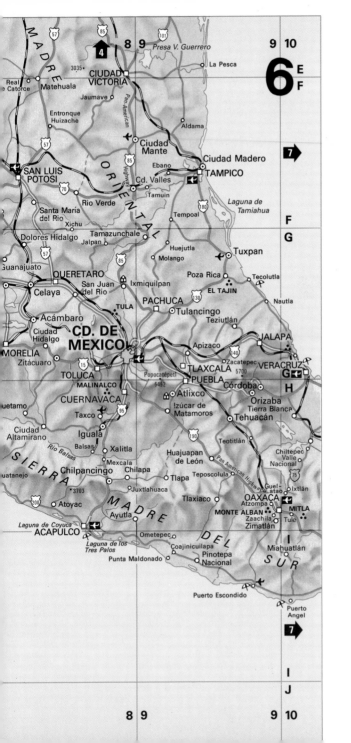

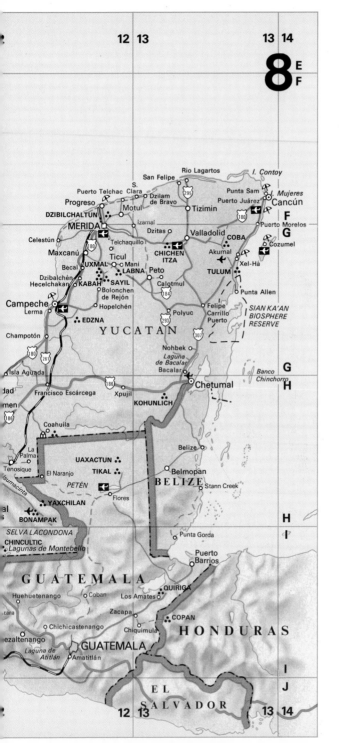

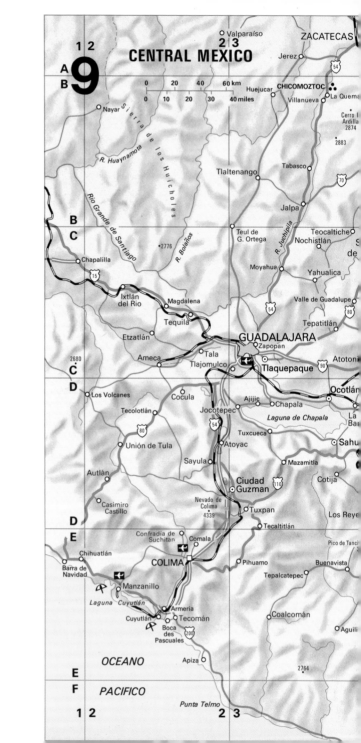

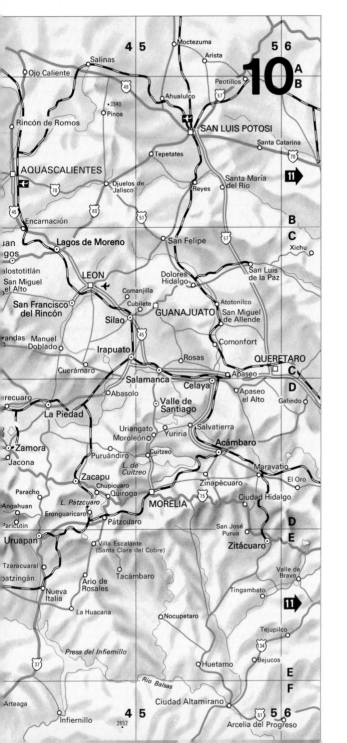

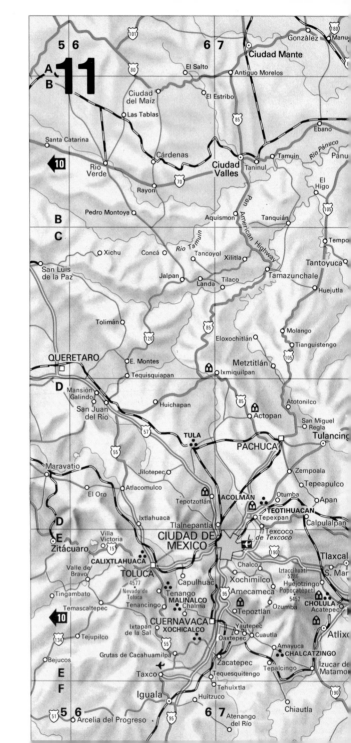

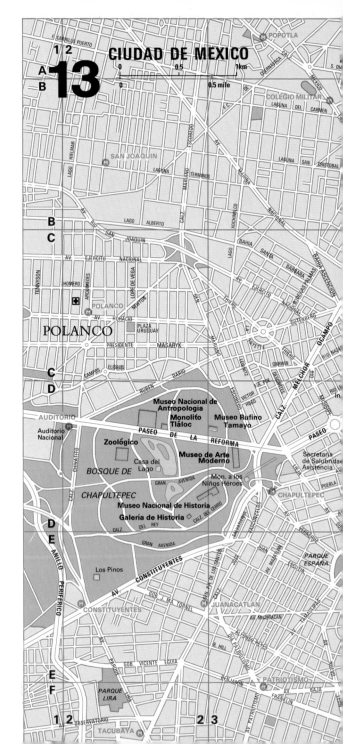

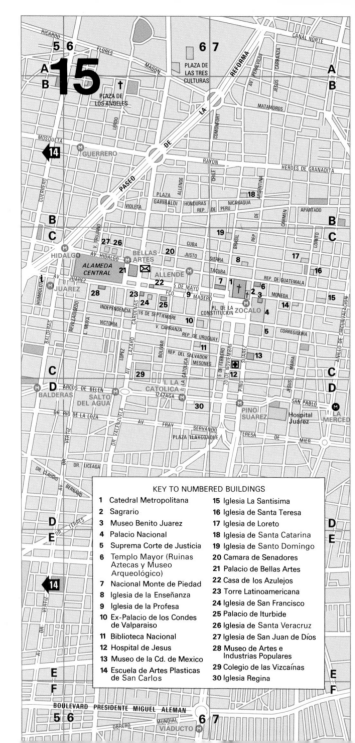

KEY TO NUMBERED BUILDINGS

1 Catedral Metropolitana
2 Sagrario
3 Museo Benito Juarez
4 Palacio Nacional
5 Suprema Corte de Justicia
6 Templo Mayor (Ruinas Aztecas y Museo Arqueológico)
7 Nacional Monte de Piedad
8 Iglesia de la Enseñanza
9 Iglesia de la Profesa
10 Ex-Palacio de los Condes de Valparaiso
11 Biblioteca Nacional
12 Hospital de Jesus
13 Museo de la Cd. de Mexico
14 Escuela de Artes Plasticas de San Carlos

15 Iglesia La Santisima
16 Iglesia de Santa Teresa
17 Iglesia de Loreto
18 Iglesia de Santa Catarina
19 Iglesia de Santo Domingo
20 Camara de Senadores
21 Palacio de Bellas Artes
22 Casa de los Azulejos
23 Torre Latinoamericana
24 Iglesia de San Francisco
25 Palacio de Iturbide
26 Iglesia de Santa Veracruz
27 Iglesia de San Juan de Díos
28 Museo de Artes e Industrias Populares
29 Colegio de las Vizcaínas
30 Iglesia Regina

What readers from all over the world say:

• "We could never have had the wonderful time that we did without your guide to *Paris*. The compactness was very convenient, your maps were all we needed, but it was your restaurant guide that truly made our stay special . . . . We have learned first-hand: *American Express — don't leave home without it.*" (A. R., Virginia Beach, Va., USA)

• Of Sheila Hale's *Florence and Tuscany:* "I hope you don't mind my calling you by your first name, but during our recent trip to Florence and Siena [we] said on innumerable occasions, 'What does Sheila say about that?' " (H.G., Buckhurst Hill, Essex, England)

• "I have visited Mexico most years since 1979 . . . Of the many guides I have consulted during this time, by far the best has been James Tickell's *Mexico,* of which I've bought each edition." (J.H., Mexico City)

• "We have heartily recommended these books to all our friends who have plans to travel abroad." (A.S. and J.C., New York, USA)

• "Much of our enjoyment came from the way your book *(Venice)* sent us off scurrying around the interesting streets and off to the right places at the right times". (Lord H., London, England)

• "It *(Paris)* was my constant companion and totally dependable . . . . " (V. N., Johannesburg, South Africa)

• "We found *Amsterdam, Rotterdam & The Hague* invaluable . . . probably the best of its kind we have ever used. It transformed our stay from an ordinary one into something really memorable . . . . " (S.W., Canterbury, England)

• "Despite many previous visits to Italy, I wish I had had your guide *(Florence and Tuscany)* ages ago. I love the author's crisp, literate writing and her devotion to her subject." (M. B-K., Denver, Colorado, USA)

• "We became almost a club as we found people sitting at tables all around, consulting their little blue books!" (F.C., Glasgow, Scotland)

• "I have just concluded a tour . . . using your comprehensive *Cities of Australia* as my personal guide. Thank you for your magnificent, clear and precise book." (Dr. S.G., Singapore)

• "We never made a restaurant reservation without checking your book *(Venice)*. The recommendations were excellent, and the historical and artistic text got us through the sights beautifully." (L.S., Boston, Ma., USA)

• "The book *(Hong Kong, Singapore & Bangkok)* was written in such a personal way that I feel as if you were actually writing this book for me." (L.Z., Orange, Conn., USA)

• "I feel as if you have been a silent friend shadowing my time in Tuscany." (T.G., Washington, DC, USA)

MEXICO CITY metro & light rail lines

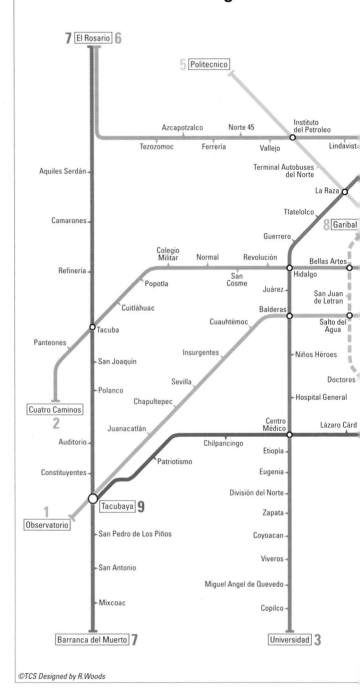

©TCS Designed by R.Woods

Metro Lines

- Line 1
- Line 2
- Line 3
- Line 4
- Line 5
- Line 6
- Line 7
- Line 8 under construction
- Line 9

Light Rail Lines

- Line A
- TL Tren Ligero

ndios Verdes **3**

6 Martin Carrera **4**

La Villa

Basílica

otrero

Talismán

Bondojito

Misterios

Valle Gómez

Rio Consulado

Eduardo Molina

Allende

Canal del Norte

Aragón

Zócalo

Morelos

Oceanía

sabel atólica

Pino Suárez

Merced

Candelaria

San Lázaro

Terminal Aérea ✈

San Antonio Abad

Moctezuma

Balbuena

Hangares

Aeropuerto

Obrera

Fray Servando

Gómez Farías

1 5 9 A

Chabacano

Jamaica

Velódromo

Zaragoza

Pantitlán

A. Oriental

iaducto

La Viga

Mixihuca

Puebla

San Juan
Tepalcates

Xola

Villa de Cortés

4 Santa Anita

Coyuya

Ciudad
Deportiva

Guelatao

Penon Viejo

ativitas

Portales

Iztacalco

Acatitla

to La Paz

Ermita

Apatlaco

General
Anaya

2 TL

Aculco

Escuadron 201

Tasqueña

Atlatilco

Iztapalapa

to Constitucion de 1917

⭕	Interchange station
7 El Rosario **6**	Terminating station & line number
✈	Station for Benito Juarez International Airport

to Xochimilco

Map authorised user number D/CAS/WW/AM/1013 V3593

What the papers say:

• "The expertly edited American Express series has the knack of pin-pointing precisely the details you need to know, and doing it concisely and intelligently." (***The Washington Post***)

• "*(Venice)* . . . the best guide book I have ever used." (***The Standard* — London**)

• "Amid the welter of guides to individual countries, American Express stands out . . . . " (***Time***)

• "Possibly the best . . . guides on the market, they come close to the oft-claimed 'all you need to know' comprehensiveness, with much original experience, research and opinions." (***Sunday Telegraph* — London**)

• "The most useful general guide was *American Express New York* by Herbert Bailey Livesey. It also has the best street and subway maps." (***Daily Telegraph* — London**)

• " . . . in the flood of travel guides, the *American Express* guides come closest to the needs of traveling managers with little time." (***Die Zeit* — Germany**)

What the experts say:

• "We only used one guide book, Sheila Hale's *AmEx Venice,* for which she and the editors deserve a Nobel Prize." (**travel writer Eric Newby, London**)

• "Congratulations to you and your staff for putting out the best guide book of *any* size *(Barcelona & Madrid).* I'm recommending it to everyone." (**travel writer Barnaby Conrad, Santa Barbara, California**)

• "If you're only buying one guide book, we recommend American Express . . . . " (***Which?* — Britain's leading consumer magazine**)

• "The judges selected *American Express London* as the best guide book of the past decade — it won the competition in 1983. [The guide] was praised for being 'concise, well presented, up-to-date, with unusual information.' " (**News release from the London Tourist Board and Convention Bureau**)

American Express Travel Guides

spanning the globe....

EUROPE

Amsterdam, Rotterdam
  & The Hague
Athens and the
  Classical Sites ‡
Barcelona, Madrid &
  Seville
Berlin, Potsdam &
  Dresden ‡
Brussels
Dublin
Florence and Tuscany
London
Moscow &
  St Petersburg ‡
Paris
Prague
Provence and the
  Côte d'Azur ‡
Rome
Venice ‡
Vienna & Budapest

NORTH AMERICA

Boston and New
  England ‡
Florida ‡
Los Angeles & San
  Diego
Mexico
New York
San Francisco and
  the Wine Regions
Toronto, Montréal &
  Québec City
Washington, DC

THE PACIFIC

Cities of
  Australia
Hong Kong
  & Taiwan
Singapore &
  Bangkok ‡
Tokyo

‡   Titles in preparation.

Clarity and quality of information, combined with outstanding maps — the ultimate in travelers' guides

Buying an AmEx guide has never been easier....

The *American Express Travel Guides* are now available by mail order direct from the publisher, for customers resident in the UK and Eire. Payment can be made by credit card or cheque/P.O. Simply complete the form below, and send it, together with your remittance. ‡ Available 1994

☐ Amsterdam, Rotterdam & The Hague
  1 85732 918 X   £8.99
☐ Athens and the Classical Sites ‡
  1 85732 308 4   £8.99
☐ Barcelona, Madrid & Seville
  1 85732 160 X   £8.99
☐ Berlin, Potsdam & Dresden ‡
  1 85732 309 2   £8.99
☐ Boston and New England ‡
  1 85732 310 6   £8.99
☐ Brussels
  1 85732 966 X   £8.99
☐ Cities of Australia
  1 85732 921 X   £9.99
☐ Dublin
  1 85732 967 8   £7.99
☐ Florence and Tuscany
  1 85732 922 8   £8.99
☐ Florida ‡
  1 85732 348 3   £8.99
☐ Hong Kong & Taiwan
  0 85533 955 1   £9.99
☐ London
  1 85732 968 6   £7.99
☐ Los Angeles & San Diego
  1 85732 919 8   £8.99
☐ Mexico
  1 85732 159 6   £9.99

☐ Moscow & St Petersburg ‡
  1 85732 349 1   £9.99
☐ New York
  1 85732 971 6   £8.99
☐ Paris
  1 85732 969 4   £7.99
☐ Prague
  1 85732 156 1   £9.99
☐ Provence and the Côte d'Azur ‡
  1 85732 312 2   £9.99
☐ Rome
  1 85732 923 6   £8.99
☐ San Francisco and the Wine Regions
  1 85732 920 1   £8.99
☐ Singapore & Bangkok ‡
  1 85732 311 4   £9.99
☐ Tokyo
  1 85732 970 8   £9.99
☐ Toronto, Montréal & Québec City
  1 85732 157 X   £8.99
☐ Venice ‡
  1 85732 158 8   £9.99
☐ Vienna & Budapest
  1 85732 962 7   £9.99
☐ Washington, DC
  1 85732 924 4   £8.99

While every effort is made to keep prices low, it is sometimes necessary to increase them at short notice. *American Express Travel Guides* reserve the right to amend prices from those previously advertised.

Please send the titles ticked above.   **MEX**

Number of titles @ £7.99	Value:	£
Number of titles @ £8.99	Value:	£
Number of titles @ £9.99	Value:	£
Add £1.50 for postage and packing		£ ___ 1 . 50

Total value of order: £_____
I enclose a cheque or postal order ☐ payable to Reed Book Services Ltd, or please charge my credit card account:

☐ Barclaycard/Visa   ☐ Access/MasterCard   ☐ American Express

Card number ☐☐☐☐☐☐☐☐☐☐☐☐☐☐☐☐☐☐

Signature_____   Expiry date _____

Name _____

Address _____

_____ Postcode _____

Send this order to American Express Travel Guides, Cash Sales Dept, Reed Book Services Ltd, PO Box 5, Rushden, Northants NN10 9YX ☎(0933) 410511.